MW00817142

PROTECTORS AND PREDATORS

GODS OF MEDIEVAL JAPAN

Volume 1:
The Fluid Pantheon

Volume 2:
Protectors and Predators

GODS *of* MEDIEVAL JAPAN

VOLUME 2
PROTECTORS AND PREDATORS

BERNARD FAURE

UNIVERSITY OF HAWAI'I PRESS
HONOLULU

Printed in China

21 20 19 18 17 16   6 5 4 3 2 1

Library of Congress Cataloging-in-Publication Data

Faure, Bernard, author.
Gods of medieval Japan / Bernard Faure.
pages cm
Includes bibliographical references and index.
ISBN 978-0-8248-3933-8 volume 1 (cloth : alk. paper)
1. Buddhist gods—Japan. 2. Buddhism—Japan—History—1185–1600. 3. Japan—Religion—1185–1600. I. Title.
BQ4660.J3F38 2015
294.3'42110952—dc23
2014046113

Volume 2, Protectors and Predators

ISBN 978-0-8248-3931-4 (cloth : alk. paper)

Publication of this book has been assisted by grants from the following:

Hiroshi Nitta Publication Fund of the Donald Keene Center of Japanese Culture, Columbia University

The School of Pacific and Asian Studies, University of Hawai'i, Mānoa

The Suntory Foundation

University of Hawai'i Press books are printed on acid-free paper and meet the guidelines for permanence and durability of the Council on Library Resources.

Designed by Mardee Melton

CONTENTS

Prologue 1

Japanese "Syncretism" 2
Honji Suijaku 4
The Rise of the *Besson* 7
Methodological Caveats 11
Synopsis 13

1. Earthly Powers 17
Bishamonten 18
Bishamonten as Protector 19
The God of Wealth 23
Bishamonten and the North 28
Once a Demon, Always a Demon 29
Tobatsu Bishamon and the Earth Deity 32
Bishamonten Mandalas 35
Tohachi Bishamon 36
The Dual-bodied Bishamon 39
Embryological Symbolism 42
Bishamonten, the Buddha's Relics, and the Jewel 43
Bishamonten as the Ox King 43
Daikokuten 45
The Demonic Mahākāla 45
Representations 46
Mahākāla as Protector of Monasteries 49
Daikokuten as a God of Wealth 52
All Too Real 54
From *Jissha* to *Honji* 55
Codetta 56
Enmaten 56
Yama and His Retinue 57
Mandalic Representations 59
The God of Death 68
The Judge 69
Changing Conceptions of the Underworld 70
Codetta 72

2. The Elephant in the Room 75
Shōten Rituals 75
Cultic Sites 76
From Demon to Deva 77
Skanda 79
Vināyaka as a Demon 81
Vināyaka and the Mothers 82
Henotheistic Tendencies 84
The Buddhist Vināyaka 85
The God of Obstacles 86
Iconography 89
Vināyaka in the Vajra Mandala 91
Other Iconographic Forms 93
Taming and Domestication 94
Kangiten 99
Functions 104
Shōten as Kōjin 104
Shōten's Network 105
The God of Yin and Yang 106
The Logic of Bipartition 107
Divination 108
The Chthonian God 111
The Demiurge 112
The Secret Lord 113
Codetta 115

3. A Stink of Fox 117
The Genealogical Model 117
The Taming of the *Ḍākinīs* 117
The Jewel in the Crown 118
From *Ḍākinī* to Dakiniten 118
Sexual Rituals 119
Dakiniten Rituals in Japanese Buddhist Literature 121
The Sectarian Background 122
Dakiniten and the Enthronement Ritual 124
The Fox and the Jewel 132
Dakiniten and the Fox 132
Dakiniten and Inari 134
Foxes and Snakes 135
Dakiniten and the Jewel 138
The Three Foxes 138
Dakiniten's Network 141
Dakiniten and Benzaiten 144
The King of Hearts, Foxes, and Jewels 148
King of Astral Foxes 148
King Shintamani 149

Dakiniten's Retinue 150
Dakiniten and Divination 152
Tarrying with the Demonic 155
Two Types of *Ḍākinī* 156
From Dakiniten to Izuna Gongen 157
Codetta 161

4. From Goddess to Dragon 163
The Vedic Goddess 164
The Buddhist Goddess 165
Genealogy and Structure 166
The Warrior Deity 170
The Music/War Polarity 171
The Esoteric Benzaiten 178
The Beauty and the Beast 179
Benzaiten as a Female Immortal 179
Benzaiten as a *Gandharva* 180
Benzaiten as a Water Deity 181
Nāgas and Dragons 184
The Hidden Side 188
Codetta 189

5. From Dragon to Snake 191
The Hybrid Deity 192
Animals and Hybridity 195
The Tendai Synthesis 200
Benzaiten and the Jewel 202
Nonduality and Ambivalence 203
Territorial Expansion 205
Chikubushima 210
Itsukushima 212
Enoshima 213
Tenkawa 214
Minō 215
Ise 216
Iconography 217
Benzaiten's Entourage 217
The Fifteen Attendants 218
The Benzaiten Constellation 224
Dakiniten 224
Daikokuten 225
Amaterasu 226
Benzaiten as an Astral Deity 227
A Deity of the Third (or Fourth) Function 228
Benzaiten as an Earth Deity 231
Ugajin, Kōjin, and Shukujin 232
Codetta 233

6. The Three Devas 235
The *Yakṣa* of Tōji and the Ritual of the Three Devas 236
Expansion of the Cult 237
The Three Devas at Mount Inari 238
Beyond Inari 239
Iconology and Interpicturality 240
"Simple" Representations 240
Complex Mandalas 247
The Tenkawa Benzaiten Mandala 250
Interpicturality 258
The Three-faced Daikoku 259
Individuals and Institutions 261
The Triadic Structure 264
The Broader Context 266

7. The Face of the Snake 269
Ugajin and Benzaiten 271
Early Studies 273
Virtual Origins 275
The Problematic Use of Etymology 276
Ugajin and Inari 277
The Snake 278
The Generic and the Individual 279
Appearance and Iconography 280
The Old Man as Landlord Deity 282
Symbol of Fundamental Ignorance and Awakening 283
Functions 285
Jewels and Prosperity 285
The Snake, the Toad, and the Three Poisons 286
Ugajin and Suwa 288
Directions 292
Identities 293
The Warp and Woof of Heaven and Earth 295
Codetta 297

8. Matricial Gods 299
Naming the God 299
Nature and Functions 300
Dark Origins 303
Symbolic Network 305
The Demonic Matarajin 305
Matarajin in Tendai 310
Matarajin's Cohort 310
Sekizan Myōjin 312
Shinra Myōjin 314

Matarajin's Evolving Functions 318
Protector of the Jōgyōdō 318
The God on/of the Threshold 319
Taming the *Tengu* 320
The God of the Genshi Kimyōdan 321
Another Matarajin 324
The Epidemic Deity 324
Matarajin on the Ground 325
Susanoo, Gozu Tennō, Konpira, Miwa Myōjin 326
Codetta 327
No Country for Old Men? 328

Coda 330
The Two-tiered Model 332
Buddhas and *Kami* 334
Back to the "Real" 336
Hybrids 343
Animal Deities 345
The Fourth Function 347
The Spandrel 348
Out of the Rut? 349

Abbreviations 353

Notes 355

Bibliography 435

Index 489

THE ESOTERIC PANTHEON

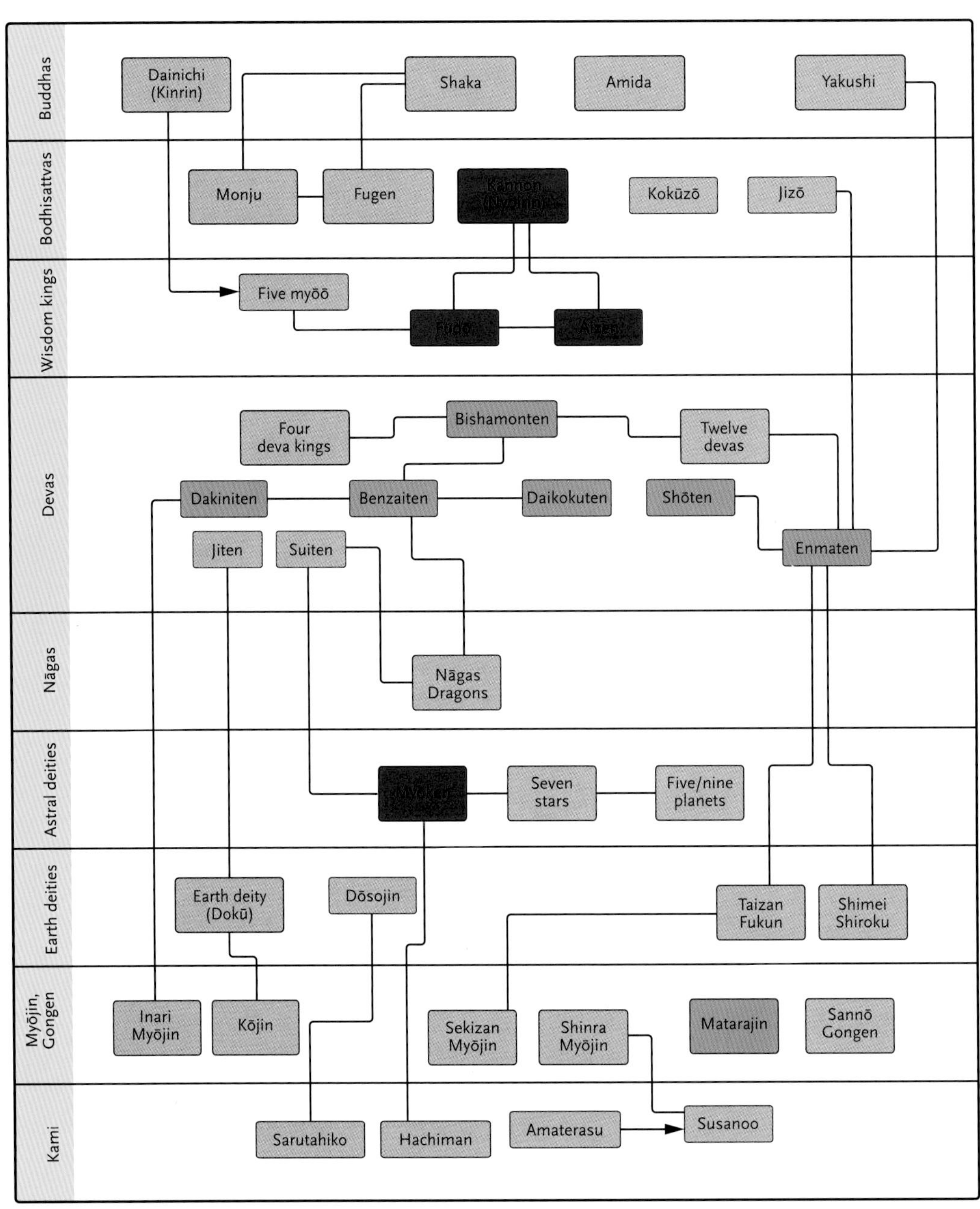

Deities discussed in *The Fluid Pantheon* appear in red; those discussed in *Protectors and Predators*, in blue.

PROLOGUE

Those who look for happiness worship Daikokuten, Benzaiten, Bishamonten . . . , and Ugajin; those who fear demonic obstacles worship Fudō Myōō; those who look for love worship Kangiten and Aizen Myōō . . . . Human desires are of all kinds, and the gods that people worship are also of all kinds.

SHŌGAKU MONDŌ[1]

There are many sects among the pagans and the oldest is that of the kami, the lords and kings of old times. . . . This sect has three gods: one is called Benzaiten, another is called Bishamonten, while the third is known as Daikoku. These are the gods to whom they pray for wealth. . . . They have a multitude of other gods and I would never finish describing them, but you can judge them from the others.

GASPARD VILELA, S.J.[2]

The Japanese Middle Ages—a term broadly defined here as referring to the period extending from the twelfth to the sixteenth century—is often perceived from the religious standpoint as the heyday of the *honjui suijaku* 本地垂迹 model of esoteric Buddhism, a model in which Indian buddhas are paired with Japanese *kami*. Following that model, which is said to reflect a process of Buddhist syncretism or "acculturation," all Japanese gods are "traces" (*suijaku*) or manifestations of Indian buddhas and bodhisattvas, who constitute their "original ground" (*honji*) but have "softened their light to mingle with the dust" (*wakō dōjin* 和光同塵).

Yet something occurred in that period that considerably affected the model's operation: at all levels of the esoteric pantheon, certain deities morphed, transforming from mere traces or provisional manifestations (*gongen* 権現) into "real" entities (*jissha* 実者). This change is most evident in the case of devas like Daikokuten 大黒天, Shōten 聖天, Dakiniten 荼吉尼天 (var. 茶枳尼天,拏枳尼天), and Benzaiten 弁才天, deities who are usually described as inhabiting "the gray area between Shinto and Buddhism," in Carmen Blacker's phrase.[3] Far from being a gray area, however, their domain is brightly colored, and it is not located "between Shinto and Buddhism"—it permeates them through and through. Nevertheless, while the cults devoted to these deities form a rich tapestry in Japanese religious practice, they have been largely neglected in Western scholarship, probably because the "hybrid" or "moot" category to which they have been assigned tends to fall through the cracks of Buddhist ideology and is harder to conceptualize. I have trawled through Buddhist and non-Buddhist literature to retrieve information about them.

Yamamoto Hiroko has called these deities "strange" or "alien" gods (*ijin* 異神), emphasizing their foreign origin. In the prologue to her book entitled, precisely, *Ijin,* she says that this term refers neither to the *kami* of ancient Japanese mythology nor to buddhas and bodhisattvas, but to a variety of gods that constitutes a third category.[4] In her account, the *ijin* reached their maturity during the Insei 院政 period (1086–1192) and declined in the early modern period. Because of their obscure origins, these deities were either rejected or domesticated by Buddhist and Shintō orthodoxies.

While greatly indebted to Yamamoto's work, my own research has developed along slightly different lines. Indeed, her emphasis on the "alien" nature of the *ijin* prevents her from explaining why certain of these deities came to be perceived as autochthonous. In other words, while she may be right to point out their radical novelty, she tends to exaggerate their foreign character and heterodox nature. If foreignness, then, is not always an attribute of these medieval deities, what are their main characteristics and functions? I submit that they are Janus-faced deities, gods of obstacles as well as controllers of human destiny. Even when integrated as "protectors" in esoteric Buddhism, they still retained their demonic and threatening nature, aspects that elude the grasp of the *honji suijaku* framework.[5] The relative neglect of these "hybrid" deities in traditional scholarship has much to do with an uncritical acceptance of that framework.

JAPANESE "SYNCRETISM"

The story of medieval Japanese religion is that of a mythical and ritual proliferation—and of theological and scholarly attempts to control that proliferation and subsume it under broad formulae such as esoteric Buddhism, Shintō, Shugendō 修験道, and Onmyōdō 陰陽道. The term *syncretism,* while useful to describe a conscious effort to reconcile diverse ideas and doctrines, is itself problematic in the Japanese context.[6] It suggests the merging of two distinct, preexisting, and allegedly "pure" traditions, instead of making clear that such traditions were never a given, but the outcome of a painstaking ideological process of "purification." In other words, in order to obtain a "syncretistic" effect, one must first "separate" two religions, a doctrinal perspective that is only available from certain ideological heights.[7] One does encounter, in various corners, a discourse that brings together traditions perceived as distinct. Often it is militant syncretism, aimed at establishing the superiority of one tradition over the others. A case in point is Kūkai's grand doctrinal synthesis, an heir of earlier Chinese Buddhist doctrinal classifications (Ch. *panjiao* 判教). The beliefs and practices of ordinary lay people and clerics, on the other hand, were not "syncretistic" inasmuch as they did not see the buddhas as fundamentally different from gods of all stripes.

While the word "syncretism" may describe the religious situation of sixth and seventh century Japan, when Buddhism was still perceived as a foreign religion, it becomes misleading in later periods, when most Japanese were at least nominally Buddhist and the buddhas were no longer perceived as foreign. It is not as if two full-fledged religions ever merged (the usual meaning of syncretism), nor was there a "fusion" of gods and buddhas. Among the great variety of gods available (including buddhas), people simply turned to those who they felt were most relevant to them. The buddhas were no more "alien" to them than the *kami* of the ruling elite.[8] It was only with the centralization of the state during the Nara period—in particular, with the creation of the Great Buddha of Tōdaiji 東大寺—that Buddhism began to be perceived as a radically different type of discourse: universalist, absolutist, and particularly appropriate for the nascent imperial ideology. But even then, at the grass-roots level, buddhas were not seen as ontologically distinct from autochthonous *kami.* The emergence of the "bodhisattva" Hachiman (Hachiman Bosatsu 八幡菩薩) as a new oracular deity during the construction of Tōdaiji, for example, cannot be understood as the expression of a dualistic framework of buddhas and *kami.* The same is true of the medieval deities that constitute the subject of this book.

Recent studies have preferred to use the term "combinatory" to describe the logic of medieval Japanese religion.[9] While this term does account for the ideological activity of official Buddhist theology (or rather "polytheology," as a discourse on the gods), it tends to overemphasize a systematic aspect of the process, as well as ascribe to it a dualistic nature ('combination' deriving from 'binary'). Esoteric Buddhism is not simply an *ars combinatoria.* While it relies heavily on analogical thinking, its tangle is vastly more complex and unpredictable than any combinatory system. It relies less on mechanical association and permutation than on imagination, which, in Samuel Taylor Coleridge's words, "dissolves, diffuses, dissipates in order to recreate."[10] Instead of combination or *bricolage,* we have constant reconstruction or recreation, in which elements reconstitute themselves into a new whole. If Japanese religion were purely combinatory, it would be easily understandable through the structuralist method, since in structuralism "nothing is really transformed, it's simply combined."[11] Bruno Latour emphasizes the "abyss" between a structure and a network, however.[12] Although the context and methodology of this work have little to do with the sociological theories of Latour and other proponents of actor-network theory, I have found in their description of networks the same patterns that I encountered in my analysis of the ritual and mythological "structures" of esoteric Buddhism: there is something that circulates, which is constituted by semantic and symbolic associations and which in turn constitutes social associations.

The classic scenario of Japanese religious history is that of a gradual takeover of indigenous cults by Buddhism during the ancient and medieval periods, followed by a sharp decline of Buddhism and a revival of the "native" religion (Shintō) in the Edo period, an evolution that culminated in the forceful separation of Buddhism and Shintō (*shinbutsu bunri* 神佛分離) during the so-called Meiji Restoration. This political "separation," however, was only the distant outcome of the ideological discrimination between buddhas and *kami* implied by their reunion in the *honji suijaku* model, or their fusion in the so-called *shinbutsu shūgō* 神仏習合 model—a term which, incidentally, was coined in the nineteenth century and is therefore contemporary of its antithesis. This alleged "fusion," just like the separation, is a dated historical and ideological product.

The "conquest" model, inherited from Erik Zürcher's classic work on Chinese Buddhism, is itself highly problematic, if only because it denies agency to the populations that were supposedly "converted" to Buddhism.[13] This is akin to what Michael Baxandall has characterized as the "billiard ball" model of causality.[14] In the present case what we actually find on the ground is something quite different—namely, the creativity of the Japanese (and others) who selectively adopted and adapted Buddhist ideas to their own use.[15] As powerful symbols, Buddhist and non-Buddhist figures alike were "arenas of contention," evolving stakes in relationships between individuals and groups.[16] Most Japanese were Buddhists, and, apart from a few immigrants, most Buddhists were Japanese. While it is often said that Buddhist monks "converted" local gods, one could just as well argue that these gods "diverted" Buddhism. Perhaps one should rather speak of a "mutual capture," to use a term coined by Gilles Deleuze.[17] In fact, the place of the buddhas was already inscribed (*en creux,* as it were) in the Japanese religious landscape. Just as modern freeways follow medieval roads, which themselves followed prehistoric pathways, Buddhism followed the tracks of Japanese religion, even when it claimed to ignore them.

HONJI SUIJAKU

The linchpin of the *honji suijaku* architectonic is the proclaimed identity between the sun goddess Amaterasu 天照 and the Buddha Vairocana (J.

Dainichi 大日 'great sun'), which led to the institution of Ryōbu shintō 両部神道 and the identification of Ise's Inner and Outer Shrines with the two great mandalas of esoteric Buddhism.[18] Despite its mythological proliferation, the *honji suijaku* theory was initially a demythologizing attempt in which the gods became increasingly abstract entities.[19] Yet, paradoxically, this process also led to a proliferation of relations and correspondences between all kinds of supernatural beings and sacred sites, and to a remythologizing of Japanese religion.

Let us briefly retrace the evolution of that concept.[20] While modern Japanese scholars shared the same premise—that of the existence of two distinct currents (Buddhism and Shintō)—they derived different conclusions from it: Tsuji Zennosuke 辻善之助 (1877–1955), the main proponent of the *honji suijaku* model, described premodern Japanese religion as culminating in a harmonious fusion of the *kami* and the buddhas (*shinbutsu shūgō* 神佛習合). He outlined a process of gradual co-optation of the gods, who became protectors of Buddhism, then proceeded to obtain deliverance, becoming bodhisattvas, and eventually were redefined as manifestations of the buddhas.[21] After Tsuji, the established view has been that, from the eighth century onward, Japanese gods were first reinterpreted as local variants of the Indian devas, that is, the divine beings still subject to karma and saved by Buddhism. With the identification of Hachiman as a protector of the Dharma, then as a bodhisattva, a new stage was allegedly reached, paving the way to *honji suijaku*.[22] Tsuji's thesis of a natural evolution was criticized on specific points but rarely questioned as a whole.[23] Despite their divergences, all his critics agreed that the "fusion of *kami* and buddhas" developed following its own inner dynamics. This viewpoint presupposed the "harmonizing" nature of Japanese culture and its power to assimilate a foreign religion. One significant exception was Tsuda Sōkichi 津田左右吉 (1873–1961), who emphasized the fundamental difference between Chinese and Japanese thought, and argued that in Japan there never was such a fusion, because of strong resistance on the part of local cults.[24] According to Tsuda, the Buddhist notion of protecting deities was unrelated to real popular cults. His thesis inspired Kuroda Toshio's seminal essay on Shintō and, indirectly, the revival of medieval Shintō studies that followed.[25]

Beginning with the work of Alicia Matsunaga, whose book on the topic is essentially a translation of Tsuji's, Western scholarship has on the whole uncritically accepted Tsuji's linear model.[26] Yet this model never addresses the question of whether the *kami* existed as a clearly established conceptual unit before fusing with or into Buddhism. The word *kami,* written with the Chinese character 神 (read *shin* in Sino-Japanese), designates a vast array of entities ranging from the highest powers to the most humble.[27] Should one, then, assume any specificity for the *"kami"* vis-à-vis Indian and Chinese gods? As to the category "buddhas," it is itself far from stable and homogenous. The word designates in many cases just another kind of god; read *hotoke,* it refers to the spirits of the dead.[28] Ultimately, both buddha and *kami* are shorthand for highly polysemic, fluid, and elusive realities.[29] A closer look at the context reveals that metaphysical buddhas, by becoming local, tend to become "gods," whereas certain local gods can rise to the status of bodhisattvas or buddhas. Conversely, other local deities, when they (or the groups they represent) refuse to convert to Buddhism, are degraded to the status of demons. Thus, *kami* can be (alternatively) gods, genii, demons, spirits, and even bodhisattvas and buddhas. A two-tiered model that recognizes only buddhas and *kami* forces us to classify the majority of the deities as hybrid or residual. In reality, as medieval vows (*kishōmon* 起請文) and other similar documents show, these deities constituted the mainstream of medieval religion.[30]

The last stage of this hypothetical Buddhist assimilation of the gods, and its paradoxical outcome, has been relatively neglected.[31] Around the eleventh to twelfth centuries, certain of these gods were promoted from the subaltern rank of "traces" and recognized as "essences" (*honji*), that is, as embodiments of Dainichi's ultimate enlightenment.[32] In the Tendai tradition, especially, they are seen as manifestations of "fundamental awakening" (*hongaku* 本覚) and move from a peripheral position to the center of ritual space as *besson* 別尊, the main deity and object of worship (*honzon* 本尊) of specific rituals. No longer merely local manifestations in a distant, tiny land in the degenerate age of the Final Dharma (*mappō* 末法), the gods have become primordial manifestations in the Great Land of Japan (Dainipponkoku 大日本国)—a land that is divine (*shinkoku* 神国) because it is the "original land of Dainichi" (Dainichi 大日 *no honkoku* 本国). This wordplay on Japan and Dainichi is found in many texts of this period, one notable example being the *Keiran shūyōshū* 渓嵐拾葉集 by the Tendai monk Kōshū 光宗 (1276–1350).[33] As a development in ideology, most evident in the work of Kōshū's contemporary, the Tendai monk Jihen 慈遍, this notion was to lead ultimately to the emergence of a Shintō religion antithetical to Buddhism.[34]

But in the medieval period, instead of two clearly defined categories constituting the warp and woof of Japanese religion, gods and buddhas, what we find (or are eluded by) are multiplicities that constantly crisscross into increasingly complex figures. To counter dualistic notions of the relationship between buddhas and *kami,* we might contrast two interpretations of the interplay between warp and weft: the first describes a regular intertwining that produces a grid-like surface, or what Deleuze and Guattari call a "striated space," in which diverse things are laid out each in its assigned location (as in the esoteric pantheon); to this, they oppose "smooth" space, which has no layout and presents a patchwork of continuous variation. The difference is like that between felt and linen, "the one matted from a swirling morass of fibres that have no consistent direction, the other woven through the regular intertwining of warp and weft."[35] In this interpretation, warp and woof can only represent a dualistic order. Yet Tim Ingold suggests another, nondualistic interpretation when he explains that "it is in the nature of weaving, as a technique, that it produces a peculiar kind of surface that does not, strictly speaking, have an inside and an outside at all."[36] He also emphasizes the skill needed for weaving, a "close up, immediate, muscular and visceral engagement" with the fabric, which counterweighs and complements the regular intertwining of the warp and the weft.[37]

To return to Deleuze and Guattari's terminology, we could speak of the rhizome-like structure of medieval Japanese religion as formed of "a thousand plateaus"—connecting buddhas, gods, astral deities, demons, various religious movements (Onmyōdō, Shugendō), epistemologic levels (folklore, scholasticism), and social groups, all in nonlinear fashion. If the tree under which the Buddha reached awakening belonged to the *ficus* species, as we are told, so Buddhism, in its development, resembles another Indian *ficus,* the banyan, whose aerial prop roots grow into trunks, allowing it to spread over a large area.[38] One can also conceive of the *bodhi* tree along the rhizomatic lines of the banyan.[39] In the same fashion, the present text has tended to proliferate: at all points of its tree-like structure, excrescences appeared, which rapidly grew into a rhizome. As the author, I felt compelled to eliminate them, or at least to prune them in order to keep the sap of the argument flowing. As Foucault has pointed out, authors, by their very function, attempt to "discipline" ideas, associations, transformations, and try to limit the proliferation of discourse or the dissemination of meaning.[40] Caught between these antithetic, agonistic, perpendicular constraints, I have been forced to proceed diagonally, obliquely, in crab-like fashion, trying to maintain a fragile balance between too much order (which betrays the complexity of reality) and not enough (which makes a book unreadable).

THE RISE OF THE *BESSON*

The "conversion" of Indian gods to Buddhism had led to an impoverishment of their mythological personalities. Yet they regained their full power in Japanese esoteric Buddhism, owing in particular to the worship of individualized "separate worthies" (*besson* 別尊). This development seems to have derived from the notion of the "primary god" (Skt. *iṣṭadevatā*) in Indian Tantrism and reflects the rise, in Japan, of specific cults that took as their central object of worship (*honzon* 本尊) deities that had until then occupied a relatively peripheral position in the esoteric mandalas (or had a subaltern rank in the Buddhist pantheon).[41] While this phenomenon would eventually affect the entire pantheon, it was initially concentrated at the lower and intermediate levels. As a response to human needs (beginning with the mitigation or elimination of the calamities and dangers constantly threatening the individual and society), the new cults focused on gods and buddhas who specialized in that type of function—the Healing Buddha Yakushi 薬師 (Skt. Baiṣajyaguru), in particular, among the buddhas. As *besson,* we also find a rather abstract group called emanations of the Buddha's crown (Skt. *buddhoṣṇīsa,* J. *butchō* 佛頂)—in particular, Ichiji Kinrin 一字金輪 (the Golden-wheel Buddha [Emanated from] the One Letter), reputed for his apotropaic power.[42] Among the bodhisattvas, we of course find Kannon 観音 (Skt. Avalokiteśvara); above all, certain forms of the esoteric Kannon known to subdue demonic powers. Although the bodhisattva Jizō 地藏 (Skt. Kṣitigarbha) was perceived essentially as a savior in the other world, his name (Womb of the Earth) suggests his chthonian nature. His counterpart Kokūzō 虚空藏 (Skt. Ākāśagarbha) was associated with astral cults and their apotropaic functions, and in particular with the "bodhisattva" Myōken 妙見, god of the pole star.

From a cultic standpoint, the growing emphasis on gods of lower rank reflected a judgment that they were more apt to serve as mediators in matters perceived as too mundane or inappropriate (e.g., involving sex or power) for a buddha or bodhisattva. But there was also the sense that because the new gods were lower in rank, they were more easily *obliged* (in both senses of the word) by ritual. The interesting point here is that the intermediaries had become increasingly powerful, turning into full-fledged mediators endowed with agency.[43] These mediators themselves eventually reached a kind of apotheosis, becoming the main deity or *honzon* of specific and often complex rituals.

The emergence of such deities in medieval Buddhism was marked in esoteric iconography by the creation of mandalas for the "separate worthies" (*besson mandara* 別尊曼荼羅).[44] Like the *honji suijaku* paradigm, the *besson* phenomenon can be interpreted from two different perspectives: as the emergence of a new deity, through its transfiguration and integration at a higher level; and as a subversion of the classificatory system. Between deities of various categories, particular affinities existed, allowing multiple resonances, a network of correspondences, an exchange of attributes and functions, and a circulation of power across strict classificatory boundaries. These symbolic exchanges paved the way to their elevation to the rank of "separate worthy" with a position at the heart of specific rituals that every so often verged on heterodoxy. A rapid examination of a few of these deities will allow us to bring out some of these correspondences.

Every type of esoteric ritual (for prosperity, subjugation, seduction, and so on) had its specialized mandala and *honzon.* The deities invoked included bodhisattvas such as Kṣitigarbha; wisdom kings (*vidyārājas*) like Acala, Yamāntaka, Trailokyavijaya, and Āṭavaka; devas like Mahākāla, Sarasvatī, Vaiśravaṇa, and Yama; and even former demons like Vināyaka and Hārītī. Despite those who would prefer to see them as an archaism, a mere survival of Brahmanism, these deities actually played a central role in East Asian Buddhism. Indeed, the medieval period could be called the Age of the Devas. Admittedly, these transfigured devas are not the faded gods of early Buddhism. Adding new colors to their restored image, they constitute in many respects novel deities who shared certain functions—chief among them the capacity to cause *or* remove obstacles and the power to control human destiny. Being neither buddhas nor *kami,* they challenge that overly simple distinction—and in the end, must be understood in the context of medieval Japanese religion, a setting in which their non-Buddhist origins had by and large been forgotten.

The devas are divided into various categories—for instance, the twelve devas (*jūniten* 十二天) ruling over the twelve directions (Fig. 1), or the twenty-eight devas (*nijūhachibu* 二十八部) forming Senju Kannon's retinue. The recognized leaders of the devas are Brahmā (J. Bonten 梵天) and Indra (J. Taishakuten 帝釈天), two Vedic gods who made their way into early Buddhism. Foremost among their number are the four deva kings (*shitennō* 四天王), who protect the four directions (Fig. 2). Bishamonten 毘沙門天 (Skt. Vaiśravaṇa), in particular, the protector of the north, became the object of an important cult. Many of the devas who ascended to the status of "separate worthies" are like Bishamonten in having demonic origins. Such was the case with Daikokuten, Dakiniten, and Shōten.

As Friedrich Max Müller put it, "True, all Devas must have started from one small nest, but they soon took wings and soared away, far and wide."[45] By an ironic turn of events, these Indic deities—who had been humiliated, coerced into conversion, and even killed (as was Śiva/Maheśvara) by Buddhist wisdom kings—became the dominant figures of Japanese esoteric Buddhism. The importance of the devas in medieval Japanese religion is brought out in a section of the *Keiran shūyōshū* entitled "About the fact that the devas can free us from *saṃsāra,*" which states: "Worldly people think that the devas can bring worldly happiness. In Tendai, the deva category constitutes the deepest mystery. . . . The devas take good fortune as their front, ultimate awakening as their back."[46] Referring to a specific pairing of devas, it states that "generally speaking, the male deva is a god of obstacles symbolizing the virtue of wisdom, while the female deva is a fortune deity symbolizing the virtue of compassion."[47] Yet, for all its emphasis on the efficacy of the devas, the *Keiran shūyōshū* warns its readers at the same time that they are vulgar and dangerous and should be left alone.[48] Significantly, it is the devas who appeared more frequently than the buddhas and bodhisattvas in dreams.[49]

FIGURE 1. The twelve devas. Detail of Dakiniten mandala. Muromachi period. Hanging scroll, color on silk. Tokyo National Museum.

As we shall see, the symbolic appeal of the devas was due in part to their Janus-faced nature. This ambiguity facilitated their integration into the binary structures of both esoteric Buddhism and Onmyōdō, since the Buddhist notion of nonduality conveniently overlapped with yin-yang theory and its popular variants. To give just one example, the dual-bodied deva called Kangiten 歓喜天 (or Sōshin Binayaka 双身毘那夜迦) is said to represent not only the blissful sexual union of the demon Vināyaka with his consort Senāyaka, but also the subduing of the former by the latter (an incarnation of Avalokiteśvara), as well as the nonduality of the Womb and Vajra realms, and so on. Yet it would be misleading to reduce these dual figures to mere symbols of the yin and yang: their apotropaic function, in

FIGURE 2. The four deva kings. Kamakura period, 13th century. Ink and color on paper. *Jikkanshō*. Nara National Museum.

particular, resists any simple assignation to predetermined harmony. The ambiguity of most of these deities reveals their uncanny or whimsical nature and expresses their devotees' hope for rapid gratification, mixed with the fear of an impending curse.

METHODOLOGICAL CAVEATS

In *The Fluid Pantheon,* I adopted a methodological approach partly inspired by structuralism but I also attempted to take into account certain aspects of religious phenomena which structuralism, more focused on ideology, tends to neglect.

Alongside the *explicit* pantheon of esoteric Buddhism, I emphasized the presence of an *implicit* pantheon, a complex and active network that greatly differs from the official hierarchy as described by the *honji suijaku* model. I do not intend for all that to discard old "maps" as if they have become useless or without referents, nor do I mean to affirm that what I described is the true "territory" of medieval Japanese religion. There is no longer any difference in nature—*pace* Skorupsky, Van Vogt, and J. Z. Smith—between map and territory.[50] The territory, in this case, is just another map, and every map, in turn, becomes a territory. Nevertheless, certain differences remain, and I want to believe that all descriptions or inscriptions are not born equal. I contend that the implicit mythology that I have tried to tease out, as well as certain recurring structures of Japanese mythical and ritual thought, are closer to real practices than official doctrine and mythology, even if the latter eventually imposed themselves, through sheer repetition and persuasion, as the only available reality.

In order to follow more closely these representations and practices, I found the "network" paradigm (even if it has become a little too fashionable) more useful than those of system and structure. Even Lévi-Strauss, the founder of anthropological structuralism, came close to the network with his notion of *bricolage,* in contrast to his earlier, all-too-Leibnizian concept of structure as an abstract *combinatoire.*

Although I have made a rather broad use of this notion of network, it does not satisfy me entirely insofar as the network, like the net from which it derives etymologically, claims to capture in its meshes a fundamentally fluid and evanescent reality. There is indeed a part of reality that flows along the lines of the network, but there is another part that escapes its meshes and is excluded by the network—an interstitial thought, as it were. But here my project reaches its limits. Language needs to identify entities—for example, to collect under the proper names Vināyaka and Benzaiten a multitude of various entities or modes of existence that perhaps only share a family resemblance. Structuralism helps us to see beyond simplistic identifications and to avoid the "individualist fallacy." We should keep in mind, however, that "individuated" deities remain alive in the experience of individuals (who are themselves constituted, as we now know, by networks). When it yields to its own proclivities, structural analysis tends to dissolve the phenomenological reality of such entities, and to bypass the resilient evidence of religious phenomena. I will therefore continue to speak, without worrying too much about contradictions, of gods like Vināyaka and Benzaiten 弁才天 as if they were close (or distant) relatives of mine.

I have tried to point beyond the systemic or structural aspects of the Japanese pantheon by contrasting an implicit, virtual pantheon with the explicit, established pantheon of orthodox Mikkyō. But even the notion of an implicit pantheon quickly reaches its limits, inasmuch as it re-territorializes (to speak like Deleuze and Guattari) even as it de-territorializes esoteric discourse. Here is, obviously, my major caveat. That being said, all categories do not have the same value for such a project. Thus, the category of the devas seemed more useful for "soliciting" (that is, undermining) the religious system of esoteric Buddhism than did more conspicuous traditional categories like buddhas and *kami,* or bodhisattvas and wisdom kings. Even if these categories are "open" and fluid—as I have shown in the case of bodhisattvas like Myōken and Nyoirin Kannon, and wisdom kings like Aizen 愛染 and Fudō 不動—they nevertheless remain closer to an orthodoxy bent on imposing its binary thinking and on trapping reality in its theoretical and doctrinal meshes. For that reason, the devas that will serve as our stepping stones into the religious world of medieval Japan are both the cornerstones and the stumbling stones of the Buddhist system.

Building on the work of Georges Dumézil, Marcel Detienne has emphasized the importance of the details that reveal a god's specific mode of action. Applying this insight to Japanese religion, one could for example distinguish a group of deities that is defined by a significant detail: they are all said to "follow humans like their shadow." These deities—Myōken, Shōten, and Dakiniten among them—usually share the functions of a god of obstacles and ruler of human destiny. Another significant aspect of their mode of action is *secrecy:* they tend to work in the dark. They can perhaps be seen as the long shadow projected by humans (and in particular by Buddhist monks). But, just like Peter Pan's shadow, they have their own life—becoming at times unruly and malevolent doppelgängers.

Another detail that will catch our attention is that these deities often have an embryological function, acting as protectors of the fetus in the mother's womb. I will refer time and again to that aspect, following Voltaire's method in one of his letters to the king of Prussia, where he speaks of certain repetitions as "toothing stones."[51] My intention is to return to the embryological theme and give it fuller treatment in a forthcoming book, *Lords of Life*.

SYNOPSIS

This book suggests that the *gekokujō* (world turned upside down) model that informed and transformed medieval Japanese society also applied, *mutatis mutandis,* to the religious sphere. It therefore emphasizes the role played by certain deities that have generally been treated as marginal while remaining relatively silent about the traditional protagonists of Japanese religious discourse (the great buddhas like Dainichi and Amida and *kami* like the sun goddess Amaterasu). It also de-centers traditional Japanese religious history by shifting the focus from purely Japanese Buddhist figures to their Indian and Chinese prototypes and to their non-Buddhist (and also non-Shintō) elements, showing how, even as Japanese religion became increasingly "national" (not to say nativist), it remained heavily indebted to foreign influences. Indeed, more often than not, native gods were *heterochthonous.* Their foreign origin, quite visible in gods like Shinra Myōjin 新羅明神, the "bright deity of Silla," did not at all prevent them from becoming local protectors—through the ideological legerdemain that consists in arguing that even foreign gods were originally a manifestation of Japanese gods (i.e., Susanoo 須佐之男 in Shinra Myōjin's case).

Chapter One, "Earthly Powers," focuses on three devas—Bishamonten, Daikokuten, and Enmaten—emphasizing their demonic origins and ambiguous nature. For all their differences, these three gods shared strong affinities with one another and with another triad that will form the core of this work, namely, Shōten, Dakiniten, and Benzaiten.

Chapter Two, "The Elephant in the Room," focuses on Vināyaka (a.k.a. Shōten), the Buddhist version of Gaṇeśa and the paradigmatic demon of obstacles. After a quick survey of Vināyaka's Indian origins, I examine the process through which this demon, once tamed by the bodhisattva Avalokiteśvara, with whom he then formed a dyad known as Kangiten (Bliss Deva), was eventually promoted to the status of a demiurge. Yet Shōten's demonic nature was never entirely erased, and his ambiguity is reflected in the fact that, even today, his cult is surrounded by a deep cloud of secrecy.

Chapter Three, "A Stink of Fox," focuses on Dakiniten, a complex deity derived from the Indian *ḍākinī,* a demoness feeding on the vital essence of human beings. It shows, by way of association with the fox and with the Japanese deity Inari, how she tempered her demonic tendencies to become a god in charge of human destiny. This chapter also examines the affinities that Dakiniten shares with Bishamonten, Benzaiten, and Ugajin 宇賀神, in large part through their common symbol, the wish-fulfilling jewel (Skt. *cintāmaṇi,* J. *nyoi hōju*).

Chapter Four, "From Goddess to Dragon," adopts a genealogical approach to describe the trajectory of the goddess Benzaiten from an Indian river goddess named Sarasvatī to a Japanese dragon deity. It also follows the development of her cult in Japan, based on her function as the goddess of music and the arts. This, however, is only half the story of Benzaiten.

Chapter Five, "From Dragon to Snake," examines the symbiotic relationship that Benzaiten formed with the Japanese snake god Ugajin, a hybrid deity represented with the body of a snake and the head of an old man. The new deity they formed was named Uga Benzaiten.

Chapter Six, "The Three Devas," focuses on a weird-looking deity formed by Shōten, Dakiniten, and Benzaiten. I try in this chapter to understand how a triad of devas was transformed into a single, three-headed deity riding a fox. Mention of the Three Devas first appears in the thirteenth century, in a record about a protecting deity of Tōji, a major Shingon temple in Kyoto. It resurfaces, after an apparent eclipse of three centuries, in a Tendai context and rapidly expands, outside Mikkyō, in Onmyōdō, Shugendō, and Shintō circles. In a section on iconography, I connect this triune deity to another figure, Tenkawa Benzaiten 天河弁才天, a snake-headed representation of the Buddhist goddess of music.

Chapter Seven, "The Face of the Snake," takes up the case of Ugajin as an independent figure, distinct from Benzaiten. In spite of his archaic features and his relationship to the ancient *kami* Uka no Mitama, Ugajin and his cult are essentially a product of medieval Mikkyō. Like other deities studied in this book and in *The Fluid Pantheon,* Ugajin came to be associated with prosperity and the wish-fulfilling jewel—indeed, he is represented as dwelling inside a jewel. Yet he also has an atropopaic and soteriological function as a predator of toads, that symbolize the three poisons or passions that hinder the practitioner. This aspect was particularly pronounced at Suwa 諏訪 (in Nagano prefecture), and I therefore examine in some detail the role of Ugajin in the rituals of Suwa Shrine. I conclude with a discussion of Ugajin's function as a directional deity and his elevation to the status of a primordial deity, "the warp and woof of heaven and earth."

Chapter Eight, "Matricial Gods," focuses on the god Matarajin 摩多羅神. It combines a diachronic or genealogical approach with a synchronic one. Through the former, I follow the trajectory leading from the Indian god Mahākāla, leader of the vampire-like *ḍākinīs*, to the Japanese Matarajin, protector of *nenbutsu* practice in Tendai monasteries and patron of the performing arts; through the latter, I examine Matarajin's symbolic network, keying on the figures of Sekizan Myōjin and Shinra Myōjin, protectors of two rival branches of Tendai.

In the Coda, I consider the consequences of a still dominant dualistic conception of medieval Japanese religion that relies on a simplistic version of the *honji suijaku* model. I also examine the nature and status of "moot" deities like the devas in light of heuristic notions such as the "fourth function" (added to Dumézil's trifunctional model) and the "hybrids" of actor-network theory.

In sum, starting almost randomly from three popular Japanese gods that seem to reflect the diversity of the deva category (Bishamonten, Daikokuten, and Enmaten), I began perceiving lines of force, incipient structures connecting these deities. At first glance, apart from their status as members of a neglected category, nothing seemed to predispose these motley characters to the formation of a significant grouping. Bishamonten and Daikokuten, worshiped as gods of fortune, turn out to be former demons, while Enmaten, the terrible judge of the underworld, becomes in turn a god of longevity and happiness. In contrast, the next group of devas (Shōten, Dakiniten, and Benzaiten) seemed from the outset to share affinities. The first two belong to Enmaten's entourage, while Benzaiten is said, in some sources, to be Enmaten's sister. These devas partially fuse in the composite figure popularly known as the Three Devas, whose history and iconography provide a striking example of how an emergent deity can overflow the ternary model from which it sprang.

This sample of Japanese religion may strike some as arbitrary, and that is indeed how it appeared to me at first. The deva category, which in Hinduism referred to a clear-cut group of gods defined by their opposition to the asuras, found its way into early Buddhism and was taken up with enthusiasm in esoteric Buddhism, where it became considerably more messy. From Mikkyō, it eventually passed into local religion. With Benzaiten and Ugajin, who merge in the figure of Uga Benzaiten 宇賀弁才天, and with Matarajin, we witness the transition from a medieval Buddhist ideology still largely indebted to India to an early modern religiosity where the discourse of Mikkyō informs—and is gradually superseded by—other cultural forms, particularly the performing arts.

1

EARTHLY POWERS

Bishamonten, Daikokuten, Enmaten

This chapter brings together three devas—Bishamonten 毘沙門天 (Vaiśravaṇa), Daikokuten 大黒天 (Mahākāla), and Enmaten 閻魔天 (Yama). This grouping may seem arbitrary at first, but these devas, while appearing very different at first glance, share strong affinities and are connected by a number of links. All three are chthonian deities, and their relation to the earth explains both their ambiguity and the fact that they were all worshiped as gods of wealth. Bishamonten and Daikokuten, in particular, were frequently paired because they shared associations with the northern direction in the traditional cosmological scheme, and with prosperity, eventually becoming two of the Seven Gods of Fortune (Shichifukujin 七福神) after the Muromachi period.

In the Bishamonten section, after examining traditional descriptions of the god as a martial deity, tamer of demons, god of wealth, and symbol of the north, I draw out the implicit chthonian and demonic characteristics that are expressed in figures such as Tohachi Bishamon and the dual-bodied Bishamon.

In the Daikokuten section, I briefly describe as a domestication the complex process by which the flesh-eating Mahākāla (the Great Black One, the dark aspect of the Hindu god Śiva) eventually became the pot-bellied god of fortune Daikokuten. I first discuss the transformation of the Buddhist Mahākāla into a god of the kitchen and protector of Buddhist monasteries, particularly after his legendary encounter with Saichō 最澄 (767–822), who made him a protector of Enryakuji 延暦寺 on Mount Hiei. I then describe how, through the influence of Tendai and his identification with the Miwa deity Ōmononushi, Daikokuten was transformed into a symbol of prosperity and fecundity, finally becoming one of the Seven Gods of Fortune.

In the Enmaten section, I examine the transformation of the Indian Dharma-king Yama into a Chinese judge of hell, and the coexistence of the two images in medieval Mikkyō. To understand the nature of the esoteric Buddhist Enmaten, I focus on the retinue of the Indian deva Yama as it was depicted in the Enmaten mandalas; in that group, it is Dākinī, Vināyaka, and Cāmuṇḍā who stand out. I then turn to the judiciary function of King Yama and more precisely to his function as a ruler of human destiny, a role he inherited from the ancient Chinese deity Siming (who still appears, split in two, as Yama's two assistants, Siming 司命 and Silu 司録). I conclude with an examination of changing conceptions of the Buddhist underworld.

BISHAMONTEN

Among the devas in the strict sense, chronological precedence goes undeniably to the twelve devas who protect the twelve directions. They form the framework and protecting enclosure of most esoteric rituals. They are also perceived as the source of all other esoteric deities. As one text puts it: "The twelve devas subsume all the devas, *nāgas,* demons, stars, and hell officials."[1] Only one of them, however, became the object of a thriving cult: it is Vaiśravaṇa, the guardian of the north. Indeed, Vaiśravaṇa is a complex deity who deserves a monograph—but this is true of all the deities discussed in this book. As it is only possible to discuss him briefly here, I describe his main features while also bringing out certain apparently marginal aspects that are more relevant to my purpose.

Vaiśravaṇa was originally hardly distinguishable from the other three deva kings or the twelve *yakṣa* commanders. And yet, just like Acala (Fudō) in the *vidyārāja* (wisdom king) group—with whom he will indeed be paired—he distinguished himself from his cohort and rose to the highest rank of the Japanese pantheon as a Dharma protector, a god of battles, and a deity of fortune. I will not dwell on those functions, which, while important to explain Bishamonten's popularity, belong to official mythology (or theology) and express its manifest content. My contention is that these functions do not suffice to explain why Bishamonten was chosen to join groups such as the Three Devas. We need to explore instead the latent associations between Bishamonten and deities such as the earth goddess (Jiten 地天), Kichijōten 吉祥天, and Benzaiten 弁才天, to name just a few.

In early Buddhist mythology, the four deva kings were said to dwell on the four sides of Mount Sumeru and to protect it from demonic intrusions. They came to be seen as regents of the four spatial quarters and rulers of the demonic crowds that populate those quarters. Vaiśravaṇa (Tamonten) controlled the *yakṣas* in the north, Dhṛtarāṣṭra (Jikokuten 持国天) the *gandharvas* and *piśācas* in the east, Virūḍhaka (Zōchōten 増長天) the *nāgas* and the *kuṃbhāṇḍas* in the south, and Virūpakṣa (Kōmokuten 広目天) the great *nāga* kings in the west. In these roles, the four deva kings appear as protectors of the state in the *Golden Light Sūtra Suvarṇaprabāsottama-sūtra (Ch. Jinguangming zuishengwang jing* 金光明最勝王經*).*

Yet Vaiśravaṇa is occasionally presented as a *yakṣa* himself, so he is not just a deva king but also a demon king. With his ninety-one sons who roam over the ten directions riding animals and humans, and with the *yakṣas, rākṣasas, kuṃbhāṇḍas, pretas, piśācas, nāgas,* devas, and constellations that form his retinue, he protects Buddhism and subdues evil.[2] In the magnificent painting in Boston's Museum of Fine Arts (Fig. 1.1), he is represented as standing on the hands of the earth deity and surrounded by female attendants and a motley group of demons, among whom, in the lower right corner, one figure wearing an elephant head as headgear may represent a *vināyaka* demon.

It is not clear how Tamonten became Bishamonten—in other words, how Vaiśravaṇa broke free from the group of four deva kings. Actually, the independent vs. collective aspects in Vaiśravaṇa, which we see as contrasting, were not always clearly distinguished, and the two images of him coexisted.

Vaiśravaṇa is easy to recognize among the martial figures that are commonly found in esoteric Buddhism because of the stūpa-reliquary or pagoda he holds on the palm of his left hand—or sometimes his right hand. He also holds a jeweled club (occasionally a halberd or a trident) in his other hand. (See Figs. 1.2–1.8.) Vaiśravaṇa is mostly known as a protector—of Buddhism, of the state, of the individual—and as a god of wealth. In the medieval period, this last role became increasingly important, and from the Muromachi period onward, he was regarded as one of the Seven Gods of Fortune. Observers have differed on the question of which of these aspects—protection or wealth—is the most fundamental. Let us consider them briefly before widening our view to include other roles and functions.

Bishamonten as Protector

Bishamonten is first and foremost a demon subduer who subjugates maleficent entities—namely, his putative brothers, such as the *gandharvas,* the *piśācas,* the *kumbhāṇḍas,* the *pretas,* the *nāgas,* and *tutti quanti.* More precisely, he is the leader of the *yakṣas* and the *rākṣasas.* He is also a protector of the Buddha's relics and, by extension, of the Buddha Dharma and the Buddhist state.

The military function ascribed to Bishamonten derives from his apotropaic role in driving off demons that threaten the Dharma and its earthly embodiment, the Buddhist ruler. Thus, his image as a god of battles is an extension of his role as demon tamer, a function that he shares with the three other deva kings, as well as with Mahākāla (Daikokuten) and Mārīcī (Marishiten 摩利支天). In the *Golden Light Sūtra,* Vaiśravaṇa vows to protect all those, beginning with the ruler, who will uphold that sūtra. But already Vaiśravaṇa stands alone. Images of Vaiśravaṇa in the caves of Dunhuang attest to the early popularity of his cult.

One of the main legends attesting to his prowess as a martial god in China is his rescuing of the town of Anxi in 742, when the town was

FIGURE 1.1. Vaiśravana and his retinue. Late 12th–early 13th century. Panel, ink, color, gold, and silver on silk. Museum of Fine Arts, Boston.

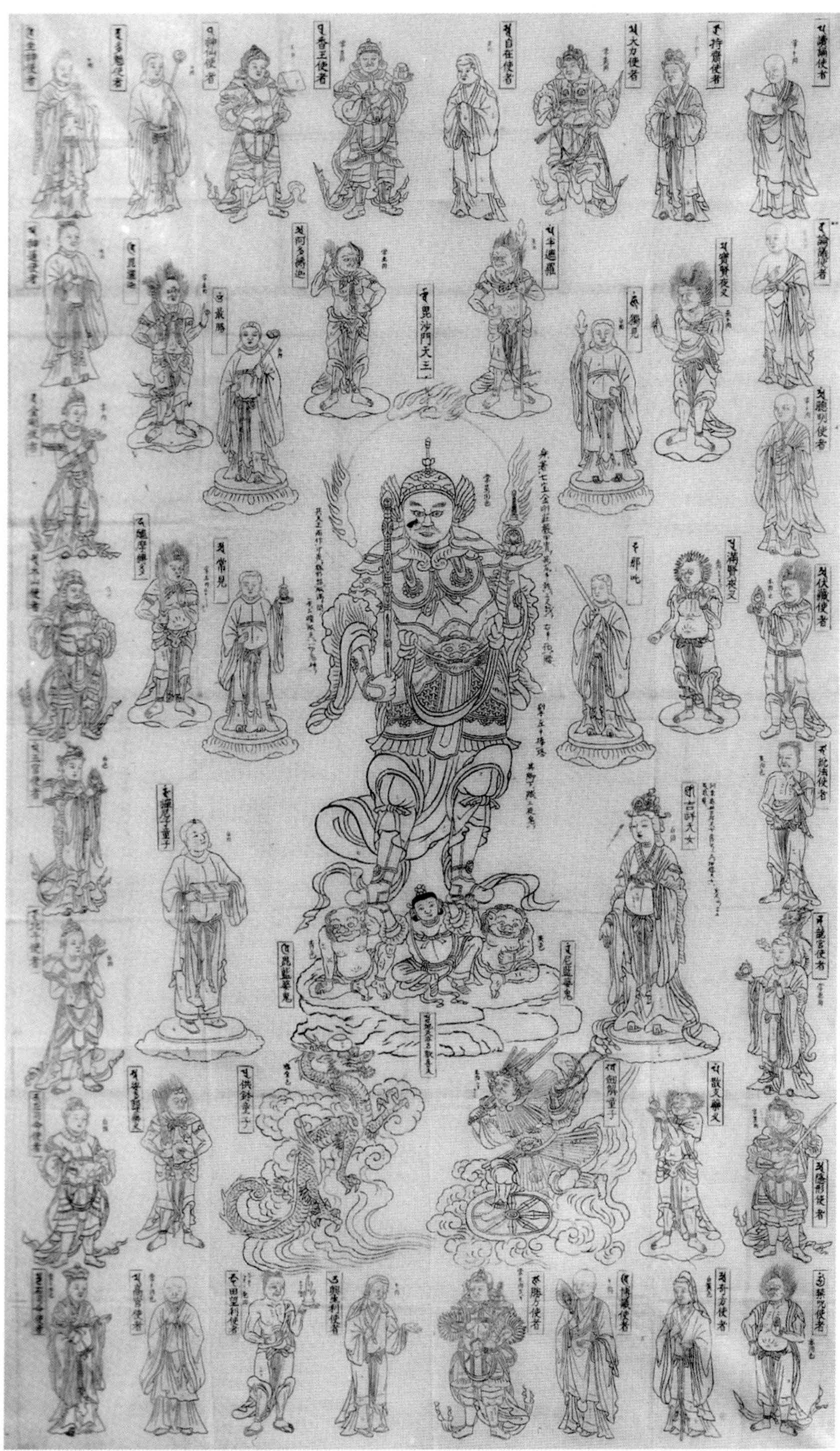

FIGURE 1.2. Bishamonten mandala. Edo period. Sheet, ink on paper. University Art Museum, Kyoto City University of Arts. *BZS* 1072.

FIGURE 1.3. Bishamonten (one of twelve hanging scrolls representing the twelve devas). 1127. Ink and color on silk. Kyoto National Museum.

besieged by a coalition of "barbarians" (Arabs, Sogdians, and Tibetans).[3] In Japan as well, where the *Golden Light Sūtra* (J. *Konkōmyō kyō* 金光明經) became widely known in the Nara period, the first image of Bishamonten was that of a protector. As early as the seventh century, the group of the four deva kings (*shitennō*) was already prominent, as evidenced by the founding of Shitennōji 四天王寺 (known as Tennōji 天王寺 in present-day Osaka). This monastery owes its name to the legendary appearance of the four kings to assist Shōtoku Taishi 聖徳太子 in the decisive battle against his enemy Mononobe no Moriya 物部守屋 (d. 587).[4] On this occasion, Shōtoku Taishi allegedly put an image of Bishamonten on his headgear. As a result, the cult of Bishamonten grew with the legend of Shōtoku Taishi in subsequent periods.

During the Heian period, Bishamonten was regarded essentially as a protector, and in this role he was usually seen as one member of the group of four deva kings. Temples dedicated to these four deities were built in western and northern Japan, regions facing possible foreign intrusions. Following the Chinese precedent just mentioned, the image of the four kings was placed in the Rashōmon 羅生門 Gate at the southern extremity of the capital.[5] As protector of the state, Bishamonten also appeared in a dual-bodied form, known as Sōshin Bishamon 双身毘沙門, in one of the four great rituals of Tendai, the so-called Chinshō Yasha 鎮将夜叉 ritual. He was also the *honzon* or main deity of one of the four "sudden rituals" of Mount Hiei, the other three being centered on the devas Daikokuten, Benzaiten, and Shōten.[6] It was of course the martial aspect of Bishamonten that made him a favorite of the emerging warrior class, and he became the patron deity of warriors. Taira no Kiyomori 平清盛 (1118–1181), for instance, ordered a large statue of Bishamonten to be made in order to defeat the Minamoto. Kusunoki Masasashige 楠木正成 (1294–1336), one of the staunchest supporters of Emperor Go-Daigo 後醍醐 (r. 1318–1339), was also a fervent devotee of Bishamonten.[7]

The God of Wealth

Bishamonten was also worshiped as a god of wealth.[8] Tanaka Hisao and others consider this development to be a relatively late one, dating mostly from the Muromachi period.[9] Tanaka sees it more specifically as a development of the protecting function associated with gold, particularly at Kuramadera on the northern outskirts of Kyoto. Kida Teikichi (var. Kita Sadakichi), on the other hand, derives the wealth-related function from Bishamonten's identification with Kannon in the Kurama legend.[10] Yet Vaiśravaṇa had already taken on the attribute of a god of fortune in India and central Asia. From early on, he had been identified with Kubera, an Indic god of wealth who controlled precious metals and pearls. The fusion of the two deities probably resulted from their

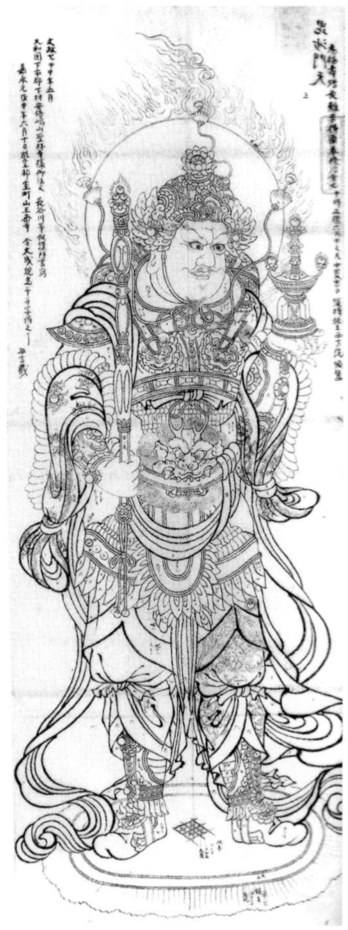

FIGURE 1.4. Bishamonten. Edo period. Sheet, ink on paper. University Art Museum, Kyoto City University of Arts. *BZS* 2247.

FIGURE 1.5. Bishamonten. *Nijū hachibushu*, *TZ* 7: 498, fig. 16.

FIGURE 1.6. Bishamonten (trampling on demon). Heian period, 12th century. Color on wood. Fugen-in, Kōyasan (Wakayama prefecture).

FIGURE 1.7. Bishamonten (trampling on demons). Kamakura period, 13th century. Ink and color on paper. *Shoson zuzōshū*. Kanazawa bunko.

FIGURE 1.8. Ten-armed Bishamon. Edo period. Sheet, ink on paper. University Art Museum, Kyoto City University of Arts. *BZS* 2202.

functional affinity as regents of the north. The different values assigned to the northern direction in the Indian and Chinese cosmologies explain in part the twofold nature of Vaiśravaṇa—as both a demon king and a god of wealth.[11] Kubera was also identified with Pañcika, who formed with the goddess Hārītī a couple replicating that of Vaiśravaṇa and Śrī.

Bishamonten became the object of specific cults at Kurama and Shigisan 信貴山 (in Yamato province). The origin story or *engi* 縁起 of Kuramadera identifies Bishamonten as an emanation of Shō Kannon 聖観音, who was worshiped as a dispenser of blessings.[12] Local nuances were added to this foundation—for instance, the associations with gold and metallurgy—as the cult developed around Kurama.

The *Konjaku monogatari shū* 今昔物語集 tells an interesting story about the strange methods that Bishamonten employed at times to enrich people. A monk who was too poor to stay on Mount Hiei used to go on pilgrimage to Kurama. One evening, as he returned, he met a boy (*chigo* 稚児) and took him home. This boy was actually a young woman, with

FIGURE 1.9. Bishamonten driving away demons. Detail from the *Hekija-e.* 12th century. Color on paper. Nara National Museum.

whom the monk eventually had sex. She gave birth to a child and disappeared. The "child" turned out to be a heap of gold, and the monk became rich.[13]

It is true, however, that the image of Bishamonten as a god of fortune, as reflected, for instance, in the apocryphal *Bishamon kudoku kyō* 毘沙門功徳經, became prevalent during the Muromachi period.[14] Religious specialists known as *shōmonji* 唱門師 (var. 声聞師) recited the *Bishamon kyō* at one of the gates of the imperial palace on the New Year, before going from door to door to perform a shorter version of the same ritual.[15] The menials (*tsurumeso,* var. *inujinin* 犬神人) of Gion 祇園 Shrine also performed that role.[16]

It was during that period that the apotropaic image of Bishamonten developed. In his apotropaic role, Bishamonten appears in a painted scroll known as the *Hekija-e* 辟邪絵 (Images to Exorcize Evil), together with a strange group of demon tamers including Tenkeisei 天刑星 (var. Tengyōshō), the Gandharva king Candana, and Shōki 鍾馗 (Ch. Zhong Kui), as well as a monstrous demon-devouring insect. In this scroll, he is shown aiming his bulb-arrows at two winged demons that are trying to hinder a Buddhist devotee of the *Lotus Sūtra* (Fig. 1.9).[17]

Bishamonten also appears as an apotropaic deity in the Shushō-e 修正会 ritual performed at New Year. In this ritual, it was originally specialists wearing four-eyed masks, the *hōsōshi,* derived from the *fangxiangshi*

FIGURE 1.10. Bishamonten triad. Edo period. Sheet, ink on paper. University Art Museum, Kyoto City University of Arts. *BZS* 2199.

FIGURE 1.11. Bishamonten triad. Edo period. Sheet, ink on paper. University Art Museum, Kyoto City University of Arts. *BZS* 2200.

方相氏 of the Chinese nuo 儺 exorcism (J. *tsuina* 追儺), who drove away the demons. When these ritualists, however, came to be perceived themselves as demons, their exorcistic function was taken over by Bishamonten and the *nāga* (Ryūten 龍天).[18] This evolution may be explained in part by the fact that, in their role of exorcizing the four directions, the *hōsōshi* resembled the four deva kings.[19] Toward the end of the Kamakura period, the goal of the Shushō-e ritual became that of chasing and beating the demon Vināyaka, a disrupter of cosmic order.[20]

Bishamonten was also believed to protect individuals and lead them to awakening. Already in the *Qifo bapusa suoshuo da tuoluoni shenzhou jing* 七佛八菩薩所說大陀羅尼神呪經 (Sūtra of the Divine Incantations, the Great *Dhāraṇī* Taught by the Seven Buddhas and the Eight

Bodhisattvas), Vaiśravaṇa declares: "In the past, cultivating awakening, I became the demon king for the sake of beings. Those who linger in the darkness of ignorance, I open their eyes with my golden axe. Once their eye of wisdom is open, they pass beyond life and death and ascend to nirvāṇa."[21]

Bishamonten and the North

The likely key to Bishamonten's popularity, however, lies in his association with the north. Although each direction had its own demons, the northern quarter remained, in the Chinese cosmological schema, the demonic region *par excellence,* and this contributed in large part to the importance of Vaiśravaṇa as a directional deity. In Indian mythology, the north was assigned to the god Kubera (or Kuvera), the god of wealth with whom Vaiśravaṇa came to be identified.

The symbolic association of Vaiśravaṇa with the north also explains why he is sometimes identified with the Northern Dipper or with the pole star (and its deity, Myōken Bosatsu 妙見菩薩). The identification of Bishamonten with the pole star is illustrated by the fact that in the *Yūzū nenbutsu engi* 融通念佛縁起 of Anrakuji 安楽寺 (in Nara), he becomes the central deity of a star mandala. In a Bishamonten triad preserved at Saimyōji 西明寺, on the eastern shore of Lake Biwa, Bishamonten appears, standing like Myōken on a tortoise (i.e., Xuanwu 玄武, the Dark Warrior, symbol of the north), flanked by Kichijōten and Zennishi Dōji.[22]

Bishamonten became an object of devotion for Sakanoue no Tamuramaro 坂上田村麻呂 (758–811), the general who was sent in 791 to pacify the Emishi 蝦夷, the people of northern Japan who resisted the expansion of central rule and were demonized as "northern barbarians."[23] In Tsugaru, the northermost part of Honshū, the name of the Northern Chronogram, Hokushin 北辰 (that is, Myōken), is read "Bishamonten." Tamuramaro is said to have worshiped the seven stars of the Northern Dipper, giving them the names of Bishamonten. His pacification of Tsugaru is said to have resulted from his performance of secret rituals invoking Bishamonten, Myōken, and the seven stars. Indeed, the seven temples and shrines dedicated to Bishamonten in this area are said to form the pattern of the seven stars and are connected to Tamuramaro.

Because of the symbolic equivalence of the north and the center in the case of the pole star, Bishamonten became linked to the center. In this fashion, he came to be perceived as a ruler of human destiny, like Myōken and the seven stars, or the buddha Yakushi and the twelve spirit-generals. The symbolism of the north also connects him with the cyclical sign (or deity) of the Rat, who presides over the beginning of the temporal cycle.[24] This sign came to be associated with one of Yakushi's twelve acolytes, the divine general Kumbhīra (J. Konpira 金比羅), which should not surprise us when we recall that Vaiśravaṇa was identified with Kubera.[25] At Hie

Shrine, the god Daigyōji 大行事 (whose *honji* is Bishamonten) is related to the Rat, and his shrine is called Oratory of the Rat (Nezumi no hokora 鼠の祠). According to the *Yōtenki* 耀天記, the deity of that oratory is the spirit of the Day of the Rat, and its *honji* is Bishamonten.[26]

From all these examples, it is clear that the spatiotemporal equivalence derived from Chinese cosmology and esoteric Buddhist astrology implies that Bishamonten, like the Roman god Janus and similar deities, presides to beginnings and rules over human destinies.

Once a Demon, Always a Demon

In spite of his association with the Buddha's relics, Vaiśravaṇa remained a fundamentally demonic being. He is, after all, a demon who has turned against his kin. The fiends against whom he protects humans are his own brothers, the *yakṣas,* and not surprisingly he is occasionally represented as a kind of *yakṣa* himself. His ambiguity resonates in his title of Demon King (Maō 魔王), a name initially reserved to Māra. As leader of the *yakṣas* and the *rākṣasas,* he retains from his former life a fierceness that, even though transmuted into a martial quality, is nonetheless uncanny. As one source puts it, "When Vaiśravaṇa is joyful, the *yakṣas* do not harm humans; when he is angry, they cause havoc."[27]

Judging from his appearance, however, joyfulness does not seem to be one of his prevalent states of mind (see, e.g., Figs. 12–14). In other words, Vaiśravaṇa is, at least potentially, a god of obstacles whom it is important to propitiate. The cloth may make the monk, and armor the warrior, but under his armor a demon remains dormant, subdued for the moment by the stūpa-reliquary he holds.[28] This demonic nature is suggested by his long fangs pointing downward. Another clue can be seen in his retinue, especially in his son Naḍa (Ch. Nezha 哪吒), a violent god who represents an aspect of Vaiśravaṇa.[29] Nezha protects the state by tearing out the eyes and heart of evil men and breaking their head with a *vajra* staff.[30] As in the case of the *vidyārājas,* the textbook reference to Vaiśravaṇa's Buddhist compassion must be taken with a grain of salt. Also noteworthy in this respect is the demon face that appears on the belt or belly of Tobatsu Bishamon. The same iconographic detail is found in the representation of another strongly demonic figure, the great general called Deep Sands (J. Jinja Daishō 深砂大将), an emanation of Vaiśravaṇa. This demon is sometimes linked with Āṭavaka (J. Daigensui 太元帥), Vaiśravaṇa's brother and one of the eight *yakṣa* generals in his retinue.[31] Deep Sands is said to have appeared to the Chinese monk and pilgrim Xuanzang 玄奘 (ca. 602–664) during his crossing of the central Asian wilderness and to have become his protector—after being duly tamed. This was not, however, their first encounter. A later legend has it that Xuanzang, in past attempts to go to India, had been devoured by the demon seven times, and the seven skulls on Jinja Daishō's necklace are precisely those of

FIGURE 1.12. Jinja Daishō. Kamakura period, 13th century. Color on wood. Kongōbuji, Kōyasan (Wakayama prefecture).

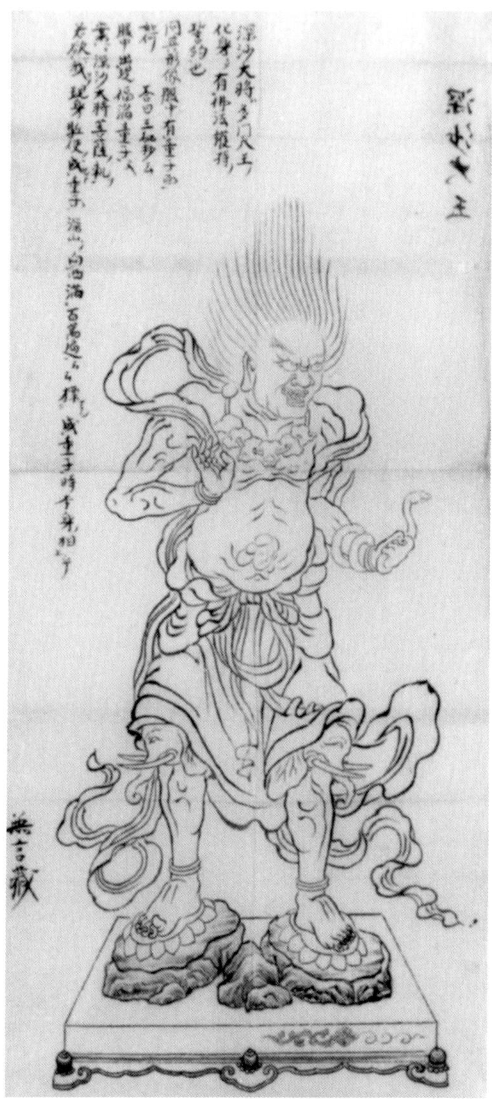

FIGURE 1.13. (*Left*) Jinja Daishō. Edo period. Sheet, ink on paper. University Art Museum, Kyoto City University of Arts. *BZS* 2204.

FIGURE 1.14. King Deep Sands (Jinja-ō). *Besson zakki, TZ* 3: 613, fig. 276.

Xuanzang's past incarnations. This legend, apparently unknown in China, became widespread in Japan during the Muromachi period. Jinja Daishō was already popular in ninth-century Japan, and he was regarded, in particular, as one of the protectors of Kongōbuji 金剛峰寺 on Mount Kōya.

A statue at Kongōbuji dated to the Kamakura period shows him half naked, with snakes coiled around his arms, and wearing a necklace of skulls and elephant-head kneecaps (Fig. 1.12).[32] This formidable figure also played an important role in Shugendō, particularly in the Nikkō tradition, where he became the protector of Rinnōji 輪王寺 and is worshipped in a small shrine at the entrance of the monastery compound (by the riverside, as seems fit).[33]

FIGURE 1.15. Tobatsu Bishamon. Heian period. Color on wood. Shinnō-in, Kōyasan (Wakayama prefecture).

FIGURE 1.16. (*Right*) Tobatsu Bishamon. Heian period, 12th century. Color on wood. Nara National Museum.

Tobatsu Bishamon and the Earth Deity

The martial attribute of Vaiśravaṇa is most obvious in the representation known in Japan as Tobatsu Bishamon 兜跋毘沙門 (see, e.g., Figs. 1.15–1.18), a form of Vaiśravaṇa that shows strong central Asian influence, and from which the kingdom of Khotan and its royal lineage are said to have descended.[34] But perhaps this martial element—typical of the explicit mythology—is less significant than the royal and chthonian symbolism. In this representation, Vaiśravaṇa is clad in long-skirted armor and his helmet is replaced by a kind of tiara. He stands on the hands of the earth goddess (Pṛthivī), whose body half emerges from the ground (Figs. 1.15–1.18).[35] She is sometimes flanked by two demons, Niranba 尼藍婆 (Skt. Nilva or Nīlavajra) and Biranba 毘藍婆 (Bilva or Vilambā/Vairambha), who are said to be Vaiśravaṇa's male and female attendants (Fig. 1.16).[36] This representation has been intensively studied by art historians and historians of religions. Phyllis Granoff, for example, has brought out the royal symbolism in Khotanese mythology, founded on a notion of

FIGURE 1.17. (*Left*) Seated Tobatsu Bishamon. Kamakura period, 13th century. Ink and color on paper. *Shoson zuzōshū*. Kanazawa bunko.

FIGURE 1.18. (*Right*) Tobatsu Bishamon. Kamakura period, 13th century. Ink and color on paper. *Shoson zuzōshū*. Kanazawa bunko.

deified royalty in which the king, represented as the husband of the earth, is supported by the earth deity.[37] The legend of Khotan is replete, too, with chthonian symbolism: Aśoka's consort, during a visit to Khotan, sees Vaiśravaṇa and becomes pregnant. When Aśoka abandons the child in the wilderness, a breast emerges from the earth to nurse the child—a detail providing an important clue to Vaiśravaṇa's chthonian nature.

Dwelling for a moment on the iconographic motif of the earth deity and the two demons that usually appear under Bishamonten's feet, we can observe that the presence of the demons complicates the picture, weakening the royal symbolism of the hierogamic image described above. Already in the *Golden Light Sūtra,* Vaiśravaṇa is depicted as closely related to the earth deity (as well as to Śrī and Sarasvatī). Śrī (Kichijōten), in particular, becomes his consort. As Madeleine Biardeau pointed out, she is a manifestation of the earth—under its beneficent aspect.[38] Benzaiten, the Japanese form of Sarasvatī, inherited several of Kichijōten's characteristics, but, as we will see, she is more complex and also represents the dark,

FIGURE 1.19. Tobatsu Bishamon. Edo period. Sheet, ink on paper. University Art Museum, Kyoto City University of Arts. *BZS* 2194.

chthonian powers of the earth. The *Asabashō* 阿娑縛抄 by Shōchō 承最 (1205–1282) explains that one should invoke Kichijōten when one prays for fertility, and Benzaiten when one has "violated" the earth.[39] The *Golden Light Sūtra* claims that Bishamonten and the two female deities are actually one single power, which manifests itself as Kichijōten for people of superior capacities, as Benzaiten for those of medium capacities, and as Bishamonten for those of inferior capacities.[40]

In several representations, Vaiśravaṇa crushes these two demons underfoot. It is important to distinguish the earth goddess, who acts here as a pedestal (hence as a kind of protector), from the demons whom Vaiśravaṇa and other similar figures usually trample, and who, from an iconographic standpoint, also serve, albeit reluctantly, as pedestals. In certain cases, however, the difference between the earth goddess and the two demons fades out.[41] Indeed, the latter are after all only another aspect of the chthonian powers represented by the former. Iwasa Kanzō argues that the two demons are actually "companion spirits" (*kushōjin* 倶生神), that is, deities who spy on humans in order to report their actions to King Yama.[42] Although Iwasa does not explain how he reached that conclusion, his interpretation constitutes an important link to the role of Bishamonten as an embryological deity—a question we will come back to explore later.

The two demons are also said to symbolize the troupes of *yakṣas* and *rākṣasas* controlled by Vaiśravaṇa. Depending on the emphasis, they can be seen as being trampled by Vaiśravaṇa or, conversely, as supporting him. In the former case they are fiends, in the latter, acolytes. That the latter is usually the case may be inferred from their grotesque, almost comic appearance, which recalls that of the two attendants of En no Gyōja 役行者, the legendary ancestor of Shugendō.

The earth deity, on the other hand, is more dignified, although her appearance too has evolved from that of an aristocratic Chinese lady to that of a local, "Shintō" deity. In these representations, she is occasionally called Kangiten 歓喜天 (Bliss Deva), a name usually reserved for the dual-bodied

Vināyaka, the elephant-headed deity represented in sexual embrace with his twin-looking consort.[43] This motif also calls to mind the figure of the earth deity in the famous episode of Māra's attack on the Buddha. As noted above, this image has been interpreted as symbolizing the "hierogamy" between the king (representing heaven) and the earth. Yet the motif is fundamentally ambiguous, and it is not always easy to distinguish the status of the earth deity from that of the demons that flank her.

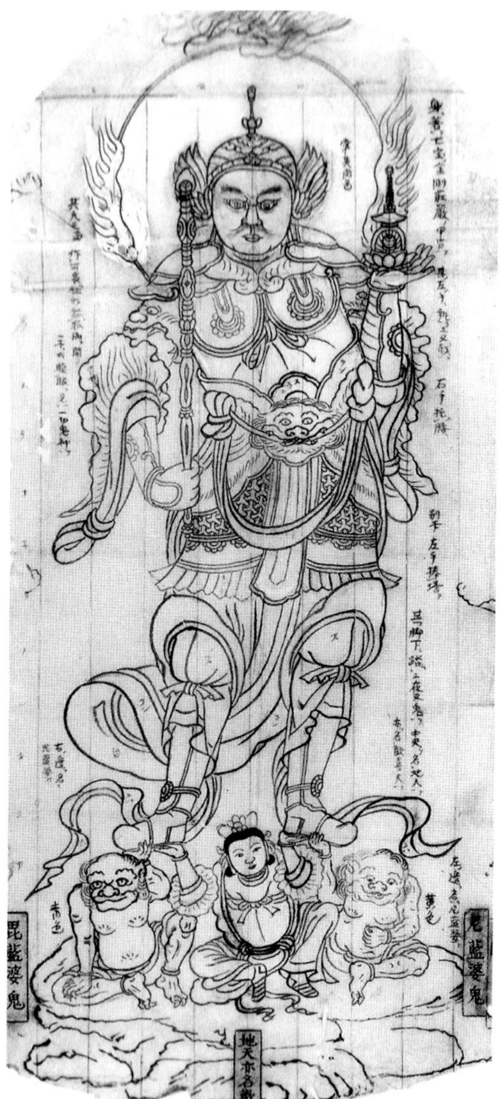

FIGURE 1.20. Tobatsu Bishamon. Edo period. Sheet, ink on paper. University Art Museum, Kyoto City University of Arts. *BZS* 2195.

Bishamonten Mandalas

As his cult developed, Bishamonten, who initially had been merely one of the four protectors—albeit the *primus inter pares*—at the periphery of esoteric mandalas, now moved to the center of his own mandala.[44] The oldest such mandala appears to be the seed-letter mandala of Enrakuji 円楽寺, as shown in the *Mandara shū* 曼荼羅集. Another interesting mandala, the *Bishamon mandara zu* 毘沙門曼荼羅図, is a printed image preserved at the Shōrin-an 勝林庵 (Bishamon-dō 毘沙門堂) of Tōfukuji 東福寺.[45] In the central court, Bishamonten holds a trident in his left hand while standing on the earth goddess and two demons (as in the representations of Tobatsu Bishamon). He is flanked by his consort Kichijōten (Skt. Śrī or Lakśmī), who carries fruit offerings, and by his son Zennishi Dōji 禅膩師童子; his four other sons are standing at the corners.[46] In the second court, we find a group of wrathful deities, namely, the eight great *yakṣa* generals, who are sometimes described as Bishamonten's brothers. In the outer court, finally, are Bishamonten's twenty-eight acolytes (*shisha* 使者), whose names refer to the kinds of wishes they are believed to fulfill. This type of popular print shows that the cult of Bishamonten and his retinue, like that of Benzaiten and her fifteen attendants, was widespread by the end of the medieval period.

In the Kuramayama mandala 鞍馬山曼荼羅, Bishamonten appears as guardian of the northern gate of the imperial capital (Kyoto). The *tengu*-like deity behind him—whose name, Maō, means "Demon King"—is actually one of his manifestations. He is flanked by Kichijōten and Zennishi Dōji, as well as by two centipedes. The latter creatures, for obscure reasons—perhaps because they are believed to kill snakes, or because of an etymological association with ore veins—became his emblematic animals in medieval Japan.

Tohachi Bishamon

The name Tobatsu Bishamon inspired another, very different representation (despite the near synonymy)—that of Tohachi Bishamon 刀八毘沙門, a figure usually traced to the Tendai priest Son'i 尊意 (859–940). The fearsome, quasi-arachnean appearance of that deity constitutes a kind of visual pun, since the swords he holds in eight of his hands derive from the aberrant transcription of Tobatsu as Tohachi 'sword eight.' This ten- or twelve-armed, one- or four-headed Bishamonten usually rides a giant lion reminiscent of Mañjuśrī's mount. His four heads look like those of Fudō 不動 and Aizen 愛染, Bishamonten and Benzaiten, while his lion headgear recalls Aizen's. This image became widespread in the Muromachi period and was still popular in the Edo period.

A recent exhibition catalogue shows some fascinating iconographic developments.[47] The oldest one, it seems, is a scroll from Imakumano Kannonji 今熊野観音寺 in Kyoto dating from the Muromachi period (Fig. 1.21). This Bishamonten has three heads, twelve arms, and rides a lion (who stands on four lotuses, on a Dharma wheel). He wears lion headgear, like Aizen, and three small acolytes are visible above his head, two of them resembling Dakiniten's fox-riding acolytes. In two of his hands he holds a jewel and a key, traditional attributes of Dakiniten and Benzaiten, and his feet rest on two turtles, a feature reminiscent of Myōken. But the most interesting detail is that his mandorla is bordered by a motif formed by eight white foxes.

The next examplar, from Fushimi Inari Shrine in Kyoto, has been somewhat misleadingly labeled Inari mandala 稲荷曼荼羅 (Fig. 1.22). Dated to the Muromachi period, it shows a four-faced Bishamonten riding a large lion. His attributes, as well as the tortoises under his feet, are similar to those of the Kannonji examplar. But the three acolytes above his headgear have been replaced by two small buddhas, and there are no foxes in his mandorla. On the other hand, five of his sixteen attendants ride white foxes, like Dakiniten's acolytes. The number of these attendants calls to mind the sixteen or fifteen youths that form the retinue of Benzaiten. Among them, one recognizes Daikokuten, two *nāga* kings, the Inari deity in the form of a man carrying rice saplings, and Bishamonten's usual acolytes, Kichijōten and Zennishi. The others seem to be the same as Dakiniten's acolytes. According to the scroll box's inscription, the painting was "transmitted" at Ryūkō-in 龍光院 on Mount Kōya. This form of Bishamonten is rare enough to be described in a catalogue as "strange and unheard of," and the commentator wonders whether it could be a secret form of the god Inari.[48]

FIGURE 1.21. Tohachi Bishamon. Muromachi period, 16th century. Color on silk. Imakumano Kannonji, Kyoto.

FIGURE 1.22. Inari mandala. Muromachi period, 14th century. Color on silk. Fushimi Inari Shrine, Kyoto.

FIGURE 1.23. Tohachi Bishamon. Edo period. Sheet, ink on paper. University Art Museum, Kyoto City University of Arts. *BZS* 2203.

Also noteworthy are two scrolls from Rinnōji in Nikkō. The first one shows Tohachi Bishamon riding a lion and flanked by two white foxes (Fig. 1.24).[49] In the upper part of the scroll is a young immortal, seated on a lotus, with a sword on his shoulder and a Dharma wheel in his left hand. Above him are two dragons guarding the wish-fulfilling jewel, flanked by sun and moon disks. The figure of the divine youth had been identified with Kūkai in Monkan's 文観 *Goyuigō daiji* 御遺告大事, and the Rinnōji scroll bears the influence of that representation.[50] This painting can therefore be seen as typical of the cult that developed in medieval Shingon around the wish-fulfilling jewel of Mount Murō—except that Tohachi Bishamon does not normally appear in this context.

The second Rinnōji scroll is a Dakiniten mandala, misleadingly labeled Izuna mandala, in which Tohachi Bishamon appears as the central deity under the alias Dakiniten. I will return to this remarkable mandala in Chapter 3, consecrated to Dakiniten.

These representations suggest that Tohachi Bishamonten, in spite of his strong-armed, over-armed appearance, was worshiped more as a god of wealth, like Dakiniten and Benzaiten, than as a warrior deity. Incidentally, it is that image that the German physician Philipp Franz von Siebold (1796–1866), visiting Japan in the early nineteenth century, encountered in an iconographic compendium entitled *Butsuzō zui* 佛像図彙 and reproduced in the ethnographical section of his work, *Nippon* (1832).[51]

FIGURE 1.24. Tohachi Bishamon (with youth). Edo period. Color on silk. Rinnōji, Nikkō (Tochigi prefecture).

The Dual-bodied Bishamon

Let us now turn to another peculiar—and to some, aberrant—form of Bishamonten, that of the dual-bodied (Sōshin) Bishamon.[52] This particular form appears in a secret Tendai ritual for the protection of the state, the Chinshō Yasha 鎮将夜叉 ritual.[53] The importance of this ritual derives from the fact that the location of Mount

Hiei, northeast of the capital, corresponds to that of the Demon Gate (*kimon* 鬼門), and its rituals were aimed at protecting the capital from demonic influences. No one was better qualified for this task than Bishamonten, the leader (and tamer) of the *yakṣas*. In this ritual, Bishamonten is flanked by his consort Kichijōten, the five great princes (*go daiōji* 五大王子), the eight great *yakṣa* generals, the twenty-eight emissaries, and two figures called Kokuni Dōji 黒耳童子 (Black-eared Youth) and Hanten Baramon 半天波羅門.[54]

FIGURE 1.25. Dual-bodied Bishamon. *Asabashō*, *TZ* 9: 429, fig. 71.

The ritual's object of worship, the dual-bodied *honzon,* consists of two addorsed figures, standing on a circular pedestal.[55] One of them holds a one-pronged *vajra* between the palms of his hands, the other a Dharma wheel (Fig. 1.25). This image is said to represent the union of Bishamonten and Kichijōten, who are indeed often described as husband and wife.[56] In the present case, they are said to symbolize the two esoteric mandalas, and they are interpreted in terms of Tendai nonduality.[57] The *Keiran shūyōshū* explains this dual figure as follows: "It means that this worthy [Bishamonten] and Kichijōten are nondual and secretly united. This expresses the teaching of the nonduality of Womb and Vajra realms, the equality of principle and wisdom."[58] Kōshū adds that Bishamonten guides beings toward awakening and rules over the supramundane realm, whereas Kichijōten attends to "worldly dharmas" such as profane happiness. Perhaps the apparent opposition between these two realms explains why the two deities are shown back to back; but the two realities they represent are actually one, because those who reach awakening get worldly happiness by the same token. We have here another expression of the notion of fundamental awakening (*hongaku* 本覚) that equates the phenomenal world with ultimate reality.[59]

All this would make (some kind of) sense if the two figures were not actually male: but the alleged Kichijōten, like her partner, is clad in armor, and she has a red face, three eyes, and even fangs—a far cry from her usual seductive appearance. This dual-bodied Bishamon is also called the Eight-fanged Deva King (Yatsuge Tennō 八牙天王). Conscious of the discrepancy, Kōshū mentions a tradition that sees them as two brothers, Hanten Baramon and Tamonten:

> "Hanten Baramon and Tamonten mean a nondual body." According to the origin story (*engi*), in the past Tamonten produced the thought of awakening (*bodhicitta*) at the same time as Hanten; but whereas the former was diligent, the latter was not. Out of resentment, Hanten vowed to become a god of obstacles. Tamonten symbolizes the Dharma nature (Skt. *dharmatā,* J. *hosshō* 法性), while Hanten symbolizes ignorance (*avidyā,* J. *mumyō* 無明). Because the two dharmas are interdependent, in this dual body [Tamonten and Hanten] stand back to back. . . . Because ignorance and the Dharma nature are in essence the same, (these two bodies) are inseparable.[60]

Apparently the ambiguity of Bishamonten as a god of obstacles made it necessary to provide him with an evil twin. Thus, not only does the interpretation of the dual-bodied Bishamon as symbolizing the sexual union between Bishamonten and Kichijōten seem counterintuitive, given their unnatural back-to-back position, but it also differs from that of a moral opposition between Bishamonten and Hanten. This difference, however, is glossed over by a metaphysical reduction in which both pairs (Bishamonten/Kichijōten and Bishamonten/Hanten Baramon) simply express the opposition between the mundane and supramundane realms.

The *Asabashō* describes the ritual centered on the dual-bodied Bishamon as aimed at seduction (*keiai* 敬愛) and the obtaining of happiness (*fukutoku* 福徳). This interpretation, of course, fits better with the couple formed by Bishamonten and Kichijōten than with the agonistic relationship between Bishamonten and Hanten Baramon, but it bluntly contradicts the iconography. The latter might refer to another ritual aimed at subjugation, and might have resulted from a confusion.

The figure of Hanten Baramon, symbolizing here Bishamonten's evil twin—and his non-Buddhist (Brahmin) rival—does not appear elsewhere. Its prototype may be the demon Rāvaṇa, who is presented in the *Laṇkāvatāra-sūtra* as Vaiśravaṇa's sworn enemy. Lalou argues that Vaiśravaṇa/Kubera had another twin brother, namely Gaṇeśa, and what looks like fangs in this representation may actually be tusks.[61] Thus, the motif of the dual-bodied Bishamonten might be related to that of the dual-bodied Vināyaka (Kangiten 歓喜天). The affinities between Bishamonten and Gaṇeśa/Vināyaka (J. Shōten) are also suggested by the fact that the dual-bodied Bishamon is sometimes called "dual-nosed" (*sōbi* 雙鼻).[62] Rolf Stein considers the two dual-bodied figures (Bishamonten and Kangiten) as a further bipartition of the pair formed in Hinduism by Skanda and Gaṇeśa. For him, this logic of bipartition is inherent to the motif of the gatekeepers. The fact that Bishamonten and his partner stand back to back would then signify that they protect the northern and southern directions, and it would have nothing to do with the sexual model implied by the identification of the two figures as Bishamonten and Kichijōten. Another link between Bishamonten and Shōten can perhaps be found in a ritual that consists in bathing an icon of the god in oil. In Tendai, one bathes the dual-bodied Bishamon; in Shingon, the dual-bodied Kangiten.

If Vināyaka (Shōten) is the leader of all the *vināyakas* (animal-headed demons), Bishamonten is their tamer. In the *Ungadaya giki,* for instance, after vowing to protect the Dharma, Vaiśravaṇa offers an incantation that protects beings against all *vināyakas.*[63] Again, Tobatsu Bishamon is sometimes said to trample *vināyakas*—although he is usually shown trampling ordinary (and rather caricatural) demons, whose elemental nature is suggested by their confused form (sometimes they look hardly distinguishable from a lump of earth).

Lalou has emphasized the hybrid (bovine and divine) origins of Vaiśravaṇa (the son of a cow and of Brahmā), as well as his androgynous nature and his propensity to change gender.[64] Perhaps the dual (addorsed) Bishamonten (said to represent the couple Vaiśravaṇa/Śrī) is a repetition of his primitive androgyny. In this case, however, the two figures are the same—the only changes being the position of their arms, and the attributes they hold.[65] One may also speak of twinship—the two interpretations are not exclusive. Alfred Foucher noted that Kubera and Gaṇeśa look like twins, whereas Gaṇeśa looks very different from his brother Skanda, the handsome youth.[66] Lalou also emphasized the motif of the fangs (in the case of Kubera/Vaiśravaṇa) and tusks (in the case of Gaṇeśa) as symbols of wealth.

Another example of the twin motif is the pairing of Fudō and Bishamonten in various contexts, most notably in the so-called Ox King ritual.[67] Fudō is said to protect Dainichi's Dharma, while Bishamon protects Shaka's Dharma. In the *Taiheiki* 太平記, however, the two "youths" (*dōji*) Fudō and Bishamonten protect the devotees of the *Lotus Sūtra.* The *Keiran shūyōshū,* too, by pairing Fudō and Bishamonten, seems to consider them Dharma protectors (*gohō* 護法), and therefore to downgrade them to the status of young attendants (*dōji* 童子).[68]

Embryological Symbolism

Since sexual and embryological symbolism are often paired, do we find any of the latter in Bishamonten? I would point to one iconographical detail of the dual-bodied image: the two figures are standing back to back on a large lotus leaf, turned downward. Two lotus buds grow from it, their stalk half-hidden by their bodies, and emerge above their head. The embryological symbolism of the lotus is evident. The downward lotus leaf is a frequent symbol of the placenta, and here the lotus stalk seems connected to the figures' lower body, as if it were an umbilical cord. In the *Keiran shūyōshū,* the robe (or armor) of Bishamonten is explicitly compared to a placenta.[69] Likewise, the lotus bud that emerges from the two figures' head symbolizes the unborn fetus. In other words, the two deities may, at a subliminal level, represent two twins in the womb and symbolize the "deities born at the same time" (*kushōjin*), who are said to follow people throughout their life. In the absence of textual confirmation, however, this must remain speculation.

Bishamonten, the Buddha's Relics, and the Jewel

Bishamonten is said to owe his alias Tamonten ([He Who] Has Heard Much) to the fact that the stūpa he holds on the palm of his left (sometimes right) hand contains the entire Buddhist canon. However, there are other far-fetched etymologies for that name. The importance of the stūpa as his attribute is reflected in the fact that his symbolic (*samaya*) form is an iron stūpa or tower, which is identified with the Iron Tower in southern India. This tower, the *fons et origo* of all esoteric teachings, is also the origin of the wish-fulfilling jewel allegedly brought to Japan by Kūkai.[70] For all these reasons, Vaiśravaṇa was from very early on closely associated, and eventually identified, with the relics of the Buddha. By the same token, he benefited from the cult of the relics that was significantly boosted by the association of the relics with the wish-fulfilling jewel.[71] In certain medieval texts, Bishamonten is identified with the jewel.[72] His seed-letter (Skt. *vai,* J. *bi*) is said to produce all things; for that reason, it is the seed-letter of the wish-fulfilling jewel.[73] In the Ox King ritual—a ritual specially performed at the beginning of the year and centered on Bishamonten and Fudō Myōō—Bishamonten was identified with the Buddha's relics and with the jewel, both of which, like the two horns of an ox, were said to symbolize nonduality.[74] The ox king is also contrasted with the deer king (*rokuō* 鹿王) in terms of a contrast between the "jewel of the earth" and the "jewel of space."[75] Perhaps this identification with the wish-fulfilling jewel led to Bishamonten's identification with Dakiniten—as expressed, for instance, in the Izuna mandala of Rinnōji.

Bishamonten as the Ox King

Another interesting, albeit less visible association is that between Bishamonten and the ox, in the so-called Ox King (*goō* 牛王) ritual. We recall that Lalou has emphasized the bovine origins of Vaiśravaṇa (as Kubera). There is indeed an ox-headed manifestation of Bishamonten, although its representation was not widespread.[76] The *Asabashō* also mentions a legend that once, when an epidemic broke out in the country of Tohatsura (Tokhara?), the Eleven-faced Avalokiteśvara manifested himself as an eleven-fold ox-headed Vaiśravaṇa.[77]

The *Keiran shūyōshū* affirms the identity between the ox king and the relics of the Buddha or the wish-fulfilling jewel on the ground that they all symbolize nonduality.[78] It also explains why, in Tendai, Bishamonten is related to the Ox constellation (Go-shuku 牛宿), one of the twenty-eight lunar lodgings: they both rule over the northeast (corresponding to the Demon Gate)—as does Mount Hiei, located to the northeast of the imperial palace. This directional symbolism justifies the importance of the Ox constellation in the Ox King ritual. In Indian esoteric Buddhist cosmology, however, the northeast has a more positive connotation, since it is the first of the twelve directions and therefore symbolizes the beginning of things, the union of yin and yang, and the nonduality of the mind and its objects.[79]

The Ox King ritual also shared affinities with rituals centered on Daiitoku Myōō 大威徳明王 (Skt. Yamāntaka) and Enmaten (Yama), because both deities ride a bull or buffalo, and both were perceived as emanations of the earth deity.[80] Iconographically, the image of Bishamonten does resemble certain representations of the male earth deity, Kenrō Jijin 堅牢地神. The *Sange yōryakki* 山家要略記, after a passage claiming that Kenrō Jijin "is the father and mother of the 84,000 demons (*kijin* 鬼神)," adds that this passage establishes the identity between that deity and Bishamonten.[81] The conflation of these various rituals was possible because the Japanese language does not always distinguish between ox, bull, and buffalo. Śiva/Maheśvara's mount is a bull (Nandi); Yama's, a water buffalo; and Yamāntaka's, a bull. At any rate, all these animals were seen as having an essentially chthonian nature.

Bishamonten was also linked with the pestilence god Gozu Tennō (the bull-headed divine king). In the *Hoki naiden* 簠簋内伝, seven of Gozu Tennō's eight princes (Hachiōji 八王子) have the same names as the great *yakṣa* generals, all of whom are emanations or children of Bishamonten. In the *Ungadaya giki* and in the *Shintōshū* 神道集, they are all the same. The fact that the retinue of two gods is the same suggests that these two gods share deep affinities, even if they remain distinct. In another context, Tohachi Bishamon shares his acolytes with Dakiniten.

One significant, albeit latent association is that between Bishamonten and the archetypal god of obstacles, Kōjin 荒神. We have already noted the link between Vaiśravaṇa and Jinja Daishō, a typically "wild" deity (*kōjin*). Bishamonten is also said to be the *honji* of Hata no Kawakatsu 秦河勝, the ally of Shōtoku Taishi in his fight against Mononobe no Moriya. Kawakatsu is mentioned in the *Nihonshoki* 日本書紀 as the founder of Kōryūji 広隆寺 in Uzumasa (Kyoto), and he is also celebrated in the Nō tradition as the ancestor of *sarugaku* 太秦. In his legend, we learn that after his death he became a wild deity, worshiped under the name Ōsake Daimyōjin 大避大明神.

The case of Bishamonten recalls the importance of the directional grid as a generating schema that fosters various associations of ideas and deities. This kind of schema, however, is both a way to domesticate resilient deities and notions and to make them "wildly" proliferate. Therefore, the structural or systemic aspect of that schema should not make us forget the demonic, untamed aspect of Bishamonten, or the symbolic proliferation of this and related figures in the interstices of the esoteric system—like weeds growing between cobblestones. We will find a similar ambiguity in all the devas, beginning with Mahākāla, to whom we now turn.

DAIKOKUTEN

In this section, I examine the process of domestication of a god that is Fear itself: Mahākāla, the Great Dark One.[82] Unlike Vaiśravaṇa, Mahākāla is not a deva king, yet he was singled out as the *primus inter pares* among the devas. This is why, the *Keiran shūyōshū* tells us, he is called "great" (*mahā*). He is identified with Śiva (or with one of his sons) and more specifically with Śiva's Buddhist forms, Maheśvara and Īśāna. Despite a humiliating conversion enforced by Vajrapāṇi (or similar Buddhist bullies), Śiva remained the ruler of the gods.[83] He became one of the directional devas under the name Īśāna, and he ruled over the northeast, the first and foremost direction, while Vaiśravaṇa ruled over the northern quarter.

The Demonic Mahākāla

Because Mahākāla (through his double Pāñcika or Kubera) was also associated with the north, he came to be perceived as related to Vaiśravaṇa and to the cyclical animal that symbolizes the north in Chinese cosmology, namely, the rat.[84] This shared directional attribute also explains why both gods were associated with wealth and why they were found side by side, centuries later, under their Japanese names Daikokuten and Bishamonten, among the Seven Gods of Fortune.

Iyanaga Nobumi has discussed the Indian Mahākāla and his transformation into the Japanese Daikokuten.[85] Mahākāla was initially the male counterpart of the great goddess Kālī, although he never reached the latter's gruesome popularity. Buddhist texts describe him as a dark and fierce deity, called the "demon who steals the vital essence [of people]" (*dasshōki* 奪精鬼). In the *Daikoku Tenjin-hō* 大黒天神法, he is a manifestation of Maheśvara (Śiva) who lives near a town in the country of Ujjayinī, roaming in the forest all night long with a horde of demons that feed on the flesh and blood of humans.[86] As a god of the dark night, Mahākāla was sometimes assimilated to Kālāratri (J. Kokuanten 黒暗天), the consort of King Yama.[87] Madeleine Biardeau argues that Mahākāla (or Rudra-Śiva) "is the part of danger and impurity that Hinduism had to integrate as part of its system starting with the Veda, in order to make it viable."[88] His darkness reflects the realm of the nightmarish beings that form his retinue.[89]

The *Kakuzenshō* 覚禅鈔 has a short section explaining why one must offer blood and flesh to Daikokuten. It quotes the following gloss by the Shingon priest Ejū 恵什: "He is Daijizaiten [Maheśvara], who enjoys

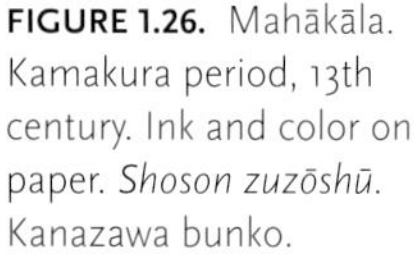

FIGURE 1.26. Mahākāla. Kamakura period, 13th century. Ink and color on paper. *Shoson zuzōshū.* Kanazawa bunko.

feeding on blood and flesh."[90] This unpalatable habit is turned into a Dharmic quality when we learn that Mahākāla only devours those who have committed sins against the Three Jewels.[91] In the *Kakuzenshō,* the notion that Daikokuten feeds on flesh and blood is placed just before a section describing him as "father and mother" to all beings.[92]

Representations

Despite the existence of Chinese texts about Mahākāla, this god does not seem to have been represented in Tang and Song iconography very often. However, he was at the center of a flourishing cult after the ninth century in the Nanzhao 南詔 and Dali 大理 kingdoms (in modern Yunnan), a region bordering Tibet, where his cult was also widespread.[93] His importance in metropolitan China increased during the Yuan dynasty, owing to Tibetan influence on Mongol rulers.

Mahākāla is often represented as a three-headed, six-armed deity holding an elephant skin over his shoulders (Figs. 1.26 and 1.27). This motif can be traced back to a mythical episode in which Śiva, appearing as Mahākāla, kills the demonic elephant Gajāsura.[94] According to a variant, the asura Nīla tried to kill Śiva by taking the form of an elephant. Nandin, the guardian of Śiva's palace, killed him and offered his skin to Śiva. Covering himself with it, as a kind of armor, Śiva went to fight another asura, the demon king Andhaka, to punish him for desiring

Pārvatī, Śiva's consort. Because the blood of the wounded Andhaka, as it fell to the ground, produced clones of him, Śiva and the other gods created female forms (*śakti*) of themselves—the seven or eight Mothers (*mātṛkās*)—to drink this blood before it touched the ground.[95] Andhaka eventually repented and took refuge in Śiva, who magnanimously gave him to Pārvatī as her son. Andhaka then became the leader of Śiva's troupe, that is, Gaṇeśa. This quasi-Oedipal myth thus describes the birth of the Seven Mothers and their relation to Vināyaka.[96]

FIGURE 1.27. Mahākāla. Kamakura period, 13th century. Ink and color on paper. *Shoson zuzōshū*. Kanazawa bunko.

In traditional representations of Śiva as Andhakāsura-vadhamūrti (that is, Śiva as the tamer of the asura Andhaka), the god is shown holding a trident on which Andhaka is impaled. The representation of this episode at Ellora also shows a *ḍākinī*—represented as a hybrid creature, half bird and half woman—asking for her share of Andhaka's blood. In the Mahākāla mandala, the god is surrounded by the Seven Mothers, to whom is added an eighth female figure, called Bontenmo (Brahmā mother, i.e., Brahmāṇī).[97]

Mahākāla is frequently represented as trampling on the elephant-headed deity Vināyaka (the demonic aspect of the god Gaṇeśa), for reasons we will examine later.[98] Yet Mahākāla and Gaṇeśa were closely related and occasionally perceived as identical. The affinities (and antagonism) between Mahākāla and Gaṇeśa may explain, on the formal plane, the exchange of certain of their features (such as Gaṇeśa's pot belly) after they enter the Japanese pantheon. Like Gaṇeśa, Mahākāla was related to female demons such as the Seven Mothers and the *ḍākinīs*.[99]

An important source for the iconography of the Buddhist Mahākāla is a description found in the *Sound and Meaning of All Sūtras* (*Yiqiejing yinyi* 一切經音義), a dictionary of the Chinese canon by the central Asian monk Huilin 慧琳 (737–820).[100] Mahākāla is described as a six-armed deity, standing on the hands of the earth goddess. He holds an elephant skin above his head with his upper hands; a trident horizontally

FIGURE 1.28. Daikokuten mandala (Mahākāla). Edo period. Sheet, ink on paper. University Art Museum, Kyoto City University of Arts. *BZS* 1076.

with his lower hands; and a human figure and a goat with his median hands. This representation seems to have provided the model for the image of Mahākāla in the Womb Realm mandala. It is also found in one of the mandalas of the *Liqu jing* (J. *Rishukyō* 理趣經), in which eight Mothers are shown around Mahākāla.[101]

Japanese representations show a six-armed Mahākāla, seated, wearing a necklace of skulls (Fig. 1.28). The details are the same as in Huilin's description, apart from the fact that he holds a sword, not a trident, in his lower hands.[102] Although only medieval line drawings (*zuzō* 図像) of this figure are extant, they still served as models for statues made during the Edo period, at a time when Mahākāla had moved beyond monastic circles to become the jovial Daikokuten, one of the Seven Gods of Fortune.

FIGURE 1.29. Seated Daikokuten. Color on wood. Onjōji, Ōtsu (Shiga prefecture).

Mahākāla as Protector of Monasteries

One of the keys to Mahākāla's popularity as a god of fortune is found in the following passage of Yijing's diary of his journey to India:

> There is likewise in great monasteries in India, at the side of a pillar in the kitchen, or before the porch, a figure of a deity carved in wood, two or three feet high, holding a golden bag, and seated on a small chair, with one foot hanging down towards the ground. Being always wiped with oil its countenance is blackened, and the deity is called Mahākāla or the Great Black One. . . . Those who offer prayers to him have their desires fulfilled.[103]

Yijing 義淨 further comments: "The efficacy of that deity is undeniable."[104] Mahākāla (Daikokuten) is described here as a god of the kitchen who brings prosperity to the monastery (Fig. 1.29). As such, he came to be associated in Japan with another "wild" god, Kōjin, whose domain was domestic fire. A Daikokuten pillar or Kōjin pillar used to be found in many Japanese kitchens, near the stove. Daikokuten's affinities with Kōjin paved the way to many symbolic associations.

As a protector of the monastery, Mahākāla was regarded as a manifestation of the earth deity, Kenrō Jijin 堅牢地神 (or Kenrō Jiten 堅牢地天),[105] and the blackness of his color was perceived to be that of the earth itself.[106] He is sometimes depicted as standing on the hands of the earth goddess, whose body half emerges from the ground—an image recalling certain forms of Vaiśravaṇa, such as that of Tobatsu Bishamon.

FIGURE 1.30. Bearded Daikokuten. *Kakuzenshō, DNBZ* 50: 267.

FIGURE 1.31. Bearded Daikokuten. *Kakuzenshō, DNBZ* 50: 266.

FIGURE 1.32. Sanmen Daikoku. Color on wood. Mount Haguro (Yamagata prefecture).

FIGURE 1.33. Sanmen Daikoku. Color on wood. Keishōji, Matsusaka (Mie prefecture).

The three-faced Daikoku of Mount Hiei is also said to have come out from the earth.

Over time, Daikokuten came to be perceived as a landlord deity (*jinushi* 地主). The foundation story of Enryakuji 延暦寺 recounts that when Saichō 最澄 first climbed Mount Hiei, Daikokuten appeared to him in the form of an old man and offered his protection to the new monastic community envisioned by Saichō, thus becoming the tutelary deity of Mount Hiei. This legend led to the development of the figure called the Three-faced Daikoku (Sanmen Daikoku 三面大黒), which we will take up when we consider the Three Devas.[107]

As the protector of Mount Hiei, Daikokuten was identified with Sannō Gongen 山王権現, that is, the god of Miwa (Ōkuninushi 大国主), who was also worshiped at Ōmiya 大宮, the western main shrine (Nishi Hongū) of Hie Taisha 日吉大社, at the foot of Mount Hiei. The fusion (or confusion) of Daikokuten with Ōkuninushi is traditionally attributed to a

FIGURE 1.34. Sanmen Daikoku. Edo period. Color on wood. Tōji, Kyoto.

FIGURE 1.35. Sanmen Daikoku. *Ofuda.* Hieizan. Personal collection.

lapsus calami, an error committed by Kūkai when he wrote the Sino-Japanese name of Mahākāla, Daikoku 大黒 (Great Black One), as Daikoku 大国 (Great Country, also read as Ōkuni).[108] The alleged confusion took place much later, however, during the medieval period. At any rate, the fusion of the two figures would probably have taken place without Kūkai's "error," owing to the functional affinities shared by the two gods. Deliberate or not, the play on words confirmed a preexisting situation. As the "original landlord" (*jishū* or *jinushi* 地主) of Japan, Ōkuninushi—also known as Ōmononushi 大物主, a former demonic figure (as master of the *mono* 'ghosts')—was indeed predisposed to merge with Daikokuten. Tendai monks were familiar with such symbolic associations, and they did not need the typo of a Shingon priest to turn the perceived affinities between two gods into an identity. Whatever the case, certain features of Ōkuninushi passed to Daikokuten, reinforcing his character as a god of the third function, that is, a purveyor of wealth and fecundity.[109]

FIGURE 1.36. Daikokuten. *Ofuda*. Mount Haguro (Yamagata prefecture). Personal collection.

FIGURE 1.37. Daikokuten as Miwa Daimyōjin. *Ofuda*. Nishinomiya Shrine (Hyōgo prefecture). Personal collection.

Mahākāla was thus identified with Miwa Myōjin. The latter is said to have been invited to Mount Hiei in 668 on the order of Tenji Tennō 天智天皇, and it is he who appeared to Saichō in the form of Mahākāla, according to the *Keiran shūyōshū*.[110] In the *Miwa daimyōjin engi* 三輪大明神縁起 (1318), a text of the Miwa tradition influenced by the Ritsu 律 priest Eison 叡尊 (1201–1290), Miwa Myōjin does appear in the form of Mahākāla (Daikokuten).[111] The same Eison, on the basis of a vision, had a statue of Daikokuten carved at Saidaiji 西大寺. Interestingly, a board representing the goddess Benzaiten has recently been found inside this statue. In the section "Miwa Daikokuten" of the *Jingi shūi* (ca. 1525) by Yoshida Kanemitsu 吉田兼満 (the successor of Yoshida Kanetomo 吉田兼倶), Saichō is also said to have carved a three-faced Daikokuten (Sanmen Daikoku 三面大黒). But the names of Bishamonten and Benzaiten do not appear, and Daikokuten is said to have come from Mount Hiei to Miwa, not the contrary.[112]

Daikokuten as a God of Wealth

One can easily imagine how, from a kitchen god, Mahākāla went on to become a god of fertility and fecundity. Under the name Mohouluo 摩睺羅,

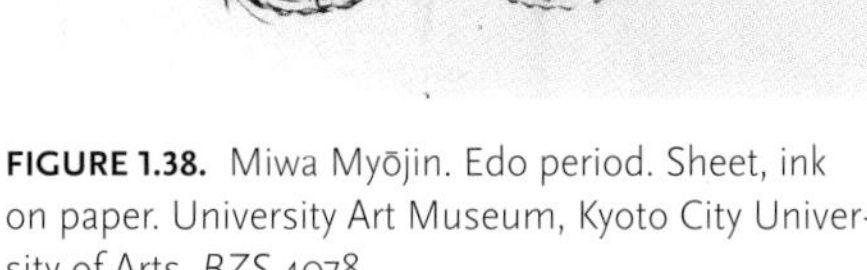

FIGURE 1.38. Miwa Myōjin. Edo period. Sheet, ink on paper. University Art Museum, Kyoto City University of Arts. *BZS* 4078.

FIGURE 1.39. Daikokuten and Uzume. *Ofuda.* Kasuga Shrine. Personal collection.

Mahākāla was worshiped in China on the day when one prays for children during the Festival of the Seventh (Month), known as the Tanabata Festival in Japan. Daikokuten (or rather, one of his prototypes, Pañcika) and his wife Hārītī (J. Kariteimo 訶梨帝母 or Kishimojin 鬼子母神) were probably also worshiped as a couple at that time.[113]

Toward the fourteenth century, with the rise of the merchant class, Daikokuten began to gain weight (literally) and to be depicted as standing on two big balls of rice, holding the mallet that "brings riches" (see, e.g., Figs. 1.36 and 1.39). He also acquired strong sexual characteristics. In the *Byakuhō shō* 白宝鈔, for example, Chōen reports an oral tradition to the effect that if a woman wishes to seduce a man, she must pray to Daikokuten.[114] The *Mahāpratisarādhāraṇī-sūtra* (Ch. *Suiqiu tuoluoni jing* 隋求陀羅尼經, translated into Chinese by Amoghavajra) describes various deities to be worshiped by women who desire a child. A pregnant woman, for instance, should make a drawing of Mahākāla.[115] In his *Playful Essays* (*Kiyū shōran* 喜遊笑覧, 1830), Kitamura Nobuyo 喜多村信節 (1784–1856) explains that Makora (that is, Mahākāla) became a protector of children owing to his relations with Hārītī.[116] At the

Wakamiya 若宮 Shrine of Kasuga, Daikokuten (or rather Ōkuninushi) is worshiped today as part of a couple, together with Okame お亀 (a.k.a. Otafuku お多福, the popular version of the goddess Ame no Uzume 天宇受売). The shrine also sells votive wooden plaques (*ema* 絵馬) for female lactation, on which a female breast is crudely drawn. During the Edo period, Daikokuten was at times depicted as making a hand gesture with strong sexual connotations, the so-called *manofica* (from *manus* 'hand' and *fica* 'fig', a symbol of the female organ).[117] An illustration on a fan, representing Daikokuten carrying a forked radish over his shoulders, clearly has a similar meaning.[118] At Mount Haguro 羽黒 and elsewhere, Daikokuten is often plainly represented by a wooden phallus.[119]

The vexing question of Daikokuten's transformation from a bloodthirsty demon into a jolly good fellow and a god of fortune has been studied by Iyanaga and others. It is difficult to find any clear precedent for the popular image which Daikokuten came to assume in the medieval period: if not his black, dwarf-like, pot-bellied appearance, since the Tantric Mahākāla was sometimes represented as a stout fellow, then at least his attire (consisting of a layman's dress and a strange hat) and demeanor (carrying a big bag on his left shoulder and holding a mallet in his right hand). Iyanaga has compared Daikokuten's bag, a symbol of abundance, to that of the Chan monk Budai (J. Hotei 布袋), better known as the Laughing Buddha.[120] The image of that trickster may indeed have influenced that of Daikokuten, but the motif of the bag could just as well be a distant iconographic echo of Mahākāla's elephant skin. The bag has also been described as a symbol of the eighth consciousness (Skt. *ālaya-vijñāna*, J. *arayashiki* 阿頼耶識).

Daikokuten's mallet is usually described as a magic tool, a kind of wish-fulfilling jewel (*cintāmaṇi*); but it is also a magic weapon, used in connection with epidemics. In the Madarijin 摩怛哩神 ritual centered on the Seven Mothers (Skt. *Śaptamātṛka,* J. *Shichimo* 七母), the seven deities each hold a mallet, and this attribute is explained by their role as epidemic deities.[121] Another interesting, albeit marginal and heterodox, aspect of the medieval cult of Daikokuten is an oral tradition regarding the so-called *tsubute* 礫, a term usually referring to "stone throwing." In this case, however, the object thrown does not seem to be a stone, and the throwing does not constitute any kind of Buddhist intifada; rather, the goal is to steal the wealth from a rich house by throwing into it, at the hour of the rat (around midnight), a talisman in the form of a wish-fulfilling jewel dedicated to Daikokuten.[122]

All Too Real

As Mahākāla's roles as an earth deity and protector of Japanese Buddhist monasteries moved to the forefront, smoothing the way for his evolution into a god of fortune, his dark, nocturnal side was downplayed and progressively forgotten.[123] In Tendai esotericism, the Great Dark One continued to be perceived as a symbol of fundamental ignorance ("great darkness").[124] But his name lent itself to a Tendai exegesis based on the *hongaku* notion of the identity between defilement and awakening; in this interpretation, the first character of his name, *dai* 大, designates ultimate reality, the realm of awakening, whereas the second character, *koku* 黒, refers to the darkness of ignorance. *Dai* is also said to refer to the cosmic buddha Ichiji Kinrin 一字金輪, and *koku* to Īśāna (Maheśvara), who is not only one of the twelve directional devas, but also a god of obstacles.[125] In this way, Daikokuten came to symbolize the principle that transcends all such oppositions.[126] Yet, even as he was being redefined as a supreme and somewhat abstract deity, an embodiment of ultimate reality, he remained a god of obstacles, a very concrete and potentially dangerous deity. That is, while he no longer needed to be "tamed" like Maheśvara, he still needed to be converted by receiving the Tendai precepts.

This ambiguity was not limited to Daikokuten, as it reflected the paradox of the Indian devas (and other functionally related deities) who symbolize the three poisons and are fundamentally limited by ignorance, yet still become symbols of awakening, owing to the nondual logic of innate awakening (*hongaku*), and rise to the top of the Buddhist pantheon. We will observe the same paradox at work in the arc traced by the so-called Three Devas (Shōten, Dakiniten, and Benzaiten).

Thus, despite Daikokuten's rise in the Buddhist pantheon, the darkness explicit in his name was seen as an anchor pulling him back toward the lower realm of ignorance. The *Keiran shūyōshū* explains that he is called Daikokuten because his fundamental nature is that of the three poisons (ignorance, anger, and greed).[127] Indeed, he was often designated as a "real one" (*jissha* 実者) in rituals, because of the stigma related to his origins. This is probably how the couple formed by Daikokuten and Benzaiten also came to symbolize various forms of nonduality—of passions and awakening, conventional and ultimate truth, and exoteric and esoteric teaching.

From *Jissha* to *Honji*

In a move typical of its monistic tendency, medieval esoteric Buddhism posits a "higher" Daikokuten who manifests himself in various guises—one of which is the conventional Daikokuten. Whereas the latter represents ignorance, the former transmutes that ignorance into awakening. For example, Daikokuten is called the "global body" of the seven planets, which in turn have the seven stars of the Northern Dipper as their essence.[128] According to the *Daikokuten kōshiki* 大黒天行講式, a liturgical text attributed to Kūkai: "When [Daikokuten] tames demons, he is called Dōro Shōgun 道路将軍 (Road General). When he dispenses wealth, he is called Daikoku Tenjin 大黒天神. He is also identical in substance to Ugajin. His body is that of a male because he is a manifestation of Tamon Tennō 多聞天王. He is black because he can transform the world of darkness."[129] Likewise, in the *Daikoku tenjin shiki* 大黒天神私記, Daikokuten is the "trace" (*suijaku*) of Fudō and of the earth deity.[130]

A similar view is expressed in the caption for an image of Daikokuten written by the Zen master Genko Shikei 原古志稽 (1401–1475): "At times he becomes the earth deity, at other times Benzaiten; he also transforms into Maheśvara, or into Dōso Shōgun 道祖将軍.[131] His manifestations, numbering hundreds of millions, are a very deep mystery. He is called 'Tathāgata king of awakening, Dainichi of the central lotus dais [of the Taizōkai mandala],' 'Worthy Fudō of the Vajra section,' and 'Buddha of the jewel trove of the Buddha section.' He is also called the earth deity in the universe of the lotus treasure, and the luck-bringing deity in the palaces of Tuṣita heaven."[132]

Codetta

Like other devas, the wrathful Daikokuten was eventually bowdlerized, becoming a god of wealth and one of the Seven Gods of Fortune.[133] The same evolution occurred with Bishamonten. This should not surprise us, as both deities, while being linked to war, were also from the outset perceived as chthonian gods, and more precisely as manifestations of the earth deity.[134] The fact that Mahākāla's retinue includes the Seven Mothers suggests affinities between him and Yama. The latter is not simply the judge of the dead, he is above all the cause of their death, and as such he is associated with (and surrounded by) the ghouls that ravish the individual's vital essence—a category that includes not only Mahākāla's retinue (the Mothers, the *ḍākinīs*) but also Mahākāla himself. Indeed, Mahākāla is coupled with Yamuna, the Black One, who also happens to be Yama's consort.

A common link between Mahākāla and the *ḍākinīs,* on the one hand, and Yama and his acolytes (in particular, the *kushōjin* or companion spirits), on the other hand, may be found in the "rites to call back the soul." A coma or apparent death was attributed to a loss (or rather theft) of the vital spirit, and Yama and Mahākāla were not always considered neutral. Like Mahākāla/Maheśvara, Yama was represented as seated on a buffalo—and at times the two figures can be distinguished only by their respective attributes. To better understand this commonality, we now turn to the figure of Yama, the deva who rules over the southern quarter, just as Vaiśravaṇa rules over the northern quarter.

ENMATEN

In East Asia, Yama (J. Enma 閻魔) is usually seen through a Chinese prism as one of the ten kings of hell. He is represented as a stern, awe-inspiring Chinese magistrate, a figure that was apparently influenced by the Daoist image of the Taishan deity, Taishan Fujun 泰山府君 (J. Taizan Fukun). Whereas the Indian Yama was a multifunctional deity, in China it was his judicial function that came to the forefront, and it is essentially that Chinese image that has been studied by Stephen Teiser.[135] When we consider the Japanese image of Yama, the figure of Enmaten shows us the resilience, in medieval esoteric texts, of certain aspects that were all but erased from the Chinese sources. We are fortunate to have, in the case of esoteric Buddhism, a large commentarial literature in both Japan and Tibet, whereas the canonical literature in the Taishō collection practically stops with Yixing 一行 (683–727), Vajrabodhi (662–732), and Amoghavajra (705–774).

The main purpose of esoteric Buddhist ritual is to obtain worldly benefits by inviting deities into the ritual arena. It therefore implies that the beneficiary is still alive, differing in this respect from funerary rituals that imply a departed beneficiary and a ritual journey to the other world (for instance, to "break the gates of hell"). Thus, the esoteric ritual's main tendency is quite different from that found in texts on funerary rituals, which are looking at a postmortem situation and trying to alleviate Yama's verdict. In this "worldly" conception, the main punishment is the shortening of a person's lifespan. Of course, the two approaches are not mutually exclusive, and the emphasis on "hungry ghosts" (*pretas*) can also be found in Chinese Tantric texts.[136] Indeed, much of the discourse on Yama is about the afterlife, and the most popular texts were those on the Buddha's disciple Mulian 目蓮 (Skt. Maugdalyāyana (J. Mokuren)) rescuing his mother and on the Ghost Festival (Yulanpen). As Stephen Teiser has shown, the Yulanpen literature, and the tale of Mulian in particular, spare us no details about the horrors of the Buddhist hells.[137] Esoteric Buddhist texts, on the other hand, are more concerned with death itself, and they insist on the judicial function of Yama and his acolytes. But the first mention of these acolytes (as companion spirits or *kushōjin*) is really about ritually rescuing the dying from Yama's grip, rather than alleviating death's aftermath.[138] It is this "this-worldly" version of that religious system that will be my focus here.

Yama and His Retinue

In Brahmanism, Yama was essentially a Dharma king.[139] As the first man who died, he was correlated with the deceased (the "fathers," *pitṛ*). In the Vedas, Yama is never called a god, bearing the title of king instead. While he is the ruler of the underworld, his realm is also said to be in the highest heaven, and in the southern region of the world.[140] As one of the twelve directional devas, Yama seems to have superseded Indra as the god of the southern direction.

As his name suggests, before becoming the god of the dead, and Death itself, Yama was first and foremost a twin. He has a sister, named

FIGURE 1.40. Enmaten. Edo period. Sheet, ink on paper. University Art Museum, Kyoto City University of Arts. *BZS* 2257.

FIGURE 1.41. Enmaten. Kamakura period, 13th century. Ink and color on paper. *Shoson zuzōshū*. Kanazawa bunko.

Yamī, who was also identified, probably through alliteration, as the goddess of the Yamunā River.[141] According to some later Buddhist sources, Yama rules over the male dead, his sister over the female dead. This is why one calls them the "double kings" (or "twin kings," *shuangwang* 双王).[142] As Kāla (Time), Yama is associated with Śiva-Mahākāla. As the child of the solar deity Visvavant, he is also sometimes identified with the sun.[143]

Yama also has a demonic aspect, however.[144] In Purāṅic literature, he is said to present a frightening face to sinners, a benign face to the innocent.

In the *Padma Purāṇa,* for instance, he looks terrifying to the culprit, whereas he assumes the pleasant aspect of Viṣṇu for meritorious people.

The esoteric Buddhist Yāma inherited from his Brahmanic prototype his three functions as guardian of the south, god of death, and judge of the dead.[145] As a Dharma king, he became closely identified with the working of karma, and lost some of his individuality. In theory at least, the theory of karmic retribution seems to make him redundant, verging on irrelevant. In actual practice, however, just the opposite was true, and the figure of Yama came to loom very large in Buddhist visions of the otherworld. While Indian Mahāyāna, with its emphasis on emptiness, apparently undermines the reality of the Buddhist hells, in Chinese Buddhism King Yama becomes the central figure of funerary rituals, together with Kṣitigharba (Dizang 地藏).[146] In the Chinese bureaucratic conception of the underworld, King Yama (Yanluo wang 閻羅王) becomes a stern, awe-inspiring magistrate, and is dressed and addressed as such.

FIGURE 1.42. Enmaten. Kamakura period, 13th century. Color on silk. Kyoto National Museum.

From the esoteric viewpoint, the points of emphasis are his deva characteristics (Yamadeva, J. Enma-ten 閻魔天), both as king of hell and as ruler of the southern quarter. Rituals centered on Yama in esoteric Buddhism were not merely funerary rituals concerned with the afterlife; they were aimed at worldly benefits such as the avoidance of calamities and longevity. By meeting these needs, Yama temporarily regained the status of "king of equality" (*pingdeng wang,* J. Byōdō-ō 平等王) and ultimate ruler of the underworld, and he became a god of destiny and fortune, bringing above all the worldly benefit of longevity. The Japanese image of Yama fluctuated between these two—Indian and Chinese—models. In the esoteric mandalas, however, he is usually represented as an Indian deva.[147]

Mandalic Representations

The Indian Yama was said to "possess the earth in its breadth."[148] The esoteric Buddhist Yama first appears as a subaltern deity in the southern quarter of the Womb Realm (Taizōkai, Skt. Garbhadhātu) mandala, in the so-called section outside the *vajras* (*wai jingang bu* 外金剛部).[149]

FIGURE 1.43. Enmaten and daṇḍa staff. 12th century. *Kontai butsuga chō.* Tokyo National Museum.

FIGURE 1.44. *(Opposite)* Enmaten mandala. Kamakura period, 13th–14th century. Color on silk. Kyoto National Museum.

He rides a water buffalo and holds a scepter as his emblem.[150] He is surrounded by his consorts Kālāratri and Mṛtyus, and the Seven Mothers.[151] (See Figs. 1.44–1.47.) Despite being a deva, he shows strong demonic features. He is said to cut or steal the "root of life" of all beings, and is to be feared for bringing sudden death.[152] We are told that when he rejoices, people do not die suddenly, but when he is angry, epidemics make numerous victims. One must therefore perform a ritual to placate him and avoid sudden death. For Yixing, however, Yama's killing is not "true killing"—to cut the root of life merely means to cut off fundamental ignorance.[153] Yama's ambiguity is reflected in the fact that he both gives death and provides access to a realm beyond death.

Yama is described as follows in the *Mahāvairocana-sūtra:* "On the right side [of the mandala] is King Yama, holding a scepter in his hand and seated on a water buffalo, which is the color of black clouds when shaken by thunderbolts. He is surrounded by the Seven Mothers, Kālāratri, Mṛtyu, and the others."[154] The scepter is an important iconographic feature, to which I will return. It is also called a *daṇḍa* staff, appearing as a staff surmounted by a human head.

The other members of Yama's retinue are described differently in the *Mahāvairocana-sūtra* and its commentary. The sūtra mentions a "Queen [of] Yama" and the names of five of the Seven Mothers. Yixing's *Commentary* replaces Yama's queen with the Seven Mothers.[155] The *Mahāvairocana-sūtra* also describes a semi-circular mandala that is said to correspond to the wind element (hence its name, "wind altar," *fengtan* 風壇).[156] For a diagram of this mandala, we have to rely on Japanese sources (Fig. 1.49). While this is an important caveat, the rather archaic content of Yama's wind altar seems to point to a Chinese source.

FIGURE 1.45. Enmaten mandala. 14th century. Hanging scroll, color on silk. Kanazawa bunko.

FIGURE 1.46. Enmaten mandala. Detail of Aizen Myōō portable shrine. Kamakura period, 13th–14th century. Hinoki wood, lacquered. Tokyo National Museum.

FIGURE 1.47. Enmaten mandala. Edo period. Sheet, ink on paper. University Art Museum, Kyoto City University of Arts. *BZS* 1075.

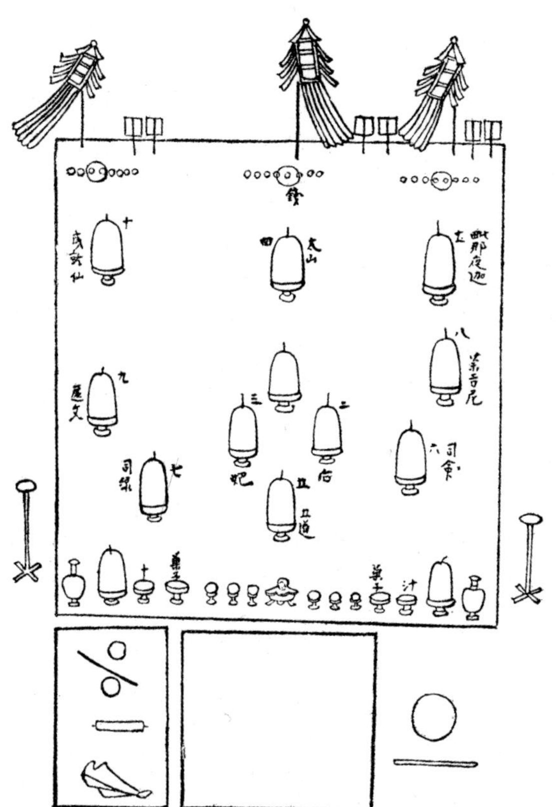

FIGURE 1.48. Enmaten's Altar. *Kakuzenshō*, *DNBZ* 50: 317.

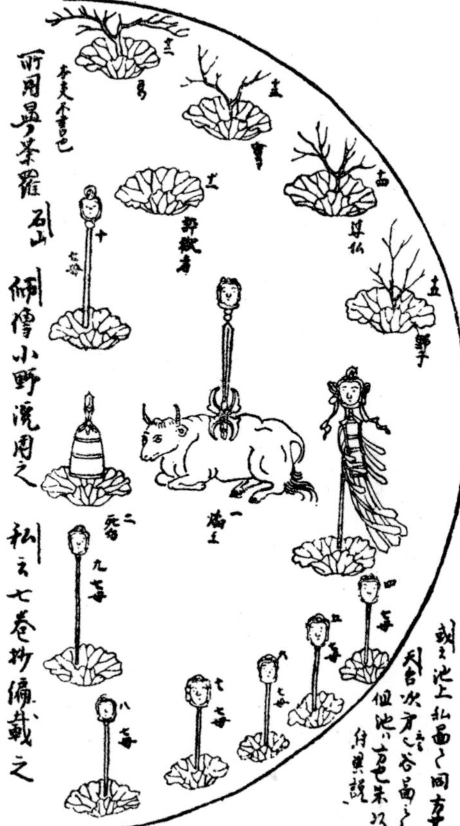

FIGURE 1.49. Yama's wind altar. Detail of Fūten mandala. *Kakuzenshō*, *DNBZ* 50: 305.

It is in fact a *samaya* (symbolic) mandala, in which Yama and his retinue are represented in the form of symbols (or "seals"), such as the small heads on the tops of the *daṇḍa* staffs or swords. It includes Yama and his two consorts, his assistant Citragupta, the Seven Mothers, and the four kinds of animals (vultures, crows, *basu* birds, and jackals or foxes) that form their retinue. This type of mandala is visually dominated by the Mothers and the animals. Some sources, even more detailed, mention other bloodthirsty demons such as the *piśacas* and *piśacīs,* creatures that devour the human spirit.[157]

Another type of Japanese mandala that was popular in the medieval era can probably be traced back to Chinese models. Containing eleven deities, it is already a hybrid mandala, reflecting a compromise or a transition between the Indian and Chinese conceptions of Yama.[158] The god and his immediate retinue are represented as Indian devas, whereas his assistant Citragupta is replaced by (or merges with) the Chinese god of

FIGURE 1.50. Enmaten and acolytes. *Kakuzenshō*. Collection Mantokuji, Inazawa (Aichi prefecture).

Taishan, Taishan Fujun, and his assistants—all dressed in official Chinese garb. This type of mandala appeared in China around the sixth century, and is said to have been imported in Japan by the ninth century.[159] Yama is represented at the center riding a buffalo, and he is flanked by two consorts. On his right is a boar-headed demoness called Cāmuṇḍā, on his left a long-haired *ḍākinī.* Above (or behind) him is Taishan Fujun, holding a *daṇḍa* staff and writing on a register. On his sides are a youth called Siddha-vidyādhara (Chengjiu xian 成就仙, Perfected [Mantra-holding] Ascetic), and the elephant-headed Vināyaka (J. Shōten). Below Yama is the Great god of the five paths (Wudao dashen 五道大神), a.k.a. General of the five paths (Wudao jiangjun 五道将軍). The latter is flanked by his assistants, Siming 司命 (Officer of the Lifespan) and Silu 司禄 (Officer of the Registers).[160] His court is the last gate through which beings must pass before being reborn.

Yama is actually at the center of two groups, composed respectively of Indian and Chinese deities, which represents two different conceptions

FIGURE 1.51. Cāmuṇḍā. Central India, 11th century. Sandstone. Staatliche Museen zu Berlin, Museum für Indische Kunst.

FIGURE 1.52. Cāmuṇḍā triad. *Daihi taizō daimandara. TZ* 1: 781.

of death—magical and karmic. The first group, demonic in nature, represents the dark powers that attack people's vital essence. The second represents the judicial (and karmic) processes that can shorten (or lengthen) their lifespan. This mandala was used in life-prolonging rituals, not in funerary rituals.

The God of Death

The members of Yama's retinue illustrate (and complement) two of Yama's aspects: as god of death and as judge of the dead. Among Yama's two consorts, Queen Death (Mṛtyus) is death personified, and in that sense she is perceived as identical with one aspect of Yama. Kālarātrī (Black Night) rules over the dark realm of the forests and cemeteries, a realm haunted by bloodthirsty beings like the *ḍākinīs*.[161] The name *ḍākinī* refers to a kind of ghoul that haunts charnel grounds and feeds on human flesh and blood. In the *Mahāvairocana-sūtra,* they are said to have been tamed by Mahākāla.[162] In the Womb Realm mandala, three of them are depicted eating human flesh next to a corpse (see Fig. 3.1).

The *ḍākinīs* are closely related to the Seven Mothers. In Yixing's *Commentary,* the Seven Mothers are attendants of King Yama.[163] They were originally animal-faced (often bird-faced) demonesses.[164] But as they became integrated into the official pantheon, their appearance became more human. As Brahmāṇī, Maheśvarī, Vaiṣṇavī, Kaumarī, Indraṇī, Vārāhī, and Cāmuṇḍā, the Seven Mothers became consorts of the major Hindu gods (Brahmā, Maheśvara, Viṣṇu, Kumāra, etc.) and were depicted as handsome maidens. This evolution led to a distinction between two types of Mothers, the old (malevolent) and the new (benevolent).[165] Yuvraj Krishan argues that when the term *mātṛkā* came to be appropriated by the new, benevolent Mothers, the term *ḍākinī* was applied to the old ones. In other words, the later *ḍākinīs* (and Cāmuṇḍā) represent the earlier (pre-Gupta) Mothers.[166] Thus, the ancient, frightening *mātṛkās* continued their demonic ways under the name of *ḍākinīs*. As a result, even when depicted as peaceful consorts of the great Hindu gods, they retain some disturbing features (like their fangs), and their demonic nature continues to lurk just below the surface.

Cāmuṇḍā (J. Shamonda 遮文陀), even when she is grouped with the Seven Mothers, occupies a special position. Unlike the Mothers, who were eventually domesticated and able to join mainstream Hinduism, Cāmuṇḍā remained wild and always retained a frightening appearance. She is usually represented as an emaciated hag (Fig. 1.51), sometimes with a dog and an owl, at the foot of a corpse. Sometimes she is described as a pestilence god. In esoteric Buddhism, she is often depicted as a woman with a sow's head and a protuberant belly (Fig. 1.52).[167]

Cāmuṇḍā and the Seven Mothers also share a special relationship with Vināyaka (Gaṇeśa). In the Ellora caves, Vināyaka is represented together with Cāmuṇḍā and the Seven Mothers (see Figs. 2.3 and 2.4 below). He was also seen as the leader of the demons called *vināyakas.* While in India, Gaṇeśa, like his half-brother Skanda, entered mainstream Hinduism and came to be worshiped as a benevolent god; in East Asian Buddhism, he retained his demonic aspects.[168]

As we can see, there were intimate ties between Yama, the seven, eight or twelve Mothers, Cāmuṇḍā, Vināyaka (and the *vināyaka* demons), and the *ḍākinīs.* Thus it is not surprising to find them together in the early Yama mandalas.[169] Indeed, we are dealing here with a fairly structured network, to which were added other demons such as the *piśacas* and *piśacīs,* and so on. The Yama rituals, centered on the Yama mandala, were aimed at prolonging life—mainly by exorcising soul-stealing demons and by erasing the names of people from the register of the dead. In both cases, the emphasis was on *this* life, not on the afterlife—as in later rituals focused on the ten kings.

The Judge

In the hybrid mandalas mentioned above, a group of Chinese-looking underworld officials—Taishan Fujun and his assistants—have been inserted into the Indian—and more specifically Shivaic—demonic retinue of Yama. The demonic aspect was not entirely covered by the judiciary aspect, however, and it can still be found in Chinese conceptions of hell—for instance, in the definition of Taishan Fujun as a deity feeding on human blood and flesh. Again, in the (apocryphal) *Sūtra of the Ten Kings* (*Jūō kyō* 十王經), Yama's three emissaries are called "soul-stealers."[170]

The Indian Yama has an assistant called Citragupta, who records good and evil actions. His name appears in Yixing's *Commentary* as that of an underworld official.[171] Even before that, however—by the third century—the lord of Taishan had been linked to Buddhist hells in popular Buddhism, and he came to supersede Citragupta, eventually becoming one of the ten kings of hell.[172] In Chinese Tantrism, however, he remains an attendant of King Yama. His image was in turn influenced by that of Yama, and he acquired similar features as a god of fortune and a protector of individual destiny.[173]

The God of the five paths is also recording the good and evil deeds of humans. He is said to dwell at the crossroads of the various paths of rebirth (the path of the devas, the path of men, and the path of the three evil destinies).[174] In certain Chinese Buddhist texts, however, a more demonic god (or general) of the five paths appears, one who is associated with "lewd" cults and animal sacrifice.[175] As Glen Dudbride points out, "in sixth-century Buddhist China the General of the five paths was indeed perceived as a powerful and threatening figure outside the Buddhist system, yet still dimly associated with the gates of death."[176]

Yama's retinue played an important role in exorcisms such as the Danuo 大儺 (Great Exorcism), aimed at driving away the demons of the four directions, but also the spirits of destitute people that were not included in the regular ancestor cult: poor literati, peasants, artisans, slaves, bandits, rebels, monks and nuns.[177] The famous demon king Zhong Kui 鍾馗 played an important role in this exorcism, as well as the General of the five paths, who is said to appear at the head of a troupe of ten thousand soldiers on the night of the exorcism. He brings the demons to Taishan Fujun, who performs an inquiry before sending them to Yama.[178]

All the underworld officials under Yama—the three pairs formed by Siming and Silu, the so-called companion spirits (*kushōjin*), and Taishan Fujun and the God of the five paths—have as their main function the reporting of good and evil actions of people.[179] Actually, they do not merely inform Yama, they represent his all-pervading knowledge of human nature. From the esoteric Buddhist standpoint, they are not merely his assistants, but more specifically his emanations, and their dual function is therefore that of Yama himself, as a panoptical twin deity. The same can be said of a number of devices that can be found in Yama's palace—for instance, the karmic mirror and the scale of deeds, which are panoptical devices that reveal the hidden truth of people's actions. But it is especially true of the strangest of all, the so-called *daṇḍa* staff—a kind of scepter surmounted by a live human head. This staff personifies Yama's judiciary function: his omniscience, his royal status, and his verdict (*daṇḍa* also means "punishment"). It is Yama's symbolic (*samaya*) form, as well as that of several members of his retinue. The head on its top is said to represent Yama's spirit.[180] It expresses rage in front of a sinner, benevolence in front of a virtuous person. At times the *daṇḍa* is a banner pole erected in the inner court of Yama's underworld palace. In medieval Japan, a two-headed type of staff developed, with one wrathful face, and one benevolent, representing the *kushōjin* or companion spirits.[181]

CHANGING CONCEPTIONS OF THE UNDERWORLD

The Indian Yama was a multifunctional deity. He was not just a deva or a Dharma king, but also a demon king who was said to "cut off the root of life" of humans. In this role, he was structurally identical to Skanda and Vināyaka (two deities related to the Seven Mothers), on the one hand, and to Mahākāla (who was himself related to the *ḍākinīs*), on the other. As a panoptical judge and god of destiny, Yama was close to deities like Brahmā and Indra, but also, more importantly, to the companion spirits (*kushōjin*) who watch over human life from beginning to end.

In Chinese Buddhism, the Yama mandalas constituted an "arena of contention"—to borrow Prasenjit Duara's term—in which various

Indian and Chinese deities vied for recognition.[182] The disappearance of Cāmuṇḍā and other "Mothers" corresponds to the sinicization of Yama and his retinue, but it may also reflect the fact that, in Japanese esoteric Buddhism at least, some of these deities (Dakiniten, Shōten, and the like) continued to develop independently, eventually ascending to the summit of the pantheon.[183] In China, however, with the development of the cult of Kṣitigarbha (Ch. Dizang 地藏, J. Jizō) and of the ten kings, Yama himself was essentially reduced to his juridical and inquisitorial functions, and his realm limited to the afterlife.[184] The departure of his demonic acolytes caused Yama to lose some of his mediating, Janus-faced qualities and to become a kind of ogre, an image of fear more than of justice. The symbolic impoverishment of Yama's retinue, despite its growth in size, led to a shift from a live, complex mandala to a representation characterized by grotesqueries and moral platitude. Esoteric Buddhism had preserved Yama's ambiguity, but Chinese conceptions of hell lost it. Originally, Enmaten mandalas served as a matrix for various deities that eventually developed independently, leaving Yama alone with demons, *pretas,* and judiciary officials.

In medieval China, the deva Yama and King Yama seem to have become distinct. This bifurcation is visible in the mandalas transmitted by Śubakarasiṃha and Amoghavajra. For example, the fact that, in the *Taizōkai kyūzuyō* 胎藏界旧図様 copied by the Tendai monk, Enchin 円珍 (814–891), at the Kaiyuansi 開元寺 in Yuezhou, Enma-ō and Enmaten appear in different hells, reflects the influence of Amoghavajra. This difference, however, was reconciled in the Genzu mandala 現図曼荼羅 introduced in Japan by Kūkai.[185] Thus we end up with two different aspects of the same god, not to say two different gods: the deva Yama (Enmaten), a deity who grants longevity and prevents calamities, and King Yama (Enma-ō), the ferocious judge of the dead.[186] Teiser argues that in the Chinese Buddhist conception of hells, "gods of both Indian and Chinese origin participate in a unitary system in which exclusivizing questions of cultural origins have no meaningful place."[187] True enough, but we should keep in mind that the coexistence of Indian and Chinese deities in Yama's retinue (and in Yama's figure itself) may reflect an enduring tension between two different conceptions of his role as much as a synthesis.

A significant shift in the conceptions of death and the afterlife took place in medieval China. In the earlier conception, death is relatively immoral. Humans are victims of bloodthirsty demons and/or angry gods. In the later conception, the judiciary framing, while apparently more keen on justice, gives way to a rather sadistic description of infernal torments, and guilt is elaborately staged—actualization of the sins through various panoptic devices, wrath of the judges, and so on. This conception, aimed at scaring the populace, reflects an attempt by Buddhists to strengthen their hold on Chinese society. Eventually it may have backfired, but the images unleashed have continued to rule over the Chinese imagination. To prevent people from falling into despair, Yama's excessive severity had to be counterbalanced by the unconditional compassion of the bodhisattva Dizang. With the development of a bureaucratic conception of hell centered on trials and tortures, King Yama (Enma-ō), the wrathful magistrate, came to supersede Yama, the impassive deva of esoteric Buddhism (Enmaten). Yet, as Teiser points out, he continued to play at least one of the major roles that he had earlier played in India: as ruler of the underworld, he kept records of people's actions in their previous lives.[188]

Another significant development took place in medieval Japan, where Enmaten came to be identified with Amaterasu, and more precisely with Amaterasu's "rough spirit" (*aramitama* 荒御霊), Seoritsuhime 瀬織津姫.[189] In the *Nakatomi no harae kunge* 中臣祓訓解, this deity, issued from Izanagi's ablution, is perceived as "emanating" from Enmaten when, in the service of Amaterasu, she manifests the aspect of Amaterasu called the "heavenly emperor manipulating the brutish force" (*ara-tenshi* 荒天子), which was believed capable of precipitating the forces of evil into the deepest hells.[190] Enmaten has here replaced Susanoo, the autochthonous ruler of the underworld. Likewise, the *kami* of the ocean Haya-akitsuhime 速秋津比売 is identified with the great God of the five paths (Godō Daijin 五道大神) and Kangiten (Vināyaka), two members of Enmaten's retinue.[191]

Thus, the esoteric Enmaten is not only a judge of the dead, as he became in popular religion. Like his alter ego Taizan Fukun, he is above all a god of destiny, and this function removes him from his underworldly abode and transforms him into an astral deity, akin to the pole star deity (Myōken) and to the solar king Aizen.[192] His chthonian nature (which identifies him with Jizō, the earth-store bodhisattva) is counterbalanced by his astral nature (which identifies him with Kokūzō, the space-store bodhisattva).

As such, he becomes a symbol of the deepest Buddhist reality, the storehouse consciousness (*ālaya-vijñāna*).

CODETTA

Like Vega, Altaïr, and Deneb in the summer sky, Bishamonten, Daikokuten, and Enmaten form a rather conspicuous triangle in the firmament of medieval Japanese Buddhism, although they were never grouped in the same constellation. It is indeed surprising that they were not brought together in this fashion, although Bishamonten and Daikokuten were often paired. Enmaten, on the other hand, remained independent, whereas his Chinese variant, Enma-ō, became subsumed in the group of ten kings (as the fifth king)—several of whom are merely his doublets.

These three devas allow us, as it were, to triangulate medieval Japanese religion. Esoteric Buddhism loved triads, and in this I seem to merely add another case to an already long list. I believe this is justified, however, by the affinities that bring these gods together in the implicit pantheon of medieval Buddhism. Yet I also want to question that triangular model, as fundamentally ideological. This triadic tendency, already at work in the grouping of the Three Worthies (Aizen, Fudō, and Nyoirin Kannon), and of the three-faced Daikoku, will become more evident when we come to the Three Devas (Shōten, Dakiniten, and Benzaiten). Despite their different origins and contexts, Daikokuten, Bishamonten, and Enmaten share the same demonic powers and chthonian nature. They provide a first approximation of a symbolic field that came to be more neatly defined with—or a network that came to extend to—the Three Devas.

Yama, Vaiśravaṇa, and Mahākāla seem to illustrate Georges Dumézil's three functions: sovereignty, war, and wealth. King Yama represents sovereignty and jurisdiction (like the Vedic god Varuna), Vaiśravaṇa war, and Mahākāla, as a kitchen god, wealth and abundance.[193] Things are not so simple, however: Vaiśravaṇa is also a god of wealth, and Mahākāla a god of battles. As Dumézil points out, functional gods are often paired with a multifunctional goddess who covers the three functions: in this case, it is the earth goddess.

Contrary to the too-well-defined trifunctional schema in the Indian model, in medieval Japanese esoteric Buddhism, each of these three devas overflows the limits of his explicit function and disseminates into other gods and functions. Even when they share the same function, however, they come to it differently, from different angles. It is their mode of action that must be taken into account, rather than a too-abstract function or domain.

It is difficult to hold them enclosed in their canonical definition. Bishamonten overflows into Inari Daimyōjin and Dakiniten; Daikokuten into Matarajin 摩多羅神, the Seven Mothers, and Dakiniten; Enmaten into Amaterasu, Susanoo, and Aizen. They are, in a sense, *enveloping* deities.

Enmaten and Daikokuten share the same retinue and reveal a dark, sinister, bloody world, which, while being Buddhist, seems closer to a demonic darkness than to the bright realm of awakening. And yet it is the heart of darkness, the unfathomable horror, which, in the *hongaku* paradigm, comes to represent the ultimate truth, the deep source of the mystery of human life. It is in order to attempt to think that unthinkable reality that esoteric Buddhism, in the margins of its doctrinal developments, extended the network of its mythological thought. The three devas in question are standing at the edge of the woods of medieval mythology and ritual, or roaming deep inside them.

The Hindu devas transformed themselves when passing over into Indian Buddhism, and they transformed again when becoming integrated into Chinese and Japanese religions: Daikokuten became Matarajin, Enmaten becomes Amaterasu or Jizō, Bishamonten became Kōjin.

The deepest transformation was that of Yama, whose Chinese version relegated the Indian deva Yama to the background. But the latter continued to exist in the form of the ruler of human destiny, not only in the other world but in this world, not only after death but during life.[194] Enmaten, the god that follows us everywhere while never leaving his underworldly realm, is not only the distant and impassive (or irate) functionary, he is the secret that sleeps within our very being.

An important point to note is that these devas, who in the traditional framework of *honji suijaku* thought are merely "traces" of the buddhas and bodhisattvas, were in fact conjointly perceived as emanations of the earth deity, which paradoxically ranks them on the side of the "real" deities (*jissha*) rather than with the "provisional" ones (*gonsha* 權者)—because, as one text puts it, the earth deity itself is a *jissha*.[195] This chthonian characteristic allowed them to break out from the all-too-controlled group of the twelve devas, and to entertain a subversive tendency that we are also going to see at work in the Three Devas: Shōten, Dakiniten, and Benzaiten.

2

THE ELEPHANT IN THE ROOM

Shōten

> *In the South suburb of the Elephant*
> *Is best to lodge.*
>
> Sebastian, in Shakespeare's *Twelfth Night*

SHŌTEN RITUALS

In 1329, Emperor Go-Daigo 後醍醐 (r. 1318–1339) performed a subjugation ritual in which he poured oil over a statue of the god Shōten 聖天 (var. Shōden, a.k.a. Vināyaka and Kangiten). The ritual was intended to "quickly dispel evil men and evil acts"—in other words, to get rid of the warrior government, the bakufu 幕府.[1] Amino Yoshihiko sees in this episode of a sovereign's resorting to black magic to defeat his opponents an illustration of the "weird" (*igyō* 異形) nature of Go-Daigo and of medieval kingship.[2] But evil is in the eye of the beholder, and Go-Daigo thought himself perfectly justified in trying to subjugate demonic warriors. A fundamental ambiguity of magic is that it usually looks "black" (i.e., aimed at destruction) to the recipient (or observer) while seeming "white" (i.e., aimed at protection) to the performer. "Le mal c'est l'autre"—the demon is always the other.[3]

This was by no means the first Shōten subjugation ritual performed at court and elsewhere, nor the last. In 1333, the monks of Mount Hiei performed a Shōten rite against the sixth Ashikaga 足利 shōgun, Yoshinori 義教 (r. 1429–1441).[4] Again, in the Warring States (Sengoku 戦国) period, monks performed many malediction rituals that invoked Shōten. Since the end of the Heian period, Shōten occupied a privileged seat in the imperial chapel, owing to his perceived efficacy in curbing enemies.[5] A famous case was the ritual of subjugation performed by the Tendai priest Son'i (866–940) at the time of the rebellion of Taira no Masakado 平将門 (940). Although the main deity of that rite was Fudō Myōō, tradition has it that, at one point, a statuette of Shōten on a lateral altar suddenly flew away, and Masakado's head fell on the main altar.[6] Son'i also attempted to subjugate the vengeful spirit of Sugawara no Michizane 菅原道真, with the help of Shōten. As is well known, Michizane died in exile after being accused of a plot, and the calamities that struck the palace and the capital after his death were attributed to his vengeful spirit (*onryō* 怨霊). The attempt to placate that spirit led to Michizane's deification as a "heavenly god" (tenjin 天神).[7] Interestingly, he is said to have been a devotee of Shōten, and one of the *engi* or origin stories that describe his demonization and subsequent divinization is actually an account of Shōten's miraculous powers. The demonic power attributed to Shōten perhaps explains why he came to be connected, and at one point identified, with Michizane.[8]

Shōten appeared in official rites such as the Latter Seven Day ritual and those centered on the *Benevolent Kings Sūtra* (*Ninnōkyō* 仁王經). Indeed, the Shōten altar is one of the altars of the standard program for any grand ritual.[9] Shōten was also invoked at court in rites for easy childbirth, but these rites were essentially exorcisms. For instance, when a Fudō rite was performed for the delivery of the imperial consort (*chūgū* 中宮) in the sixth month of the year 923, Kangiten appeared on the fourth day, and when a Shōten offering was performed, the prince was born safely.[10]

These rituals were to remain an imperial prerogative. As early as 785, an edict prohibited individual rites focused on Shōten and a number of other deities.[11] Yet Shōten was also invoked against the imperial house. In the *Hōgen monogatari* 保元物語, for instance, Fujiwara no Yorinaga 藤原頼長 (1120–1156) asks the Miidera priest Shōson 勝尊 to perform rituals centered on Shōten, Ususama Myōō 烏瑟沙摩明王, and Kongō Dōji 金剛童子 against Emperor Go-Shirakawa 後白河.

Regarding the Shōten cult among the people, only few documents exist. Perhaps in reaction against the popularity of that cult, various sources emphasize the danger of performing the rites privately, without resorting to the good offices of a priest. In the *Shin sarugaku ki* 新猿楽紀 (Record of New Sarugaku) by Fujiwara no Akihira 藤原明衡 (989–1066), an aging woman performs a Shōten ritual to win back her husband's love, but to no avail. Yet Shōten's rites were reputed for their efficacy. The concubine of Uda Tennō 宇多天皇 (r. 887–897) is said to have ascended to the rank of imperial consort because of her faith in Shōten.[12] Shōten also figured in private rites for easy childbirth, and, as we will see, he came to be worshiped as a placenta deity.

CULTIC SITES

Shōten's cult experienced a revival during the Edo period, owing to the influence of priests like Tankai 湛海 (1629–1716), who in 1678 restored Hōzanji 宝山寺 on Mount Ikoma 生駒, one of Shōten's major cultic centers. Paradoxically, at the founding of a Shōten Hall there was a concession on the part of Tankai, who was abandoning his worship of a jealous Vināyaka in favor of Fudō, who was enshrined as the *honzon* of the Fudō Hall. Even so, it is the worship of Vināyaka that has led the prosperity of that cultic center, up to the present.[13]

Shōten was (and still is) worshiped in many temples throughout Japan. One of his cultic centers, Hōkaiji 宝戒寺 in Kamakura, is very close to the Tsurugaoka Hachiman 鶴岡八幡 Shrine. After the suicide of the shōgun Hōjō Takatoki 北条高時 (1303–1333), Ashikaga Takauji was ordered by Emperor Go-Daigo to establish a memorial temple there, in 1335, to placate the spirit of his enemy. This temple is located next to the Kangiten Hall, and the custom of bringing the shōgun's funerary tablet to Kangiten's altar on the anniversary day of the god is still observed today. Ironically, Hōkaiji's founder, the Tendai priest Enkan 円観 (1281–1358), was one of the monks who had performed subjugation rituals on behalf of Emperor Go-Daigo with the aim of causing the fall of the Hōjō regime. At any rate, after the Kenmu restoration, this particular Shōten became the object of worship of the Ashikaga shōguns and of the Hōjō family.[14] Another important cultic center is Katsuoji (also read Kachio-dera 勝尾寺), north of Osaka, which is said to enshrine a "peerless" Shōten. This temple is also the cradle of the Kōjin cult, and the place where the linking of Shōten with Kōjin took place.[15]

The cult of Shōten has been traced to Kūkai, who brought to Japan ritual manuals translated by the esoteric masters Śubhakarasiṃha, Vajrabodhi, and Amoghavajra. Kūkai is also said to have authored a ritual manual, the *Shōten Procedural* (*Shōten shidai* 聖天次第). The cult developed in Shingon with the *Shōten kōshiki* 聖天講式 of Kakuban (1095–1143). In Tendai too, one finds a *Ritual of the Dual-bodied Vināyaka, the Great Saintly Deva of Bliss* (*Dai Shōten Kangi sōshin Binayaka-hō* 大聖天歓喜双身毘那夜迦法) among the texts listed by Ennin (793–864) in his *Catalogue of the Sacred Teachings Recently Sought in the Tang (Nittō shingyū shōgyō mokuroku* 入唐新求聖教目録). It was Annen 安然 (b. 841), however, who was instrumental in developing the cult.[16]

FROM DEMON TO DEVA

Shōten, also known as Binayaka 毘那夜迦 (a Japanese reading of his Sanskrit name, Vināyaka), Kangiten, or Daishō Kangiten 大聖歓喜天, is traced back to the Indic god Gaṇeśa. His name or title, meaning "Saintly Deva," appears paradoxical in view of his ambiguous nature, unless one reads it as an allusion to Shō Kannon (one of the figures that constitute the dual-bodied Kangiten).[17] Although Shōten never became as visible in Japan as Gaṇeśa in India, Wendy Doniger's remark about the latter could just as well apply to him and Japanese culture: "One can start from

Gaṇeśa and work from there in an unbroken line to almost any aspect of Indian culture."[18] Indeed, much the same could be said of practically all the deities studied in this book. As Lévi-Strauss once noted, "The earth of mythology is round."[19]

Scholars who try to describe Vināyaka (let alone explain him) resemble the blind men in the fable who try to describe an elephant—only the task is more difficult for them because, instead of dealing with a regular elephant, they are dealing with a hybrid beast, partly anthropomorphic. To begin with, to simply tell when and where the lord of beginnings began is a tall order. Tracing back the Buddhist Vināyaka to the Hindu Gaṇeśa (or the other way around) only pushes the question one step back, because Gaṇeśa's origins are just as obscure. Some scholars claim that he originated outside India, in the region of Kapiśa (present-day Afghanistan).[20] Others think that he derived from the merging of two distinct deities, a non-Indian demon called Vināyaka, and a more positive elephant-headed deity.[21] For the present purpose, I will consider that Gaṇeśa and Vināyaka refer to the same god, and use the two names interchangeably.

Gaṇeśa (or Gaṇapati) is the lord of obstacles in the sense that he is both the creator of obstacles (*vighnakartā*) and their remover (*vighnahartā*). This is why he must be invoked at the beginning of every ritual.[22] The well-known stories regarding Gaṇeśa's birth and his hybrid form reflect a late development of Purāṇic legend, and they actually obscure Vināyaka's demonic origins. They have many variants, and a brief outline will suffice here. Gaṇeśa is usually described as one of the two children of Śiva and Pārvatī, the other being Skanda.[23] In the standard myth, he is the guardian of Pārvatī, who created him from the secretions of her body.[24] In some variants he is produced by Śiva alone, or by the union of Śiva and Pārvatī. In later Hinduism, he is also said to be self-born (*svayambhū*): being the creator, he has no father or mother.[25]

One should emphasize the point that, technically speaking, Gaṇeśa is not Śiva's son, since he was produced from the filth of Pārvatī's bath; in the same way, his half-brother, Skanda, was born from Śiva's semen, outside his mother's womb.[26] It is paradoxical that this "parthenogenetic" god would become a god of sexual union. This characteristic puts the two brothers in the broader category of gods who are not born from a mother's womb, one of the motifs to be studied in a companion volume. For now, let us keep in mind the idea of twinning, however imperfect, as another toothing stone.

Gaṇeśa's elephantine appearance is said to have originated in the following episode. On one occasion, having been told by his mother to guard the door of her bathroom while she was taking a bath, he incurred his father's wrath for refusing him entrance. Śiva's looks can kill, and in this case his angry third eye reduced Gaṇeśa's head to ashes. To placate Pārvatī's wrath, or perhaps feeling some remorse, he managed to replace the child's head with that of an elephant, which happened to be nearby. In some versions of the myth, the confrontation between Śiva and Gaṇeśa turns into a real fight; in others, it is not Śiva but the fire god Agni (or Saturn, Śani) who burns and restores Gaṇeśa's head.

In spite of the myth, the motif of the elephant head remains difficult to explain. Perhaps one should see there a sign or remembrance of the demonic aspect of the god. Michel Strickmann attempts to explain it by citing the obedient nature of the elephant, but to be precise, Vināyaka is anything but obedient. I believe that the elephant head points to the uncanny nature of that god. On the other hand, the motif of the substitution of heads can be interpreted simply as an allusion to his non-brahmanical (lower caste, village) origin.[27]

FIGURE 2.1. Dancing Ganesha. Northern Bengal, 11th century. Grayish-black schist. Staatliche Museen zu Berlin, Museum für Indische Kunst.

In another version, Śiva creates Gaṇeśa to help the devas in their fight against the asuras; hence the new god's names: Vināyaka (the one who removes [obstacles]) and Vighneśvara (the lord of obstacles)—obstacles created, precisely, by the demonic *gaṇa* horde. In this version, it is Pārvatī herself who gives Gaṇeśa his elephant head. In another version, the beheading of Gaṇeśa occurs after a fight with Śiva that calls to mind the fight between the higher (divine) and the lower (demonic) orders. Once beheaded, Gaṇapati submits to Śiva (!), who makes him the leader of the *gaṇa* (hence his name Gaṇapati).[28] We will retain from this myth not only Gaṇeśa's antagonistic, albeit not simply Oedipal, relationship with his "father" Śiva, but also his function as guardian of the door (and keeper of secrecy).[29]

SKANDA

Rolf Stein and Michel Strickmann have emphasized the sibling relationship between Gaṇeśa and Skanda (a.k.a. Kārttikeya, Kumāra), the handsome young warrior (Fig. 2.2). In the *Suśruta Saṃhita,* Skanda is

FIGURE 2.2. Skanda-Karttikeya. Orissa, 13th century. Staatliche Museen zu Berlin, Museum für Indische Kunst.

the lord of planets (*grahādhipati*), a function that is also attributed to Gaṇeśa. According to Krishan, the two gods first existed independently, and both were essentially demons (asuras). The functional parallelism between the two "brothers" was broken when Skanda was appointed chief of the armies of the devas in their fight against the demons, thus becoming a deva himself, or even better, the leader of the Brahmanic gods. As Skanda was "brahmanized," becoming the god of war, his demonic nature was increasingly glossed over in silence. However, his success was relatively brief: his cult was eventually absorbed into that of Śiva, and he became a secondary deity again (particularly in northern India). Skanda's eclipse allowed Gaṇeśa to move to the forefront, although Skanda's cult remained widespread in southern India. In northern India, Gaṇeśa became the paradigmatic "demon of obstacles."[30] But, as we have seen, he eventually followed the same road toward Brahmanic orthodoxy.

Thus, the resilience of the structural dyad formed by Gaṇeśa and Skanda, whose variants, according to Stein, permeated East Asia, hides the animosity that existed between them from the outset, as it did between Gaṇeśa and Śiva. A clue to that animosity is the representation of the "fight" between the two brothers. That structural polarity was already threatened in India itself, and the two gods continued to develop independently in China and Japan. It is all the more surprising, then, to find that this polarity eventually reconstituted itself under another form in these countries. By emphasizing the "gatekeeper" function, however, Stein tended to downplay the demonic origins and nature of these two deities, as revealed in particular by their association with the Seven Mothers.

The case of the Gaṇeśa/Skanda pair shows the extent to which the structural duality, which always tends to reassert itself, hides the historic tensions (the rivalry between them, and the fact that Gaṇeśa eventually superseded Skanda) as well as their demonic aspects—which resurfaced in Mikkyō. What is true for these two figures, reduced to their gatekeeping function, is also true for other pairs of guard figures, such as Aizen and Fudō, the male and female crossroads deities (*dōsojin* 道祖神), and the companion spirits (*kushōjin*).

Like many other protectors of the Dharma, Skanda started his Buddhist career as a demon that torments children.[31] According to the *Mahābhārata,* it is from Skanda that the Seven Mothers borrow their power.[32] It is also from him that the "seizers" (*grahas*) emerge. In China, the image of Skanda split into two different versions, owing to an error in the transcription of his name.[33] While he became an important protector of Chinese and Japanese monasteries under the names of Weituo 韋駄 and Idaten 韋駄天, he carried on a parallel existence in medieval Buddhist esotericism. Mikkyō iconography inherited the Indian representation of Skanda as a six-headed god riding a peacock. Like Mañjuśrī, he is described as a handsome youth (*kumāra*). While Mañjuśrī's usual mount is a lion, and Samantabhadra's an elephant, Mañjuśrī is sometimes depicted riding a peacock. Thus, if Mañjuśrī's peacock evokes Skanda's mount, similarly, Samantabhadra's elephant evokes Gaṇeśa's.[34]

Together with the twelve Mothers, the demonic Skanda became one of the fifteen demons in a pediatric text known as *Kumāra-tantra* (and in its Japanese version, the *Dōjikyō* 童子經).[35] In fact, the Gandharva king who is the *honzon* of the *Dōjikyō* mandala inherits a role that should have remained Skanda's if the latter had not been "mobilized" under another form (as Weituo/Idaten, the guardian of the monastery gate).

VINĀYAKA AS A DEMON

Vināyaka, whose name means obstacle or impediment, is fundamentally a demon, as well as the leader of the *vināyakas,* his emanations. In one variant of his origin story, the head used to replace that of the child Gaṇeśa belonged to the demon Gajāsura (an asura). While Gaṇeśa is usually depicted with a craving for sweets, initially his propitiation included offerings of meat, fish, and liquor. In the *Brahmāṇḍa Purāṇa,* for instance, he is described as the lord of *pramathas* (night wanderers, killers), a trait reminiscent of Mahākāla.[36]

Gaṇeśa was also known as Gaṇapati, leader of the *gaṇas* (who are essentially malevolent, fierce, and destructive spirits). Yet Gaṇeśa, son of Pārvatī, is distinct from these *gaṇas,* who are thought to have issued from Śiva and form his retinue. As far as demons go, Vināyaka remains an ambiguous demon. According to the *Skanda Purāṇas,* Gaṇapati, by

FIGURE 2.3. Vināyaka and the Mothers. Ellora caves, India. Photo Bernard Faure.

polluting the minds of people, diverts them from the path of emancipation. At the same time he is said to fulfill all worldly desires, in this way keeping people in this world (like the Buddhist Māra). In the *Agni* and *Skanda Purāṇas,* however, the gods use Vināyaka to frustrate people in their activities and prevent them from going to heaven (which is already overpopulated) or attaining deliverance (*mokṣa*). In other sources, Vināyaka creates obstacles for the actions of the unrighteous—in other words, those who oppose us—and brings *mokṣa*.[37]

VINĀYAKA AND THE MOTHERS

As we have seen, Vināyaka shares with Skanda close relations with the Seven Mothers, on the one hand, and with the nine seizers (*navagrahas*), on the other. In the *Vāmapurāṇa,* Śiva puts into Gaṇeśa's service both the Mothers and the *bhūtas,* the spirits of the dead.[38] The threatening aspect of Gaṇeśa (or rather Vināyaka, who is not yet the cute Gaṇeśa) appears clearly in certain early representations—for instance, at Ellora, where he is depicted with the Seven Mothers and Cāmuṇḍā. The Buddhists, who lived side by side with the Hindus and the Jains at Ellora during the sixth and seven centuries, were familiar with that representation. A good example of this can be found in cave 6 at Aurangabad, where a massive Gaṇeśa (Vināyaka) is seen in proximity with Cāmuṇḍā on the western wall, with Vīrabhadra and six other Mothers on the southern wall, and with the Buddha on the northern wall.[39]

FIGURE 2.4. Vināyaka and the Mothers. Ellora caves, India. Photo Bernard Faure.

We recall that the seven or eight Mothers (*mātṛkās*) form Mahākāla's retinue in the *Mahāvairocana-sūtra.* At Ellora and Aurangabad, it is Vināyaka who has taken over the role of Mahākāla (that is, Śiva) himself. He is occasionally described as a member of Maheśvara's retinue, or even as Maheśvara (Śiva) himself.

Krishan has shown how the same process of "brahmanization" and ennobling that characterized Gaṇeśa and Skanda also applied to the Mothers. The latter were originally depicted with animal heads. But they evolved, from frightening animal- and bird-faced figures, to more benign, human-faced ones. Around the Gupta period, they came to be represented in the form of gorgeous young women. In other words, they changed from demons to goddesses, becoming the consorts of brahmanical gods. It was only then that their number settled to seven or eight.[40]

Among the Mothers, however, Cāmuṇḍā constituted an exception. Always on the periphery, and at times exterior to the group, her frightening appearance seems to preserve the dreadful nature of the ancient Mothers. Significantly, she is often paired with Vināyaka, at the head (or sometimes the end) of the list. She is also said to be Yama's sister or consort (*śakti*), suggesting a functional equivalence between Yama and Vināyaka.

In the Enmaten mandala, Vināyaka appears as a member of Yama's retinue.[41] Although Yama's emissaries are called Ox Head and Horse Face in Chinese Buddhism, nowhere is there any mention of an "elephant-headed" emissary, or of any other animal-faced demons (unlike in the Tibetan intermediary world, or *bardo*).[42] According to certain scriptures, bad karma could lead to rebirth in hell with an elephant head, but that does not seem sufficient to explain Vināyaka's presence.[43] Chinese texts where he is called the "demon king" may have paved the way to that evolution, although the cult was eventually prohibited in China.[44] Perhaps it was his demonic status alone that guaranteed him a place in Yama's retinue, since all demons are said to dwell in Yama's domain.

Vināyaka is thus a part (or rather the leader) of a cohort that includes the seven attractive and benevolent *mātṛkās* and the malevolent, wrathful Cāmuṇḍā. When Krishan argues that Vināyaka, having become beneficent, is no longer associated with the *mātṛkās* and *ḍākinīs,* he seems unaware of Vināyaka's role in Yama's retinue.[45] We find a similar structure in the Japanese Enmaten mandala, but here Yama has displaced Vināyaka from the central position, and the latter is only one member of Yama's retinue. The structure of this mandala—with the *mātṛkās* on one side of Yama, the *ḍākinīs* on the other, and Vināyaka above—preserves ancient ties that the Hindu tradition had apparently forgotten. The spatial relation between Vināyaka and the boar-headed Cāmuṇḍā, for instance, evokes the couple formed by Vināyaka and his boar-headed consort in the representation of the dual-bodied Kangiten.

Although largely speculative, the notion that Vināyaka himself was initially a kind of "Mother" (whose image derived from the *mātṛkā* Vināyakī) has the merit of placing Vināyaka on the plane of deities or demons associated with childhood (or more precisely with prenatal life at the fetal, embryological stage). This feature will resurface in the Japanese redefinition of Vināyaka as Kōjin and as a placenta deity.

Equally significant is Vināyaka's association with the astral demons known as the nine seizers (*navagrahas*). In Hindu Tantrism, these deities, like Vināyaka himself, must be worshiped at the beginning of all rites.[46] As their alternate name indicates, the nine luminaries were "seizers" (*graha*), that is, demons that possess humans and threaten their lives, the most baleful among them being Mars, Saturn, Rāhu, and Ketu.[47] Vināyaka's association with them confirms his astral nature, another characteristic he shares with Yama.

HENOTHEISTIC TENDENCIES

As should be clear by now, Gaṇeśa, the "lord of beginnings"—who removes all obstacles but can also cause them—was not always the plump and gracious, childlike god he became in later Hinduism. As Paul Courtright puts it, "The Purāṇic texts are uncomfortably aware of the discrepancy between the malevolent, obstacle-creating powers of Vināyaka and the positive, obstacle-removing actions of Gaṇeśa, and they attempt to disguise Gaṇeśa's demon background through the clever use of false etymologies for the name 'Vināyaka.'"[48] The development of Gaṇeśa's cult (like that of his Japanese counterpart) shows henotheistic tendencies—the urge to make him a supreme god. For instance, Gaṇeśa's body comes to symbolize the manifested principle, while his head represents the nonmanifested principle. His belly is said to contain all worlds. His four hands symbolize the four *Vedas* and the four main classes of beings (devas, men, asuras, and *nāgas*). Interestingly, he is the only god to have an odd number of hands, in the sense that his trunk is interpreted as a fifth hand, which he can use expertly in love games.[49]

Krishan retraces the steps by which Gaṇeśa ascended in the Hindu pantheon. The earliest representations of the two-armed (demonic) Gaṇeśa date from the third to fifth century. He appears with multiple arms (i.e, as an orthodox god) from the fifth century onward. The appearance of his mount, the rat, spreads only toward the tenth century—although it already appears on a bas-relief of Sarnath (late Gupta period) that describes the Buddha's *parinirvāṇa.*[50] As Krishan points out, when Vināyaka became redefined in positive terms, his mount, the rat, inherited his negative aspects and had to be tamed by his master.[51] The positions of Gaṇeśa in temples (as gatekeeper, acolyte of Śiva, and so on) reflects his progressive rise. Gaṇeśa was promoted to the status of a supreme god around the tenth to twelfth centuries—for instance, in the *Modgala Purāṇa* and the *Gaṇeśa Purāṇa,* and in three *Upaniṣads* focused on Gaṇeśa.[52] His apotheosis took place in Maharashtra in the thirteenth century. Maharashtra temples to Gaṇeśa were built from the fourteenth to the eighteenth century, and that region remains until today the center of Gaṇeśa's cult. As Krishan points out, there was nothing like this in Japan—no sect that worshiped Shōten as its supreme god, as did the Gāṇapatyas in India, around the tenth century.[53] However, this is not to say that Shōten did not become a supreme deity, as we will see shortly.

The Buddhist Vināyaka

We have seen how Gaṇeśa, as he joined classical Indian mythology, lost his demonic features. From that standpoint, Japanese Buddhism appears to have preserved a more ancient (and demonic) form of Vināyaka, and, while it eventually turned him into a supreme god, it did not bowdlerize him, as Hinduism did to Gaṇeśa. The case is rare enough to be noted.

According to Krishan, "It is clear that Gaṇeśa is a minor god in the Buddhist pantheon."[54] This may be true, but the same is not as true of Gaṇeśa's Buddhist avatar, Vināyaka. Various elements of Gaṇeśa's myth have played a role in the evolution of his Buddhist counterpart, although Gaṇeśa's name is conspicuously absent in Buddhist texts, which usually call him Vināyaka and occasionally Gaṇapati.[55] In one source, the Buddha teaches Ānanda, on the Vulture Peak (traditionally located in Rajgir, Bihar), the secret mantra of Gaṇapati, the *Gaṇapati-hṛdaya.*[56] Gaṇeśa also is rarely seen in Indian Buddhist iconography. A Gupta stele of Mathura

(4th–5th century) at the Indian Museum of Calcutta shows the astral deity Rāhu, Śiva on his bull Nandin, Indra on his elephant, Skanda on his peacock, and Gaṇeśa on his rat, all gathered to witness the *parinirvāṇa* of the Buddha. In other representations, Gaṇeśa (or Vināyaka) is a member of the retinue of Māra attacking the Buddha.[57]

For all their shared features, the representations of Gaṇeśa and of Vināyaka differ in various ways: Vināyaka does not have Gaṇeśa's characteristic potbelly. He is definitely no Babar—but neither is Gaṇeśa, despite all the modern sugar-coated reinterpretations. Another difference between the Buddhist Vināyaka and Gaṇeśa is that the latter does not have a mount (Skt. *vāhana*), at least in orthodox esoteric iconography (such as the *Kakuzenshō* and the like).[58] The same is true for Benzaiten as opposed to Sarasvatī, which perhaps means that their image is anterior to that of the deities riding a mount, a relatively late development in India. However, the *Kakuzenshō* contains numerous images of deities on their mount—for instance, Skanda on his peacock, or the five manifestations of Ākāśagarbha (J. Kokūzō 虚空藏), each riding a different animal. In this sense, Krishan is wrong when he argues that none of the Indian gods is represented on a mount in the Japanese mandalas.[59] As to the Vināyaka that forms part of the Three Deva triad, he rides a white fox. It's possible that the lack of a mount indicates that one is still dealing with a demon, the mount being one of the characteristics of a god. However, when Vināyaka becomes the "demon king," the fundamental ambiguity of that term means that one no longer knows whether one is dealing with a god or with a super-demon. In many cases, it is the mount and the acolytes who inherit the negative aspects of the deity, allowing it to "evolve" by retaining only positive features. Such was the case with Gaṇeśa's mount, the rat. In the long run, however, the positive nature of the deity tends to carry over to its mount, and conversely. Unlike other gods of obstacles (beginning with Gaṇeśa), the Buddhist Vināyaka never lost his dark or ambivalent nature, and perhaps that is why he never became potbellied. In this sense, he does not fit the *gaṇa*/gatekeeper paradigm as neatly as Stein suggests. Yet he remained a keeper of secrecy.

THE GOD OF OBSTACLES

Like his Hindu counterpart, the Buddhist Vināyaka is a god of obstacles, or rather, the god of obstacles *par excellence.* Unlike Gaṇeśa, however, he remains essentially a demon who needs to be tamed or propitiated. Although his name initially meant "remover of obstacles," Buddhists reinterpreted him as the cause of obstacles. Initially, Vināyaka and his troupe were like "demons of small things," embodying the "everyday power of evil."[60] What he developed into was a powerful demon, the leader of a demonic horde consisting of *vināyakas* (causing obstacles) and animal-headed *gaṇas* (possessing people).[61] According to the *Kakuzen-shō*'s definition, based on the *Mahāvairocana-sūtra:* "One calls *vināyakas* [those] who cause obstacles to all dharmas. All these obstacles arise from false thinking."[62] In particular, the *vināyakas* were deemed responsible for nightmares.[63]

As is often the case, the name Vināyaka can refer to a class of demonic beings or to an individual who has emerged from his cohort and become its leader (or its tamer, as the case may be). The distinction between the collective and the singular is not always clear, and when possible (in English) I refer to the individual deity by capitalizing the initial letter of its name. The gradual elevation of this deity, from demon to deva (and beyond), is reflected in the changes in his name (or title), from Vināyaka to Kangiten to Shōten (or Daishō Kangiten).

According to the *Shōtenbō engi* 聖天法縁起 by Ken'i 兼意 (1072–?), the abbot of Jōren-in 成蓮院 on Mount Kōya, Shōten dwells with his vast cohort on a mountain called Mount Vināyaka, or Mount of the Elephant Head (Zōzu-sen 象頭山), or again Mount of Obstacles (Shōge-san 障礙山).[64] He has been ordered by Maheśvara to ravish the vital breath of beings and to cause obstacles. The text specifies that this order was given before Maheśvara's conversion to Buddhism, but it does not say whether Maheśvara's conversion led to that of Vināyaka.[65] Vināyaka shares a number of features with Mahākāla (J. Daikokuten): both are closely related to Śiva, and both grant similar wishes to the practitioner—in particular, wishes of a sexual or monetary nature (we recall that Daikokuten became a god of wealth in Japan). They also share symbolic attributes such as the radish, although in Shōten's case this radish is sometimes replaced by a broken tusk, which seems to be its prototype (see Fig. 2.9).[66]

In esoteric Buddhist literature, Vināyaka is an awe-inspiring demon, an intimate enemy of the practitioner, whose practice he impedes by creating all kinds of obstacles.[67] The *Muli mantuoluo shou jing* 牟梨曼荼羅呪經 and the *Azhapo guishen dajiang shang fo tuoluoni jing* 阿吒婆拘鬼神大将上佛陀羅尼經, for instance, treat Vināyaka as a demon and teach mudrās and mantras to expel him.[68] The *Guanzizai pusa suixin zhu jing* 観自在菩薩随心呪經 also gives mudrās and incantations to expel Vināyaka.[69] The same sources, however, also contain incantations that reveal a change in perspective, even if Vināyaka remains a demon of obstacles. Instead of confronting him as an enemy, practitioners are enjoined to soothe him with offerings, and to increase their strength by eating those offerings themselves. Once propitiated, the demon of obstacles may become a protecting deity. Not everyone agreed with that optimistic vision, however.

The *Sūtra of the Divine Incantations of the Eleven-faced* [*Avalokiteśvara*] (*Shiyimian shenzhou xin jing* 十一面醋神呪心經, T. 20, 1071), translated by Xuanzang in 656, expounds the rite of Vināyaka's bath with perfumed water. Subsequently, various ritual manuals centered on Vināyaka were translated by Bodhiruci (between 693 and 713), by Śubhakarasiṃha (between 717 and 725), by Vajrabodhi (between 723and 730), and by Amoghavajra (between 746 and 774). Although they still contain incantations aimed at expelling Vināyaka, they include a number of texts centered on the dual-bodied Bliss Deva (Nandikeśvara, J. Kangiten).

When duly propitiated, Vināyaka can hold his elephants off and remove all obstacles. Evidently, the Tantric Vināyaka has not experienced the transformation that affected Gaṇeśa. Of all the deities studied here, he is the one who has been the least affected by the euphemizing process that characterizes the evolution of Japanese deities from the Muromachi period onward. Perhaps this is because the elephant remained, for the Japanese, the most extreme image of otherness. The dissociation that took place in India between two images of the elephant-headed god, a positive one (Gaṇeśa) and a negative one (Vināyaka), is not found in Buddhism; it has simply given rise to the image of Vināyaka as Kangiten, a deity whose animal lovemaking, while synonymous with prosperity, is still perceived as "weird" (*igyō* 異形).

The East Asian Vināyaka is said to fulfill all wishes, even immoral ones. According to the *Keiran shūyōshū,* his elephant head means obedience, because the elephant obeys his master's orders blindly, to the point of swallowing a burning iron ball.[70] But even when he acts as a deity of fortune, Vināyaka retains his malevolent, demonic nature; he remains dangerous, difficult, and deceptive. Thus his cult developed in relation with the belief in malevolent spirits (*onryō* 怨霊).

In the *Record of the Miraculous Powers of the Bliss Deva* (*Kangiten reigenki* 歓喜天霊験記), Shōten defeats the resentful spirit of Sugawara no Michizane 菅原道真 (the statesman later deified as Tenjin 天神).[71] This illustrated text, dating from the Kamakura period, is known by an exemplar preserved in the collection of the Kondō 近藤 family in Hyōgo. It tells the legend of Michizane (hence its traditional title, *Tenjin engi* 天神縁起), but it is in fact a recounting of Shōten's prodigies.[72] The first scroll is focused on the relations between Michizane and the Tendai priest Son'i 尊意 (866–940?), a fervent believer in Kangiten. The second scroll tells how Son'i subjugated Taira no Masakado, and how Jikaku Daishi 慈覚大師 (Ennin) received a secret Shōten rite during his stay in China; then, after being helped by Shōten during his return trip to Japan, how he made a metal statue of the god and enshrined it in his newly founded monastery. The fourth scroll focuses on Shōten's vow to save beings and on his virtues. (This emphasis on Shōten's virtues is conspicuously absent in the *Kitano Tenjin engi* 北野天神縁起.)

Makabe Toshinobu introduces another Kitano Shrine document of the Muromachi period, the *Kami no ki.* The first section of that text identifies

Shōten's five *honji* as Amida, Jūichimen, Bishamon, Daishō Kangiten, and Benzaiten.[73] On this account, strangely enough, Shōten seems to be his own *honji* (Daishō Kangiten). The text also says that the Kangiten worshiped in that shrine is an avatar of Daijizaiten (Śiva), because the so-called Daijizaiten is none other than Shōten, a deity in essence identical with Daikokuten, who brings happiness and knowledge. Iyanaga Nobumi has discussed the identity between Kitano Tenjin and Daijizaiten 大自在天.[74]

Vināyaka is a powerful demon king, the "king of the hundred demons." These demons usually have animal heads (some have elephant heads; others, however, have the heads of sheep, monkeys, dogs, oxen, and horses).[75] The dark, demonic nature of this god—as reflected in his animal features—and his love for secrecy militated against his becoming too readily a popular god of fortune. Even when he is acknowledged as particularly efficacious, his demonic stigma marks him as dangerous and heterodox. Although this image may have been, in part, a way to preserve the monopoly of his cult for the monks who claimed to be the necessary mediators, something else seems at stake here. The case of the priest Tankai, a reluctant worshiper who had to fight all his life against the threats posed by Vināyaka and his troupe, suggests that—for certain monks at least—the threat was perceived as very real. Indeed, Vināyaka belongs to the category of the "real" gods (*jissha*), who have their own powerful agency and cannot be explained away simply as manifestations of higher (or lower) principles. The dual nature of Kangiten, a composite deity formed by the union of Vināyaka and Senāyaka, may be a theological response to that threat: while the male figure is described as a "real" one, the female is said to be a "provisional manifestation" of the bodhisattva Avalokiteśvara. Thus their union expresses the nonduality of real and provisional.[76]

ICONOGRAPHY

In Japanese esoteric iconography, the elephant-headed god is mainly represented in two ways: when standing alone, he is usually called Shōten or Vināyaka (J. Binayaka 毘那夜迦) (see Figs. 2.5–2.8); when in sexual embrace with a consort, he becomes the dual-bodied Kangiten, the Bliss Deva (or devas). Textual sources mention other names as well. In canonical texts, however, the names Gaṇapati, Shōten, Kangiten, and Daishō Kangiten seem to be used interchangeably. The *Byakuhō shō,* for instance, declares: "Because he is perfectly free in the six supranormal powers and secret dharmas, he is called Shōten. Because he is perfectly free in wisdom, he is called Daijizaiten. Because he achieves love (*keiai*), he is called the dual-bodied Vināyaka king. Because he produces the five cereals, he is called the six-armed deva."[77]

FIGURE 2.5. Vināyaka. Late Heian period, 12th century. Color on paper. *Zuzōshō*. Kanazawa bunko.

FIGURE 2.6. Vināyaka. Late Heian period, 12th century. Color on paper. *Zuzōshō*. Kanazawa bunko.

FIGURE 2.7. Vināyaka. Late Heian period, 12th century. Color on paper. *Zuzōshō*. Kanazawa bunko.

FIGURE 2.8. Vināyaka. Edo period. Sheet, ink on paper. University Art Museum, Kyoto City University of Arts. *BZS* 000.

FIGURE 2.9. Vināyaka holding a radish. *Daihi Taizō daimandara, TZ*, Fig. 375.

FIGURE 2.10. Three-headed Vināyaka. *Kakuzenshō, DNBZ* 50: 118.

Shōten is usually represented with two, four, or six arms, holding various attributes such as a *vajra,* an axe, a noose, a trident, a wheel, a tusk or radish, and so on. He sometimes looks perfectly anthropomorphic—like a deva, a brahman, or a youth.[78] The *Jikkanshō* and the *Kakuzenshō* show different images of Shōten: as a three-headed seated Vināyaka (Fig. 2.13), or as a four-armed, standing, youthful Vināyaka, wearing a leopard skin around his waist (Fig. 2.8), and so on.[79]

Vināyaka in the Vajra Mandala

Once tamed and integrated into the esoteric mandala, *vināyakas* (at least some of them) become protectors, a status marked by the addition of the prefix Vajra- (J. Kongō) to their name. The external Vajra section of the Vajra Realm (Skt. Vajradhātu, J. Kongōkai 金剛界) mandala contains four groups of five deities distributed along the four directions, each group containing one Vināyaka. These Vināyakas are said to be emanations of the buddha Vairocana, which, following the Tantric rule "It takes one to tame one," adopt the form of *vināyakas* precisely in order to tame the obstacle-causing *vināyakas.* They are said to belong to the category of the space devas (*kokū-ten* 虚空天) or "devas who go in the sky" (*kūgyō-ten* 空行天)—a feature they share, as we will see shortly, with Dakiniten and her acolytes. These deities, who are represented as seated on lotus leaves, are:

1) In the east: Kongō-zaisaiten 金剛摧砕 (Skt.Vajravikirana), whose name means that he destroys all the obstacles caused by the demonic *vināyakas.* He is also called Sangaiten 傘蓋天 (Deva with a parasol), because of the parasol he holds, which is said to symbolize his ability to cover and protect all beings (Fig. 2.12).[80]

2) In the south: Kongō-jikiten 金剛食天 (or Skt. Vajrabhakṣana; var. Kongō-onjikiten 金剛飲食天 'deva of drink and food'); also called Kongō-keman (Vajramāla), because he holds a garland of flowers in his right hand, and sometimes a noose in his left hand.[81]

3) In the west: Kongō-eten 金剛衣天 (Vajra Robe, or Kongō-ebukuten 金剛衣服天, Skt. Vajravāsin), the "deva of clothing"; also called Kongō-ai 金剛愛, perhaps because his name, Vajra Robe, is said to express the notion that the placenta protects the fetus from the cold and heat produced by the mother's body. Like Aizen Myōō, he holds a bow and an arrow aimed at demonic *vināyakas.*[82]

4) In the north: Chōbukuten 調伏天 (or Kongō-jōbukuten 金剛調伏天, Skt. Vajrajaya), the "subduing deva"; also known as

Zōzuten, the "elephant-headed deva," Hōto Binayaka 抱刀毘那夜迦, the "sword-holding Vināyaka" (because he holds a sword in his left hand), and Konjiki Ganahattei, the "golden Gaṇapati."[83] (See Fig. 2.13.) In the *Kakuzenshō,* he holds a staff in his right hand, a jewel in his left (Fig. 2.11). In this text, he is the only one of the four directional Vināyakas represented with an elephant head. The others are anthropomorphic figures wearing an elephant head (or a dragon head, in the case of Kongō-ebukuten) as their headgear. In the Vajradhātu mandala and other sources, however, the four Vināyakas all have elephant heads.

Sometimes a fifth figure, specifically called the "deva Vināyaka" (Binayaka-ten 毘那夜迦天), probably representing the center, is added. He holds four attributes: a pastry (*modaka*), an axe, a winnowing fan, and a radish (or a broken tusk).[84]

FIGURE 2.11. Four directional Vināyakas. *Kakuzenshō, DNBZ* 50: 119.

FIGURE 2.12. Vināyaka with parasol. Heian period, 12th century. Ink and color on paper. *Kontai butsuga chō*. Tokyo National Museum.

FIGURE 2.13. Vināyaka with sword. Heian period, 12th century. Ink and color on paper. *Kontai butsuga chō*. Tokyo National Museum.

Finally, a sixth figure, called Kongōmen-ten 金剛面天 (Vajra-faced Deva), Kongō-chozuten (Boar-headed Deva), or Kongōku-ten 金剛拘 (Skt. Vajraṇkuśaṅ 'deva with the hook'), is represented in the northern sector of the Vajra Realm mandala. Since it is boar-faced, it is perhaps related to Cāmuṇḍā, but it could also be the female protagonist of the Kangiten couple, a manifestation of Kannon, who is represented with a sow head.[85]

Other Iconographic Forms

Another popular representation, found in various scrolls and talismans (*ofuda*), shows Kangiten as a four-armed goddess seated on a platform,

FIGURE 2.14. *(Opposite)* Shōten mandala. Edo period. Color on silk. Collection of Adrian and Judith Snodgrass.

holding a jewel staff and a small halberd in two of her hands and two radishes in her other hands, and wearing two small elephant heads—white and red—as her headgear.[86] An example is a talismanic picture preserved at Ichigami Shrine 市神神社 in Yōkaichi City (Shiga prefecture) (Fig. 2.22). The caption above the image says: "My manifestation harmonizes its light to bring benefits to beings. Fusing principle and phenomena, I pervade the entire Dharmadhātu. I protect the Three Jewels and save all beings. I am the Great Saint, the Bliss Deva (Daishō Kangiten)."[87]

As noted earlier, a Vināyaka also appears in the Yama (Enmaten) mandalas, next to Ḍākinī and Cāmuṇḍā. Here they probably represent categories in the formation of Yama's retinue rather than individual deities. In medieval Japan, however, Vināyaka became the *honzon* of a distinct Shōten mandala in which all the deities are elephant headed.[88] In the line drawing of the Shōten mandala in the *Bukkyō zuzō shūsei* 佛教図像集成, the two elephant-headed deities at the center of a four-petaled lotus are not shown embracing, as in the usual representations of Kangiten, but rather are arm in arm, as if dancing (Fig. 2.16). They are surrounded by the four directional Vināyakas, seated on four lotus petals, and by various symbols that are the *samaya* forms of the twelve devas. At the bottom, outside the central court, are two six-armed Vināyakas.

We also have two painted versions of the same mandala. One, represented by the exemplar in the Snodgrass collection (Fig. 2.14), is basically the same as the line-drawing reproduced in the *Butsuzō shūsei* 佛像集成 (Fig. 2.16). Its four directional Vināyakas are white in color. They hold the same attributes as their homologues of the Kongōkai mandala, with some slight variants. One of the six-armed Vināyakas at the bottom is white, the other red. Above the northern Vināyaka is a buffalo-riding deva, probably Ishana-ten (i.e., Śiva).

Another exemplar, the *Shōten himitsu mandara* 聖天秘密曼荼羅 (Shōten's secret mandala) preserved at Kongōbuji on Mount Kōya, is slightly different (Fig. 2.15). The four Vināyakas are colored according to the standard color code for the four directions in Chinese cosmology: the eastern Vināyaka is green, the southern red, the western white, the northern blue/black. The twelve directional devas that surround them are depicted in anthropomorphic form, following the traditional spatial order: thus, Enmaten, who rules the south, is placed just below the red Vināyaka, while Bishamonten, the ruler of the north, is placed above the blue/black Vināyaka.

Taming and Domestication

The demonic image of Vināyaka fuses with that of Gajāsura, the elephant demon killed by Śiva (or by Gaṇeśa himself in certain versions).[89] In Buddhist iconography, the theme of that subjugation is picked up in the motif of the elephant skin which Mahākāla holds above his head, and in

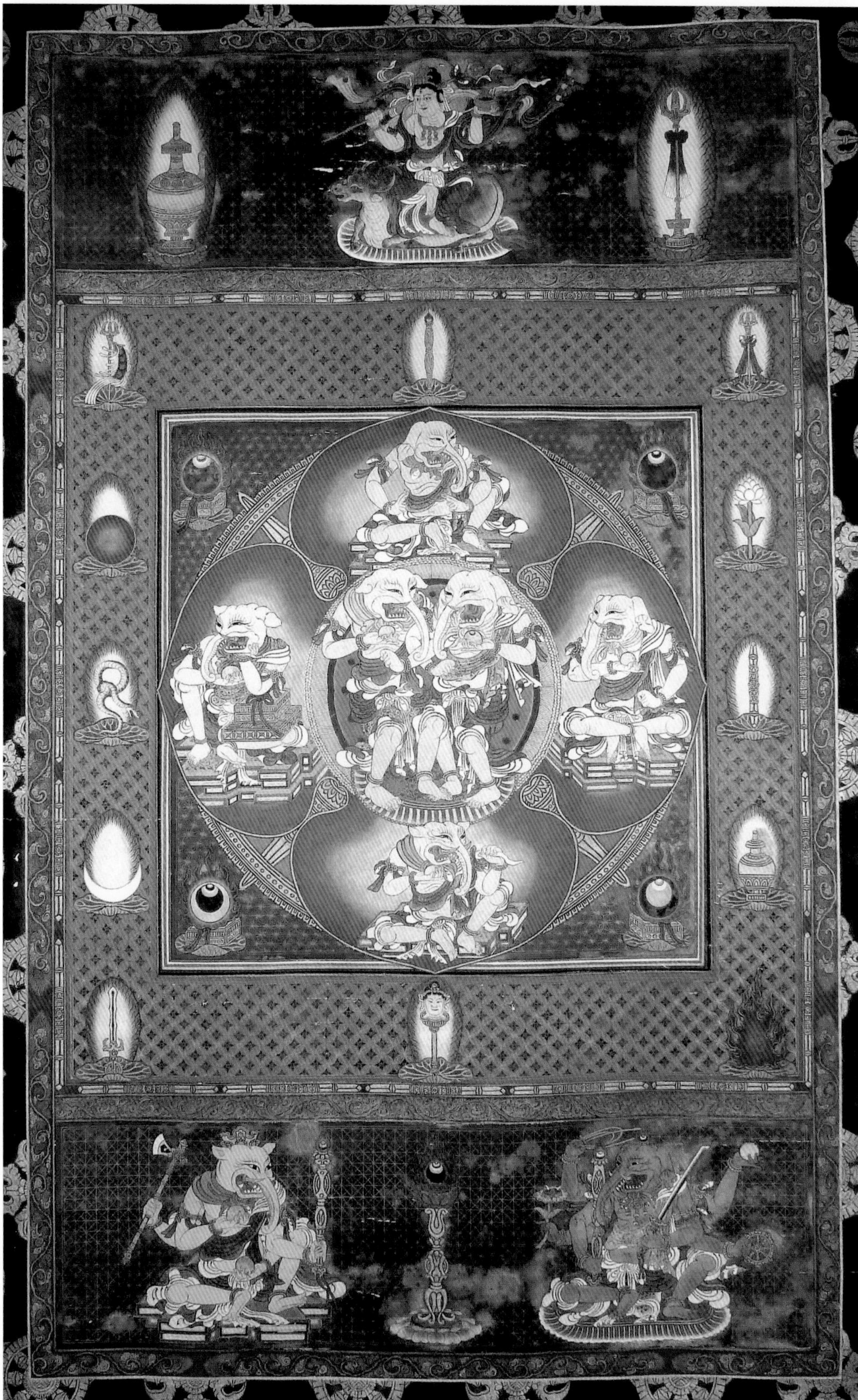

FIGURE 2.15. Shōten's secret mandala. Edo period, 17th century. Hanging scroll, color on silk. Kongōbuji, Kōyasan (Wakayama prefecture).

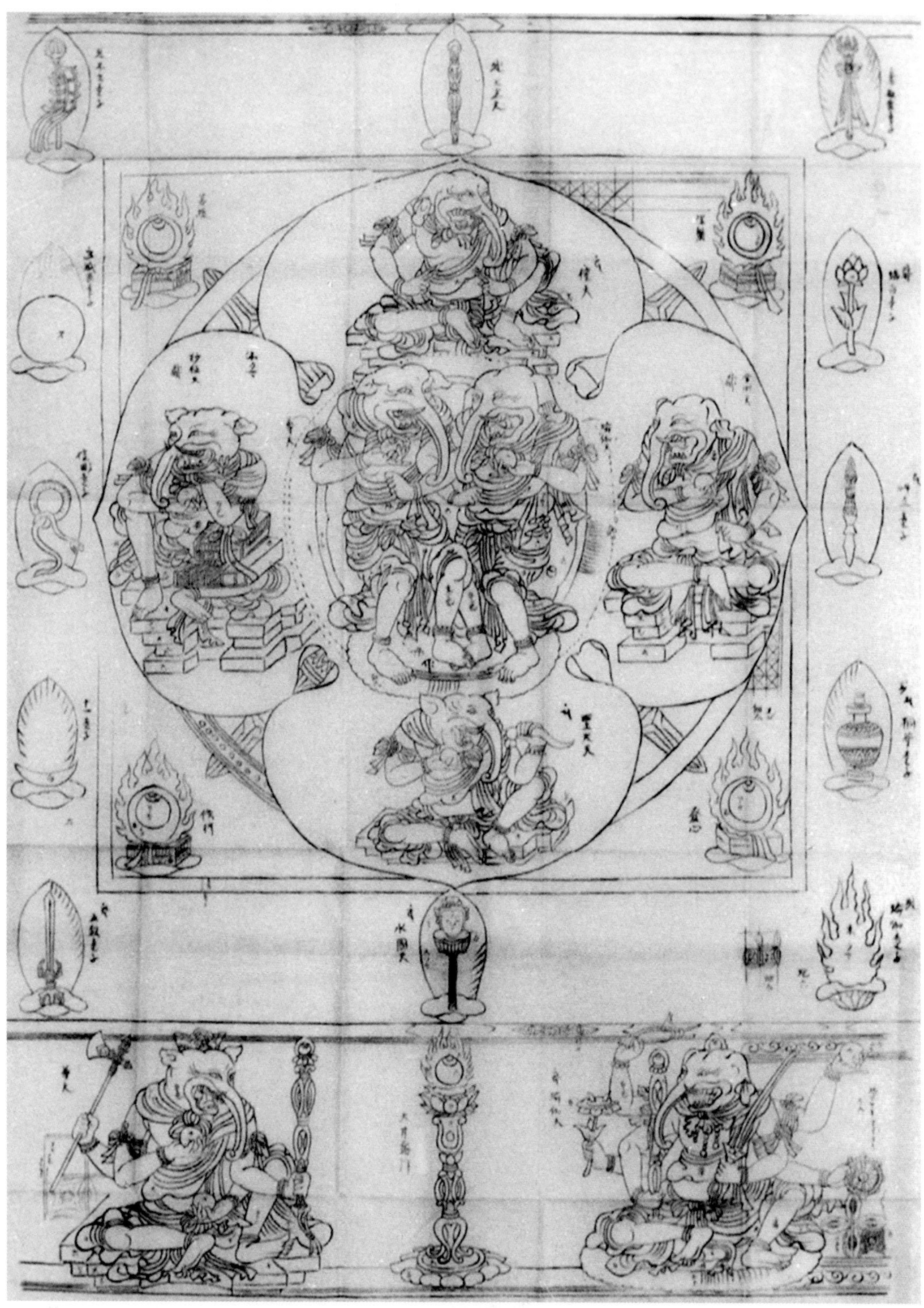

FIGURE 2.16. Kangiten mandala. Edo period. Sheet, ink on paper. University Art Museum, Kyoto City University of Arts. *BZS* 1078.

the depictions of Vajrapāṇi and his doubles (Trailokyavijāya, Ācala, and Ucchuṣma) trampling supine Vināyakas (instead of Maheśvara and his consort).[90] In a Dunhuang painting, for example, the blue-faced Vajrapāṇi and the red-faced Ucchuṣma, flanked by two other doubles, are trampling two identical Vināyakas.[91]

According to Krishan, when Vināyaka is being trampled, "he is only an imp and not a god; thus it is no evidence of Hindu animosity toward Buddhism."[92] Krishan seems to transpose Hinduism and Buddhism here, as the image is usually read as an expression of Buddhism's animosity toward Hinduism. Whether or not this is the case, it is difficult to interpret it as a form of Buddhist "ruthless compassion," as is often claimed.[93]

Another tamer of Vināyaka, the great general Deep Sands (Ch. Shensha Dajiang 深沙大将, J. Jinja Daishō), is presented as an avatar of Vaiśravaṇa. As a demon tamer, Deep Sands, like Mahākāla, wears the hide of the *vināyakas* he has killed. Significantly, in a late Daoist text by Bo (var. Bai) Yuchan 白玉蟾, he is flanked by a pair of *vināyakas,* one with an elephant head, the other with a sow head.[94] Along the same lines, the incantation known as "Wisdom Queen, Great Protectress of Great Strength" (Skt. Mahābala-mahārakṣa-vidyārajñī), uttered before the consecration rite of the Womb Realm mandala, was said to drive away all obstacles caused by *vināyakas* and *rākṣasas.*[95]

Vināyaka is trampled by a staggering number of Buddhist deities: most notably by the Thousand-armed Avalokiteśvara (while the Eleven-faced Avalokiteśvara resorts to seduction); by Ucchuṣma (J. Ususama); by Vajrakumāra (J. Kongō Dōji 金剛童子); by Ācala (Fudō); and by Amṛtakuṇḍalin (Gundari 軍荼利).[96] In light of his repeated humiliation at the hand (or rather, the feet) of Dharma protectors, Vināyaka's importance in esoteric mandalas is paradoxical, and all the more significant. Because the demon of obstacles, as he grew in stature, could no longer be simply trampled and humiliated, he had to be ritually propitiated and turned into a protecting deity, the Saintly Deva (Shōten) or Bliss Deva (Kangiten). Consequently, he was supposedly no longer the leader of the demonic *vināyakas,* but a glorious manifestation of Dainichi and/or Kannon. In spite of this attempt at co-optation, his demonic characteristics never entirely disappeared, and the two images of the deity (the negative Vināyaka and the positive Shōten or Kangiten) continued to coexist, leading sometimes to a belief in two different deities.

In the representation of Vaiśravaṇa known in Japan as Tobatsu Bishamon, the earth goddess who supports Bishamon on the palms of her hands is called Kangiten, a name usually reserved for the dual-bodied Vināyaka. Vināyaka is also sometimes described as a demoness called "Mother of Demons" (Ch. Guizimu, J. Kishimo 鬼子母)[97]—a name usually reserved for Hārītī (J. Kishimojin, or Kishibojin 鬼子母神). The latter, in turn, was sometimes called Mother of Bliss (Ch. Huanximu,

J. Kangimo 歓喜母).[98] In a representation from Dunhuang, the demon on the left of the earth goddess is Vināyaka, while the worshiper has taken the place of the demon on her right.

Shōten's ambiguity was momentarily solved for the priest Tankai when the god appeared to him in a dream and told him: "Vināyaka has an elephant head and a human body, and he looks like Shōten, but he is actually a deity of obstacles. It is not my original name. I prevent him from causing obstacles. I am a metamorphic body of Dainichi, and I have a sovereign power in the three worlds. I can free all beings from suffering and give them felicity. Because of your insufficient practice, you have ended up confusing me with Vināyaka. If you have doubts concerning me, examine the ancient documents held by the Mandaraji of the Ono [school]." Three years later, Tankai obtained a copy of the *Kakuzenshō,* where he discovered a "secret teaching" about the Mandaraji 曼陀羅寺 that confirmed his dream and solved his remaining doubts. But his troubles, caused by Vināyaka and his minions, persisted until Fudō eventually put an end to them.[99]

In medieval Japan, Shōten was also often included in composite deities whose theriomorphic elements derive from their status as assimilation bodies (*tōrujin* 等流身) of the buddha Vairocana. As we will see shortly, he was often associated with Dakiniten and Benzaiten in particular, in a triad or composite figure called the Three Devas that played an important role in consecration rituals (J. *kanjō* 灌頂, Skt. *abhiṣeka*).

KANGITEN

The dual form of Vināyaka, called Nandikeśvara or Lord of Bliss (J. Kangiten or, more precisely, *sōshin* 双身 'dual-bodied' Kangiten), is what insured the elevation of that deity as a god of fortune.[100] The name refers to the couple formed by two elephant-headed deities embracing each other. They are distinguished by various features (see, e.g., Fig. 2.18): the female wears a crown; she has small eyes, her mouth is open, her trunk and tusks are short, and she holds a rice ball (a female symbol); the male wears no crown; he has large eyes, his mouth is closed, his trunk and tusks are long, and he holds a radish (a male symbol). Both have their right tusk broken, like Gaṇeśa. The figure they form, sometimes described as an "assimilation body" of the buddha, also illustrates the esoteric notion that the tamer takes the form (and several functions) of the tamed.[101] The sexual relationship implies in this case the seduction and subjugation of the male (Vināyaka) by the female (Senāyaka, a manifestation of the Eleven-faced Avalokiteśvara).[102] In certain representations, the elephant-headed male is called Bina (Vina), while his sow-headed consort is called Yaka.[103]

Nomina numina: Stein has described the splitting process by which a god's name, split into two, gives birth to two different gods. The fact

FIGURE 2.17. Dual-bodied Vināyaka. Kamakura period, 13th century. Ink and color on paper. *Shoson zuzōshū*. Kanazawa bunko.

that these two figures are sometimes called Father of Demons (Guifu 鬼父) and Mother of Demons (Guimo 鬼母), respectively, in Chinese paintings suggests that they were perceived as forming a couple—reminiscent of the couple formed by Gaṇeśa and the sow-headed Cāmuṇḍā in India. Yet Gaṇeśa and Cāmuṇḍā are never represented in sexual embrace, as in Japan (see, e.g., Fig. 2.19).

Most scholarly studies have focused on the dual aspect of Vināyaka and emphasized the sexual elements in its cult. Michel Strickmann and James Sanford, among others, describe its connection with the allegedly heterodox Tachikawa branch of Shingon (Tachikawa-ryū 立川流), although Kangiten was not particularly conspicuous in that branch. This dual form is specific to East Asia, and it is absent in South Asia, despite the abundance of lovemaking deities in India and Tibet. Indeed, it may be the only common representation of Buddhist deities in sexual embrace in China and Japan, and this representation is markedly different from the erotic Indian *śakti* and the Tibetan *yab-yum* figures. The two elephant-headed deities stand facing each other, fully clothed. The male wears a surplice on his shoulder, the female has shorter tusks and trunk, and she wears a wreath on her head. Yet, they are said to reach great bliss, through contact of six erogenous zones.[104]

The dual-bodied Kangiten illustrates the theme of taming through seduction, rather than mere sexuality.[105] The origin of this representation is found in several myths in which a bodhisattva (Avalokiteśvara) assumes a female, semi-animal form in order to tame an elephant-headed demon. In one of these narratives, the main protagonist is the evil minister of a southern Indian kingdom.[106] This character, called "Long-nose Minister" (*bichō daijin* 鼻長大臣), has had sexual relations with the queen. Upon discovering this, the king becomes furious and poisons him. The queen tells her lover to run away and to find a counterpoison in the mountains. Having recovered, the minister is in turn enraged and vows to become a "demon of obstacles." He manifests himself as Vināyaka and raises an army against the king. The queen convinces her husband to let her deal with him, and she is able to seduce and tame him through the power of sexual bliss (*kangi*); hence the name Kangiten given to the couple they form.[107]

FIGURE 2.18. Dual-bodied Vināyaka (Kangiten). *Kakuzenshō, DNBZ* 50: 112.

FIGURE 2.19. Kangiten (elephant and sow). *Kakuzenshō, DNBZ* 50: 120.

Another myth describes the incestuous relationship between Vināyaka and Senāyaka as follows: "Maheśvara had three thousand children. He made King Vināyaka the elder of the fifteen hundred children on the left, entrusting him with all evil deeds; he made Senāyaka Jizenten the elder of the fifteen hundred children on the right, and made him cultivate good practices. This god, who is an avatar of Kannon, in order to control Vināyaka's evil deeds, produced a body of the same kind, and they became elder brother and younger brother, husband and wife, manifesting the form of 'identical bodies in embrace.'"[108]

According to Kakuban 覚鑁 (1095–1143): "[In the dual form] the male deva is a transformation body of Maheśvara. He drives off both celestial and earthly demons and distributes profit in this world and the next. The female figure is a transformation of Avalokiteśvara's eleven-faced form, the most potent of her thirty-three forms. These two standing in conjugal embrace represent the union of yin and yang. That they have elephant heads and human bodies is to show the interpenetration of all ten realms."[109]

The *Kakuzenshō* reports a strange variant of the subjugation of Gaṇapati by the Eleven-faced Avalokiteśvara. It runs as follows: In the country of Marakeira, there was a king who used to eat only beef and radishes. When all the oxen had disappeared, the king began to eat human corpses; when corpses in turn could no longer be found, he began to eat people.[110] Eventually the people revolted, and were about to kill their king when he transformed himself into a great *vināyaka* demon who continued devastating the country. The people then prayed to Avalokiteśvara to save them. Avalokiteśvara then transformed into a female *vināyaka* and seduced the demon. By mating with him, she also tamed him, so that he ceased his ravages.

In his "blissful" state, the dual-bodied Vināyaka came to be associated with sexual harmony and fecundity. The iconographic dualism of his representations expresses a symbolic ambiguity, namely, the opposition/complementarity between the procreative and apotropaic functions of sexuality. The sexual symbolism is relatively muted in the iconography of Kangiten, whereas it can be quite explicit in certain Indian images of Gaṇeśa. Thus, the "Gaṇeśa of the Leftovers" (Ucchistā Gaṇeśa or Ucchistā Gāṇapati) is represented drinking wine and plunging his trunk between the thighs of his consort.[111] In a chapter of *Mantras et mandarins* entitled "L'amour chez les éléphants" (Love among Elephants), Strickmann analyzes the sexual imagery concerning the elephant and emphasizes the symbolic overdetermination of this animal, endowed not only with a pachydermic sexual organ, but also with an eminently phallic trunk and a pair of tusks—whose powder, even today, is widely believed to be an aphrodisiac.[112] Strangely, however, Vināyaka's consort or tamer is never traced back to Gaṇeśa's consorts, Buddhi and Siddhi, both of whom have human faces and are interpreted allegorically as Awakening and Realization; nor to his elephant-headed consort (*śakti*) called, precisely, Vināyakī. The latter is related to the Mothers, and she is one of the sixty-four yoginīs of Indian Tantrism. She holds a lute (*vina*) in her right hand and forms the *mudrā* of fearlessness (Skt. *abhaya*) with her left hand.[113]

Although the sexual frankness of this representation was initially free of procreative connotations, Kangiten eventually became a god of the third function (to use Dumézil's terminology), that is, a god of fecundity and prosperity. This role is represented by the two crossed radishes that not only symbolize Kangiten but are one of his favorite foods. In this way, the Kangiten coupling came to be identified with the dual deities of the crossroads, the *dōsojin;* and with the divine progenitors of Japan, Izanagi and Izanami. As the lord of the "world of desire," he also became functionally identical with Māra.

Shōten's demonic origins bring into question the nature of the two deities that form the Kangiten dyad. Medieval esoteric texts distinguish three types of Kangiten rituals:

1) In the first, the male is a *jitsurui* 実類, a "real type" (i.e., a demon), while the female is a provisional manifestation (*gongen* 権現); its *honzon* is therefore called "provisional and real devas" (*gonjitsu no ten* 権実の天).

2) In the second, both the male and the female deities are "real" (*jitsuirui,* i.e., demonic), so the *honzon* is called "devas both real" (*kujitsu no ten* 倶実の天).

3) In the third, both deities are provisional manifestations; its *honzon* is therefore called "devas both provisional" (*kugon no ten* 倶権の天).[114]

Actually, these distinctions only reflect the perspective of the practitioner, and the image itself does not change. The ritual centered on the two "real devas" is said to be very wild and dangerous, but also the most efficient. The Tendai priest Kōgei 皇慶 (977–1049) warned that while the benefits brought by this dual god are very real, negligent practitioners are easily cursed, so it is better for people of the Final Age to leave this god alone.As noted earlier, the cult of Shōten/Kangiten developed during the medieval period among the ruling classes on the basis of a dozen "canonical" texts (most of them of Chinese origin).[115] In the Edo period, the cult spread more widely with its god of fortune, but it remained relatively arcane. Here is what Tsumura Masayuki 津村正恭 (Sōan 淙庵, d. 1806), in his *Sea of Information* (*Tankai* 譚海), has to say about Vināyaka (Kangiten):

> Kangiten is an Indian god, and because he brings many benefits, many are those who perform his rite by themselves. But even if one's spirit of faith is deep, it is better not to perform by oneself, by chanting *dhāraṇīs* and the like. Whatever their spirit of faith, ordinary people, when they practice without sufficient respect, commit a severe offence. One must ask a monk to recite prayers. . . . Kangiten is the lord of the world of desire. As he made a vow to help even evil people abandoned by the Worthies and the Buddhas, when evil people address their prayers to him, even if they are about to be beheaded, he can save them. Because he is the lord of the world of desire, he fulfills all prayers, even those made with a thought of desire. (But because there are in his retinue unruly gods that are easily offended by lack of respect, he must be approached with caution.) Even among Ritsu monks who perform the ritual of Kangiten, many fall into sexual desire. Generally speaking, in India, this is a rite performed by profanes.[116]

FUNCTIONS

The goals of the Vināyaka ritual, as described in the *Great Sūtra of the Rituals and Incantations of the Envoy* (*Da shi zhou fa jing* 大使呪法經, *T.* 21, 1268), are diverse, although they all aim at quickly obtaining pleasure, power, wealth, and honor. According to the *Kakuzenshō,* this ritual allows one, among other things, to obtain a child or a high official position, to catch a thief, to win at gambling, and to overcome various obstacles; it also puts an end to nightmares caused, precisely, by *vināyaka* demons. The ritual procedure emphasizes Vināyaka's idiosyncrasies: the oil bath, the offering of wine and sweets, and so on. Since Shōten allegedly gave Kūkai a cup of wine as medication, much ink has been spilled about these offerings, and Enchin's "trivial questions" about his appearance and his ritual oil bath have not yet received clear answers.[117] But perhaps they are just a form of red herring after all, distracting scholars from more serious issues about Vināyaka's nature and function.

As a god of obstacles, Vināyaka needs to be propitiated at the beginning of all rituals. Indeed, rituals dedicated to other deities would fail if Vināyaka had not been propitiated first. He thus becomes a god of beginnings, and this chronological priority tends to become a ritual precedence, helping him to move from the periphery to center stage of the ritual or mandala. Thus, while Vināyaka as a subaltern deity was initially worshiped for mundane purposes at the outer edge of sacred space, he eventually became a "hidden buddha" (*hibutsu* 秘佛), a transcendent being worshiped in the inner sanctum, out of profane sight. As Kakuban puts it: "King Daishō Kangiten is the root source of the yin and yang. The ten thousand forms are born from him."[118]

SHŌTEN AS KŌJIN

In the *Kangiten reigenki,* Vināyaka is described as a "raging deity" (*kōjin*) who creates obstacles for the Buddha Dharma. A similar characterization is found in the *Kakuzenshō,* which traces this idea to the Ritual of Vināyaka in Four Sections (Shibu Binayaka hō 四部毘那夜迦法), a text attributed to the Tendai priest Annen (841–915).[119] According to this text, the founding of the Jetavana monastery had been prevented by a series of calamities. As Śāriputra, perplexed, meditates to find the cause of such ill luck, a monstrous being with eight faces appears to him and claims to be the "Rough King of the Three Treasures."[120] A gloss adds: "It is Kōjin, or Vināyaka."[121] The demon, which calls himself a deva, warns that those who do not worship him suffer all kinds of calamities, and that Śāriputra, in order to avoid disaster, must fabricate his image and make offerings to it. The story reappears in the *Shintō zatsuzatsusho* 神道雜雜書, which gives a more specific description of Kōjin: he is of gigantic size and accompanied by eight acolytes. He identifies himself as Sanbō Kōjin

Vināyaka and claims to have a fabulous number of followers (also called *kōjin,* rough gods)—nine billion forty-three thousand four hundred ninety *kōjin,* to be exact. Śāriputra, baffled, apologizes for having ignored his existence and promises to worship him henceforward.[122] In his "Section on the Sixty-two *kōjin*" of the *Shinzoku zatsuki mondō shō,* Raiyu 頼瑜 (1226–1304) quotes the words of his master Kenjin 憲深 (1192–1263): "In the external scriptures, one calls him Kōjin; this is why Yin-Yang masters speak of 'Kōjin offering.' In Buddhist scriptures, one calls him Vināyaka, and one speaks of 'Shōten offering.'"[123]

SHŌTEN'S NETWORK

In the apocryphal *Bussetsu saishō gokoku Ugaya tontoku nyoi hōju-ō darani-kyō* (hereafter *Ugajin darani-kyō*), the serpent deity Ugajin (a god closely related to Benzaiten) manifests himself as Dakiniten, Daishōten (Vināyaka), and Aizen Myōō. His "original nature" (*honji*) is said to be Nyoirin Kannon. In the above text, Ugajin is said to be identical with the couple formed by the two Vināyakas, symbolized by crossed radishes (Kangiten's emblem).

In a secret tradition of Miidera 三井寺 (Onjōji 園城寺), Shōten is also identified with Aizen Myōō. This tradition describes the triad formed by Aizen and two elephant-headed figures. One of them is white and male, and has a solar disk above his head; the other is red and female, and has a lunar disk above her head.[124] On the "Shintō" side, Izanagi and Izanami are sometimes represented as embracing Vināyakas. Shōten is said to be the "original ground" of the sun goddess Amaterasu.[125] This is why, we are told, all the priests and priestesses of Ise worship him.[126] Shōten was also identified with the *kami* Sarutahiko 猿田彦, because, like the union of Sarutahiko and Ame no Uzume, the coupling of the two elephant-headed deities that form the dual Kangiten symbolize the sexual union of earth and heaven, yin and yang, and the nonduality of the Womb and Diamond realms. But this identification was also probably due in part to the fact that Sarutahiko's long nose calls to mind Shōten's proboscis.[127]

A Tendai text entitled *Sange yōshū ki* 山家要集記 identifies Shōten with the goddess of Itsukushima 嚴島 (who was herself identified with Benzaiten), with the Hie 日吉 Shrine deity Jūzenji 十禅師, with Kōjin, and with King Yama (Enma-ō).[128] The *Kangiten reigenki* 歓喜天霊験記 also identifies Vināyaka with the dual-bodied Bishamon, the bicephalous Aizen Myōō, the dual deities of the crossroads (*dōsojin*), and the two acolytes of Enmaten, the twin devas Shimei and Shiroku.[129] Kangiten was also identified with the epidemic deity Gozu Tennō 牛頭天王.[130] While it is not always explicit, we can also posit a functional link between Shōten and various other deities (Myōken, Nyoirin, Dakiniten, Fudō, and Kokūzō) as *honzon* of rituals centered on the divination board (*shikiban* 式盤).

In his *Meishuku shū* 明宿集, the Nō playwright Konparu Zenchiku 金春禅竹 links Shōten with Marishiten 摩利支天, a deity who is said to dwell in the sun; with the water/music goddess Benzaiten; and with the pair formed by Aizen and Fudō, symbolizing the inner realization expressed by the formula "One buddha, two wisdom kings (myōō 明王)."[131] An episode in Zenchiku's life also suggests a relation between Kangiten and the Inari 稲荷 deity. Zenchiku is said to have had from his youth a deep faith in Kangiten. At the end of June 1467, just about the beginning of the Ōnin 応仁 war, the 63-year old Zenchiku went to Inari Shrine with his wife, Zeami's daughter, and performed a retreat there.[132] He describes the event in his *Record of a Visit to Mount Inari* (*Inarisan sanrō ki* 稲荷山参籠記). On that occasion, he prayed for the fulfillment of the "harmonious union of yin and yang, husband and wife," and more specifically for the "strengthening of his male yang breath." He remained in reclusion in the Monju Hall for twenty-one days, during which he drank a talisman of Kangiten. Yet the priest eventually told him that he had no karmic connection with the god and therefore did not receive his protection. Zenchiku then reflected: "I have met [Kangiten] by chance in the past, and until now I have not been neglectful, but from the time I was a layman I have been lacking in practice and faith." He now renewed his vow, and eventually obtained from Kangiten an auspicious dream that deepened his faith. According to another source, a talisman fell from heaven as a result of his prayers.[133] Tanaka Noriyuki has argued that Zenchiku's play "Teika" 定家 was inspired by the image of Kangiten as a god of love.[134] It tells the story of the tragic love between the poet Fujiwara no Teika (var. Sadaie) 藤原定家 and a palace lady (*naishinnō* 内親王), and it takes place in the Kangi-ji 歓喜寺 near Senbon 千本 in Kyoto, a temple dedicated to that god.

THE GOD OF YIN AND YANG

Zenchiku emphasized Kangiten's nature as a protector of the Way of Yin and Yang (Onmyōdō 陰陽道). In popular religion, too, Kangiten became increasingly popular as a god of yin and yang, presiding over the sexual union of man and woman in the secrecy of the bedroom. Yanagita Kunio 柳田国男 has suggested that one of the reasons for this was the identification of Kangiten with the crossroads deities (*dōsojin*) and with phallic deities called *shaguji* or *mishaguji,* a term he relates to Shukujin 宿神, the astral deity that governs human destiny.[135] Yanagita finds a clue in the toponymy of places called Zōzu-san 象頭山 (Mount of the Elephant Head), which he links etymologically with *shōgejin* 障碍神 (god of obstacles) and *shaguji.*[136] The functional similarity with the *dōsojin* is clear from the fact that these deities were "gods of obstacles" (*sai no kami* 塞の神) placed at the limits of towns and villages to block the intrusion of maleficent forces (epidemics, bandits) from the outside. These paired deities, representing the saving power of fecundity and prosperity, were originally marked by a strong sexual, phallic symbolism, which explains why they were eventually replaced by less offensive representations (Jizō, Kōshin 庚申, and Sarutahiko 猿田彦). Along the same lines, Gakkō Yoshihiro has emphasized—albeit without any conclusive evidence apart from a general sexual symbolism—the affinities in Kantō between the cult of Shōten and that the *oshirasama* オシラ様, obscure deities represented by a pair (male-female) of mulberry-wood or bamboo figurines.[137]

A variant of the Kangiten-as-*dōsojin* motif appears in an *ofuda* where a male-female couple appears—the male wearing an elephant head on his headgear, the female a dragon head—below a disk on a cloud containing their seed-letters (Fig. 2.20. They are standing inside a winnowing fan, a symbol associated with Shōten.[138] The female holds a radish (Shōten's symbol), the male a key (Benzaiten's symbol), suggesting that the two deities could be associated with Shōten and Benzaiten.

FIGURE 2.20. Kangiten (human-faced). *Ofuda*. Eifukuji, Okayama. Private collection.

The Logic of Bipartition

As Rolf Stein has shown, the image of Shōten is based on a logic of bipartition that is symbolized by the gate and its guardians. One cannot therefore understand Shōten by studying him alone. One must take into account the binary structure in which he is inscribed, namely, that of the pair Skanda/Gaṇeśa, or of the bipolarity/complementarity of the functions of war and wealth. Stein argues that unlike the Dumézilian analysis of the three Indo-European functions, which tends to correlate each deity with a specific (or at least dominant) function, in the present case, owing to various cross-fertilizations and exchanges of attributes, each deity covers the two functions (whereas the third one—or rather the first one, sovereignty—is missing, unless it is expressed in the notion of secrecy).[139] Stein's analysis shows in particular how the pair formed by the figures of Skanda and Gaṇeśa, the young warrior and the pot-bellied protector, after being dissociated in Buddhism, reconstituted itself partially in other pairs such as Mahākāla and Hārītī, Vaiśravaṇa and Kubera, Mañjuśrī and Piṇḍola, Vajrapāṇi and Vināyaka, and above all, Weituo 韋駄天 and Mile 弥, the gatekeepers of Chinese monasteries. In the present context, it is the case of Kangiten, a dual deity formed by Vināyaka and the Thousand-armed Avalokiteśvara (Senju Kannon 千手観音), and that of the dual-bodied Vaiśravaṇa (Sōshin Bishamon) that are the most significant. We seem to have here a double split—that of each element of the pair formed by Vaiśravaṇa (avatar of Skanda) and Vināyaka (avatar of Gaṇeśa). Stein's explanation, while convincing, does not sufficiently take into account the demonic nature of Vināyaka (and of Vaiśravaṇa—let alone that of Gaṇeśa and Skanda), nor the way in which the keeper of the gate came to take the place of the essential secret. While Stein rightly insists on the sexual and alimentary codes, and on the motifs of filth and leftovers that link Vināyaka to Ucchuṣma and Hārītī, he neglects the embryological aspect of Vināyaka, which is just as important in my opinion to explaining this god's popularity in medieval Japan.[140] The motifs of impurity and leftovers, found in the myths of Gaṇeśa and similar figures, do not fit in the schema of the three functions. They constitute an excess, precisely, that which overflows the economic or symbolic system. Rather than perceiving such leftovers as the unpalatable products of that system, we should perhaps see them as its hidden source.

To understand the figure of Vināyaka, and the system that it both transcends and reinforces, we cannot simply say that in his case two functions merge into one single deity—although this is also true. We should not overemphasize the figure of the dual Kangiten, which is merely another expression of the theological "thought by couplings" (*pensée par couples*). Beyond Kangiten, Shōten is perhaps the figure that resists and transcends binary thinking (of the type human vs. animal, male vs. female, demonic vs. divine, war vs. wealth). If Gaṇeśa is the god of the beginnings, Vināyaka may be the god who refuses to leave, or, to use an appropriate French expression, "demande son reste."

DIVINATION

Paradoxically, in spite of his manifest Indian origins, Shōten became the *honzon* of rites revolving (literally) around an instrument, the divination board (*shikiban* 式盤), which had been used since the former Han (2nd century B.C.E.) by Chinese astrologers and later on was at the center of the so-called *liuren* 六壬 method of divination.[141] The existence of such rites in esoteric Buddhism can be traced back to the *Sheng Huanxitian shifa* 聖歓喜天式法 (*T.* 21, 1275) allegedly compiled by the Central Asian monk Prajñācakra (fl. 847–882), who was a disciple of Amoghavajra and the master of the Japanese Tendai priest Enchin. According to the *Asabashō,* the ritual in question was performed in Indian monasteries; however, the fact that the text is known only by a Japanese recension preserved at Hōbōdai-in 軍荼利 (in Toji) (Kyoto) raises questions as to its authenticity.[142] It even contains two Daoist talismans and uses the ritual formula of Daoist texts: *Jiji rulü ling* 急急如律令 (Quickly, quickly, in observance of the ordinances, obey!). At any rate, it provides us with fascinating materials about the Shōten cult as it was performed in Japanese esotericism. This scripture is now supplemented by medieval texts from Shōmyōji preserved at Kanazawa bunko, which were recently introduced by Nishioka Hideo on the occasion of an exhibition, held in 2007 in that institution, centered on the relations between esoteric Buddhism and Onmyōdō. The texts provide more concrete details about the structure of esoteric divination boards, which are no longer extent, and their use.

The *Sheng Huanxitian shifa* begins with instructions on how to construct a divination board on a particularly auspicious day and how to animate it. According to these instructions, the divination board centered on the Bliss Deva (Ch. Huanxitian, J. Kangiten), which consisted of two parts linked by a median axis: the upper part, called the heavenly board (Ch. *tianpan,* J. *tenban* 天盤), was cylindrical or rather conical; the lower part, called the earthly board (Ch. *dipan,* J. *chiban* 地盤), was square. They represented the heavenly and earthly realms, respectively. In each of the four cardinal points of the *tenban,* the officiant visualizes a seed-letter (*oṃ* in the east, *jaḥ* in the south, *hrīḥ* in the west, and *mā* in the north). These four *bījas* transform into four Vināyakas named Sun King (J. Nichiō 日王), Love King (Ai-ō 愛王), Moon Love (Getsuai 月愛), and Excellent in Discussion (Gitoku 議特), whom the text then proceeds to describe with their attributes.[143]

The eight directional devas (Sk. *lokapāla*) are distributed on the *chiban* (starting clockwise from the east): Śakra (J. Taishakuten 帝釈天), Agni (Katen 火天), Yama (Enmaten), Rākṣasa (Rasetsuten 羅刹天), Varuna (Suiten 水天), Vāyu (Fūten 風天), Vaiśravaṇa (Bishamonten), and Maheśvara (Daijizaiten 大自在天). Around them the officiant visualizes the twenty-eight lunar mansions and thirty-six animals (*sanjūrokkin* 三十六禽), the demonic spirits that preside over the hours of day and night.

Then he invokes all these deities and their retinue through appropriate mudrās and mantras, followed by a long list of the conjunctions, obtained by pivoting the *tenban* over the *chiban,* between their respective deities, the "heavenly" Vināyakas and the "earthly" devas, in accordance with the purposes of the ritual. The logic behind these conjunctions is apparently relatively simple, although the specific links are not always clear: thus, if one desires to obtain an official rank, one links the sun deva (Nichiō, presumably) to Taishakuten 帝釈天, the king of the gods.

Presumably, the conjunction of these powers will eliminate all obstacles. If one desires to give fever to a person, one conjugates the power of the solar Vināyaka with that of Agni, the deva who controls fire. To convince others, one brings together Gitokuten 議特天, the Vināyaka who excells in discussion, with Yama. To bring together husband and wife, one links the Vināyaka of lunar passion, Getsuai 月愛, with Taishakuten; to separate husband and wife, Gitokuten and Suiten. Or again, if a pregnant woman wants a quick delivery, one links Getsuai with Enmaten. To return a curse to its sender, one links the solar Vināyaka with Rasetsuten, the killer. And so on.[144] One gets the idea. From this description, it looks as if we are not dealing here with divination properly speaking, but with one of those magic rituals that are the standard fare of Tantrism. In other words, with a straightforward Tantric rite (if there is such a thing) whose goal is not to find out the fate of a person, but to bring about wanted results by manipulating occult forces. The text actually opens with a reference to the attainment of spiritual powers through the Vināyaka ritual.

Another point to note is that while the text is entitled *Divination Method of the Saintly Blissful Deva* (J. *Shō Kangiten shikihō* 聖歓喜天式法), its *honzon* is conspicuously absent. The four Vināyaka, of course, are his emanations, but it is strange that he is not described at the center (and top) of the *shikiban* in the same way as he is represented in his mandala, namely, as a dual-bodied deity. Perhaps this mandala itself is essentially an illustration of the *shikiban.* In the scripture, however, we are simply told that the four Vināyakas are one—in other words, that they are emanations of Kangiten. The equivalence between this invisible *honzon* and the overarching power of Chinese cosmology, the pole star, is made implicitly through the addition of the astral symbols (the lunar mansions and cyclical animals).

Various medieval texts give more details, confirming the Tantric interpretation of the ritual. One of them is the *Shōten shikihō* 聖天式法 (dated 1281) by the Shingon priest Kenna 劔阿 (1261–1338). According to it, the officiant must visualize the two boards of the divination board as the upper and lower part of his own body, and as the Womb and Diamond Realm mandalas. He thus becomes one with the cosmos, and allegedly masters all the cosmic forces. The goal of the ritual is to obtain "rapid realization" (Skt. *siddhi,* J. *shitsuji* or *shijji* 悉地). Significantly, the fact that we have here a kind of divination board instead of a classical mandala reveals the interpenetration of Indian and Chinese cosmological systems. It also identifies a Tantric deity (here Shōten, but in other cases Fudō, Nyoirin, or Dakiniten) with the pole star, that is, with Myōken Bosatsu. The Kanazawa bunko texts also provide a description of eight talismans inserted between the heavenly and earthly boards, which are not mentioned in the Chinese scripture. They further describe how the divination board is to be sealed by five-colored threads, as well as similar (often obscure) other details. For instance, a preliminary step of the ritual involves the invocation of a Yin-Yang deity known as the Jade Woman (Gyokujo 玉女), bowing to the Demon Gate, and the absorption of the pneumas of the twelve months.[145] The text also mentions, next to the spatiotemporal deities discussed above, the seven stars of the Northern Dipper. The visualization now begins with the seed-letter *do* in the center, which turns into the *honzon* Daishōten, followed by the four seed-letters *oṃ, jāḥ, hrīh, and ma* in the four directions, turning into the four Vināyakas, all manifestations of Shōten. The sequence for the animation of the *chiban* is the same as above. It is followed by various mudrās and mantras, including those of the Jade Woman, the earth deity, and the seven stars, as well as mudrās for binding all the demons and for producing the assistant spirits (*shikigami* 式神). The Buddhist aspect of the rite is underscored by offerings of scented water, repentence, transfer of merits, and by placing a canopy (*tengai* 天蓋) over the *honzon.*[146] The *Shōten shikiban kessa-hō* 聖天式盤決作法 contains a similar sequence and adds the twelve cyclical animals and the five dragon emperors of Onmyōdō with their 84,000 soldiers. It also mentions a Daoist rite, the Pace of Yu, but leaves it to the discretion of the officiating priest.[147] The *Shōten shikihō kuden* 聖天式法口伝 explains that, when the purpose of the rite is subjugation (*chōbuku-hō* 調伏法), the heavenly board must be rotated counterclockwise, and clockwise in the case of a rite aimed at averting calamities (*sokusai-hō* 息災法).[148]

THE CHTHONIAN GOD

While explicit Buddhist theology has tried to interpret Shōten as a manifestation of the cosmic buddha Dainichi, and his female consort as a manifestation of the bodhisattva Kannon, the implicit theology points to a Yin-Yang reading in which Shōten, as lord of this world, is described both as a heavenly deity identical with the pole star deity, Myōken, and as a chthonian deity. Like Fudō, Shōten tends to merge and exchange attributes and functions with non-Buddhist, chthonian deities.

Thus, Tankai's hesitation between Fudō and Shōten may have represented at one level a difficult choice between orthodoxy and heterodoxy, or between a higher practice aiming at illumination (*bodhi*) and a more this-worldly type of practice; yet perhaps it was not a true dilemma after all, inasmuch as both deities belong to the same symbolic field. What came to be represented in Tankai's hagiography as a rivalry between the two deities, a rivalry eventually displaced into (and solved by) a hierarchy—with Fudō above (or at the center) and Shōten below (or at the periphery), hides a more essential identity between two chthonian deities. In fact, the true object of worship at Hōzanji on Mount Ikoma, the temple founded by Tankai, is the hidden Shōten just as much as the conspicuous Fudō.

The Demiurge

While Zenchiku's faith in Shōten was apparently motivated by worldly (and more specifically sexual) desires, Shōten eventually grew in his mind into a demiurgic figure. Zenchiku identifies him with the old-man deity Okina, the tutelary deity of the Nō tradition, whom he redefines as a cosmic deity, Shukujin 宿神.[149] We seem to have here a Japanese version of what Friedrich Max Müller (1823–1900), after Schelling (1775–1854), called, in the case of Indian religion, "henotheism," that is, a form of polytheism in which the various gods are seen as variations or manifestations of one higher deity. In the present instance, this henotheistic tendency can be traced back to Chinese translations in which Shōten was already identified with Maheśvara (the Buddhist form of Śiva). According to the Chinese monk Jingse 憬瑟 (Tang dynasty), for example: "Owing to his sovereignty with regard to the six supranormal powers, he is called Shōten; owing to his sovereignty in knowledge and wisdom, he is called Maheśvara; because he achieves 'seduction' (*keiai* 敬愛, Skt. *vaśikaraṇa*), he is called the Dual-bodied Vināyaka; because he causes the five cereals to grow, he is called the Six-armed Deva."[150]

The rise of Vināyaka is already evident in early Chinese texts like Hanguang's *Pinayejia Enabode yuqie xidipin miyao* 毘那夜迦我那鉢底瑜伽悉地品秘要, which emphasizes that he is the Buddha Vairocana and is therefore a provisional manifestation, not a real (i.e., demonic) god.[151] Thus, the mating of the two deities actually represents the union of a buddha (Vairocana) with a bodhisattva (Avalokiteśvara). The same text emphasizes that *vināyakas* come in all kinds of forms—in particular, those of man and woman. But Vināyaka manifests himself precisely as a *gongen* with an elephant head so as not to be confused with other *vināyakas,* although he also appears as a man with a long nose (a Buddhist Cyrano de Bergerac!). As Gaṇapati (leader of the *gaṇa* troupes), he provokes thoughts of bliss in other *vināyakas,* to stop them from causing further obstacles.[152]

The *Kangiten reigenki* 歓喜天霊験記 identifies Kangiten with various twin deities such as the dual-bodied Bishamonten, the two-headed Aizen, the crossroads deity or deities (*dōsojin*), and the acolytes of King Enma, Shimei and Shiroku: "As the dual-headed King Aizen, he gives instructions for attaining love and happiness; to give love-seduction to people, he becomes the Dōso dōgyōjin 道祖道行神; to report good and evil to King Enma, he manifests himself as the deities Shimei and Shiroku. His benefits are not of one single form, his profits are wide."[153]

The tendency is also apparent in the *Bikisho* 鼻歸書, according to which: "Shōten is King Enma is the nether world, Shōten among the devas, the companion deities (*kushōjin*) among men, and Susanoo among the gods. All these are transformations of Shōten."[154] Here the name Shōten no longer simply designates a particularly powerful deva (and former demon king), but a transcendent god, source of all the other gods. Shōten is on his way to becoming the Shukujin.

The henotheistic interpretation of Shōten reaches its apogee in a late text, the *Chōseiden* 窕誓伝, compiled by a Katsuoji priest known as Ikū Shōnin 以空上人 (d. 1670).[155] This text, first published in 1687 and reedited in 1909, claims that Shōten has a retinue of 107,000 demons, whose leaders are the four deva kings. Because the latter also rule over the stars, Shōten is said to be the leader among all stars.[156] This is reminiscent of the fact that in India Gaṇeśa was often represented together with the nine luminaries (a.k.a. the "nine seizers," Skt. Navagraha) as their leader—taking precedence over Surya, the sun.[157] The name of these planets (*graha,* "seizer") is a clear allusion to their demonic nature. Thus, those who worship him no longer have to fear wild beasts or divine curses. But the two main points of the *Chōseiden* are probably Shōten's identity with Kōjin and the fact that he is the *honji* of Amaterasu. Shōten is also identified with the two deities that control human destiny, the so-called companion deities. In the framework of *hongaku* thought, his identification with fundamental ignorance is no longer a flaw, but the very mark of his transcendent status.

Again, according to the *Shinbutsu ittai kanjō shō* 神佛一体灌頂鈔, Daishō Kangiten, presented as the divine body of Mount Hakone 箱根, is also said to be "the manifested form of the union between man and woman, and the avatar of the harmonious union of principle and knowledge." This deity, "through his joy and pain, acts as father and mother nurturing all beings."[158]

This form of Shōten is represented at times as a four- or eight-handed, human-faced deity with one or two elephant-heads on his/her headgear. (See above, Figs. 2.21–2.23). In the Ichigami Shrine painting (Fig. 2.22), a caption reads: "My manifestation harmonizes its light to benefit all things; perfectly fusing the principle and phenomena, it pervades the entire dharma-realm; it protects the Three Jewels and saves sentient beings. Thus I am called Daishō Kangiten "the Great Saintly Deva of Bliss."

THE SECRET LORD

This brings us to another recurring motif, that of secrecy: the secrecy surrounding sexuality of course, but also that of gestation, the mysterious process taking place in the dark recesses of the womb. Kangiten, the "lord of bliss," is not only the guardian standing on the threshold of the most secret ritual, the esoteric unction or consecration (Skt. a*bhiṣeka, J. kanjō*), he is also a "hidden Buddha"—and this not only, as became the case with the so-called Meiji Restoration, for reasons of public decency.

The root metaphor behind Shōten's image is that of secrecy. Not only is he worshiped in a secret, hidden place, but this secrecy is

FIGURE 2.21. Kangiten. *Ofuda*. Shōten-in. Private collection.

FIGURE 2.22. Kangiten. Edo period, 19th century. Color on paper. Ichigami Shrine, Yōkaichi City (Shiga prefecture).

overdetermined by a number of symbolic factors—among them his unbridled sexuality and the belief in his "evil eye," from which humans must be shielded. However, in the last analysis, it is essentially the pervading symbolism of embryonic gestation that explains his transformations from a mere demon into a blissful deva and ultimately into the primordial, secret *kōjin,* the "hidden god" of medieval Japan. These henotheistic tendencies, however, should not be read teleologically, as steps toward a form of monotheism. Japanese religion, in spite of its monotheistic tendencies, remained strongly polytheistic.

FIGURE 2.23. Kangiten as Japanese *kami. Ofuda.* Kasuga Shrine, Nara. Personal collection.

CODETTA

In Japan, the Buddhist Vināyaka (Shōten), like the Hindu Gaṇeśa, became increasingly interiorized, becoming first the demon of inner obstacles, then the god who can protect the practitioner against all spiritual impediments. During the medieval period, Shōten eventually ascended to the top of the pantheon as a primordial god, again just like Gaṇeśa in Hinduism, and at about the same time. But whereas Gaṇeśa's promotion was essentially due to a sect of worshipers, the Gaṇapatiya, it does not seem that Shōten benefited from the support of a group whose members defined themselves exclusively as his worshipers.

Vināyaka's career—from mere demon to god of obstacles, and then onward from gatekeeper to "great saint" (Shōten) and "lord of bliss" (Kangiten), to god of yin and yang, god of the origins, and finally controller of human destiny—provides a paradigm of the gods of obstacles (*shōgejin*) category. We have also shifted from a god of obstacles, invoked at the beginning of rituals to insure their smooth performance, to a god that is the source of all ritual efficacy: the *para-site* who diverted to his advantage the flow of the origin has become the original site, the source and dispenser of all resources.

In his multivalent role, Vināyaka harks back to the mysterious god called Shukujin (god of destiny). With Zenchiku, the latter name came to designate a primordial, cosmic deity subsuming all the various gods of Japan. As guardian of the threshold between being and nonbeing, Vināyaka is also the first manifestation of that reality, and the god who controls access to it. His "evil eye" is the third eye that opens onto that realm of secrecy, or that brings its intrinsic violence out into the open. On a more serene note, that realm is also described in metonymic fashion, and in embryological terms, as a secret, womb-like world in which incubation takes place. As the power that rules over that hidden world, Vināyaka, the "secret buddha," is even more secret in a sense than Dainichi himself (in this sense too he is perhaps the "elder brother" of the Buddha). Thus, he was perceived in the end as a placenta deity, the god who protects human life during the liminal period of gestation that leads human consciousness from the invisible to the visible world.

3

A STINK OF FOX

Dakiniten

Till, with a sudden sharp hot stink of fox
It enters the dark hole of the head

TED HUGHES, "THE THOUGHT-FOX"

In their worst nightmares—traditionally inspired by the demons known as *vināyakas*—the medieval Japanese felt prey to invisible beings that devoured their vital essence. In the esoteric Buddhist pantheon, the most dangerous among these demons of the night were the *ḍākinīs,* a type of ghoul that frequented charnel grounds and fed on human blood and flesh.[1] From their ghastly alimentary habits they were said to derive their power to fly.[2] Like other aerial beings such as the *apsaras* and the *gandharvas,* they could cross over between realms—heaven and earth, the human and animal realms, the worlds of the living and the dead.[3]

THE GENEALOGICAL MODEL

The Taming of the *Ḍākinīs*

The Buddhist locus classicus regarding the *ḍākinīs* is the story of their subjugation by Mahākāla in the *Mahāvairocana-sūtra* (J. *Dainichikyō* 大日經).[4] Commenting on that text, the Chinese monk Yixing 一行 (683–727) writes that Mahāvairocana, assuming the form of Mahākāla, tamed the *ḍākinīs* by swallowing them. Mahākāla then agreed to free them on the condition that they stop eating human flesh. When they complained that this would condemn them to starvation, he relented and allowed them to consume the vital essence of humans, the so-called human yellow. He also taught them a method enabling them to know of a person's impending death six months in advance, in order to get to that precious substance before all other demons.[5] According to certain sources, however, they play a more active role in a person's natural or karmic demise: the gradual withering a person undergoes is indeed due to the *ḍākinī*'s invisible action, although that action is no longer a theft, since the Buddha himself has authorized it. In return for the favor, in what may be seen as the Tantric version of the Buddhist "transfer of merits" (*pariṇāma,* J. *ekō* 廻向), the *ḍākinīs* will share with the humans who worship them some of the power they have thus acquired. Thus, the taming of the *ḍākinīs* by Mahākāla should not hide the fundamental identity between tamer and tamed. Indeed, both are avatars of the bodhisattva Mañjuśrī (J. Monju).[6] We recall that the "god of battles" Mahākāla, just like the *ḍākinīs,* devours the vital spirit of humans.[7] Yet there was another rite, centered on Acala (J. Fudō), which allowed one to counter the *ḍākinīs'* attacks and postpone the time of one's death beyond the fatal period.[8] Likewise, Aizen Myōō was believed to protect his worshipers by holding their vital principle (the human yellow) in one of his hands.

The Jewel in the Crown

Unlike *yakṣas* and *rākṣasas,* however, the Japanese *ḍākinīs* were never content to simply feed on human flesh and blood. As demonic gourmets, what they really craved is the delicacy known in esoteric Buddhism as the "human yellow" (*ninnō* 人黄), a substance equated with the *hun* 魂 and *po* 魄 souls of the Chinese tradition.[9] This substance was also believed to transform itself into semen, allowing sexual reproduction.[10] Moreover, as we observed in *The Fluid Pantheon,* the human yellow also corresponded symbolically with the relics of the Buddha and the wish-fulfilling jewel (*cintāmaṇi*).[11] Whereas earlier texts had placed it in the human heart, some later commentators, taking their cue from the Tendai priest Annen (b. 841), shifted its location to the top of the head. Thus, it was usually represented as six, seven, or ten grains (or drops) located in the heart or in cruciform pattern at the top of the head. These grains, resembling grains of millet, dewdrops, or particles of white jade, were thought to control the six sense organs.[12] When people lose one of them, their vision darkens; when a second is lost, their hearing is affected. Finally, when all six grains have disappeared, they die. At that point, rituals are of no avail, except those centered on Fudō, because, like Mahākāla (Daikokuten), he is the master of the *ḍākinīs.*[13]

FROM ḌĀKINĪ TO DAKINITEN

The first mention of *ḍākinīs* appears in a stone inscription from Gangadhar in Rajasthan.[14] The Indian *ḍākinīs,* after converting to Buddhism and becoming protectors of the Dharma, were incorporated into the two great mandalas of Tantrism as manifestations of the five great buddhas. In Japan, they merged into a single deity called Dakiniten.[15]

In the Womb Realm mandala, *ḍākinīs* appear in the southern part of the external Vajra section, in the court of King Yama, next to the Seven Mothers (*mātṛkās*) and other similar deities.[16] The *samādhi* of the *ḍākinī* is said to be the first gate through which the buddhas of the Womb Realm mandala enter, in the process that will eventually lead to their identification with Mahāvairocana.[17] Yet iconographic sources show a representation of three *ḍākinīs* naked to the waist, seated on circular mats, next to a corpse; one of them is devouring the leg and arm of a human body; the others hold skulls in their right hands, and one of them holds a chopper in her left hand (Fig. 3.1).[18]

FIGURE 3.1. Flesh-eating *ḍākinīs*. Detail of Taizōkai mandala. *Daihi taizō daimandara. TZ* 1: 775.

A single *ḍākinī* (not yet the medieval Dakiniten) appears in the Enmaten mandalas of the late Heian period—for instance, in mandalas drawn by Chōen 澄圓 (1016–1081) and by Kakujin 覚乗 (1012–1081).[19] She is represented as a woman with long hair, holding a bag. Strangely, she looks exactly like Jōjūsen 成就仙 (Skt. Siddhavidyādhara), an enigmatic figure who appears in the upper left corner of the same mandalas. *Ḍākinīs* were also part of the Enmaten rituals performed around the same time within the context of the large-scale exorcism known as the Nakatomi harae.[20] Clearly, elements of the Dakiniten rite were already present in the Dakiniten Offering that formed a part of the Enmaten ritual. The latter, elaborated between the end of the Fujiwara period and the Insei period, was a large-scale ritual in which Dakiniten was worshiped as one member of Enmaten's retinue. After the Insei period, however, the deified *ḍākinī*, under the name Dakiniten, became the focus of specific rites performed outside the Enmaten ritual. Thus, she was no longer perceived simply as a demon: she had become a deva (hence her name, Dakini-*ten*). As such, she entered the Inari cult as both a deva and a fox spirit.

Sexual Rituals

In India and Tibet, *ḍākinīs* eventually became divine maidens, and they are often represented with the idealized bodies of voluptuous young women—although something demonic often remains in their features. They are sometimes compared to the *yoginīs* who protect yogis like Padmasambhava, and whose participation was essential in the psychosexual rites of the *Yoginī-tantra*.[21] As initiatory goddesses, they can bestow *siddhis* (powers). Sometimes they are represented with theriomorphic features, as in the case of the two animal-headed females seated side by side in the Berlin Museum collection (Fig. 3.2).

According to the Chinese monk Huilin 慧琳 (737–820), the name *ḍākinī* refers to deities that can bewitch men and have sexual relationships with them.[22] In Japan, *ḍākinīs* did not, as a rule, become the initiators and sexual consorts of Tantric practitioners. Even in the Tachikawa-ryū 立川流 they do not seem to have become the main object (*honzon*) of sexual rituals—a supposedly conspicuous feature of that school. A notable exception is that of the so-called Skull Ritual, known only from the "description" given by its detractors. The alleged goal of that ritual of ill repute was to create a kind of zombie that could foretell the future.

FIGURE 3.2. Two jackal-headed *yoginīs*. Central India, 10th–11th centuries. Stone. Staatliche Museen zu Berlin, Museum für Indische Kunst.

The animation of the skull was effected by a long process of coating it with the blood and semen resulting from sexual intercourse between the practitioner and his female partner. As one source puts it, "Taking care that the skull is kept warm and nourished for seven years is a secret ritual for the *ḍākinīs* who live in the *honzon*. These *ḍākinīs* are manifestations of Mañjuśrī and of Nāgakanyā, the serpent-girl. Nāgakanyā is an earthly form of the *ḍākinī-deva* [Dakini-ten]. She attained enlightenment at the age of eight and the *honzon* mirrors her example. That is why one has to wait eight years for its efficacious powers."[23]

According to the *Juhō yōjinshū* 受法用心集 by Shinjō 心定, a critic of the Tachikawa-ryū, followers of that "heterodox teaching" believed that if they deposited as an offering on the altar the skull bones of a man or of a fox, Dakiniten would come to dwell in them and, using their *hun* and *po* souls as her emissaries, would manifest all kinds of prodigies and confer magical powers on them. The *Keiran shūyōshū* echoes some of this account. That these beliefs were actually put into practice is suggested by the recent discovery of a fox tail and a fox skull, together with two Dakiniten scrolls, inside a statue of Monju at Keirinji in Tenri City.[24]

DAKINITEN RITUALS IN JAPANESE BUDDHIST LITERATURE

The cult of Dakiniten flourished from the Insei period onward, and its rite was believed to be particularly efficacious for obtaining power and good fortune. The subversive, black magical aspects of the ritual, however, secured for it the reputation of a "heterodox rite" (*gehō* 外法). Because of its essential secrecy, it rarely appears in official documents, and we must turn to literary sources and legends to find more information about it. The impression we get from these sources is that the Dakiniten ritual was a powerful instrument for upward mobility, and was consequently attractive to ambitious people in spite of its perceived dangers. In the *Kokon chōmonjū,* for instance, we are told that Fujiwara no Tadazane 藤原忠實 (1078–1162) performed this ritual for seven days as he was about to be sent into exile. At the end of that period, a fox came to eat his offering, a rice cake. Seven days later, during a nap, he was visited in his dream by a handsome young woman. When she was getting ready to leave, he grasped her hair to hold her back and suddenly woke up with pains in his belly, realizing that what he was holding was not the hair of a woman but a fox's tail. The next day, instead of being sent on his way to exile, he was suddenly promoted to a high rank. Attributing this turn of events to Dakiniten, he began to worship the fox tail as the symbolic form of that deity.[25] Another well-known story is that of the Shingon priest Ningai 仁海 (951–1046), who ascended the ecclesiastic hierarchy so rapidly that he came to be known as the monk who "became *sōjō* (prefect) in a single step" (*ikkai sōjō*). This rise to prominence was attributed to the one thousand days of austerities he had completed on Mount Inari in order to gain Dakiniten's support.[26]

Likewise, Taira no Kiyomori 平清盛 (1118–1181) is said to have owed his political ascension to Dakiniten. As the story goes, Kiyomori once shot an arrow at a fox during a hunt. The fox suddenly turned into a beautiful woman who begged for her life, promising that she would grant Kiyomori all his desires. Kiyomori spared her and began to worship Dakiniten, despite his awareness that the benefits obtained through such a heterodox rite would not be passed on to his descendants.[27]

Another well-known worshiper of Dakiniten was Kōshin 弘真 (better known as Monkan 文観, 1281–1357), a Ritsu priest whose name came to be associated with the Tachikawa-ryū.[28] (His affiliation with this supposedly heretical current of Shingon has recently been called into question.) Monkan's name is said to have derived from his devotion to <u>Mon</u>ju and <u>Kan</u>non.[29] He is known to have performed several secret rites in support of Emperor Go-Daigo's attempt to restore imperial power, yet his own rise to power is attributed solely to his performance of the Dakiniten rite. Monkan's enemies compounded his negative image by emphasizing the heterodox nature of the rites he performed. In a petition recorded in the *Hōkyōshō* 宝鏡鈔 (1376) by Yukai 宥快 (1345–1416), we read: "Formerly there was a demonic jackal (*śṛgāla*) that wore heavenly cloths, sat opposite Kauśika (Indra), and preached the Dharma. Now we have Monkan making offerings to the *ḍākinīs* and conjuring dragons while he is reporting to the throne."[30] According to the *Taiheiki* 太平記, Monkan "gathered together arms of war and kept soldiers in very great numbers."[31] While the case against him has clearly been exaggerated, Monkan was definitely a charismatic priest, and his description as a warrior-monk does not appear too far fetched. Against such a background, his devotion to Dakiniten, an avatar of Monju, the main object of worship of the Ritsu school, sounds plausible.

In the above examples, the Dakiniten ritual is presented as a two-edged weapon. Stories of rapid success followed by an equally rapid decline imply a criticism of the heterodox nature of this rite. Even Kōshū, the author of *Keiran shūyōshū,* wavers in his judgment of the ritual: on the one hand, he writes that "he who worships animals is worthy of being a master. He who worships a fox is worthy of becoming a king."[32] On the other hand, he warns his readers about the dangers of the Dakiniten cult.

THE SECTARIAN BACKGROUND

It is difficult—and perhaps irrelevant—to trace the cult of Dakiniten to specific historical actors, since the growth of such cults involves a complex combination of elements reflecting various historical and geographical settings. Yet certain circles were clearly instrumental in promoting that cult. The *Inari kechimyaku* 稲荷血脈 gives a transmission lineage for the Dakiniten ritual starting with Amoghavajra and reaching the Shingon priest Dōnin (d.u.), through a series of intermediaries like Kūkai and the Yoshino ascetic Nichizō 日藏.[33] According to a variant in the *Tonjō shitsuji kuketsu mondō* 頓成る悉地口訣問答, the lineage started with Vajrabodhi and reached the monks Dōgon 道嚴 and Dōshun 道舜 (d.u.). This lineage may more plausibly be traced back to Shingon masters such as the Jingoji priest Kengyō 鑒教 or the Tōji abbot Kanshuku 観宿 (fl. 926–930).[34]

Esoteric Buddhist priests like Ningai 仁海 (951–1046) and Monkan performed the Dakiniten ritual. Even if the latter was not the patriarch of the Tachikawa-ryū as claimed, the Dakiniten ritual clearly played an important role in that Shingon branch. Several apocryphal scriptures centered on Shinkoō Bosatsu 辰狐王菩薩 (i.e., Dakiniten) are mentioned in a list of lost Tachikawa texts. The influence of Onmyōdō on the Tachikawa-ryū may also explain the role played by Dakiniten in divination techniques preserved at Shōmyōji 称名寺, a major Shingon center of eastern Japan.

The second Shōmyōji abbot, Kenna 釼阿 (1261–1338), and his disciples were instrumental in the transmission of these Dakiniten texts. The Shōmyōji reached its apogee at the end of the Kamakura period under Kenna and his patron, the head of the Kanazawa Hōjō 金沢北条 clan, Sadaaki 貞顕 (1278–1333), and Kenna worked hard to spread the esoteric teachings in Kantō. The Shingon enthronement ritual (*sokui kanjō* 即位灌頂) proved very useful to his patron, who served the court as a supervisor, and probably contributed to his promotion to regent (*shikken* 執権) of the bakufu in 1326. Yet a ritual that brought quick worldly benefits and was known to be "heterodox" was not without risks. Hardly seven years later, in 1333, the bakufu was destroyed, and the Kanazawa Hōjō clan with it. Under such circumstances, what became of the Dakiniten ritual? All we know is that, in 1359, under abbot Jūson 什尊 (a.k.a. Kiin 熙允), one of Kenna's favorite disciples, a shrine was built at Shōmyōji and Shinkoō Bosatsu was invited to dwell in it. Judging from the documentation available, Shōmyōji had already lost its patronage and had steadily declined. Thus, the enshrinement of Shinkoō Bosatsu reflected the hope that, owing to the deity's power, the temple could be restored.[35] This hope was apparently fulfilled, as Shōmyōji and its secret teachings have survived to this day.

Dakiniten's influence extended mainly through the network of Inari worship—and conversely. (See, e.g., Figs. 3.3–3.12). The *honzon* of Toyokawa Inari, for instance, is a representation of Dakiniten riding a white fox, carrying a bundle of rice stalks on her left shoulder while holding a jewel in her right hand. She wears a diadem ornamented with a jewel and a white snake (Ugajin). This form is based on a vision experienced by the Sōtō Zen monk Kangan Giin 寒巌義尹 (1217–1300) as he was returning from China in 1267.[36] In this vision, he was given a *dhāraṇī* by Dakiniten, who vowed to protect him. The *dhāraṇī* was transmitted to Giin's successors and eventually to Tōkai Gieki 東海義易 (1412–1497), the founder of Myōgonji 妙厳寺 (Toyokawa Inari 豊川稲荷) in Mikawa province (present-day Aichi prefecture).[37] As this example indicates, it was Sōtō Zen priests, next to Shingon priests, who contributed to the transformation of Dakiniten into a goddess of fortune.[38]

In popular religion, the name Dakiniten also referred to a deity of love known as Akomachi 阿小町, Tōme 専女, or Myōbu 命婦—all names referring to a powerful female fox dwelling at Inari. By extension, the god of Inari itself came to be described as a deity of love.[39] The *Dakini no saimon* 荼吉尼の祭文, a short liturgical text preserved at Kōzanji 高山寺, consists of two prayers addressed to Akomachi in order to find a partner, the former to be recited by a "woman without a man," the latter by a "man without a woman." The person concerned asks to be possessed by the goddess, and to initiate the possession he or she has to imitate the cry of the fox (*kou, kou*—which could also mean "I beg you, I beg you").[40]

FIGURE 3.3. Dakiniten. Edo period. Sheet, ink on paper. University Art Museum, Kyoto City University of Arts. *BZS* 2223.

FIGURE 3.4. Dakiniten. Edo period. Sheet, ink on paper. University Art Museum, Kyoto City University of Arts. *BZS* 2224.

DAKINITEN AND THE ENTHRONEMENT RITUAL

As noted above, it is precisely by stealing the vital essence of humans that the *ḍākinī* (or Dakiniten) became so powerful, and paradoxically it is through the same agency that she is able to bring benefits to humans. That element was not lost on those who were performing the Dakiniten rite to get some of this formidable power. In its discussion of the enthronement ritual, for example, the *Keiran shūyōshū* quotes a passage of the *Sūtra on Benevolent Kings* (*Renwang jing* 仁王經) which refers to the human yellow.[41]

Although the precise origins of the Shingon enthronement ritual (*sokui kanjō*) are difficult to establish,[42] one tradition holds that it was the Shingon priest Seison 成尊, a disciple of Ningai, who was the first to perform it, at the time of Go-Sanjō Tennō's 後三条天皇 enthronement

FIGURE 3.5. Dakiniten (Inari). Edo period. Pigment on wood. Hildburgh Collection. American Museum of Natural History.

(r. 1068–1072).[43] If that were the case, the ritual could probably be traced back to Ningai himself. What is certain is that, owing to it, the Ono branch founded by Ningai played a major role in the constitution of the so-called Insei rule by retired emperors,[44] and that Dakiniten, as the *honzon* of the ritual, became linked with Ise Shrine and the imperial house.[45] The ritual was soon to become the prerogative of Fujiwara regents (*sekkanke* 摂関家), who secretly transmitted the mantras and mudrās of Dakiniten to the new emperor during the accession ceremony.[46] Indeed, the legendary source of Fujiwara power, according to the story of the youth who would grow up to become Nakatomi no Kamatari 中臣鎌足 (614–669), the ancestor of the Fujiwara clan, is that he had been abducted by a she-fox. It was she who initiated him (spiritually and perhaps sexually) and gave him the scythe (*kama* 鎌) with which he later beheaded his sworn enemy, Soga no Iruka 蘇我入鹿 (d. 645).

The enthronement ritual flourished after the thirteenth century, together with other accession rituals.[47] The Shingon rite was focused on two small fox figures in gold and silver. The *Bikisho* reports that when this ritual was performed in the imperial palace, its two *honzon* were disposed to the left and right of the altar, and the new ruler was consecrated through a ritual aspersion with the water of the four oceans.[48]

Why did the enthronement ritual center on the transmission of Dakiniten's mantras? The references given in the *Keiran shūyōshū* to canonical passages such as the *Mizōukyo* 未曽有經—in which the god Indra, outwitted by a fox, takes the latter as his master—and the *Nirvāṇa-sūtra*—in which the gods Brahmā and Indra revere animals—sound like

FIGURE 3.6. Dakiniten. *Ofuda*. Color on paper. Ise, Asamagatake. Columbia University, Starr Library. Photo Gaelle Faure.

FIGURE 3.7. Dakiniten. *Ofuda*. Color on paper. Toyokawa Inari, Myōgonji, Toyokawa (Aichi prefecture). Columbia University, Starr Library. Photo Gaelle Faure.

rationalizations, and the real motivations must lie elsewhere.[49] The Kamatari legend itself might suggest a dark relationship involving animality, sexuality, murder, and power, and a number of scholars have emphasized the role of sexuality in the imperial mystique of medieval Japan.[50] However, it's more likely that Dakiniten became *honzon* because of the power she had accrued by stealing the human vital essence.[51] Despite the disapproval of some members of the orthodox clergy, who looked down on heterodox rituals, the Dakiniten rite was elevated (together with the fox deity at its center) to the highest and most sacred spheres of kingly power, and it became a ritual identification of the ruler with his ancestral goddess Amaterasu in her manifestation as the "divine fox."[52]

Nakazawa Shin'ichi claims that Amaterasu and the divine fox represent two different sources of royal or imperial power. Amaterasu represents the sun, the logos, and through the ritual of enthronement, the new king inherits from her the "spirit of rice," a benign power. However, as this power alone would not suffice to rule the world, he also receives a more substantial power from the animal deity. Whether or not these two aspects were originally different, they clearly fused in the later tradition.[53] It is not clear, however, that Amaterasu originally represented a benign agricultural power.

In any case, under the name "Fox King," Dakiniten became a manifestation of the sun goddess Amaterasu, with whom the new emperor united during the enthronement ritual. In other words, just as the emperor symbolically became a fox, the fox (or Dakiniten) became a king. The Buddhist ritual allowed the ruler to symbolically cross over the limits separating the human and animal realms in order to harness the wild and properly superhuman energy of the "infrahuman" world, so as to gain full control of the human sphere. In this conception, the animal also served as a metaphor for the nonhuman (*hinin* 非人) elements at the margins outside society, as well as the outcasts living on those margins, the *kawaramono* 河原物.[54]

Another type of enthronement ritual centered on Dakiniten took place at Ise Shrine. Because its symbolism was essentially that of the consecration (*abhiṣeka*) of the *cakravartin* king, the presence of Dakiniten seems incongruous at first glance. In Yamamoto Hiroko's view, it was appropriate because the god who receives the offerings is none other than Dakiniten. This ritual was performed every morning and evening by the *kora* 狐良 (young female shrine attendants) of the Outer Shrine of Ise when they presented their daily offerings of rice, salt, and water to the deity.[55] This ultra-secret ritual is described in the *Bikisho* and in the *Tenshō daijin kuketsu* 天照大神口訣 (Shingū Collection). There are two traditions related to its origins, one claiming that it goes back to Amaterasu herself (through her priestess Yamato-hime 大和姫, the ancestor of the *kora*), the other that it originated with Kūkai.[56] In this way, the *kora,* and through them Amaterasu, came to be identified with Dakiniten, and this probably explains why the *ko* in their name is written with the ideograph meaning "fox." The *Bikisho* states: "Based on this [ancient practice of worshiping animals with special powers] at these [Ise] shrines, the shrine maidens (*kora*) perform the Ritual of the Astral Fox after presenting divine food. Its meaning is to show that the promise made in ancient times has not been forgotten. Therefore, the emperors, who are the descendants of the great deity [of Ise], are initiated in this method as part of their enthronement."[57]

FIGURE 3.8. Dakiniten mandala (with Bishamonten and Kichijōten). Muromachi period, 15th century. Color on silk. Ichigami Shrine, Yōkaichi City (Shiga prefecture).

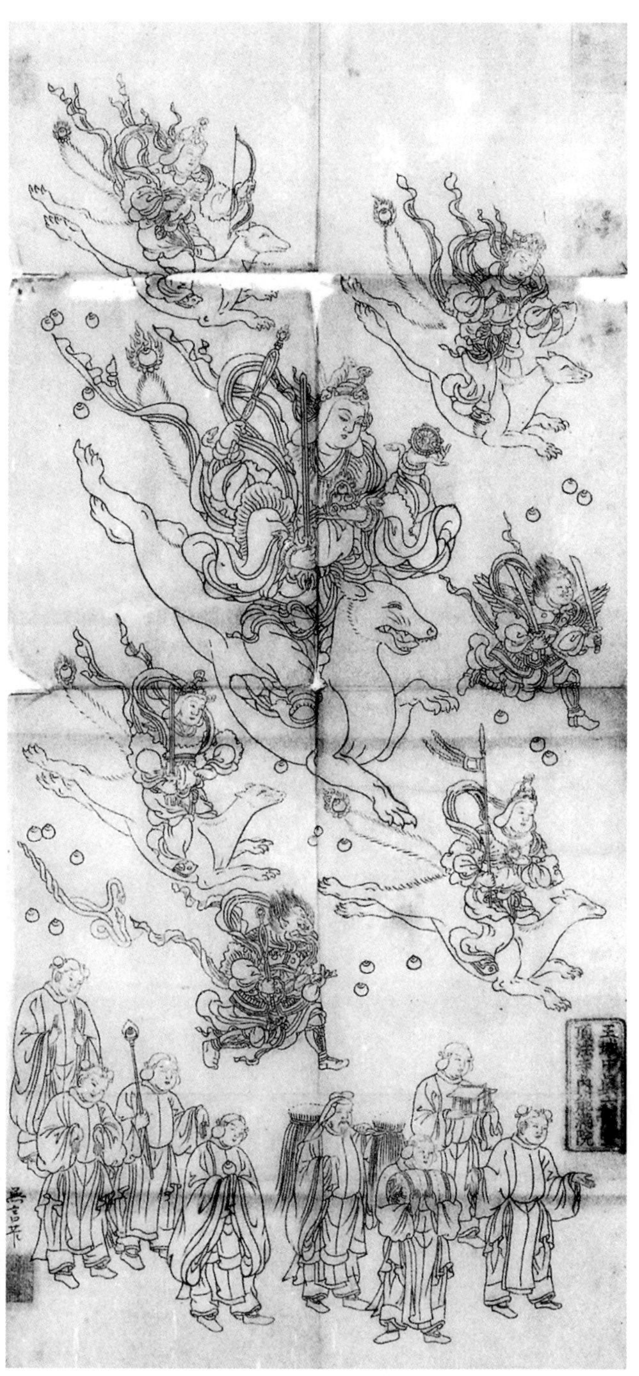

FIGURE 3.9. Dakiniten. Edo period. Sheet, ink on paper. University Art Museum, Kyoto City University of Arts. *BZS* 2225.

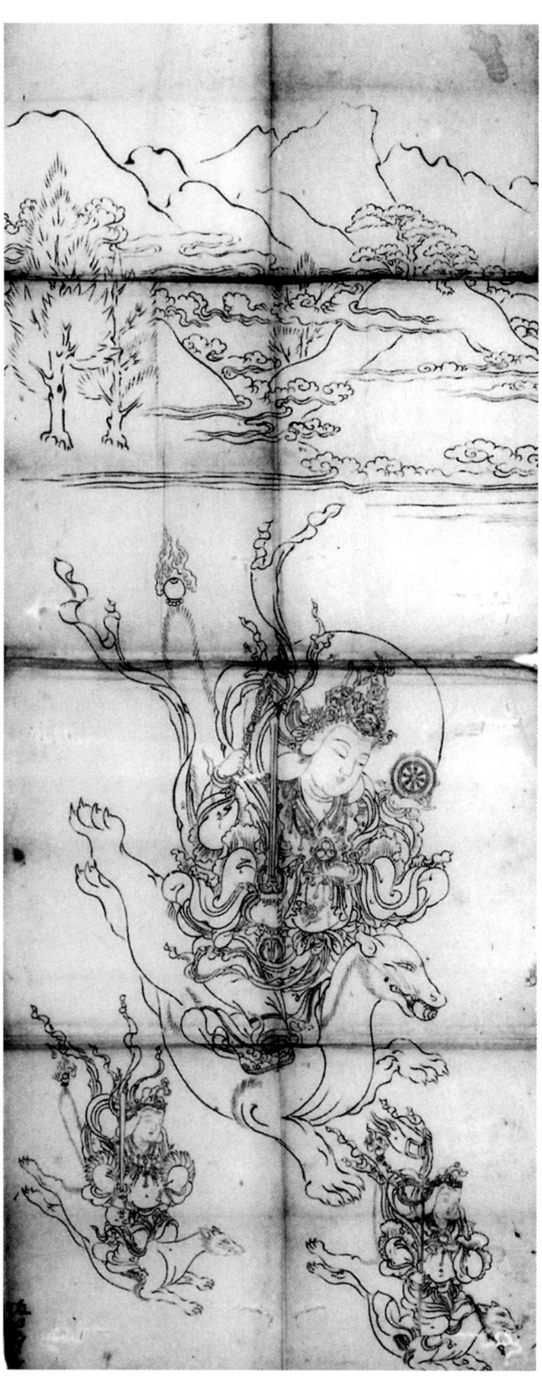

FIGURE 3.10. Dakiniten. Edo period. Sheet, ink on paper. University Art Museum, Kyoto City University of Arts. *BZS* 2226.

FIGURE 3.11. Dakiniten mandala. Edo period. Sheet, ink on paper. University Art Museum, Kyoto City University of Arts. *BZS* 1077.

FIGURE 3.12. Dakiniten mandala. Edo period, 17–18th century. Hanging scroll, ink, color and gold on silk. Museum of Fine Arts, Boston.

This *cakravartin* ordination (*rinnō kanjō* 輪王灌頂) was centered on the transmission of the mantras and mudrās of Dakiniten.[58] In terms of ritual structure, it was quite similar to other Dakiniten rites. Initially aimed at the fulfillment of wishes and realization of happiness, it eventually crystallized into a specific enthronement ritual, apparently on the basis of a scriptural passage according to which the person who worships a fox can become king. Apart from being an enthronement ritual, the *shinko* ritual described in the *Kora no daiji* 狐良大事 also served as a monastic rite of initiation. As the *Tenshō daijin kuketsu* puts it: "If he does not receive this ritual, the ruler's power is light and it cannot hold the four oceans. This is why this ritual is not limited to the king; monks of the various temples and profanes, too, when they perform it, can obtain a high rank and be perfectly free."[59]

Even though Dakiniten disappeared from the public scene when the esoteric accession rite was abandoned during the so-called Meiji Restoration, her cult left deep traces on the geographical and religious landscape of Japan through its fusion with Inari worship. Indeed, the importance of Inari "syncretism" can hardly be overstated when the Inari cult, even today with some 3,000 shrines all over the land standing resolutely outside the National Association of Shrines (NAS) and its "pure Shintō" ideology, remains what could perhaps be called the main religion of Japan.[60]

THE FOX AND THE JEWEL

Until now, we have followed what I call the "genealogical" model, which relies on an official mythology. In this model, we saw how a female demon gradually became a goddess and made its way into the official pantheon. I now turn to a different model, the "relational" model, to shed light on an implicit mythology. This relational model is defined by the transformation of the relatively well individualized figure of Dakiniten into a complex network involving such disparate elements as animals (foxes and snakes, primarily), jewels, and other wild things that burn bright in the night.

Dakiniten and the Fox

The Indo-Tibetan *ḍākinī* is essentially a "sky-goer." In Japan, Dakiniten retained the flying powers of her Indian sisters, as shown by the representations in which she appears traveling through space at the speed of light on the back of a fox. The aerial elements, however, are counterbalanced by chthonian elements. The demonic *ḍākinī*—initially a bird-like spirit—has become an earthly deity bringing fertility and fortune.

Perhaps the most important factor in this evolution, which started in China, was her association with the fox, a chthonian animal known for its psychic powers and ability to communicate with the underworld. In the

Mahāvairocana-sūtra and its Chinese commentary by Yixing, the *ḍākinīs* are associated with various scavengers, including the *yakan* 野干 (Ch. *yegan,* a translation of Skt. *sṛigāla* 'jackal,' which in Chinese designates an animal associated with the fox that eats human flesh). Yixing is of the opinion that *yegan* and *hu* 狐 (fox) refer to the same animal.[61] While the cult of the fox was not widespread in China, many stories attest that the Chinese perceived the fox as a "spiritual" animal that could transform itself into a *femme fatale.*[62] This was an innovation, however, as this identity is not found in the Indian and Tibetan pantheons. As Jean Lévi points out regarding the Chinese case, "between foxes and the dead the relationships are more than metonymical, there is a similarity, or even an identity. Like ancestors, foxes have an ambiguous nature—both earthly and heavenly, beneficent and maleficent. The graves where they take up residence are believed to give access to heaven. Thus, the lower world communicates with the beyond, and the 'wild fox' (*yehu* 野狐) becomes a 'heavenly fox' (*tianhu* 天狐)."[63]

The *ḍākinī* came to be assimilated to foxes in China, while the image of the "heavenly fox" developed fully in Japan, where foxes were believed to be the messengers of the god of Inari.[64] The *Bikisho* emphasizes the ancient, and possibly pre-Buddhist, origins of the Japanese cult of foxes: "In ancient times, people simply had faith in animals with special powers, and prayed to them to increase their worldly treasures."[65] The slopes of Mount Inari, for instance, are occupied by hundred of graves, and the image of the fox has merged with that of the ancestors.[66] The image of Dakiniten in Japan grafted itself onto a real and thriving popular cult, that of the god of Inari, through its association with Inari's messenger, the fox. In some respects, the Dakiniten cult could be considered only a Buddhist version of the old Japanese fox cult. In other respects, however, without ever losing its ties to the fox cult, it became something quite different.

Dakiniten's vulpine mount became in medieval Japan an independent and powerful deity known by the strange name of "astral fox" or "dragon fox" (*shinko* 辰狐, also translated as "gleaming fox"), closely related to the sun goddess Amaterasu.[67] According to the *Keiran shūyōshū:* "After the great goddess Amaterasu descended and secluded herself in the heavenly cave, she took the form of a dragon fox. It is because only the fox among all animals emits a light from its body that she manifested herself in this form."[68] As the earthly foxes becomes "astral," Dakiniten becomes their ruler, and by the same token Master of the Cintāmaṇi—under the name of King Shintamani (Shindamani-ō 真陀摩尼王).

Although Dakiniten and the fox were strongly connected by the thirteenth century, this does not mean that they fused perfectly. It is a very particular type of preternatural animal, the astral or dragon fox, a combination of aerial and earthly elements, that became the mount and symbol of Dakiniten.[69] The postface to the Edo-period *Reflections on Inari Shrine*

FIGURE 3.13. Inari Myōjin. Edo period. Sheet, ink on paper. University Art Museum, Kyoto City University of Arts. *BZS* 4076.

(*Inari jinja kō* 稲荷神社考) declares: "Fearing to worship openly fox spirits, one calls them Dakiniten, Matarajin, Izuna Gongen, Yashajin, or Fuku daijin, and one worships them. All of them, these Matarajin and wild foxes, their [true] form is [that of] a three-faced and six-armed [deity]. . . . This is why Dakiniten takes the form of a heavenly maiden and her cult has been transmitted in the esoteric school."[70]

Dakiniten and Inari

By the end of the Heian period, the Indian *ḍākinī* had merged into the single figure of Dakiniten, represented as a fox-riding deity. This Dakiniten was said to be an emanation of the bodhisattva Mañjuśrī (J. Monju).[71] Many factors must have been at work in that evolution. In the case of Shingon, a particularly important element, to which we will return, was the symbolic association of the fox with the wish-fulfilling jewel (*cintāmaṇi*).[72] Perhaps the most important association, however, was with Mount Inari, a site long connected with foxes.

A good part of the popularity of Inari Shrine derived from its reputation of efficacy in answering prayers for fertility. This efficacy was reflected in the sexual symbolism of the site, as revealed by the shape of its platform, which is supposedly that of the Chinese character *kai* 開 'open,' symbolizing the vagina. We recall that the Inari deity was characterized as a deity of love.

The god of Inari is usually represented as an old man (see Figs. 3.13–3.15), but it was also depicted with the features of a young woman, in which case it is identified with Uka no Mitama 宇迦之御魂 or Toyouke 豊受, two goddesses of cereals.[73] The image of that goddess must have influenced the representation of Dakiniten.[74] In some images, the old man joins Dakiniten's retinue as one of the so-called eight youths (*hachi dōji* 八童子). Dakiniten's rise was thus due in large part to her identification, through the intermediary of the fox, with Inari Myōjin 稲荷明神, a god of rice, and by extension, of food and wealth.[75]

In the *Inari ki* 稲荷記 the five peaks of Mount Inari are distributed as follows: the central peak corresponds to the king of the dragon foxes, named Shinkoō 辰狐王, the eastern peak to Dakiniten, the western peak to Benzaiten, the southern peak to Gōzanze Myōō 降三世明王, and the northern peak to Fudō.[76] The fact that the king of the dragon foxes and Dakiniten are perceived here as distinct suggests that toward

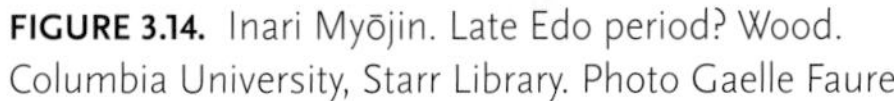

FIGURE 3.14. Inari Myōjin. Late Edo period? Wood. Columbia University, Starr Library. Photo Gaelle Faure.

FIGURE 3.15. Inari Myōjin, riding a fox, with a bundle of rice and a wish-fulfilling jewel. Late Edo period? Wood. Columbia University, Starr Library. Photo Gaelle Faure.

the beginning of the fourteenth century, when that text was compiled, the fox and Dakiniten had not yet perfectly fused. But because of his central position, the king of the dragon foxes does not seem to be a mere acolyte or emissary of Dakiniten—it is Dakiniten herself.

Foxes and Snakes

In Japan, foxes and snakes were often worshiped together. The merging of the two animals symbolizing Dakiniten (or Dakiniten's two aspects) was achieved in the image of her mount, a fox around whose neck and legs snakes are coiled (Fig. 3.4). At the heart of this cult, then, we find a nexus of the deities Dakiniten, Benzaiten, and Ugajin against a background of fox and snake worship and the worship of *kami* like Uka no Mitama and her "sisters" Toyouke and Ukemochi 保食.

Foxes were, of course, the messengers of the Inari deity (Fig. 3.17). The intimate relationship between them is illustrated in an origin story of Inari Shrine, which also throws an interesting light on the murky relations between the Hata 秦 clan, the Korean immigrant group that sponsored the Inari cult, and the Korean peninsula. In the story, we are told that the Inari deity manifested itself on the side of the Japanese army in the form of two foxes, one white, the other red, during a battle that took place

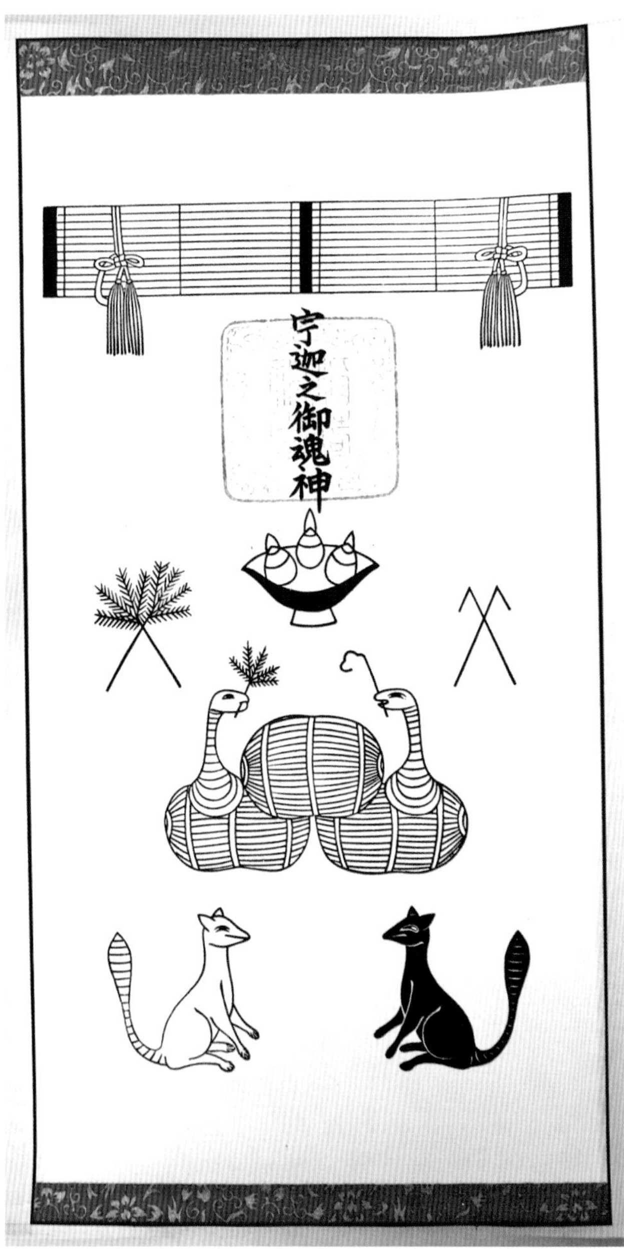

FIGURE 3.16. Uka no Mitama. *Ofuda*. Color on paper. Fushimi Inari Shrine, Kyoto. Columbia University, Starr Library. Photo Gaelle Faure.

in Kōrai (K. Goryeo). The red fox was killed by the enemy, and its body was brought back to Japan, to be worshiped as Inari.[77] Here the deity and its messenger have become one.

The identification of Dakiniten with Inari also led to an association with the snake—and its deified form, Ugajin. This in turn reinforced the link between Dakiniten and Benzaiten. Through these associations, foxes and snakes have come to be regarded as bringers of wealth and happiness (unless it is the other way around).

The talismans (*ofuda*) of the Saijō Inari 最上稲荷 Shrine in Okayama prefecture show a goddess called Saijōōkyō Daibosatsu 最上王經大菩薩 (Great Bodhisattva King of the *Saijōōkyō,* i.e., the *Lotus Sūtra*). She rides a white fox that is flying on a cloud, and holds a scale with rice sheaves in her left hand and a scythe in her right hand. She has the dual function of bringing prosperity (like Inari Myōjin) and protecting the *Lotus Sūtra.*[78] This image nicely reflects the two currents constituting the Inari tradition: the agricultural deity of Korean origin worshiped by the Hata clan, and the esoteric Buddhist deity Dakiniten. Additional elements were borrowed from the *kami* of cereals Uka no Mitama (who came to be confused with the Buddhist snake deity Ugajin) and from local beliefs about snakes and foxes (see, e.g., Fig. 3.16). The fact that Uka no Mitama is one of the deities enshrined at Inari Shrine clearly contributed to the eventual fusion of Ugajin, Dakiniten, and the fox.[79]

The *Inari ichiryū daiji* 稲荷一流大事, a document copied by the priest Tenna 天阿 (d. 1674), contains severals texts, including the *Inari*

FIGURE 3.17. Fox as messenger of Inari. Saijōji Inari (Okayama prefecture). Photo Bernard Faure.

wasan 稲荷和讃, the *Inari shingyō* 稲荷心經, and the *Ototari shinku saimon* 乙足神供祭文.[80] The last is traced back to a legendary figure called Shin (i.e., Hata) no Ototari 秦乙足, an old man credited with bringing the cult of Inari Myōjin to Japan. In it, we are told that "the deity appears as an astral fox to fulfill the vows of beings in the two worlds, and to give them love (*keiai*)."[81] Again, in the *Inari Daimyōjin saimon* 稲荷大明神祭文 of the Sanbōin-ryū 三宝院流, we read that Inari Daimyōjin received the help of Ototari to come to Japan and spread the cultivation of rice among the people, and that this deity, who holds a wish-fulfilling jewel, eliminates all troubles and brings good fortune. In a variant, the same old man saves Dakiniten's emissaries or children from the belly of a monstrous catfish (*namazu* 鯰).[82]

The shared identity of Inari, the wish-fulfilling jewel, and the Buddha's relics is well established. In the *Keiran shūyōshū,* we read that when Kūkai buried the jewel on Inari Peak, the Inari deity brought him the relics of the seven buddhas of the past. In fact, there are many tumuli (*kofun* 古墳) on Mount Inari. The bones that were deposited in them were described as "silver relics," and the wish-fulfilling jewel(s) as rice seedlings (*ina* 稲). This association between death and fertility is one of the reasons Mount Inari was perceived as a sacred wealth-bringing site. Moreover, the agricultural symbolism of Inari further connects that site and its deities with the jewel. In the *Buchū kanjō hongi* 峰中灌頂本記, a text dated to the mid-Muromachi period, the jewel is identified with the seed-letter *a* and the earth element, from which the five cereals grow.[83]

Fushimi Inari was from very early on a place of religious practice, and more specifically a cultic center for the Hata clan. In the *Honchō shinsenden* 本朝神仙伝, for instance, we read that Taichō 泰澄 (682–767), the founder of the Hakusan 白山 cult, once practiced for several days at Inari shrine, and that Kannon appeared to him in a dream in the form of Inari Daimyōjin. The Shingon priest Ningai (951–1046) performed a thousand-day reclusion on Mount Inari.[84] Another case was that of the Enryakuji abbot Son'i (866–940), who, after making a pilgrimage to Fushimi Inari Shrine, was visited in a dream by the Inari deity (in her female form). On the basis of that dream, he built the Shrine of the Holy Lady (Seijo-gū 聖女宮) inside the precinct of Hie Shrine. The original form (*honji*) of that goddess was said to be Nyoirin Kannon, providing another link between Inari and the wish-fulfilling jewel.[85]

Dakiniten and the Jewel

Another element that contributed to Dakiniten's rise in the Japanese pantheon was her transformation into King Shintamani (or Cintāmaṇi King). In other words, her symbolic (*samaya*) form became the wish-fulfilling jewel.

This image of Dakiniten developed against a symbolic background formed by relics of the Buddha and wish-fulfilling jewels, and it was part of a broader network including deities such as Aizen, Nyoirin, Benzaiten and Ugajin.[86] The notion of "silver relics," a metaphor for rice, was based on these associations, and it contributed to bringing the wish-fulfilling jewel (and therefore Dakiniten) into the symbolic sphere of Inari. As is well known, Kūkai is said to have buried a wish-fulfilling jewel on Mount Inari after the Inari deity appeared to him in the form of an old man carrying sheaves of rice (*ina*).

Elaborating on the relationship between Dakiniten and Inari, the *Keiran shūyōshū* declares: "Dakiniten is called 'Cintāmaṇi Jewel.' Because the beings of the realm of desire are full of desires, she makes the ten thousand treasures rain on them—hence her name. The *ina* (of Inari, meaning "rice") corresponds to the *cintāmaṇi* in the jeweled banner. Thus it is said in the *Da*[*zhidu*] *lun:* 'The relics of the ancient buddha transform into rice grains.' Reflect deeply on this."[87]

According to the origin story of the Dakiniten Hall at Shinnyo-dō 真如堂 in Kyoto, Kōson Shōnin 公尊上人, was a worshiper of Dakiniten and he had just finished reciting the 600-scroll *Prajñāpāramitā Sutra* when a white fox appeared on the altar, holding a *cintāmaṇi* in its mouth. The fox then transformed into a youth, who declared that he was the god Uka no Mitama and that his jewel could fulfill all wishes. This jewel came to be worshiped as "Uka's jewel" (based on the word-play allowed by the reading of *mitama* in the name Uka no Mitama as "jewel").[88] In the talismans sold today at Shinnyo-dō, the youth is represented as riding a fox.[89]

The Three Foxes

The transformations of the divine fox, however, do not end there. Soon the dragon fox developed into a composite figure called Sankoshin 三狐神 or "Three-fox God."[90] Sometimes this name refers to three separate figures, and at other times, to a single deity. It is said to derive from *miketsu no kami* 御食津神 'god of the Miketsu (dono)'—a building that served as a granary at the Outer Shrine of Ise. The term *miketsu* was apparently misread as *mi-ketsu* 三狐 'three foxes' (which can also be read *sanko*). According to the *Ise nisho kōtaijin gochinza denki* 伊勢二所皇太神御鎮座伝記, the god of the Mikura (August Granary) is Uka no Mitama 宇賀之御魂, and it is also called *miketsu no kami* 三狐神 (written as "three-fox god").[91] This god of the August Granary was the tutelary god of the Hata clan at Fushimi Inari—thus he was not originally a fox. This

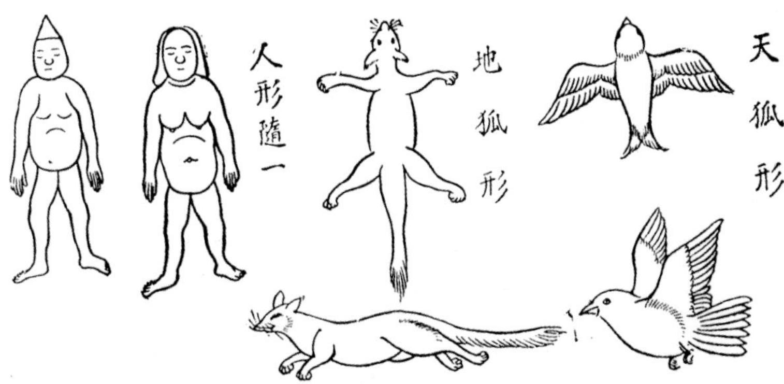

FIGURE 3.18. Three foxes (variants). *Besson zakki* 11, *TZ* 3: 152.

etymological drift was allowed by the fact that the fox (*kitsune* 狐) was also called *ketsu.*[92] Thus, Uka no Mitama, the deity of Fushimi Inari and of the Outer Shrine of Ise, came to be seen as a fox, and to be associated with Dakiniten. This hermeneutic legerdemain apparently took place not at Fushimi, but at Ise, where the dragon fox (*shinko*), under the name Sankoshin 三狐神, was at the heart of rituals performed by the priestess (*saigū*) and her attendants, the *kora.*[93]

This misreading would hardly deserve any mention had it not contributed to the associations between Inari, Ugajin, and the fox, thereby giving birth to the Sankoshin. The "three foxes" were interpreted, following the Chinese *heaven, earth, man* model, as the heavenly, earthly, and human foxes, respectively.[94] In spite of their name, however, they hardly looked like foxes. In texts such as the *Kakuzenshō* and the *Gyōrinshō* 行林抄, the three foxes appear in connection with the *goma* 護摩 ritual, and the heavenly fox (*tenko* 天狐) is actually represented as a bird (Fig. 3.18). Sometimes the interpretation can differ: of the three figures employed in the ritual—bird, human, and fox—the two animals are said to be the demons that possess the person, represented by the human figurine, on behalf of whom the ritual is performed. These paper figurines were thrown into a stream, following the practice of the Shintō purification ritual (*harae* 祓え). In the *Nihongi Miwaryū* 日本紀三輪流, the Tenkojin is mentioned as representing the path of demons and animals, next to the crossroads deity (Dōsojin), who represents the dark path of the underworld (*meidō* 冥道), and to King Yama (Enma-ō 閻魔王), representing the path of Māra's armies.[95]

As noted, the Sankoshin enjoyed a parallel existence as a single deity. According to the *Tamakisan gongen engi* 玉置山権現縁起 (copy of 1350), an account of the origin of the cultic site on Mount Tamaki near Totsugawa (Kii peninsula), this deity, also called the "king of heavenly foxes" (Tenko-ō 天狐王), was worshiped at the Zaō Hall on Kinpusen 金峰山 (var. Kinbusen). It was a three-faced, six-armed, six-legged deity with Daishō Kangiten and Dakiniten as its *honji.*[96] The central face was that of Kannon, while its right face was that of the heavenly fox, and its

FIGURE 3.19. Monju, Fugen, and the fox. Edo period. Sheet, ink on paper. University Art Museum, Kyoto City University of Arts. *BZS* 2072.

left face that of the earthly fox.[97] Since Kangiten and Dakiniten were presumably the *honji* of the heavenly and earthly foxes, respectively, Kannon here appears to be standing in for Benzaiten (who is often linked with this bodhisattva) in a prototype or variant of the so-called Three Devas (Santen 三天), a composite deity to which we will return.[98] We should also note, however, that the name Sankoshin is also used in the same text to designate an individual deity dwelling at Asuka Shrine in Shingū (Kumano).[99]

The fox-like mythical animal called *shinko* no longer has much to do with the ordinary foxes that roam through forests and moors. According to the *Keiran shūyōshū* (T. 76, 2410: 520c): "The astral fox (*shinko*) is a manifestation of Nyoirin Kannon. Because it takes the wish-fulfilling jewel (*cintāmaṇi*) as its essence, it is called King Shintamani. Because the *cintāmaṇi* always shines at night, one takes it as one's lamp when one recites the various mantras and makes offerings (T. 76, 2410: 520c)." Although the astral fox appears to be distinct from the demonic "three foxes" expelled in exorcisms, the difference between them is not clear. Nevertheless, from the Sankoshin emanated a host of supernatural animals—among them the heavenly, earthly, and human foxes. Because of the homophony, the heavenly foxes (*tenko*) came to be confused with the *tengu* 天狗, while the earthly foxes, fusing with the earth god, became rulers of the earth.

The *Inari saimon* 稲荷祭文, a ritual text contained in the *Inari ichiryū daiji,* begins with the words: "I invoke the green emperor of the east, the earthly fox, the august child (*miko*) of the wood spirit." A similar invocation is repeated for the deities of the other three directions and the center, and the other four elements or phases. The text continues: "The various members of King Dakini's retinue, depending on their capacities, benefit beings. . . . Those who take pity on beings are called heavenly foxes; those who benefit sentient beings are called earthly foxes."[100]

The Izuna mandala of Rinnōji, which is actually a Dakiniten mandala, is striking for the profusion of foxes that surround the central figures and their acolytes, who are themselves riding foxes (Fig. 3.20). It can be further noted that some of these foxes are hybrid figures: on the top of the picture, one figure has the head of an old man (perhaps the Inari deity) and another that of a youth, suggesting that Dakiniten and her human acolytes may themselves be hybrids after all.[101]

DAKINITEN'S NETWORK

Dakiniten rarely appears alone in legend, rituals, and iconography. She is usually surrounded by a variety of acolytes and emissaries, as well as by other deities (mostly devas). Like other medieval Buddhist deities, in fact, she can only be understood as part of a network.

Let us first look at her relations with the other deities that constitute her cohort before examining the symbols they share. In the official *honji suijaku* framework, Dakiniten's essence or *honji* is usually considered to be the bodhisattva Monju (Mañjuśrī), but it can also be Nyoirin Kannon or Bishamonten.[102] The fact that she has other *honji* apart from Dainichi/Monju has often been invoked as proof that she outshines all other devas—although she is by no means the only deity in that category.

In some sources, Dakiniten is an assimilation body (*tōrujin* 等流神) of the buddha Dainichi. Far from being a mere "trace" or manifestation (*suijaku*), however, she is at times described as the essence or "original ground" (*honji*) of other deities. In one intriguing document, Dakiniten herself is a *honji* endowed with four bodies (that is, three types of manifestations): a body of self-nature, symbolized by the lunar disk and corresponding to the Dainichi of the Womb realm; a function body, corresponding to Monju; a metamorphosis body, corresponding to the fox; and an assimilation body, corresponding to a bird.[103]

We have already noted Dakiniten's fusion with the Inari deity and her privileged association with devas such as Daikokuten, Shōten, and Benzaiten. I will return to this matter shortly in my discussion of the Three Devas. Next in importance are Dakiniten's links with Aizen, Myōken, Amaterasu, and Shinra Myōjin.

FIGURE 3.20. (*Opposite*) Izuna mandala. Nanbokuchō period, 14th century. Color on silk. Rinnōji, Nikkō (Tochigi prefecture).

The rituals centered on Aizen and on Dakiniten dealt with the vital essence of humans, their "human yellow." Both rituals, actively promoted by the Ono school of Shingon, grew from attempts to reinforce royal power during the Insei period.[104] As a result, the two deities were also believed to give the ruler "control over the four seas."

In the Jimon 寺門 tradition, Shinra Myōjin, he is the protector of Onjōji (Miidera), is said to be a manifestation of Dakiniten, whose *honji* is Sonjōō 尊星王 (i.e., Myōken Bosatsu), and whose emissaries are the astral foxes. The *Keiran shūyōshū* explains that "the fundamental nature [of this deity] is Sonjōō, and its trace is called Shinra Myōjin. He is none other than Dakiniten. This is why divine foxes (*shinko*) are considered to be the emissaries of his trace, Shinra [Myōjin]."[105] This is also why the seven stars are sometimes represented on (or above) the tail of Dakiniten's fox.

Dakiniten was also linked or identified with Bishamonten. The *Tamon dakini kyō* 多聞吒枳尼經, an apocryphal scripture (dated 1139 and preserved at Ninnaji 仁和寺 in Kyoto), after explaining the origins of the *ḍākinīs,* mentions the conversion of a fox who had come to the Buddha to complain that it was persecuted by a dog. The Buddha then reveals that the fox was in a past life a wealthy man who once refused to feed a starving man. As a result, he was reborn in vulpine form, while the starving man was reborn as a dog, its current nemesis. However, the Buddha continues, because the fox had also been the Buddha's master in another past life, it is in essence one with the buddha Dainichi, and its manifest body is that of the bodhisattva Monju. Upon hearing these words, the fox obtained deliverance and, transforming into Bishamonten (a form known as Tamon Dakini), began to preach the dharma of sudden realization to beings.[106] This legend provides a context for the Inari mandala, where Bishamonten appears, riding a lion (like Monju) and surrounded by foxes and fox-riding acolytes, in a form known as Tohachi Bishamon. In the *Dakini hyakutai henge kyō* 吒枳尼百躰變化經, Dakiniten is said to turn into a "many-armed" Bishamon (Tahi no Bishamon 多臂の毘沙門). Indeed, Dakiniten's acolytes are said to be the same as those of Tohachi Bishamon.

In the Izuna mandala of Rinnōji (in Nikkō) (Fig. 3.20), Bishamonten is also called Dakiniten, and he seems to be an emanation of the latter.[107] This densely populated mandala, dated to the Nanbokuchō period, is an important document. One of its characteristics is the presence of cartouches next to the deities, which suggests that it was used in preaching. Unfortunately, a number of the cartouches have been erased. Significantly, three deities on the central vertical axis are accompanied by two cartouches each (as opposed to the one cartouche for other deities). The deity on the top, surrounded by a halo of flames, rides a seven-headed fox and wears a lion diadem. The cartouche on the left reads "The Worthy Monju," the one on the right (a mixture of Siddhaṃ letters

and Sino-Japanese characters), "Heavenly King Dakini." The same treatment is given to the two other deities, Tamonten (Bishamonten) and Jūichimen Kannon 十一面観音, who are also identified as King Dakini.[108] All these figures are riding foxes, and they are clearly assimilated to Dakiniten. Strangely, the latter is represented, under the name Shinkoō Bosatsu, only as one of five fox-riding deities (the others being her four acolytes) around Bishamonten. Here not only is Bishamonten (in his late manifestation as Tohachi Bishamon) identified with Dakiniten, he is also surrounded by Dakiniten (Shinkoō Bosatsu) and her acolytes, the four princes and the eight *dōji*.[109]

According to the *Keiran shūyōshū,* the sun goddess Amaterasu sometimes appears in vulpine form as an "astral" or "gleaming" fox that is said to be an avatar of Nyoirin Kannon, and to have the wish-fulfilling jewel as its essence. He has one such jewel on each of his three tails.[110] In the Shingon tradition, Dakiniten becomes the *honji of* Amaterasu. In the Ise Consecration (Ise kanjō) section of the *Tenshō daijin kuketsu* 天照大神口訣, we read: "The *honji* [of Amaterasu] is Daten (i.e., Dakiniten). Hence she manifested herself as Kashima Daimyōjin 鹿島大明神, who in turn manifested itself as Kasuga [Daimyōjin]. The Kashima deity, appearing as Daten, gave birth to the Taishokan 大織冠 (Fujiwara no Kamatari 藤原鎌足, 614–669). First it abducted [the youth], took him around, and slept with him."[111] Thus, in a rather circular fashion, it is Dakiniten who manifests herself as the Kashima and Katori 香取 deities. The Kashima deity, in turn, manifests itself as the fox (Dakiniten) that gave birth to Kamatari and to the Fujiwara lineage.

As a soul stealer, Dakiniten was also assimilated to the demonesses known as *rākṣasī* (J. Rasetsunyo 羅刹天女). In the oral traditions of Tendai, one of the ten *rākṣasīs* who protect the *Lotus Sūtra* is called Sarvasattvōjāhārī (J. Datsu-issai-shujō-seiki 奪一切衆生精気 'ravisher of the vital energy of all beings'), and she is none other than Dakiniten.[112] Furthermore, as we will see shortly, one of Dakiniten's eight *dōji* is called Dakkonjin 奪魂神 or "Soul-stealing deity." In the *Keiran shūyōshū,* Mahākāla is also assimilated to an "essence-stealing demon" (*dasshōki* 奪精鬼).[113]

DAKINITEN AND BENZAITEN

Among the deities that influenced the development of Dakiniten, none is more important than Benzaiten. Medieval tales often suggest the identity shared by the two goddesses by apparently confusing their mount or messenger, the fox and the dragon or snake, respectively. In the *Heike monogatari* 平家物語, for instance, after Kiyomori's encounter with a numinous fox that transforms itself into a maiden (supposedly Dakiniten), he concludes that he must henceforward worship Benzaiten. In the Yamato-bon

大和本 version of that text and in the *Genpei jōsuiki* 源平盛衰記, when the Taira warrior Tsunemasa 經正 visits Benzaiten's cultic center at Chikubushima 竹生島, the goddess, moved by the sound of his lute, manifests herself as a white fox.[114] In another version, Benzaiten manifests herself as both a white fox and a white dragon.[115] In yet another version, Tsunemasa first sees a white snake, then a divine youth, and finally a white fox.

Similarly, three fox cubs are said to have appeared on the altar when the Ritsu priest Ninshō (1217–1303) 忍性 (Ryōkan Shōnin 良観上人, 1216–1303) performed a ritual in the dragon cave at Enoshima 江ノ島, another cultic center of Benzaiten.[116] The cubs then transformed into a white snake. Ninshō's vision reflects a widely shared motif.[117] According to Namami Hiroaki, this legend points to the performance of a Tendai ritual centered on both Benzaiten and Dakiniten. He argues that a similar ritual was performed in the fourteenth century at the Shrine of the Holy Woman (Seijo-gū) on Mount Hiei, a site that was a gathering place for blind mediums like the *biwa hōshi* 琵琶法師, the recitants of the *Heike monogatari* (in which, precisely, the story of Tsunemasa appears). As noted earlier, the founding of that shrine is traced to a dream of the Tendai priest Son'i.[118] The deity worshiped there, while being a manifestation of the Inari deity, and as such associated with foxes and Dakiniten, also came to be identified with Benzaiten.

Another trace of this kind of joint ritual is found at Tenkawa 天河 Shrine near Yoshino 吉野. In the *Eishun onkikigaki* 英俊御聞書 (dated 1554), the record of a pilgrimage to Tenkawa by the priest Eishun 英俊 of Tamon-in 多聞院, a subtemple of Kōfukuji 興福寺 in Nara, we are told that the seven auspicious signs of Benzaiten include visions of a white fox and a white snake. In the Tenkawa Benzaiten mandala, which was produced around the same time, white foxes and snakes are represented side by side.

The *Keiran shūyōshū* argues that the Dakiniten ritual was specific to Shingon and did not exist in Tendai.[119] At the same time, it mentions that a secret text entitled *Geppei nenju hiketsu* 藥陛念誦秘訣 was transmitted in the Kurodani-ryū 黒谷流, a branch of the Anō-ryū 穴生流. This text claimed to be a collection of secret teachings from Kūkai and Saichō. Thus, in spite of the widespread belief that the Dakiniten ritual disappeared from Tendai after Saichō declared it to be heterodox, it is Saichō himself who is said to have secretly transmitted it.[120] Even today, there is a shrine dedicated to Dakiniten near the Main Hall (Konpon chūdō 根本中堂) of Enryakuji.[121] The Dakiniten ritual was also transmitted at Miidera, where it was said to bring about awakening, wisdom, and good fortune.[122]

Remarkably, one of the rare explicit textual links between Dakiniten and Benzaiten appears in an Onmyōdō 陰陽道 text. According to the *Hoki naiden* 簠簋内伝, the three major cultic centers of

Benzaiten—Itsukushima, Enoshima, and Chikubushima—were places where the three daughters of an Indian fox king had landed after flying from India to Japan.[123] These three deities are elsewhere described as Dakiniten's main acolytes, and it is therefore significant that they are linked here with three forms of Benzaiten.[124]

But it is above all the iconography that reveals the close link between Benzaiten and Dakiniten. Sometimes the two goddesses are hardly distinct, particularly when they exchange attributes, acolytes, or mounts. In the Dakiniten mandala, for instance, Dakiniten is often surrounded by Benzaiten's usual acolytes, the fifteen *dōji.* Sometimes Benzaiten rides a dragon, while Dakiniten usually rides a fox. But there are exceptions.

In a scroll reproduced in the catalogue *Tenbu no shoson* 天部の諸尊, Benzaiten is shown riding a dragon. An X-ray image of that scroll, however, reveals that she was initially riding both a dragon and a fox.[125] This is confirmed by a line drawing from Nōman-in in Kyoto, reproduced in the *Butsuzō shūsei.*[126] Likewise, in a Dakiniten scroll at the Metropolitan Museum of Art, Dakiniten is riding a fox, but the latter is standing on two dragons. The synthesis of fox and dragon seems complete with the notion of a dragon fox (*shinko* 辰狐, a term I also translate as "astral fox").

In the Dakiniten mandala in the *Butsuzō shūsei* collection, a relatively late image drawn by a priest on Mount Atago in 1858, Dakiniten is shown riding a fox as usual. In her four pairs of hands, she holds a jewel and a sword, a wheel and a key, a bow and an arrow, and a trident and a jeweled club (Fig. 3.21). The snake god Ugajin appears in her headgear, and she is accompanied by fifteen youths who stand next to a horse, an ox, and a cart on a river bank—all motifs usually associated with Benzaiten. The merging of Dakiniten and Benzaiten is also present in another drawing in the same collection (fig. 3.4), where the goddess is represented holding a jewel and a sword in her two hands. She rides a fox that has snakes coiled around its legs, and Ugajin appears on her headgear. One cannot rule out the possibility that all we are actually dealing with here is a representation of Benzaiten riding a fox, surrounded by her usual acolytes. In either case, the identity between the two goddesses is suggested through the symbols they share—the fox, the snake, and the jewel—in a word, through Ugajin.

The existence of joint rituals for Benzaiten and Dakiniten, that is, the parallel development of the two deities (and their tendency to merge into each other or at least exchange attributes and characteristics), is well illustrated in an undated scroll that shows them side by side: Dakiniten, riding a fox, holds a sword and a single jewel; Benzaiten stands, holding a sword and a triple jewel in two of her eight hands. Their two faces and demeanor are identical. A fox is visible in Dakiniten's headgear, while the snake on Benzaiten's headgear appears in the form of Ugajin.[127]

FIGURE 3.21. Dakiniten (or Benzaiten) with fifteen attendants. Edo period. Sheet, ink on paper. University Art Museum, Kyoto City University of Arts. *BZS* 2217.

THE KING OF HEARTS, FOXES, AND JEWELS

The *Inari Daimyōjin saimon* includes the following passage: "Thus, Daten [Dakiniten] is a trace of the bodhisattva Monju. . . . Among the bodhisattvas, she is Jūichimen and Nyoirin; among the wisdom kings, Fudō and Aizen. The heavenly youth [*sic*] Benzaiten, Shōten and Daikokuten, all are none other than this Daten."[128] Even in the *Inari ichiryū daiji,* supposedly centered on Inari Myōjin, it is Dakiniten who appears at center stage. The urge to turn Dakiniten into a supreme deity is also evident in the "Inari saimon" section, where the priest invokes the foxes of all directions as members of King Dakini's retinue.[129] According to an incantation traditionally attributed to Kūkai:

> King Dakini is the mother of all the buddhas of the three periods. She transforms herself into Ranba and the nine other *rākṣasīs.* She manifests herself in space as the seven stars, the nine seizers, the twenty-eight mansions—the so-called heavenly [devas]. On earth, she manifests herself as the twelve [cyclical] deities and the thirty-six animals—that is, the devas who constantly follow [people]. Daijizaiten, Bonten, King Śakra [Indra], the deities of the three luminaries [sun, moon, and stars], the kings of the *yakṣas* and *rakṣasas,* Enmaten and Taizan Fukun, all are the physical bodies that King Dakini manifests through skillful means.[130]

Here Dakiniten is no longer simply one of the devas, but their *fons et origo.* She has become a primordial deity, and she is even redefined, like Amaterasu, as an abstract first principle, the equivalent of the cosmic buddha Dainichi—or rather, of the pole star deity, Myōken Bosatsu. We will come back to this astrological symbolism and to the divinatory practices associated with it.

King of Astral Foxes

In her apotheosis as a divine king, Dakiniten received different titles, most notably Bodhisattva King of Astral Foxes (Shinkoō Bosatsu 辰狐王菩薩) and King Shintamani (Shindamani-ō 辰陀摩尼王). In this manner, Dakiniten transcended not only her demonic nature, but also her gender; or rather, she revealed a certain ambiguity in this regard: with the exception of Jade Woman (Gyokujo 玉女), the titles she received downplay her female gender and emphasize maleness and kingship. Yet in the iconography Dakiniten remains a goddess.

In the *Inari Ichiryū no daiji,* Dakiniten has become a cosmic ruler, standing at the center of the five-phases spatiotemporal system like Pan Gu (J. Banko 盤古), the cosmic man of Chinese mythology. Among her retinue, we find the earth deity, Kenrō Jijin. The five emperors or dragons that symbolize the five phases were also called "earthly foxes," and they were assimilated to the earth deities (Dokōjin 土公神) of Onmyōdō. In other words, Dakiniten has become the "warp and woof of heaven and earth." She rules over heaven as the heavenly fox, and over the earth as the earthly fox, projecting her emanations into the upper and lower reaches of the Japanese cosmos.

In the "Inari Daimyōjin" section of the *Shintōshū,* the Bodhisattva King of Foxes (Shinkoō Bosatsu) is a demiurge who controls the five agents and the cycle of changes.[131] In this new, astrological incarnation, the earthly foxes that are his vassals replace the five emperors or dragon kings of classical Chinese cosmology.[132] Thus, under the title of King Shindamani, Dakiniten progressively detached herself from earthly constraints to become a primordial deity that rules over heaven and earth and controls the five phases of Chinese cosmology.

A traditional formula attributed to Enchin and Annen explains that this ruler of astral foxes is the "global body" of Shingon and Tendai; its power branches into yin and yang and into the Womb realm and the Vajra realm. It becomes the Northern Chronogram (Hokushin) and, dividing into the seven stars, constitutes the root of life of all beings. This deity appears in the world to reveal good and bad omens. In other words, it controls the happiness and longevity of all beings.[133]

King Shintamani

The source of King Shintamani's supernatural powers is said to lie in the strength of human desires and the *cintāmaṇi* jewel's capacity to fulfill them. As the *Keiran shūyōshū* puts it: "[In] all the beings of the world of desire, desire is powerful and flourishing. This is why King Shintamani appears and makes all wishes come true."[134] Yet the animal origins of that deity were never forgotten, as can be inferred from the reasons invoked to worship it. Various canonical sources are marshaled, to emphasize that the god Indra in India, the heavenly emperor in China, and Fujiwara no Kamatari in Japan all took a fox as their master.

In some texts, the title "king of astral foxes" or King Shintamani refers, not to the fox-riding Dakiniten herself, but to her mount. In the *Shintōshū,* for example, we are told: "The rider has the form of a delicate heavenly maiden of golden complexion. Her white mount is the supreme king of astral foxes. Rider and mount symbolize the unity of concentration and wisdom."[135] Fundamentally, then, Dakiniten and the fox are one.

The apocryphal *Sūtra of the Realization of the Great King of Dragon Foxes* (*Shinko daiō jōjukyō* 辰狐大王成就經), a text clearly inflenced by apocryphal scriptures centered on Ugajin, reports that when the householder Sudatta tried to feed a mendicant, all his alms vanished. When he asked the Buddha about this, the Buddha answered that it was a karmic retribution caused by the fact that the mendicant died of starvation in a past life. He then asked if someone in the assembly could give him alms, and a bodhisattva called Great King of the Astral Foxes stood up. The divine general Ugajin emerged from his side. The bodhisattva said that in a distant past he had vowed to manifest himself as Ugajin. He then offered an incantation that could bring good fortune to the needy. He added that he always dwells in the northwestern corner of human houses and brings prosperity to them. The Buddha praised him and called this discourse the *Cintāmaṇi Sūtra.*[136]

DAKINITEN'S RETINUE

The nature and function of a deity are frequently revealed by its attributes, and also by its retinue. In a mandala reportedly used by the Shingon master Ningai, Dakiniten is represented in the central circular court, with four acolytes in the first rectangular court, the eight great youths (*hachi daidōji*) in the second, and the twelve cyclical signs or deities in the third.[137] The presence of the cyclical signs calls to mind astral mandalas and the divination boards of Onmyōdō. Another such mandala, probably dated to the late fourteenth century, shows Dakiniten on her fox flying from the upper left to the lower right of the painting, together with her four acolytes, also on foxes, as well as two *tengu*-like emissaries and eight youths at the bottom of the picture. According to Shirahara Yukiko, the painted landscape in the background represents Mount Inari. She therefore argues that this painting depicts the Inari deity and her attendants and should be called the Fushimi Inari mandala.[138]

Dakiniten's retinue is usually formed of three groups: the first consists of four acolytes, the second of eight youths (*dōji*), the third of two emissaries. The four acolytes—three female, one male—are known as the four princes, and they are also riding foxes. The male figure is sometimes considered apart from the others and seen as a mere emissary (*shisha* 使者). In that case, the three female acolytes are called the three princes. Of the three, the heavenly maiden (Tennyoshi 天女子) holds a bow and arrows, the red maiden (Shakunyoshi 赤女子) holds a "seduction jewel" (*aikei-gyoku* 愛敬玉) and a halberd, and the black maiden (Kokunyoshi 黒女子) a black jewel and a sword."[139] We recall that in the *Hoki naiden* 簠簋内伝 they are said to have flown from India and landed in Japan at Itsukushima, Chikubushima, and Enoshima, three sacred sites of Benzaiten, respectively.[140] The male deity is called Taishaku Shisha 帝釈使者 (Indra's emissary) and he has the paraphernalia, if not the look, of an underworld official: holding a brush and a tablet or register, he writes down the good and evil deeds of people in order to report them to the king of astral foxes. The latter will punish them accordingly, assuming thereby the role of King Yama (Enma-ō).[141] The figure of Taishaku Shisha provides another link between Dakiniten and Onmyōdō: he is identified with

Ten'ichi 天一, an ambulatory deity charged with periodically inspecting the actions of humans.[142] He is also said to be a god of wisdom, a characterization that probably derives from the fact that Dakiniten's *honji* is the bodhisattva Monju. He is in essence a "companion spirit" (*kushōjin* 倶生神).[143] Yet his benign expression contrasts with the threatening aspect of Enmaten's acolytes.

The eight youths are already mentioned in the *Keiran shūyōshū* and the *Shintōshū*.[144] A ritual text, the *Otorari no saimon* 乙足祭文, describes their origins as follows: they are the children of a noble lady of Tang China (var.: of an Indian king) who sent them as emissaries to Japan in the form of divine foxes. After their ship wrecked, they were swallowed by a monstrous catfish (*namazu*) but eventually rescued by a fisherman, Shin no Ototari 秦乙足, the ancestor of the Hata clan.[145] Out of gratitude, they promised to protect his descendants, and this legend explains why Ototari's descendants have served, generation after generation, as priests of Inari Shrine.[146]

The *Tonjō shitsuji hō shidai* 頓成悉地法次第, a Shōmyōji document, names the eight *dōji* (along with their associated directions). In this document, Shutakujin 守宅神 (House-protecting deity) wears a red layman dress; Inari-jin 稲荷神 (Inari deity) carries rice sheaves; Meijishin 米持神 (Rice-holding deity) is depicted as a woman holding a rice bag on her head; Aikei-shin 愛敬神 (Love-subduing deity) joins his hand in respect (*gasshō*); Hajuso-shin 破呪詛神 (Spell-breaking deity) looks like a red *yakṣa;* Datsukonpaku-shin 奪魂魄神 (Spirit that steals the *hun* and *po* souls) looks like Bishamonten and holds a jeweled staff; Kushi-jin 駆使神 (var. Kenshi-jin 驗使神) looks like a youth; and Gonin daijin 護人大神 (Great deity that protects humans) looks like a woman. These names are somewhat different from those given in the *Shintōshū,*[147] and it is not clear if Datsukonpaku-shin is the same as Datsukonpaku-ki 奪魂魄鬼 (Demon that steals the *hun* and *po* souls), a name that of course calls to mind not only Dakiniten herself, but also one of the ten *rākṣasīs* who protect the *Lotus Sūtra.*[148] In the Izuna mandala of Rinnōji, these eight *dōji* surround the central *honzon,* a ten-armed manifestation of Bishamonten, in a sequence identical to that of the Shōmyōji document. One of these "youths" is actually represented as a mature or old man holding rice sheaves, and he may be a duplicate of the traditional Inari deity, whose name also appears as that of a figure on the list, Inari-jin. The name of the first on that list, Shutakujin, is also one of the names that Ena Kōjin 如来荒神, the placenta deity, receives when it continues to protect the child after birth. According to the *Shintōshū,* the seventh of the eight acolytes specializes in the technique of yin and yang to benefit beings.[149]

The two emissaries of Dakiniten (and sometimes of Benzaiten) are two *tengu*-like warriors, named Ton'yugyō 頓遊行 and Shuyuchisō 須臾馳走. The former is said to bring happiness, the latter longevity.[150] They are mentioned in the *Keiran shūyōshū*'s section on Dharma protectors (*gohō* 護法). They are also called *shikijin* or *shikigami* 式神, the Onmyōdō equivalent of *gohō*—all terms designating elemental spirits that assist a deity or a saint. Their name emphasizes their main virtue, namely, the amazing speed with which they roam the world in order to bring benefits to all beings (but also, implicitly, to report on their deeds, like Taishaku Shisha).[151] This aspect links them functionally to the so-called companion spirits (*kushōjin*).[152]

In the Dakiniten mandala associated with Ningai, the emissary on the right has wings and holds a sword, the one on the left has a bird head and holds a jewel staff. A fox head is shown above their heads. In the Dakiniten mandala in the Clarke Collection, Dakiniten is flanked only by these two warriors, one of whom has what looks like a rooster's head and holds a jewel club and a red bag.[153]

The Kasuga Inari mandala 春日稲荷曼荼羅 (private collection) adds Kojima Kōjin 小島荒神 and Aizen Myōō to the group of the Dakiniten mandala. The standard image of Kojima Kōjin is said to derive from a vision of the Kōfukuji priest Shinkō 真興 (934–1004).[154] This mandala suggests ties between Kasuga Shrine and Fushimi Inari. A line drawing from Nōman-in in Kyoto shows, instead of the four fox-riding acolytes, five officials—the five emperors—riding lions, under the image of a bodhisattva-like deity, Nyorai Kōjin 如来荒神, who holds two jewels—one white, one red.[155]

DAKINITEN AND DIVINATION

Dakiniten's acolytes were reputed to ward off calamities and bring good fortune. The three princes were equated with Buddhist rubrics such as the three sections (Buddha, Lotus, Vajra) of the mandala and the Three Treasures (Buddha, Dharma, and Sangha). In rituals, however, where the spatial dimension is important, quaternary symbolism tends to predominate and the "four princes" are distributed in the four directions (southeast, southwest, northwest, and northeast) that correspond in Chinese cosmology to the "four gates" (of earth, of humans, of gods, and of demons). In textual descriptions, the four acolytes are said to appear complete with their own retinue (composed of 13,758 spirits).[156]

The influence of Onmyōdō on the Dakiniten cult is clearly evident in the *Keiran shūyōshū*'s discussion of the Buddhist swastika (interpreted as a variant of the Sanskrit letter *a*, the source of all things). This text provides a diagram of the twelve cyclical signs distributed around a square (itself divided into four sections marked by the characters for *goat, dog, dragon,* and *tiger*). It adds the following commentary: "The hare deity is Indra's emissary (Taishaku Shisha). The horse deity is the red maiden (Shakunyoshi). The rooster deity is the heavenly maiden (Tennyoshi).

The rat deity is the black maiden (Kokunyoshi). The ox, goat, dragon, and dog [deities] correspond to Shinkoō Bosatsu. The five great elements and five phases are all Dharma gates contained in the single body of the practitioner."[157]

An exhibition held in 2007 at Kanazawa bunko on the links between esoteric Buddhism and Onmyōdō allows us to better understand the role which Dakiniten, as the king of astral foxes, played in medieval divination rituals. The Kanazawa bunko corpus presented in the exhibition catalogue *Onmyōdō kakeru mikkyō* 陰陽道X密教, consisting of 26 documents, is important because the paucity of information regarding Onmyōdō divination techniques obliges us, paradoxically, to turn to esoteric Buddhism for complementary information.[158]

A divination method centered on Dakiniten was apparently cultivated at Shōmyōji, and a number of related documents was compiled by Kenna (1261–1338), the second abbot of Shōmyōji, or by his disciples.[159] The distinguishing characteristic of that method, based on the Chinese technique of the *liuren* 六壬, is that it replaces yin-yang Onmyōdō deities with esoteric Buddhist ones (devas like Dakiniten and Shōten, or bodhisattvas like Nyoirin and Kokūzō, or *vidyārājas* like the five wisdom kings).[160]

These rituals used a wooden divination board (*shikiban*) whose structure resembled that of the Chinese compass, while also drawing on esoteric Buddhist symbolism, namely, the figure of Dakiniten and her acolytes. Until recently, Japanese art historians who have studied the Dakiniten mandalas and the Inari mandalas have largely ignored the use of the *shikiban*—with the significant exception of Nishioka Yoshifumi. Except for a *shikiban* from Tamon-in (Shimomatsu City, Yamaguchi prefecture), there are no extent exemplars of the esoteric Buddhist *shikiban,* probably because these rituals did not survive beyond the medieval period.[161] Fortunately, some of the Kanazawa bunko documents contain diagrams that give us a good idea of what these devices looked like.

The use of the *shikiban* in esoteric Buddhism reflected the same mutual influence between esoteric Buddhism and Onmyōdō that led to the creation of astral rituals centered on the seven stars, Myōken, and Rokuji Myōō 六字明王 (a deity representing the fusion of Myōken and the Six Kannon). The *shikiban* was constituted of three parts: a conical top, symbolizing heaven; a cylindrical or conical revolving part, symbolizing the realm of men; and a square foundation, symbolizing the earthly realm. At the top or center, Dakiniten as the king of astral foxes was depicted holding a jewel and a sword, while her four acolytes appeared on the side of the cylindrical section. On the square board were drawn the eight youths, the twenty-eight lunar constellations, and the thirty-six animals—exactly as in star mandalas.[162] Furthermore, below the square board were drawn images of the five emperors and of the earth deity (Kenrō Jijin). Between each part were inserted "wheels," upon which were put talismans (called *toraen*), with diagrams, spells, and representations of bodhisattvas on the upper one, wrathful deities on the lower one. Once animated through the invocation of all the deities represented, the *shikiban* was sealed with five-colored threads.

While the *shikiban* is well described, the divination technique itself is unfortunately not explained, and it may be that in some cases the board itself was taken as the *honzon* of a typical esoteric ritual, without any divination actually taking place. At any rate, it is strange that the texts are so detailed about the ritual sequence (which in principle is secret), while they remain silent on the divination proper that was supposed to accompany it. Judging from the titles of these documents, the goal of that ritual was to obtain "sudden realization" (*tonjō shitsuji* 頓成悉地), that is, the immediate fulfillment of all wishes. On that point, Dakiniten was seen as supremely efficacious (like Shōten, who also appears in Kanazawa bunko documents as *honzon* of a similar ritual of "sudden realization" centered on a *shikiban*). At any rate, this kind of ritual divination device suggests the extent of the Dakiniten cult in the medieval period, and of the interaction it allowed between esoteric Buddhism and Onmyōdō.

While the *shikiban* is sometimes described as consisting of three parts—corresponding to the traditional Chinese rubrics of *heaven, man,* and *earth*—the human realm is in fact subsumed by the earthly realm, leaving us with two parts that correspond to the Womb and Diamond realms. The *shikiban* is thus identified with Mount Sumeru, the *axis mundi* of Buddhist cosmology, and with the wish-fulfilling jewel. It is also perceived as the body of the practitioner—its three parts corresponding, respectively, to the head, the chest, and the lower body.[163] Apparently, bones (together with various things like feathers and so on) were inserted into the *shikiban* to emphasize that corporeal symbolism.

As in a classical mandala, the goal was to bring into one's body (thereby animating and protecting it) all the divine powers of the universe, viz., all the cosmic deities represented on the *shikiban*—following the classical Shingon notion of the interpenetration of self and deity (*nyūga ganyū* 入我我入). By the same token, the practitioner transforms his vulnerable body into a cosmic adamantine body. The texts indeed state that, in the visualization technique that lays the ritual ground, the practitioner's body becomes a wish-fulfilling jewel that is none other than the divination board. To do this, one first visualizes one's body as a universe inhabited by all the gods, then one invokes the *honzon* (Dakiniten) and her four acolytes. The eidetic sequence varies slightly, but it can be described in outline as follows: one visualizes the seed-syllable *ro,* which turns into a *cintāmaṇi* jewel, with which one's body merges; then the jewel transforms into a three-part *shikiban*—a symbolic replica of Mount Sumeru, where the main deity and his retinue dwell; again, one's body merges with the *shikiban.* Finally, the *honzon* and the practitioner merge into each other. One must also "open" the eyes of the *shikiban,* as one would open the eyes of an icon, to animate it. Finally, one seals it with threads. This rite, described as "extremely secret," was performed during the enthronement ceremony, as well as during regular consecration (*kanjō*) rituals.

The *shikiban* is described as a "worldly" mandala, in the sense that it contains all the beings of the world (including the worldly devas), whereas the two great mandalas of Shingon contain all the otherworldly deities. Yet the two are in fact identical—in other words, the heavenly board corresponds to the Vajra realm, while the earthly board corresponds to the Womb realm.

At this point, a disciple may raise an objection: how did Dakiniten, who was initially a marginal deity in the Womb Realm mandala, come to dwell at the top of the heavenly board (i.e., the center of the Vajra realm)? The master replies that because the twin mandalas are centered on the buddha Dainichi, it is normal to place Dainichi's assimilation bodies, including Dakiniten, at their periphery. In the "worldly" mandala of the *shikiban*, however, it is appropriate to place that deva at the top. Furthermore, astral deities like the twenty-eight mansions are placed on the earthly board to express the idea that heaven and earth interpenetrate harmoniously. In the Chinese divination board, the heavenly part is centered on the pole star—suggesting that in the esoteric *shikiban,* Dakiniten corresponds to the pole star and its deity, Myōken Bosatsu. A similar *shikiban*—one of the rare divination boards preserved in Japan—is centered on Nyoirin Kannon (Tohyō Nyoirin 都表如意輪), another deity symbolizing the pole star.[164]

TARRYING WITH THE DEMONIC

Even after becoming a deva, Dakiniten retained the demonic nature of a *ḍākinī* and remained at the center of black-magic rituals focused on the vital essence of humans or "human yellow." The ambiguity of the Indian *ḍākinī,* reinforced by fear of the East Asian fox, a spirit-animal known for its shape-shifting talent and its capacity to possess humans, created a lingering problem for worshipers and ultimately led to an attempt to distinguish between two types of *ḍākinī*—although no explicit distinction seems to have been made between two forms of Dakiniten, as was the case with other devas like Benzaiten and Daikokuten.

It is worth reiterating that the transformation of Dakiniten into a god of good fortune was never entire. Her apotheosis should not be seen as a chapter in her "biography," even when narratives tend to give that impression. Once again, we must resist our inveterate tendency to subsume a complex set of symbols under a single name—Dakiniten—and to entertain the belief that it refers to a real individual. Behind the name that gives the illusion of individuality, we must be attentive to the existence of a vulpine constellation, an extended family of heavenly and earthly foxes. Beside the auspicious image of Dakiniten—who is so close to the Inari deity that she practically fuses with it—another, more nefarious image lingered. Even as Dakiniten became the auspicious Shinkoō Bosatsu (a.k.a. King Shintamani), the fox spirits under her command continued to inflict harm on humans. Ironically enough, it was often Dakiniten herself who was invoked to exorcise possessing spirits. We have here a kind of homeopathic ritual, in which Dakiniten was said to cure an illness induced by her own kin. The *Keiran shūyōshū,* for example, prescribes a series of methods for curing possession by foxes—or what was actually called "possession by Dakiniten." Similarly, the so-called three foxes remained the object of exorcisms such as the Six-letter Riverside Ritual (Rokuji karin-hō 六字河臨法) even when they were collectively seen as a powerful deity named Sankoshin, each having maintained a separate and parallel demonic existence. The priest who performed the Dakiniten ritual was believed to be able to make them his servants, and thus to cure fox sickness.[165]

Heavenly foxes, in particular, were said to cause something called *dada* illness (*dada-byō*).[166] This strangely named disease was also attributed to one of Dakiniten's eight attendants, Datsukonpaku-ki (or Dasshōki 奪精鬼), the "demon that steals the *hun* and *po* souls." Interestingly, worship of this demon was seen as a way for sages and the wellborn to deflect the illness toward commoners.[167] The most interesting part of the exorcism is probably its object of worship, which varied depending on the size of the province: for a large province (of more than one hundred *li*), one had to use the head of an astral fox (*shinko*), whereas in a smaller province, one could use the head of a dog or a *tanuki*.[168]

Two Types of *Ḍākinī*

During the Edo period, Unshō 運敞 (1614–1693), author of the *Jakushōdō kokkyōshū* 寂照堂谷響集, was at pains to distinguish between two types of *ḍākinī,* the "real" ones (*jissha*) who devour the human yellow but also provide happiness to those who worship them; and the *ḍākinīs* of the esoteric mandala, who are avatars of the buddha Mahāvairocana. The latter only devour the defilements found in humans' hearts, in order to lead them to nirvāṇa.[169] Similarly, we read in the *Kiyū shōran* 嬉遊笑覧 by Kitamura Tokinobu 喜多村節信: "Regarding the so-called devouring of the heart, there are two kinds of *ḍākinīs:* the real type (*jitsurui* 実類) and the mandala type. The former are those that devour the heart of humans. Although people who worship them obtain happiness, that ritual is heterodox. The mandala type refers to the 'traces-responses' of the Tathāgata, which devour all the dust in our hearts and lead us to the great nirvāṇa."[170]

The protector of Jōgyōdō 常行堂 on Mount Hiei, the god Matarajin 摩多羅神, was also a kind of flesh-eating demon who eats the liver of humans. But a secret oral transmission argues that the *ḍākinīs* and

Matarajin, by eating the liver of beings afflicted by heavy, undigested karma, only help them to reach the Pure Land. This positive reinterpretation of Dakiniten's soul stealing is well illustrated by the *Rinnō kanjō kuketsu* 輪王灌頂口決:

> [When] the wild fox sucks out the vital spirit of beings, it sucks on their eight-petaled heart lotus. 'Sucking' means that it sucks dry the obstacles created by ignorance of life and death, and makes them return to their source, the heart lotus of the Dharma nature [Skt. *dharmatā*]. This is why the one called Dasshōki (essence stealer) among the ten *rākṣasīs* is none other than Shinkoō Bosatsu.[171]

In the *Shin[koō] bosatsu kuden jō kuketsu* 辰菩薩口伝上口決, we also read: "As the Northern Chronogram, [Dakiniten] divides into the seven stars and gives the root of life to all beings. As the dragon fox, she manifests as the northern and southern [Dippers] and tells the good and bad luck of the [people of the] world. Thus, because longevity and happiness depend on this worthy, she must be accorded extreme respect." The text then explains that the name "Woman who steals the essence of all beings" is another name for Shinkoō Bosatsu (Dakiniten):

> When she steals the *hun* and *po* [souls] of beings, or when she goes to the charnel ground to devour the flesh and bones of the dead, she dispenses longevity and fortune. And at the time of death, because she eats [the corpse], it returns to its principle. It is said in a very secret tradition: 'It is only that, by licking the *hun* and *po* souls [that cause] the ignorance of beings, she manifests the heart lotus of the Dharma nature, and by eating the flesh and bones of beginningless *saṃsāra,* she makes us realize the profound principle of nirvāṇa.'[172]

The *Keiran shūyōshū* concludes: "These blood-drinking and horned types are [manifestations of] the primordial, eternal Dainichi. Thus, [to worship them] is not like worshiping worldly devas. That is why in Tendai one interprets the devas as expressing the ultimate meaning. (This is the most secret of all teachings.)"[173]

FROM DAKINITEN TO IZUNA GONGEN

As noted above, the Izuna mandala of Rinnōji is actually a Dakiniten mandala in which Dakiniten is assimilated to Monju, Bishamonten, and Jūichimen Kannon. As Dakiniten's popularity extended beyond imperial rituals and the search for power, she increasingly became a deity of good fortune. Along with this image, new legends developed.[174] In the

FIGURE 3.22. Akiba Gongen. Edo period. Sheet, ink on paper. University Art Museum, Kyoto City University of Arts. *BZS* 4085.

FIGURE 3.23. Akiba Gongen. Edo period. Sheet, ink on paper. University Art Museum, Kyoto City University of Arts. *BZS* 4086.

Shintōshū, for example, Dakiniten is a savior deity better adapted to the declining world of the Final Age (*mappō*), and she has now become the "father and mother" of deluded people.[175]

Dakiniten's two emissaries, represented as *tengu*-like warriors (see Figs. 3.22 and 3.23), constitute the first iconographic link between the fox-riding Dakiniten and the *tengu.* Unlike other acolytes of Dakiniten, they are not riding foxes. The link between the fox and the *tengu* (more precisely the beaked or crow *tengu, karasu tengu* 烏天狗) finds its fullest expression in the cult of Izuna Gongen. In the *Izuna Daimyōjin yurai no engi* 飯綱大明神由来之縁起, this deity is described as a warrior god standing on a white fox.[176] Starting from Mount Izuna in Shinshū (present-day Nagano prefecture), the Izuna cult spread throughout Japan toward the end of the medieval period, probably through the mediation of the mountain ascetics (*shugenja* 修験者) on neighboring Mount Togakushi 戸隠, and quickly took on the characteristics of a martial tradition.[177] Apart from Mount Izuna in Nagano, Izuna Gongen is worshiped on Mount Izuna in Sendai and on Mount Takao 高尾山 in Hachiōji City, on the western outskirts of Tokyo.

Izuna Gongen is represented as a winged *tengu* holding a sword in his right hand and a noose in his left; he is standing on a white fox and surrounded by an aura of flames.[178] When snakes coil around his young body, he is said to have manifested himself in the form of the snake god Ugajin in order to destroy karmic obstacles and dispense bliss. In sum, he looks like a collage of attributes of other deities: not only is he standing on Dakiniten's fox, his sword and noose, as well as his standing posture, immediately evoke the image of Fudō. Sometimes, in fact, he was even depicted *as* Dakiniten, with whom he was said to be identical. Thus, through the figure of Izuna, Dakiniten's function as the king of astral foxes was subsumed in the image of the *tengu*, due in part to the homophony between *tenko* 'heavenly fox' and *tengu.*

Mount Izuna was famous for its rites, a combination of martial techniques, divination techniques, and medical and magical recipes. These rites came to be linked with Dakiniten rituals and the cult of Shōgun Jizō 将軍地蔵 (Atago Gongen 愛宕権現).[179] Soon the Izuna cult developed into a martial cult, and the Izuna deity became a god of battles. According to legend, Izuna Gongen (a.k.a. Chira Tenko 智羅天狐 or Chira the heavenly fox) was originally one of the eighteen children of an Indian king. Among them, eight became monks who settled on Mount Tiantai to spread the Dharma in China, while the ten others flew to Japan on the backs of white foxes. They landed at Akitsushima during the reign of Kinmei Tennō 欽明天皇 (r. 539–571) and settled on ten mountains (Atago, Hira 比良山, Togakushi, Fuji, Hakusan, Ontake 御岳, Haguro, Ōyama 大山, Nikkō 日光山, and Hakone), where they came to be worshiped as *tengu.* Chira Tenko first appeared as Iizuna Daimyōjin 飯綱大明神 on Mount Myōkō 妙高 (or Togakushi) in Shinano province (Nagano prefecture). As a directional deity, he was said to come from a different direction at the beginning of each season to protect his followers from demons. Depending on circumstances, he could also manifest himself as a buddha, a bodhisattva, or a wisdom king; or again, as the gods Marishiten, Kōjin, Ugajin, and *dōsojin*.[180]

The name Izuna had already appeared in the *Asabashō* (1279) in connection with the origin story of Togakushi-dera 戸隠寺, and, as we have seen, it reappeared in the name of the Izuna mandala of Rinnōji (Nikkō). The *honji* of Izuna Gongen is said to be Jizō, which allowed (or resulted from) an amalgamation with the cult of Shōgun Jizō on Mount Atago.[181] Although the cult of Izuna spread among mountain ascetics, Izuna shugendō developed in relative independence from—and even rivalry with—Togakushi shugendō. Very early on, it demonstrated a characteristic emphasis on martial and magical techniques. The tradition traced its lineage to two warriors, Itō Tadatsuna 伊藤忠縄 and his son Moritsuna 守綱, who, because of their thousand-day austerities on Mount Izuna, came to be known as Sennichi Dayū 千日大夫 and were ultimately identified with *tengu.* It was this martial aspect that earned for Izuna Gongen the veneration of warriors like Takeda Shingen 武田信玄 (1521–1573) and Uesugi Kenshin 上杉謙信 (1530–1578).

Izuna Gongen assumed different (and mostly demonic) identities and functions depending on the season. In this respect, he is reminiscent of the earth deities. He was actually identified with Kōjin, appearing as the fundamental Tathāgata to reward good people and as a demon to punish evil ones. Standing on a white fox, he guides all the beings of the demonic world.[182] Like Fudō, he holds in his right hand a sword to tame the demons of obstacles, and in his left hand a noose to tame the demons of famine.

It is probably owing to the influence of the Dakiniten cult that the figure of the fox moved to the forefront of the Izuna cult. Izuna Gongen's mount, identified as Dakiniten's white fox, was related to a specific feature of the Izuna rites. Actually, the animal used in those rites, called *kuda-gitsune* 管狐 'pipe fox,' was a fox only in name: it was a kind of weasel, which the practitioner kept inside a bamboo pipe.

Because the *shugen* group on Mount Izuna was not able to organize itself as well as the rival group on neighboring Mount Togakushi, the Izuna tradition remained somewhat marginal and its magical component, perhaps inherited from the "heterodox" Dakiniten rites, became predominant, to the point that *izuna* became a generic term for magic.[183] Another reason for that drift toward heterodoxy may have been the close relationship between Izuna and the martial tradition, particularly after the end of the medieval period when the Tokugawa government put an end to feudal warfare. The various elements that had fused in the Izuna cult also continued to develop independently. The figure of the *tengu* as the "master of fire," for instance, survived in Akiba Gongen 秋葉権現, an iconographic double of Izuna Gongen, and in the Izuna cult of Mount Takao (Figs. 3.22 and 3.23).

Apart from the three main components (Dakiniten, Fudō, and *tengu*) informing the image of Izuna Gongen, one can discern the influences of figures such as Garuḍa (a bird deity that is, with the kite, one of the prototypes of the bird *tengu*), Kangiten (Shōten), and Ugajin. On Mount Takao, there is a Shōten Hall next to the main hall dedicated to Izuna Gongen. The influence of the Ugajin cult has been cited to explain the motif of the snakes coiled around the arms and legs of Izuna. This motif, however, may also derive from esoteric strongmen figures like Gundari Myōō, as well as illustrate the awe-inspiring power of Izuna Gongen.

In the Edo period, Dakiniten and Izuna Gongen were sometimes lumped together, as shown in a discussion between Hirata Atsutane (1776–1843) 平田篤胤 and his young informant Torakichi 寅吉, who claimed to have been abducted and initiated by a *tengu*. Torakichi declares that his master has a strong dislike for the worship of Dakiniten, Izuna, and Shōten, "because they are served and worshiped by *tengu,* foxes, demons, and things like that."[184]

CODETTA

Although the name (if not the image) of Dakiniten was erased from Mount Inari, probably during the Meiji Restoration, the popularity of the Inari cult cannot be explained without acknowledging the catalyzing power of Dakiniten.[185] Indeed, the name Inari is frequently used to designate Dakiniten. Conversely, while the Dakiniten cult initially developed in Shingon (and to a lesser degree in Tendai), it eventually spread to other schools (Zen, Nichiren, Jōdo) as well. One of Inari's two main cultic centers, Toyokawa Inari 豊川稲荷, is actually a Sōtō Zen temple, while the other, Saijō Inari, is a Nichiren temple.[186]

Ironically, the process that transformed Dakiniten into a god of fortune stemmed from a symbolic—and initially much less auspicious—association between the vital essence of beings, the relics of the Buddha, and the *cintāmaṇi* jewel. Other symbolic elements such as fire, the color red, blood, the sun and the moon, the red and white drops of Buddhist embryology (signifying blood and semen), and the human yellow were also woven into this rhizome-like symbolic network, one we have already encountered in the discussion of Aizen Myōō and Nyoirin Kannon in *The Fluid Pantheon*.

In the first part of this chapter, we followed the rise to prominence of an ambiguous and protean deity who was initially a demoness haunting cemeteries, then a sky spirit of sorts in Indo-Tibetan Tantrism, an avatar of the bodhisattva Mañjuśrī (J. Monju) and a flying fox spirit in East Asian esotericism, and, in Japanese religion specifically, the true form of Amaterasu in medieval Shintō, and ultimately a universal, absolute deity, named the king of astral foxes and King Shintamani, who governed the five cosmic phases. Yet the question of the linkage between these episodes, or whether indeed they are episodes of a single narrative at all rather than heterogeneous stories bearing a family resemblance, remains open.

Despite Kōshū's claim that the Dakiniten ritual is only for stupid commoners, this ritual (or a version of it) played a central role in imperial ideology and liturgy. The attempt to distinguish between two types of *ḍākinī* and two types of ritual—orthodox and heterodox—cannot mask the deep continuity, or even identity, between the two. Indeed, through the Dakiniten ritual, it is the ancient fox cults—with their possession rituals, supplemented by new rituals centered on the *cintāmaṇi*—that perpetuated themselves. These rituals were two-edged affairs, drawing on the hidden power of animality and revealing the latent demonic nature of the enthronement ritual.[187] It isn't simply that the fox, a parasitic animal, came to feed on imperial ritual. Through the performance of her secret rites, Dakiniten gradually left the wilderness, the usual haunt of foxes and other creatures of the night, to become the ruler of this world, Shinkoō Bosatsu. A similar apotheosis occurred with deities like Fudō, Kangiten, Benzaiten, and Kōjin, so it can hardly be surprising that they came to be considered as the various names and aspects of a single primordial deity. While contiguous with Dakiniten, Shinkoō Bosatsu has already morphed into another hybrid deity, known as the Three Devas (or Three Deva deity). With the titles of King Shintamani and Shinkoō Bosatsu, the image of Dakiniten, having apparently reached its apogee, changes drastically, and her cult ramifies into an increasingly complex, multiform network. But perhaps that change is merely an optical illusion created by a selective use of sources, giving the impression of a linear evolution from the Indian *ḍākinī* to the Japanese Dakiniten. Probably the situation was always entangled, and the fact that our focus on the Muromachi period seems to yield a more intricate picture may not be so different from what went on before. Yet we reach here a kind of threshold in complexity where Dakiniten seems to merge with Shōten and Benzaiten, or with Inari Myōjin, Ugajin, and Izuna Gongen—where, in a word, she becomes truly herself by becoming increasingly other.

4

FROM GODDESS TO DRAGON

Benzaiten

The origins of the Japanese goddess Benzaiten are usually traced back to the Indian river goddess Sarasvatī, who was also worshiped as a goddess of eloquence and music. Like her Indian prototype, Benzaiten is often represented as a beautiful maiden playing the lute (*biwa* 琵琶 in Japan, *vīnā* in India), and her shrines are usually located on small islands on ponds or rivers, or by the waterside. These similarities give the impression of a straightforward transmission from India to China and Japan. However, things are rarely simple in the mythological realm, as everywhere, and the smiling face of the goddess might only be a mask. Medieval Japanese Buddhists were well aware of that possibility, having been counseled repeatedly that "a woman . . . outwardly may look like a bodhisattva, but in her heart she is like a *yakṣa*."[1] In certain cases, however, their wariness might have been as much a realization of the profound ambiguity of divine power as an expression of misogyny. For these Buddhists, the image of Benzaiten distilled—and symbolized—an even greater ambiguity: she was not only a woman, but a dragon and snake as well.

The standard description of Benzaiten, as found in most Buddhist ritual or iconographic texts, includes her various names, her scriptural sources, her place in esoteric mandalas, her mudrās and mantras, her conventional attributes and symbolic form(s), her acolytes or attendants (*kenzoku* 眷属), her ritual functions, and, last but not least, her main cultic centers and the local traditions related to them. With Benzaiten, Japanese art historians usually identify two types of images: the two-armed Benzaiten and the eight-armed.[2] That distinction, however, lumps together several different iconographic types: consider a two-armed Benzaiten playing the *biwa* vs. a two-armed Benzaiten holding a sword and a wish-fulfilling jewel;[3] or the eight-armed Benzaiten of the *Golden Light Sūtra* vs. the so-called Uga Benzaiten. In medieval Japan, it was only the last Benzaiten, as described in apocryphal sūtras, that can properly be described as the medieval Benzaiten.

The canonical description of Benzaiten aimed at establishing a few stable features. Most secondary sources, by repeating them uncritically, end up glossing over the complexity of the image. To get a better sense of that complexity, we need to destabilize the image and question the canonical sources. The casual assertions of the textbooks actually conceal many misgivings, doubts that are occasionally mentioned in passing as "variants." When they are taken into consideration, an image of Benzaiten emerges that is quite different from the canonical one. Only then does it become clear that this deity, who has been claimed by Buddhist and Shintō (not to mention Onmyōdō) ideologues alike, always transcended sectarian affiliations.

THE VEDIC GODDESS

The Indian goddess was said to be the personification of the river Sarasvatī. While she may have been an agrarian deity dispensing fertility, her name also came to designate the powers of wisdom, eloquence, and music. From the outset, as it were, we are confronted with multiple origins, and with an essential ambiguity.

In her study on the topic, Catherine Ludvik describes Sarasvatī's evolution from a river goddess to the goddess of sound and music, identifying four aspects of the pre-Buddhist Sarasvatī: (1) her original, physical presence as the river; (2) and (3) her functions as goddess of speech and of music; and (4) her relationships as daughter-consort of Brahmā, reflecting a wider mythological context. The functional aspects are familiar from the iconography, as in the four-armed Sarasvatī who holds both a manuscript and a vīnā.[4] Ludvik summarizes the development of the image of Sarasvatī as follows: "[In the *Vedas*, the] mighty river goddess, through the association, on the one hand, with the recitation of hymns accompanying rituals performed on her banks, and, on the other hand, with inspired thoughts inseparably tied to the composition of these hymns, was identified with speech. Through speech, embodying knowledge, most particularly of the *Veda,* Sarasvatī became goddess of knowledge in her own right. . . . She also became goddess of music . . . and was connected with the vīnā."[5]

In the commentaries on the *Vedas* known as the *Brāhmaṇas,* Sarasvatī is identified with the goddess Vāc (Speech). In Vedic India, Vāc was both the daughter of the primordial god, Prajāpati, and his consort, who united with him in an incestuous union to create all beings. The relations between Brahmā and Sarasvatī in the Hindu *Purāṇas* derive from that relationship, since Prajāpati has become Brahmā.[6] In Ludvik's words: "Prajāpati-turned-Brahmā falls in love with his daughter Sarasvatī and takes her for his consort."[7] In the *Ṛg Veda,* Vāc shows strong warrior characteristics, declaring: "I stretch the bow for Rudra so that his arrow will strike down the hater of prayer. I incite the contest among the people. I have pervaded sky and earth."[8] Ludvik also points out that in the *Vedas* Sarasvatī was called a slayer of strangers and was associated with the storm gods (Maruts), "with whom she shares might and a certain wild, fighting spirit."[9] In the *Yajur Veda,* she takes on a fierce, combative character and is described as the Vṛtra-slayer.[10]

The powers of speech and war point to the first two functions in Georges Dumézil's tripartite analysis of Indo-European ideology. The third function, abundance, is also a power that was attributed to the Vedic Sarasvatī.[11] As a "variable goddess," Sarasvatī subsumes all three functions and at the same time transcends or eludes them. She is associated with the horse-headed Aśvins (also called the Nāsatya twins), with whom she collaborates to bolster Indra's strength by telling him how to kill the demon Namuci.[12] (I note in passing that the third function of abundance and fecundity is usually represented by pairs of deities, often twins like the Vedic Aśvins or the Greek Dioscuri.) Sarasvatī and the Aśvins are also among the gods mentioned in the *Ṛg Veda* in connection with incantations for safe pregnancy and delivery. In other Vedic texts, Sarasvatī "is specifically invoked to grant progeny and to place the embryo in a woman's womb."[13] As consort of the Aśvins, moreover, she bears the newly formed embryo of Indra within her own womb, and becomes both his surrogate mother and his consort.[14] However, "like her wild, raging waters, this mother takes on a fierce, wrathful appearance," a reminder of her role as a deity of the second function.[15]

THE BUDDHIST GODDESS

The locus classicus for the Buddhist Sarasvatī is the *Golden Light Sūtra* (Skt. *Suvarṇaprabhāsa-sūtra, T.* 663, 664, and 665), a text that played an important role in Japan during the Nara and Heian periods.[16] This sūtra actually devotes an entire chapter to Sarasvatī. Of the three extant Chinese versions, it is the translation of the *Suvarṇaprabhāsottamarāja-sūtra* (*T.* 665) by Yijing 義浄 (635–713) that most strongly emphasizes her warrior characteristics. In this text, the goddess appears before the Buddha's assembly and, addressing the Buddha according to a well-established pattern, vows to protect all those who put their faith in the sūtra, recite it, or copy it. In particular, if a Dharma master recites it, she vows to increase his intelligence and his eloquence; she will help him understand and remember all the incantations (*dhāraṇīs*), and she will ensure his longevity and ultimately his awakening.[17] Then she teaches the assembly how, by bathing in scented water and reciting incantations, one can heal all illnesses, defeat one's enemies, escape all demons, curses, ill luck, and baleful astral influences, prolong one's life, and become rich. Finally, she promises to help beings cross the ocean of *saṃsāra* and reach supreme

FIGURE 4.1. (*Opposite*) Eight-armed Benzaiten (with Yama, Indra, Vasu, Nanda, and animals). Edo period. Sheet, ink on paper. University Art Museum, Kyoto City University of Arts. *BZS* 2219.

awakening. Thereupon, the brahmin Kauṇḍinya praises her and compares her to Nārayaṇī (that is, Śrī Lakṣmī), Viṣṇu's consort.[18] Significantly, he points out that she can manifest herself not only as a benevolent deity, but also as Yamī, the sister of Yama, a terrifying deity who haunts the wilderness. He describes her eight-armed form, with all its attributes—bow, arrow, sword, spear, axe, *vajra,* iron wheel, and noose.

Yijing's translation goes on to emphasize that wild animals often surround Sarasvatī's appearance. Compared to a lioness, this Sarasvatī is strikingly different from the elegant vīnā player of the classical Hindu tradition, and takes up a position next to the goddess of fortune Śrī (Mahaśrī, Lakṣmī, J. Kichijōten 吉祥天) and the earth goddess Dṛdha (a.k.a. Pṛthivī, J. Jiten 地天). Śrī is often described as a daughter of Hārītī (J. Kariteimo 訶梨帝母 or Kishimojin 鬼子母神) and a wife of Vaiśravaṇa (J. Bishamonten).[19] In this text, Śrī, Sarasvatī, and Vaiśravaṇa are described as different facets of the same divine power, which manifests itself as Śrī for people of higher capacities, as Sarasvatī for those of medium capacities, and as Vaiśravaṇa for those of lower capacities. It stops short of explicitly associating Sarasvatī with the wish-fulfilling jewel, however, as she will come to be seen in Japan.

In a Japanese representation based on the *Golden Light Sūtra*, the goddess appears near a river, against a background of mountain and forest, and is surrounded by Basu sennin (Vasu), Enmaten (Yama), the water god Nanda (Nanda suishin), and Taishakuten 帝釈天 (Indra), as well as various animals including the tiger, lion, buffalo, fox, rooster, and goat (Fig. 4.1).

Sarasvatī also appears in the *Mahāvairocana-sūtra* (and its commentary by Yixing 一行).[20] In the Womb Realm mandala based on that scripture, Sarasvatī's position is among the devas of the western court external to the Vajra section, between Nārayaṇī and Kumāra. This section also contains Indic deities such as Brahmā, Viṣṇu, Skanda, Yama, and their retinue, as well as other lesser deities. Keeping such company may seem strange for a goddess of music and a provider of wealth. One should bear in mind, however, that in the *Golden Light Sūtra,* too, Sarasvatī is associated with a number of dark female deities who surround Yama—among them the Seven Mothers, Cāmuṇḍā, and the *ḍākinīs.*[21]

GENEALOGY AND STRUCTURE

In Japan, as Ingrid Fritsch has shown, the image of Benzaiten (Sarasvatī) as a goddess of music and of the arts in general was favored not only by court musicians but also by the blind musicians called *biwa hōshi* who sang the legend of the Heike. Eventually her popularity spread, and she became a protecting deity for other groups of the blind as well, including minstrel monks (*mōsō* 盲僧) and the female mediums and massage specialists of northern Japan.

最勝王經辨才天
閻魔天
帝釋天
婆藪仙人
難陀水神
無言藏

FIGURE 4.2. Benzaiten. Kamakura period, 13th century. Ink and color on paper. *Shoson zuzōshū*. Kanazawa bunko.

However, the logic of Sarasvatī's development into Benzaiten may not have been as linear as it appears. In particular, the image of Sarasvatī as a warring deity is reminiscent of that of the Indian goddess Durgā. According to Ludvik, this aspect might have been a response to a new Buddhist concern for state protection, the atmosphere in which the *Golden Light Sūtra* was promoted.[22] Yet the emergence of a martial Sarasvatī may also have obeyed a more fundamental structural logic, inasmuch as Vāc, the Vedic goddess of speech, had already displayed martial characteristics. As Georges Dumézil points out, Sarasvatī (like Vāc and Durgā) belongs to the group of trifunctional deities whose activities include war. Already in the *Vedas,* it is said that she destroys the enemies of the gods, the asuras. Admittedly, later sources seem to omit or downplay that aspect of her powers, but this does not mean that its importance in religious practice was lost. Dumézil argues that Sarasvatī is a multifunctional deity not by accident, as the result of a more or less random evolution, but structurally, as a complete expression of the trifunctional ideology of the Indo-Europeans. Judging from the extant documentation, these functions resurfaced at various times in the "career" of the deity, inflecting it like the meanders of the river Sarasvatī and contributing to the definition of its course.

FIGURE 4.3. Benzaiten. *Jūnihachibu narabini jūnishinshō zu, TZ* 7: 494, fig. 12.

The Japanese goddess Benzaiten, in contrast, moves freely between functions (and manifestations), transforming from a woman into a dragon, a snake, or even a fox. The structural approach, while taking diachronic developments into account, emphasizes a contrasting synchronic approach, in which Benzaiten is grasped in her relationships with her "paradigmatic others." Although Dumézil considered that the three functions he identified were specific to Indo-European ideology, one of his students, Yoshida Atsuhiko, has argued that they were also operative in Japanese mythology.[23] As the protector of warriors and musicians, Benzaiten spanned the first and second functions of sovereignty and war. In the Muromachi period, she increasingly became a goddess of wealth and fertility, the third function.

As Ingrid Fritsch remarks, Benzaiten resists categories, and to study her one must place at the center the communities that worshiped her. Fritsch's perspective encourages a sociological approach to understanding the changes in the deity's image. Ludvik focuses instead on the figure of the eight-armed Benzaiten, emphasizing the ways in which that warrior deity departs from the traditional image of Sarasvatī as a goddess of eloquence and music. The insights provided by Ludvik and Fritsch are complementary but still leave aside aspects of Benzaiten that may be equally important, aspects with specifically Japanese characteristics that come to the forefront in the cult of Uga Benzaiten.

As noted above, the goddess Sarasvatī was from the outset a multifunctional deity: one could therefore posit, at the origins, a more abstract

Sarasvatī, the product of Vedic theological speculation, for whom a merging with Vāc was not a simply random or ancillary development. At the other end of Asia, the course of her development was not random either: metaphorically speaking, the river Sarasvatī flowed into the riverbed prepared for her by the Japanese religious landscape.

Despite the common assertion that Benzaiten *is* Sarasvatī, many things changed in the passage from India to Japan. Admittedly, certain motifs can be surprisingly resilient from one culture to another. Yet the most obvious features are not always the most significant for understanding the hidden dynamics of such a richly layered figure. I will therefore start from the relatively simple, static, and visible opposition between the woman and the *nāga* in order to show how the same symbolism, reinscribed into various contexts, became enriched with new values, eventually forming, with the reemergence of motifs that had been muted, a kind of a symbolic polyphony.

The Warrior Deity

Like her mythological cousin, the Alpheus river, Sarasvatī disappeared into the ocean of Indian myth to resurface in Japanese mythology. But in the meantime a momentous change had taken place. The deity that emerged from Lake Biwa bore little resemblance to her Hindu prototype. She was now an eight-armed goddess, whose image and features were strongly influenced by Yijing's translation of the *Golden Light Sūtra.* The apparition of the eight-armed Sarasvatī in that sūtra had already signaled the emergence (or perhaps merely the resurgence) of the warrior function. This martial figure appealed to the warriors of medieval Japan, who took her as one of their protecting deities. The distance between that deity and the "classical" two-armed Benzaiten did not go unnoticed: indeed, it led to a bifurcation into two distinct identities, Myōonten 妙音天 and Benzaiten.

While the features of the eight-armed Benzaiten were clearly indebted to the *Golden Light Sūtra,* the impact of this text alone is insufficient to explain the development of her cult. Certain essential aspects of Sarasvatī's cult, emphasized in that scripture, seem to have been almost forgotten (for example, the ritual of the perfumed bath), whereas other features of the Indian cult (like the choice of islands in rivers and ponds for her shrines, or the immersion of her icons during festivals) seem to have reached Japan by other—textual or iconographic—means.

As Ludvik points out, "a study of India . . . goes a long way in revealing what is to be found in China and Japan, while a study of China and Japan can show something easily missed in India."[24] For instance, "it is from China that we learn of the impact of the Durgā cult on the Buddhist Sarasvatī in India."[25] Ludvik argues that the Japanese figure of Uga Benzaiten may reveal another aspect of Sarasvatī that the Indian materials no longer allow us to perceive.[26] This is an important point, to which I will return.

While Sarasvatī may be, as Ludvik claims, "Durgā under the guise of Sarasvatī," perhaps she is equally the earth deity in the guise of Sarasvatī, or Vāc in the guise of Sarasvatī. Or maybe none of the above. In spite of all the analogical links, she is not just a mask put on by other deities; she was perceived as a living power, different from (albeit related to) all the other deities with whom she may have a family resemblance. The strands revealed by historical and sociological research in the magnetic field surrounding Sarasvatī/Benzaiten emphasize the development of certain important features. Yet they do not clarify the relations between Benzaiten and snakes or dragons, or why Uga Benzaiten became so prominent in medieval Japan.

The Music/War Polarity

The usual description of Benzaiten as a goddess of eloquence and music overlooks other features—in particular, her warrior function. Actually, her domain encompasses what the Chinese called the spheres of the literary (*wen* 文) and the military (*wu* 武). The image of Benzaiten developed around a number of polarities—between the musical goddess and the warrior goddess, for instance, and between the dragon deity and the young maiden.

In medieval Japan, it was not always clear whether the names Myōonten and Benzaiten represented a single figure or two distinct ones. Even when Myōonten and Benzaiten coexisted as distinct entities, they constantly exchanged certain of their attributes and functions. According to the *Keiran shūyōshū,* "because there is no duality between Knowledge and Principle, [Myōon Benzaiten] can also assume the body of Ugajin. . . . Her 'trace' is a white snake, who dispels the poisons of the three sufferings."[27]

Benzaiten's two functions—war and music—come together in the legend of the Heike warrior Tsunemasa, as related in the *Heike monogatari.* Having come to the shore of Lake Biwa, Tsunemasa sees Chikubushima island in the offing and decides to visit it. Upon landing, he prostrates himself before the shrine of Benzaiten and declares: "Daibenkudokuten 大弁功徳天 is none other than Śākyamuni Buddha; she is a bodhisattva who manifests the absolute nature of the Buddha mind. Two are the names Benzai and Myōon, one is the true form of this divinity, who brings salvation to sentient beings. It is said that those who worship here a single time will have every wish granted: thus I face the future with hope." When he completes his recitation of scriptures, the resident monks bring him one of the shrine's lutes and convince him to play.[28] The suave melody moves the goddess to appear in the form of a white dragon (var. a white snake or fox). Tsunemasa interprets this manifestation as a clear sign that the rebel forces (the Minamoto) will soon be defeated.[29] This passage weaves together motifs of the numinous lute, the island of

嘉永五壬子五月十三日清書之　大成藏
吉祥天
辯財天女
寶藏天女

the immortals, and the messenger animal(s) or animal manifestation of Benzaiten. The lute motif was of course important for the *biwa hōshi,* the main propagators of the *Heike monogatari.* The belief that Benzaiten was the protector of the Taira is a leitmotiv of that work.

FIGURE 4.4. (*Opposite*) Benzaiten (bottom left) as acolyte of Kichijōten (with Hōzō tennyo, bottom right). Edo period. Sheet, ink on paper. University Art Museum, Kyoto City University of Arts. *BZS* 2206.

Myōonten

The figure of Myōonten initially developed toward the end of the Heian period as an object of worship among powerful aristocrats like Fujiwara no Moronaga 藤原師長 (1137–1192).[30] He was a renowned musician, known as Myōon-in 妙音院 because he had transformed a part of his residence (near present-day Shijō Kawaramachi in Kyoto) into a temple of the same name, dedicated to Myōon. He had a wooden statue of Myōon made and enshrined it there. That statue served as the model for a number of later representations, including the Myōonten of Ninnaji.[31]

The name Myōon is traced to the bodhisattva Gadgadasvara (J. Myōon Bosatsu 妙音菩薩), who appears in the *Lotus Sūtra.*[32] This bodhisattva, originally unrelated to Sarasvatī, is said to have obtained his extraordinary powers as a reward for playing music on countless occasions for the buddha Meghadundubhisvara-rāja (J. Unraionnō butsu 雲雷音王佛). (See, e.g., Figs. 4.5–4.8, where Myōon is depicted playing a stringed instrument.) One such power is his gift of metamorphosis: to preach the Dharma, he can assume all kinds of forms, including those of the gods Brahmā, Indra, Iśvara, Maheśvara, and Vaiśravaṇa. His metamorphic capacity, as well as his awakening through music, facilitated his identification with Sarasvatī. Not surprisingly, he became the protector of professional groups such as court musicians and blind singers.

The spread of Myōonten's following in medieval Japan was due in part to a cultural (and technical) factor, namely, the growing popularity of the lute (*biwa*) among musicians.[33] The expanded influence of the *biwa hōshi* was probably due to the decline of court music, brought about by the destruction of the capital during the Ōnin war (1467–1477). The image of Myōonten spread by these wandering musicians was not merely that of a goddess of music and a protector of the arts, but also that of a goddess of fortune. The *biwa* itself was seen as a good-luck instrument, associated with prayers for prosperity. Thus, as Fritsch points out, if Myōon Benzaiten became the protecting deity of the *biwa hōshi,* she served as both a goddess of fortune (through the influence of performing arts, *geinō* 芸能) and a goddess of music (through the influence of *gigaku* 伎楽).[34]

Next to the *biwa hōshi,* we must emphasize the role of another group of minstrels known as the "blind monks of the earth deity" (*jishin mōsō* 地神盲僧), who were influenced by Korean musical traditions.[35] This group was particularly widespread in western Japan (Kyūshū and Chūgoku), but also present in Yamato.[36] In contrast to the *biwa hōshi,* who specialized in the recitation of epics (principally the *Heike monogatari,*

FIGURE 4.5. Myōon Benzaiten. Kamakura period. Hanging scroll, color on silk. Nezu Museum, Tokyo.

FIGURE 4.6. Myōon Benzaiten. Kamakura period, 13th century. Ink and color on paper. *Shoson zuzōshū*. Kanazawa bunko.

but also the *Soga monogatari* 曽我物語 and the like), the *jishin mōsō* were more religiously oriented. The distinction should not be pressed too far, however: the recitation of the *Heike monogatari* was sometimes performed to placate the spirits of the defeated Heike warriors, whereas the *jishin mōsō* also performed songs for entertainment. As a result, a certain rivalry developed between the two groups. This rivalry eventually led to a famous lawsuit in the seventeenth century. The *biwa hōshi* won, owing to the political strength of their guild, the Tōdōza 当道座, and the *jishin mōsō* were forced to limit themselves to the recitation of the *Earth Deity Sūtra* (Jishin-kyō 地神經).[37] Despite (or because of) that feud, the two groups influenced each other in many ways, and the mutual impact is reflected in many of their legends and symbols. Both groups, for example, traced their lineage back to a blind prince, variously identified as Amayo 天夜 (var. 雨夜), Komiya 小宮, or Semimaru 蝉丸, who was held to be an incarnation of Myōonten (or Myōon Bosatsu).[38] Conversely, as we will see shortly, certain beliefs related to the earth deity were probably transmitted from the *jishin mōsō* to the *biwa hōshi*. At any rate, it was perhaps among these blind musicians that the amalgamation between Myōon-Benzaiten and the earth deity took place.[39]

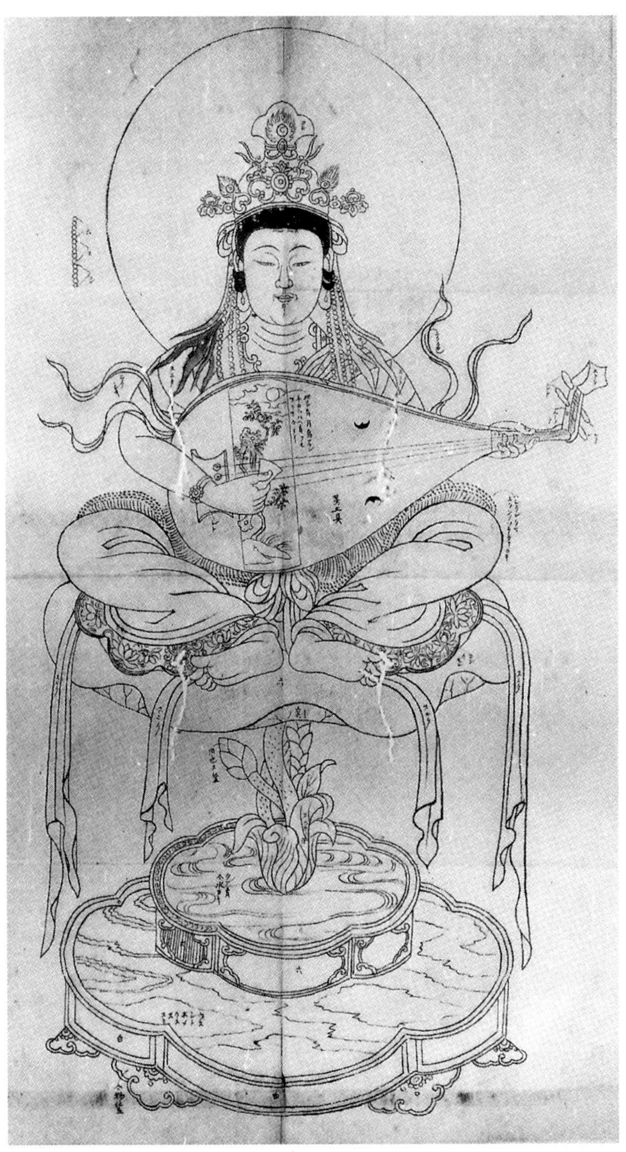

FIGURE 4.7. Myōon Benzaiten. Edo period. Sheet, ink on paper. University Art Museum, Kyoto City University of Arts. *BZS* 2208.

There were close ties between the Tōdōza and the Enryakuji–Hie Shrine complex on Mount Hiei, where the doctrinal synthesis involving Myōon, Benzaiten, and Ugajin was elaborated. Another group of artists, the *sarugaku* troupe of Ōmi, was closely related to Hie Shrine (while yet another troupe, in Ōtsu city's Kasuga-chō, was related to the Kasuga-Kōfukuji complex in Nara). Thus, the image of Benzaiten first evolved among the monastic circles of Mount Hiei (and to a lesser extent, Kōfukuji) before spreading via the artistic milieux of blind monks, *sarugaku* actors, and other outcasts (*hinin*). It was probably in this context that the relationship between Benzaiten and the Sannō deities (principally Jūzenji 十禅師), on the one hand, and the Kasuga deities on the other was established.

Let us return to Myōonten. Besides the legend of Prince Amayo, the Tōdōza had another origin story going back to the blind prince Komiya, an avatar of the Kamo deity (Kamo Daimyōjin 加茂大明神).[40] In the *Komiya taishi ichidaiki* 小宮太子一代記, the prince's divine identity is revealed to him by Myōon Benzaiten, who becomes his protector. Komiya is also initiated by a blind monk named Ekan, who had himself been initiated by Benzaiten after a hundred-day retreat at Chikubushima.[41]

According to a variant found in the *Zachō shidaiki* 座長次第記, it was Myōon Benzaiten who was born as Prince Chiba (Chiba Taishi 千葉太子), the blind child of Kōkō Tennō 光孝天皇 (830–889), and it was the Kamo deity who revealed to this prince his divine nature and his destiny as leader of the blind.[42] In certain versions of the *Heike monogatari,* it is suggested that the imperial consort Kenreimon'in 建礼門院, one of the few survivors of the Heike clan, was an avatar (*keshin* 化身) of Myōon.

The idea is usually implied by the comparison of her two ladies-in-waiting with the *nāga* princess of the *Lotus Sūtra* (who is herself often identified with Benzaiten), but in the Nagato-bon 長門本 recension of the *Heike monogatari,* it is explicitly stated that Kenreimon'in is none other than Myōon Bosatsu (and hence Benzaiten herself, the protecting deity of the *biwa hōshi*).[43] Thus, Kenreimon'in's sūtra offerings in memory of her relatives can be seen as an anticipation of the recitation of the *Heike monogatari* by the *biwa hōshi.*[44]

FIGURE 4.8. Myōon Benzaiten. Stone carving. Okayama prefecture. Photo Bernard Faure.

Myōon also figures in the tradition of the blind female singers (*goze* 瞽女) of Tōhoku.[45] The legendary founder of that tradition is now a princess, named Sagami or Sakagami逆髪, again an avatar of Kamo Daimyōjin. Her brother, Semimaru, is himself described as an avatar of Myōon Bosatsu. A spurious imperial edict preserved in that tradition says, for example: "The *honzon* Nyoirin Kannon turned into Myōon Bosatsu. The faithful must therefore constantly pray to Myōon Bosatsu, as well as to Benzaiten and Shimogamo Daimyōjin 下加茂大明神, because they are the deities who protect their livelihood. Those who neglect that point will be immediately punished."[46]

Benzaiten was believed to cure blindness and eye disease, as can be seen in a legend involving the Tendai priest Ennin 円仁 (a.k.a. Jikaku Daishi, 793–864). After Ennin had long suffered from eye disease, the goddess appeared to him in a dream and gave him a remedy, requiring in exchange that he worship her at Chikubushima. When he awoke, he found a small image of Benzaiten near his pillow, together with some medicine. As soon as he ingested the medicine, his eyes were healed. Out of gratitude, he enshrined the image at Chikubushima, where it came to be worshiped as the main deity.[47] In another popular tale, Benzaiten manifests herself as the young girl Sayohime 佐用姫, who sacrifices herself to restore her blind mother's eyesight.[48]

THE ESOTERIC BENZAITEN

A new phase in the development of Benzaiten was marked by her introduction into esoteric Buddhist discourse—which opened a new set of possibilities. As Myōonten, this deity was also (and perhaps primarily) related to Tantric speculations about sound. We recall that Sarasvatī appeared in the *Ṛg-veda* as a motherly, protecting figure, ensuring the efficacy of the prayers of sacrifice. Very early on, however, she was identified with speech (Vāc), and this aspect was emphasized in the *Brāhmaṇas.*[49] Thus, she simultaneously represents the Word and the Mother, the source of creative power. In the Vedic age, the murmur of her waters evoked the sounds of music. As Vāc, she was the consort (or daughter) of Brahmā. She became the inventor of Sanskrit, the goddess of grammar, eloquence, intelligence, knowledge, and craft—hence her name Benzaiten, "Deva of eloquence and talent." As the *Keiran shūyōshū* puts it: "Because Myōon Benzai is the wisdom of many buddhas, she pervades various worthies. . . . She can be the *honji* of Shaka, Yakushi, and Amida, as well as of the bodhisattvas Kokūzō, Jizō, and Miroku."[50]

While the image of the Buddhist Sarasvatī was based on the same water imagery as that of the Vedic Sarasvatī, she had already become quite different. She was now the object of several *sādhanās* (means of accomplishment), that is, visualizations through which the practitioner becomes identical with a specific deity and "accomplishes" that deity's nature. The *samaya* or symbolic form of Sarasvatī used in such visualizations was either the lute or the wish-fulfilling jewel.[51] Another important element of the ritual was the vessel in which she was said to dwell. This motif derives from the legendary invitation proffered by the Tiantai patriarch Zhiyi 智顗 (538–597) to Sarasvatī to take up her abode in a special vase. This vase was said to have been brought to Japan by Saichō.[52]

Medieval Japanese esoteric rituals usually began with a "contemplation of the ritual area" (*dōjōkan* 道場観), during which the main deity was invoked through seed-letters (*bīja,* J. *shuji* 種字), mantras and mudrās, and symbolic forms. In the case of Benzaiten, the seed-letter could be, depending on the purpose of the ritual, *a, ban* (Skt. *vaṃ*), *on* (Skt. *oṃ*), or *sa.*[53] Benzaiten rituals were performed in the Shingon-Ritsu school, as shown by the *Secret Ritual of Benzaiten,* compiled by the Vinaya master Eison. This manual describes the visualization of the ritual area as follows: one must visualize the seed-letter *sa* (first syllable of the name Sarasvatī) on a lotus seat at the center of the altar; that letter then transforms into a *biwa,* which eventually transforms into Benzaiten. The practitioner must then identify himself with the deity, who in this case is Myōon Benzaiten.[54] In the rituals of Uga Benzaiten, the symbolic form that is visualized is a wish-fulfilling jewel rather than a *biwa.*

One ritual, described in the *Keiran shūyōshū,* involved the use of a ladle and the seed-syllables *a* and *vaṃ*. In the cosmological system built around the five elements, the letter *vaṃ* is the symbol of water. We are told that water is the element in which Benzaiten dwells as a water deity, that is, as a *nāga.* Since the five elements are the basic constituents of the human body, Benzaiten also dwells within the human body, and more precisely in the lungs, the organ most closely related to the water element. According to the *Keiran shūyōshū:*

> Inside the water wheel [in our body] are the lungs, which contain golden water. In that golden water dwells a three-inch snake. It is our sixth [consciousness], called the mind-king. The lungs are the locus of the Wisdom of wondrous discernment, in the western direction [of the mandala]. It corresponds to the sixth consciousness, which discerns good and evil; it is our faculty for affirming the right and rejecting the wrong. Its seed-letter is *un* (Skt. *hūṃ*). It is the seed-letter for Benzaiten. Thus, our unconditioned, fundamentally awakened body has the form of a snake.[55]

Benzaiten both symbolizes and emanates from the "wisdom of wondrous discernment" (*myōkanzatchi* 妙観察智, Skt. *pratyavekṣana-jñāna*), one of the five wisdoms of the buddha Mahāvairocana. Following the psychogenetic schema of medieval esoteric Buddhism, she is said to correspond to the sixth consciousness (Skt. *mano-vijñāna*), out of which the five sense-consciousnesses evolve.

THE BEAUTY AND THE BEAST

Even more than Sarasvatī, Benzaiten is a Janus-faced deity. A primary aspect of her fundamental ambivalence has to do with the fact that she is not only a goddess but also a *nāga*—that is, an animal. As a woman, Sarasvatī plays a number of roles: she is both a lover and a mother figure. She is also a daughter (of Brahmā), a sister (of Yama or Vasu), and a wife (of Viṣṇu or Brahmā). Although Benzaiten is usually presented as the consort of Daikokuten, she is also paired with Bishamonten, a god of war and wealth.[56]

Benzaiten as a Female Immortal

Benzaiten is often depicted as a female immortal, as in the origin story of Chikubushima. In the section on immortals of the *Honchō monzui* 本朝文粋 (mid-eleventh century) and the *Jikkinshō* 十訓抄 (ca. 1252), and in the Nanto-bon 南都本 recension of the *Heike monogatari,* Benzaiten exchanges a poem with Toryōkō 都良香, a man who was said to be an immortal. The motif of the island of the immortals (Penglai, J. Hōrai 蓬萊) reappears in the *Genkō shakusho* 元亨釈書 in its account of the legend of the nun Nyoi 如意. Nyoi, Benzaiten's human double, is described as a female immortal, and the purple box in her possession is related to the box brought back by the fisherman Urashima 浦島 from his visit to Penglai (identified here with the *nāga* palace).[57] This legend also emphasizes the essential unity of Myōonten and Benzaiten.

In the Ise tradition, the origins of the building called Sakadono 酒殿 are explained by a legend inspired by the folkloric theme of the feather robe (Hagoromo 羽衣), in which a female immortal is stranded on earth after a man hides her feather robe. The Tendai priest Jihen, in his *Tenchi jingi shinchin yōki* 天地神祇審鎮要記 (1333), tells us how, when eight female immortals came down to earth, an old man of Tango province stole the feather robe of one of them. Unable to return to heaven, the stranded maiden became his daughter (or wife) and was eventually deified as Toyouke, the deity of the Outer Shrine of Ise.[58] The Ise tradition weaves several mythological strands together, including one of Benzaiten as a heavenly maiden who teaches humans how to fabricate sake, and the image of Ugajin (Uka no Mitama) as the spirit of rice. When the maiden eventually goes back to heaven, she leaves behind her a flask of pure sake in which Uka no Mitama (var. Toyouke) is said to dwell. According to Jihen, the deity of Sakadono is both Benzaiten and Toyouke.[59] The *Minō Benzaiten no koto* 弁才天の事 gives a doctrinal exegesis of Benzaiten's name and interprets the expression "heavenly maiden" (*tennyo* 天女) in the name Benzaitennyo as an allusion to sexual union. It also mentions the origin story of a heavenly woman called Princess First Flower (Hatsuhana-hime 初花姫), who was said to be a manifestation of Benzaiten.[60]

Benzaiten as a *Gandharva*

In the *Asabashō,* Benzaiten is also identified with the *gandharvas,* although this point was apparently a matter of debate.[61] In another passage, the *Asabashō* states: "Among the devas, she is the one who specializes in poems, songs, and beautiful sounds. She is not a *gandharva.*"[62] Since there are several other extant mentions of Benzaiten as a *gandharva,* the author of the *Kakuzenshō* feels obliged to examine the question and to determine whether Benzaiten belongs to the *gandharva* or *nāga* category.[63] In the *Keiran shūyōshū* as well, she is identified with the *gandharva* Bion 美音 (Sound of Beauty), but the associations actually played out are those with the *nāgas.*[64]

The question of Benzaiten's relations with the *gandharvas* derives from the Indian myth of the barter for Soma, when the gods exchanged Vāc (i.e., Sarasvatī) for Soma, who had been stolen by the *gandharvas.*[65] However, when Vāc is asked to choose between the *gandharvas* and the devas, she prefers the music performances of the latter to the former's recitation of the *Vedas.* Interestingly, this episode marked the very first mention of the vīnā (J. *biwa*) in connection with Vāc/Sarasvatī. It also reinforced a sexist interpretation according to which Vāc, being a woman, is naturally seduced by deceptive music. As a female (and later as a *nāga*), Sarasvatī became linked to delusion and ignorance, like the musical arts over which she presides.[66]

The possible identification of Benzaiten with the *gandharvas* presupposed Myōon Benzaiten's function as a goddess of music, since in Buddhism the *gandharvas* were usually reduced to a subaltern role as celestial musicians. However, as Georges Dumézil has shown, the Vedic *gandharvas* were complex figures, and it may be worthwhile to examine more closely the connection between them and Sarasvatī.[67]

According to Dumézil, *gandharvas* and their Indo-European relatives (in particular, the centaurs of Greek mythology) derived from the carnival masks of the new year, and they represented the demons, the spirits of the dead, and the regents of time.[68] If we follow this line of thought, what we find in the description of Benzaiten as a Janus-faced deity turns from a simple colloquial English expression into a quite appropriate symbolic expression: like Janus, the Roman god who presides over the change of year, Benzaiten becomes a deity presiding over the new year's rituals. Indeed, her main ritual took place on the fifteenth of the first month, the so-called little New Year (*ko-shōgatsu* 小正月).[69]

Benzaiten as a Water Deity

Beyond her early definition as a river deity, Sarasvatī's redefinition as a *nāga* or dragon proceeded through the logic of association. According to the *Benzaiten engi* 弁才天縁起 quoted in the *Keiran shūyōshū:* "Benzaiten is a water deity. Dragon gods are the quintessence of the water element, and this is why they dwell at the bottom of the ocean. The wish-fulfilling jewel is produced by the water wheel, and it is the source of all beings. Dragons are also the essence of the water wheel. This is why dragon gods see the essence of the relics (*śarīra*) as the vital (*hun* and *po*) spirits of water."[70] In the *Keiran shūyōshū*'s section on the *nāga* maiden and Benzaiten, the identity both share is established through their *honji,* Nyoirin Kannon, and through their primary symbol, the wish-fulfilling jewel.[71]

Benzaiten was also identified with other water deities such as Varuna (J. Suiten 水天). Varuna was originally the god of the ocean and one of the twelve directional devas. As guardian of the west, he became in Buddhism one of the four guardians of the Vajradhātu mandala. In female form, this deity was said to bring rain and to protect against sea disasters. Resembling a celestial woman, she is often shown holding a *cintāmaṇi* in each hand. Benzaiten's affinities with Suiten (Fig. 4.9) also link her to Myōken Bosatsu.

Four of the five great cultic centers of Benzaiten, as well as countless smaller ones, are located on islands: Chikubushima, Enoshima, Miyajima (Itsukushima, Hiroshima prefecture), and Kinkazan 金華山 (Miyagi

FIGURE 4.9. Suiten. Edo period. Sheet, ink on paper. University Art Museum, Kyoto City University of Arts. *BZS* 2228.

prefecture). Two other well-known sites are Aojima 青島 (Miyazaki prefecture, Kyushu) and the Benten-dō 弁天堂 on Shinobazu Pond 不忍池 in Ueno Park (Tokyo).

When Taira no Kiyomori attempted to develop seaways in the Inland Sea, he chose Benzaiten as the protector of navigation. As told in the *Heike monogatari,* however, the story takes on greater religious significance: when Kiyomori went to Mount Kōya to pay reverence to the Great Stūpa, which had just been restored, an old monk with hoary eyebrows told him that he should restore Itsukushima Shrine. When the monk suddenly vanished, Kiyomori, struck with awe, decided to follow his instructions. He conveyed the story to the retired emperor and received an order to repair Itsukushima. When the shrine was repaired, he visited it and spent the night in prayer. He dreamed that a divine youth, acting as a messenger from the goddess, handed him a short spear with a silver snake-coil pattern on the hilt, saying: 'With this blade, bring peace to the realm and protect the imperial house.' Kiyomori awakened to find the weapon on his pillow. This *In illo signe vinces* is nuanced by a further apparition—that of the goddess herself, who warns him that his good fortune will not extend to his progeny if he commits wicked deeds.[72] This is a transparent foreshadowing of the Heike's fall, to be caused by Kiyomori's hybris.[73]

The famous *Sūtra Offered by the Heike* (*Heike nōkyō* 平家納經), a magnificent series of thirty-three illustrated scrolls of the *Lotus Sūtra* and two smaller sūtras (the *Muryōgikyō* 無量義經 and the *Kan Fugen kyō* 觀普賢經), allegedly copied by Kiyomori and members of the Taira clan, was offered to Itsukushima Shrine in 1164. In the dedicatory vow (*ganmon* 願文), Kiyomori mentions his dream on Mount Kōya, gives a list of the thirty-two Taira members who have shared the task of copying the thirty-two scrolls, and asks, in return for the accumulated merits which he now offers to Benzaiten, that she protect the state, vouchsafe the realization of his wishes and those of others, and lead him to awakening and rebirth in the Pure Land.[74]

In 1174, the retired emperor Go-Shirakawa went on pilgrimage to Itsukushima with the Taira clan. A few years later, in 1180, retired emperor Takakura 高倉 twice made the trip himself, to pray that the goddess would soften Kiyomori's rebellious spirit, which was keeping Go-Shirakawa prisoner.[75] The shrine was destroyed in the years 1222–1224 but rebuilt in 1241. In the Muromachi period, the third Ashikaga 足利 shōgun, Yoshimitsu 義満, visited the shrine, and it subsequently prospered. In the meantime, the goddess Ichikishima 市杵嶋 had become Benzaiten.

We recall how Taira no Tsunemasa, visiting Chikubushima, interpreted his vision of Benzaiten as a sign of the Heike's victory against the Minamoto. His interpretation of this event turned out to be wishful thinking, however, as the Heike were defeated soon afterward. The purported auspiciousness of his vision is already contradicted in the *Heike monogatari* by the report of a portentous dream in which another young warrior saw a group of senior officials gathered in a hall of the imperial palace and expelling someone who seemed to be a member of the Heike. When the dreamer asked who this person was, he was told that it was the Itsukushima deity. Then the main official, an emanation of the bodhisattva Hachiman, declared that the sword that had been entrusted to the Heike would now be given to Minamoto no Yoritomo 源頼朝. Another official, an emanation of the Kasuga deity, added that the sword should go to his grandson afterwards. When this dream was reported to the novice Nariyori 成頼 on Mount Kōya, the latter commented: "Ah! The Heike will not last much longer! It was reasonable that the Itsukushima deity should have sided with them. But I had always heard that that divinity was feminine, the third daughter of the *nāga* king Sāgara."[76] Nariyori perhaps alludes to the supposedly fickle nature of women, and he apparently attributes the demise of the Heike to the Itsukushima deity's inconstancy, but in an earlier section of the *Heike monogatari,* it is clear that the blame has been placed on Kiyomori's hubris. At any rate, the Itsukushima deity—that is, Benzaiten—literally takes a back seat and her protection of the Heike is no longer perceived as a sign of enduring prosperity for that clan. The Heike's relationship with Itsukushima also led to the belief that Benzaiten herself had been reborn in the imperial house as Antoku Tennō 安徳天皇, the child emperor and Kiyomori's grandson, who drowned in the sea at the battle of Dan-no-Ura 壇ノ浦 (1185) with one of the Three Regalia, the divine sword.[77]

If Benzaiten's loss of status in the *Heike monogatari* affected (or reflected) the fate of the Heike, the eventual demise of that clan did not have long-lasting repercussions on the goddess's popularity. On the contrary, she became the protecting deity of the shōgunate founded by the former rebel Yoritomo, and her images were enshrined in the Tsurugaoka Hachiman Shrine in Kamakura, as well as on the nearby Enoshima island.

After the death of Yoritomo, Benzaiten became the protector of the Hōjō family. According to the *Taiheiki* 太平記, at the beginning of the Kamakura period, Hōjō Tokimasa 北条時政 (1138–1215) secluded himself on Enoshima to pray that his descendants would be blessed forever. On the night of the twenty-first day, a fair and stately lady suddenly appeared before him. Acknowledging the meritorious karma he had

FIGURE 4.10. Detail of the *Scripture on Praying for Rain* mandala (*Shōugyō* shiki mandara). Edo period. Sheet, ink on paper. University Art Museum, Kyoto City University of Arts. *BZS* 1045.

gained while a monk at Hakone shrine (by making exemplars of the *Lotus Sūtra* to present to sacred places in each of the sixty-six provinces), she predicted that his descendants would rule over Japan; but their prosperity would not extend beyond seven generations if they lacked righteousness. Having said this, the lady turned into a great snake two hundred feet long, which entered the sea. The text concludes: "Thus was it owing to the divine favor of Enoshima Benzaiten and to the effect of a past good cause, that still the Sagami lay monk (i.e., the shōgun Takatoki) ruled the realm after more than seven generations [until the time of Go-Daigo's Kenmu Restoration]. But as regards the strange doings of Takatoki, may it not be that the time was come for the Hōjō to be cut off? For already the seventh generation was past, and the ninth generation was reached."[78]

Nāgas and Dragons

So Benzaiten came to be perceived as a female *nāga* or dragon—a deity controlling rain, fecundity, and wealth. (Figs. 4.10 and 4.11 are examples of the association of *nāgas* and dragons with rain-making.) Given the importance of the *nāga*/dragon motif in the development of her cult, it may be useful to delve into the role of these divine animals in Japan, as well as the mythological topos of the *nāga* palace. Although Benzaiten is not mentioned in M. W. de Visser's classic study on *nāgas,* the goddess had a long history of association with those mythical beings in China and Japan.[79] The first thing to note is that this was another Buddhist

FIGURE 4.11. Mandala of the *Scripture on Praying for Rain* (*Shōugyō* shiki mandara). Edo period. Sheet, ink on paper. University Art Museum, Kyoto City University of Arts. *BZS* 1046.

innovation, since the Vedic river goddess Sarasvatī had not been associated with those water-controlling deities. Indeed, the Indian *nāgas,* figures of autochthony, and as such representatives of local, pre-Buddhist deities, seem to have developed only within the framework of Buddhism.

A complex mythology extends far beyond the few points I can mention here. As an animal, the *nāga* remained subject to the sufferings of karma. According to Buddhist tradition, the *nāgas* were constantly afflicted by the three fevers (*sannetsu* 三熱). This paradoxical image is also found in the "Consecration" chapter (Kanjō no maki) of the *Heike monogatari.* In this chapter, one of the survivors of the Heike defeat at Dan-no-ura, the imperial consort Kenreimon'in, tells retired emperor Go-Shirakawa that all the members of the Heike clan had been reborn as *nāgas:* "I dozed off, and in a dream I saw the Former Emperor and the Taira senior nobles and courtiers, all in formal array, at a place far grander than the old imperial palace. I asked where we were, because I had seen nothing like it since the departure from the capital. Someone who seemed to be the Nun of Second Rank answered, 'This is the Nāga Palace.' 'What a splendid place! Is there no suffering here?' I asked. 'The suffering is described in the *Ryūchikukyō Sūtra.* Pray hard for us,' she said. I awakened as she spoke."[80]

In East Asia, the figure of the Indian *nāga* came to merge with local water deities, especially the dragon, a positive symbol often associated with highborn women.[81] According to Edward Schafer, "in China, dragon essence is woman essence. The connection is through the mysterious powers of the fertilizing rain, and its extensions in running streams, lakes, and marshes. In common belief as in literature, the dark, wet side of nature showed itself alternately in women and in dragons. The great water deities of Chinese antiquity were therefore snake queens and dragon ladies."[82]

In China, the yin-yang theory is expressed symbolically by two emblems, the dragon and the tiger, standing for water (yin) and fire (yang), respectively. The dragon is also the symbol of heaven (yang), although there are heavenly dragons and earthly dragons. The snake, which is not always distinguished clearly from the dragon and the Buddhist *nāga,* is more specifically chthonian. At any rate, the dragon/snake, associated with earth and water—and, as we will see later, with sacred jewels and relics—is a symbol of fertility and fecundity. The earthly dragon usually lives in ponds, caves, or waterfalls. Many Buddhist temples were built near ponds or waterfalls. Famous examples include Ishiyamadera, Hasedera 長谷寺, and Murōji 室生寺, all centers located near a "dragon hole."[83] The story of Kūkai's inviting the dragon king Zennyo 善女 to Shinsen'en is also well known.[84] The mythology of the dragon and the symbolism of water thus came to play an important role in medieval Buddhism and in its discourse on sexuality. An emblematic image is that of Guanyin/Kannon riding a dragon. Another widespread symbol of yin and yang is Kurikara 倶梨伽羅, a representation of Fudō as a dragon coiled around a sword and swallowing its tip. The dragon king Zennyo (Fig. 4.12) is said to have offered one of his scales to Kūkai when the latter initiated him. The motif of the scale reappears in the legend of Benzaiten's apparition to the second shōgun, which is described below.

The association of Benzaiten with dragons is particularly explicit in the *Keiran shūyōshū,* which uses it to reinforce the link between Benzaiten and the wish-fulfilling jewel. In his attempt to interpret esoteric Buddhism within the framework of the fundamental scripture of Tendai, the *Lotus Sūtra,* Kōshū also links Benzaiten with the *nāga* maiden of the *Lotus Sūtra.*

In the *Heike monogatari,* when a monk on pilgrimage reaches Itsukushima and asks a hunter about the shrine's deity and its relation

FIGURE 4.12. The dragon king Zennyo. Edo period. Sheet, ink on paper. University Art Museum, Kyoto City University of Arts. *BZS* 2186.

to the sea, the hunter replies: "Our principal deity is the *nāga* king Sāgara's third daughter, a manifestation of the Womb realm Vairocana."[85] In his *Ga'un nikkenroku batsuyū* 臥雲日件錄拔尤, Zuikei Shūhō 瑞溪周鳳 (1391?–1473) reports an oracle from the goddess of Itsukushima describing how her two younger sisters (i.e., the *nāga* maiden of the *Lotus Sūtra* and the Enoshima Benzaiten) manifested themselves on Mount Katori 笠取山 in Yamashiro and at Enoshima in Izu, respectively.[86] Here, as in other sources, Benzaiten becomes one of the daughters of the *nāga* king Sāgara. In the *Keiran shūyōshū,* she is also described as a dragon.

The Nāga *Palace*

In the *Jingi hishō* 神祇秘抄, Benzaiten is described as the ruler of the *nāga* palace.[87] The *nāga* palace was thought to be a submarine or subterranean world that could be reached from any cave or waterfall.[88] As the repository of the Buddha's relics, the wish-fulfilling jewel, and other Buddhist sacra,[89] it gradually came to be seen as the origin and ultimate destination of all Buddhist treasures, as well as a source of legitimacy for both the Buddhist law and the secular law. Thus, in the *Heike monogatari,* the sacred sword, lost in the waters of Dan-no-ura, returns to the *nāga* palace when the Heian world, which had seen the flourishing of Buddhism and the rise of the Taira warriors, comes to an end. The *nāga* palace is sometimes identified with the palace of the bodhisattva Maitreya or with the heavenly cave of the sun goddess Amaterasu; it can also be described as the source of ignorance and passions.[90]

Tendai mythological discourse went one step further, interpreting the *nāgas* allegorically as the part of human nature that dwells in the water element of the body. The *nāga* palace thus becomes the source of the mind, the ultimate reality of all things. Furthermore, the *nāga* king came to be identified with the sea king of classical Japanese mythology, who gives to the young god Hoori 火遠理 his daughters Toyotama-hime 豊玉姫 and Tamayori-hime 玉依姫, together with two jewels controlling the tides. The relationship between Benzaiten and her younger sister (the *nāga* maiden of the *Lotus Sūtra*) is patterned after that between the two daughters of the sea king.[91]

The Taming of the Dragon

A number of local traditions describe Benzaiten as taming (and/or mating with) a dangerous dragon. At times this taming involves a sacrifice, either of Benzaiten herself or of a maiden who is her substitute. According to legend, on a mountain near Chikubushima lived a giant centipede that required the yearly sacrifice of a young girl. In the end, only one maiden remained. Taking pity on her, Benzaiten appeared in a dream to Fujiwara no Hidesato 藤原秀郷 (popularly known as Tawara Tōda 俵藤太 or Rice-bag Tōda), telling him to kill the monster and leaving a bow and arrows near his pillow. With her protection, the young man was able to fulfill his mission and save the maiden. Another legend, that of Matsuura Sayohime 松浦佐用姫, involves Benzaiten's own sacrifice.[92] Sayohime was the daughter of the headman of Matsuura village. Having lost her father at the age of three, she lived in poverty with her mother. Lacking the financial means to celebrate the thirteenth anniversary of her husband's death, the mother secretly sold Sayohime to a man named Gonga no tayū, who intended to offer the girl to a local dragon as a substitute for his own daughter. When Sayohime is led to the monster, she recites the Devadatta chapter of the *Lotus Sūtra,* thereby saving both herself and the dragon, and she is eventually able to return home. In the meantime, however, her mother has become blind, because of the tears wept over her lost daughter. With the jewel given to her by the dragon, Sayohime restores her mother's eyesight and later reveals her true nature as the Benzaiten of Chikubushima.[93] In this legend, at least, the heroine is not simply "married" (that is, sacrificed) to the dragon to put an end to human sacrifices, and the predominant motif of blindness obviously reflects the concerns of the blind musicians (*mōsō*) who spread Benzaiten's cult.

The Hidden Side

As a *nāga*/dragon, Benzaiten was still subject to the afflictions of her animal nature. After the Muromachi period, this aspect went under concealment, and she became more plain as she turned into one of the Seven Gods of Fortune. But in the medieval period, she retained her mystery, her ambiguity, her uncanniness.[94] Schafer's characterization of water goddesses in Tang literature seems to apply equally to Benzaiten: "However glossed they may be with gauze and rouge, however remote they seem from their fierce and powerful originals, however much—in short—they may resemble tinted photographs or fashionably painted dolls, [they] remain pitiless spirits and lethal sirens underneath.[95]

Benzaiten's dark side is emphasized in a number of medieval tales. In "Yoritomo no saiji," for instance, the Benzaiten of Enoshima offers fish to the Chinese Zen master Rankei Dōryū 蘭渓道隆 (Ch. Lanqi Daolong, 1203–1268 or 1213–1278), the abbot of Kenchōji 建長寺 in Kamakura. When the second shōgun, Minamoto no Yoriie 源頼家 (1182–1204), invites Benzaiten to Kenchōji, a fine-looking lady appears and listens to Rankei's sermon. Seduced by her beauty, Yoriie asks her to reveal her true form. Suddenly, a putrid wind fills the room as she turns into a large horned snake, which then begs Rankei to free it from its karmic hindrances in exchange for its protection of the shōgunate.[96] Here the contrast between her female beauty and her animal ugliness is striking, and could perhaps be read as an allusion to the true nature of women.[97]

Kyōen 慶円 (var. Keien, 1140–1223), a priest who lived near the famous dragon hole of Murōzan 室生山, is reported to have experienced a similar mishap. Once, as he was crossing a bridge, a noble lady appeared and asked him for a mudrā that would allow her to reach buddhahood. When Keien asked who she was, she replied that she was the *nāga* Zennyo (the same *nāga* whom Kūkai once invited to Shinsen'en). When he asked her to show her true nature, she replied: "My shape is so frightening that no man can look upon it. Yet I cannot refuse your wish." She then rose into the air, but the only thing Keien could see before she disappeared was a long claw.[98] *Ex ungue draconem.*

The negative image of Benzaiten is more obvious in the following story reported by the *Keiran shūyōshū.* When the Dharma master Dōchi 道智 went to Enoshima to read the *Lotus Sūtra,* a woman came every day to bring him food and listen to his sermons. Wondering about her real identity, he covered himself with a wisteria cloth and followed her to a cave, where she resumed her animal form. When she found out that she had been followed, she became angry, but, instead of punishing him, she declared that wisteria would no longer grow at Enoshima—a rather puzzling curse. Here the *nāga* goddess reveals her ambiguous nature: although she seeks deliverance, she can be draconian, and one cannot trespass upon her privacy without danger.[99]

CODETTA

I have been using a genealogical approach to describe the gradual transformation of Sarasvatī into Benzaiten. This method can be problematic, however, if it naively assumes a single origin of the deity. In the mythological field, origins are never that simple. Just as many streams flowed into the river Sarasvatī, the goddess who bears that name is herself the confluent of many deities, with Vāc, the goddess of speech, prominent among them. That fundamental plurality, which had been temporarily subsumed under the Sarasvatī/Vāc (water/music) polarity, diffracted again into a number of streams—which, for the sake of an illusory simplicity, I have tried to harness under such polarities as war and the arts, animality and femininity, and so on.

The logic of this deity's evolution (and involution) is thus much less linear than is implied by the genealogical approach that claimed to take us from Sarasvatī to Benzaiten. Besides her aquatic aspects and musical function, the Buddhist Sarasvatī acquired a warrior's role and other more sinister aspects, to the point that Ludvik sees her as a mere stand-in for the wrathful Hindu goddess Durgā. One of the main changes along the way was her transformation into a *nāga,* which opened the floodgates to a rich water symbolism. Another, more marginal development, deriving from her feminine image and that of the heavenly musician (*gandharva*), was the folkloric motif of the heavenly maiden, which linked her to folkloric legends.

At the crossroads of various religious trends and mythological traditions, the figure of Benzaiten constitutes not only a shared symbol, but also an arena of contention. Her name is shorthand for a complex network that links such variegated motifs as the lute (*biwa*), the snake, the dragon, and the jewel. Because of her multifunctional nature, she does not fit neatly—and actually undermines—the traditional distinction between buddhas and *kami.* Under the name Uga Benzaiten, she becomes part of a broad mythological field that includes devas such as Bishamonten, Kichijōten, Daikokuten, Dakiniten, Kangiten, and the earth deity (Jiten). To understand the emergence of this complex deity, the genealogical approach proves less efficient than a structural one, to which I now (re) turn.

5

FROM DRAGON TO SNAKE

Uga Benzaiten

> Conforming to the capacity of beings, [Benzaiten] manifests all kinds of secret bodies. At times she appears as the Thousand-tongued Deva and dispenses unobstructed eloquence; at other times she becomes the Virtuous Deva (Kudokuten, i.e., Śrī) and confers unlimited happiness. At times she is called Karitei (Hārītī) and leads the five hundred demons in order to eliminate diseases; at other times she is called Deity of the Firm Earth (Kenrō Jijin 堅牢地神) and dispenses food and drink, clothes, and palaces and pavilions. At times she is called the Great Black God (Daikokujin 大黒神, i.e., Mahākāla) and brings happiness to [the beings of] the three thousand great worlds; at other times she becomes the deity [called] Jade Maiden (Gyokujo 玉女) or the crossroads deity (Dōsojin 道祖神) and travels in all directions, dispensing love and respect.[1]

The major turning point in the Benzaiten tradition was not the appearance of the eight-armed Sarasvatī but rather the emergence of the so-called Uga Benzaiten, the focus of the present chapter. I have long hesitated as to whether I should discuss this hybrid deity together with Benzaiten or with Ugajin. In the end, I believe that she is, at least in many contexts, distinct from both the classical Benzaiten and from Ugajin, while being clearly indebted to both. I have therefore decided to give her a separate chapter, although I am aware of the difficulties and the arbitrary nature of such a treatment.

When focusing on the dragon aspects of Benzaiten and Ugajin, in particular, it is difficult to make a clear distinction between the two. However, because of Sarasvatī's history as a water deity, I have found it more convenient to interpret these dragon-related characteristics as a Japanese continuation of the Indian Sarasvatī rather than an appropriation of East Asian (be it Japanese or otherwise) dragon-related symbolism. Likewise, I trace the geographic expansion of the Uga Benzaiten cult despite the fact that many Uga Benzaiten cultic centers are associated

FIGURE 5.1. Uga Benzaiten. Nanbokuchō period, 14th century. Wood. Seto Shrine (Kanagawa prefecture).

with other forms of Benzaiten as well: the island of Chikubushima was home to Myōon prior to Uga Benzaiten's dominance there, two forms of Benzaiten coexist at Itsukushima, and at Enoshima the dragon aspect of Benzaiten is most prominent (although today the so-called naked Benzaiten, i.e., Myōon, is enshrined next to Uga Benzaiten).

I begin, then, with a general discussion of Uga Benzaiten's characteristics and symbolism before turning to the Tendai transformation in which she became a deity in her own right rather than a simple variation on Benzaiten. This transformation was largely carried out by the Tendai chroniclers (*kike* 記家), and the results are most evident in the *Keiran shūyōshū,* a work that has been frequently cited in earlier chapters. As we will see, the resulting Uga Benzaiten was deeply informed by an emphasis on dualities—heaven and earth, good and evil—matched by the solvent of nonduality.

I also address the geographical expansion of the cult to six sites: Chikubushima in the northern part of Lake Biwa, Itsukushima (present-day Miyajima, on the Inland Sea), Enoshima (off the coast of Kamakura), Tenkawa (about halfway between Nara and Kumano), Minoo 箕面 (on the northern outskirts of modern-day Osaka), and Ise. We then consider the iconography of Uga Benzaiten, with special attention to the fifteen *dōji* so often depicted alongside Benzaiten. Finally, I draw the reader's attention to links between Uga Benzaiten and other deities, especially Dakiniten, before concluding with observations on Uga Benzaiten's character and function.

THE HYBRID DEITY

Any discussion of Uga Benzaiten (Figs. 5.1–5.3) must begin with (and depart from) the canonical Benzaiten. The nature of Benzaiten changed drastically between the Nara period—when she was worshiped together with Kichijōten in repentance rituals inspired by the *Golden Light Sūtra*—and the Kamakura period.[2] At first, Kichijōten was more popular than Benzaiten, due to her centrality in the rites performed in state-sponsored provincial temples (*kokubunji* 国分寺), but toward the end of the Heian period, Benzaiten came to the forefront and her status continued to rise during the Kamakura period.

As noted earlier, the *Keiran shūyōshū* contains a number of stories about Uga Benzaiten and establishes a parallel between Myōonten and Uga Benzaiten, but in so doing it actually reinforces the latter's doctrinal status. During the Kamakura period, Kenchū 鎌忠 (fl. mid-thirteenth century), a monk of the Anō-ryū 穴太流 branch of Tendai esotericism, compiled a collection of esoteric practices entitled *Saishō gokoku ugaya tontoku nyoi hōju-ō shugi* 最勝護国宇賀耶頓得如意宝珠王修儀 (cited

FIGURE 5.2. Detail of Uga Benzaiten. Nanbokuchō period, 14th century. Wood. Seto Shrine (Kanagawa prefecture).

FIGURE 5.3. (*Right*) Uga Benzaiten. *Ofuda*. Color on paper. Chikubushima. Personal collection.

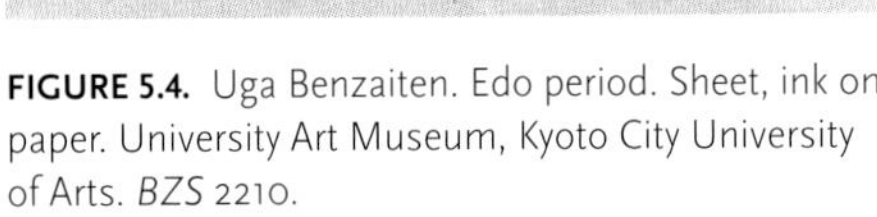

FIGURE 5.4. Uga Benzaiten. Edo period. Sheet, ink on paper. University Art Museum, Kyoto City University of Arts. *BZS* 2210.

FIGURE 5.5. Uga Benzaiten. Edo period. Sheet, ink on paper. University Art Museum, Kyoto City University of Arts. *BZS* 2212.

hereafter as *Benzaiten shugi*).[3] The contents of this collection suggest that the Tendai teachings regarding Uga Benzaiten were largely systematized by this time. But in addition, several medieval apocrypha focus on Uga Benzaiten.[4] They depict the deity as an eight-armed goddess, holding various attributes (a jewel and sword, spear and club, wheel and key, bow and arrow) in her four pairs of hands (Fig. 5.3 and 5.4). The god Ugajin, represented as a white snake with the face of an old man, can be seen under a small torii in her headgear (Fig. 5.3), and she is accompanied by fifteen youths. The torii is sometime interpreted as meaning that she is a Shintō deity, but it rather indicates that she is neither a buddha nor a *kami.*

The Tendai reinterpretation of this figure opened the gates to a proliferation of interpretations and explanations of Uga Benzaiten's significance, which appeared in ritual sources and as origin stories. They also emerged in popular forms such as the *honjimono* 本地物, which developed on the margins of Buddhist institutions—among the blind monks (*biwa hōshi*) associated with Mount Hiei, for example. Thus, instead of the linear development we are familiar with from iconographic textbooks, we have a complex growth pattern, radiating from multiple sources—geographical, mythical, ritual, and doctrinal.

Animals and Hybridity

At the risk of muddying the clear waters of the Sarasvatī river, I want to focus on the earth and animal elements in the figure of Uga Benzaiten. In the *Golden Light Sūtra,* the eight-armed Sarasvatī is surrounded by lions, tigers, and other wild animals. While the eight-armed Benzaiten closely follows the canonical description, in Japan she is never represented in the company of such animals, but rather with foxes, dragons, and snakes—all chthonian spirits in the medieval Japanese religious world. This Benzaiten's animal nature is nowhere represented more vividly than in the Tenkawa Benzaiten mandala: dressed in long robes and wearing jewelry, she resembles an elegant Chinese lady; the three serpent heads emerging from the neck of her dress, however, reveal her true nature. I will come back to this striking representation, but for the time being, suffice it to say that there is no other known representation of Benzaiten with three snake or dragon heads. The only image I know of that resembles it is that of the *nāga* goddess Dasheng Fude Longnü 大聖福德龍女 (a.k.a. Baijie 白姐 'white sister') in the *Fanxiang juan* 梵像卷 or *Long Roll of Buddhist Images* of Dali 大理 (in modern Yunnan).[5] In this splendid iconographic document, three white snakes rise above the head of Fude Longnü, who is paired with Mahākāla and flanked by four female attendants (each with a snake on her head) and two male acolytes (one with a snake head, the other with a rooster head).[6]

As opposed to the canonical and rather abstract Benzaiten—whether in her exoteric, two-armed form or her esoteric, eight-armed form—Uga Benzaiten is often described as the "living" (*shōjin* 生身) Benzaiten. This term brings with it a sense of awe and uncanniness, which resonates with the descriptions of Benzaiten as a dragon. While it can be traced back to the Heian period, the hybridization or partial transformation of Benzaiten into an animal is one of this deity's most significant developments during the medieval period. It places her at the confluence of a number of symbolically significant symbols—e.g., the *nāgas,* the dragons, the snake, the fox, and the wish-fulfilling jewel—which we must briefly address.

FIGURE 5.6. Snake deity. *Daigo-bon Yakushi jūni shinshō*, *TZ* 7: 439, fig. 52.

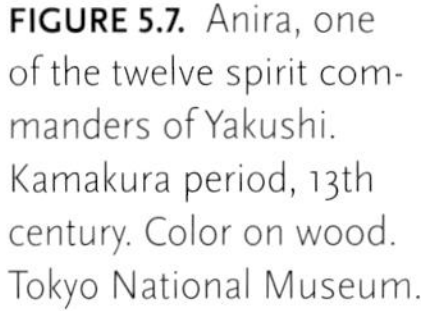

FIGURE 5.7. Anira, one of the twelve spirit commanders of Yakushi. Kamakura period, 13th century. Color on wood. Tokyo National Museum.

FIGURE 5.8. Detail of Anira, one of the twelve spirit commanders of Yakushi. Kamakura period, 13th century. Color on wood. Tokyo National Museum.

One aspect of the iconography of Uga Benzaiten that has not received sufficient attention is the apparent incongruity of the presence in Uga Benzaiten's diadem of Ugajin, a visibly hybrid figure: his face is that of an old man, his body that of a snake, and he sits coiled behind or below a torii.[7] Theriomorphic images are not unique in Buddhist iconography, but they are rather rare. Buddhist mythology and iconography contain numerous subaltern, animal-headed deities (e.g., the horse-headed *gandharvas*).[8] Among them, the *nāgas* are usually classified as animals who can assume a human appearance and who have fallen into an animal's destiny because of their karma. Unlike them, however, Ugajin is said to symbolize buddhahood. In the Chinese tradition, the twelve zodiacal animals are often represented with a human body and an animal head. One of them in particular, the snake, has a snake head (see, e.g., Figs. 5.6 and 5.10), and in Buddhism it came to be identified with Anira, one of the twelve spirit commanders (Jūni shinshō 十二神将) of Yakushi's retinue (Figs. 5.7 and 5.8).[9]

FIGURE 5.9. Fu Xi and Nü Wa. John C. and Susan L. Huntington Photographic Archive.

Yet the figure that Ugajin most closely resembles is the Chinese representation of the primordial mythic couple Fu Xi 伏羲 and Nü Wa 女媧—human-headed snakes with their tails interlocked (Fig. 5.9). Similar representations appeared in medieval Japan, one such being a document of Hasedera describing the seven generations of heavenly gods, in which the male figures in the last three hybrid couples strikingly resemble Ugajin (Fig. 7.5).[10]

But Benzaiten was not simply a manifestation of Ugajin. She formed a dyad with him, and it is precisely the dual nature of that deity (reminiscent of the dual-bodied Kangiten) that defined it as ultimate and transcendent. This pairing is quite different from the traditional *honji suijaku*

FIGURE 5.10. Snake-bodied *kami*. Susa Shrine, Izumo (Shimane prefecture). Photo Bernard Faure.

model, in which the "original ground" and its "traces" remain hierarchically related and distinct. Not surprisingly, this dual nature was criticized by Edo scholars such as Amano Sadakage 天野信景 (1663–1733), who in his *Shiojiri* 塩尻 rejects Uga Benzaiten as unorthodox and insists that Ugajin and Benzaiten must be kept distinct, as indeed they were in some cases.

Although Benzaiten herself is occasionally referred to as Ugajin, that name usually designates the snake-headed deity. It is the relationship between Benzaiten and Ugajin that raises the crucial question: are we confronted with a variant of Benzaiten or with a radically new hybrid deity? The figure represented in the crown of Buddhist worthies (bodhisattvas or *myōō*) usually represents the particular buddha who is said to be the worthy-in-question's *honji* or original nature. However, it is not at all clear that this is the case when it comes to Uga Benzaiten. Ugajin's presence could indicate that he is the true nature—the *honji*—of Benzaiten, and that she serves as a mediator, safely transforming his dangerously powerful energy. But it could just as well be the other way around, the reptilian figure being Benzaiten's "trace" (*suijaku*). Various commentaries suggest that we have here a couple representing the yin and yang principles, like the couples formed by Fu Xi and Nü Wa, by the Dōsojin in Japanese folklore, and by Vināyaka and Avalokiteśvara in the figure of the dual-bodied Kangiten. Although the woman in the present example (Benzaiten) is not represented in reptilian form, she is also thought of as being a snake or dragon.

The dual Uga Benzaiten is not merely a pair, however, and we cannot speak merely of combination or pairing. In the process, Benzaiten herself becomes a white snake. Things are therefore more complicated than standard Tendai theolology, with its binary and ternary models, would have us believe. The presence of Ugajin on Benzaiten's head is not merely an iconographic detail: it points to a fundamental difference, both in nature and function, with the canonical eight-armed Benzaiten. Despite the common (and usually late) interpretations, Uga Benzaiten is not merely a "syncretistic" representation, combining a *honji* and a *suijaku;* rather, she is suggestive of a hybrid, pluralistic deity (of the same type as the hybrid, three-headed Matarajin of Tōji and other representations of the Three Devas in one). In this process, it is Benzaiten who changes into a snake: the snake is no longer merely Ugajin, but a new deity named Uga Benzaiten.

Unlike Fudō, a chthonian deity who is sometimes represented allegorically as a dragon coiled around a sword, Benzaiten, who was initially a water deity and by extension a *nāga* or dragon, came to be perceived predominantly as a snake deity. Of course, snakes and dragons are closely related in Japanese mythology, and yet the Edo-period *Shiojiri* emphatically asserts that Benzaiten is *not* a snake.[11] However, such isolated voices did not prevent the shift in popular perception that brought about an emphasis on Benzaiten's snake-like nature, a shift that occurred, most likely, as a result of her association with Ugajin. This is not just an instance of the expression "Beginning like a dragon, ending like a snake," used in reference to someone who fails to fulfill her promises. On the contrary, Benzaiten's power and prestige as a snake god greatly increased.

As noted earlier, Benzaiten acquired some of the characteristics of her "sister" Kichijōten. The assimilation of Benzaiten to Ugajin (or Ugajin to Benzaiten) served to emphasize her fecundity, a motif associated with earth and water. In the *Benten gobukyō* 弁天五部經, a collection of five Japanese apocrypha centered on Benzaiten, the process by which she merged with Ugajin (and Inari) and her subsequent transformation into a fortune deity is complete. The symbolic forms of Uga Benzaiten (the wish-fulfilling jewel, the sword, and Ugajin) are explained in the *Keiran shūyōshū* as the most efficient means to subdue the demons of the three poisons. The torii, however, is passed over in silence.

To give an idea of the complex mythico-ritual system formed by Benzaiten and Ugajin, it might be enough to mention just one ritual text from the Kanazawa bunko archives, the *Ugajin-ku saimon* 宇賀神供祭文 (1400), which describes an offering to Ugajin (a name referring here to Uga Benzaiten). In the ritual, the priest first invokes the main deity (or deities, depending on whether one considers the title "Benzaiten Uga shinshō bosatsu" 弁才天宇賀神将菩薩 as referring to a single figure or two distinct ones)—and its (or their) incalculable retinue(s). He then invokes the *ugajin* (used as a collective name) of all directions, as well as the fifteen princes (*ōji* 王子) of the spirit commander Uga; then the "three devas" and their countless following, the three devas being the heavenly maiden Daibenzai, Daten (i.e., Dakiniten), and Shōten in a single body.[12] The goal of the *saimon* is to obtain the power of realization (*siddhi*) in this life and after.[13] That such rituals were seen as particularly efficacious can be seen in a section of the *Keiran shūyōshū* dated 1318, which tells of the exorcisms performed by the priest Ryūyu 隆愉 at the imperial palace during the Kenchō era (1249–1256). After several failures, Ryūyu resorted to the Uga ritual, at which point snakes arrived from the ten directions and crowded the ritual area, scaring off the demons.[14]

The Tendai Synthesis

Like the Shingon *gumonji* 求聞持 ritual centered on the bodhisattva Kokūzō 虚空藏 (Skt. Ākāśagarbha), the Tendai Benzaiten ritual was originally intended for use in memorizing sūtras; it entailed visualizing Myōonten, with her *biwa,* against a background of caves, cliffs, and rivers (as described in the *Golden Light Sūtra*). All this changed with the Uga Benzaiten ritual as described in the *Keiran shūyōshū,* which was used not to memorize sūtras but to obtain worldly benefits (*genze riyaku* 現世利益). It seems that Kōshū was determined to elevate Benzaiten—or, rather, Uga Benzaiten—to the status of Myōonten. In describing Benzaiten's cultic sites, he lists Tenkawa first, as a site of "Jizō Benten," Itsukushima second, as a site of "Myōon Benzaiten," and Chikubushima third, as a site of "Kannon Benzaiten." Whereas Myōon Benzaiten is said to symbolize wisdom, Uga Benzaiten, as a transformation of Kannon, symbolizes (and brings about) happiness. According to Nanami Hiroaki, this image of Benzaiten served as a basis for the Nanto-bon 南都本 recension of the *Heike monogatari.* In the process, the *honji* of the Chikubushima deity shifted from Senju Kannon to Nyoirin Kannon, which had been made possible by Kōshū's identification of Benzaiten with Kannon. Other recensions of the *Heike monogatari* (e.g., the Sasaki-bon 佐々木本) did not inherit this identification.[15] Kōshū also tried to link the Tendai doctrinal interpretation of Benzaiten to her cultic and mythological aspects, but only with relative success, as evidenced by the discrepancy between the two chapters on Benzaiten in his *Keiran shūyōshū.*

As noted earlier, the cradle of the Uga Benzaiten cult was Mount Hiei. One of the earliest promoters of the cult was the Tendai priest Kōgei 皇慶 (a.k.a. Ikegami Ajari 池上阿闍梨, 977–1049), the presumed author of the *Origin Story of Enoshima (Enoshima engi* 江ノ島縁起). Kōgei is also credited with labeling Uga Benzaiten (or Ugajin) as a placenta deity (*ena kōjin* 胞衣荒神) and identifying her with both the pole star deity Myōken and Jūzenji 十禅師, one of the gods of Hie Shrine.[16] He is also reported to have had a vision of Oto Gohō 乙護法, the mountain god of Sefuri-san in northern Kyūshū, who would eventually become his protector and be included among Benzaiten's retinue as her lastborn (and favorite) child.[17]

The embryological aspect of Benzaiten was further developed in Shugendō. In the *Buchū hiden* 峰中秘伝, for instance, Benzaiten is described as the mother, and the bodhisattva Jizō as the father, of all beings: "The father brings from the upper world the yang spirit, which becomes a 'rough deity' (*aragami, kōjin* 荒神) and creates the five forms. The mother brings from the lower world the yin spirit, which becomes a deity of life and generates the flesh."[18]

Another important Tendai proponent of Uga Benzaiten was the Vinaya master Kenchū, a resident of Sannō-dō 山王堂 in Kamakura, who is said to have compiled the *Benzaiten shugi* 弁才天修儀 under the direct inspiration of Benzaiten.[19] According to legend, once, when Kenchū performed a Benzaiten ritual at Sannō-dō, a dragon emerged from the pond in front of the hall. After his death, Kenchū is said to have been reborn as Benzaiten's fifteenth attendant (namely, Oto Gohō).[20]

Kōshū and his disciple Unkai 運海 attempted to forge a synthesis between the doctrinal and mythological aspects of Benzaiten's manifestations. From the doctrinal standpoint, the main distinction was that between Myōonten and Uga Benzaiten. Kōshū chose to see them as one, and emphasized Benzaiten's dual nature. He mentions Kyūkai's 救海 criticism of Kenchū for emphasizing Uga Benzaiten at the expense of Myōonten: "Kenchū of Sannō-dō only knows Uga Benzai; he does not know Myōon Benzai."[21] As Nanami Hiroaki points out, Kyūkai's criticism shows that he found Kenchū's belief in Uga Benzaiten somewhat heterodox. In his criticism, Kyūkai mentions a passage quoted from a *Benzaiten saimon* 弁才天祭文 found at Inari Shrine. This text exhibits the Shingon combination of a Dakiniten ritual with the Inari cult. The identification of Uga Benzaiten with Inari Myōjin in Tendai presupposed the mediation of the Dakiniten ritual. The transformation of Dakiniten into Inari Myōjin, based on Shingon rituals, paved the way for this synthesis.

If such is indeed the background of Kyūkai's remark, the Uga Benzaiten ritual of Kenchū, too, must have been a joint performance of the Benzaiten and Dakiniten rituals. Judging from Kyūkai's words, one can infer that, even in Tendai (and in particular with Kenchū), the joint rituals of Uga Benzaiten and Dakiniten were important. It is significant that Kōshū, who was probably feeling more inclined toward Kenchū, felt obliged to mention Kyūkai's criticism. The intimate relationship between these two aspects of Benzaiten (which were sometimes perceived as distinct deities) can be inferred from the fact that Kōshū, when he speaks about Myōonten, ends up by endowing her with characteristics of Uga Benzaiten.

Kōshū's interpretation is typical of the chroniclers of Mount Hiei, who were straddling two interpretive traditions: a mythological (concrete) one and a cosmological/doctrinal (abstract) one. The classical mythology which they reinterpreted was permeated by the Chinese five-phase cosmological theory, and it was an already "disenchanted" *mytho-logy,* in which Tendai principles (Tendai's *logos*, as it were) conflicted with (but at times also reinforced) local beliefs (*mythos*). This may explain the structure of the Benzaiten section of the *Keiran shūyōshū,* which is pulled in two opposite directions: that of the demythologizing theories of Tendai scholasticism, influenced by Shingon doctrine and yin-yang thought, and that of local traditions, full of topographical *mirabilia.* This tension can be seen at work in the interpretation of Benzaiten as a snake: not only is she a symbol or an emanation of the water element, she can also become a real, potentially threatening snake.[22]

Although the institutional spread of Tendai throughout Japan (from Kunisaki in Kyūshū to Tsugaru in Tōhoku) and the influence of itinerant Tendai monks like Kōgei reinforced the coherence of that doctrinal and symbolic network, this process was never completed. Local beliefs and practices proved resistant to attempts at doctrinal integration and prevented the network from turning into a closed system. Instead it was transformed into a rhizome, with its own local dynamics reflecting specific places and social groups, as well as doctrinal, ritual, mythological, artistic, and psychological components.

The image of Uga Benzaiten developed further with the legend of En no Gyōja 役行者 (634–ca. 701), the founder of Shugendō. In the early versions of the legend, En no Gyōja's performance of austerities at Ōmine 大峰 causes three deities to appear successively in front of him: Benzaiten, Jizō, and Zaō Gongen 藏王権現.[23] In a later version, in which Shaka and Amida have replaced Benzaiten and Jizō, En no Gyōja seems unimpressed by their appearance, explaining that these two buddhas look too gentle to convert the hard-boiled Japanese, and that only Zaō's fierce appearance will do the trick. In the *Yamato Tenkawa Daibenzaiten engi* 大和天河大弁才天縁起, however, Benzaiten is by no means "nice." She appears to En no Gyōja in her living form, with a female body and three snake (or dragon) heads. Yet the vision is auspicious, as the stones surrounding them are transformed into jewels, and all other objects into treasures.[24] This awe-inspiring vision is reflected in the Tenkawa Benzaiten mandala, to which I will return.[25]

Benzaiten and the Jewel

In the *Keiran shūyōshū,* Benzaiten is associated with two triads of *honji:* the buddhas Śākyamuni (Shaka), Baiṣajyaguru (Yakushi), and Amitābha (Amida); and the bodhisattvas Ākāṣagarbha (Kokūzō), Kṣitigarbha (Jizō), and Maitreya (Miroku).[26] These triads reflect the Three Truths of Tendai, namely, the absolute, the relative, and the middle way. In the figure of Uga Benzaiten, however, it is yin-yang symbolism that becomes most prominent: she is said to symbolize the binary sets of heaven and earth, the two mandalas, and principle (*ri* 理) and knowledge (*chi* 智). She is a goddess of fortune, whose essence is the wish-fulfilling jewel. As Myōonten, she is the goddess of wisdom and eloquence, qualities common to all the buddhas. Her manifestation as a white snake is said to symbolize the six paths of rebirth, with the snake representing the three poisons or three evil destinies, and the color white, the three good destinies.[27] The sword in her right hand symbolizes the destruction of all things—in other words, the truth of emptiness—while the jewel in her left hand symbolizes the rebirth of all things—that is, the provisional truth. Her manifestations at Tenkawa, Itsukushima, and Chikubushima are symbolized by three jewels linked to form a triangular shape.[28] That triangular shape is further likened to the three dots that form the Sanskrit letter *i*, and the three eyes of the god Maheśvara (Śiva).

The interpretation of Benzaiten as the embodiment of a supreme metaphysical principle is typical of a general tendency toward abstraction in esoteric Buddhism.[29] A similar process is at work, for instance, in the transformation of the ghoulish *ḍākinī* into the ethereal goddess Dakiniten.[30] But this tendency hides the fact that the deity called Benzaiten was originally plural, resulting from the accretion of different deities, whose cults developed in situ—indeed, in the very different settings of seas, lakes, and mountains.

Nonduality and Ambivalence

The figure of Uga Benzaiten is marked by the same kind of ternary symbolism that we saw in the cases of Aizen, Nyoirin Kannon, and the wish-fulfilling jewel, and will encounter again with the hybrid deity known as the Three Devas. The jewel in Uga Benzaiten's left hand, the sword in her right hand, and the white snake (Ugajin) in her headgear symbolize the Three Truths and the taming of the three poisons (personified as three demons). An oral tradition adds that this image encapsulates the Tendai teachings on the Three Truths (*santai* 三諦) and the Three Contemplations (*sangan* 三觀).

The presence of this fundamental hermeneutic and perceptive grid in Tendai doctrine also explains why Benzaiten became the symbol of the Susiddhi realm (the Tendai synthesis of the Womb and Vajra realms). Like her *honji,* Nyoirin Kannon, and the wish-fulfilling jewel that symbolizes both, Benzaiten came to be seen as a preeminent expression of nonduality.[31] This is why the Sōji-in 総持院 on Mount Hiei, symbol of nonduality, is discussed in the Benzaiten chapter of the *Keiran shūyōshū* next to the so-called three luminaries (sun, moon, and stars), three powers (heaven, earth, and man), and three seed-letters (*a, vaṃ,* and *hūṃ*), all symbolized by the shapes of the three torii of Hie Shrine.[32] This ternary structure, however, was ultimately subverted by the image of the "living" Benzaiten. In the same way, the notion of the three poisons began to permeate the mythological forms of the gods of obstacles like a swarm of snakes—indeed, as emanations of the more concrete Ugajin, or Uga Benzaiten.

While this "new" Benzaiten emerged from within Tendai, it soon deviated from the image of that deity as established in Chinese esoteric Buddhism (Zhenyan 真言). Not surprisingly, Uga Benzaiten became the object of criticism on the part of Shingon monks despite (or because of) the fact that a similar hermeneutical and cultic drift was also taking place within Shingon.

Benzaiten's ambiguity as both provisional (*gonsha*) and "real" (*jissha*) became a particularly apt way to express the Tendai theory of fundamental awakening (*hongaku*). In its section on the living body (*shōjin* 生

身) of Benzaiten, the *Keiran shūyōshū* states that the bodies of dragons are replete with the three poisons. Because these poisons are the cause of people's drowning in the sea of birth and death, the dragons that symbolize them dwell at the bottom of the sea.[33] Although "real" entities (*jissha*) and "wild gods" (*kōjin*) are limited by their ignorance and other karmic impediments, it is precisely this aspect that explains why the paradoxical reality of fundamental awakening is better expressed in figures like them. Thus, according to Kōshū, "the deluded minds of dragon-beasts, as such, are the unconditioned, originally existing mental body—the body of immovable, unconditioned original enlightenment. The snake mind expresses the unconditioned." Ultimately, Kōshū argues, the complete body of unconditioned original enlightenment takes the form of a snake. This means that all the gods manifest themselves as snakes.[34]

Another type of ambivalence has to do with the idea that ritual efficacy increases in proportion to the risks taken in performing the ritual. Worshiping Benzaiten can thus be a form of playing with fire (or water, as the case may be). As a real and essentially demonic deity, she must be tamed, and ideally receive the Buddhist precepts. Only then will she become a protector of those precepts. When the deity is perceived as a provisional manifestation (*gonsha*), there is of course no need for that kind of ordination. Confirming Benzaiten's relationship with the precepts, Yamamoto Hiroko observes that Benzaiten played an important role in the transmission of the precepts (*kai kanjō* 戒灌頂, Skt. *śīla-abhiṣeka*) by the Tendai chroniclers. Indeed, the cult of Uga Benzaiten initially developed among these Vinaya specialists, one of whom was Kōshū.[35]

While attempting to allegorize Benzaiten as a *gonsha* and to integrate her into orthodox doctrinal networks, the *Keiran shūyōshū* allows oral traditions to speak for themselves, at the risk of subverting its classificatory attempts. That is, Kōshū strives to explain all the aspects of this deity in terms of Tendai doctrine, trying to fit Benzaiten into a Procrustean bed of esoteric teaching, but then goes on to report miscellaneous legends on dragons, snakes, and *nāgas*—local traditions that in their uncanny concreteness both revitalize and subvert his abstract model, and challenge the coherence he attempted to create in early parts of his work. The Benzaiten section, for example, ends with bizarre stories related to the living or "real" Benzaiten. Kōshū was not only a Tendai ideologue; he was also an ethnographer of sorts, who could not resist telling an interesting story, even if it sounded bizarre and did not contribute to his argument. All was grist to his mill, and that is why we are indebted to him.

In any case, these legends, in their raw form, constitute a precious document on medieval religiosity. Kōshū's inclusive approach was criticized in the Edo period by the Shingon monk and Vinaya master Jōgon 浄嚴 (1639–1702) in his *Daibenzaiten hiketsu* 大弁才天秘訣 (colophon dated 1713). In the name of Shingon orthodoxy, Jōgon also rejected all the Ugajin scriptures as mere apocrypha, and endeavored to return to the canonical Sarasvatī.[36] He dismissed in particular the motif of the fifteen *dōji,* which had come to play such a prominent role in Benzaiten's cult.[37] Indeed, judging from iconographic evidence, it was precisely that form of Benzaiten which attracted popular, devotional fervor, even if the deity's strange appearance raised some questions at times.

But the *Keiran shūyōshū* section on Benzaiten reveals another, deeper, tension. Benzaiten is at first exalted (and at the same time domesticated) and promoted to the rank of primordial deity: as Myōon Benzaiten, she is the primordial sound from which the sixteen vowels (symbolized by the sixteen *dōji*) of the Sanskrit alphabet emanate. As Uga Benzaiten, she is the primordial origin of all things, the "warp and woof of heaven and earth." In this way, her fearsome aspect is downplayed, and she becomes more abstract, more easily reintegrated into the cosmic order. At the same time, however, evil receives an ontological reality that it did not previously possess, for the primordial deity is also the source of the three poisons and of fundamental ignorance. The power that governs human life has some decidedly dark aspects; the association between defilement and enlightenment, based on the doctrine of fundamental awakening, has perverse effects. After the medieval period, however, Benzaiten's ambiguity was increasingly downplayed until she was reduced to her auspicious function and eventually reintegrated as one of the Seven Gods of Fortune (Shichifukujin 七福神).

TERRITORIAL EXPANSION

As Benzaiten's popularity grew, new cultic centers passed under her aegis, many of which had traditionally been dedicated to water deities. Depending on one's viewpoint, the story of Benzaiten can be understood as that of a foreign water deity who, by successfully merging with Japanese deities, eventually became increasingly chthonian, to the point of becoming autochthonous. Alternatively, one could instead focus on local deities which, by co-opting a foreign deity (Buddhist or otherwise), succeeded in raising their status to that of national deities, so to speak. In either case, we should note that Benzaiten was usually worshiped in caves, on mountains, by rivers, or on small islands (Fig. 5.11) like Itsukushima (a.k.a. Miyajima, near Hiroshima), where the main shrine, isolated from the mainland by the tide, was said to be the palace of the *nāga* king.

At Tenkawa, Benzaiten's abode shifts from an island to a mountain setting, although the site is still close to water and was said to have originally been a lake. The mountain is called Misen 弥山, after the cosmic mountain, Mount Sumeru. At Chikubushima, analogies are drawn between Mount Hiei and Misen, and Lake Biwa and the sea. The combination of mountains and waters symbolizes the union of yin and yang,

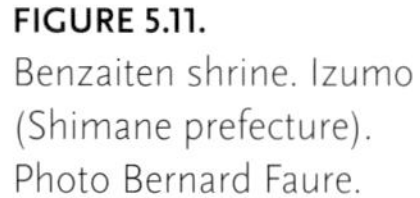

FIGURE 5.11.
Benzaiten shrine. Izumo (Shimane prefecture). Photo Bernard Faure.

and the esoteric fusion of the Womb and Vajra realms. The same is true at Itsukushima, another site combining an island and a mountain (also called Misen). According to Kōshū, Kūkai banned women from this mountain. Like Sakadono at Ise, it was associated with the elixir of immortality, and was said to be the gate to the palace of the immortals (J. Horai, Ch. Penglai).[38]

Often, these cultic centers came to be linked by the discovery (or creation) of kin relationships between their respective tutelary deities. Kōshū goes one step further: using the symbolism of the jewel, he argues that these centers were linked not only conceptually but also physically. The *Keiran shūyōshū* lists Tenkawa, Itsukushima, and Chikubushima as the three pure lands of Benzaiten, and claims that the caves found at these three sites are physically linked by subterranean passages (like Daoist grotto-heavens), forming a triangular network, which is symbolized by Benzaiten's three jewels (Fig. 5.12). Kōshū futher asserts that all caves are Benzaiten's pure land and that the goddess sometimes dwells on mountains to express the exalted nature of her "true essence" (*honji*), and at the bottom of the ocean, at other times, to express the depth of her concentration.[39]

In his Benzaiten chapter (as well as in two other chapters), Kōshū describes Japan as a one-pronged *vajra* with Lake Biwa at its center (Fig. 5.13). He identifies the five parts of the *vajra*—the center plus the cardinal directions—with the five sections of the Vajra Realm mandala, and with the five great shrines: Hie 日吉 (Sannō 山王) in Ōmi (center, Buddha section), Ise in Kinki (south, Jewel section), Sumiyoshi 住吉 in Settsu

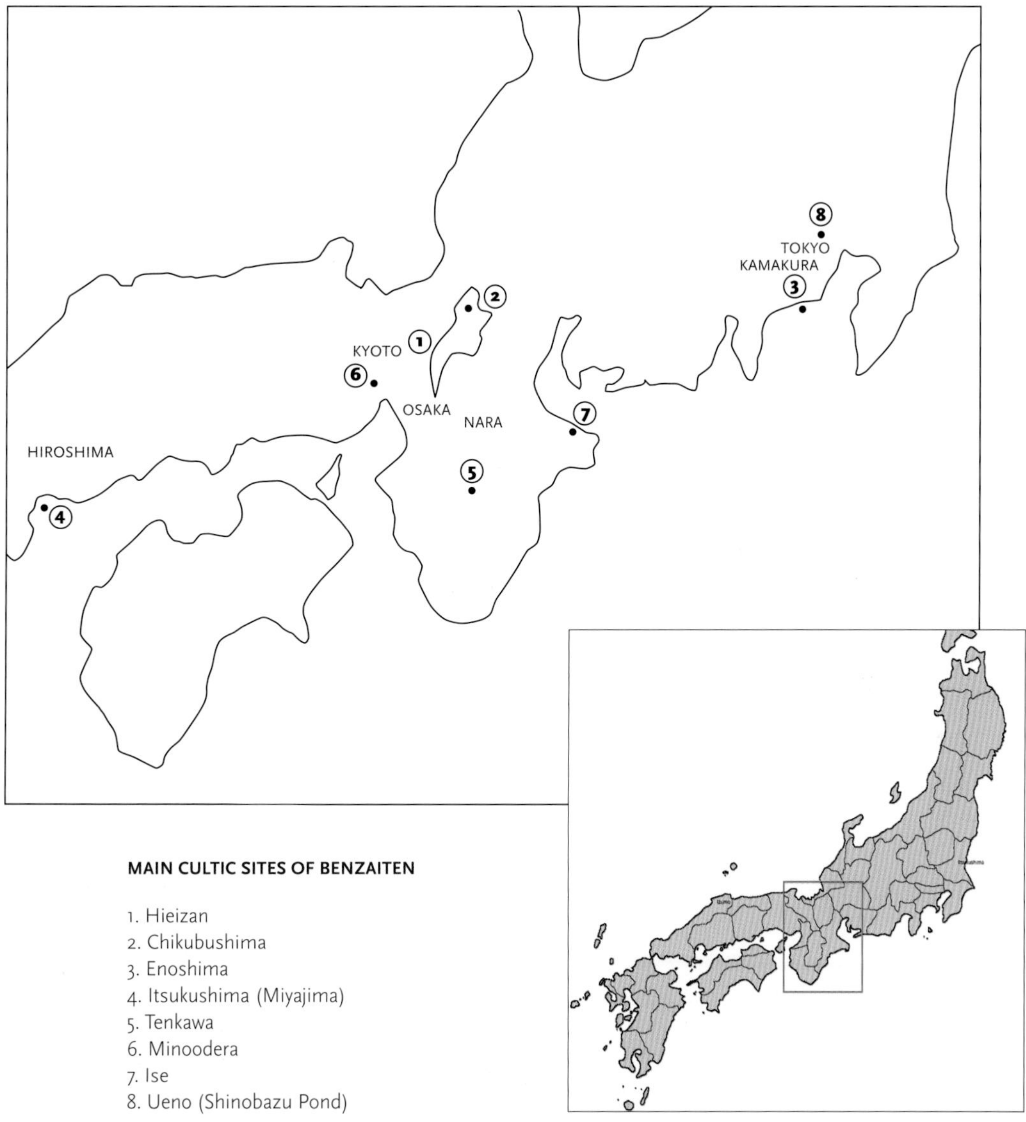

MAIN CULTIC SITES OF BENZAITEN

1. Hieizan
2. Chikubushima
3. Enoshima
4. Itsukushima (Miyajima)
5. Tenkawa
6. Minoodera
7. Ise
8. Ueno (Shinobazu Pond)

(west, Lotus section), Kehi 気比 in Echizen (north, Karma section), and Suwa 諏訪 in Shinano (east, Vajra section).[40] Here Kōshū is drawing on several maps, attributed to the priest Gyōki 行基 (668–749), that circulated during the medieval period and depicted Japan as a one-pronged *vajra.* Only six are currently extant, and they bear the inscription: "The country of Japan is shaped like the point of a one-pronged *vajra.* This is why Buddhism continues to flourish. The shape resembles that of a wish-fulfilling jewel (*cintāmaṇi*), therefore [Japan] is blessed with such treasures as gold, silver, copper, and iron; and the five kinds of cereals are harvested in abundance."[41]

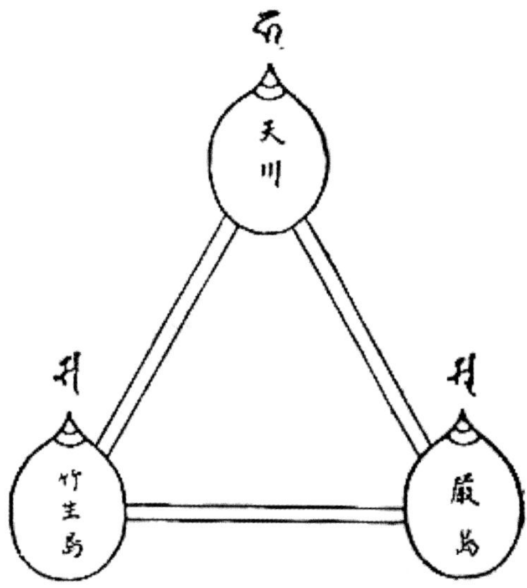

FIGURE 5.12. Benzaiten's three jewels (clockwise from top): Tenkawa, seed-letter *ha;* Itsukushima, seed-letter *a;* Chikubushima, seed-letter *sa. Keiran shūyōshū, T.* 76, 2410: 625b.

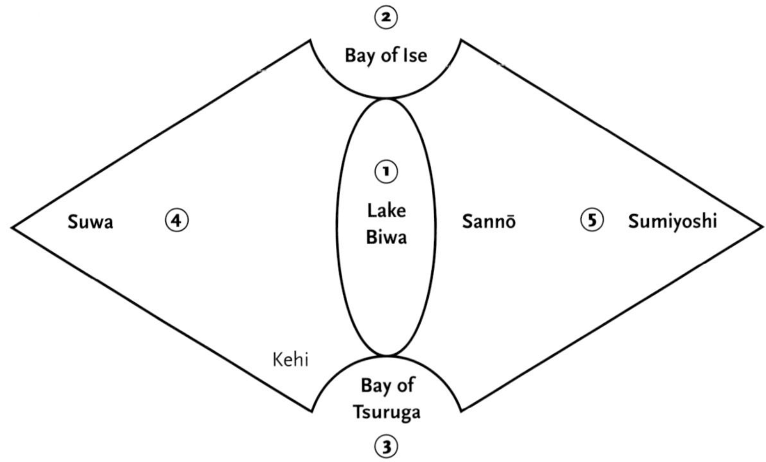

FIGURE 5.13. Japan as a one-pronged *vajra. Keiran shūyōshū, T.* 76, 2410: 626b.

SITE	MANDALA (BUDDHA-FAMILIES)	SHRINE/DEITY
1. Biwa Lake (Center)	Buddha	Sannō
2. Ise Bay (South)	Jewel	Ise (Amaterasu)
3. Tsuruga Bay (North)	Karma	Kehi
4. Suwa (East)	Vajra	Suwa
5. Sumiyoshi (West)	Lotus	Sumiyoshi

These maps reflect the medieval claim that Japan, far from being a small peripheral country in a Buddhist universe centered on India, was the "fundamental land of Dainichi" (a meaning derived from reading the phrase Dai 大 Nippon 日本 *koku* 国 as Dainichi 大日 *honkoku* 本国), the cradle of esoteric Buddhism. Japan is also described as a wish-fulfilling jewel and as the Vajra Realm mandala.[42] The connection between Japan's own understanding of its place in the world and Benzaiten was based largely on the belief that Japan was protected (but also threatened) by a giant dragon (or catfish), a belief that also led to the use of these maps as talismans against earthquakes, a natural phenomenon thought to be caused by the movement of this giant beast.

In this country lying, as it were, in a dragon's bosom, dragons (and Benzaiten) were worshiped in a number of power spots. The original cultic center for Benzaiten was Mount Hiei itself, where Benzaiten was worshiped at each of the so-called three pagodas (Eastern Pagoda, Western Pagoda, and Yokawa 横川). Among them, the main one was the Benzaiten shrine at the Eastern Pagoda, near Mudōji 無動寺 (a temple dedicated to Fudō), and founded by Sōō 相応 (831–918). This particular Benzaiten was (and still is) worshiped as a dragon, and her shrine is located against a cliff.

At the eastern foot of Mount Hiei, Benzaiten was also worshiped at two of Hie Shrine's oratories: the Iwataki 岩滝 and Seijo 聖女 shrines. Records found in the *Hie hongi* 日吉本記, a work attributed to Kenchū, attest to a Benzaiten cult at Iwataki Shrine as early as 1235.[43] It was in front of this shrine that the founder of the Shinshū sect of Japanese Pure Land Buddhism, Shinran 親鸞 (1173–1263), is said to have vowed to spread the Dharma. Behind the shrine, a "stone of manifestation" (*hyōgoseki* 影向石) can be seen, where Benzaiten is said to have manifested herself as a white snake. Her cult at the Seijo Shrine is said to go back to a dream of the Tendai abbot Son'i 尊意 (866–940), in which a noble lady appeared, declaring that she was the Inari deity and that her *honji* was Nyoirin.[44] Jihen 慈編 (fl. 14th century), a contemporary of Kōshū, further identifies her with Ugajin and with the Ise deity Toyouke in his *Tenchi jingi shinchin yōki* (1333).[45] By Ugajin, he clearly means Uga Benzaiten, and therefore links her with Inari and Nyoirin Kannon. This is precisely what Kōshū was attempting to do. The Edo-period *Hie Sannō Gongen chishinki* 日吉山王権現知新記 retains the identity between Uga Benzaiten and Nyoirin, but fails to mention the name of Ugajin, which by that time may have smacked of heterodoxy.[46] Thus, the cult of Uga Benzaiten was apparently disseminated as part of Sannō shintō by Tendai practitioners, from Mount Hiei to Chikubushima and Mount Inari (on the southern outskirts of Kyoto), and further on to Enoshima (near Kamakura), Minō (near Osaka), and Tenkawa (near Yoshino).

Chikubushima

Chikubushima is a small island in the northern part of Lake Biwa, in modern-day Shiga prefecture.[47] The development of a Benzaiten cult on that island came about as a result of the growing influence of Mount Hiei. A commentary quoted by the *Keiran shūyōshū* states: "Ōmi province has a numinous island. Because it is the dwelling place of Benzaiten 'in the flesh' (lit. in her 'living body,' *shōjin*), the Buddhist teachings have prospered on Mount Hiei."[48] Chikubushima was also likened to the island of the river goddess Sarasvatī, mentioned in the *Avataṃsaka Sūtra.* Even before the advent of Buddhism, it was a cultic site, appearing to worshipers as the island of the immortals (Ch. Penglai, J. Hōrai). As the *Heike monogatari* puts it:

> Even thus must have been the appearance of Mount Hōrai, the unattained goal of those boys, girls, and magicians dispatched by Shihuangdi and Wudi to seek the elixir of immortality, who frittered away their lives in ships on the vast ocean, pledged not to return without having reached their destination. A sūtra says, "In the world of men, there is a lake, and in that lake, emerging from the bowels of the earth, there is a crystal isle where heavenly maidens dwell." This was that very island.[49]

The ancient tutelary deity of the island was a goddess named Asaihime. Under Tendai influence, her place was taken by Myōon Benzaiten, initially. According to tradition, a heavenly maiden once appeared to Emperor Shōmu (r. 724–749), who ordered Gyōki to build a shrine there. The identity of this "heavenly maiden" became clear only in 834 when the Tendai priest Ennin, who had been suffering from an eye ailment, had a vision of her. In his dream, she gave him a remedy for his failing eyesight and told him that she was the Benzaiten of Chikubushima.[50] By the thirteenth century, however, the main deity of the shrine had become Uga Benzaiten, despite the traditional association of the lake with the *biwa* or lute, the favorite musical instrument of the two-armed Myōonten.[51]

Because the island was under the jurisdiction of the Tendai school, many eminent Tendai priests, beginning with Saichō and Ennin, are said to have visited it and to have obtained visions of the goddess. The list given by the *Keiran shūyōshū* actually begins with En no Ozunu 役小角 (better known as En no Gyōja), the legendary founder of Shugendō. At the turn of the tenth century, the Tendai abbot Ryōgen 良源 (a.k.a. Jie Daishi 慈恵大師 or Ganzan Daishi 元三大師, 912–985) is said to have initiated the famous Lotus assemblies (*renge-e* 蓮花会) of the sixth month—water festivals reminiscent of the dragon boat festivals of China.[52] According to Kōshū's rather cryptic explanation, these assemblies "entail the making of a stately boat in the shape of a big bird [presumably a phoenix]. Upon completion of the ceremonies, this boat is capsized so that it sinks to the bottom of the lake."[53]

Chikubushima is replete with legends of snakes and dragons. The Shingon novice Shinzei 信西 allegedly found dragon's eggs, described as "Benzaiten's living body," while swimming under moonlight in a pool on the island.[54] The deity of Chikubushima was said to be a catfish (*namazu* 鯰) or "fish dragon."[55] In Kōshū's account:

> According to a past transmission, a great catfish circled (or coiled around) the island seven times. This was a manifestation of the seven Yakushi buddhas. Mount Hiei and Lake Biwa represent Mount Sumeru and the Great Sea, respectively. The two parts—yin and yang, wisdom and blessing—are the two ornaments [on the corresponding mandala]. Chikubushima is in truth referred to as the island of wisdom and fortune (Chi-fuku-shima).[56]

It is hard to imagine such a monster (said to be 1,000 *jō* 丈 in length—1 *jō* being roughly equivalent to 3 meters) circling the island seven times in the shallow Lake Biwa. At any rate, the numerological symbolism allows Kōshū to interpret the event as a manifestation of the seven Yakushi buddhas, although there is no obvious relationship between Benzaiten and the Healing Buddha (Skt. Baisajyaguru)—apart from the fact that the latter was the *honzon* of Enryakuji.

Kōshū's "past transmission" may have been the *Chikubushima engi* 竹生島縁起, the origin story in which a huge catfish is said to coil itself around the base of the island seven times. The story continues: from the summit of the island, a white snake then descends to the water's edge and lowers its head to drink. At that instant the catfish lifts its head to the surface, takes the snake's head in its mouth, and pulls the snake into the water.[57]

A variant appears in the Nō play *Chikubushima.* At the beginning of that play, a courtier comes on pilgrimage to the island, and a shrine attendant reveals to him the island's sacred treasures. According to Royall Tyler, the play's theme (and the island's mystery) is the conjunction or nonduality between Benzaiten, who descends from the heights of the rocky island, and the dragon god, who ascends from the (shallow) depths of Lake Biwa. This mystery of the island is revealed to the courtier by the shrine attendant when he jumps off a high rock into the lake, whence he emerges sneezing—thereby demonstrating that above and below are nondual.[58]

As a dragon, Benzaiten is the protector of the center, but she is also, in her catfish form, the power that threatens the center by causing earthquakes.[59] This motif of the catfish was already present at Chikubushima in the medieval period, but its elaboration occurred later, during the Edo period.[60] The island came to be seen as a kind of *omphalos,* a place that could not be shaken by earthquakes, because of the *kaname-ishi,* the erected stone that was believed to pin down the head of the earthquake-causing catfish or dragon.[61] As one text puts it: "This Chikubushima is a diamond rock coming out of the diamond wheel (*kongō rinsai* 金剛輪際)."[62]

Itsukushima

The main cultic center of Benzaiten, as a water deity, was the island of Itsukushima (present-day Miyajima in Aki province), near Hiroshima, on the Inland Sea. The Itsukushima Shrine was originally dedicated to the three goddesses of the Munakata 宗像 Shrine in northern Kyūshū, the daughters of the mythic siblings Amaterasu and Susanoo. One of them, Ichikishima-hime 市杵嶋姫, was said to have come to Itsukushima island by boat, and to have become the eponymous deity of the place. In the *Engishiki* 延喜式, the site is called Itsukishima Shrine. The ophidian nature of that deity is described in the origin story of Itsukushima, noted in his diary by a Zen priest of Shōkokuji 相国寺, Zuikei Shūhō 瑞溪周鳳 (1392–1473), writing toward the middle of the fifteenth century: "At the time of Empress Suiko 推古 (r. 593–638), an attractive woman arrived by boat. The ancestor of the Itsukushima clan asked her where she came from. She said: 'I have looked at the sea, there was no cave like the one on this island; I have therefore wanted to leave my traces there.' Saying this, the woman changed into a great snake."[63]

The relationships between Benzaiten and the Itsukushima deity appear clearly in the origin story of Itsukushima, whose gist is as follows: After falling in love with an image of the goddess Lakṣmī (Kichijōten), an Indian king asks for the hand of the princess Ashibiki no miya, the most beautiful woman in the kingdom. During the king's absence, the other consorts, jealous of her, accuse her of adultery, and she is eventually executed. Owing to the intercession of a holy man, Ashibiki returns to life and takes revenge on the other consorts. She then leaves India by boat and eventually lands in the province of Aki in Japan, where she comes to be worshiped as the *kami* of Itsukushima. At the end of the tale, this *kami* is revealed to be identical with Benzaiten. This *engi,* which belongs to the medieval *honjimono* type, is just part of a symbolic network linking Benzaiten with the Itsukushima deity, the *nāga* maiden of the *Lotus Sūtra,* and *nāgas,* dragons and water deities in general.[64]

The Itsukushima Shrine was a tutelary shrine for the Heike clan, famous after the dream that Kiyomori had during a night vigil there in 1178, in which he received a dagger as a token from the deity. After the Meiji Restoration, the two deities (Itsukushima Myōjin and Benzaiten) were separated, and Benzaiten is now worshiped in a Buddhist temple adjacent to the shrine.

Enoshima

Enoshima is often paired with Chikubushima. If Buddhism flourished on Mount Hiei owing to the Chikubushima deity, it prospered in Kamakura owing to the Enoshima deity. Both were identified with Benzaiten. Actually, it is the Benzaiten of Chikubushima which Minamoto no Yoritomo, at the demand of the priest Mongaku 文覺 (1139–1203), is said to have invited at Enoshima in 1182.[65] Two other important cultic centers developed in Kamakura itself, the so-called Zeniarai Benzaiten 銭洗弁才天 and the Benzaiten cave (Benten-kutsu 弁天窟) at Hasedera.[66] Another famous image of the goddess is preserved at Tsurugaoka Hachiman Shrine, with an inscription dated 1266.[67]

Enoshima is famous for its caves, the traditional dwellings of dragons.[68] According to the *Enoshima engi emaki* 江島縁起絵巻, the island of Enoshima in Sagami Bay resulted from an earthquake in 552, during the reign of Emperor Kinmei 欽明. At that time, a heavenly maiden appeared in the clouds and descended on it. She was the third daughter of the dragon king of Munetsunō(chi) 無熱悩(池) Pond (also called Munecchi 無熱池), and the elder sister of King Yama. She seduced and tamed the five-headed dragon of the Tsumura 津村 Lake, who had devastated the area. Subsequently, his misdeeds ended, and the mountain called Tatsunokuchi emerged. After becoming the "bright" deity of Enoshima (Enoshima Myōjin), Benzaiten appeared to a series of eminent ascetics and monks who subsequently fabricated images of her.

This cult is said to go back to an oracle given by the deity in 543. The oracle commanded that the local people build a shrine in the cave on the southern cliff of the island and perform two rituals there every year. According to another tradition, a man by the name of E no chōja 江ノ長者 (headman of E village) lived in Sagami province with his wife, with whom he had sixteen children. In the neighborhood was a very deep lake in which a five-headed dragon lived. Every year, this dragon devoured one of the couple's children. When they had only one child left, Benzaiten, out of compassion, vowed to become the dragon's consort and to placate him.[69] She created an island called E-no-shima. Thereafter, many eminent Tendai priests and Shugendō practitioners came to perform austerities on that island, and they all obtained visions of the goddess or of her acolytes.[70]

Although today two images of Benzaiten, one with two arms (Myōon Benzaiten) and one with eight (Uga Benzaiten), are enshrined side by side in the Enoshima Shrine, this is a recent arrangement. The eight-armed statue was allegedly brought to Enoshima at the request of Mongaku, on the occasion of rituals for the subjugation of Fujiwara no Hidehira 藤原秀衡.[71] The two-armed statue, popularly known as the "naked Benten," is made of colored wood. She has the breasts and genitalia of a young girl. She was initially adorned with sumptuous clothes and employed in a ritual whose specifics have long been forgotten. There are other examples of naked Benten, albeit not as famous.[72] Apparently, most of them were stripped of their clothes (and their mystery) during the Edo period, when the figure of Benzaiten, losing its dark side and its disturbing ambiguity, gradually became that of the ideal maiden. The kind of voyeurism to which they are subjected, in a country where, contrary to practices in India, deities have always been fully clothed, is perhaps a sign of the times and a sad testimony to the decline of medieval deities.

Tenkawa

Surprisingly, the *Keiran shūyōshū* presents Tenkawa 天河 as the first and foremost cultic site of Benzaiten. It claims that this ranking is a "very profound" esoteric teaching, due to the fact that "Tenkawa in Yoshino is [the dwelling place of] Jizō Benten 地藏弁天," i.e., the Benzaiten who has Jizō as her *honji*.[73] Actually, Tenkawa is usually not included on lists of Benzaiten's three most famous cultic centers (most often they are Chikubushima, Enoshima, and Itsukushima), and it comes last in an expanded list of five Benzaiten sites (consisting of the above three, plus Kinkazan 金華山 and Tenkawa). Sometimes, a sixth one (Asama Shrine on Mount Fuji) is added. Thus, it is strange that in a Tendai text like the *Keiran shūyōshū* Tenkawa moves to the first rank, particularly since this shrine was a dependent of Kōfukuji, not of Mount Hiei. From an orthodox Tendai viewpoint, the main cultic center had to be Chikubushima, because of its proximity to Mount Hiei. But Kōshū was apparently influenced in his ranking by the *Kinpusen himitsuden* 金峰山秘密伝 of the Shingon priest Monkan. The *Keiran shūyōshū* quotes a "Record of Tenkawa," according to which there once was in Tenkawa a great lake in which two dragons lived: a male, who was evil, and a female, who was good. The evil dragon was eventually killed by the gods Ōnamuchi 大己貴 (or 大穴牟遅) and Sukunamuchi 小名牟遅. When it fell into the lake, the water rose up to the sky, congealing to form a great mountain, known today as Tenkawa (Heavenly River, that is, the Milky Way). The good dragon was none other than Benzaiten, and the evil one was her husband, the great king Tokuzen 徳善, and they had fifteen children.[74]

Unlike the other major cultic sites of Benzaiten, Tenkawa, which was regarded as the inner sanctum (Oku-no-in 奥の院) of Yoshino, is not located on an island, but at the bottom of a mountain called Misen 弥山 (an abbreviation of Shumisen 須弥山, or Mount Sumeru). This Misen was perceived by esoteric Buddhist monks as the point of contact of the Vajra Realm and Womb Realm mandalas, which correspond to the Yoshino and Kumano regions, respectively. That mountain and the deity that dwells on it, Benzaiten, therefore symbolize their nonduality.

In the *Kinpusen himitsuden* by Monkan, it is said that the shrine of this Benzaiten is called Yoshino-Kumano Shrine (Yoshino-Kumano-gu

吉野熊野宮) because it is located between Yoshino and Kumano. Furthermore, this Benzaiten is the essence of the Susiddhi realm, which symbolizes the union of man and woman and the nonduality of the Womb and Vajra mandalas,[75] and brings prosperity and longevity (i.e., the seven felicities).[76]

Kōshū argues that the Tenkawa Benzaiten is the most fundamental manifestation of the deity, and that Tenkawa's origin is anterior to that of her other cultic sites.[77] In order to explain why this Benzaiten dwells not on an island but on a mountain, Kōshū distinguishes between two aspects of Benzaiten—the earthly (or aquatic) and the heavenly—and divides the six sacred sites into two groups, the "insular" and the "mountainous" sites.[78] The association of Tenkawa with Shugendō explains this. The Tenkawa tradition, with its devotion to a "mountain-dwelling" Benzaiten, reflects the influence of Shugendō on the development of Benzaiten's legend.[79]

Although the cult of Benzaiten as a protective deity of Ōmine is traditionally traced to the legend of En no Gyōja and to Kūkai's alleged visit to that site, in fact the origins of this cult can only be traced back to the early Kamakura period.[80] The Vinaya master Eison reportedly made a pilgrimage to Tenkawa Shrine. During the Nanbokuchō period (1334–1392), which saw retired emperor Go-Daigo take refuge in Yoshino, this shrine naturally took the side of his Southern Court. After the reconciliation, it flourished owing to the resumption of pilgrimages. During the Muromachi period, Kōfukuji took over its administration.

With the radical changes in the iconographic image of Tenkawa Benzaiten during the Muromachi period, the shrine's function also gradually changed. Because of its growing emphasis on worldly benefits, the number of pilgrimages increased.[81] The Tenkawa guides (*oshi* 御師), like those of Ise and Kumano, traveled throughout Japan and expanded their shrine's economic base. They distributed talismans, whose popularity probably explains Tenkawa's temporary inclusion on the list of Japan's three main Benzaiten sites (along with Chikubushima and Itsukushima).

During the Muromachi period, musical and theatrical representations were performed in honor of the goddess at Tenkawa, and later on, a Nō troupe was founded there. A Nō mask, allegedly carved in 1430 by Zeami's son Kanze Motomasa 観世元雅 (d. 1432) as an ex-voto to Benzaiten is still preserved at the shrine. This period of prosperity came to an end when the shrine was destroyed by fire in 1586.

Minō

The influence of Shugendō is also conspicuous in the origin story of Minoodera 箕面寺 in Settsu, on the outskirts of modern-day Osaka. Here again, Benzaiten is worshiped at the heart of a mountain, near a waterfall, and not on an island.[82] As the legend goes, when En no Gyōja first ascended that mountain, he was initiated by the bodhisattva Ryūju 竜樹

FIGURE 5.14. *(Opposite)* Benzaiten and her fifteen attendants. Muromachi period, 14th–15th century. Hanging scroll, ink, color and gold on silk. Museum of Fine Arts, Boston.

(Skt. Nāgārjuna) into the secret topography of the place, and was led to the palace of King Tokuzen 徳善. The latter appeared to him with his consort Benzaiten and their fifteen children. En no Gyōja subsequently built a hall in which he enshrined the images of Ryūju, Benzaiten, King Tokuzen, and the fifteen *dōji* as protectors.[83] Afterwards, as En no Gyōja continued his practice of ascesis near the waterfall, he had a vision of a wrathful eight-armed, eight-faced Kōjin, who offered to protect him.[84]

This origin story is closely related to that of the nearby Katsuoji 勝尾寺, which was a stronghold of Kōjin, particularly the form known as Kojima Kōjin, which came to be worshiped in the Kojima-ryū 小島流 after a vision recorded by the monk Shinkō 真興 (a.k.a. Kojima Shōnin 小島上人, 934–1004). This probably explains why, in some Benzaiten mandalas, Kojima Kōjin appears among the acolytes of Benzaiten. In a number of sources, Benzaiten and Kōjin are seen as two faces of the same divine power, and they serve as the media through which that power relates to good and evil people.

Ise

Another stronghold of Benzaiten was Ise, on the Kinki peninsula. Benzaiten was present at both the Inner and the Outer Shrines even though it was the deity of the Outer Shrine, Toyouke, who is usually associated with Benzaiten, while the deity of the Inner Shrine, Amaterasu, is associated with the fox and with Dakiniten.

In a Ryōbu shintō text of the Watarai 度会 family, the *Kōko zōtō hishō* 高倉藏等秘抄, one of the caves of Mount Takakura 高倉, behind the Outer Shrine, is compared to Ama no Iwato 天岩戸, the Heavenly Rock Cave in which Amaterasu hid herself. It is also said to symbolize the Womb and Diamond Realm mandalas. Its "divine body" (*shintai* 神体), Uga Benzaiten, was worshiped on the day of the snake, allegedly since the eleventh century. This cult, mixing elements of nascent Shintō, yin-yang theory, and star worship (centered on the bodhisattva Myōken), remained popular well into the Edo period.[85]

At the Outer Shrine, Benzaiten was said to be the protecting deity of Sakadono 酒殿, a building consecrated to Toyouke. Next to (or above) other sacred sites of Benzaiten, Sakadono is said to be the most secret dwelling place of Benzaiten.[86] In the *Toyouke kōtaijin gochinza hongi* 豊受皇太神御鎮座本紀, we read that the protector of the Tsuki no mikura 調御倉, a pavilion attached to Sakadono, is a white dragon, a statement that immediately evokes Benzaiten. Obviously Uga Benzaiten, owing to her name, came to overlap with Uka no mitama, the deity worshiped at the Outer Shrine, and especially at the granary formed by the Sakadono and Tsuki no mikura buildings.[87] We recall the legend (a variant of the Hagoromo motif) by which Sakadono traces its origin to a heavenly maiden. This heavenly maiden came to be identified with Benzaiten.

At the Inner Shrine, the so-called Heart Pillar (*shin no mihashira* 心御柱), a small pillar partly buried in the ground, is a kind of *axis mundi* symbolizing Mount Sumeru, and below it lies a white snake that is none other than Benzaiten.[88] The notion of the Heart Pillar as a kind of *omphalos* also calls to mind Chikubushima, said to be the unmoving center of Japan. As noted earlier, another *axis mundi,* Mount Misen (i.e., the Mount Sumeru of Indian lore) above Tenkawa, was the abode of Benzaiten.[89] As we have seen, Benzaiten has been said to dwell on or near a number of other mountains called Misen (in Itsukushima, Tenkawa, and so on). The relationship between Benzaiten and Mount Sumeru also links her with the two *nāga* kings Nanda and Upananda, who in traditional Buddhist cosmology are coiled around and protect the sacred mountain. In medieval Japan these two *nāga* kings often appeared in the context of relic worship, in which they were usually depicted protecting the stūpa-reliquary, which symbolizes Mount Sumeru.

ICONOGRAPHY

Benzaiten's Entourage

Most of the painted representations of Uga Benzaiten extant today date to the fourteenth and fifteenth centuries. In them, Benzaiten, clad in blue, stands on a rock, facing sideways; her stature is majestic and of a size that could well fill the entire island (Chikubushima) that floats above and behind her, in the top part of the picture (Figs. 5.14 and 5.22). The lower part of the picture is usually divided in two by a stream that flows toward a lake or sea. On the banks of that stream stand the fifteen *dōji,* as well as several acolytes of the goddess, usually Daikokuten and Bishamonten, but sometimes Dakiniten, Kojima Kōjin, and others as well. This representation seems to have been inspired by the depiction of Sarasvatī in the *Golden Light Sūtra,* where she is said to dwell in caves or near rivers.

The *dōji* are usually carrying offerings, and one of them (Gyūba Dōji 牛馬童子) pulls an ox and a horse, another (Sensha Dōji 船車童子) a boat and cart. In the catalogue *Shinbutsu shūgō* 神佛習合, four of the *dōji* seen in fig. 183 hold musical instruments.[90] Fig. 184 shows a frontal view of Benzaiten, flanked by the fifteen *dōji,* as well as by Bishamonten, Daikokuten, and Kojima Kōjin on the left, and Dakiniten, Kichijōten, and Shōten on the right. Fig. 185 shows Benzaiten seated on a lotus atop a cliff, under a red torii. Around the torii's pillars, two dragons are coiled, emphasizing the dragon-like and jewel-like aspects of Benzaiten's nature (dragons usually protect the wish-fulfilling jewel, the symbol of nonduality). Above her are the sun and moon, a variant of the same motif. She is also flanked by two old men who hold a kind of scepter (*shaku*). The one on the left looks like an underworld official, the one on the right, judging from the fact that a white snake coils around his head, is an anthropomorphic representation of Ugajin.

An interesting painting featured in a recent Kanazawa bunko exhibition shows a "running Daikokuten" (Hashiri Daikokuten 走り大黒天), seen in profile, carrying a huge round bag on his back.[91] In the golden disk formed by the bag, Benzaiten is seated, flanked by the fifteen *dōji* and a fox-riding Dakiniten. Fig. 8 in the same catalogue shows Benzaiten wearing a helmet (instead of the usual diadem), against a background of three mountains (one of them possibly Misen, above Tenkawa). She is surrounded by her fifteen youthful attendants and Daikokuten. In front of her (at the lower center), a dragon offers her a jewel.

All the paintings discussed so far represent Benzaiten as a heavenly maiden. The Tenkawa Benzaiten mandala, in which Benzaiten is depicted as a hybrid deity (half-woman, half-snake), will be discussed later. Finally, Uga Benzaiten with her fifteen attendants was often represented in small votive pictures and portable shrines (*zushi* 厨子), several exemplars of which can be found in Western ethnographic museums, such as those in Vienna, Munich, and New York.

The Fifteen Attendants

The fifteen *dōji* came to play an important role in the representation of Benzaiten. (See Figs. 5.15–5.22.) They first appear in an apocryphal sūtra, the *Uga daranikyō* 宇賀陀羅尼經. Initially, they were not regarded as protectors of guilds but seem to have been perceived as individual protectors (*gohō dōji* 護法童子). In Monkan's *Kinpusen himitsuden* 金峰山秘密伝,

FIGURE 5.15. Benzaiten and her fifteen attendants. Muromachi period, 15th century. Hanging scroll, color on silk. Ichigami jinja, Yōkaichi City (Shiga prefecture).

FIGURE 5.16. Benzaiten and her fifteen attendants. Muromachi period, 15th–16th century. Hanging scroll, ink, color and gold on silk. Art Gallery of New South Wales, Sydney.

for example, Zaō Gongen is surrounded by the eight great Kongō Dōji 金剛童子 (Skt. Vajrakumāra) and fifteen youthful servant spirits when he finally reveals himself to the ascetic En no Gyōja.[92]

The fifteen attendants are said to be the foremost among the 508,000 youths (*dōji*) that form Benzaiten's retinue.[93] Last among these fifteen but not least, Sensha Dōji is actually a *primus inter pares*. According to

FIGURE 5.17. Benzaiten and her fifteen attendants. Muromachi period, 14th century. Hanging scroll, color on silk. Senshōji, Osaka.

FIGURE 5.18. Benzaiten and her fifteen attendants (under torii). Edo period. Sheet, ink on paper. University Art Museum, Kyoto City University of Arts. *BZS* 2214.

FIGURE 5.19. Benzaiten and her fifteen attendants. Edo period. Sheet, ink on paper. University Art Museum, Kyoto City University of Arts. *BZS* 2215.

FIGURE 5.20. Benzaiten (on fox and dragon) and her fifteen attendants. Edo period. Sheet, ink on paper. University Art Museum, Kyoto City University of Arts. *BZS* 2216.

Kōshū, he is the last-born child of Benzaiten, Oto Gohō 乙護法, who served initially as the protecting deity of Sefuri-san 背振山 in northern Kyūshū. Oto Gohō is a kind of *shikigami* 式神 or helper spirit.[94] Kōshū retells a legend about an Indian king found in the *Sefuri-san engi* 背振山縁起. When the youngest of his fifteen children disappears, the king asks the bodhisattva Ryūju 龍樹 (Skt. Nāgārjuna) to find him, and Ryūju, entering *samādhi,* perceives that the prince has reappeared on Sefuri-san in Japan. Taking along his fourteen other children and Ryūju, the king departs for Japan and becomes the avatar of Sefuriyama (Sefuri-san Gongen 背振山権現).

The motif of the king and his fifteen children is presented in the *Keiran shūyōshū* as an allegory for the primal sound *a* and the fifteen vowels

FIGURE 5.21. Benzaiten and her fifteen attendants. *Ofuda*. Chikubushima. Private collection.

FIGURE 5.22. Benzaiten and her fifteen attendants. Edo period. Terra cotta. Hildburgh Collection. American Museum of Natural History.

of the Sanskrit alphabet, which are also the seed-syllables (*shuji* 種子, Skt. *bīja*) of the Tantric cosmic emanation process.[95] Here is how Kōshū describes the process known in Indian Tantrism as *nyāsa* (J. *fuji* 布字, i.e., putting the seed-syllables over the body in order to "seal" it): "When the [*bīja* of] the fifteen children are drawn [on the body], the first one, In'yaku Dōji 印鑰 (var. Inkan Dōji 印鑑童子), is placed on the crown of the head, and the fifteenth, Sensha Dōji 船車童子, is placed on both feet. Placing the fifteen children on the practitioner's body protects [his body]."[96] In some cases, a sixteenth *dōji* is added: Zenzai Dōji 善財童子 (Skt. Sudhana), the young protagonist of the *Gaṇḍavyuha-sūtra.* His apparition (as a vanishing figure) also illustrates esoteric speculations about Sanskrit phonemes.[97]

In spite of their auspicious nature, the fifteen *dōji* may have had a demonic origin, as is pointed out in at least one legend. According to the *Soga monogatari,* a queen named Benzaiten laid five hundred eggs and abandoned them. The eggs then hatched and gave birth to five hundred children, who became demons and tried to rob the queen. The number five hundred resonates with Hārītī's one thousand children (five hundred heavenly demons, five hundred earthly demons).[98]

Toward the end of the medieval period, as Benzaiten became redefined as one of the gods of fortune, the fifteen *dōji* came to be worshiped as protectors of various professional guilds. They also became identified with the first fifteen days of the month. The *Ugajin ku saimon* 宇賀神供祭文 lists their virtues and functions.[99] In one of the Tenkawa Benzaiten mandalas, they are shown riding various animals, some of them purely imaginary.

THE BENZAITEN CONSTELLATION

Dakiniten

As noted earlier, Benzaiten came to be identified with Dakiniten, in part through the association between Benzaiten and Ugajin, who was himself identified with Inari and therefore Dakiniten.

Another interesting association made by the *Keiran shūyōshū* is that between Benzaiten, on the one hand, and Aizen and Fudō on the other. Benzaiten came to be linked with Aizen through the wish-fulfilling jewel—the symbolic form they shared—and the seed-syllable *hūṃ*. The jewel symbolism, derived from the representation of Benzaiten as a *nāga,* also explains why she became the "master mind"—the sixth consciousness—of all beings.

The shared identity of Benzaiten and Dakiniten, in the group (and composite deity) known as the Three Devas, provided a link between Benzaiten and Inari Myōjin, as can be seen at the Seijogū on Mount Hiei. Another link was provided by the semantic and cultic associations between Ugajin and Uka no mitama (or Ukemochi 保食), a food deity worshiped at Inari.[100]

Dakiniten and Benzaiten exchanged not only their attributes, but also their acolytes. In a Kanazawa bunko text entitled *Benzaiten,* we find a diagram of a ritual altar where Benzaiten's two acolytes are the *tengu*-like figures called Shuyuchisō and Ton'yugyō, both of whom were traditionally Dakiniten's acolytes.[101] In several representations, we can see a fox-riding female (Dakiniten or Benzaiten) surrounded by the fifteen *dōji* (Fig. 5.20). There are also instances where Benzaiten herself becomes Dakiniten's acolyte. Thus, among the four emissaries of Dakiniten, the three female ones are said to be the Benzaiten of Chikubushima, Enoshima, and Itsukushima.[102]

The identity between Benzaiten and the Inari deity finds its literary expression in the *Genpei jōsuiki*, in an episode where Taira no Kiyomori, while hunting, encounters a fox. Kiyomori is about to shoot the fox when it turns into a handsome maiden, who tells him that she will fulfill all his wishes if he spares her life. She then reveals to him that she is none other than the "king of the seventy-four ways." When Kiyomori dismounts his horse to worship her, she regains her animal form and disappears.

Struck with awe, Kiyomori concludes that the fox was none other than Benzai Myōon, and that the Dakiniten ritual is the best method to get rid of all "violent deities" (*kōjin*) that might cause obstacles. The point here is that he identifies the fox king with Benzaiten. This passage further suggests that one can worship Benzaiten with a Dakiniten ritual. The text adds, however, that because of its heterodox nature, the effects of the ritual will not carry over to one's descendants.[103] This statement looks like a veiled prediction of the fall of Kiyomori and his clan, which recalls the prediction made by Benzaiten to Kiyomori during his visit to Itsukushima.

The Benzaiten section in the *Keiran shūyōshū* has an interesting passage entitled "How Ryōkan Shōnin invited the god of fortune." It tells how Ryōkan Shōnin 良観上人, otherwise known as the Ritsu master Ninshō 忍性 (1217–1303), a disciple of Eison, secluded himself in the dragon hole of Enoshima to perform a jewel ritual.[104] After seven days, three fox cubs appeared on the altar. Although the text does not report why and how the foxes died, it states that Ryōkan buried one of them under the abbot's cell at Gokurakuji 極楽寺, another at Tahōji 多宝寺, and the third at a monastery in Mimura 三村. Subsequently, these three monasteries prospered. However, when the abbot of Gokurakuji died and his cell was restored, a small white snake emerged from the ground and was slain. This event was followed by a series of calamities. A commentary explains that this snake was a transformation of the fox that had been buried there, and that the latter's apparition had been due to Ryōkan's performance of the ritual of the two-armed spirit king, as explained in the *Uga otome kyō*.[105] Nanami Hiroaki has used that passage to trace the expansion of the Uga Benzaiten cult from Chikubushima to Enoshima. According to him, the presence of foxes and snakes suggests that Ninshō used Uga Benzaiten and Dakiniten as the *honzon* of the joint ritual he performed at Enoshima.[106] Judging from the presence of foxes in the Tenkawa Benzaiten mandala, the same combination must have been used in the Tenkawa Benzaiten ritual.

Daikokuten

The intimate relationship between Benzaiten and Ugajin has been perceived as a relationship between Benzaiten and Daikokuten. We recall that Daikokuten, representing the earth deity (Kenrō Jijin 堅牢地神), appeared to Saichō in the form of an old man. It is therefore not surprising that, in this form, Daikokuten was explicitly assimilated with Ugajin. As the Tendai priest Kōen 興円, Kōshū's master, puts it: "On the crown of Benzaiten, there is a white snake with the head of an old man. It is Daikoku Tenjin. Daikoku[ten] and Benzai[ten] correspond to the yin and the yang, the father and the mother, the source of all things."[107] The link between the two deities is also suggested by the fact that, according to a record of pilgrimage to the seven great temples of Nara, hundreds of statuettes of Daikokuten, allegedly fabricated by Kūkai himself, were buried under the Benzaiten Shrine of Kōfukuji during what was probably an earth-quelling ritual.[108]

Daikokuten was not only the protector of Mount Hiei; he was also the patron deity of the Kurodani-ryū 黒谷流, a branch of Tendai that specialized in esoteric reinterpretations of the Vinaya. In this branch, the couple formed by Daikokuten and Benzaiten is said to represent the (quasi-sexual) union between the practitioner (who identifies himself with Daikokuten) and the goddess. In this way, Benzaiten and Daikokuten came to symbolize the yin and yang principles united in the practitioner's body.[109] The pairing of Daikokuten and Benzaiten is a specific feature of medieval Japanese documents. In Tendai esotericism, this pairing came to symbolize the coupling of esotericism and exotericism.[110] The doctrinal conjunction established by *kenmitsu* Buddhism was in this way reinforced by a "mythological" and "rito-logical" logic. Thus, a Daikokuten statue allegedly carved by the Vinaya priest Eison at Saidaiji in 1276 contains a small copper figurine (*kakebotoke* 賭け仏) of Benzaiten.[111]

Amaterasu

Benzaiten is often associated and even identified with Amaterasu. According to the Chikubushima tradition, she manifested herself (as Myōon Benzaiten) in the sixth year of the reign of Emperor Kinmei (r. 539–571) and declared herself to be an emanation (*wake mitama* 分霊) of Amaterasu.[112] In the *Taiheiki,* the warrior Nitta Yoshisada 新田義貞 declares: "I have heard that the Sun Goddess of Ise . . . conceals her true being in the august image of Vairocana, and that she has appeared in this world in the guise of a dragon god of the blue ocean."[113] We recall that Amaterasu was said to appear in vulpine form, and sometimes also as a snake or dragon. This should not surprise us, since her offspring, the three deities of Munakata, were themselves perceived as water deities associated with Benzaiten. Benzaiten also shared affinities with Uhō Dōji 雨宝童子, a Buddhist form of Amaterasu. For instance, in the *Uhō Dōji no keibyaku* 雨宝童子敬白, a text attributed to Kūkai, she is described as the essence of the sun, while Dakiniten is the essence of the moon.[114]

The link between Benzaiten and the solar deity Amaterasu is further reinforced by her identification with Aizen Myōō, a solar deity whose fierce splendor makes the stars (and astral deities) fade out.[115] As the wheel-commanding body (*kyōryōrin-shin* 教令輪身) of the buddha Mahāvairocana, Benzaiten is technically identical to the wisdom kings (*myōō* 明王).[116] As a solar or stellar deity, she dwells at the apex of the cosmos; as a water deity, she lies in the innermost recesses of the human microcosm—in the form of a small snake.

BENZAITEN AS AN ASTRAL DEITY

The *Keiran shūyōshū* transformed the image of Benzaiten by adding new features and making latent ones explicit. Such was the case with its interpretation of Benzaiten as an astral deity. In the *Golden Light Sūtra,* Sarasvatī had already promised that those who uphold that sūtra would be protected from all astral "disasters" and calamities caused by demons. Her astral nature was tied into her apotropaic function.

Actually, Kōshū stops short of calling Benzaiten an astral deity: he merely suggests it by inserting into the chapter he dedicates to her a long discussion of astral rituals performed at Sōji-in (Dhāraṇī Pavilion) on Mount Hiei and their *honzon,* Ichiji Kinrin, as well as other astral deities such as Aizen Myōō (like Ichiji Kinrin, a deity of the solar wheel) and Kokūzō. Kōshū connects Benzaiten with the Blazing Light Ritual (Shijōkō-hō 熾盛光法) performed at Sōji-in to ensure the longevity of the ruler and the prosperity of his kingdom. The figure of Uga Benzai is said to control the three main aspects of human life: happiness, emoluments, and longevity. The number of her attendants (i.e., fifteen) is explained in allegorical fashion as resulting from the combination of these three aspects (or levels of reality) with the "three talents" (heaven, earth, and man) and the five phases.

Harada Nobuo mentions the worship of a form of Benzaiten holding the sun and moon in her hands at Zenkōji 善光寺 in the Ryūkyū Islands.[117] This figure calls to mind one of the standard representations of Myōken Bosatsu. Benzaiten also shares iconographic affinities with the deity of the planet Venus, who is usually represented as a court lady holding a lute.[118] Harada further suggests a possible connection between this form of Benzaiten and the asuras Rāhu and Ketu, two astral deities who were thought to cause lunar eclipses.[119] In this context, it is perhaps worth recalling that the Vedic Sarasvatī was the deity who vanquished the asuras. Benzaiten also appears in the Ryūkyū Islands as a three-faced, six-armed deity, which Harada compares with the famous *Asura* statue at Kōfukuji 興福寺.[120] He notes that Benzaiten, under the name Tobo 斗姥 (Old Woman of the Dipper), came to be assimilated with Doumu 斗母 (Dipper Mother), a Chinese deity identified with the esoteric Buddhist deity Mārīcī (J. Marishiten 摩利支天).[121]

In the *Jingi kan'yo* 神祇鑒輿, a medieval text attributed to Ennin, Benzaiten, identified with the *kami* Masaya-akatsu as the main deity of Itsukushima Shrine, is listed as *kami* of the stars (next to Amaterasu as *kami* of the sun and Ketsujin (a.k.a. Miketsu no kami) as *kami* of the moon). The text adds that Myōken transforms himself into Ugajin, the "god of longevity and happiness of all beings," and into the companion deity (or deities) that protect the fetus in the womb and individuals throughout their life.[122] The affinity (and virtual identity) between Uga

Benzaiten and Myōken is perhaps one of the reasons why Toyotomi Hideyoshi, after worshiping Benzaiten at Chikubushima, secluded himself on Mount Arakami 荒神 in Ōmi and sponsored a ritual centered on Chintakureifujin 鎮宅霊符神 (God of the Numinous Talismans to Placate the House), that is, Myōken.

Benzaiten's role as an astral deity that controls human destiny may also derive from her status as Yama's sister. As the god of primordial sound, Sarasvatī, or (the later) Myōonten, was already seen as the source of all beings. In the *Golden Light Sūtra,* she became the mother of the world. According to Kōshū, her "partner" Ugajin is also a cosmic deity that constitutes the "warp and woof of heaven and earth."

A DEITY OF THE THIRD (OR FOURTH) FUNCTION

In the *Golden Light Sūtra,* the Buddhist Sarasvatī was no longer simply—if she ever was—a river goddess and a goddess of music; she had become the great mother who gives birth to all beings. She was, in other words, a deity of Dumézil's third function, who dispenses fertility, fecundity, and abundance. Nothing surprising here, since, as we have seen, this was already the case with the Vedic Sarasvatī. Situated at the origin of heaven and earth, Benzaiten alternates between her functions as a heavenly (astral) deity, as an earth deity and water deity, and also as a chthonian (underworld) deity. Even the eight-armed Benzaiten cannot be interpreted simply as a representative of the second function (war). According to Harada Nobuo, the three functions are symbolized by the three types of weapons that Benzaiten holds: the bow and arrows stand for sovereignty, the sword for war, and the halberd for prosperity. The pairing of Benzaiten with Ugajin (or Daikokuten) led to their identification with the yin and the yang, emblems of fecundity.[123] In the preface of the *Zatsuzatsushū* 雑々集 by the Tendai abbot Chūjin 忠尋 (1065–1138), a citation attributed to Ennin presents Benzaiten and Makeishura 摩醯首羅 (Skt. Maheśvara, i.e., Śiva) as the two primordial progenitors, the ancestors of all the devas, as well as the source of the two types of karmic retribution and the origin of the Womb and Vajra mandalas.[124] In the *Onjōji denki* 園城寺伝記, Benzaiten is said to be a manifestation of Shō Makaraten 聖摩迦羅天 (probably another variant of Mahākāla, i.e., Śiva); she is the consort of Daikokuten (Mahākāla), and the mother of fifteen children. She also gives birth to the twenty-eight devas, whom she offers to the bodhisattva Kannon. She then manifests herself as the spirit commander, King Uga (Uga shinshō-ō 宇賀神将王), and, taking Kōjin now as her husband, she gives birth to twelve deities (symbols of the twelve months), whom she entrusts to the buddha Yakushi. Finally, she gives birth to "sixteen good deities," whom she bequeathes to the bodhisattva Monju to help him protect the Perfection of Wisdom (Skt. Prajñāpāramitā).[125]

FIGURE 5.23. Kariteimo (Kishimojin, Hārītī). Edo period. Sheet, ink on paper. University Art Museum, Kyoto City University of Arts. *BZS* 2221.

In other words, Benzaiten is the *fons et origo* of all gods. She can manifest herself directly, in her "living" body, but also in the form of "traces" (*suijaku*) or "provisional manifestations" (*gongen*), or even more indirectly, by procreating gods. This last method reflects the impact of maternal imagery in medieval Japan and the rewriting of mythology in terms of kinship ties.[126]

Uga Benzaiten is a goddess with a vast progeny.[127] This capacity links Benzaiten to Hārītī (J. Kariteimo, Kishimojin), another emblem of fecundity, who is usually depicted surrounded by her infant children (Fig. 5.23). Benzaiten's children, on the other hand, are always represented as youths, not infants, even in the case of her last-born.[128] In Hārītī's case, the children seem to represent both her own children and the human children that this former ogress now protects (instead of devouring them). Sometimes these divine children have had a prior existence as local deities before being integrated into Hārītī's or Benzaiten's retinue, and they seem to have remained the objects of an independent cult afterwards. This is particularly the case with their last-born children—Piṇgala and Oto Gohō, respectively. Interestingly, both were at one point separated from their mothers: Piṇgala was abducted by the Buddha, who wanted to teach a lesson to the ogress Hārītī, while Oto Gohō simply disappeared, leaving his parents in despair. He was found again in the distant land of Japan by the esoteric patriarch Nāgārjuna, who, owing to the translation of his name as Ryūju 龍樹 'dragon tree,' came to play a significant role in Japanese *nāga* lore and in Benzaiten myths.

In the Minō tradition, Benzaiten is the consort of King Tokuzen (or sometimes the king himself) and the progenitrix (or progenitor) of fifteen (or sixteen) children.[129] In another oral transmission influenced by Onmyōdō, Benzaiten is the name of a king who fathered five princes (who correspond to the five dragon kings ruling over the four cardinal directions and the center).[130]

As a spouse and a mother, Benzaiten (like Hārītī) is sometimes represented in the company of Daikokuten (Mahākāla). In the Nichiren tradition, Kishimojin's retinue is formed by the ten *rākṣasīs* (J. *rasetsunyo* 羅刹女), with whom she protects the *Lotus Sūtra.* These female demons are usually represented as handsome maidens, but in Hārītī's case, the two representations (woman and demon) have persisted until today. Admittedly, the demonic nature of Hārītī—who is the "deity mother of demons" and the leader of the *rākṣasas*—is emphasized to a greater extent than that of Benzaiten. The close relationship between Benzaiten and Hārītī is also clear from the fact that the latter is often represented as one of Benzaiten's two female attendants. Sometimes she is even presented as an avatar of Benzaiten.[131]

There is also a legend, told in the *Soga monogatari,* in which a queen named Benzaiten laid five hundred eggs and abandoned them. The eggs hatched and five hundred children were born.[132] Also noteworthy, in this context, is Benzaiten's relationship to the goddess of silkworms.[133] Her sericultural function was particularly conspicuous in central Japan (modern-day Fukui, Nagano, and Gunma prefectures) and the area of northern Japan that is now Yamagata prefecture, where blind female mediums called *goze* 瞽女 were active. A similar relationship had already existed in China, where Biancaitian 弁才天 was identified with the goddess of sericulture Canniu.[134] Although the *goze* do not seem to have worshiped the silkworm goddess Oshirasama オシラ様, her cult spread widely among the female mediums of northeastern Japan. These blind mediums often associated Oshirasama with Myōonten in their worship, because both were perceived as healers of eyesight. However, Myōonten was no longer a musical deity for them, and the *biwa* had lost its symbolic significance.

Benzaiten as an Earth Deity

As noted above, Benzaiten's symbolic form, the wish-fulfilling jewel, is a symbol of abundance related to the earth. As a mother and nurturer, Sarasvatī was intimately related to the earth, a symbol of the third function. In the *Golden Light Sūtra,* the Sarasvatī chapter is followed by chapters on Śrī (J. Kichijōten) and the earth deity Dṛḍha (J. Jiten). As Iyanaga Nobumi points out, rather than simply listing Śrī, Sarasvatī, and the earth deity as figures appearing in the *Golden Light Sūtra,* one should instead speak of Śrī-like and Sarasvatī-like earth deities as manifestations of the earth deity proper. In the *Kakuzenshō* and the *Byakuhō kushō* 白宝口鈔, it is Jiten, the earth goddess, who is said to resemble Benzaiten.[135] Among the three, she is the least individualized. However, she may be the most important, inasmuch as she is the *honji* (original ground) *ante litteram* of the other two.

In Vedic India, Śrī and Sarasvatī both participated in the third function, whereas in classical Hinduism Śrī alone retained that function. In Japan, however, Benzaiten gradually superseded Kichijōten as a goddess of abundance and fecundity. In other words, as Iyanaga Nobumi has pointed out, while Hinduism apparently forgot the third-function characteristics of the Vedic Sarasvatī, Buddhism (and more particularly Japanese Buddhism) retrieved them.[136]

But the earth goddess is an ambiguous figure, to say nothing of her retinue (consisting of various earth deities) and manifestations or avatars (Mahākāla, Daikokuten, and Bishamonten among them). Benzaiten's role as an earth deity was not always positive; it encompassed dark, chthonian aspects as well. In the *Keiran shūyōshū,* Benzaiten is identified with Dokū 土公 (var. Dokku, Ch. Tugong), an irascible deity who often needs to be placated.[137] The *Asabashō* describes earth-quelling rituals that must be performed when one has violated the earth, pointing out that "when one prays for abundance, one invokes Kichijōten; when one has violated the earth, one invokes Benzaiten."[138] Thus, Benzaiten's place in the medieval imagination wasn't only as a goddess of fortune; it also owed to her chthonian nature.

These aspects of Benzaiten are evoked in the Shingon work *Bikisho* 鼻帰書 (1324). In the *Kakuzenshō,* the image of the earth deity (with sickle and other attributes) is also said to have taken Benzaiten as its model. This earth deity was the main object of worship of the blind monks of Kyūshū, who were known for that reason as *jishin mōsō* 地神盲僧. Accompanied by a lute, they would recite the so-called *Earth Deity Sūtra* (*Jishin-kyō* 地神經), which was said to have derived from the *Golden Light Sūtra*'s chapter on that deity.[139] Actually, it is a different work, an apocryphal scripture strongly influenced by Onmyōdō. The ritual they performed was essentially an earth-quelling ritual, similar to the pacification rituals (*anchin hō* 安鎮法) associated with Fudō and the dragon kings of Onmyōdō. These dragon kings were identified with the demonic assistants (*shikigami*) of Onmyōdō masters.[140] In the *Shiko ōji,* for instance, the five dragons or five princes are the children of King Benzai and his consort Kirisai Nyorai; they preside over the five quarters and the five phases.[141] This male Benzaiten plays the role given in Onmyōdō documents to King Banko (derived from Pan Gu, the Chinese primordial man) or to Dokō, who is another—male—aspect of the earth deity. Dokō was known to be a particularly dangerous god, who fortunately could be placated with a Benzaiten ritual. The *Keiran shūyōshū* reports, for example, that during excavation works at Jufukuji 壽福寺 in Kamakura, the workers fell victim to a strange disease and madness. After a ritual was performed, golden sand in the shape of an ox (a symbol of Dokō) was found on the ground. At this point, the diary of the monastery's founder, the Zen priest Myōan Eisai 明菴栄西 (var. Yōsai, 1141–1215), indicated that during the initial earth-quelling rituals, golden sand had been buried in a vase during a ritual dedicated to Benzaiten. This golden sand, cast into the shape of an ox, had become the earth deity. Apparently, objects were buried in the ground at the time of the founding of temples and other buildings as offerings to the earth deity, or as symbols of that deity.

As noted earlier, Benzaiten was also said to be a small snake dwelling under the central pillar of the Sakadono at the Outer Shrine of Ise. The snake or earthly dragon symbolizes not only the telluric forces but also the spirits of the dead who have not yet been saved, and it must therefore be placated.[142] They also represent the "wild spirits" (*araburu kami, kōjin* 荒神) of mountains and rivers, the autochthonous powers of the land. The fact that Benzaiten, originally a foreign deity, became a figure of autochthony may seem paradoxical, but it is not an isolated case.[143]

Ugajin, Kōjin, and Shukujin

Benzaiten is also related to another territorial deity, the crossroads deity (or deities) known as Dōsojin 道祖神. The connections are complex, and one example may suffice. As the protecting deity of blind monks, Benzaiten was said to have incarnated herself as a blind prince called Shigū 四宮 ("fourth prince," because he was the fourth child of an emperor). This prince was later perceived to be an emanation of Dōsojin. When "Shigū" is read "Shinomiya," the name also designates the place on the eastern outskirts of Kyoto where he is said to have secluded himself. The term evokes Shukujin 宿神 (god of the *shuku*)—and Shinomiya was indeed a *shuku* or post station. But the term *shukujin* is polysemic, as it can also mean "astral god" or "god of destiny" (both meanings being related to Benzaiten). As one document from Higo province puts it: "Until the end of our days, we dwell in the womb of the goddess, unknowingly and without feeling any gratitude."[144]

Nanami Hiroaki quotes the *Zachū tenmon ki* 座中天文記 (1540), according to which the notion of *shukujin* originated at Hie Shrine, perhaps as a patron deity of the *biwa hōshi.*[145] According to him, Mount Hiei monks intent on fundraising (*kanjin* 勧進) tried to control the doctrinal content of the *Heike monogatari* recited by the *biwa hōshi.* The Nanto-bon version of the *Heike monogatari* would represent that copyedited text, permeated by Tendai ideology as it is, whereas other versions seem to lack this feature.[146]

Thus, through her symbolic and iconographic associations with Ugajin, Benzaiten was naturalized and localized, as well as (to a certain extent) demonized.

CODETTA

Benzaiten's transformation into a *nāga* essentially followed from her early function as a water deity. Her apotheosis as a wild spirit or *kōjin,* while still taking place within a theological framework, undermined that framework in a way that reflected the inner dynamics of the medieval imagination. It also reflected the reciprocal process of myth formation: from the top down (in theological speculations) and also from the bottom up (through local myths, legends, and practices).

The figure of Uga Benzaiten is not merely a case of Shinto-Buddhist "syncretism," as is too often said, or of the resurgence within Buddhism of subterranean currents originating in local cults—Indian ones in the case of the *nāga,* Chinese in the case of the Onmyōdō dragons, and Japanese in the case of food-god cults, the worship of snakes and foxes, and the cult of Kōjin.

An emphasis on Benzaiten's chthonian nature, probably under the influence of Onmyōdō, brought about the transformation of her image as an aquatic *nāga* to that of a (terrestrial) dragon and snake. Unlike the Indian Sarasvatī, a relatively individualized goddess, Uga Benzaiten, as a god representing earthly powers, became increasingly complex and elusive. She does not simply act as an intermediary between the buddhas and the *kami;* she is a god of a new kind, whose manifestations span the entire spectrum of the Japanese pantheon. In this way, she became the "warp and woof of heaven and earth." Shedding her foreign nature, she became one of the tutelary gods (*jinushigami* 地主神) of Japan, a *vajra*-shaped land in which "dragons dwell."[147]

José Ortega y Gasset's words seem appropriate when trying to pin down this deity: Benzaiten is an "ontological centaur, half immersed in nature, half transcending it."[148] It is precisely the fact that she is "stuck in nature" that affords her a transcendental power and enduring appeal.

6

THE THREE DEVAS

This chapter focuses on a composite deity formed from a combination of Dakiniten, Benzaiten, and Shōten (or sometimes Daikokuten). The composition of this set was never static, however, and while I discuss the specific attributes of the individual deities involved, the chapter also considers the general theme of ternary deities, including those with three faces, each representing a different deity. In the Edo period, Daikokuten, Marishiten, and Benzaiten were worshiped as a tripartite set, popularly known as the Three Devas (Santen 三天).[1] My use of the term "Three Devas" refers primarily to the set formed by Dakiniten, Benzaiten, and Shōten, and also at times to other premodern triads that involve at least one of those deities. When I refer to the Three-Deva deity, however, I have in mind something different, namely, the composite fox-riding, three-headed, six- or twelve-armed deity whose heads are those of the Three Devas.

There are three crucial questions that need to be answered when it comes to the Three Devas. First, why did medieval Japanese thinkers combine multiple deities into a single form? Second, why the number three? Third, why did they choose the deities that they did in any given instance? I leave my answers to these questions for this chapter's conclusion, as it is important to first present what we do know about the religious developments that led to the appearance of the Three Devas.

I begin with a discussion of rituals involving the Three Devas performed both at the Shingon redoubt of Tōji and within Tendai. An examination of these rituals makes clear the esoteric Buddhist foundation for the institution of the Three Devas. Next, I look at the expansion of the Three Devas cult beyond the confines of Buddhist orthodoxy into religious traditions that we now refer to as Onmyōdō, Shintō, and Shugendō. Following this, a large section comprising half the chapter focuses on questions of iconography and interpicturality related to the Three Devas.[2] In the context of iconography, I look at depictions of Dakiniten as a ternary deity, the Tenkawa mandala, and the three-faced Daikokuten. I end by piecing together some of the facts discussed in order to address the aforementioned questions.

THE *YAKṢA* OF TŌJI AND THE RITUAL OF THE THREE DEVAS

The *Shūyōshū* 拾要集, a ritual text compiled by the imperial priest Shukaku Hōshinnō 守覚法親王 (1150–1202), contains an interesting passage concerning the image of the protecting deity of Tōji, the headquarters of the Shingon school.[3] This image, unfortunately no longer extant, was of a *yakṣa* deity (*yashajin* 夜叉神) called Matarajin, who is described as a strange deity (*kishin* 奇神) with three faces and six arms.[4] Its central face (golden in color) was that of Shōten, its right (red) face that of Benzaiten, and its left (white) face that of Dakiniten. This *yakṣa* was a messenger of the Inari deity, and it was believed that he could predict future events, eliminate calamities, and bring good fortune.[5] He was also described as being extremely compassionate and free of resentment—a statement that sounds more like a pious wish than a description, given the general reputation of *yakṣa*s. According to the Shingon priest Gōhō 杲宝 (1306–1362), he was actually a kind of ogre, whom people attempted to placate by consecrating their children to him.

While lacking a proper canonical definition, the deity of Tōji was apparently the central icon of a ritual in which the Three Devas were worshiped together.[6] This ritual also existed in Tendai. According to a later ritual text preserved at Eizan Bunko, the Santen gōgyō-hō 三天合行法, the Joint Ritual of the Three Devas began with the following visualization of the ritual area: "In the middle of the great altar is the lion's seat, on which one visualizes the seed-syllable *ro*. This letter then transforms into a *cintāmaṇi* jewel, which in turn becomes the bodhisattva Shinkoō 辰狐王 (Dragon-fox King, that is, Dakiniten]. Two seed-syllables, *giri-gyaku,* appear on it, which transform and become the dual-bodied Kangiten. Above is the letter *kya,* which transforms into Benzaiten."[7]

While the protecting deity of Tōji was specific to Shingon, the composite deity later known as the Three Devas and formed from Shōten (or Daikokuten), Dakiniten, and Benzaiten was a natural fit for the ternary logic of Mikkyō. These devas were said to represent the Three Truths of Tendai, and to correspond to the Womb realm, the Vajra realm, and the Susiddhi (Realization) realm, respectively. According to the *Keiran shūyōshū,* these Three Devas (here Daikokuten, Dakiniten, and Benzaiten) symbolize the three mysteries (of body, mind, and speech) of the buddha Dainichi. Daikokuten also represents the ultimate mystery of the dharmas of form, Dakiniten that of mind, and Benzaiten that of speech and sound.[8]

Dakiniten, Benzaiten, and Shōten were of course also worshiped individually. Indeed, they serve as the *honzon* of three of the four "sudden rituals" (*shitonpō* 四頓法) of Tendai and Shingon, the fourth one being centered on Bishamonten.[9] According to Tendai tradition, Sange Daishi 山家大師 (i.e., Saichō) took Mahakara-ten (Mahākāla-deva, i.e., Daikokuten) as his protecting deity (*gohō*), the great master of Zentōin (Zentōin Daishi 前唐院大師), i.e., Ennin (794–864) took Benzaiten, and Enchin performed the two secret rites of Daikokuten and Benzaiten. The Joint Ritual of the Three Devas, however, is said to be the most secret tradition.[10]

The Three Devas played an important role in medieval enthronement rituals (*sokui kanjō*).[11] The *Jindaikan hiketsu* 神代巻秘決 credits Kūkai with creating the Joint Ritual of the Three Devas as a special enthronement ritual and provides the following account of it:

> In the Hirosawa [branch], the joint worship of the Three Devas is called the "special enthronement ritual." It was created by the great master [Kūkai]. In spite of this, it is not the correct enthronement ritual as regards the fundamental destiny of the Son of Heaven, but only a secret private rite. . . . It takes Shōten, Daten [i.e., Dakiniten], and Benzaiten as a single worthy. Because it combines their worship, it is called the Joint Ritual of the Three Devas. This is why [its *honzon*] has three faces. . . . They symbolize the three poisons (greed, ignorance, and anger) and the tripartite jewel. They correspond also to the three shrines (upper, middle, lower) of Inari. It is the most secret among the secret, the most sudden among the sudden rituals. . . . It is the body of the *honji* that preaches the way in the three periods (past, future, and present). You must keep it very secret.[12]

In this enthronement ritual, Shōten, Dakiniten, and Benzaiten merge into a single entity, and their rituals are performed together—hence the name Joint Ritual of the Three Devas. This name suggests a relationship between this ritual and the Joint Ritual of the Three Worthies (*Sanzon gōgyō-hō* 三尊合行法), centered on the triad formed by Nyoirin Kannon, Aizen, and Fudō, discussed in the preceding volume, *The Fluid Pantheon*. In the case of the *santen gōgyō-hō,* however, the *honzon* is a composite deity rather than the central deity of the triad. Its central face is that of Shōten. The three worthies are linked to a series of ternary groupings: the three poisons, the three jewels, and the three shrines (upper, middle, and lower) of Inari. This ritual is said to be the highest and most sudden ritual, representing the preaching of the original body (*honji shin* 本地身) of the great master (here meaning Kūkai) in the three periods.[13] For example, the *Shake shiryō* 社家史料, a collection of documents from Suwa Shrine, states that at that shrine the enthronement ritual was "the ritual of the joint practice of the three worthies Daikokuten, Benzaiten, and Dakiniten."[14]

EXPANSION OF THE CULT

The Three Devas were also worshiped at, and even beyond, the margins of Buddhism in loosely organized traditions that later came to be known as Onmyōdō, Shintō, and Shugendō. The important Onmyōdō work *Hoki naiden* 簠簋内伝, for example, reveals that the "three mirrors" were identified with a series of triads, including the three luminaries (sun, moon, and stars), the three talents (heaven, earth, and man), the three bodies of the Buddha, the three fundamental seed-letters (*a, vaṃ,* and *hūṃ*), the three sections of the mandala (Buddha, Lotus, and Vajra), the three buddhas (Dainichi, Amida, and Shaka), and, last but not least, the Three Devas (Dakiniten, Shōten, and Benzaiten).[15]

The Three Devas at Mount Inari

As noted above, the *yakṣa* deity of Tōji was seen from early on as a messenger of Inari Daimyōjin. The Three Devas came to be inscribed in the landscape of Inari Shrine, on the so-called Peaks of the Three Devas, where Kūkai allegedly buried three wish-fulfilling jewels. The mounds of the Three Devas are compared to the tripartite wish-fulfilling jewel. The three deities, once associated through the three jewels, came in turn to symbolize the three treasures of the Buddha, the Dharma, and the Sangha. At Inari's three shrines, the lower corresponded to Dakiniten, the middle to Benzaiten, and the upper to Shōten.[16] According to the *Keiran shūyōshū,* among the manifestations (lit. "trace bodies") of the Buddha, the higher one is Benzaiten, the middle one is Shōten, and the lower one is Dakiniten.[17] In the section "Inari Daimyōjin no koto" of the *Shintōshū* 神道集 (1358), the Three Devas are worshiped as *honji* of Fushimi Inari's three main *kami*. Shōten is worshiped on Mani Peak (Mani-hō 摩尼峰), Benzaiten at Taki no Mine, and Dakiniten at the Kōjin Mound (Kōjin-zuka 荒神塚, also known as Daten 荼天／陀天／吒天 Peak. In a document included in the *Inari kōshi* 稲荷講志, the Aizenji 愛染寺 abbot Tenna 天阿 is said to have compared the Shōten, Benzaiten, and Dakiniten of the upper, middle, and lower shrines to the sun, moon, and stars (specifically the stars of Ursa Major, that is, the Northern Dipper), respectively, and to have worshiped them collectively at Aizenji as a single "worthy [resulting from] the harmonious union of the Three Devas" (*santen wagō-son* 三天和合尊).[18] Another source specifies that three shrines were built on Mount Inari in 908: the southern shrine was dedicated to Shōten and Nitten 日天 (the sun deva), the northern shrine to Benzaiten and Gatten 月天 (the moon deva), and the central shrine to Dakiniten and the Northern Dipper. The composite figure formed by the union of the Three Devas, the Three-Deva deity, is also called the Bodhisattva King of Astral Foxes (Shinkoō Bosatsu), a name that initially referred to Dakiniten proper.[19] Although Dakiniten is now only one component of this hybrid deity, she remains the *prima inter pares.*[20]

The *Busshin ittai kanjōshō* 佛神一体灌頂鈔 gives an interesting embryological reading of Dakiniten and Shōten. Dakiniten is the numinous water that gushes forth from a spring in the mountain, symbolizing the fusion of the two drops (red and white, blood and semen), the merging of the two seed-letters *raṃ* and *vaṃ,* and the nonduality of the Womb and Vajra realms. Her messengers—the red fox and the white fox—are manifestations of the sun and moon deities, who must be worshiped on the morning and evening of the first and the third days of the first month.[21] The divine body of the mountain is Daishō Kangiten (i.e., Shōten), who symbolizes the union of husband and wife. He is a provisional manifestation (*gongen*) that harmonizes principle and knowledge. The text adds that the union between husband and wife began with the deities Izanagi and Izanami's experience of pleasure and pain. This is why Daishō Kangiten, by experiencing pleasure and pain, becomes the father and mother of all beings.[22]

Beyond Inari

The Three Devas were also important in Shugendō, a fact that can easily be seen in the symbolism of the *shugenja*'s attire. The *Keiran shūyōshū* explains:

> The physical appearance of the *yamabushi* corresponds to the appearance of the Three Devas. The so-called persimmon dress symbolizes the color of the astral fox (*shinko*) [i.e., Dakiniten]; the Fudō robe (*kesa*) symbolizes the coiled Kurikara [i.e., Fudō]; it is Benzaiten [in her dragon form]; the *tokin* 頭巾 on the *shugenja*'s head symbolizes the Lotus of the Womb realm, that is, Shōten's symbolic (*samaya*) form. Thus, the *shugenja*'s physical appearance is patterned after the sacred ritual of the joint worship of the Three Devas (*santen gōgyō*).[23]

The importance of the fox at Inari and the role of the three foxes in apotropaic rituals perhaps paved the way for the representation of the Three Devas as a single, fox-riding deity. The *Jingi hishō* 神祇秘抄, for instance, has an interesting discussion on the *kora* 子良, the female attendants at Ise Shrine. The term *kora* itself is said to derive from the word *ko* 狐 'fox', and these shrine maidens were perceived as avatars of Dakiniten.[24] The text elaborates:

> The heavenly fox (*tenko* 天狐) is the acolyte of the great goddess Amaterasu, the earthly fox (*chiko* 地狐) that of Kasuga Daimyōjin. In heaven and on earth, these two deities protect the originally unborn jewel. The heavenly fox becomes Shōten, the earthly fox Dakiniten, and the jewel that they guard is called Benzaiten. The three fuse together and become three jewels. They also correspond to the three luminaries in the sky (sun, moon, and stars), the three eyes in the [god's] face, the three acts of body, speech, and mind, as well as the three points that summarize the Dharma.[25]

While the textual record sheds some light on the deity seen as the product of that fusion, one has to turn to the iconographic record to get a better idea, and to scrutinize it in what may seem excruciating detail. If there is any key, it may be found in these images, although, apart from the key that this deity holds in one of its twelve hands, perhaps there is none.

ICONOLOGY AND INTERPICTURALITY

The Three Devas appear as a single deity in a series of painted scrolls often called *Image of Dakiniten* or *Dakiniten Mandala.* Only one of them, preserved at Hōju-in 宝珠院 (Wakayama Prefecture), is actually called *Image of the Three Devas.* These representations flourished during the Nanbokuchō and Muromachi periods, and they were still being produced during the Edo period.

The Dakiniten mandala usually depicts a three-faced deity riding a fox. While the three faces are those of Dakiniten, Shōten, and Benzaiten, their disposition varies.[26] The deity is usually identified as Dakiniten (or, more specifically, Shinkoō Bosatsu) because of its mount, the fox. However if we take into account its central face, as well as its attributes and acolytes, it would be just as appropriate, in many cases, to identify it as Benzaiten or Shōten.[27] In at least one example, additional faces (both human and animal) are visible on the sides of the head (see Fig. 6.4 below).

Let us first look at two types of depictions of the Three-Deva deity. First are the art works in which it appears either by itself or with a small number of acolytes. Second, there are the so-called Dakiniten mandalas, which situate the deity in a complex scene populated by a large number of acolytes and an assortment of other creatures. These two types overlap chronologically, so the mandalas cannot be considered a later development of the depictions of the Three-Deva deity by itself.

"Simple" Representations

The first type is exemplified by several painted scrolls preserved on Mount Kōya. Here I address each of them in turn.

(a) The first scroll is from Hōju-in (Fig. 6.1). It is dated to the Muromachi period and is commonly known as the *Three-Deva [Deity] Riding a Fox.* Its *honzon* is strongly reminiscent of the *yakṣa* of Tōji, since the distribution of the three faces (with that of Shōten at the center) is the same. Although the color symbolism that characterized the Tōji image has disappeared (possibly due to the fading of the pigments over time), other symbolic elements are visible. The deity is winged, and snakes are coiled around its neck and arms.[28] The face of Shōten is grinning, while the other two faces appear more serene. Above them are three disks: the red solar disk above Shōten displays the traditional three-legged crow in the sun;

FIGURE 6.1. *Three-Deva [Deity] Riding a Fox.* Muromachi period, 15th century. Hanging scroll, color on silk. Hōju-in, Kōyasan (Wakayama prefecture).

the white lunar disk above Dakiniten's head, the hare in the moon; and on the left, the empty disk above Benzaiten's head is partly filled by the head of the snake god Ugajin.[29]

The twelve-armed deity holds various attributes (different types of jewels, a small *shakujō* staff, a small *vajra* staff, a noose, a *vajra* bell, a five-pronged *vajra*) in eight of its hands; the two remaining pairs of hands are joined together in front of its chest and navel making the gesture called *gasshō* 合掌. Around it are four acolytes—small figures riding foxes—who are so close to the legs of the central fox that they appear to be standing on its paws.

The *Hōjuin monjo* 宝城院文書 contains a section entitled "The Four Bodies of the Three Devas" that forms a textual counterpart to the scroll. It gives a metaphysical interpretation of the four bodies in question, correlating the four with the bodies of self-nature (*jishōshin* 自性身), function (*juyōshin* 受用身), metamorphosis (*hengeshin* 変化身), and assimilation (*tōrūshin* 等流身) of the buddha Vairocana (Dainichi). This list represents an expansion of the traditional theory of the Buddha's three bodies. In principle, the Three Devas should represent the lowest type of hypostasis, the assimilation body. Here, however, they seem to be at the center of the classificatory scheme. In addition, the *Hōjuin monjo* presents the following correlatory scheme, shown here as a table matching the four bodies (columns) to the Three Devas (rows).[30]

THE FOUR BODIES OF THE THREE DEVAS

	self-nature body	function body	metamorphosis body	assimilation body
Shōten (also called Heavenly Fox)	Dainichi of the Vajra realm, symbolized by the sun	Kannon	three-legged bird (traditional symbol of the sun)	lightning and thunder
Dakiniten	Dainichi of the Womb realm, symbolized by the moon	Monju	fox	bird
Benzaiten	Dainichi of the Susiddhi realm, symbolized by Venus	Kokūzō	white snake	bee or wasp

This list is very strange. Usually, devas are considered to be the metamorphosis bodies or the assimilation bodies of the buddha Vairocana (Dainichi); here, however, they seem to share his ontological reality while their animal forms become their metamorphosis body. This still makes some kind of sense. Their assimilation bodies—lightning and thunder, bird, and bee or wasp—don't (at least to me).

(b) In the second exemplar, from Tōji, the white face in the center is Dakiniten, the pink face to the right is Shōten, and the white one on the left is Benzaiten (Fig. 6.2).[31] No animals are visible in the sun and moon disks above Shōten and Benzaiten. The deity wears strange headgear, on which several other faces appear (one red rooster face, two green demonic faces, and two female bodhisattva-like faces crowned by smaller buddha heads). It holds two disks in his upper hands, which also represent the sun and moon. The attributes held in eight of its twelve hands are slightly different from those in the previous scroll—two astral disks, a sword and a noose (traditional attributes of Fudō), as well as a tray and a tripartite jewel, a *vajra* and a *vajra* bell (traditional attributes of Aizen)—while the four others are joined in two *gasshō* gestures.

FIGURE 6.2. Three-Deva deity (a.k.a. *Manifestation of Inari Daimyōjin*). Hanging scroll, color on silk. Tōji, Kyoto.

The four figures riding foxes are Dakiniten's acolytes. They are distributed in the usual fashion and hold similar attributes, but their faces seem more friendly than usual. The male figure on the right, "Indra's emissary" (Taishaku Shisha 帝釈使者), holds his brush and sheet of paper in a gesture that suggests joviality. The deity's mount is smaller, less impressive; it holds a jewel in its mouth, and a smaller fox head appears above its head. A snake is coiled around its neck, and it has a *vajra* at the tip of its tail. A geometric pattern is also visible, which may be the form of a constellation (although it looks slightly different from the usual pattern of the Northern Dipper). The group is set on a red, irregularly shaped lotus leaf, which is itself set on a cloud above a geometric design.

A slightly different representation is a so-called Dakiniten mandala in the collection of Boston's Museum of Fine Arts (Fig. 6.3). The *honzon* is surrounded by large images of four fox-riding acolytes, with two

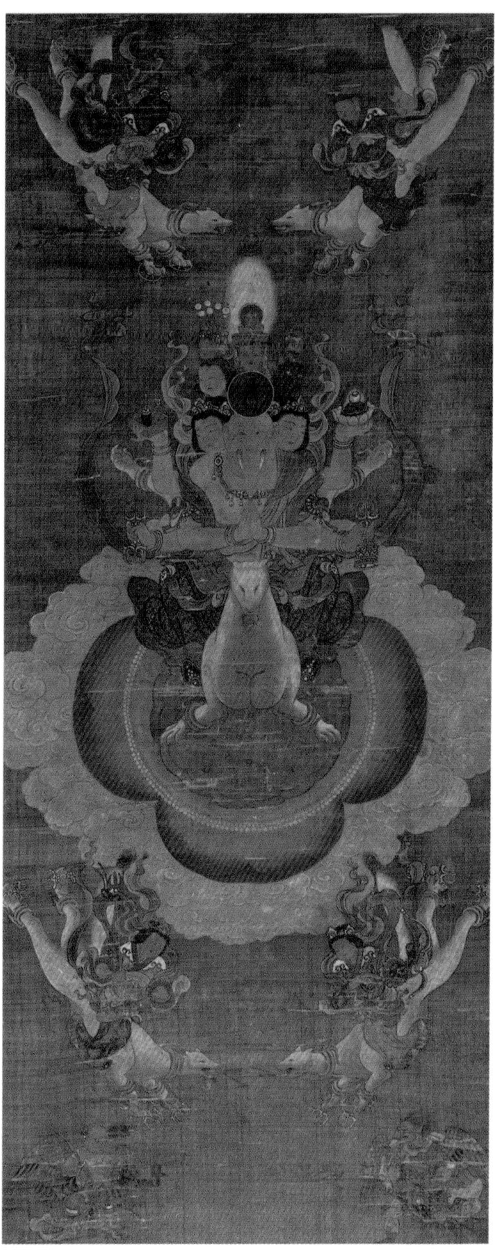

FIGURE 6.3. Dakiniten mandala. Edo period, 18th century. Hanging scroll; ink, color and gold on silk. Museum of Fine Arts, Boston.

warrior-like *tengu* at the bottom of the scroll. In spite of the museum's label, the central face of the *honzon* is not that of Dakiniten, but Shōten. It has a red solar disk with a three-legged crow above its head, while the other two faces, Dakiniten and Benzaiten, have nothing. It has only six arms—its two upper hands hold a box with a key and a lotus dais with three jewels on it; its median hands hold a three-pronged *vajra* and a *vajra* bell; its lower hands are joined in *gasshō*. The idiosyncrasy begins with the additional heads, on either side of the solar disk: one is red and wears a lion diadem (like Aizen); the other looks like a bodhisattva, and has another head on it. Above the solar disk is another head, which wears what looks like a diadem, but on closer inspection consists of two ranks of smaller heads (ten in all, with one more above, calling to mind the Eleven-faced Kannon). The identity of these figures eludes me, and the mystery remains. In spite of the baroque composition, the general impression is one of harmony.

(c) A further development of the same motifs can be found in another scroll, from Yochi-in 桜池院 (Edo period) on Mount Kōya, labeled simply *Dakiniten* (Fig. 6.4). Ugajin appears above the central head, which may be that of Dakiniten, just as he does in representations of Uga Benzaiten. The two flanking heads, Shōten and Benzaiten, have the sun and moon above them, and next to them are two *more* heads—that of a lion next to Shōten, an eagle next to Benzaiten—which have no counterpart in any other image or text. Furthermore, to the left of Ugajin is a large goat head, and above them are two small buddhas. Small figures also appear above the heads of the lion and the eagle. The deity has twelve arms: ten of its hands hold the usual attributes (wheel and key, sun and moon disks, noose and sword, jewel and staff, *vajra* and *vajra* bell), while two hands are held in *gasshō* in front of its chest. Another striking detail is the strange perspective that places two of the four minuscule acolytes as well as the mount's hind legs and tail at the top of the picture. Finally, a constellation pattern appears on the fox's tail, on which there is

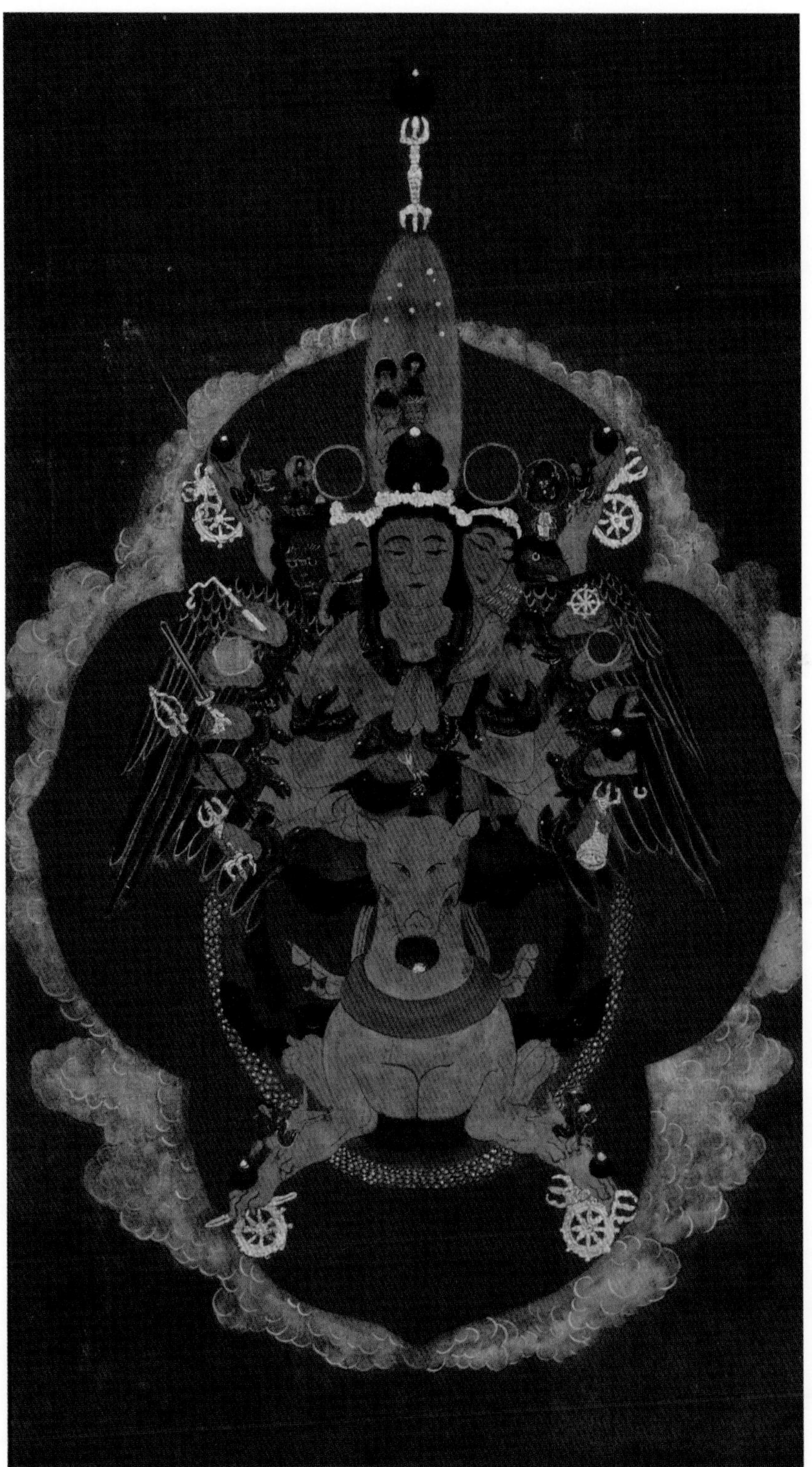

FIGURE 6.4. Three-Deva deity (a.k.a. *Dakiniten*). Edo period. Hanging scroll, color on silk. Edo period. Yochi-in, Kōyasan (Wakayama prefecture).

FIGURE 6.5. Three-Deva deity (a.k.a. *Jade Woman Deity*). Edo period. Sheet, ink on paper. University Art Museum, Kyoto City University of Arts. *BZS* 4114.

a three-pronged *vajra* and jewel, adding to the verticality of the picture. The fox's paws rest on jewels, *vajras,* and dharma wheels. The whole painting is teeming with esoteric Buddhist symbolism.

Also worth mentioning is a line drawing from the Nōman-in 能満院 collection of the Chōhōji 頂法寺 in Kyoto (popularly known as Rokkakudō 六角堂) (Fig. 6.5). It is a simpler composition, surprisingly called *Jade Woman Deity* (*Gyokujo-shin* 玉女神), a name that suggests an Onmyōdō influence. The twelve-armed deity, flanked by only two fox-riding acolytes, has Shōten's face at the center. Its lower hands hold Shōten's traditional attributes, a kind of cake and a radish (*daikon*), while its other pairs of hands hold three jewels and a sword, a trident and a key, a wheel and a jeweled staff, and a bow and set of arrows. Two hands are also joined in *gasshō.* Unlike paintings of the same type, no sun and moon are visible above the deity's head(s), nor other heads. The fox on which it is mounted has a snake coiled around its neck. It is flanked by two fox-riding youths, facing each other, their hands also joined in *gasshō.*

A striking element in all these representations is the frontal position of the fox, which is seen in plunging view, as if the viewer were positioned slightly above and in front of the scene. This feature is accentuated by the unusual form of the lotus on which (or above which) the god and his mount are set: in the various exemplars, the four large petals of this lotus surround the *honzon* according to different perspectives that correspond to the elevation of the viewer's vantage point. This lotus is lined with a fringe of clouds, which indicates that the scene takes place in the sky.[32] The cloud trailing behind the fox legs gives a sense of great speed. In most cases, the fox is drawn in a frontal fashion that gives its body a massive and uncanny appearance. At times it is represented sideways, plunging toward the lower right of the painting—although the god standing on it still faces the viewer.[33] The astral symbolism of the sun and moon is reinforced by the diagram of a constellation (usually the Northern Dipper) above it.

Complex Mandalas

So much for scrolls depicting the composite Three-Deva deity in relative isolation. The viewer's feeling of uncanniness may increase by several degrees with the second type of representation I want to discuss, the so-called Dakiniten mandalas. (One of them, misleadingly labeled Izuna mandala, has already been mentioned in relation with Dakiniten.) These works are far more complex than the aforementioned scrolls and are characterized by a significant increase in the size of the deity's retinue. The feeling of something preternatural—due in part to the proliferation of snakes, foxes, and other animals, depicted alongside auspicious symbols—introduces a dimension of trouble (or even threat) in a painting that is supposed to center on good fortune. Despite the diversity of the surroundings, the representation of the *honzon* remains basically the same as that of the simpler images: a frontal vision of the deity riding a fox, on a large lotus lined with clouds. In addition to the multiheaded deity surrounded by four acolytes, some or all of the following elements can usually be found:

1) Two attendants, at the feet or in front of the main deity: according to oral tradition, they are the devas Suiten 水天 (Sk. Varuṇa) and Katen 火天 (Sk. Agni).

2) Two goddesses bringing offerings, flanking the main deity. They are identified as Kichijōten 吉祥天 (Skt. Śrī or Lakṣmī) on the left and Kariteimo 訶梨帝母 (a.k.a. Kishimojin 鬼子母神, Skt. Hārītī) on the right.

3) Fifteen or sixteen divine youths (*dōji*), disposed in rather linear fashion on each side of the main deity. They clearly represent (or are patterned after) the "children" or acolytes of Benzaiten. Most of them ride animals (fish, crane or heron, horse, ox, deer, fox, and snake) and hold specific attributes.

4) In cases where we find only eight *dōji,* they are the acolytes of Dakiniten rather than those of Benzaiten. In the Fushimi Inari mandala, their group includes an old man.

5) At the bottom of the image, two armored generals of the bird *tengu* variety are visible; they seem to be running toward each other or toward the viewer.

Let us start with a particularly rich scroll, a Kasuga mandala preserved at Boston's Museum of Fine Arts (Fig. 6.6).[34] In the upper part of the image, a deer, traditional messenger of the Kasuga deity, can be seen standing at the foot of Kasuga mountain (Fig. 6.7). Below it are two goddesses

FIGURE 6.6. Dakiniten mandala, Kasuga Shrine. Muromachi period. Panel, ink, color, and gold on silk. Museum of Fine Arts, Boston.

with offerings: Kariteimo, on the right, is surrounded by her children; Kichijōten, on the left, rides what appears to be a phoenix (Fig. 6.8). Below them, the three-faced *honzon* rides a white fox and is flanked by two female acolytes, who are also riding foxes. Despite its being identified as Dakiniten, its central face is that of Shōten. It has a coiled Ugajin over its head.

The other figures in the mandala together constitute an epitome of Japanese Tantric iconography: below the *honzon* is a dual-body Kangiten, flanked by two unidentified figures (the one on the left could be Myōken). Further below, Aizen Myōō is seated on a vase inside a fiery circle. On the left is one of the *tengu*-like figures that usually accompany Dakiniten. On the right, however, is a standing, black figure (Mahākāla, J. Daikokuten) holding an elephant-skin over his head. At the bottom, various offerings of food are arrayed, a feature reminiscent of the Tenkawa Benzaiten mandala, to which we will return shortly.

Along the same lines, I would like to mention a Dakiniten mandala in the collection of the Tokyo National Museum (Fig. 6.9). The central face of the *honzon,* again, is that of Shōten. Its main point of interest is that the *honzon* is surrounded by the fifteen *dōji* bringing gifts, together with a small Daikokuten just under the fox, in the lower part of the scroll (Fig. 6.10), while the upper part is filled with an impressive representation of the twelve directional devas.

Another particularly fine exemplar is a mandala dated from the Nanbokuchō period, belonging to the Osaka Municipal Museum of Art (Fig. 6.11). The main figure is a three-faced, twelve-armed deity. The white face at the center is probably that of Dakiniten, surmounted by Ugajin. The red face on the left is Benzaiten, surmounted by a moon disk; the elephant face

FIGURE 6.7. Detail of Dakiniten mandala, Kasuga Shrine. Muromachi period. Panel, ink, color, and gold on silk. Museum of Fine Arts, Boston.

FIGURE 6.8. Detail of Dakiniten mandala, Kasuga Shrine. Muromachi period. Panel, ink, color, and gold on silk. Museum of Fine Arts, Boston.

on the right is Shōten, surmounted by a sun-disk. Further up, the seven stars of the Northern Dipper are visible. This mandala lacks the four fox-riding attendants found in other mandalas. The *honzon* is surrounded by Benzaiten's sixteen *dōji,* several of whom are riding foxes or other animals.[35] Equally prominent are the four acolytes and the two running, warrior-like emissaries of Dakiniten: a bird *tengu* holding a spear, and a red-faced, winged goblin holding a sword.[36]

An intriguing detail in this scroll is the presence of a couple of hybrid deities standing below (or in front of) the main deity. Both are naked to the waist: the man's body is red, and he wears a black hat; the woman's body is white. They hold each other around the waist with one arm and hold up an unidentified object in their free hand. Even more unexpected, the male

FIGURE 6.9. Dakiniten mandala. Muromachi period. Hanging scroll, color on silk. Tokyo National Museum.

has a fish tail and the female a fox tail. They are flanked by two foxes that are plunging toward these tails and apparently biting them.

The Tenkawa Benzaiten Mandala

The strange couple in the Dakiniten mandala of the Osaka Municipal Museum of Art, whose role and identities remain mysterious, provides a bridge to a second iconographical series consisting of variations on a theme—that of the so-called Tenkawa Benzaiten mandala. As noted above, the Tenkawa Shrine near Yoshino is one of Benzaiten's cultic centers. The Tenkawa Benzaiten mandala is known mainly through four scrolls, all dated to the Muromachi period: a set of two scrolls preserved at Nōman-in 能満院, a *tatchū* 塔頭 or subtemple of Hasedera in Nara prefecture (not to be confused with the aforementioned Nōman-in in Kyoto) (Figs. 6.12 and 6.15), a single scroll preserved at Shinnō-in 親王院 (Wakayama prefecture) (Fig. 6.16), and a fourth scroll preserved at Ishiyamadera 石山寺 (Shiga prefecture).[37] According to writing appearing at the end of the first Nōman-in scroll, it was painted in 1546 by Rinken 琳賢 (an *e-busshi* 絵佛師 from the Nara-based Handaza 吐田座 guild). The second Nōman-in painting is attributed to a certain Takuma Hōgen 琢磨法眼. Nothing is known about him, but he was most likely a painter from Nara.

The central subject of these mandalas is Benzaiten, dressed as an elegant Chinese lady. Yet her elegance is belied by the three serpent (or dragon) heads that replace her feminine face. Their mouths emit clouds of dark vapor, in the midst of which three wish-fulfilling jewels are visible

FIGURE 6.10. Detail of Dakiniten mandala. Muromachi period. Hanging scroll, color on silk. Tokyo National Museum.

(Fig. 6.13). This haunting image has neither a textual counterpart nor any equivalent in Japanese iconography. It has no clear Indian or Chinese antecedent either, although Indian *nāginīs* can be represented with snake hoods emerging above their heads. The closest representation I have found is that of the dragon goddess Fude (Fude Longnü 福得龍女) in the so-called Long Scroll of the Dali kingdom.[38] This *nāginī* was identified with the Dali deity Baijie Shengfei 白姐聖妃 (Holy Consort White Sister), who was said to be the consort of Mahākāla. She was also identified with Hārītī and Śrī. An inscription dated 1461 reads: "The three snakes above her head express her mastery over the three realms."[39] Benzaiten is often paired with Daikokuten, but in the Tenkawa mandala her two female attendants are Kichijōten (Skt. Śrī) and Kariteimo (Hārītī). I have, however, no clue as to how a Dali image might have resurfaced in the vision of a Japanese monk of the Muromachi period. Although numerous foxes appear in the picture, the three-headed *honzon* is shown standing instead of riding a fox, as in the Dakiniten mandala. The sixteen youths are visible in the two Nōman-in scrolls (although not in the Shinnō-in scroll). Three snake-headed guardians also appear; in oral tradition they are referred to as the three princes.

A woodblock print of the Tenkawa Benzaiten mandala in the *Bukkyō zuzō shūsei* corresponds to the painting by Rinken (Fig. 6.12), but it also contains inscriptions that are unfortunately illegible (Fig. 6.17). It shows that this representation of the Tenkawa mandala proliferated during the Edo period as a mandala of Mount Misen, the peak behind Tenkawa Shrine.[40]

One of the Nōman-in scrolls contains another striking (yet by now familiar) element, linking it to the Osaka Dakiniten mandala: not just one, but two couples of half-naked, hybrid deities appearing toward the bottom of the picture, bringing to mind the fauns of ancient Greece (Fig. 6.16). Their amorous postures also give the scene a vague resemblance to Bosch's *Garden of Delights.* The male of the couple on the left wears a black hat, and he holds the female by her waist. She has a fox tail, he has

FIGURE 6.11. Dakiniten mandala. Nanbokuchō period, 14th century. Hanging scroll, color on silk. Osaka Municipal Museum of Art.

FIGURE 6.12. Tenkawa Benzaiten mandala, by Rinken. Muromachi period, 1546. Hanging scroll, color on silk. Nōman-in, Sakurai (Nara prefecture).

FIGURE 6.13. Tenkawa Benzaiten mandala, attr. Takuma Hōgen. Muromachi period. Hanging scroll, color on silk. Nōman-in, Sakurai (Nara prefecture).

bird legs. She holds a cone of white rice or sugar in her right hand while he holds an open fruit in his left. They are flanked by two foxes, which are depicted in the same plunging posture as those in the Dakiniten mandala.

The couple on the right stands on snake skins and the two partners face each other. The female deity has four arms and holds what look like sugar cones in three of her hands; a white fox tail emerges from under her skirt. The male deity holds a tray of fruit, and he has bird legs. Their are flanked by a seated fox and two coiled snakes. Further below are what appear to be two large insects, a rat, and a centipede or caterpillar.

The two Nōman-in mandalas seem to form a set, and their differences are limited to color and minor details. In Fig. 6.13, the dominant color is green (the color of Benzaiten's dress and of the three snake/dragon heads), whereas in Fig. 6.12 brown tones are more important, a contrast that could be related to specific spring and autumn rituals.[41] This interpretation is reinforced by another shared characteristic: the presence of large ritual objects—in particular, vases filled with jewels, a motif reminiscent of Aizen Myōō representations. The *Inori no michi* 祈りの道 catalogue explains that these objects evoke the seven treasures of the *cakravartin* king, but this is not very convincing. Another significant element is the proliferation of wish-fulfilling jewels.

FIGURE 6.14. Tenkawa Benzaiten mandala. Muromachi period. Hanging scroll, color on silk. Shinnō-in, Kōyasan (Wakayama prefecture).

In one scroll, the two snake-headed guardians at the top of the picture are connected by an arc of jewels that emanates from their mouths, giving the impression they are juggling; similarly, the offerings just mentioned are outlined by *cintāmaṇi* jewels. At the top of the picture, the three mountains in the distance are themselves crowned by large wish-fulfilling jewels. They probably represent the three peaks of Yoshino, with Misen (Mount Sumeru), the mountain behind Tenkawa Shrine, at the center; Kinpusen is on the Yoshino side, and Ōmine on the Kumano side.

FIGURE 6.15. Detail of Tenkawa Benzaiten mandala, by Rinken. Muromachi period, 1546. Hanging scroll, color on silk. Nōman-in, Sakurai (Nara prefecture).

FIGURE 6.16. Detail of Tenkawa Benzaiten mandala, by Rinken. Muromachi period, 1546. Hanging scroll, color on silk. Nōman-in, Sakurai (Nara prefecture).

The Shinnō-in mandala has a simpler structure.[42] The *honzon* is not surrounded by the fifteen or sixteen youths. The two deities on whose hands she stands are identified as Suiten (Skt. Varuṇa) and Katen (Skt. Agni), the water and fire devas; the two goddesses making offerings are Kichijōten and Kariteimo.[43]

For the sake of comparison, we should look at the Tenkawa Benzaiten mandala housed in the Nezu Museum in Tokyo.[44] Also from the Muromachi period, its central deity is an anthropomorphic figure, the traditional eight-armed Benzaiten, surrounded by the fifteen *dōji* and Daikokuten. The two protectors found at the top of the other Tenkawa mandala scrolls have been replaced by Zaō Gongen (on the left) and En no Gyōja (on the right), two mythical figures associated with Yoshino Shugendō. No snake-headed deities are visible. The *dōji* are grouped in a more natural way and do not ride animals. Although this picture was produced around the same time and in the same place, it entirely lacks the unsettling characteristics of the other pictures I have discussed.

FIGURE 6.17. Tenkawa Benzaiten mandala. Edo period. Sheet, ink on paper. University Art Museum, Kyoto City University of Arts. *BZS* 2218.

The Tohachi Bishamon 刀八毘沙門 mandala of Shinnō-in (Muromachi period) provides another interesting contrast.[45] The *honzon* here is a four-headed, ten-armed Bishamonten who wears a lion headgear above which two small, seated buddhas are visible. His four faces are alike. He holds a spear and a stupa in his two upper hands, a key and a jewel (the usual attributes of Benzaiten) in the next pair of hands, and eight swords in the remaining hands. He rides a lion, which stands on four lotuses. The god's feet rest on two tortoises (emblems of the north). The lion's frontal view is strongly reminiscent of that of the fox in the Dakiniten mandala (in contrast to Monju's lion, usually depicted in profile).[46] The fox-riding acolytes of Dakiniten are also found here, and Bishamonten's mandala is clearly influenced by those of Dakiniten and Benzaiten. As noted, he holds several of Benzaiten's attributes, and several of the sixteen deities around him seem to belong to the retinues of Benzaiten and Dakiniten. A few of them carry a large bag over their shoulders, not unlike Daikokuten, although the latter is rarely depicted atop a fox. Daikokuten also seems to be invoked by one of the figures: a youth holding a ball of rice above his head (also found in the Dakiniten mandala). This youth resembles one of the six manifestations of Daikokuten. Also worth mentioning are two red, wrathful deities: one holding a bow and arrows (like Aizen), the other two spears. (The latter also appears in several Dakiniten mandalas.) In addition, there are two warrior-like *tengu* (who seem to be Dakiniten's emissaries), a *nāga* king presenting a fruit offering, and a man wearing a hat and carrying two bundles of rice stalks (a motif usually associated with the Inari deity).[47]

Interpicturality

I have presented these paintings in such detail not only because "the god is in the details," but also because these motifs reveal the *interpicturality* (an iconological equivalent of the literary term "intertextuality") at work in the composition of these pictures. Many of their features remain incomprehensible, and perhaps they have no "signification" in the strict, symbolic sense of the term but are merely there to create or reinforce a certain atmosphere. They plunge the viewer into an oneirical or visionary milieu in which the deities cannot be reduced to their shared, pragmatic function as gods of fortune, even if it was the same circulation of symbols, transfer of attributes, and network of identifications that allowed both the Three-Deva deity and other ternary figures such as the Three-faced Daikoku (Sanmen Daikoku 三面大黒) to develop.

Every viewer selects specific motifs in a painting on the basis of his or her own neuronal library. The details that struck me the most are the half-naked hybrid deities in the Osaka Dakiniten mandala and in the foreground of one of the Nōman-in mandalas. As Yves Bonnefoy points out, when a detail invades the foreground of a scene—for instance, the horse in

Carravagio's famous *Conversion of Saint Paul*—"it is no longer a detail, its status changes, it expresses some unavoidable necessity."[48] Without denying the register of symbolic and ritual relevance, I want to emphasize here a "noninterpretive interpretation" that resonates with Michel de Certeau's discussion of Bosch's *Garden of Delights.*[49] I would argue that here, after paying due attention to ritual and historical contexts, the interpreter must take the risk of committing an anachronism. It could be that the painting, in de Certeau's words, "organizes, aesthetically, a loss of meaning" which no interpretation (whether historical, socioeconomic, mythological, ritual, or psychological) can come from without to fill in.[50] Like Bosch's *Garden,* the Tenkawa Benzaiten mandala may not be reduced to the univocity of a master narrative. Perhaps "it not only establishes itself within a *difference* in relation to all meaning; it produces its difference in *making us believe that it contains hidden meaning.*"[51] There is no denying that many of the iconographic, mythological, and ritual elements in this painting do in fact *make sense.* But perhaps that sense, if not purely illusory, lies merely at the level of conventional truth while the painting conveys not a deeper doctrinal truth, but a more immediate affect—namely, its uncanniness, obtained by the merging of the divine, human, and animal registers, and by the commingling of auspicious signs of wealth and natural sexuality together with an ugly, threatening, reptilian presence. As de Certeau remarks, "the painting seems both to *provoke* and *frustrate* each one of these interpretive meanings. . . . It does not cease *withdrawing,* thanks to the *secrecy effect* it produces."[52] In other words, we should not even ascribe to this painting "the status of an enigma, a statement that tells 'the truth' to the extent, and only to the extent, that it means what we make it say." Perhaps its aesthetics "does not consist in generating new lights for intelligibility but in extinguishing it."[53] While recognizing the importance of the aesthetic and ritual levels, I want to suggest here in passing the possibility that we need temporarily to withdraw from our conventional interpretive mode in order to yield to the fascination that this representation (or more exactly, "presentification") exerts on us, and to realize that this uncanniness, in the Freudian sense, brings us closer to the reality of the devas than any hermeneutic rationalization, any doctrinal or cultural recuperation.

THE THREE-FACED DAIKOKU

The Three-Deva deity has been compared with the Three-faced Daikokuten,[54] but in the case of the latter, one seems rather to be dealing with a process of reduction and fixation, a symbolic impoverishment, an erasure of ambivalence. That process eventually led to the formation of the Seven Gods of Fortune, a set of dignitaries in whom all shadows and suspicions of ambiguity have disappeared, and the dark side, which lent

Dakiniten and the deities of her entourage an air of heterodoxy, has been all but erased.

The legend of the Three-faced Daikoku (Sanmen Daikoku) is relatively late, probably dating from the Muromachi period. In the *Sōgi shokoku monogatari* 宗祇諸国物語, for instance, Daikokuten appears to Saichō in response to the latter's request that he protect his future monastery, and he first offers to provide sustenance for one thousand monks per day. Saichō, however, is concerned that this will not suffice for his envisioned community of three thousand monks. Daikokuten then manifests himself in his three-faced, six-armed form.[55]

It may be said that Daikokuten's three faces reflect the taste of Tendai scholars for ternary models. Such models, however, fail to explain why two of these faces, which initially belonged to the same Daikokuten, eventually became those of Bishamonten and Benzaiten. Apparently, at the time of the compilation of the *Keiran shūyōshū,* the name Sanmen Daikoku did not yet refer to three distinct deities: the three faces were those of the wrathful Mahākāla, as this deity was depicted in the Womb Realm mandala, and they simply symbolized the trifunctional nature of the god. As Iyanaga points out, "although this form is specific to Japan and somewhat late, there are reasons to think that the choice of these three deities was not arbitrary, but on the contrary stems from a coherent system of beliefs, whose origins can perhaps be traced back to Central Asia."[56] The transformation of Daikokuten's three faces also presupposes the notion of the Three Devas as forming a single deity.

Another element that must have played a role is the symbolism of the wish-fulfilling jewel, common to these three deities. In a painting of Danrinji 大林寺 (Kyoto prefecture), Sanmen Daikoku (with Bishamonten and Benzaiten as lateral faces) is represented inside a large, pink transparent jewel (like Ugajin, the deity lurking behind both Daikokuten and Benzaiten). Both Ugajin and Daikokuten were indeed identified with the wish-fulfilling jewel. Although his convential attributes are the mallet and sack, in esoteric rites it is the jewel.

Certain scholars see the Three-faced Daikoku as the prototype for the Seven Gods of Fortune.[57] According to Nakagawa Zenkyō, for example, he represents a new, purely Japanese type of deity, quite distinct from the six-armed, three-faced Mahākāla of the early esoteric mandalas. Nakagawa thinks that this new deity was created to be the ideal god of fortune, formed by combining Daikokuten, Bishamonten and Benzaiten.[58] Iyanaga has expressed doubts about this interpretation: even if the auspicious new god has masked the blood-thirsty deities that preceded him—the *ḍākinīs* and other *yakṣas*—those demons are never that far away.

There also exists a three-faced Bishamon (with Bishamonten at the center, Kichijōten on the left, and Daikokuten on the right). The deities represented are the same as those that make up the Three-faced

Daikokuten; only the order of precedence differs, which is similar to the Three Devas, wherein each deity takes its turn at the center. In the present case, however, there is no known example of Kichijōten at the center. The above image reflects a late development, perhaps triggered by the growth of Bishamonten's cult at Kurama.

While the tendency to fuse multiple deities into a single one to obtain a superdeity seems relatively natural, it remained a relatively rare phenomenon in medieval Japan—the dual-body Bishamon, two-headed Aizen, and dual-body Kangiten being examples that come to mind. In other cases (such as Bonten), the various faces merely express multiple facets or functions of the same god.

Although Benzaiten is often represented as flanked by Bishamonten and Daikokuten, she is practically never the central figure of a three-faced statue. A significant exception is the Benzaiten triad of Rinshōji 林昌寺 (Gunma prefecture), dated 1703. Here the central face is that of Benzaiten, the right one that of Bishamonten, the left one that of Daikokuten.

INDIVIDUALS AND INSTITUTIONS

Although a motif as widespread as the Three Devas cannot be attributed solely to localized efforts by individuals and institutions, a few can be identified as having been particularly instrumental to its emergence and development. First, in Insei-period Shingon, particularly in the Ono branches of Daigoji 醍醐寺 and Kajūji 勧修寺, there was an elaboration of the mystique of the jewel and of the emperor, organized around the legend of Kūkai. Influential Shingon masters of the period include Ningai 仁海 (951–1046) and his disciples Seison 成尊 (1012–1074), Gihan 義範 (1023–1088), Hanjun 範俊 (1038–1112), and Shōken 聖賢 (1083–1147). The last two, like Kūkai himself, are said to have produced wish-fulfilling jewels.[59] The fact that precisely three masters produced jewels is of course not accidental in a history governed by ternary logic. Hanjun also developed an Aizen rite centered on the jewel in 1080.[60] It is also in these branches of Shingon that the cult of Nyoirin developed, leading to the Joint Ritual of the Three Worthies (Nyoirin, Aizen, and Fudō), a development that occurred around the same time that Shukaku Hōshinnō described the *yakṣa* of Tōji as a combination (and culmination) of the Three Devas.

Another important figure was the Kōfukuji monk Shinkō 真興 (934–1004), founder of the Kojima branch of Shingon, who played a critical role in the synthesis of the Hossō and Shingon teachings. Shinkō's dreams and visions contributed to the development and assimilation of the figures of Shōten, Benzaiten, and Kōjin. He was particularly instrumental in the elaboration of the embryological symbolism that later became so important in medieval esotericism (particularly in the Tachikawa-ryū). The so-called Kojima Kōjin also became a regular figure in the Benzaiten mandalas of the Muromachi period. Shinkō is said to have had a vision in which he received a "sudden realization" (*tonjō shitsuji* 頓成悉地) rite, a ritual usually associated with Dakiniten or with the Three Devas, but which seems in this case to be referring to Shōten.[61]

The Aizen ritual also developed in Tendai with Kōgei, a.k.a. Ikegami Ajari 池上阿闍梨 (977–1049), the "systematizer of Tendai," who is also credited with the elaboration of the Six Kannon Ritual. Equally important is Kōgei's role in the development of Benzaiten's cult. He was, among other things, the author of the *Enoshima engi.* It was Kōgei who created the association between Ugajin, Kōjin, and Jūzenji (the child god of Hie Shrine) and identified these figures as placenta deities.[62] Kōgei was the nephew of Shōkū 性空 (?–1007), the famous monk of Mount Shosha 書写. He was himself a kind of *shugenja,* who had lived and practiced in Kyūshū before settling in Tanba province and then returning to Mount Hiei late in his life. Through him the impact of local Kyūshū cults (influenced by Korean immigrants) was strongly felt. Like the blind monks of Kyūshū, he is said to have performed powerful earth-quelling rituals. Another case in point is the cult of Oto Gohō, the deity of Sefurisan in northern Kyūshū, who became one of Benzaiten's fifteen *dōji.*[63] Kōgei's influence concerning this cult is made clear in the *Keiran shūyōshū.*

Between the Insei period and the end of the Kamakura period, and perhaps linking Kōgei and the *Keiran shūyōshū,* we find the alleged founder of the Miwa-ryu, Kyōen 慶円 (1140–1223) and his disciples. Although it is not clear whether Kyōen himself practiced at Miwa, he was clearly well connected with the Mount Murō cult focused on the dragon and the wish-fulfilling jewel.[64] He was indeed well versed in both the Shingon and Tendai doctrines, and in that sense provided a good synthesis of both schools. He also contributed to the development of the figure of Kōjin and the cult of snake deities like Ugajin (and the Miwa deity itself).[65] One of Kyōen's disciples was Rendōbō Hōkyō 蓮道房宝篋 (fl. thirteenth century), a monk connected with the Tachikawa-ryū.

Another monk of the Shingon-Ritsu school that contributed to the development of the Joint Ritual of the Three Worthies, and perhaps to that of the Dakiniten cult as well, is Monkan.

We have already noted the important role that Kōshū and his disciple Unkai 運海 played in Tendai mythology. In fact, as Tanaka Takako has shown, the sections of the *Keiran shūyōshū* relative to Shōten, Dakiniten, and Benzaiten integrated an independent work by Unkai, the *Himitsu yōshū* 秘密要集. Unlike his eclectic master Kōshū, Unkai merely recorded the rituals related to these three (or four) devas. This may be due to the fact that, while Kōshū was primarily a chronicler (*kike*), Unkai was a Vinaya master (*kaike* 戒家) of the Kurodani-ryū, a branch of Taimitsu centered on these devas and their rituals. In other words, priests of the

Kurodani-ryū, and more specifically Unkai, seem to have been instrumental in transforming the Three Devas into a single deity, following the precedent established two centuries earlier by Matarajin, the protecting deity of Tōji.[66]

If we turn to the groups and institutions represented by these monks, we have the Shingon monasteries—in particular, Daigoji, Murōji, and the Tōji-Inari complex—on the one hand, and the Tendai monasteries Enryakuji and Onjōji (Miidera) on the other. In between, we find the constellation formed by the Kōfukuji-Kasuga and the Yoshino-Tenkawa complexes (in the northern part and at the southern tip of the Nara basin, respectively), and Katsuoji 勝尾寺 (also read Katsunoo-dera) and Minoodera in Settsu province (modern-day Osaka). Many of these places were Shugendō centers.

The Miwa-ryu can be seen as an extension of the influence of Mount Murō, on the one hand, and of Saidaiji and Shingon-Ritsu on the other. Saidaiji is well known for its Aizen and Nyoirin statues. As noted above, one of the monks who performed the combined Benzaiten-Dakiniten rituals at Enoshima was the Ritsu monk Ninshō 忍性 (Ryōkan Shōnin).

The influence of these groups is also visible in (and through) texts such as the *Bikisho,* the *Jindaikan hiketsu,* and the *Tenshō daijin kuketsu* 天照大神口訣.[67] Many of these texts were preserved at Shinpukuji (Ōsu bunko) in Nagoya, a temple founded by Nōshin 能信 (1291–1354), and at Shōmyōji (Kanazawa bunko) in Yokohama. The *Jindaikan kuketsu,* for instance, contains sections on Nyoirin Kannon and the jewels, on Aizen and Fudō, on the Three Devas, and on embryological symbolism.

Finally, the figure of Dakiniten as Shinkoō Bosatsu developed at the Tōji-Inari complex, probably under the influence of Shugendō. As can be seen from the *Inari ki,* the combination of the Three Devas with the deities of Inari was already achieved by the mid-Kamakura period. However, it was after the destruction of Inari Shrine during the Ōnin War and its restoration by Buddhist monks in 1474 that the Buddhist presence was institutionally affirmed at Inari with the founding of Aizenji. Its first abbot, Tenna 天阿 (1598–1674), also became the abbot of Shinkoō-ji 辰狐王寺 in Edo and of Keihōji 慶法寺 in Ise. He contributed to the elaboration of Ryōbu shintō theories related to Inari and was also a devotee of Kangiten. His hagiography is replete with stories of the manifestations of foxes.[68]

Outside of monastic institutions proper, we should also take into account the influence of *sarugaku* groups centered around Kasuga and Mount Hiei, as well as that of the *biwa hōshi* of Mount Hiei and other blind monks in the Kyūshū tradition. Other external influences include the actions of yin-yang masters. We have seen that the three-faced deity was also called Jade Woman, and the Dakiniten cult apparently developed in

Onmyōdō. This influence was already clear by the Insei period with the emergence of Myōken Bosatsu and this deity's transformation (in Hanjun's circle) into the figure of Rokuji Myōō, a development that paved the way for Shinkoō Bosatsu.

THE TRIADIC STRUCTURE

Having presented a brief history of the Three Devas and their changing and complex iconography, I want to return to the questions posed at the outset of this chapter. First, what led medieval Buddhists to worship the Three Devas as a single composite deity? It would appear that the grouping of several deities perceived as having functional or symbolic similarities within a single ritual (or parallel ones) such as the Joint Ritual of the Three Devas may have been part of a strategy for obtaining greater ritual efficacy. As noted above, Sasama thinks that the grouping of Daikokuten, Benzaiten, and Bishamonten into a single deity called Sanmen Daikoku was simply an aggregation of three gods of fortune.[69]

If that is true, then we have a specialization of function (within a larger meta-function, namely, bringing happiness) that prefigures the Seven Gods of Fortune. This type of analysis, however, falls short of a full explanation. First, as Iyanaga points out, reducing ambiguous deities to a single function—bringing good fortune, in this case—obscures those deities' multifaceted character. Even if that was in fact the case for Sanmen Daikoku, things might not have been so simple in the case of the Three Devas, which developed at an earlier date. Furthermore, it does not explain why we have *three* devas and why these three in particular were chosen.

As for the second question—Why the number three?—the answer is at the same time obvious and unsatisfying. The number three has a particular symbolic value in esoteric Buddhism: the Three Truths of Tendai, three mysteries of Shingon, and three bodies of the Buddha are but a few of the central doctrines for which the number three was crucial. Symbolically, the triangle stands in for the fire of *goma* rituals, and represents the shape of the hearth used for subjugation rituals. It is also evokes the three dots of the Siddham letter *i*, which plays an important role in Tantric ritual, and the three eyes of Śiva, a god who in his Buddhist incarnations as Mahākāla and Maheśvara is the paradigmatic representative of the deva category. The triangular form can also represent the so-called threefold jewel (*sanben hōju* 三辨宝珠), an omnipresent symbol in Japanese Buddhism. As noted earlier, this threefold jewel is associated with many medieval deities, e.g., Benzaiten, whose three main cultic centers are represented as three jewels that form a triangle when linked.

Actually, the Three Devas, like the three musketeers in Alexandre Dumas's novels, are usually *four*, although the identity and status of the fourth member of the set varies. At times it becomes part of the triad, replacing one of the triad's usual members, while in other cases it remains in the background as a multifunctional deity serving as a link between the other three or as their synthesis (as in the case of the Matarajin at Tōji). Iyanaga has argued that the Indic god Śiva lurks behind many devas, particularly when appearing as Matarajin (another name for Mahākāla). Several other "synthetic" deities come to mind, however, such as Aizen Myōō, Yama (as a chthonian deity), and Ugajin.

So the reasons for the combining of deities and for the choice of the number three are not particularly complicated.

While the third question—In any given combination, what criteria informed the choice of specific deities?—is more difficult to answer, in the case at hand the answer seems to be found in symbolic links between, and in characteristics held in common by, Matarajin, Dakiniten, Daikokuten, and Benzaiten. First, although Matarajin (i.e., Mahākāla), Dakiniten, and Daikokuten each have their own separate history, all three initially shared an important characteristic: they all steal the vital essence of humans. In this respect, they are closely related (and opposed) to another deity that symbolizes this vital essence, namely, Aizen Myōō. This characteristic also makes them (almost by default) deities that control human destinies. Following that symbolic thread, we see that they are also related to embryonic gestation and childhood.

From a doctrinal standpoint, the three faces of Matarajin, the protecting deity of Tōji, symbolize the three poisons (hatred, concupiscence, and anger) that subsume all human passions.[70] Iyanaga notes that the three deities were all symbolically related to Aizen Myōō. We recall that in one representation Aizen is flanked by two elephant-headed figures, with the sun and the moon appearing on their diadems, respectively.[71] Like Aizen, the snake god Ugajin is said to dwell in the sun disk. He manifests himself as Dakiniten to grant people longevity and happiness, as Kangiten to remove obstacles in present and future lives, and as Aizen to bestow love on all beings and lead them to enlightenment.[72]

Just as important, however, is the link that connects the Three Devas to the earth deity and to the subterranean realm of Yama. The Three Devas were regarded as part of Yama's retinue, and two of them—Shōten and Dakiniten—are closely related to Mahākāla, an avatar of the earth deity and of Maheśvara (Śiva). Yama is also said to be the "global body" of all the earth deities. The two types of connections are of course not exclusive; on the contrary, they reinforce each other. In the apocryphal *Dhāraṇī Sūtra of Ugaya's Wish-fulfilling Jewel* (*Ugaya tontoku nyoi hōju darani-kyō*), for instance, Uga Benzaiten is related to Amaterasu (called here Nichirin 日輪 'sun wheel'), Dakiniten, Shōten, and Aizen Myōō.[73]

Admittedly, these affinities do not in themselves justify the temporary fusion of the Three Devas into a single deity like Matarajin, the *yakṣa* of Tōji. The link between Benzaiten and Shōten may have been achieved through the intermediary of Hārītī, the "mother of demons" (Kishimojin), who shares with Benzaiten various iconographic features, including numerous offspring.

The iconography thus merely expresses and brings the associative logic to its conclusion. To understand this logic, we must understand each of these devas in its complex singularity and realize that beyond their similarities and constant permutations, it is their differences and their own dynamics that have allowed the three (or four) devas to coexist without being reduced to a single "personality." Yes, the boundaries between them are admittedly blurred at times. By passing through the three-in-one stage, each of the Three Devas was enriched by a variety of features that contributed to its promotion within the medieval pantheon. The same is true of the deity under whose name they were for a time gathered, namely, Matarajin.

THE BROADER CONTEXT

However, the development of the Three Devas paradigm cannot be explained simply by the role of individuals, groups, or institutions. It represents the interconnection of several orders of reality: ideas like the notion of fundamental awakening (*hongaku*), teaching and theories on duality and nonduality, texts, objects (e.g., mandalas, portable altars (*zushi*), divination boards (*shikiban*), relics, and jewels) and technologies, myths, legends, icons, and symbols (e.g., the three jewels, triangles symbolizing fire, the tripod stove, the three-legged solar crow).

Why did it take three centuries for this paradigm to flourish, when its image was already present at Tōji at the end of the eleventh century, and the model of the Joint Ritual of the Three Worthies was already fully developed by that time, in large part owing to Monkan's ternary genius (or obsession)? There is no clear answer to this question at the current time. In the case of the Tenkawa Benzaiten mandala, a circumstantial reason is that it was only after the Nanbokuchō period that the Tenkawa Shrine, which had sided with the Southern Court, was able to flourish again as a pilgrimage center. The mandala drawn by Rinken in 1546 represents the culmination of a long process.

But perhaps at the symbolic level the center of gravity had first to shift from a hierarchical or vertical model to a horizontal one in which the Three Devas could become interchangeable. The goal of rituals in the two models differs, the first focusing on exorcism, the latter on "realization" (Skt. *siddhi,* J. *shitsuji* or *shijji* 悉地). Again, the linkage of the Three Devas was also permitted by the development of the figures of Kōjin and Aizen. Although these figures were already present at the time of Shinkō and Hanjun, their real impact came later, perhaps under Tachikawa-ryū influence, as can be seen by the importance of the *Shinkō musōki* among the Shōmyōji documents copied by the second abbot, Kenna. In this text,

Shōten is not only identified with the placenta deity known as Ena Kōjin, he is also identified with Ugajin. While the Nyorai Kōjin was identified with Aizen, it is only during the Muromachi period that the Kojima Kōjin dreamed by Shinkō was included regularly in the Benzaiten mandalas.[74] Kōjin also constitutes a common ground between Shinkō, Kōgei, Kyōen, and Kōshū. At this point, the distinction between Shingon and Tendai is moot. This is particularly true of Kyōen: he seems to have been a kind of shamanistic type and is said to have received a Kōjin ritual from Kōjin himself (or from Māra).

The ternary logic expressed in the Santen gōgyō-hō ritual first entered the imperial mystique as an extension of the Dakiniten ritual used in the enthronement ceremony.[75] As Iyanaga points out, however, there was an important element of gender in this notion of "three combined" (two male, one female; or two female, one male). Perhaps it is significant that the change in the male-to-female ratio between the Three Worthies and the Three Devas is also a shift from a predominance of the male to the female element.

In the triangular pattern formed by the Three Worthies (Nyoirin, Aizen, and Fudō), we still find the traditional hierarchical model of the *honzon* flanked by his two acolytes. In the case of the Three Devas, however, one observes a permutation of center and acolytes. Each deva takes the central position in turn. They are therefore in a relationship of equality, and the *honzon* is only the *primus* (or *prima*) *inter pares*. Furthermore, the triangular pattern in the *sanzon gōgyō-hō* involved a structure of production (two elements engendering the third) or of emanation (one element engendering the other two, much as the Dao produces yin and yang). The dominant metaphor was that of duality merging into nonduality. Although this pattern is fundamental in medieval Japanese theology, it can be found in other mythological traditions as well, as R. Stein has shown in his discussion of beliefs related to the three stove deities found throughout Asia.

However, I want to stress that the figure of the Three Devas is not simply the combination of three clearly defined deities; actually, as the iconography shows, it overflows the ternary model—more heads appearing in almost random fashion next to or on top of those of the Three Devas. It is rather the progressive convergence or emergence of bundles of features—a mangling and tangling of ideas, myths, symbols, and rituals resulting in the concentration and contraction of a nebula that we then perceive as some sort of core. We never obtain a neat structure à la Lévi-Strauss, but an entangled knot that leaves the viewer himself confused and bewildered. The networks of associations and permutations determine a field of potentialities, within which a precise and composite image becomes fixed.

The iconographic representation of the Three Devas as a single composite deity adds another dimension, relatively absent from the Three

Worthies model. The hybrid bodies of these emergent deities, like those of the people in the paintings of Markus Lüpertz, bring to my mind images of ancient Egyptian deities like the lion-headed goddess Sekhmet (with a solar disk above her head), who fused with Mut, the consort of Amon Merseger, represented as a serpent with a female-head. As Hegel says in his work on Egyptian art (in his *Philosophy of History*), the human is represented, but only as part of a being that remains largely animal. I will, however, not follow Hegel when he sees the spiritual or human as silent and enigmatic, existing "shut up within and dulled by the physical organization and [sympathizing] with the brute."[76] On the contrary, the conjunction of the human and the animal is what defines the divine in this case.

The Three Devas form the pictural equivalent of a musical "tonic triad," the key that frames a song. But the present book, while it follows this model to a certain extent, is more like an attempt to depart from the traditional structure (to continue the musical metaphor, its "model" would be Stravinski's *Rite of Spring*). As Wittgenstein would say, the second part of the book, the most important, is the one that is not written. Likewise, the most important aspect of Japanese esotericism—I dare not say its "essence"—is the part that falls through the cracks or porous mesh of the triadic model.

7

THE FACE OF THE SNAKE

Ugajin

I don't know if the serpent has a face.

EMMANUEL LÉVINAS[1]

Every man worthy of the name
Has in his heart a yellow Snake
Installed as if upon a throne,
Who, if he says: "I will!" answers: "No!"

BAUDELAIRE, *FLOWERS OF EVIL*

Apart from a simple iconographic description, it is nearly impossible to provide a concise and definitive account of the deity Ugajin. As we have already seen, Ugajin is so closely associated with Benzaiten that in many cases it is unclear whether he is anything more than a variant of Benzaiten. Still, there are enough examples of Ugajin appearing in isolation to warrant a separate chapter on this evasive but important deity.[2]

Since the preceding two chapters have addressed Benzaiten, I shall begin by clarifying Ugajin's relationship to Benzaiten before taking up scholarly conjectures about the origins of this deity. Although many scholars claim to see a proto-Ugajin in various food-related Japanese gods, I argue that Ugajin as we now know him is a product of medieval Japan and that it is therefore meaningful to call him (and study him as) a medieval deity, one that was intimately associated with snakes, foxes, and Inari. When we look at his origins, we confront the fact that the name Ugajin can refer to both a specific deity and a certain type of deity. Sometimes Uga-jin means the god Uga, while at other times it refers to a type of deity called an *uga* (though we have yet to reach a point where Anglophone scholars can speak of "an *uga*" as they might of "a *tengu*" or "a *gongen*"). What appears to be the case is that, like Dakiniten, the individual deity Ugajin developed from the category of the *ugajin,* and not the other way round.

Ugajin's iconography revolves around his status as a hybrid being—part snake, part human—and this aspect can be traced to Chinese and Japanese mythologies. By focusing on one particular iconographic feature—his face, usually that of an old man—I explore Ugajin's relationship to the figure of the old man (*okina* 翁) so prevalent in Japanese myth and legend. The web of associations leading to and from Ugajin, however, requires an examination of both the esoteric doctrinal understanding of Ugajin and the functions he was thought to possess. Like Aizen, Nyoirin Kannon, Dakiniten, and Benzaiten, Ugajin was identified with the wish-fulfilling jewel and was therefore thought to bring about prosperity. But he also served a more directly soteriological purpose as a predator of toads, seen as one or more of the three poisons that obstruct the individual's progress toward awakening. (The toad metaphor is obviously related to Ugajin's association with snakes, which commonly feed on toads.) The depth of the snake identity in Ugajin's makeup leads us back to the historical relationship between Ugajin and Suwa (in modern-day Nagano prefecture). Suwa had long been a stronghold of snake cults, and sometime after the Suwa shrines came under the jurisdiction of Shingon institutions in the early Kamakura period, Ugajin was conflated with the Suwa deity, Suwa Daimyōjin 諏訪大明神.

In the last part of the chapter, I address Ugajin's role as a directional deity; his identification with esoteric Buddhist deities such as Dakiniten, Myōken, Jūzenji, and Daikokuten; and his portrayal in Tendai as a primordial deity—aspects that are less apparent in the iconography and found instead in the ritual and exegetical literature. I conclude by noting that it might be more useful and accurate to think of Ugajin not as a clearly identifiable figure but rather as a sort of symbolic repository that assimilated reptilian aspects of other deities, especially Benzaiten. Through this assimilation, Ugajin came to be closely associated with those deities but in such a way that no matter how great his influence on a particular deity's character, he remained hidden in the background. In this way, his relationships with other members of the esoteric pantheon are quite different from the vertical *honji-suijaku* model we are so accustomed to discussing in medieval Japanese Buddhism, and remain elusive.

Some readers will inevitably be frustrated by my reluctance to reduce both *ugajin* (as a type of deity) and Ugajin (the individualized deity) to something whose parameters, function, and identity are clear and stable. To do so, however, would be to present an inaccurate picture of how Ugajin was understood and how he actually functioned in medieval Japan. I hope that those readers will find comfort in knowing that medieval Tendai exegetes had a similar problem trying to fit Ugajin into their own conceptual models.

UGAJIN AND BENZAITEN

As we have seen in the figure of Uga Benzaiten, Ugajin is so closely associated with Benzaiten that their relationship is the first topic we need to untangle. As was the case with the cults of Daikokuten and Benzaiten, Ugajin's cult was actively promoted by Tendai priests.[3] In medieval Tendai texts, Benzaiten and Ugajin are difficult to dissociate: the name Ugajin often refers to Benzaiten in her goddess form, whereas references to Benzaiten in her snake (or dragon) form appear to be veiled references to Ugajin.[4] When the *Bikisho* tells us about the white snake that dwells at the base of the Heart Pillar (*Shin no mihashira*) of Ise, we are certainly dealing with Ugajin.[5] And yet their symbiosis—the fact that Ugajin is unfailingly suggestive of Benzaiten (and vice versa)—did not prevent them from leading separate lives as well, at least in certain rituals, minds, and visual representations.

It was through a metonymic drift that the name Ugajin came to designate Benzaiten. In the origin story of Oka 乎加 Shrine (Maibara City, Shiga prefecture) on the eastern shore of Lake Biwa, just east of Chikubushima, it is told that a noble woman appeared with fifteen children in a poor village one rainy night and asked for hospitality, promising to reward her host. When a farmer took her in, the noble woman turned into a white snake. The farmer subsequently became very wealthy and built a shrine dedicated to Uga Daimyōjin.[6] Uga Daimyōjin's appearance in this *engi* is identical to that of Benzaiten as the latter is represented in the apocryphal *Ugajin darani-kyō,* in which the spirit king Uga (Uga jinnō 宇賀神王) is described as a snake with an old man's face.[7] In the *Uga Daimyōjin engi* 宇賀大明神縁起, we are told of a woman who becomes a white snake. The Uga jinnō described in that text is a female deity of agricultural abundance, holding a wish-fulfilling jewel in her left hand and a sword in her right. This makes it clear that both the old man *and* the young woman were symbols of overflowing energy. By changing into a white snake, the woman does not simply become Ugajin; rather, this is a clue that she is none other than Uga Benzaiten. Although the two deities are inextricably intertwined, there is a danger of downplaying the Ugajin component in this symbiosis, and forgetting that Ugajin is also found in close association with other deities. In other words, Ugajin cannot simply be reduced to an aspect of Benzaiten, even though the frequent assocation between these two can mistakenly lead one to such a conclusion.

On this note, it is difficult to determine whether Uga Benzaiten is a form of Benzaiten, or of Ugajin. This ambiguity, or thorough merging, is perhaps a distinguishing feature of these two deities. Nevertheless, just as Uga Benzaiten is distinct to the extent that she requires a separate chapter, so too must Ugajin be treated as a separate entity.[8]

Ugajin occasionally appears as an independent (albeit subaltern) figure in representations of Benzaiten. In a painting of Benzaiten with the fifteen *dōji,* for instance, the goddess is seen on a cliff, seated on a lotus under a red torii around which two dragons are coiled. The white snake coiled around the head of the old man to her left reveals that man to be Ugajin, while the figure on Benzaiten's right looks like a underworld official. Both hold a kind of scepter (*shaku*).[9]

While both Benzaiten and Ugajin were perceived as ophidian deities, the latter's usual representation inverts the figure of Tenkawa Benzaiten, who has a human body and three snake (or dragon) heads. (Tenkawa Benzaiten's attendants are also snake headed; these might in fact be *ugajin.*) Although Ugajin and Tenkawa Benzaiten are both human-ophidian hybrids, there is nevertheless an important difference: given the importance of the head, it is clear that in Tenkawa Benzaiten the ophidian element is dominant, where as in Ugajin the human (or divine) nature is most prominent. Ugajin's face also links him to old-man deities such as Inari Myōjin. This distinction, however, is only a relative one.

Ugajin appears in the origin story of the Kamakura shrine popularly known as Zeniarai Benzaiten Ugafuku Jinja 銭洗弁才天宇賀福神社 (a misreading for Uga fukujin sha 宇賀福神社 'Uga Fukujin shrine'). According to this story, on the snake day of the snake month of the year 1185, the new shōgun, Minamoto no Yoritomo (1147–1199), dreamt that an old man revealed to him the existence of a sacred site to the northwest of Kamakura. It was the dwelling place of Benzaiten, and there was holy water there that would bring prosperity. The old man claimed to be Ugajin, the lord of a "hidden village" (*kakurezato* 隠れ里). Yoritomo worshiped him, found the place mentioned by the old man, and had a cave dug in which he enshrined Ugajin. Peace ensued. Later, during the fall of another snake year (1257), the regent Hōjō Tokiyori 北条時頼 (1227–1263) also worshiped Ugajin, the deity of the hidden village. Around this time a belief developed that money washed in the spring would multiple hundreds or even thousands of times. The temple subsequently became extremely popular, as it remains today, although the temple's modern-day priests conveniently interpret the money washing as a symbolic act that signifies the purification of the worshiper.

Another instance in which Ugajin appears as a distinct figure is in the *engi* of Minoodera, which tells of En no Ozunu's 役小角 (a.k.a. En no Gyōja) vision of Benzaiten and her husband, King Tokuzen 徳善. In this story, En no Ozunu climbs Mount Minō and discovers a deep dragon cave, where he performs austerities. He eventually meets King Tokuzen, who guides him through a mysterious city. They reach a magnificent hall where Ryūju 竜樹 (Nāgārjuna) and Benzaiten are seated next to each other, guarded by Ugajin and fifteen attendants. En finally receives the esoteric initiation (*abhiṣeka*) from King Tokuzen and Ryūju.[10] According to the *Kōkozōtō hishō* 高倉藏等秘抄, the Takakura 高倉 cave contained images of Benzaiten and of Uga Shinnō next to each other.[11] In certain invocations in which the invoked gods are separated into two groups—heavenly and earthly—Benzaiten is designated as "above," Ugajin as "below."[12] Yet in a number of sources Ugajin is the *honji* of Benzaiten. In the *Sanbōin-ryū dōsen sōjō kuketsu* 三宝院流洞泉相承口訣, a collection of oral traditions from Sanbō-in, we read that "this Ugajin is the *honji* of Benzaiten. It is the formless dharma body (*musō hosshin* 無相法身). This formless dharma body is the beginningless form. The white [color] of his snake body expresses fundamental being (*honnu* 本有). The old-man form of his head is the beginningless form."[13]

EARLY STUDIES

In an article published in 1940, the art historian Alice Getty writes that it was while visiting Engakuji 円覚寺 in Kamakura that she first came across the *ofuda* (talisman) of a god "with the body of a coiled serpent and the head of a bearded man."[14] (Fig. 7.1 shows a comparable specimen.) After describing the secrecy surrounding this god, she adds: "Curiously enough, this strange god has been found in several countries in the Near East; but unlike the god, Gaṇeśa, whose worship may be traced step by step from India to Japan, the cult of Uga-jin has furnished no element by which we may trace its provenance. And still, the resemblance between the serpent-god of Japan and the god of fertility worshipped in Iraq, Babylonia and Mesopotamia 3000 years ago is unmistakable."[15] She further argues that the cult may have been introduced to Japan by Kūkai himself, and goes on to examine examples on Babylonian cylinder-seals.[16] She even extends her comparative studies to Mexican deities like the Mexican god Quetzalcoatl, who, in her eyes, is undeniably "a contemporary of Uga-jin, while both are linked without question but in a way that at present escapes us, with the mysterious serpent-god of fertility of the Near East."[17] While I admire her confidence and optimism, I am not ready to follow her into the subterranean realms of serpentine world mythology. And yet she was on to something, for it seems that Ugajin's origins are not as Japanese as Edo period scholars argued, or at least there was significant foreign influence at play in the creation of this deity. Getty is right to mention Ugajin together with Gaṇeśa (or rather, his esoteric Buddhist equivalent, Vināyaka/Shōten), for there is indeed an association between Vināyaka, a paradigmatic *kōjin,* and Ugajin. In the *Shinkō musōki* 真興夢想記, for example, Ugajin is said to be identical with Shōten, the "wisdom god of Tōji."[18] Like Shōten, Ugajin belongs to the category of theriomorphic (or, more accurately, "therio-cephalic") deities—a specific group among a larger class of gods associated with animals (e.g., Dakiniten and Benzaiten).

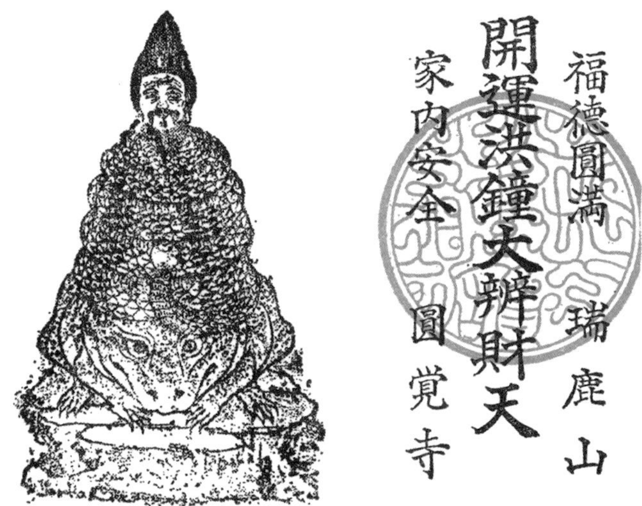

FIGURE 7.1. Ugajin on toad. *Ofuda*. Zuirokusan, Kamakura. Personal collection.

Ugajin's uncanny image looks out of place in the esoteric context. After the glorious visions of buddhas and bodhisattvas and the terrifying visions of wrathful deities such as the deva kings or the wisdom kings, Ugajin does not look very impressive at first glance. However, with the exception of Tenkawa Benzaiten, this hybrid deity has something, a *je-ne-sais-quoi* impossible to define, that even the most awesome deities cannot match. And in terms of Ugajin's real power and influence on medieval Japanese religion, there is definitely more than meets the eye. In one of the apocryphal sūtras centered on this deity, the Buddha himself warns his listeners against the temptation to belittle Ugajin because of his appearance, and reveals that he is in fact the Ur-deity that is the source of all the gods.[19]

Apart from his symbolic and iconographic association with Benzaiten, the fact that from the Edo period on both Buddhism and Shintō advocates claimed Ugajin for their own tradition suggests the problematic nature of that deity (or rather, of that Shintō-Buddhism divide). On the Buddhist side, Ugajin was above all a protecting deity, and in particular a protector of the placenta. On the Shintō side, he was a rice god identified with Toyouke and Inari, and with chthonian animal spirits like the fox and the snake. His role as a deity of fortune was emphasized from early on, due in part to the motif of the wish-fulfilling jewel. His geriatric features linked him to the symbolism of the tutelary god and suggest his pre-Buddhist nature, although his image appears only in Buddhist contexts, as was the case with so many deities claiming to be pre-Buddhist or autochthonous.

Ugajin was first studied by Yanagita Kunio (1875–1962) and Kida Teikichi 喜田貞吉 (1871–1939).[20] According to Yanagita, "Uga is a god of caves and at the same time a god of wealth. He takes the temporary form of a young woman, but his fundamental body is a snake body. Snakes and dragons originally formed a single group, but if one distinguishes them according to their dwelling places (water and land), Uga's ophidian body belongs rather to the dragon category."[21] Yanagita points out the relations between the stove god (*kamadogami* 竈神) and Ugajin.[22] Kida emphasizes Ugajin's nature as a "god of fortune" (*fukujin*). More recently, Yamamoto Hiroko has described in detail Ugajin's affinities with Kōjin.[23]

VIRTUAL ORIGINS

The pre-Buddhist past of Ugajin is what Lévi-Strauss calls a "virtual origin"—like the Kantian thing-in-itself, it is at best a regulating horizon forever out of our reach, even though archeological findings might give us a few tantalizing clues. We never encounter Ugajin face to face, as it were: our relations with him are always already mediated by Buddhism. Yet, because of his undeniably archaic features, it is easy to forget that he is a Buddhist creation. Thus, the torii above Ugajin must not mislead us into mistaking him for a purely Shintō or autochthonous deity. This is precisely what distinguishes him from conventional Shintō (and Buddhist) deities, who are *never* represented under a torii.

While the cult of the snake clearly antedates the arrival of Buddhism in Japan, there is in the case of Ugajin a danger of falling into anachronism or archaism (à la Alice Getty).[24] There is no indication that Ugajin existed prior to Buddhism, and, while his status as an autochthonous deity is clearly affirmed, his case may be similar to that of the Indian *nāgas,* whose cult as "ancient gods" actually began with Buddhism. The same is true, *mutatis mutandis,* of many "ancient" Shintō deities.

Admittedly, a number of sources clearly link Ugajin with Shintō. In the *Jinnō keizu* 神皇系図, for instance, we are told that "Izanagi is the deity of the east called . . . Yugajin 由賀神." But, as if to signal its Buddhist context, our text adds: "In Sanskrit he is also called Ishanaten 伊舎那天."[25] In the *Mudai shō* 無題抄, Ugajin is identified with Toyouke and Uka no Mitama.[26] But these are later sources, which, like the Edo-period *Shiojiri,* reflect an attempt to naturalize Ugajin. The supposed archaic nature of Ugajin is perhaps an optical illusion—it is a trompe-l'oeil effect, an anachronism, that makes the Shintō reading look more ancient and authentic. Even if the snake cult can be traced back to prehistoric times, Ugajin himself does not appear before the medieval period, and then only in a Buddhist milieu. This is not to deny the existence of older strata, but merely to acknowledge that, whatever his ancient origins, Ugajin, as we know him, is a medieval deity. Nor is it to say that a tide of "autochthonous" resistance could not have invested in certain symbols perceived to be less typically Buddhist, like Ugajin, and used them in an attempt to subvert Buddhist hegemony. Nonetheless, while the image of Ugajin points to an ancient and probably pre-Buddhist cult, it is hard to dissociate him from his medieval Buddhist setting.

The mysterious Ugajin, an elusive and swarming deity, was somehow caught in the nets of the metaphysical dialectic of esoteric Buddhism, and a god of rice became *par excellence* a deity of the rhizome. His symbolism snakes in many directions: he is a dragon (an earthly, heavenly, and aquatic deity), a *nāga,* a tortoise, and a variety of other reptiles. And in the most physical sense he is a snake, who eats mice, frogs, and toads.

THE PROBLEMATIC USE OF ETYMOLOGY

Attempting to understand the historical development of Ugajin, Japanese scholars have resorted to folk etymology despite the problematic nature of such an approach. The first thing to note is the semantic imprecision of Ugajin's name, combined with a relative iconographic poverty. Regarding the name, two traditions can be found, which are reflected in later sources such as the *Jinten ainōshō* 塵添壒囊鈔 (1532) and the *Shiojiri* 塩尻 (early eighteenth century). The latter, relying on apocryphal texts like the *Ugaya daranikyō,* insists on the autochthonous nature of the god and distinguishes him from Benzaiten while tracing the name back to a Sanskrit word, *uraga.* The author, Amano Sadakage 天野信景, writes: "Although [Ugajin] is at times different from Benzaiten, since the medieval period, when one fabricates an image of Benzaiten, one puts a white snake over her head. But she is not a snake. Likewise, today, one puts a monkey on the head of Shōmen Kongō 青面金剛, but this is a Japanese creation. . . . It is based on the words of esoteric monks."[27] According to him, "Ugaya is translated as white snake, or god who confers wealth; it was originally a dragon god."[28]

Another (perhaps more widespread) tradition emphasizes the deity's function. Relying on phonetic similarities (*uga, uka, uke*), it associates Ugajin with the Japanese *kami* Uka no Mitama, Ukemochi, and Toyouke.[29] In the *Kojiki,* the goddess Uka no Mitama 倉稲魂 represents the spirit of rice (*inadama* 稲玉). She is the daughter of the god Susanoo. In the *Nihon Shoki,* she is the child of Izanagi and Izanami.[30] Her elder brother is Ōtoshigami 大年神 (a.k.a. Taisaijin 太歳神 'great year deity'), the deity in charge of crops. She was worshiped at Ise and Inari and was a tutelary deity of the Hata clan.

Ukemochi 保食神 (a.k.a. Ōgetsuhime オオゲツヒメ) is also the daughter of Izanami and Izanagi and is the source of food. In the *Nihon Shoki,* she is killed by the moon god Tsukuyomi 月読 when he is offered food that has come out of her body. (In the *Kojiki,* it is Susanoo rather than

Tsukiyomi.)[31] In the *Kojiki* account, silkworms come from her head, rice from her eyes, and so forth, while in the *Nihon Shoki* the food exits from her mouth.

Toyouke 豊受, whose name means "abundant food," is the daughter of Wakumusubi 稚産霊 (var. 和久産巣日), a *kami* born of Izanami when she died giving birth to the fire god. Like Ukemochi, Toyouke is connected to childbirth and to death and rebirth. She is also described as a female immortal and a medicine god (related to sake brewing).[32] She was originally a subaltern deity of the Outer Shrine in charge of the offerings to the Inner Shrine deity, Amaterasu.[33] She was in particular the protector of the Miketsudono, a kind of rice granary.[34] However, with the political and economic rise of the Outer Shrine, and its ensuing rivalry with the Inner Shrine, Toyouke was promoted to a status equal or superior to that of Amaterasu. In the process, she was redefined as a primeval water deity, a development that brought her into association with *nāgas* and Benzaiten. We should therefore not be surprised to learn that the protecting deity of the Tsuki no mikura is a white dragon, and that the deity of the adjacent pavilion, Sakadono 酒殿, is Benzaiten herself.[35]

At times Toyouke and Uka no Mitama seem to merge into a single entity. Both were apparently called Miketsu no kami 御食津神 (Deity of the August Granary). Confusing the matter further is the existence of a deity called Miketsu no kami 三狐神 'three fox deity' (better known by the name's Sino-Japanese reading, Sankoshin), whose emergence was due to an erroneous (but probably voluntary) misinterpretation based on the homophony between *ketsu* 'granary' and *kitsu* 'fox'—another illustration of the Latin saying *nomina sunt numina.* This deity was related to and sometimes identified as Dakiniten. The point is that Ugajin, by being identified with Toyouke, took on the symbolism of the fox and of Inari. Ugajin's rise in the esoteric Buddhist pantheon paralleled that of Toyouke at Ise. In the process, both acquired astral characteristics: Toyouke became identified with the primordial Chinese god Taiyi 太一, and Ugajin with Myōken (both Taiyi and Myōken being symbols of the pole star). While Ugajin clearly shares a family resemblance with Uka no Mitama, Ukemochi, and Toyouke, he cannot simply be derived from them—his nature and function clearly set him apart, and the phonetic similarity seems to be a red herring. For all his alleged Shintō origins, Ugajin is essentially an esoteric Buddhist deity.

UGAJIN AND INARI

Yet because of his perceived affinities with Uka no Mitama, Ugajin came to be associated with Inari's messenger, the fox, and by extension with Dakiniten. As already mentioned, the Inari Shrine was not originally dedicated to the fox, this assocation being the product of a semantic drift whereby the name Sankoshin 三狐神 'three fox deity' developed from the name Miketsu no kami (written as 三狐神). The Inari deity thus became associated with the divine or astral foxes called *shinko* 辰狐, possibly explaining how Ugajin was in turn associated with foxes.

In Japan, foxes and snakes are closely linked as bringers of wealth and happiness, to such an extent that they are at times interchangeable in the popular imagination. We recall the story of the Ritsu monk Ninshō, who, as he was worshiping Dakiniten, saw a white fox appear from below the altar, holding a jewel in its mouth. The fox transformed into a youth, who claimed to be Uka no Mitama (written here with the characters *hōju* 宝珠 'jewel'). Before disappearing, he declared that this jewel would fulfill all wishes; in other words, it was a *cintāmaṇi*.[36]

As a god of fortune and a chthonian deity, Ugajin was also identified with Daikokuten.[37] In his *Enkai jūrokujō* 円戒十六帖, the Tendai priest Kōen, Kōshū's master, identifies the snake god on Uga Benzaiten's diadem with Daikokuten, and describes Benzaiten and Daikokuten as the two primordial deities of yin and yang.[38]

Coming back to Inari, however, this deity was known to manifest itself as both a woman and an old man (*okina*).[39] To Kūkai, it appeared as an old man, the mountain god Ryūtōta 竜頭太. As for the female manifestation, this form may have derived from connections with the female food deities mentioned above. The distinctive elements that constitute the Inari deity (or deities)—the food *kami* Uka no Mitama, the Dakiniten cult, fox and snake cults, and Ugajin—appear on the *ofuda* (talisman) of Fushimi Inari shrine as stylized jewels, snakes, and foxes, all flanking the name Uka no Mitama, as in Fig. 3.16 above. From as early as 1624, *ofuda* called "Inari taisha Ugajin shinpu" 稲荷大社宇賀神神符 (divine talismans of Ugajin of Inari Taisha) were distributed at Aizenji, the Buddhist temple on Mount Inari, where they are still in use today.[40] A red screen (*sudare* 簾) is drawn on the upper part of the *ofuda,* which gives the visual impression that the name Ugajin at the bottom is actually above the altar.[41] Below the *sudare* are ten wish-fulfilling jewels (divided into three sets: three small, two large, and five large), as well as two snakes and two foxes. The snakes have rice bags for bodies; one holds a twig in its mouth, the other a key. One of the foxes is black, the other white. This pairing of foxes and snakes, two chthonian animals, expresses the true nature of the Inari deity, and it also provides a link between Dakiniten and Benzaiten, two gods associated with the fox and the snake, respectively.

THE SNAKE

As noted above, the name Uga is said to derive from the Sanskrit word *uraga,* designating the snake.[42] Even if this etymology is dubious, the ophidian nature of Ugajin is clear. Ugajin and Benzaiten, as deities, were associated specifically with the white snake, a variety that is practically nonexistent in Japan.[43] In other words, the white snake of medieval texts, like the white fox, is an imaginary animal whose whiteness indicates its divine nature. Yet many predatory features common in Japanese snakes were attributed to this imaginary white snake.[44] As for the toad that occasionally serves as Ugajin's mount, it was regarded as a symbol of both evil and longevity (an ambivalence also found in premodern Western views).[45] A similar ambivalence characterized views of the snake. On the one hand, it was perceived as a protector of granaries and rice, and a tutelary deity of houses. This view, closely associated with Inari Shrine, may have been brought to Japan by immigrant clans like the Hata, who played an important role both in the development of riziculture and in the founding of Inari Shrine. On the other hand, the earlier view of the snake as a dark, autochthonous, fearsome being also shaped the medieval understanding of the white snake.

THE GENERIC AND THE INDIVIDUAL

Ugajin, like Kōjin/*kōjin* and similar names, can refer either to the individual deity named Uga or to a category of deities called *uga*. The textual history is as follows. The figure of Ugajin was developed in a group of apocryphal scriptures attributed to the Indian master Amoghavajra (Ch. Bukong 不空, 705–774) but actually produced in medieval Japan. These scriptures, known as the "five Ugajin sūtras," are in form and content clearly modeled after the *Golden Light Sūtra*.[46] In these works, Ugajin is referred to as Uga Shinnō (Spirit King Uga) and Uga Shinshō (Spirit Commander Uga). Of course, if we understand *uga* as referring to a type of deity (*jin*), then these titles can be read as "King of *uga* spirits" (Ugajin-ō) and "Commander of *uga* spirits" (Ugajin-shō). The term "spirit commander" recalls the twelve spirit commanders (Jūni shinshō) that form the retinue of the buddha Yakushi; like them, Ugajin is a directional deity, associated with the southeast (the direction *mi* 巳 'snake').

Uga as a type of deity apparently predates Ugajin the individual deity I have been discussing, who belonged to a category of gods characteristic of medieval Japan—a category that includes Myōken, Jūzenji, Matarajin, and Kōjin. Indeed, he is as intertwined with Kōjin as he is with Benzaiten. Ugajin represents the positive pole, Kōjin the negative—but things of course are not so simple, and roles tend to be reversed with time.[47] I will examine elsewhere the role of Kōjin in medieval Japanese demonology and beyond; for now, let us stay with Ugajin.

If we are to understand *uga* as a type of deity, then the relationship between Benzaiten and Ugajin could simply mean that Benzaiten belongs to the *ugajin* category—that is, that she is a reptilian entity. Ugajin can also refer not just to a single deity of the *uga* variety but to a large group of *uga* spirits. In the *Benzaiten shugi ki* attributed to the Tendai master Kenchū, for example, we read: "The *uga* of the five directions and the eight general kings . . . are the five dragon kings and the eight great dragon kings . . . that dwell in the heaven and earth of one's own nature. The eight deities are seated together on an eight-petaled lotus, the so-called secret repository of one's own mind."[48] Here the *uga* correspond to the directional dragons of Onmyōdō, and they are further identified with the five dragon kings of one's own (or self) nature. [49]

In various other ritual texts, including an *Ugajin saimon* 宇賀神祭文 attributed to Kūkai, the *ugajin* correspond to the *nāga* kings of the eight directions.[50] In earth-quelling rituals as well, the *ugajin* seem to correspond to the *shikijin* 式神 of Onmyōdō, and they are invoked next to deities such as Gozu Tennō, Shōten, and Dakiniten and her emissaries (the four princes).[51] We also find mention of the Uga generals of the ten directions, a notion reminiscent of the eight dragons of Onmyōdō.

The *ugajin* are also said to dwell in large numbers in the human body, just like the *kōjin* (a term that perhaps in certain cases is a synonym). The term *ugajin* becomes at times an epithet for a certain category that includes well-known deities. In the *Private Notes on the God Daikokuten* (*Daikokutenjin shiki* 大黒天神私記), for example, it is said that Daikokuten, Shōten (Kangiten), Dakiniten, Benzaiten, and the Dōsojin are invoked together as "all the *ugajin*."[52]

As for gender, both the generic *uga* deity and Ugajin proper were portrayed in both male and female form.[53] The female Ugajin may be linked to the *kami* Ugahime 宇賀姫: "The *kami* Ugahime is of same essence as Matsunoo Myōjin 松尾明神 of Nishinokyō 西ノ京. In other words, it is a *kami* of sake."[54] This deity is reminiscent of Benzaiten in her guise as the heavenly maiden who brings the knowledge of sake brewing to humans.

Although my focus in this chapter is on Ugajin the individual deity, understanding his emergence from the *uga* category of deities can help us understand what he became during the medieval period. We now turn to his iconography.

APPEARANCE AND ICONOGRAPHY

The standard image of Ugajin is rather striking. In particular, the fact that Ugajin is represented as a hybrid deity—half human, half snake—sets him apart from other medieval deities. We have to go relatively far back in Chinese and Japanese mythology to find similarly hybrid deities.

Ugajin is a human-faced snake, the face usually being that of an old man (Figs. 7.2–7.4) but sometimes of a younger woman. The appearance of these human-faced snakes is reminiscent of the Chinese primordial deities Fu Xi 伏羲 and Nü Wa 女媧.[55] The primordial man Pan Gu 盤古 was occasionally depicted as a *red* snake with a human face. The *Shanhai jing*

山海經 (*Guideways through Mountains and Seas*) depicts similar deities.[56] Marcel Granet also mentions the rebellion of Gonggong 共工, who had a human head and a serpent's body and fed on the five cereals. He rebelled against Nü Wa and was defeated, eventually becoming the water official (*shuiguan* 水官). His descendants rebelled in turn against Emperor Shun 舜 but were defeated and exiled to the periphery of this world, specifically to the Dark Hill of hell.[57] Hybridity also marked the god of Bell Mountain (Zhongshan 鐘山): "When he is watchful, it is daytime; when he is asleep, it is night. He is a red snake with a human head."[58]

On the Japanese side we find medieval representations of the heavenly *kami* as snakes with human heads.[59] The five generations of

FIGURE 7.2. Ugajin. Edo period. Onjōji, Ōtsu City (Shiga prefecture).

FIGURE 7.3. (*Left*) Ugajin on toad inside a portable shrine. Edo period. Hildburgh Collection. American Museum of Natural History.

FIGURE 7.4. Ugajin. Hildburgh collection. American Museum of Natural History.

heavenly *kami* (*amatsukami* 天神), for example, were described as ten snakes (organized into five couples) with human faces.[60] According to one legend, Shinra Myōjin (another form of Susanoo) manifested himself in reptilian form as the god of Mount Song 嵩.[61] As the story goes, when the Tendai priest Enchin visited the Shinra Myōjin shrine on Mount Song, a terrible storm suddenly broke out. From the darkness, a strange being emerged, with a snake's body and a human head. It turned out to be a manifestation of Shinra Myōjin, who appeared again as an old man to Enchin during the latter's return trip to Japan, eventually becoming the protecting deity of Onjōji (Miidera).[62]

If the snake cult has deep roots in the rich soil of ancient Japan, the image of Ugajin, like that of the primordial *kami,* was influenced by Chinese models. In this sense, Getty's attempt at crosscultural comparison was not completely off the mark, even though her speculations went too far and missed the Chinese clue.[63] Unlike the images of the primordial couple Nü Wa and Fu Xi and the primordial *kami,* however, Ugajin was rarely associated with cosmogony.

THE OLD MAN AS LANDLORD DEITY

All of this does not explain the old man's face, however. Although the image of Ugajin as a hybrid figure is the most common, one also finds a representation in which the old man's head *emerges* from the body of a snake coiled around him.[64] In the Edo period, the Sōtō temple Senryūji 泉龍寺 (Komae, Tokyo) sold talismans for preventing smallpox on which appeared a coiled snake with a woman's head positioned beneath a torii.[65]

An intriguing case is that of the deity of Yanagisawa 柳沢 Pond, known as Yanagisawa Myōjin 柳沢明神. He is represented as a coiled snake with an old man's head, and he wears a diadem (Fig. 7.6). The snake rests on a red lotus flower in the midst of a pond, under a willow tree (hence the god's toponym). On the bank of the pond is a hunter holding a bow and arrows and flanked by two dogs (one black, one white); it is Kariba Myōjin 狩場明神, one of the landlord deities of Mount Kōya.

From the snake god arises a cloud, in which the Siddhaṃ letter *vaṃ* (a symbol of the Vajra realm Dainichi, but perhaps also of Kūkai in this case) is represented on a lotus dais. Because Kariba Myōjin is usually paired with Niutsuhime Myōjin 丹生都比売明神, the snake god in this picture is also associated with Nihutsuhime Myōjin (Niu Myōjin 丹生明神), a deity identified with Wakahirume 稚日女, Amaterasu's younger sister. This image, dating from the late Edo period, belongs to Yanagisawa Shrine, which is on the precincts of Amano 天野 Shrine, at the site where Niutsuhime Myōjin is said to have manifested herself to Kūkai. Although the catalogue in which it is reproduced does not identify the deity as Ugajin, it is clearly derived from the Ugajin representations.[66] The relationship between Ugajin and Niu Myōjin reveals the former's chthonian nature, which is related to the latter's association with cinnabar and metal, as well as to the "water of life" (sake, but also the water of youth, like the water of Wakasa) and rain rituals.[67]

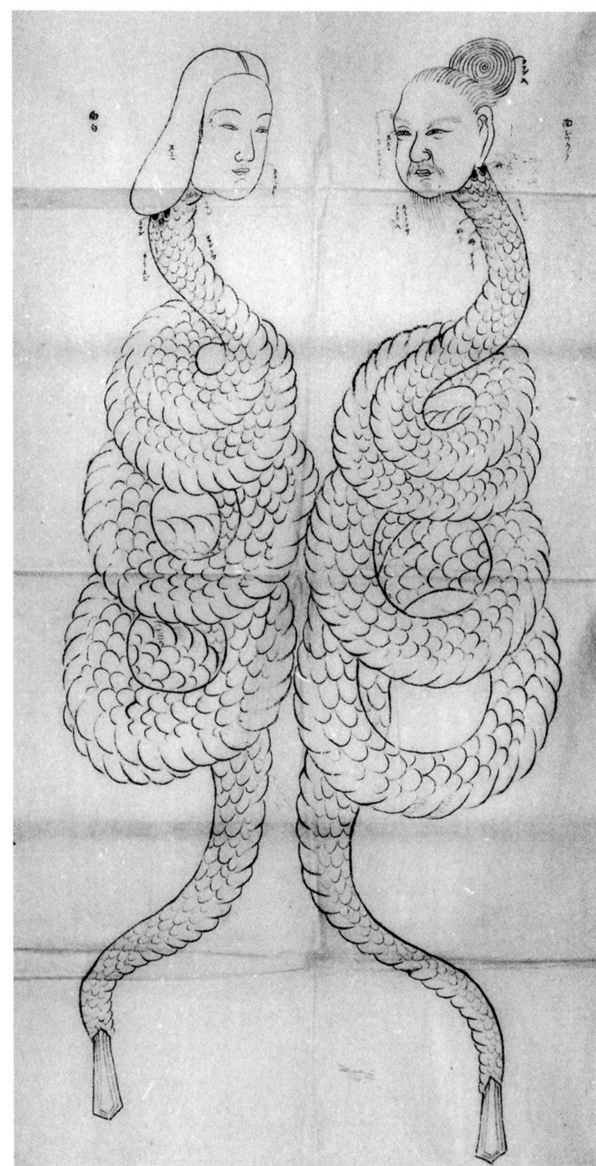

FIGURE 7.5. *Kami* in reptilian form. Edo period. Sheet, ink on paper. University Art Museum, Kyoto City University of Arts. *BZS* 4028.

SYMBOL OF FUNDAMENTAL IGNORANCE AND AWAKENING

While I have already made reference to some of the doctrines associated with Ugajin in the context of discussing his iconography, here I want to address in greater detail the ideas that are reflected in descriptions and visual representations, as well as the functions traditionally attributed to him. To begin with the obvious, there is the snake, which in esoteric Buddhism is a symbol of both delusion and fundamental ignorance. As a representative of delusion, Ugajin obstructs; but as a predator of toads (themselves symbols of ignorance), he destroys obstacles. The *Keiran shūyōshū* emphasizes the importance of the snake as a symbol of the gods: "The deities (*jinmei* 神明) always manifest in a

FIGURE 7.6. Yanagisawa Myōjin. Late Edo period. Color on paper. Private collection.

snake body."[68] It explains that the venomous snake is the extreme form of the three poisons, and that it dwells in the human body: "Inside our lungs, there is a fundamentally existing snake body."[69]

In esoteric ritual, Ugajin—or more precisely Ugaya in the shape of a white snake—is sometimes invoked among other protectors with a specific mudrā (the so-called snake-shaped mudrā), in association with the solar wheel; in such cases the officiating priest must be turned toward the sun.[70] At the same time, owing to the ambivalent nature of the snake, Ugajin is said to symbolize ignorance. The same is true for Aizen when he appears in the form of a snake, and for Susanoo 須佐之男 (素戔嗚), a deity related to dragons. Ugajin, in this negative role, is also identified with Vināyaka. The ophidian image of Ugajin is also occasionally confused with that of the "Peasant Aizen" (Denpu Aizen 田夫愛染) in a special consecration (*kanjō* 灌頂) ritual of the Ono-ryū, which is centered on Aizen's seed-letter *hūṃ,* this letter being a symbol of Fudō, Ugajin, and the wish-fulfilling jewel.[71]

Aizen appears as the *honzon* of the *shintō kanjō* 神道灌頂 in a Ninnaji painting based on the *Tenchi reikiki* 天地麗気記, which shows a green snake on a red lotus, with a *cintāmaṇi* jewel on top of its head (or rather, on the back of its neck). The shape of its body resembles that of Aizen's seed-letter in the Kanazawa bunko painting.[72] In the *Reiki kanjō* 麗気灌頂, this image accompanies instructions for a consecration ritual in which a priest is to visualize the *honji* of Aizen in the form of a snake, shaped like the seed-letter *hūṃ*. Ugajin is linked to Aizen through the image of the green snake, as it developed in the Denpu Aizen tradition.[73] In the apocryphal *Uga shinshō bosatsu*, Ugajin appears in front of the Buddha in the form of a white snake, which is actually a metamorphosis of the dragon king of Lake Anabadatta 阿那婆達多 (Skt. Anavatapta), one of the eight dragon kings dwelling north of the Himalayas.[74]

FUNCTIONS

Jewels and Prosperity

We have already seen that Aizen, Nyoirin, Dakiniten and Benzaiten were symbolically connected through the wish-fulfilling jewel. To them we can add Ugajin, whose dominant function was to bring prosperity. Arguably, Ugajin could even be considered the paradigmatic jewel deity: while the others have the wish-fulfilling jewel as one of their attributes, Ugajin is represented as actually *dwelling* inside the jewel.[75] In one apocryphal Ugajin text, Ugajin appears before the Buddha and his assembly and offers a *dhāraṇī* called *Cintāmaṇi* that will protect all beings.[76] Ugajin *is* this *dhāraṇī;* in other words, he is none other than the *cintāmaṇi.* He is, indeed, the snake in the jewel.[77] Thus, while Uka no Mitama was worshiped as the spirit of rice, Ugajin came to be regarded as the spirit of the wish-fulfilling jewel. The shift from the former to the latter was facilitated by the symbolic equivalence among rice, the relics of the Buddha, and the jewel.[78]

The Snake, the Toad, and the Three Poisons

In the *Ugaya daranikyō,* the three emissaries of Kōjin—three demons named Greed, Obstacle, and Famine—are tamed by a *dhāraṇī* called *Cintāmaṇi.* In a variant of that story, when Ugajin presents this *dhāraṇī* to the Buddha, the latter objects that this may not suffice for the protection of beings, for there are three powerful demons that will continue to harm them despite the recited *dhāraṇi.* Ugajin responds by providing further means to tame these demons, at which point the demons in question appear in front of the assembly and declare that they will cease harming beings.

The apocryphal Ugajin sūtras emphasize not only Ugajin's role as bringer of prosperity, but also his protective function. Like the wisdom king Trailokyavijaya (J. Gōzanze 降三世 'tamer of the three worlds'), Ugajin is said to tame the three demons (*kōjin*) impersonating the three poisons (which in these texts differ slightly from the traditional Buddhist formula). The relationship between Ugajin and the three poisons—which was alternatively one of equivalence and of opposition—was further developed in Tendai esotericism and interpreted through the doctrine of fundamental awakening (*hongaku*).[79] As an ophidian deity, Ugajin embodied not only ignorance, but also, at a deeper level, the ultimate identity between ignorance and fundamental awakening.

In one of these Ugajin apocrypha, the deity is indeed called Spirit Commander Uga (Uga shinshō 宇賀神将). An illustration of Ugajin's exorcistic power can be found in a story entitled "How the Monacal Rector Ryūyū Invited Uga":

> During the Kenchō [era, 1249–1256], evil spirits in the palace afflicted the ruler. Although wonder-working monks of various monasteries were called to perform incantations (*kaji* 加持) [Skt. *adhisthāna* 'empowerment'], they had no effect. The *mononoke* 物の怪, speaking of themselves, declared: "Presently, no monk can perform incantations against us except the monacal rector Ryūyū.' When Ryūyū was called and was ordered to perform incantations, the imperial affliction ceased. However, despite the efficacy [of Ryūyū's rituals], the [demons] remained in the emperor. When [Ryūyū's] disciples tried to persuade him to perform the ritual of Uga, he replied: "Because I aim at supreme enlightenment, I do not rejoice in fortunate retribution with outflows." At that moment, his disciples thought: "How can he speak so cleverly in the presence of the ruler!" Eventually Ryūyū performed the Uga ritual. During the first phase of the invocation, snakes came from the ten directions

> and filled up the platform. Furthermore, in the palace, too, the room was full [of them]. The [demonic] children and their roommates were scared. Thus, he expelled them without even having to perform the offerings.[80]

Ugajin is also said to eat toads, one of the favorite prey of snakes. The toad usually symbolizes one or more of ignorance, greed, and/or anger, the three poisons. According to a description in the *Benzaiten shugi shiki* 弁才天修儀私記, when a practitioner forms the mudrā called Seal of the Form of the Live-body Snake: "the water finger of the left hand is the ocean. The middle and small fingers of the right hand are the head and the tail of the white snake. The middle finger of the left hand is the toad. This means that the white snake of the *honzon* tames the toad, which symbolizes the spirit of greed." Thus, the idea that Ugajin, in the form of a white snake, tames the batrachian-looking demon of greed can be traced to texts on Uga Benzaiten.[81] In talismans, Ugajin is often represented riding a toad.[82] In at least one account, he himself turns into a frog.[83]

As we noted, Ugajin was at times confused or identified with the ophidian form of Aizen, which symbolized both the quintessential ignorance residing within beings and fundamental awakening (*hongaku*). Those two aspects were usually represented by the toad and the snake, respectively. Sometimes, however, it is the snake or the *nāga* that represents ignorance. Another common symbol of ignorance in the hermeneutics of fundamental awakening is the god Susanoo, who has a dragon nature and is sometimes depicted as a snake with a human face. Judging from the rituals described in the Ugajin apocrypha, Ugajin's main function was seen as the taming of demonic forces, represented by three powerful demon kings. The mudrās of these rituals are particularly revealing: the officiating priest snaps his fingers three times to tame the demons. In one apocryphal text, the Buddha snaps his fingers three times toward the northwest to make Uga Benzaiten appear. Prior to the main ritual, in which Ugajin is the principal object of devotion, the officiating priest performs a preliminary ritual outside the primary ritual space in order to placate the *kōjin,* and invokes the *ugajin* of the eight directions to protect the ritual space. In this instance, it appears that the term Ugajin refers both to the main deity of the ritual and to a group of directional deities (the *uga* deities) that may or may not form his retinue. The ritual interiorizes the nature of the god(s), in the sense that they are said to be born from the mind of the practitioner.[84]

One last example of Ugajin's association with snakes can be gleaned from a secret Uga shinnō (Ugajin-ō) ritual that was performed under the floorboard of the *ushirodo* 後戸 of the Eastern Golden Hall of Kōfukuji. The *honzon* of this ritual was an image of Ugajin, flanked by Daikokuten and the twelve spirit commanders that form the usual retinue of the buddha Yakushi. The ritual area was located right under the triad of Shaka, Kannon, and Kokūzō on the main floor. The fact that this Ugajin ritual was performed underground (or at least under the floor) seems to suggest that it was being entrusted to snakes.[85]

UGAJIN AND SUWA

The cult of Ugajin implanted itself, probably rather easily, at Suwa in Shinano province (present-day Nagano prefecture), a site that had long been a stronghold of snake cults. The god of Suwa, Takeminakata 健御名方 (a.k.a. Suwa Daimyōjin 諏訪大明神), was believed to be a snake-dragon deity (*ryūjashin* 龍蛇神). His ophidian or dragon-like nature is clearly attested in classical mythology and medieval sources. He occupies, however, a rather singular position in the myth. We are told that, when all the *kami* of Japan, in the form of snakes, attempted to go to Izumo during the tenth month (as they now supposedly do every year), their path was obstructed by Takeminakata, whose snake body was so monstrous that its head was already in Izumo while its tail was still in Suwa. For that reason, Suwa Daimyōjin was henceforward forbidden to go to Izumo, a distinction that is unique to this deity (despite the fact that he is still the main deity of the Suga Shrine 須我 in Izumo).

The cult of Ugajin (and of Uga Benzaiten) in the guise of Suwa Daimyōjin seems to have been particularly important at the Upper Suwa Shrine (Kamisha 上社) and its *jingūji* 神宮寺. In spite of the repression of Buddhism during the Meiji Restoration, which erased the *jingūji* of Kamisha from the map, a number of documents allow us to describe the symbiosis that occurred in the medieval period between between the Suwa god and Ugajin.

Originally under Tendai obedience, the Lower and Upper Suwa shrines and their respective *jingūji* came under the influence and control of Shingon esotericism during the Insei period when they were restored by Seison 成尊 and his disciple Meizan 明算 (1021–1106). Seison and his master Ningai, founder of the Ono-ryū of Shingon, were instrumental in promoting the cult of Aizen, another deity associated with snakes and wish-fulfilling jewels.[86]

The domain of Suwa passed under the jurisdiction of Hachijōin 八条院 (1137–1211), the third daughter of Emperor Toba and his consort Bifukumon'in. After the defeat of the Heike, it became a domain of Minamoto Yoritomo. After the Jōkyū 承久 Disturbance (1221), the Hōjō 北条 regents established close links with Suwa and made its god one of the protectors of Japan. In medieval documents such as the *Hachiman gudōkun* 八幡愚童訓 (also read *Hachiman gudōkin*), the Suwa deity, along with Sumiyoshi Daimyōjin, is one of the two martial deities that assist Empress Jingū in her conquest of the Korean peninsula.

Furthermore, Hokkeji 法華寺, the Tendai temple that had been the predecessor of the *jingūji* of the Upper Suwa Shrine, became a Zen temple under the direction of the Chinese master Rankei Dōryū 蘭渓道隆 (Ch. Lanxi Daolong; 1213–1278).

Until the Meiji period, the Suwa shrines remained under the jurisdiction of the *jingūji* monks (*shasō* 社僧). The *honzon* of the Suwa *jingūji* was the bodhisattva Fugen 普賢 (perhaps due to the fact that the Suwa basin was perceived as a Womb Realm mandala, and that the Upper Suwa Shrine, in the southeast quarter of that mandala, was governed by Fugen. Indeed, Buddhist presence was so dominant that the *shintai* (abode of the *kami*) of the Upper Suwa Shrine was said to be an iron stūpa 鉄塔, which was of course meant to represent the Iron Tower of Southern India in which Nāgārjuna received the esoteric teachings from Vajrasattva, a manifestation of the cosmic buddha Vairocana (Dainichi). During (or before) the Meiji cultural revolution, this stūpa was moved to the Zen temple Onsenji 温泉寺 in Suwa City, where it remains to this day.

In order to understand Ugajin's place within the cultic system of the Suwa shrines, a few words on this complex system are in order. First, this cult was characterized by the presence of a "living god" (*arahitogami* 現人神) called Ōhori 大祝, a youth who, after an elaborate ritual of possession and enthronement, was said to embody the Suwa deity (and therefore Ugajin). I will come back to this ritual in a moment.

As for the relationship between Suwa Daimyōjin and Ugajin, there are several elements that reinforced this mutual identification: the symbolism of the wish-fulfilling jewel, seen as proof of Buddhist orthodoxy and as a harbinger of prosperity; and the symbolic pair comprising tamer (the snake/Ugajin) and tamed (the toad/Kōjin). Kōjin was of course perceived as a demon of obstacles, and more specifically the demon of desire. This motif perhaps led to the reinterpretation of local frog-hunting rituals within Suwa-related Mikkyō lineages.

The identity between Suwa Daimyōjin and Ugajin found expression in various local traditions and rituals. One of them, known as the Mimuro 御室 Ritual, took place in Kōbara 神原 (present-day Maemiya 前宮). In this archaic-looking incubation ritual, a youth was cloistered for the three winter months in a building called the Mimuro or August Room (or in cases where *mi* 巳 is used in place of *mi* 御, the Snake Room), together with three straw snakes representing the Suwa deity. At the end of this ritual, he was reborn as the Ōhori, or living god, the process being facilitated by these snake gods. In the *Moriya-ke shokirokurui* 守屋家諸記録類 and the *Keiran shūyōshū,* the Mimuro god is called *kōjin* and "Ugajin of the snake-boar direction"—that is, of the SE-NW axis, which was associated with Ugajin and his evil twin, Kōjin (or *kōjin* in the plural).[87] In other words, the Ōhori could be seen as a human manifestation (or messenger) of Ugajin *qua* Suwa Daimyōjin. The main rituals of the Upper

Suwa Shrine were also performed on the snake and boar days, which were associated with Ugajin and Kōjin (or *kōjin*), respectively.

In a tradition related to the so-called August Seat-stone (Gozaseki 御座石), we hear of the taming by Suwa Daimyōjin of a divine toad that had become a "great *kōjin*" and caused all kinds of calamities in the world. This toad lived in a hole that was said to lead to the *nāga* palace. The Suwa god destroyed his abode by filling the hole with stones and then sitting—coiled—on the highest stone, keeping the toad, as it were, under pressure.[88]

In a recent book, Hara Naomasa has linked this myth to the story, told in the *Keiran shūyōshū,* of Ugajin controlling the Kōjin of Ignorance, represented as a toad (*gama* 蝦蟆).[89] (Notice that the compound word 降魔 'demon subduing' can also be read as *gama.*) Indeed, even today Ugajin's *ofuda* depict him seated (or coiled) on a huge toad. Hara further connects this myth with the interesting, and somewhat abject and infantile ritual of frog hunting (*kawazugari shinji* 蛙狩神事) that takes place at the Upper Suwa Shrine on New Year.

A word on the *shintai* of the Upper Suwa Shrine may also be in order. This shrine does not have a wooden main hall (*honden* 本殿). The function normally attributed to this building, common to most shrines, is instead performed by the rock called Gozaseki, the seat of the god who tamed the toad demon. According to Hara, this rock is essentially identical to one that appears in other sources and goes by the name Frog Stone (*kaeru ishi* 蛙石) or *kō-ishi* 甲石, an obscure term that perhaps means "the *A* stone." The Frog Stone was said to shine like a star (or a jewel) at night, just like the jewel associated with Ugajin that it came to symbolize. On it was erected the "iron stūpa" (also called Tahōtō 多宝塔 in reference to Prabhūtaratna's stūpa in the *Lotus Sūtra*).[90] As noted above, this stūpa, allegedly erected by Kūkai himself and restored by Yoritomo, was later transferred to Onsenji 温泉寺 in Suwa City. According to tradition, the exemplars of the *Lotus Sūtra* that were deposited yearly in that stūpa disappeared by the following year, which was interpreted as proof that the dragon god of Suwa had taken them to the *nāga* palace, the repository of the Buddha's teachings during the final age of the Dharma (*mappō* 末法). According to a related tradition, the ruler of the *nāga* palace is none other than Benzaiten.[91]

At the same time, as we have seen, that rock is precisely the object with which the Suwa god sealed the demonic toad's hole, burying it temporarily (rather than swallowing it, as did Ugajin). It is also on that rock that frogs (representing the toad) are sacrificed during the New Year ritual, after being caught on the banks of the nearby river. They are shot at close range by the shrine attendants—young boys called *ōko* 神使, who are equipped with small bows and arrows.[92] This derisory ritual is only one of the animal sacrifices for which Suwa Shrine was famous, the other involving the killing on a grand scale of larger animals such as deer and boar. On the other hand, it must be said that the cult of the snake (and of Ugajin) has led to the preservation in Japan of some thirty-three snake species, including venomous snakes such as *mamushi* and *habu*.

The structural resemblance between the two stone monuments is significant: whereas the rock itself, by obstructing the divine toad's hole, interrupted communication with the *nāga* palace, the iron stūpa restored it. According to Hara, we have here the sedimentation or fusion of several mythological strands. In the end the rock becomes one with Ugajin himself and with his symbol, the jewel.

Over that mythico-ritual structure is laid the *hongaku* theory according to which fundamental ignorance is none other than Dharma nature (Skt. *dharmatā;* J. *hosshō* 法性), defilements are none other than awakening. In that sense, the toad is none other than the snake, or rather, once tamed, it becomes the snake, and Kōjin becomes Ugajin. Whereas in other (or similar) contexts it is the snake that symbolizes ignorance, here it represents the principle that destroys (or transmutes) ignorance. By dwelling on the rock that symbolizes the toad, the Suwa god (Ugajin) becomes one with the toad, which becomes, as it were, his mount (as seen on Ugajin's *ofuda*). We have here the theory, derived from the fundamental-awakening school of thought, that the gods assume the most efficacious form, including that of a snake or dragon, in order to save beings. In Suwa, those forms ironically symbolize the three poisons of greed, hatred, and ignorance themselves.

According to the *Togakushi-san shugen monogatari* 戸隠山修験物語 (1561), "Suwa Myōjin manifests himself as Fugen in the Upper [Suwa Shrine], and as Senju [Kannon] in the Lower [Suwa Shrine]. It is in order to guide beings that he manifests himself in the form of a snake."[93]

Similarly, the Mimuro in Kōbara—the abode of the god and his representative, the Ōhori—is located to the southeast of the Upper Shrine. Their spatial relationship can thus be drawn on a SE-NW axis. As noted, the southeast is the direction of the threatening *kōjin,* tamed by Ugajin, who abides in the northwest and faces the southeast.[94] Related to this is a passage in the *Jadoku shinkyō,* in which Dokū Kōjin is said to dwell in the northwest corner (*inu-i*), and to transform into Ugajin to protect the six periods of day and night and the four directions, and to fulfill all wishes.[95]

Thus, we are in the presence of a symbolic network that links Suwa Daimyōjin to Ugajin, the wish-fulfilling jewel to the Buddha's relics, and the Iron Tower of southern India to its Suwa replica and the August Seat-stone (or Frog Stone) of the Upper Shrine. Although Ugajin only comes to the forefront in a few texts like the *Moriya-ke shokirokurui*, he is in fact the secret identity of Suwa Daimyōjin. This identity, however, was erased with the Meiji Restoration and would not have come to light without the sleuthing of scholars such as Hara Naomasa. While some of Hara's arguments remain speculative, this does not diminish the validity of his main point, namely, that Ugajin was central to the Suwa cult in the medieval period. The *Ugajin ku saimon* 宇賀神供祭文, for instance, includes Suwa as one of the sites where Ugajin manifested himself as a dragon.[96]

DIRECTIONS

It should be obvious by now that for the purpose of exorcisms the directional symbolism of Ugajin was of utmost importance. If the *uga* deities come from the eight directions, like the dragon gods of Onmyōdō, Ugajin himself was said to dwell in the northwest (*inu-i* 戌亥), facing the southeast (*tatsu-mi* 辰巳), the latter being the direction from which the *kōjin* are said to appear. In this iteration of Chinese cosmology based on the eight directions, with its main axis running northwest-southeast, the northwestern direction represents the Gate of Heaven, and the southeastern direction the Gate of Earth, while the northeastern direction represents the Gate of Demons, and the southwestern direction the Gate of Humans.[97] In Japan, the Gate of Demons (*kimon* 鬼門) was particularly important. Consequently, we should not be surprised to find Ugajin "standing" at that gate to confront the demonic aggression arising from the northeast. Mount Hiei, where the figure of Ugajin developed, is situated to the northeast of Kyoto, capital of Japan for almost a millennium. In the *Genealogy of Divine Rulers* (*Jinnō keizu* 神皇系図), Ugajin is identified with the directional deva Ishana (Skt. Īśāna), guardian of the northeast, whose name was linked to that of Izanagi due to the phonetic similarity of their names.[98]

However, according to a passage in the Daikokuten chapter of the *Keiran shūyōshū* entitled "About the fact that the three evil gods of obstacles dwell in the southeast, while Ugajin dwells in the northwest": "The southeastern direction is [also called] the Gate of Humans (*ninmon* 人門). . . . This is the meaning of 'endowed with the three poisons.' The northwestern direction, on the other hand, corresponds to the heavenly gate (*tenmon* 天門)."[99] The southeast and northwest are also associated with the two phases of spiritual practice, cause and fruition. The same idea is expressed by the Tendai priest Kōgei when he explains the identity between Ugajin and Jūzenji: "This Ugajin dwells in the northwest, facing the southeast, that is, the quarter where the deities of trouble (*soranshin* 麁乱神) dwell. The lord Jūzenji, to pacify the wild deities (*kōjin*), faces the southeast."[100] We recall that the Benzaiten ritual, as described in the *Benzaiten shugi ki,* includes a preliminary rite in which a symbolic offering of rice is made and the officiating priest performs an exorcistic mudrā while facing southeast in order to placate Kōjin's three emissaries.[101]

The relationship between Inari and Ugajin also has a directional facet. Of the three great shrines of Yamashiro province (Kamo, Matsunoo, and Inari), Inari was said to be the one that protects the southeastern direction. The same spatial grid is applied to Benzaiten's cultic centers; Uga Daimyōjin says: "I dwell in the west, but my heart communicates with the southeast."[102] Here west refers to Chikubushima, southeast of Oga 於賀 Shrine.[103] This directional aspect of Ugajin was absent in its putative prototypes such as Uka no Mitama and Toyouke.

IDENTITIES

Apart from Ugajin's identification with Benzaiten (the only one reflected in the iconography), Ugajin's counterparts among the major esoteric deities include Dakiniten, Myōken, Jūzenji, and Daikokuten. In at least one source, he is presented as the *honji* (*not* the trace) of Muryōjubutsu 無量寿佛 (i.e., Amida), Nyoirin Kannon, Dakiniten, Shōten, and Aizen.[104] The reptilian form of Ugajin may have provided a link not only to jewel deities such as Benzaiten, Dakiniten, Daikokuten, and Aizen, but also to the Ise deities Amaterasu and Toyouke. The *Daikokuten kōshiki* 大黒天講式 contains a passage similar to that of the *Ugaya darani kyō,* in which Daikokuten is said to be identical in substance to Ugajin.[105]

Medieval ritual texts reveal two types of processes at work: the identification of Ugajin with Aizen Myōō, on the one hand, and the identity of Ugajin and Daikokuten, on the other.

The association between Ugajin and Benzaiten is perhaps another expression of the (sexual) union between Daikokuten and Benzaiten. One also finds in the *Daikokuten kōshiki* 大黒天講式 a passage in which Daikokuten is said to be identical in substance to Ugajin.[106] Likewise, in the *Daikokutenjin shiki* 大黒天神私記 attributed to Kūkai, Daishō Kangiten, Dakiniten, Benzaiten, the *dōsojin* (crossroads deities), and Dokujin 土公神 (earth-governing deities) are all described as manifestations of Ugajin.[107] Indeed, the pair formed by the male and female Ugajin brings to mind the yin-yang deities and the Dōsojin couple, whose paradigmatic figure is the pair formed by the male and female *kami* Sarutahiko and Ame no Uzume. In a section of the *Kuma-gun jinja ki* 球摩郡神社記 dealing with the Dōsojin, we find a quotation from the *Urabe Kanekuni shō* 卜部兼邦抄 to the effect that Ugajin is identified with Sarutahiko and defined as a god of obstacles (*shōgejin* 障礙神).[108] Also worth mentioning in this context is the etymological link between Ugajin and Ugame (female Uga), the latter term being synonymous with Okame (that is, the goddess Uzume).[109] On Mount Hiei, the Shrine of the Sacred Maiden (Seijo-gū 聖女宮) is dedicated to the Inari goddess Toyouke, who was, as noted above, associated with Uga Benzaiten.[110]

FIGURE 7.7. Ugajin inside a tree trunk. Photo Andrea Castiglioni.

In the *Keiran shūyōshū,* Ugajin is described as a god of longevity. This function links him with astral deities like Myōken Bosatsu. We have seen that Ugajin dwells in the northwest. In medieval Japanese cosmology, this direction is also, in a sense, the higher plane of the *axis mundi,* identified with the pole star. Thus, it is not surprising to read that in certain sources Ugajin is identified with Myōken. He therefore assumes a twofold role, as both cosmic lord and controller of human destinies. According to one source, Myōken, when worshiped properly, becomes Ugajin; if he is not, he becomes Kōjin. The same ambiguous definition is characteristic of Kōjin. One of the other roles shared by Ugajin, Myōken, and Kōjin, is that of the "deity of the placenta" or "deity born at the same time [as the individual]" (*kushōjin* 倶生神). Along the same lines, Ugajin was assimilated to the "star of fundamental destiny" (or birth star) of a person, and more precisely to the birth star of one's previous life. This idea is found in a rather peculiar passage, which is worth quoting in full.

> The Northern Chronogram, Myōken Bosatsu, transforms into Uga shinshō, who is called the god of longevity and happiness (*jufukujin* 寿福神) of all beings. He is the same as the one called Lord of the Numinous Talismans (Reifujinkun 霊符神君). Thus, from the time of the five phases [of gestation] inside the womb, he becomes the deity born at the same time [as the person] (*kushōjin*), and until the single thought at the end of life, he never leaves that [person's] body, and everything is under the protection of this being [*satta,* Skt. *sattva,* perhaps an abbreviation for *bodhisattva*]. It is said in the *Last Testament* (*Yuigō* 遺告): "If you revere the Worthy of the Numinous Talismans (Reifu sonshō 霊符尊), he becomes Ugajin; if you turn away from him, he becomes the Great Raging Deity (Daikōjin 大荒神).[111]

The same source states that "the Northern Chronogram (Myōken) is the lord of heaven, who directs human destinies. Furthermore, he and Ugajin possess the same divine character, that of gods of longevity and happiness."[112] This passage indicates that Ugajin, like Myōken, was the positive face of a fundamentally ambiguous figure. This type of definition is found again in the case of Kōjin and similar medieval deities. This is even, in a sense, their fundamental characteristic. The image we get here is that of an ambiguous deity, which protects people from birth to death (and beyond), but is also extremely jealous and irascible.

According to the "Notes on the Northern Dipper Ritual" in the *Mon'yōki* 門葉記, a record of the Tendai temple Shōren-in 青蓮院 in Kyoto compiled by the princely monk Son'en Hōshinnō 尊円法親王 (1298–1356), Ugajin is identical to Kōjin, the paradigmatic deity of obstacles, and both are identical to a person's birth star: "When the birth star of a past life becomes wild, it turns into Kōjin [or: a *kōjin*] and causes obstacles. But when it is appeased, it becomes Ugajin [or: an *ugajin*] and brings happiness and wisdom. Thus, we must return to the birth star."[113]

In one of the Ugajin apocrypha, Ugajin and Kōjin are paired: they symbolize the Dharma nature (*hosshō* 法性) and ignorance (*mumyō* 無明), respectively, or the Dharma nature and the practitioner's body.[114] In the *Kōjin engi* 荒神縁起, Kōjin is identified with Maheśvara (or Vināyaka) and with Māra, the ruler of the sixth heaven, and his consort is Ugajin.[115] In certain representations, Sanbō Kōjin 三宝荒神 is shown inside a crystal globe in the form of a wish-fulfilling jewel, like Ugajin.[116]

The list of Ugajin's cultic sites, not surprisingly, overlaps with that of Uga Benzaiten's sites: Chikubushima, Mishima 三島 Shrine (in Izu), Enoshima, and Itsukushima. The *Ugajin-ku saimon* adds, however, that the deities of Suwa 諏訪, Sumiyoshi 住吉, Kashima 鹿島, and Katori 香取 all manifest themselves in dragon bodies, and that all snake bodies are transformations of Ugajin.[117]

THE WARP AND WOOF OF HEAVEN AND EARTH

Despite his elusive nature, Ugajin was integrated into Tendai metaphysics, eventually becoming a primordial deity—nothing less than "the warp and woof of heaven and earth." We have seen that *ugajin* could refer to a genus rather than to an individual deity. According to Kōshū, however, Ugajin is a unique, primordial deity who encompasses the heavenly, earthly, and human realms. The *Keiran shūyōshū* explains as follows the three syllables constituting the god's name: *u* 宇 corresponds to heaven, *ga* 賀 to the earth, and *shin/jin* 神 to humans.[118] Thus, "this spirit commander is the origin of the origin of heaven and earth, the beginning of the beginning of the yin and yang. . . . He has been hearing the Dharma since the time of the 'King of Emptiness' Tathāgata."[119] The syllables *u* and *ga* are also said to correspond to "emoluments" (*roku* 禄) and "life" (*mei* 命). In other words, Ugajin is a controller of human destiny, in charge of the three aspects of happiness (*fuku* 福), emoluments (*roku*), and longevity (*ju* 寿). This is a function he shares with Myōken, the god of the pole star, and with Okina, the paradigmatic old man deity.

As mentioned earlier in this chapter, in the apocryphal *Ugajin darani-kyō,* the Buddha warns his disciples not to despise Ugajin because of his unseemly appearance: he is actually the supreme god, manifesting in many different guises:

> He is called Muryōju-butsu 無量寿佛 (Buddha of Infinite Longevity, i.e., Amida) in the western paradise, and Nyoirin Kannon in the Sahā (J. *shaba* 娑婆) world. His living body manifestation . . . dwells in the solar wheel, illuminating the world. He manifests himself as Dakiniten to dispense fortune and longevity, as Shōten to discard the obstacles of the three worlds, and as Aizen Myōō to give love and bliss and help beings to reach ultimate awakening.[120]

Ugajin is also said to be Kokūzō in heaven and Jizō on earth, thus suggesting that these two bodhisattvas were only manifestations or "traces" (*suijaku*) of the snake god. The procreative nature of Ugajin is emphasized in various sources that call him god of the yin and yang (some actually imply the existence of two Ugajins, as a pair of yin and yang deities); this again echos the Chinese primordial couple Fu Xi and Nü Wa. In *Shinkō's Record of Dreams* (*Shinkō musōki* 真興夢想記), a visionary description of Shōten (Kangiten) by the priest Shinkō 真興 (934–1004), Kangiten's symbol, two intertwined radishes, is said to symbolize Ugajin.[121] In the *Izuna yamamawari saimon* 飯綱山廻祭文, Izuna (飯綱 or 飯縄) Gongen is represented as a winged youth with snakes coiled around his body. He is said to manifest himself in the form of Ugajin.[122]

We recall that Ugajin is depicted on the central head of the Three-Deva deity, between the sun and the moon that adorn the two lateral heads. We find here the same ternary structure we saw in the cases of Aizen, Fudō, and Nyoirin, in which the sun and the moon, the red and the white, fuse into nonduality to produce the transcendent golden jewel. This makes Ugajin the ultimate symbol of transcendence.

If, owing to his role as controller of human destinies, Ugajin encompasses heaven and earth, his snake nature brings him closer to the earth, and this telluric aspect might explain why he is worshiped in "humble" (from *humus* 'earth') places like the basement of Kōfukuji. This basement was entrusted to a snake god representing the powers of autochthony.[123] Along the same line of thinking, the old man's face, which evokes that of Matarajin and the mythical ancestor of the theatrical tradition (Sarugaku and Nō), Okina—and through him the *shukujin* (astral deity, god of destiny)—is justified by the fact that Ugajin also serves as a tutelary deity (*jinushi*).[124]

CODETTA

Whether worshiped on his own or together with Benzaiten, the medieval Ugajin was very different from ancient *kami* of cereals like Uka no Mitama and Toyouke. In addition to his close association with a host of esoteric deities, he benefited from strong symbolic connections with the snake cults (and, to a lesser extent, that of foxes). Rather than calling him a "combinatory" deity (as if all Japanese deities were not combinatory), it would be better to refer to him as an emergent deity in the sense that in him we can see the nascence of certain features that became the salient characteristics of medieval deities.

As Rob Linrothe argues in the case of the wrathful deities (*krodha*) of Indian Tantrism, there are two possible interpretations of the fight between good and evil, the divine against the demonic: either the tamer takes on the appearance of the tamed (and to an extent the nature of the tamed as well), or the demonic deity merely represents an earlier (and not yet purified or pacified) characteristic of the divine deity.[125] They are mutually distinct, antagonistic beings that come to resemble each other at the end of their struggle, like the Inquisitor and the heretic in Luis Borges's short story "The Theologians," or like two phases of a single process of domestication.[126] From this standpoint, Ugajin and Kōjin are at the same time antagonistic and identical. They constitute an attempt on the part of medieval Buddhists to understand (and to master) the intertwining of good and evil—of ignorance and awakening—through the lens of the doctrine of fundamental awakening (*hongaku*). The names Ugajin, Benzaiten, Matarajin, are Shōten are so many milestones in this effort to express, on the planes of ritual and myth, profound speculations regarding human nature and the nature of reality.

Although they do not generally have their own shrines, temples, or mandalas, Ugajin and Matarajin are, as it were, encompassing deities that seem to hang back and provide a symbolic reserve to other, relatively more individualized deities (e.g., Benzaiten, Dakiniten). The term "deity" in this case implies an ambiguous status, between individual and collective.

Perhaps we are mistaken when we try to define Ugajin as a particular deity. He serves instead as a kind of symbolic operator or shifter, to which all cases of Benzaiten and related deities turning into snakes or revealing their true reptilian nature can be assimilated. Even when this role is forced into the parameters of traditional Tendai theology, it invariably slips out again owing to Ugajin's reptilian nature. Ugajin "captures" Benzaiten and makes her more tangible in the form of a white snake. In the end, however, it may be better to speak of a *mutual capture* (to borrow a term from Gilles Deleuze).[127]

While the notions of food, wealth, and happiness—whether or not they derive from the etymological link to Uka no Mitama and the like—are clearly important, the reptilian and old-man aspects of Ugajin, as well as the jewel symbolism, are clearly of greater importance in the medieval *imaginaire*. These features allowed medieval thinkers to make Ugajin the rough equivalent of certain deities, who in turn superficially detached themselves from the Ugajin association even while remaining inextricably linked to and influenced by Ugajin. This is one of the main difficulties in any attempt to clearly grasp Ugajin: he loiters in the background, enveloping the deity in the foreground without making his presence known. Even when he does appear, he remains elusive. The relation between Benzaiten and Ugajin is therefore not of a simple, vertical nature; rather, it is something like an exponent, a connotation, the opening of a symbolic field. If Benzaiten is identified with the jewel, Ugajin is the snake inside the jewel. Here the snake, like the fox, becomes the index of a higher reality.

8

MATRICIAL GODS

Matarajin

Where does one god end, and another begin? In the case of Matarajin, that question remains as vexing as ever, owing in part to the fact that the lack of canonical sources regarding this figure allowed for a greater fluidity of its forms.[1] As is often the case in medieval Japanese religion, what looks like a proper name—here Matarajin—does not always designate a clearly individualized deity. Once again, I am trying to uncover—and possibly reinvent—a network that has long been dislocated and buried on the basis of scant documents and monuments that have barely escaped the ravages of time. Attempts of this kind are bound to remain largely speculative. What is there in common between the demonic protector of Tōji and the old man who became the god of song and dance? Can one still speak of one deity, or of family resemblances—or are we faced with radically different deities that happen to share the same name? And if so, is there any logical necessity for that homonymy? These are some of the questions I would like to address here, without raising too many expectations that they can be answered.

NAMING THE GOD

If a god does not end where another begins, neither does it begin where another ends. The problem with determining Matarajin's identity—or frustration (probably unavoidable in the case of a self-proclaimed god of obstacles)—begins with his name. The name points toward Indian and Tantric origins, while his function of impeding points toward China and Korea. It's possible that the influence of his doubles, Shinra Myōjin 新羅明神 and Sekizan Myōjin 赤山明神, will shed some light on the shift in his appearance from a wrathful Tantric deity to an old man, a ruler of human destiny and god of the arts. I will examine the Indic (or perhaps Iranian and central Asiatic) background first and then take up the artistic aspects.

We recall that Matarajin first appeared in Shukaku Hōshinnō's *Gyōki* 御記 as the protecting deity of Tōji, a composite figure that subsumed the Three Devas. This Matarajin was called a *yakṣa* god (*yashajin*)—in other words, he was perceived as a kind of subaltern deity or demon.[2] In the *Tōbōki* 東宝記 by the Tōji priest Gōhō 杲宝 (1306–1362), we learn that the two deities that guarded the central gate of Tōji were one male and one female *yakṣa* whose statues had allegedly been carved by Kūkai. Gohō quotes a commentary on the *Avataṃsaka-sūtra* by Guifeng Zongmi 珪峰宗密 (780–841) which maintains that male *yakṣas* are winged and able to fly, and eat children. He also notes that the custom of consecrating newborns to these *yakṣas* was an attempt to protect them from demonic harm.[3]

Despite his demonic origins, the *yakṣa* of Tōji must have already acquired a certain prestige to include in its composite "personality" or makeup three of the most important devas of the Japanese esoteric pantheon. When given to a *yakṣa* whose faces are those of the Three Devas, the name Matarajin could mean that the devas were perceived as belonging to the category of the "Mothers" (*matara,* Skt. *mātṛkā*), a term referring to pestilence deities. These Mothers were said to attack fetuses in the womb and children after birth. Even as an individualized deity, Matarajin could be the "god of the *matara,*" and thus his name might be an alternative name or title for Shōten, a god derived from the Indic Gaṇeśa (Vināyaka). Like Mahākāla, Vināyaka was often represented in India in the company (or as the leader) of the *mātṛkās* (and, by extension, of the *ḍākinīs*).[4] According to the *Shiojiri*'s section on Makakara-ten 摩訶伽羅天: "His mysterious function is not only one. Among his [images] is a form with three faces and six arms; it is [the one that] tames the *ḍākinīs.* By manifesting this *yakṣa* form, he subdues all categories of ghosts and demons, and he is also called Matarajin."[5]

Another opinion recently advanced concerning the origins of Matarajin's name is that of Hasuike Toshitaka 蓮池利隆, who wants to derive it from the Zoroastrian god Mithra.[6] Hasuike's argument is largely speculative and hardly convincing; furthermore, unlike the derivation of Matara from the Sanskrit *mātṛkā,* it does not find any support in medieval Japanese sources.

NATURE AND FUNCTIONS

The nature and functions of this hybrid deity also raise a number of questions, some of them already pondered by scholars of the Edo period. In his *Personal Reflections on Matarajin* (*Matarajin shikō* 摩多羅神私考, 1738), the Tendai priest Kakujin 覚深 wonders whether Matarajin is Indian, Chinese, or Japanese. Matarajin is also discussed at length—and eventually dismissed as heterodox—in Amano's *Shiojiri* 塩尻 and Myōryū's *Kūge dansō* 空華談叢 (1782).[7] However, the Matarajin that these scholars had in mind was no longer the *yakṣa* of Tōji but a quite different deity that had been promoted, together with Sannō Gongen, to the rank of acolyte of the new ancestral god of the Tokugawa, the divinized shōgun Ieyasu 家康, enshrined in his Tōshōgū 東照宮 mausoleum in Nikkō.[8] As is well known, Tōshōgū was the creation of the Tendai priest Tenkai 天海 (1536–1643), the founder of Sannō ichijitsu shintō 山王一実神道.[9] While the importance of Tenkai for the development of Tendai during the first part of the Edo period can hardly be exaggerated, one tends to overlook the fact that he drastically changed the content of the Sannō cult while shifting Tendai's center of gravity from Mount Hiei to Kantō. This may explain the continuing success of a translocal Matarajin in contrast to the relative decline of his peers or prototypes, Sekizan Myōjin and Shinra Myōjin. At any rate, we cannot assume that the Edo-period image of Matarajin corresponds to medieval conceptions of this deity.

Tenkai's attempt to provide the Tokugawa bakufu with a revived Buddhist ideology eventually failed, however, and this may be one of the reasons Myōryū and Amano criticize his promotion of Matarajin. Another reason has to do with Matarajin's association with a heterodox current of Tendai esotericism, the Genshi kimyōdan 玄旨帰命壇, which acted as an intermediary between the medieval Matarajin and the Matarajin of the Tōshōgū. This esoteric current, originating on Mount Hiei, became the main target of the *Hekija hen* 闢邪篇 (*Repudiation of Heresies*) by Reikū Kōken 霊空光謙 (1652–1739), a work that Amano and Myōryū cite as their source.[10] The Genshi kimyōdan was centered on two initiation rituals called the *genshi-dan* 玄旨壇 and the *kimyō-dan* 帰命壇, and its critics lumped it together with the Tachikawa-ryū, a Shingon current labeled as "heretical."[11] Despite the eventual prohibition of the Genshi kimyōdan, certain of its texts remained in circulation. Its suppression, however, did affect the popularity of its *honzon.* Matarajin and his two young acolytes now came under criticism for their allegedly indecent song and dance, and they became coded expressions for sexual union. The *Shiojiri* and the *Kūge dansō* criticize this development as an "aberration" engendered by the Genshi kimyōdan.[12] The cult of Matarajin even came to be prohibited on Mount Hiei, its cradle. In spite of this, it was able to survive in the shadow of the Jōgyōdō 常行堂 (Constantly Walking [Samādhi] Hall) in peripheral Tendai centers such as Hiraizumi, owing above all to Tenkai's integration of Matarajin into the Tōshōgū triad and into Sannō ichijitsu cosmology.[13]

William Bodiford has recently reexamined the case of the Matarajin cult in the Edo period, taking his cue from the work of a Togakushi 戸隠 abbot named Jōin 乗因 (1682–1739). Bodiford criticizes the "multiple personality" approach adopted by most scholars, starting with Kida Teikichi 喜田貞吉 (1871–1939). He points out that each scholarly discussion brings with it a new split-personality diagnosis of the god.[14] Why should Matarajin, of all gods, have assumed so many different roles, he asks, although Matarajin is hardly an exception in this respect, as should be clear by now. Looking for a ritual link behind Matarajin's incarnations, he finds it in the Buddhist dream technique and in Matarajin's function as a dream king (*muō* 夢王), based on the association made by Jōin between Matarajin and the bodhisattva Shinsō 信相 (Faith Appearance) in the *Golden Light Sūtra.* It should be pointed out that this connection, while interesting in itself, is a late doctrinal development, and there is no reason to privilege it over medieval conceptions of the god.[15] Bodiford's dream king is another avatar of Matarajin, and it does not provide access to the god that is more direct or clearer. Moreover, medieval images of Matarajin were not connected simply by "mere historical accidents," as Bodiford avers, nor was the medieval Matarajin "the product (or victim) of random acts of confusion." Bodiford's attempt to retrieve the inner logic of Matarajin's development is flawed by an uncritical and slightly anachronistic reliance on a single doctrinal source, the work of Jōin. He ends up reducing the Tōshōgū deity to a unidimensional figure while conveniently bypassing its medieval prototype(s).[16]

Bodiford's interpretation reflects the fact that Edo-period scholars like Jōin no longer understood (or had any use for) the medieval images of Matarajin. One reason for this is that the figure of Matarajin merged with one of the central figures of *sarugaku* and Nō, Okina 翁 (Old Man), during the Muromachi period. Although it can be argued that Matarajin survived, or even grew in prestige, on the *sarugaku* stage behind the mask of Okina, his nature changed radically as he left the darkness of his original abode, at the back door (*ushirodo* 後戸) of Buddhist temples, for the Nō stage. While his background initially expanded the symbolic range of Okina, their success led ultimately to a symbolic impoverishment of Matarajin himself.

The cult of Matarajin developed in at least six distinct yet related contexts, the last of which lies outside our field of inquiry:

1) as a god of obstacles related to Mahākāla and the *ḍākinī,* and paving the way to the cult of the Three Devas

2) as a protector of the Jōgyōdō and god of the *ushirodo* in Tendai monasteries

3) as one of the gods invoked during the Genshi kimyōdan rituals

4) as a pestilence god, invoked in particular during the Ox Festival of Kōryūji

5) as a patron god of the performing arts (*geinō*)

6) as a protector of the Tōshōgū mausoleum in Nikkō

The first three contexts, examined by Yamamoto Hiroko, essentially reflect the monastic understanding of Matarajin. With the fourth context, we begin to move beyond monastic confines. Ultimately, it was in the mountain cults of Shugendō and in popular festivals, i.e., outside the performing arts in the strict sense, that essential aspects of Matarajin—his functions as a pestilence god and god of fortune—reached their full expression.[17]

The following points—marking the origins of a number of intertwined symbolic threads—can be laid out: Matarajin is a *foreign god* who appears to the Japanese priest Ennin during his return trip from China. He is a *demon of obstacles;* like Vināyaka, he can cause obstacles as well as discard them. He resorts to spiritual blackmail in order to obtain a following; once duly worshiped, he becomes a protector of his cult. More precisely, he protects the practice of *nenbutsu* centered on the buddha Amida, and the place where it is performed, the Jōgyōdō. He has the appearance of an *old man,* linking him to conventional representations of the autochthonous *jinushi* or landlord deity. This tutelary function is only an apparent contradiction to his foreign background.[18]

Very early on, or so it appears, Matarajin lost his distinctly Tantric nature and wrathful appearance to assume the form of an old man, by which he is known today. In this traditional representation, he wears Chinese headgear and a Japanese hunting dress. He is shown striking a drum, flanked by two youthful acolytes; one of them, Chōreita Dōji 丁令多童子, holds ginger leaves and strikes a small drum, while the other, Nishita Dōji 爾子多童子, holds bamboo leaves and dances wildly. Above them, the seven stars of the Northern Dipper are visible (Figs. 8.2 and 8.3). This image led commentators to interpret Matarajin as a god of the performing arts (*geinō*) connected to the figure of Okina, a symbol of longevity and prosperity, but they chose to emphasize the lewd connotations of the song and dance. In Genshi kimyōdan texts, the dance is said to represent the twelve *nidānas* (J. *jūni innen* 十二因縁), that is, the twelve links constituting the causal chain of existence.[19] This ritual initially had an apotropaic aspect, as suggested by its performance during the Shushō-e festival at New Year.[20]

DARK ORIGINS

The question of the emergence of the medieval Matarajin remains virtually intact with no solution in sight. There is too large a time gap between the three-faced deity of Tōji and the figure worshiped under the same name on Mount Hiei, even apart from the fact that the former was a Shingon monastery protector, the latter essentially a Tendai figure. There is also a large conceptual gap between the protector of the Jōgyōdō (or Jōgyōzanmai-dō 常行三昧堂) on Mount Hiei and the pestilence god worshiped during the Ox Festival at Kōryūji 広隆寺. So again, there is a large hiatus between the hybrid *yakṣa* of Tōji and representations of the old man wearing the black hat and informal dress of a Japanese courtier.[21] Scholarly attempts to fill these gaps have failed, and in that sense Bodiford's disappointment with earlier scholarship is partially justified. Yet the problem does not seem more intractable than the case of the shift from the Indian Mahākāla to the Japanese-looking Daikokuten—although there we have a few more transitional types.

Despite his self-proclaimed foreign origins, it was only in Japan that Matarajin entered the Buddhist pantheon. If we leave aside for now the *yakṣa* deity of Tōji—which disappeared or was absorbed into the figure of the Three-Deva deity discussed earlier—the emergence of the medieval Matarajin is usually traced to the legend of the Tendai master Ennin (Jikaku Daishi, 794–864). According to the *Keiran shūyōshū:*

> When the great teacher Jikaku [Ennin] returned from China [in 847] to transmit the ritual for the extended vocalized *nenbutsu,* on his ship he heard a voice in the empty sky, which told him: "My name is Matarajin, and I am a god of obstacles (*shōgejin*). Those who do not worship me will not be able to attain rebirth [in the Pure Land]." Consequently, Matarajin was enshrined in the Constantly Walking Samādhi Hall (Jōgyōzanmai-dō).[22]

Here Matarajin does not appear in the form of an old man, as he will in later manifestations. The legend developed soon after Ennin's death, although it does not yet appear in his early biographies. It was one of his disciples, Sōō 相応 (831–918), who put the Constantly Walking Samādhi into practice at the Jōgyōdō and designated Matarajin as its protector. Sōō was instrumental in the development of many Tendai rituals and cults—for instance, those centered on Fudō Myōō and Hira Myōjin 比良明神, as well as the ritual Circling of the [Hiei] Peaks (Kaihōgyō 回峰行).[23]

Certain sources trace Matarajin's apparition farther back. He is now said to have appeared to Ennin's master, Saichō, on the boat that brought him back to Japan. In one version, Saichō is also said to have previously encountered Matarajin on Mount Tiantong 天童山 in Shandong. On this occasion, the god revealed to him that his abode is neither in heaven nor on earth, but in the citadel of the human heart—a typical doctrinal rationalization.[24] In other versions, Saichō first meets Matarajin, alias Konpira 金比羅, at Qinglongsi 青龍寺 on Mount Tiantai 天台, and later again on Mount Hiei.

The circumstances of Matarajin's apparition to Ennin constitute a hagiographic topos: Fudō, for example, appears to the same Ennin during another sea voyage and saves him from danger. In the Sōtō Zen tradition, the god Daigenshuri 大権修理 (Daigenshuri Bosatsu 大権修理菩薩) appears to Dōgen 道元 (1200–1253) in similar circumstances during the latter's return from Mount Tiantong.[25] But Matarajin's manifestion immediately calls to mind that of two other deities, Sekizan Myōjin and Shinra Myōjin, who are said to have appeared to Ennin and Enchin (814–891), respectively, during their return trips to Japan. The three manifestations are so similar that it has been argued that we are dealing here with a single deity under different names.

Matarajin's role as protector of the Jōgyōdō may have initially been a subaltern and local function.[26] With the territorial expansion of Tendai, however, the multiplication of the meditation halls—at Tōnomine, for example, and at Mōtsuji 毛越寺 in Hiraizumi and Gakuenji 鰐淵寺 in Izumo—greatly increased Matarajin's prestige and gave him a translocal dimension.

SYMBOLIC NETWORK

The Demonic Matarajin

In medieval Japan, the ritual logic that structured the figure of Matarajin merged with another, more purely mythological logic, which developed on the basis of symbolic permutations. At times, ritual similarities led to mythological connections; at other times, it could be the other way around. Yet the field of mythological production during this period remained relatively autonomous, and it needs to be examined briefly on its own terms. We begin with a genealogical or diachronic approach.

(a) We recall that the central face of the three-headed *yakṣa* of Tōji was that of Shōten (Skt. Vināyaka). In the *Keiran shūyōshū,* Matarajin is described, like Shōten, as a god of obstacles, or more precisely, as a "demon that constantly follows beings (*jōzuima* 常随魔), like their shadow."

(b) Several texts identify Matara and Mahākāla, an identification suggested or reinforced by the near homophony.[27] The *Keiran shūyōshū* states that Matarajin, *qua* Mahākāla, is the god who tames the "essence-stealing demons" (*dasshōki* 奪精鬼), a term that designates the *ḍākinīs.* As noted above, these *ḍākinīs,* once tamed by Mahākāla, receive from him a "secret method" that allows them to prolong by six months the life of humans who are about to die, so that they can feed on the humans' vital essence, or human yellow.[28] Kōshū hesitates between the two identities, however, quoting an oral tradition according to which "Matarajin is none other than the god Mahākāla, and he is also the *ḍākinī.*" The statement is at first glance confusing, since the two identities seem contradictory: is Matarajin an emanation of Mahākāla, the tamer of the *ḍākinīs,* or are we faced here with a kind of *ḍākinī*? In the first case, he protects the practitioner against soul stealers, whereas in the second, he is one of them. In other texts, Matarajin seems closer to the *ḍākinī,* since he is said to devour the vital essence of beings. Yet the *Keiran shūyōshū* clearly identifies

FIGURE 8.1. Matarajin (Mahākāla). Edo period. Sheet, ink on paper. University Art Museum, Kyoto City University of Arts. *BZS* 4062.

him with Mahākāla.[29] It seems difficult to be the tamer and the tamed at the same time—unless one considers them as two aspects of the same deity, before and after conversion. Furthermore, the distinction between tamer and tamed is itself not very clear—we recall that Mahākāla himself was originally a bloodthirsty demon, whereas the *ḍākinīs,* duly placated, can become protectors and extend the practitioner's life.[30] A document dated 1361 identifies Matarajin with Dakiniten as a deity who fulfills all wishes.[31]

Genshi kimyōdan texts go further in developing a positive spin on Matarajin's vampirism. This current tried to reform the demonic Matarajin by turning him into a manifestation of the buddha Amida and interpreting his vampirism as a way to "cut the breath" of the dying to better lead them to rebirth.[32] Paradoxically, Matarajin *has* to devour the dying person's liver before that person can be reborn in the Pure Land. His original vow reads as follows: "When people reach the time of death, I will go and devour their liver so that they will obtain the correct thought [leading to rebirth]."[33] So the "secret method" attributed to Mahākāla/Matarajin, based on a reinterpretation of certain secret breathing techniques, allows the practitioner to eliminate demonic obstacles caused by "soul stealers" and to reach at the time of death the correct thinking that will allow rebirth in the Pure Land. According to the *Keiran shūyōshū,* this teaching was so secret that it was unknown even to the monks of Jōgyōdō, who worshiped Matarajin as their *honzon.*

The *Asabashō* also gives an interesting twist to the *ḍākinī*'s vampirism by interpreting it as a meritorious and beneficial act—in the sense that, without the *ḍākinī*'s merciful devouring of the liver and other organs of the dying, they could not hope for rebirth in the Pure Land.

(c) The identification of Matarajin with Mahākāla and the *ḍākinīs* points to another demonic association (already suggested by his name), one with the Mothers (*mātṛkās*) that form Mahākāla's (and King Yama's) retinue. The difference between *ḍākinīs* and *mātṛkās* is rather subtle. Indeed, there was a Matarajin (Madarijin 摩怛哩神, 摩怛利神) ritual that was centered on the Seven Mothers. As noted earlier, the name Matarajin—or its variant, Madarijin—is traced to *mata* or *matara* (the Japanese transcription of *mātra* or *mātṛkās,* a term designating not only the demonic Mothers, but also the vowels of the Siddhaṃ alphabet).[34] One example is Kakujin's *Matarajin shikō.*[35] The Madarijin ritual is also described as an Offering to

FIGURE 8.2. Matarajin and acolytes. Edo period. Sheet, ink on paper. University Art Museum, Kyoto City University of Arts. *BZS* 4063.

FIGURE 8.3. (*Opposite*) Matarajin. Edo period. Color on paper. Ichigami Shrine (Shiga prefecture).

the Seven Mothers. According to the Chinese translation of the *Mahāvairocana-sūtra* and its commentary by Yixing, the Mothers are the sisters of Yama. According to the *Liqu shi* 理趣釈 (trans. Amoghavajra), however, the Seven (or Eight) Mothers belong to the retinue of Mahākāla.[36] They hold mallets like Daikokuten, but in their case (and perhaps in his too, initially), it is in order to drive nails into the head of a sick person.[37] The motif is derived from the Seven Mothers that appear in the Enmaten mandala. The name Matarajin (Madarijin) could thus mean a collective entity (the Seven Mothers) or the god(s) ruling over them—Yama, Mahākāla, and Vināyaka.

Yamamoto argues that the Matarajin ritual bifurcated: on Mount Hiei it was essentially a kind of *ḍākinī* ritual, but in Kantō—and in particular at Nikkō—it came to be centered on Madarijin, that is, on the Seven Mothers. As noted earlier, the confusion initially occurred in the arena of Enmaten rituals, where both the *ḍākinīs* and the *mātṛkās* figured as acolytes of King Yama. Yet the cult of Matarajin as an old man and patron of the performing arts was clearly important at Nikkō, as shown by the famous Rinnōji painting by Tenkai 天海 (1617), in which Matarajin performs a wild song and dance with his two young acolytes.[38]

The relations between Matarajin and various members of Yama's retinue may also have played a role in Matarajin's identification with the ruler of the underworld Taizan Fukun, himself a Daoist version of King Yama (Enma-ō). The other symbolic element that connects Matarajin to Yama, as well as with Taizan Fukun and his two acolytes Shimei 司命 and Shiroku 司禄, is their shared function as regents of human destiny. This function also explains in part Matarajin's evolution into a *shukujin* (a stellar deity and god of destiny) as Okina, through the mediation of performing arts like *sarugaku*. Yet, as we will see, there is little evidence for this: only one text from Tōnomine, dated 1530, actually links Matarajin and the *shukujin*/Okina. In spite of this scarcity, I would argue that the underlying logic required such an identification.

(d) One of the three faces of the Tōji *yakṣa* was that of Dakiniten, and, as we have just seen, Matarajin, described as an "essence-ravishing demon" (*dasshōki*), is at times explicitly identified with the Indian *ḍākinī*. This suggests that he may have been initially perceived as female. We recall that the *ḍākinīs* who form Mahākāla's retinue are also found in the retinue of King Yama, together with the Seven Mothers and Vināyaka. These Mothers are pestilence gods who attack children, or protect them when they have been placated.[39] They are also found in Hinduism, again in the company (or under the direction) of Gaṇapati (Vināyaka). As a demonic "mother," Matarajin is also related to Hārītī, the Mother of Demons (Kishimojin 鬼子母神). The latter is also known as Mother of Bliss (Kangimo 歓喜母)—and as such she constitutes a female counterpart of Kangiten, the Bliss Deva (i.e., Vināyaka). According to the *Inari jinja kō,* Matarajin is one of the names given to divine foxes, and this deity is represented with three faces and six arms (like the *yakṣa* of Tōji).[40]

In the *Mahāmayūri,* the twelve great Mothers (the last of which is Mahākālī, the consort of Mahākāla) are deities protecting the fetus inside the womb, which means that, before being placated or converted, they would attack it.[41] For Yamamoto, Matarajin and Madarijin began as independent deities, and it is Kakujin 覚深 who first linked them.[42] Even if that is the case, Kakujin only connected the dots, bringing to light affinities, not to say a structure, that preexisted him. The cult of the Mothers already points or paves the way to the association of Matarajin with epidemics. This association was reinforced by the links with Susanoo and Gozu Tennō.

MATARAJIN IN TENDAI

The cult of Matarajin on Mount Hiei was strongly influenced by the emerging Dakiniten cult, which explains why Kōshū mentions it in his section on Dakiniten. Yet the same Kōshū, while noting the efficacy of the Dakiniten ritual, judges it to be heterodox. Because it represents the goddess in animal form, he deems it appropriate only for inferior, stupid people. This explains why, according to him, it was not performed on Mount Hiei and was found only in a secret tradition of the Kurodani branch. Thus, the assimilation of Matarajin to Dakiniten appears limited in Tendai to the Kurodani branch, whereas it was widespread in Shingon, where it was traced back to Kūkai himself and therefore considered perfectly orthodox.

The female or hybrid Matarajin was more important in Shingon, and it is by no means clear how this image eventually gave way to the Tendai perception of Matarajin as an old man. The motif of the encounter between a Tendai monk and an old man deity is quite widespread.[43] According to Yamamoto, this motif is typical of the *ijin* (heteromorphic gods).

Matarajin's Cohort

The parallelism between the origin stories of Matarajin, Sekizan Myōjin, and Shinra Myōjin has often been pointed out.[44] Japanese scholars have long debated as to whether Shinra Myōjin's cult was promoted at Onjōji (Miidera) in response to that of Sekizan Myōjin at the foot of Mount Hiei, or the other way around. This is an intriguing but perhaps misguided question, since it tends to obscure deeper structural affinities. At any rate, the family resemblance between these three deities is significant, and it allowed certain functions and attributes to circulate between them. Sekizan Myōjin's identification with Taizan Fukun, for instance, explains in part why Matarajin himself came to be identified with this ruler of the underworld.[45] Likewise, the functional identity between Shinra Myōjin and Susanoo, *qua* pestilence gods, clearly influenced the nature of

Matarajin. Thus, according to the *Jimon denki horoku* 寺門伝記補録 (Muromachi period): "Susanoo has many traces—among them, Matarajin and Gozu Tennō in India, the god of Mount Song in China, or again Shinra Taijin (read Myōjin) in Japan."[46] Unlike Sekizan Myōjin and Shinra Myōjin, Matarajin was never called a "bright" deity (*myōjin* 明神). Yet, as a temple guardian, he acquired translocal characteristics, and his spread reflects the provincial expansion of the Tendai school. In spite of their antagonism and their reciprocal influence, however, Shinra Myōjin and Sekizan Myōjin had different origins and developed along different lines.

Whatever the case may be about their origins, both cults must be understood in the context of the sectarian rivalry between the disciples of Ennin on Mount Hiei (Sanmon 山門) and those of Enchin at Miidera (Jimon 寺門). That confrontation escalated in 993 when Miidera monks occupied Sekizan Zen'in 赤山禅院, prompting a complaint to the court by Hieizan monks.[47] The main bone of contention between the Sanmon and the Jimon was the fact that Miidera did not have its own ordination platform despite repeated petitions to the court, because of Enryakuji's opposition. The involvement of Shinra Myōjin and Sekizan Myōjin in the dispute between them was reported to be total.[48] In contrast, the main protector of Mount Hiei, Sannō Gongen, avoided intervening directly in the rivalry, probably because he was originally the protector of Enchin and continued to be worshiped at Miidera.[49] The clerical dispute between the Jimon and Sanmon was translated or reenacted at the mythological level as a rivalry between the two gods. Because there was an oratory of Shinra Myōjin at Sekizan Zen'in, Sekizan Myōjin's temple, Hieizan monks argued that Shinra Myōjin was a servant of Sekizan Myōjin. Miidera monks, of course, claimed the opposite.

The story of the two dreams of Go-Sanjō Tennō 後三条天皇 (r. 1068–1073), the first retired emperor, reveals the dilemma faced by the court when confronted by the schism that divided the Tendai school. In Go-Sanjō's first dream, Shinra Myōjin appears and orders him to build the Miidera ordination platform; in the second dream, Sekizan Myōjin appears and forbids him to do so.

Raigō and Shinra Myōjin

The *Onjōji denki* contains a fascinating passage related to the dispute. In reward for the rituals that the Miidera priest Raigō 頼豪 (d. 1084) had performed for the birth of a crown prince, Go-Sanjō promised that he would let Raigō build the ordination platform at Miidera. Sekizan Myōjin then appeared in the emperor's dream, armed with bow and arrows, and declared that he would aim his arrows at anyone who authorized the erection of this platform. The emperor, duly frightened, decided to reconsider his promise.[50] His change of attitude infuriated Raigō, who called on Shinra Myōjin to curse the emperor. In spite of his abdication and profuse

apologies, as well as all the ritual efforts of Hieizan monks on his behalf, Go-Sanjō soon died.[51] In this version, Shinra Myōjin's power is so great that he does not hesitate to strike an emperor, and the protection of Mount Hiei monks (and of Sekizan Myōjin) proves insufficient to save him. Yamamoto Hiroko has argued that the image of Raigō's malevolent spirit (*onryō* 怨霊) fused with that of Shinra Myōjin as a pestilence god who could cause epidemics as well as avert them.

Another emperor, Nijō Tennō 二条天皇 (r. 1158–1165), was caught in the same double bind. When he sided with Mount Hiei against Miidera, he is said to have been possessed on his deathbed by Hannya Dōji, 般若童子, one of Shinra Myōjin's acolytes, and by Kuroo Myōjin 黒尾明神, one of the manifestations of Mio Myōjin 三尾明神, the original protector of Miidera. According to a variant, Shinra Myōjin sent his two acolytes, who touched Nijō Tennō with their staff (*shakujō* 錫杖)—an attribute usually associated with the bodhisattva Jizō. The emperor died three days later from smallpox.[52]

FIGURE 8.4. Sekizan Myōjin. Sheet, ink on paper. Edo period. Sheet, ink on paper. University Art Museum, Kyoto City University of Arts. *BZS* 4061.

Even though the two rival groups understandably downplayed their similarities (and potential identity), their antagonism contributed to reinforce their symbolic relationship. Thus, it does not really matter who started it, since the two figures developed *de concert,* forming a kind of *duel* (in both senses of the word, grammatical and martial).

Sekizan Myōjin

A similar demonic nature is suggested by Sekizan Myōjin's appearance. He is usually depicted as a Chinese official in a dress of red brocade, seated on a high chair (Figs. 8.4 and 8.5). Pestilence gods often wear a red dress.[53] Holding a bow and white-feathered arrows, he has a rather threatening, martial look (Fig. 8.6). This motif came to supersede an earlier, more benign version of the god, and it perhaps indicates a response on the part of the monks of Sekizan Zen'in when they were attacked by Miidera monks in 993.[54] The votive tablets (*ema* 絵馬) of Sekizan Zen'in show the god accompanied by a monkey holding paper strips (*gohei* 御幣). The monkey is a symbol of Mount Hiei and a messenger of the Sannō deity.

FIGURE 8.5. Sekizan Myōjin. Edo period. Color on paper. Ichigami Shrine (Shiga prefecture).

According to the *Sekizan Myōjin engi* 赤山明神縁起, Sekizan Myōjin was originally the tutelary god of Chishan 赤山 (Red Mountain, J. Sekizan) in Mingzhou (Shandong province), where Ennin came to pray before his return trip to Japan. Perhaps owing to the proximity of Taishan 泰山, the Chinese site of hell, this god came to be assimilated to the Lord of Taishan (Taishan Fujun, J. Taizan Fukun), and his *honji* was said to be the bodhisattva Dizang (J. Jizō). According to a variant, when Ennin visited Chishan (or Wutaishan 五台山) in 840 and recited the Buddhist scriptures at the Fahua yuan 法華院, a subtemple founded by the Korean warrior and merchant Chang Pogo 張保皐 (d. 846), the god appeared to him in the form of an old man and vowed to protect him. His protection, however, was in return for Ennin's promise to build a temple for him once he returned safely home. Thus protected, Ennin escaped the anti-Buddhist repression of the Huichang era (842–846) and returned to Japan, though not without a frightening detour to the island of the *rākṣasīs*.[55] At that critical moment, the god appeared again, holding a bow and arrows, and routed Ennin's assailers.

It was only after Ennin's death that his promise was fulfilled. The Sekizan Zen'in 赤山禅院 was erected in 864 by Ennin's disciple Anne 安慧 (795–868) at the western foot of Mount Hiei, on the northeastern outskirts of the capital, the so-called Demon Gate (*kimon* 鬼門).[56] After Anne's death, this shrine was destroyed. In 884, the god appeared before the priest Sōō 相応 (831–918) in a dream to complain about this sad state of affairs. Sōō promptly restored the shrine, and soon an edict of Uda Tennō 宇多天皇 (r. 887–897) promoted Sekizan Myōjin to the

third main rank. Subsequently, the temple received important land donations from Daigō Tennō 醍醐天皇 (r. 897–930), and Sekizan Myōjin was promoted to the second rank, and eventually to the first.

Following a recurring pattern, the local god Sekizan Myōjin, once "dis-located," was redefined in translocal terms and came to assume cosmic proportions on several different registers (heaven, earth, the underworld) as an astral deity, an earth deity, and an official of the underworld. He was identified in particular with the "auxiliary star" (*hosei*) of the Northern Dipper—that is, Myōken Bosatsu—and with Taizan Fukun.[57] All these elements are connected by the god's main function, that of a ruler of human destiny.[58]

Shinra Myōjin

According to the Miidera tradition, it is Shinra Myōjin himself who advised Enchin to leave Mount Hiei.[59] He had been Enchin's protector since appearing to him on the boat during Enchin's return trip from China. On that occasion, the god had told him that he was a deity from Silla and that he would henceforward protect him. What initially may have been a generic appellation, "Silla deity," eventually became a proper name, Shinra Myōjin. The question of this god's name and origin cannot be solved easily, however, as he came to be known by a number of secret names that point toward Chinese rather than Korean origins. In particular, he was called "King of Mount Song." That he was eventually called Shinra Myōjin may have to do with the fact that Enchin's sponsors were merchants of Korean descent. According to modern Korean scholars, Shinra Myōjin represents the deification of another protector—albeit a human one—of Ennin and Enchin, the warrior and merchant Chang Pogo.[60] Whatever the reality of that Korean link, it underscores the importance of Korean immigrant groups like the Hata clan, as well as their importance in and around the capital (especially at Uzumasa, at Fushimi Inari, and in Ōmi province).[61]

FIGURE 8.6. (*Opposite*) Sekizan Myōjin. *Ofuda*. Sekizan zen'in, Kyoto. Personal collection.

Shinra Myōjin shared his function as protector of Miidera with the ancient landlord deity (*jinushi*) Mio Myōjin 三尾明神.[62] His two acolytes, the red-colored Hannya Dōji 般若童子 and the blue-colored Shukuō Dōji 宿王童子, were said to protect children dedicated by their parents to Miidera.[63] They call to mind the acolytes of Matarajin and of Fudō, another important protector of Miidera.

The origins of the Shinra Myōjin ritual can be traced to a ritual performed by Myōson 明尊 (971–1063) in 1052. In an oracle delivered during that ritual, Shinra Myōjin declared that he was also called Shukuō Bosatsu 宿王菩薩, and that he would protect Miidera monks. Shukuō (Mansion King) is also the name of one of his acolytes, Shukuō Dōji, and it points to astral worship (and perhaps already to the cult of the *shukujin*). Shinra Myōjin is also identified with Sonjōō (Myōken Bosatsu) and with the bodhisattva Kokūzō, two eminent star deities.[64]

Representations of Shinra Myōjin are relatively rare, and his statue at Miidera, commonly dated to 1052, is kept hidden.[65] This icon's appearance is very striking with its white face, oblique eyes, and three-pronged headgear. The whiteness of the face contrasts with the redness of Sekizan Myōjin's dress. The color code is obviously significant, but both colors can connote epidemics. Certain scholars have argued that Shinra Myōjin was homophonous with *shira* 'white' and that the god was therefore related to a network of white deities, including old men like Sumiyoshi or Shirahige Myōjin 白髭明神 and the *oshirasama* of popular religion.[66]

In paintings, Shinra Myōjin is usually represented as an old man wearing a Chinese dress and headgear, seated on a chair, holding a pilgrim's staff in his left hand and a scroll in his right hand (Figs. 8.7 and 8.8). His look is definitely foreign, and the staff identifies him as a traveler. The scroll is perhaps a reference to his *honji,* Mañjuśrī, the bodhisattva of wisdom, who usually holds a scripture in one of his hands. Kuroda Satoshi has pointed out the resemblance between Shinra Myōjin and certain representations of Kamatari 鎌足 (614–669), the ancestor of the Fujiwara lineage.[67] Shinra Myōjin may also have served as an iconographic model for En no Gyōja.[68] An interesting representation of Shinra Myōjin is kept at Shōgo-in 聖護院, the headquarters of Tendai shugendō in Kyoto. Although he is also represented as an old man, he is much more corpulent than in the Miidera representations.[69] The Historical Museum of Ōtsu holds a scroll in which Shinra Myōjin, seated in the same typical position, is a middle-aged man

FIGURE 8.7. Shinra Myōjin. 16th–17th century. Preparatory drawing. Hanging scroll, color on paper. Onjōji (Ōtsu, Shiga prefecture).

with dark hair (Fig. 8.8). Yet another atypical representation is a statue representing Shinra Myōjin as a lean old man standing.[70] Also worth mentioning is the Mii mandala, with Miroku at the center, flanked by Shinra Myōjin and Mio Myōjin; Sonjōō at the top, with the so-called Yellow Fudō (Ki Fudō 黄不動) and a diagram made of circles representing the deities of the eighteen shrines of Miidera on either side; and Sannō Gongen at the bottom, flanked by Chishō Daishi (Enchin) and Hārītī.[71]

Shinra Myōjin's Network

In the *Jimon denki horoku,* Shinra Myōjin is described as a man with plain (not white) hair. He is identified with Susanoo, but also with Matarajin, Gozu Tennō, and the god of Mount Song. The cult of Shinra Myōjin developed in relation to that of Sonjōō (the Miidera name for Myōken). Shinra Myōjin is also said to have come to Japan to protect the Sonjōō ritual brought from China by Enchin.[72] Eventually he himself became identified with Sonjōō.[73] Shinra Myōjin is also identified with Dakiniten, whose emissaries are the astral foxes (*shinko*).[74] The seven stars were also called astral foxes, and they were said to constitute the essence of the human body.

According to the *Shinra Myōjin mondō shō yōkun sho* 新羅明神問答抄用訓書 (1344), Shinra Myōjin is the son of the *nāga* king Sāgara and the brother of the Itsukushima deity (and, by extension, of Benzaiten).[75] The *Record of Shinra* (*Shinra no ki* 新羅記) states that the god manifested himself as Benzaiten in India, the King of Red Mountain (Zhushan wang 朱山王) in China, and Susanoo in Japan.[76] In *Stories Heard from Writers Old and New* (*Kokon chomonjū* 古今著聞集, 1254) by Tachibana no Narisue 橘成季, he is the son of the *nāga* king Sāgara (who is sometimes

FIGURE 8.8. Shinra Myō-jin. Nanbokuchō period, 14th century. Hanging scroll, color on silk. Ōtsu City Museum of History (Ōtsu, Shiga prefecture).

presented as Benzaiten's father). In the *Shinra ryakki* 新羅略記, Shinra Myōjin is identified with the *kami* Susanoo.[77] It is allegedly because the latter went to the foreign land of Silla with his fifteen children that he came to be called by the name of that country, Shinra Myōjin.[78]

In this way, through the latent associations shared with Sekizan Myōjin and Shinra Myōjin, Matarajin came to be linked, or even identified, with deities such as Taizan Fukun and Susanoo. These links often merely reinforced—while slightly redefining them—earlier associations between Matarajin and various members of King Yama's retinue, namely Vināyaka, the *ḍākinīs,* and the Seven Mothers. The association with the Seven Mothers also allowed Matarajin to be associated with the seven stars of the Northern Dipper. Finally, the fact that both Sekizan Myōjin and Shinra Myōjin were perceived as pestilence gods clearly resonated with the popular image of Matarajin as it developed at Kōryūji.

In the end, it looks as if Matarajin, Sekizan Myōjin, and Shinra Myōjin were all avatars of the same Chinese deity, Taishan Fujun (J. Taizan Fukun). According to the *Jimon denki horoku* 寺門伝記補録, Shinra Myōjin is identical with Matarajin and Gozu Tennō. Like Matarajin, Sekizan Myōjin and Shinra Myōjin may have been generic names initially (gods of Red Mountain, gods of Silla), i.e., the local gods invoked by Ennin as he departed from Shandong to return to Japan. In the end, Matarajin came to form with them an implicit triad—he stands at the top of Mount Hiei, protecting the three pagodas of Enryakuji, while they dwell at the eastern and western feet of the mountain. These *mytho-logical* and *rito-logical* associations explain in large part the functional evolution of Matarajin, to which we now turn.

MATARAJIN'S EVOLVING FUNCTIONS

Protector of the Jōgyōdō

Matarajin's claim to be a demon of obstacles is reminiscent of another paradigmatic deity of obstacles, Vināyaka/Kōjin, who claimed to be able to prevent practitioners from reaching awakening. Not surprisingly, Matarajin came to be identified with Sanbō Kōjin.[79] However, just as Kōjin, once placated, became the protector of Buddhism, Matarajin became the protector of Mount Hiei's Jōgyōdō and its Amida-centered *samādhi* practice. There were three halls called Jōgyōzanmai-dō 常行三昧堂 on Mount Hiei, one in each of the monastic centers known as the Western Pagoda (Tōtō 東塔), the Eastern Pagoda (Saitō 西塔), and Yokawa 横川. Matarajin was apparently worshiped at the back door (*ushirodo* 後戸) of these halls, a space located just behind the main altar or in the northeastern corner (corresponding to the Demon Gate). Thus, while his function was to protect the building and its occupants against demons, his localization suggests that initially he may himself have been one of them—a pattern familiar by now. The symbolic valence of the *ushirodo* reinforces Matarajin's symbolic potential as *kōjin* and directional deity.

It is not clear, however, that Matarajin was always perceived as an insider, that is, a protector enshrined inside the Jōgyōdō. Behind that hall was a torii, through which the god's palanquin was brought on certain occasions. This suggests that Matarajin was enshrined in a separate place outside the Jōgyōdō, to the northeast. In other words, he may have been the object of an independent cult.[80] The structure of the preliminary rite of welcoming implies that he was perceived as a kind of mountain god, descending on certain occasions from the mountain top to dwell in a temporary abode (what in Shintō shrines is called *otabisho* 御旅所). Two different conceptions (at least) of Matarajin seem to have coexisted in Tendai monasteries, that of a traveling god and that of a sedentary deity—and only the latter can be described as a protecting deity. The traveling god, on the other hand, is—even if temporarily—the master of the place where he comes to dwell.

Through a common inversion, Matarajin, the demon causing obstacles to rebirth in the Pure Land, became a deity that guides practitioners toward the Pure Land. One step further, and he actually became a manifestation of Amida, or, more precisely, his wheel-commanding body (*kyōryōrinshin* 教令輪身). In esoteric Buddhism, this term refers to the wrathful manifestation of a buddha, and it may surprise us to hear it in connection with Amida. Perhaps this was never more than wishful thinking on the part of his worshipers, however, as Matarajin always retained his disruptive potential. But we are not in a "pure" Pure Land context here, and the Jōgyōdō practice led to an esoteric reinterpretation of Amidist beliefs. In the Genshi kimyōdan, in particular, Amida was interpreted as the breath of life. Thus, when Matarajin "cuts the breath" of a person, he is no longer stealing the essence of that person in the same purely harmful way as the *ḍākinīs* (and the demonic Mahākāla). In this way, Genshi kimyōdan adepts were able to downplay Matarajin's perceived heterodoxy.

The God on/of the Threshold

Matarajin initially was, and remained, essentially a god of obstacles. This is a crucial point, and I believe that the radical nature of his self-introduction—at the time of his encounter with Ennin—has not been sufficiently emphasized. Matarajin's hubris is clear when he claims that, unless properly propitiated, he will prevent practitioners from being reborn in the Pure Land. This claim is particularly egregious because it downplays Amida's power and undermines his vow to take to his western paradise all those who put their faith in him.[81]

Matarajin, a typical liminal deity, is thus standing on the threshold between life and death, and depending on the viewpoint he is a spiritual parasite or the gatekeeper of the other world. He is also, according to the

Genshi kimyōdan, the regent of the twelve *nidānas*—a notion that seems to contradict or undermine the early Buddhist notion of a quasi-automatic causality (*pratitya-samutpāda*).[82]

Taming the *Tengu*

Matarajin's demonic nature resurfaces in the Tendai ritual called Placating the *Tengu* (*tengu odoshi* 天狗怖し). In this ritual, Matarajin himself was apparently perceived as a kind of *tengu* who had to be placated. The monks achieved this goal by feigning to conform to his frantic behavior, reading scriptures at random and making boisterous noise.

Yamamoto argues that Matarajin was not as important at the Jōgyōdō's Shushō-e ritual at New Year as he was at the *tengu odoshi* of the eighth month.[83] She believes that the apparition of Matarajin on the Nō stage ultimately derived from his role in that *tengu* exorcism.[84] Unfortunately, the meaning of that performance—which prefigures the so-called *modoki* もどき (parody) feature of the performing arts—had been forgotten by the time the *sarugaku* figure named Okina developed. That aspect of Matarajin can also be observed in the famous Ox Festival of Kōryūji 広隆寺 (Kyoto) and in the drinking bouts of the Matarajin ritual at Tōnomine 多武峰 (Nara prefecture).

According to Kawamura Minato, while Matarajin was essentially a protector of *nenbutsu* practice in the exoteric Tendai doctrine, in esoteric Buddhism he became one of the deities (although not the main one) worshiped during a secret ritual specific to the Genshi kimyōdan initiation, the so-called Consecration of the Original Purport (*genshi kanjō* 玄旨灌頂).[85]

Backdoor (*ushirodo*) rites rested on the premise that the regular ritual, performed in front of the main altar, attracted demonic obstructions. In ordinary esoteric ritual, the priest begins by invoking Agni, Vināyaka, and the twelve devas in order to prevent all obstructions. In the present case, this method was judged ineffective against troubles caused by *tengu,* and it was deemed more appropriate to give the devil his due, that is, to seem to yield to demonic influence by performing the ritual, sometimes literally, "under the influence." The point was to behave in a demented fashion, reading the scriptures at random and dancing and shouting—all while trying to remain perfectly concentrated and unmoved inwardly. Here we have a twofold discrepancy between frontstage and backstage: the orthodox ritual of the main hall and the slightly heterodox rite of the *ushirodo*, on the one hand, and the outwardly frantic behavior and the inwardly lucid disposition, on the other. It is not entirely clear whether the sound and fury were meant to please or scare the *tengu.* The name of the ritual suggests that the point was to drive them away, but paradoxically, this was to be achieved by creating the very type of havoc they like. Likewise, the role of Matarajin in all this is not too clear: was he attracted and aroused by the tumult, or simply distracted by it—as in the case of the *sarugaku* entertainment that was also performed at the *ushirodo*. In any event, his mere presence was deemed sufficient to scare away the *tengu* and other demons. But this implies that Matarajin was thought to be a kind of *tengu* or demon king himself. The *tengu*—and perhaps Matarajin—represented obstacles of an essentially spiritual or psychological kind encountered by the monks, rather than physical calamities—like epidemics—that can strike humans. As we will see, however, Matarajin was also considered a pestilence god.

While Matarajin's role on Mount Hiei was essentially limited to the Jōgyōdō ritual and the *tengu odoshi,* in other Tendai centers such as Mōtsuji in Hiraizumi, Tōnomine, and Nikkō, his rituals were defined in broader terms.[86] Following the homeopathic logic of "evil driving away evil," Matarajin was invoked to expel demonic influences during periods of radical change, such as at New Year or during the Great Nenbutsu of the eighth month.[87]

This *tengu* image seems at first glance quite different from that of Matarajin performing a ribald song and dance with his acolytes—but the two are connected. The Shushō-e festival at New Year, when *sarugaku* performances took place, is perhaps the context in which the figure of Matarajin gradually merged with that of Okina.[88] In these festivals, a new image of Matarajin as *shukujin* came into existence. However, even if he became the *honzon* of these particular rituals, Matarajin was not able to impose himself everywhere as a deity of the arts.[89] He was, by nature, too secret for that. He had to change radically first. Only in certain contexts, wearing the mask of Okina, did he emerge as a deity of *sarugaku.* In the process, however, he lost much of his secrecy and his ambiguity. This was not always the case: at Mōtsuji, Matarajin was (and still remains) a hidden god, whose statue can only be seen once every thirty-three years, like the relics of the Buddha.

THE GOD OF THE GENSHI KIMYŌDAN

Let us now turn to the esoteric interpretation of Matarajin in the Genshi kimyōdan, as it was perhaps influenced at least in part by the transgressive atmosphere of the *ushirodo* ritual. Because of the prohibition of the Genshi kimyōdan during the Edo period, we have few documents concerning that ritual. One of the surviving texts, the *Genshidan hishō* 玄旨壇秘鈔, was edited in Hayakawa Junzaburo's *Shinkō sōsho* 信仰叢書 (1915).[90] It provides, among other things, a sexual exegesis of the representation of Matarajin with his two acolytes.[91] Two points are worth noting here: the interpretation of the three figures in terms of sexual duality and the ultimate nonduality of defilement and awakening; and the symbolism of the seven stars of the Northern Dipper. Kageyama Haruki has emphasized the astral symbolism of the Matarajin cult.[92] For him, Matarajin is the *honzon* of the Kimyōdan ritual. Yamamoto Hiroko, on the other hand, downplays the astral aspect of Matarajin, arguing that his role in the Genshi kimyōdan initiation remained preliminary, and that the real *honzon* of that ritual was not Matarajin but rather the seven stars.

Performed with a pure mind, the song and dance of human life symbolized by Matarajin and his two acolytes bring deliverance; otherwise, they make us fall deeper into the cycle of life and death. In this sense, Matarajin is a Buddhist version of the Chinese god of destiny, who controls the process leading to birth, aging, death, and rebirth. This image paved the way to the medieval notion of the *shukujin*. The sulfurous reputation of the Genshi kimyōdan, however, comes from the enigmatic words ("shishirishi ni shishiri" alternating with "sosoroso ni sosoro") of his acolytes' song, which are perceived as an allusion (or an invitation) to sexual union.[93] Their apparent meaninglessness, akin to that of some nursery rhymes, has generated a surplus of significance. They are also said to allude to the male and female organs, and to express the sounds of pleasure uttered during sexual union. In that interpretation, "song and dance" are used as metaphors for sexual intercourse (not unlike the "clouds and rain" of Chinese poetry). In the actual description of the Genshi kimyōdan ritual, however, nothing confirms this interpretation, which seems fraught with polemical intentions.[94]

According to medieval scholastic commentaries, Matarajin and his two acolytes reveal the essence of the three paths (defilements, karma, and suffering) and of the three poisons (greed, hatred, and desire). The two youths are said to symbolize karma and defilements, or greed and hatred, respectively.[95] Their wild performance allegedly expresses the endless transmigration we experience in the world of *saṃsāra,* whereas the rhythm of Matarajin's drum symbolizes—and produces—the identity between defilements and awakening (*bonnō soku bodai* 煩悩即菩提) that constitutes the hallmark of *hongaku* thought.[96] With time, however, it seems likely that the exorcistic meaning of the raucous performance of the acolytes dwindled and was lost, giving way to mere ribaldry. Yet nothing in the surviving texts of the Genshi kimyōdan suggests the kind of orgiastic teaching of which it was accused.

Because of the fundamental *hongaku* notion identifying defilements with awakening, the two acolytes are also said to symbolize various traditional rubrics such as the ten Perfections (*pāramitā*) and the ten realms of rebirth (five earthly, five heavenly), and their dance, the self-given Dharma pleasure (*hōraku* 法楽).[97] They also correspond to the bodhisattvas Fugen and Monju.

Indeed, the rather tedious doctrinal descriptions found in Genshi kimyōdan texts are rather anticlimactic, anti-orgasmic. They sound very much like orthodox esoteric texts, such as the commentaries on the *Yugikyō* and its "horse penis *samādhi*" of Aizen. While they present Matarajin and his two acolytes as symbols of ignorance and the three poisons, and seem to point to sexual defilement, they by no means recommend sex as a shortcut to enlightenment, as certain Tantric texts do. The absence of any female figure in the triad is in itself significant.

True, the Genshi kimyōdan text does at one point interpret the triad in terms of sexual union, as the fusion of the red (blood) and white (semen), but the point here, as in texts of the Tachikawa-ryū and many other esoteric texts, is not sex per se but embryology.[98] The fetus is symbolized by the stūpa, usually the five-wheel stūpa, but here the Many Treasures Stūpa (*tahōtō* 多宝塔) of the *Lotus Sūtra;* and the descent of consciousness (*vijñāna*) into the fetus is symbolized by the buddha Śākyamuni's entrance into that stūpa. In this embryological discourse, Matarajin plays a rather minor role. Human conception is described in our text as the descent of the seven stars of the Northern Dipper (and more specifically of the star of fundamental destiny (*honmyōshō* 本命星) and the star of the primordial spirit (*ganjinshō* 元辰星). Thus, the human body is a microcosm, its seven holes corresponding to the seven stars.[99] These seven stars also correspond to the seven shrines of Hie. Matarajin does reappear briefly after a section on the Northern Dipper, which describes how, at the end of the initiation, the master reveals the seven stars reflected in a mirror. He is then identified with Sanbō Kōjin 三宝荒神, and the latter's numerological equivalence with the Three Truths of Tendai makes him worthy of being, retrospectively, the *honzon* of a ritual that apparently unfolded without him. On the basis of this rather superficial numerological symbolism, and of Kōjin's equation with fundamental ignorance, the text argues that Matarajin's ritual is the "great affair" of the Genshi kimyōdan.[100]

In other words, the "essential purport" of the Genshi kimyōdan was not sex. In fact, the *Genshidan hishō* identifies mundane sex with ignorance, not with enlightenment. The dance and song of the Matarajin triad represent a world dominated by karma and the three poisons, and they constitute the starting point of the ritual, not its culmination.[101] From a doctrinal standpoint, the Genshi kimyōdan fashions a synthesis between the images of Matarajin as protector of Tendai and a soul stealer. This synthesis paved the way to the esoteric *nenbutsu* of Tendai, derived in large part from that of Shingon.[102] This esoteric ritual constituted the metamorphosis of Matarajin, and his first appearance on the theatrical stage. It replicated the passage from Matarajin to Amida in the Jōgyōdō rituals, but by interpreting the inversion or taming in yogic terms, as a kind of breath yoga (*prāṇāyāma*). In the esoteric *nenbutsu* of the Genshi kimyōdan, Amida has become the life breath of beings, while Matarajin, the "essence-stealing demon," is reinterpreted as the mind-king, and as a kind of psychopomp deity that guides practitioners to paradise.[103] Paradoxically, it is through the rationalized teachings of the Genshi kimyōdan—even if they preserve a subversive, sexual potential—that the passage from the demonic Matarajin to the emblematic Nō character Okina was made possible.[104] It represents the ultimate doctrinal development of the medieval Matarajin, a development that opened the way to the Edo-period Matarajin, who gradually lost all his demonic character.

ANOTHER MATARAJIN

The Epidemic Deity

We have seen how, in Tendai, Matarajin lost his connection to the cult of the Mothers, as in Shingon. He became essentially a protector of *nenbutsu* practice, and his association with star rituals in the Genshi kimyōdan contributed to his redefinition as a regent of human destiny.

Yet the "real" Matarajin somehow slipped through these doctrinal interpretations. He developed a kind of trickster figure, whose ribald song and dance gives cosmic meaning to laughter and sex.[105] His demonic aspects, and in particular his role as a pestilence god, also endured, at least for a time. The Matarajin Offering (Matarajin-ku 摩多羅神供) of Senmyōji 千妙寺 (in Hitachi), for example, states that the protecting deity of the Jōgyōzanmai-dō had the power to stop epidemics.[106] The same is true of the Madarijin 摩怛哩神 of Kōryūji, whose statue, we are told, was enshrined at the rear of the Jōgyōdō, facing the northeast, as a guardian of the Buddha.[107] The priest Myōe 明恵 (1173–1232) is said to have inherited a Madarijin ritual and to have made good use of it during an epidemic in 1206.[108] In this way, Matarajin became the *honzon* of *yakujin* 厄神 festivals, rituals aimed at subduing pestilence demons. On the talismans (*gofu* 護符) of Gyokusenji 玉泉寺 in Yoshino (Nara prefecture), he appears as a wrathful deity with three faces. Similar festivals also took place in shrines like Yoshida jinja 吉田神社 in Kyoto, as shown by the talismans produced on those occasions.

The Jōgyōdō ritual of Kōryūji developed into a popular ritual known as the Ox Festival (*ushi matsuri* 牛祭), which contained carnivalesque elements strongly reminiscent of the *tengu odoshi*. This festival was traditionally performed on the twelfth of the ninth month; despite an interruption during the Meiji Restoration, it was still performed on October 12 until recently. Its outline is as follows: after nightfall, a priest wearing a mask (supposedly of Matarajin) appears, riding a black ox; he is flanked by four monks disguised as green and red demons, supposedly impersonating the four deva kings. The priest then reads a *saimon* aimed at eliminating all calamities and bringing forth peace and happiness.[109] An important element of the festival is the symbolic inversion: the priest who in some accounts rides the ox backwards is the object of jokes or insults on the part of bystanders. After the reading of the *saimon,* a sudden scramble ensues, as everyone rushes behind Matarajin, who retreats to a certain hall. This carnivalesque atmosphere has been compared to the "night parade of the hundred demons" (*hyakki yakō;* var. *hyakki yagyō* 百鬼夜行) that was believed to proceed through the streets of the capital on dark nights.[110] In this sense, Matarajin remained a demon king.[111]

Matarajin on the Ground

The name Matarajin was initially related to ill-defined entities, animal spirits such as the white fox (also identified with Dakiniten) and the *tengu.* While Yamamoto emphasizes the monastic Matarajin of Tendai, as worshiped in the exoteric tradition of the Jōgyōdō and in the esoteric tradition of the Genshi kimyōdan, she also points out that the image of Matarajin developed in other places as well—in natural sites and in mythological discourse, for example. Near the Main Hall (Konpon chūdō 根本中堂) of Enryakuji, a rock said to have the shape of a white fox and therefore identified with Dakiniten was called Matara Tenjin. Stones, rocks, and tumuli, in which foxes or *tengu* were believed to have manifested themselves, were often called *matara.*[112] At Nachi 那智 (Wakayama Prefecture), there is a Matarajin Cave (Matarajin no Iwaya) near the waterfall of Hirō Gongen 飛瀧権現. The same is true at Kumano, where the name of Matarajin is found on numinous rocks next to those of Benzaiten, Daikokuten, and Kishimojin (Hārītī). These places were cultic sites for Shugendō practitioners, who saw in Matarajin a *tengu*-like deity like Izuna Gongen.

Near the Eastern Pagoda on Mount Hiei, a deity called Ina Tenjin 移那天神 was identified with Matarajin and presented as an avatar of the Black Yakṣa (that is, Mahākāla). As the toponymy indicates, this deity was credited with the power to remove obstacles. When they reached that site, medieval pilgrims formed the mudrā of Dakiniten by licking their right palm, like a fox. It was therefore related to a cult of Matarajin as a god of obstacles. The mantra associated with that mudrā consists of a series of occult names related to Enmaten and his retinue. In other words, we are dealing here with a cohort of demons associated with the underworld.[113] Other rocks bearing the name Matarajin are related to the cults of Dakiniten, foxes, and *tengu.* Orikuchi Nobuo emphasized that Matarajin—in particular, the Matarajin of Kōryūji—far from being a foreign god like Shinra Myōjin and Sekizan Myōjin, was actually a local god, a *genius loci* or landlord deity (*jinushigami*), symbolizing the chthonian energies that must be placated through an appropriate cult.[114] But the same can be said of the two other gods just mentioned, and the fact of being perceived as foreign never prevented a god from merging with and representing "auto-chthonous" deities—on the contrary.

Susanoo, Gozu Tennō, Konpira, Miwa Myōjin

As a pestilence god, Matarajin came to be identified with Gozu Tennō and his *kami* counterpart, Susanoo.[115] In the *Jimon denki horoku,* Susanoo is said to have manifested himself as Matarajin and Gozu Tennō in India, as the god of Songyue 嵩嶽 (Mount Song) in China, and as Shinra Myōjin and Mutōjin 武塔神 (a doublet of Gozu Tennō) in Japan.[116] Kageyama has also emphasized the association of Matarajin with the seven stars of the Northern Dipper and with the bodhisattva Kokūzō. During the Shushō-e New Year ritual at Nikkō, seven masks, symbolizing the seven stars, escorted Matarajin's "Dharma body" (unfortunately, we are not told what this Dharma body may have been).[117] In Tendai esoteric rituals, the seven stars, descending to earth, give birth to sentient beings. At the end of the Kimyōdan initiation, they appear to the practitioner, reflected in a mirror.[118] As we have seen, there are parallels between the seven stars and the Seven Mothers, on the one hand, and the seven Hie shrines on the other. Kageyama argues that Matarajin was also the *honzon* of the Hachibu-dō 八部堂, a building near the Main Hall (Konpon chūdō) on Mount Hiei. This building, no longer extant, had been erected on the site where the seven stars (or, in a variant, the planet Venus) had fallen, which was called, for that reason, Kokūzō's Tail.[119]

Furthermore, the identity of Matarajin with Mahākāla—i.e., Daikokuten, the protector of the Mount Hiei community—links him to Sannō Gongen and to Konpira 金比羅, a protector of the Demon Gate in the northeast.[120] According to the *Karasaki (no) ki* 唐埼記 (1362), Konpira or Matarajin was the god of Vulture Peak before becoming the protector of Mount Tiantai and its monastery, Qinglong si. According to the *Sange yōryakki,* Konpira appeared to Saichō during the latter's stay at Qinglong si and vowed to follow him to Japan. The same source identifies Matarajin both with Susanoo and with Konpira, that is, the Miwa god Ōkuninushi (the son and/or heir of Susanoo).[121] This connection was emphasized at Nikkō at the beginning of the Edo period, and I won't dwell on it here. Let us simply note that it was for Tenkai a way to impose his brand of Tendai shintō, the so-called Sannō ichijitsu shintō, by promoting Matarajin as a Miwa god (i.e., Konpira, the god of Hie Shrine and the ancestral god of the shogunate) to a status equal or superior to that of Amaterasu, the ancestral deity of the imperial family.[122] Through this symbolic link, Matarajin gained in orthodoxy. The link with Susanoo (and Shinra Myōjin, another deity identified with Susanoo) also brought him to the frontstage as a pestilence god, on a par with Gozu Tennō.[123]

The name Konpira brings together several homonymous deities: Kubera, an Indic god of fortune, associated with the north, identified with Vaiśravaṇa (J. Bishamonten), and often paired with Hārītī (J. Kariteimo, Kishimojin); Kuṃbhīra, the guardian of Vulture Peak, and later of Mount Tiantai; and Kuṃbhira, the first of the twelve directional spirit commanders who form the retinue of Baiṣajyaguru (Yakushi), the *honzon* of the Main Hall on Mount Hiei. Konpira was also identified with the north (or more specifically, with the northeast or *ushi-tora* 'ox-tiger' direction).[124] In the Chinese system of the twelve calendar signs, he also came to be identified with the rat, and occasionally with the boar. The spatiotemporal symbolism of the northeastern direction explains why, in the Genshi kimyōdan, Konpira became the very symbol of liminality, the transition between day and night, and consequently a symbol of nonduality.[125] This directional aspect clearly links Konpira with Matarajin, a deity worshiped in the northeastern corner of the Jōgyōdō.[126]

Many clues point to a link between Matarajin and the demonic category of the *kōjin,* or the individual deity of the same name. Susanoo and Gozu Tennō are two well-known forms of *kōjin,* and we recall that Vināyaka was also called Kōjin. Indeed, Matarajin is clearly identified with Sanbō Kōjin (Kōjin of the Three Jewels) in Genshi kimyōdan texts. According to Zeami Motokiyo 世阿弥元清 (ca. 1363–ca. 1443), author of the Nō treatise *Fushikaden* 風姿花伝 (Flowering Spirit), Matarajin is a fear-inspiring *kōjin,* a deity prompt to punish those who lack respect for him. Matarajin's *kōjin* nature also comes to the forefront in the legend of Hata no Kawakatsu (also read Kōkatsu), the legendary ancestor of the Hata clan and the alleged founder of Kōryūji. In the Zenchiku's *Meishuku shū,* after identifying Matarajin with Daikōjin, who is himself a transformation of Hata no Kawakatsu, Zenchiku adds: "When he is angry, he is Sanbō Kōjin; when he is quiet, he is the fundamentally existing Tathāgata."[127]

The mention of *kōjin* should also alert us to another aspect of Matarajin, that of a placenta god. As we have seen, one specific type of *kōjin* was the placenta *kōjin* (*ena kōjin*), a god protecting the fetus within the womb. This function is shared by a number of the deities described above. According to the *Sanmon kiroku kikigaki* 山門記録聞書, Matarajin was also known on Mount Hiei as Ina Tenjin 稲那天神.[128] This god was said to be related to the *ḍākinīs,* and its name resonates with that of the placenta kōjin. Matarajin also shares many affinities, as we recall, with another placenta god, Vināyaka.[129] In particular, both are closely related to the "mothers," female demons who, depending on the circumstances, attack or protect the fetus in the womb. Yet another such deity is Ugajin, whose relationship with Matarajin has been already noted.

CODETTA

One could enumerate *ad nauseam* explicit or implicit associations between Matarajin and other deities. Tendai exegetes are always ready to invoke yet another secret teaching, yet another oral tradition that links Matarajin to a larger network. While Matarajin's transformations may appear dizzying, their *ligne de force* remains the same. It shows how Matarajin, initially a demon of obstacles, became a high god that controls human destinies on the one hand, while on the other hand, at the other end of the spectrum, it continues to manifest elemental forces, not yet individualized, such as animal spirits and other natural or sacred energies. In this respect, Matarajin resembles Kōjin, a protean deity that—like the slime mold—oscillates between a single being and a swarm. Indeed, in certain respects, Matarajin and all the other deities described earlier may be seen as manifestations of Kōjin, or simply as members of a class called *kōjin*. We have already discussed the case of Benzaiten. As Suzuki Masataka has pointed out, the figure of Matarajin/Okina that developed in *sarugaku* is only one aspect of an infinitely more complex deity (indeed, a constellation or nebula of deities)—inside which other deities circulate—the Seven Mothers and other female figures such as Hārītī, Dakiniten, as well as animal deities, and so on. Even if he remains a male deity, he includes the female principle (and the union of sexes), and as such transcends gender.

Matarajin, as an essence-stealing demon, fused with Daikokuten and Dakiniten; as a demon of obstacles, he came to merge with epidemic deities such as the Seven Mothers and Susanoo. In spite—or because—of this, he eventually rose to the status of a ruler of human destiny.

NO COUNTRY FOR OLD MEN?

The figures of Matarajin, Sekizan Myōjin, Shinra Myōjin, and Ugajin share one common feature: they are all represented as old men. This feature, which also defines the Inari and Sumiyoshi deities, as well as Shirahige Myōjin and En no Gyōja, points toward a Korean influence, and particularly toward Korean descent groups like the Hata. Fushimi Inari, Uzumasa (Kōryūji), and above all Mount Hiei and the shores of Lake Biwa were strongholds of Korean culture. Saichō himself was supposedly of Korean descent. In that sense, Shinra Myōjin assumes a paradigmatic status, inasmuch as his name openly reveals his Korean (Silla) origins.

The topos of the monk's encounter with a local god overlaps here with that of the monk encountering a demon (or god) of obstacles—this time in the midst of the sea, a spatial realm even more dangerous and alien than the mountain, far from all fixed locations. Indeed, what the demon requests is to be worshiped in a fixed location (thereby becoming a god). The paradigmatic example is the encounter between the Buddha's disciple Śāriputra and the demon of obstacles Vināyaka/Kōjin. Later on, however, in the Nō tradition, this demon of obstacles was humanized, appearing under the features of Devadatta, the Buddha's cousin, or under those of Matarajin (as Okina).

Like Dakiniten in contrast to the *ḍākinīs,* Matarajin became a much more individualized deity than the Mothers who were perhaps his prototype. In this way, he was able to ascend the esoteric pantheon. Yet his individualization also blurred the hierarchic framework of esoteric Buddhist mythology: indeed, it is hard to locate him on a status scale when he is identified with such great devas as Dakiniten, Shōten, and Benzaiten. Like them, Matarajin ends up becoming all things to all people—or almost. He enters into contact with many spirits and, through these contacts, eventually morphs into the figure of Okina.

These images, however, represent mere "fixations," which betray the deity's fundamentally metamorphic nature. Rightly enough, a god of obstacles causes obstacles above all to totalizing, abstract thought. At any rate, in the present case, one may argue that Inari Daimyōjin, Ugajin, and Matarajin are variants or ramifications, if not of the same cult or structure, then of the same ritual/mythological constellation (which also encompassed Dakiniten, Benzaiten, and a few others).

The continuity we find in Matarajin's career, by linking the dots, may be no more than a narrative facility and a perceptive illusion. The name Matarajin designates very different deities: here a female demon or a three-faced deity, there a smiling old man, a god of the performing arts. This phenomenon, however, perhaps reveals the metamorphic nature of the god, which tends to be obscured by adhesion to any single form. Thus, while the historian tends to underscore the symbolic and apparently random drift, and the structuralist analyses the structural coherence that underlies these variants, the phenomenologist will emphasize the transcendence of the divine power that manifests itself behind or through all these masks. Matarajin, like Okina, is indeed a masked god, or rather the god *as* mask.

CODA

The stone that the builders rejected has become the cornerstone.

MATTHEW 21:42

The puzzle is only complete when a piece is lacking.

PABLO DE SANTIS, *THE THEATER OF MEMORY*

The time has come to recapitulate. My contention has been that the devas, while they are conspicuously absent from accounts of medieval Japanese religion, were actually at its center—its blind spot, as it were—and that historians of religion have been affected by blindsight. The chapters of this book show what is called in computer lingo an accordion effect: when a topic (here a deity) comes to the forefront, the others recede to the background.

This recapitulation is also a capitulation of sorts. But perhaps all scholarship is after all a deferred capitulation. *In cauda venenum* (In the tail lies the venom)—the venom in this case being the lingering doubt contained in the coda (a term derived from *cauda* 'tail'). Perhaps it is the poison that the snake god Ugajin has instilled in me, in the form of a doubt about the validity of my whole enterprise. Yet this poison may also be the *pharmakon* that prevents me from reaching closure—a closure that often proves fatal to understanding and scholarship. If so, I would also like to instill that poison in others. With this caveat in mind, let me briefly restate the arguments encountered in the preceding chapters.

This book has woven together several red (or multicolored) threads into a kind of braid. These threads include, for instance, the definition of medieval deities as gods of obstacles, gods of human destiny and embryological gods (*fatum* and fetus), earth deities, both autochthonous and foreign, protectors of the natal land (*jinushi*) and of local identity. I have distinguished in these deities a certain number of characteristics that are generally ignored to the profit of more visible features:

- They are all, to one degree or another, gods of obstacles, who rule over human destiny (in a positive or negative way).

- They have an embryological aspect, and can be described at times as placenta gods.

- Despite their crucial importance, they are perceived as liminal (a characteristic of the fourth function).

- They have a secret, mysterious, hidden nature.

- They are often linked to the Buddha's relics and the wish-fulfilling jewel, understood as a mysterious principle of production and subjugation.

- They are always ambiguous and can even be malevolent—or at least they have an intimate relationship with the forces of evil, even if they cannot be reduced to them.

- They have a chthonian nature and are often explicitly related to or assimilated into the earth deity (or deities).

- They stand at the intersection of various religious currents and are therefore cross-sectarian, or rather, transcend any kind of sectarianism.

- They constitute a distinct type of deity—not entirely new—that has only recently become visible. The prototype of these gods, assuming there is one, could be Kōjin.

- Their very existence invites us to question the traditional models of medieval Japanese religion.

- While their origin is often monastic and esoteric, they moved toward the margins of society by a centrifugal movement—through the mediation of marginal groups such as the blind monks and the *hinin*. The latter, in turn, tried to establish their own orthodoxy, and the movement found its achieved expression with Zenchiku's "henotheist" interpretation, in the *Meishuku shū*.

- These gods correspond to that which, within the orthodox Buddhist structure, deconstructs that structure and lends itself to the formation of heterodox currents (*gedō* 外道) like the Tachikawa-ryū and the Genshi kimyōdan.

FIGURE C.1. *(Opposite)* Sannō mandala. Nanbokuchō period, 14th century. Hanging scroll, color on silk. Nara National Museum.

– This current of resistance, however, is reflected within and outside Buddhism by the existence of the *jissha* (in parallel with, but in reaction to, the attempts to elevate Amaterasu to the exalted status of the deity of the Dharma nature (Skt. *dharmatā*; J. *hosshō* 法性), and despite attempts to reintegrate resilient deities (like Aizen) into dualist and ternary exegeses.

THE TWO-TIERED MODEL

My study of the medieval Japanese pantheon has led me to question one of its organizing principles, namely, the two-tiered structure embedded in the *honji suijaku* model. The habitual thesis is that this theory allowed Buddhists to assimilate the "autochthonous" Japanese pantheon. This idea has been taken at face value by earlier generations of scholars, and by generations of Buddhist thinkers before them.[1] It is expressed in a number of mandalas, but perhaps nowhere more perfectly than in the Sannō mandala (Figs. C.1 and C.2), in the upper part of which the protecting deities of Mount Hiei are represented below their associated buddhas and bodhisattvas and their respective seed-letters.

It is my view, however, that this model fails to explain the role played by most deities (buddhas and *kami* among others) in medieval Japanese religion. It offers a blinkered view of religious phenomena and does not allow us to untangle the skein of the relationships between gods, humans, and other modes of existence. It does little, for instance, to elucidate the crucial role of protean deities like Shōten, Dakiniten, Benzaiten, and Ugajin.

The *honji suijaku* theory assumes transparency: gods are mere "traces" or "provisional manifestations" of the buddhas. They simply *re-present* their prototype, albeit not perfectly, since the latter is said to "hide its light." Yet this "hiding," being a skillful means, does reveal the perfection of the buddha's original enlightenment. Nothing is lost, nothing added between the two ends of the chain, the movement between *honji* and *suijaku* is unimpeded. In other words, the *suijaku* acts as a mere intermediary between the buddhas and humans. The reality is a little different, however, in that the transparent *suijaku* became gradually opaque, transforming themselves into what Bruno Latour calls "mediators," intermediaries that have acquired their own agency.[2] From this kind of active *suijaku* to the *jissha,* independent gods that are no longer mere traces, there was only one step. The system deconstructed itself, largely (but not only) as a result of its inner dynamics; its structures turned out to be dissipative structures (to borrow Ilya Prigogine's expression). If we are to continue using the *honji suijaku* theory, we need then to distinguish between its integrative or assimilative logic and its dissolving or disseminating effects.

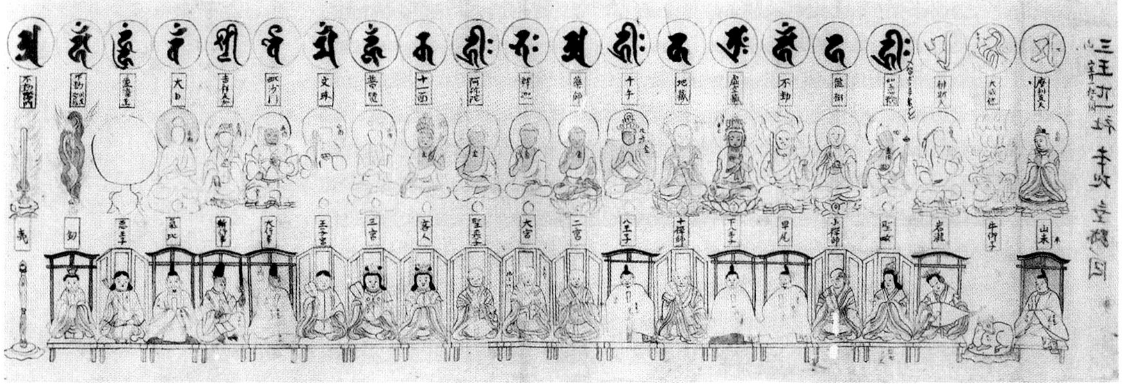

FIGURE C.2. Sannō mandala. Edo period. Sheet, ink on paper. University Art Museum, Kyoto City University of Arts. *BZS* 4003.

BUDDHAS AND *KAMI*

The resilience of the traditional dichotomy is emphasized in a recent book entitled *Buddhas and Kami in Japan*. Despite its title, the book actually suggests that the *honji suijaku* paradigm is too simplistic to describe a complex reality. According to its editors, Mark Teeuwen and Fabio Rambelli:

> When one takes into account the proliferation of cults of other, "moot" kinds of deities, one notices that a great many equations are missing from Tsuji's model [of *honji suijaku* development in four phases]. . . . This means that *honji suijaku* in the classical definition . . . was a phenomenon of limited scope. . . . Rather, *honji suijaku* took the form of a complicated network of associations, establishing links between kami and buddhas, but also between kami and other kami, kami and Yin-Yang deities, buddhas and other buddhas, Wisdom Kings, historical culture heroes both from Japan, China and India, and even demons and witch animals.[3]

Teeuwen and Rambelli conclude: "*Honji suijaku,* then, was not a simple mechanism for 'buddhifying' kami, but rather an extremely versatile tool for assembling complex divine entities of the greatest possible power."[4]

The point is important and needs some elaboration, because it suggests the self-deconstructive nature of the paradigm, that is, its disseminating aspect as opposed to its hierarchical, dualistic aspect. Teeuwen and Rambelli recognize the limitations of the *honji suijaku* model and emphasize its two sides: on the one hand, a two-tiered model; on the other, a mechanism to assemble complex divine entities. All this sounds very Derridean, though I doubt that Teeuwen and Rambelli would acknowledge that (disseminated) influence on their work. It also reinforces my distinction between "explicit" and "implicit" pantheons, the former corresponding to classical *honji suijaku* theory, the latter to its side effects.

Teeuwen and Rambelli conclude: "In this sense, a *honji suijaku* combinatory deity was often not just a dual entity (a buddha or bodhisattva and a kami), but a multiplicity in which different images of the sacred, ritual elements, myths, and narrative elements interacted in complex ways."[5] Consequently, "each of these nondual entities is multifaceted and plural, and their totality encompasses both positive and negative forces."[6] While I agree with this argument, I must point out that it is not the explicit, commonly accepted, ideological understanding of *honji suijaku*. I also object to Teeuwen and Rambelli's characterization of such deities as "moot," although the authors are careful enough to put the term in scare quotes. Yet the fact that they still rely on the dichotomy between buddhas and *kami* forces them to talk of the "patchwork-like nature of the divine realm" and to develop an extra category of residual deities (including Gozu Tennō, Shinra Myōjin, various malevolent *goryō,* and astral deities like Myōken).[7] On the contrary, so-called moot deities are the norm, the matrix, of Japanese religion, and they remain moot only for scholars who still take at face value the ideological standpoint of later "Shintō" and orthodox Buddhism. While our two authors are acutely aware of the limitations of the two-tiered paradigm, it continues to dominate their discussion.

The brocade of medieval Japanese Buddhism was made of many more strands than the simplistic distinction between Buddhism and Shintō would suggest. It took form first of all as an uneasy (and necessarily imperfect) combination of different worldviews and cosmological and mythological systems—in particular, the Indian (Tantric) and Chinese (Daoist and Confucianist). The *honji suijaku* model was above all a way of integrating the gods, reducing them to passive objects in a broader synthesis. As should be clear by now, the parallel expression "gods and buddhas" (*shinbutsu*) does not simply mean, as is often believed, "Shintō and Buddhism." Among the most important medieval gods, certain ones had roots in Hinduism (Benzaiten, Dakiniten, Shōten), others in Daoism (Myōken, the seven stars) and in Yin-Yang thought (Gozu Tennō, Taizan Fukun, Daishōgun, Kōjin). As to the *kami,* it is doubtful that they existed as clear conceptual units before the arrival of Buddhism (and even after).

Contrary to its controlling purpose, the *honji suijaku* paradigm turned into a fascinating device to produce new deities and extend the networks of preexisting ones. In this sense, it worked like another form of analogical thinking with which it was intertwined, the so-called five-phase theory of Chinese cosmology.[8] My point is therefore not that we should reject it wholesale, but that we need to subject to criticism the simplistic "classical," dualistic interpretation it fostered. The latter must be taken into account as well, as it expresses the desire for simplification and purification that constitutes one of the aspects of religiosity. No doubt the religious world of medieval Japan was structured along the lines of the *honji suijaku* model, but it was also textured in quite different ways, which academic methods of inquiry have been unable or unwilling to grasp. There is no need to posit an unspeakable pure experience at the source of these representations, but we should not forget that esoteric Buddhist priests, like the Queen in *Through the Looking Glass*, were in principle able to think (and perhaps actually experience) six impossible things before breakfast.

The multiplication of frames of reference complicates and undermines the simplistic schema initially proposed by the *honji suijaku* theory. Worldly gods, who had been looked down upon by clerics intent on purifying the Buddhist teaching, returned through the back door of ritual and the *ushirodo* of temples to the "other scene" of the imaginary. The *honji suijaku* theory, initially aimed at regulating the gods' proliferation through a clear one-to-one, hierarchical linkage with the buddhas, achieved precisely the opposite: a multiplication of transversal relationships between all categories and levels of the pantheon that opened the door to all kinds of demonic entities and the constitution of various sub-pantheons. The outcome was a considerable development of divine and demonic activity, an integration of strange and stranger deities, and an increase of their prestige through mutual contact. To give just one example, while late Heian Buddhists had equated Dainichi and Amaterasu, the late medieval period saw the Tenkawa deity identified, under the name Nichirin Benzaiten (Benzaiten of the Solar Wheel), with the deva Benzaiten and with the "rough spirit" (*aramitama*) of Amaterasu.

BACK TO THE "REAL"

Ironically, while the *honji suijaku* theory attempted to silence the alleged cacophony of the autochthonous deities, by locking them up into a closed pantheon or mandala and "mobilizing" them in an efficacious system, it allowed the emergence of new deities that were no longer mere symbols or "traces," but were perceived as quite "real" (*jissha*), that is, as deities whose actual existence was ontologically grounded—in contrast to the hypostases of the buddhas known as "provisional manifestations" (*gonsha* or *gongen*).[9] While the esoteric devas were in principle "assimilation bodies" (*tōrujin*) of the buddha Mahāvairocana (J. Dainichi), they eventually acquired a reality and agency of their own.

The distinction between *jissha* and *gonsha* adumbrates the early Buddhist distinction between "worldly" (*laukika*), usually malevolent deities lost in darkness and enlightened ones that are said to have passed "beyond the world" (*lokottara*). In the case of certain devas, however, that distinction became an inner one. Daikokuten, Dakiniten, and Benzaiten, for example, were said to encompass both aspects, real and provisional, depending on the nature of the ritual that takes took as its chief deity.[10]

The term *jissha* usually designates local deities of demonic nature, which, even when they converted to Buddhism, retained a lower status—in other words, deities that were not fully integrated into the esoteric Buddhist system and retained a degree of independence. The attitude of the Buddhists toward these symbols of autochthony was ambivalent: while usually warning people against worshiping them, they also saw in them at times the highest expression of awakening, following the paradoxical logic of *hongaku* nondualism. Even when they seem to be locale-specific, the *jissha* are mobile, elusive, and nomadic. They are often oracular deities, whose power resides in speech—which may explain why they tend to elude representation.[11] Their energy can at times be harnessed, but it represents an inherent danger. They often take an animal or hybrid form.

Thus, while the *gonsha* are said to bring profit to the people and lead them to salvation, the *jissha* are defined as heterodox or "perverse" deities (*jashin* 邪神), prone to throw curses (*tatari* 祟り) and cause people to suffer. Orthodox authors—Buddhist monks and "Shintō" priests alike—argue that it is only to placate these nefarious entities that one calls them "gods" and worships them.[12] Vināyaka is a typical *jissha,* a demon who rebels against the Buddha. Yet the love duel between him and Senāyaka (a manifestation of the bodhisattva Avalokiteśvara) gives birth to a hybrid, dual-bodied deva, Kangiten, the "Bliss Deva," half *jissha*, half *gonsha*. This example can be seen as paradigmatic of the "double capture" between buddhas and gods, and of the twofold nature of the devas (even when they are represented as single-bodied).

The *Keiran shūyōshū*, for instance, claims that "the gods always manifest themselves as snakes."[13] Following the logic of *hongaku*, it further argues that the nature of the snake is fundamentally ambivalent, expressing both Ignorance and Awakening.

In exoteric Buddhist commentaries, the *jissha* are merely demons. As one source puts it, "[People] call them *ujigami* and worship them. . . . However, the *Hikekyō* 悲華經 declares that those who worship them even only once will receive a snake body during five hundred lifetimes."[14] In certain texts inspired by *hongaku* thought, a few *kami* (most notably Amaterasu) are elevated from the status of traces (*suijaku*) to that of "original ground" (*honji*), as embodiments of Dainichi's original enlightenment. This promotion to the supreme rank is achieved at the expense of the *jissha,* who are by contrast demonized—in a kind of see-saw movement. In this way, Japanese gods came to be divided into three categories: (1) *kami* of original enlightenment (*hongaku-shin* 本覚神), such as Amaterasu, the *kami* of Ise; (2) *kami* of nonenlightenment (*fukaku-shin* 不覚神), such as the violent *kami* of Izumo Shrine; and (3) *kami* of acquired enlightenment (*shikaku-shin* 始覚神), such as Hachiman. Although this classification appeared as early as the *Nakatomi ōharae kunge* 中臣大祓訓解 (ca. 1150), it only came into full effect with the rise of sectarian

"Shintō" during the late medieval period. While it obviously reflects the agenda of Ise Shrine priests, it bears testimony to the embarrassment caused by *kami* like Susanoo, who occupies an ambiguous position in the divine hierarchy.[15] While relying on the terminology of *hongaku* (original enlightenment) thought, this threefold classification actually undermines its deeper meaning—namely, the identity of Ignorance and Awakening —by returning surreptitiously to the pre-Mahāyāna notion that certain beings, the *icchantika*, are fundamentally devoid of buddha nature and can therefore neither be converted nor reach awakening. This means that they are demons that must be tamed or eliminated. This typology, which conveniently omits problematic *jissha* like Benzaiten and Dakiniten, is in complete denial of the fluid nature of medieval gods: depending on the circumstance, the same deity can become demonic or demiurgic.

In actual practice, the difference between *gonsha* and *jissha* was never absolute. The *Jindaikan hiketsu*, for example, distinguishes between "gods who are truly deluded" (*jitsumeishin* 実迷神) and "gods who are truly awakened" (*jitsugoshin* 実悟神).[16] Yet this distinction is belied by the passage that immediately follows,[17] a long list of very concrete and eminently abstract deities reminiscent of Jorge Luis Borges' imaginary Chinese encyclopedia, quoted with obvious delight by Michel Foucault at the beginning of *The Order of Things*.[18] Evidently, the *gonsha* themselves can on occasion have the same demonic (or animal) characteristics as the *jissha*. Yet the distinction also paved the way to the "reverse" *honji suijaku* theory in which the *kami* become the original ground and the buddhas their traces. We should therefore distinguish in turn between two modes of reaction to the *honji suijaku* model: the former, being a mere inversion of the model (the so-called reverse *honji suijaku* 反本地垂迹), shares with Buddhism the same contempt for the *jissha,* while the latter, constituting a more diffuse and significant current of resistance to the model, lets the *jissha*, precisely because they are real, develop their own difference and autonomy.

Still, the *jissha* were caught up in the same dichotomic tendency that elevated the *kami* from the status of *suijaku* to that of *honji*—first as manifestations of original enlightenment, then as an alternative, and a superior one, to the buddhas, so that they were no longer local divine manifestations in a tiny, peripheral land at a time of the Dharma's decline, but rather primordial powers in the great divine land of Japan, source of the sun. Teeuwen has shown how the ideological scaffolding of Shintō "revival" (or rather emergence) was the Buddhist *hongaku* theory. The sun goddess Amaterasu now stood at the apex of the pantheon, as well as outside it (as its vanishing point), just as the cosmic buddha Dainichi sat at the apex of the esoteric Buddhist cosmos while transcending it. Dainichi and Amaterasu were no longer *honji* and *suijaku,* but equals in a horizontal, not vertical relation. Amaterasu, as deity of the Dharma nature, was raised above both *gonsha* and *jisha*, becoming the "universal equivalent" of all gods and buddhas, a kind of *dea otiosa*. But wait, things are never so simple under the sun.[19] If that was the end of Amaterasu's story, we would still find ourselves in the two-tiered model of Japanese religion, the vertical logic of the *honji suijaku* theory. Yet, not only does Amaterasu remain the trace of Dainichi in some corners, she is also, in a more problematic fashion, identified with the solar Aizen and the chthonian Yama, not to mention such demonic characters as Māra, Dakiniten, Shōten, Kōjin, and her evil twin Susanoo. Not much remains of the traditional distinctions between *honji* and *suijaku* when Amaterasu happens to be the trace of a *jissha* like Dakiniten, a former demon who, in obvious contradiction to the *honji suijaku* model, has now become the *honji* of a major Japanese *kami*. We recall how Dakiniten, transcending her demonic origins, transformed herself into a demiurge named Shinkoō Bosatsu (Bodhisattva King of Astral Foxes). A similar process can be observed in the cases of Fudō, Shōten, and Matarajin to name just a few. The functional similarity explains why these deities came to be regarded as the various names and aspects of a single primordial deity (unless the opposite is the case). To speak here of a combinatory logic does not do justice to the complexity of the phenomenon: the Three Devas are not simply the combination of three well-defined deities, but the intertwining of bundles of functional features. The emergence of a hard kernel results from the mangle and tangle of ideas, myths, and rituals. This entanglement is also that of the scholar, left in a state of bewilderment.

Amaterasu ascended to the firmament of medieval Japanese religion, but she was by no means the only one to claim such an apotheosis. Other stars rose on the horizon, and some of them at times eclipsed her. Even at Ise, Toyouke, the deity of the Outer Shrine, was put forward by the Watarai clan, which claimed for Toyouke equality, or even superiority, to Amaterasu. Similar cases were made for the Miwa deity and Sannō Gongen.

Furthermore, Amaterasu became an increasingly remote deity, a sun so distant that its rays could no longer warm up the earth, while at the same time becoming the *honji* of a long list of lesser deities. The two movements are both similar and opposite: one leads to increasing abstraction, while the other remains firmly grounded in the concrete. A similar tendency can be seen at work in the cases of devas like Dakiniten and Benzaiten. Dissemination is not the same thing as transformation into a general equivalent. In the former case, the deity remains in play, within the world of immanence; in the latter, it withdraws from the game, becoming a transcendent principle. The *honji suijaku* paradigm led to the two tendencies, but it was the first that prevented Japanese religion from falling into a kind of monotheism.

At the other end of the divine spectrum, the realm of the *kami* extended downward to elementary deities that were hardly distinguishable from demons. The schema was in constant flux: while demons were being converted and raised to the status of protectors, local deities were often demonized. Their common nature was expressed by terms such as *kijin,* meaning "demon gods." When the term *kami* is used in opposition to *buddha*, it tends to subsume a large part of the spectrum, a redefinition that significantly affects the nature of the *kami*. In that respect, we should also note in passing the importance of a deity's retinue (*kenzoku* 眷属, Skt. *parivāra*), including servants, children, and emanations or secondary aspects of a buddha or deity. The nature of these "relatives" also modifies the more or less transcendent nature of their source. We witness a kind of contamination from bottom to top—from demons to devas to bodhisattvas, which explains in part the dark side of buddhas and bodhisattvas like Yakushi, Kannon (Batō 馬頭), Monju, Fugen, Jizō, and Kokūzō. The symbolic circulation between buddhas and lesser deities explains how a pestilence demon like Gozu Tennō could acquire some of the transcendent characteristics of the buddha Yakushi, who eventually came to be perceived as his *honji*. Even the provisional manifestations (*gongen* 権現), originally mere hypostases of the primordial buddha(s), become increasingly locale specific (as in the case of Kumano Gongen 熊野権現), losing their provisional nature and gaining an absolute sacredness.

Ironically, the logic of *honji suijaku* requires that the bodhisattvas too, who remain in this world to save beings, be interpreted as mere traces, since their original ground is pure transcendence. But the same is true of the buddhas themselves, who are after all mere symbols.[20] Although the notion of "buddha" initially constituted an attempt to express that transcendence, it was eventually recuperated and localized, as the buddhas were brought down to earth through the worship of specific icons. Here the official definition of the buddhas as pure transcendence is bluntly contradicted by practices on the ground. The name Amida, for instance, comes to designate both an original ground *and* a kind of trace. There is no clear line with human patriarchs either: semi-historical figures like the Indian monk Nāgārjuna, the Chinese priest Baozhi 宝誌, or the Japanese "bodhisattva" Gyōki 行基 become *honji* or *suijaku* depending on the circumstance and are classified as "gods." Another case in point is that of the buddha Yakushi and his retinue, who become cosmic (immanent) forces governing time and space (the sun and moon bodhisattvas, the twelve spirit commanders symbolizing the twelve months, and so on). Here, as in many other cases, the entourage of a buddha transmits a subliminal message, disclosing an implicit meaning that often subverts the manifest meaning conveyed by the main deity.[21] It is the same incomprehensible reality that manifests itself as buddhas and *kami. Honji* and *suijaku* are not ultimate terms, then, but moments in an infinite chain of displacement and repetition. The *honji* is always already a *suijaku.* What we find behind the *kami* mask is not the face of the true buddha, but yet another mask.

We have here, in Deleuze's words, "a mask behind every mask, and a displacement behind every place."[22]

The most problematic aspect of the *honji suijaku* paradigm is its hierarchical structure, which was preserved, albeit inverted, in the so-called *reverse* honji suijaku theory elaborated by Shintō advocates during the fourteenth and fifteenth centuries. The model deconstructs itself in a number of ways, however. For instance, instead of having several traces (*kami*) for one original ground (buddha or bodhisattva), we have cases where a single trace leads back to several original grounds. Contrary to the usual iconographic representation, in which a buddha is flanked by several acolytes, we find that, in practice, an acolyte is correlated to several buddhas. Likewise, instead of a master having several disciples, a disciple has several masters. And then we witness, in the medieval period, the emergence of the *jissha,* demonic gods who remain outside the paradigm.

The *honji suijaku* theory was in large part an ideological attempt to co-opt local cults and to impose a certain order on their mythico-ritual proliferation. Yet it was not merely the expression of a well-planned strategy; it also reflected the penetration of Buddhism by the tendrils of local cults, a process in which Buddhism lost the initiative. The ideological device intended to assimilate local deities backfired, as essences (*honji*) and traces (*suijaku*) proliferated, blurring the neat hierarchy between buddhas and *kami:* now even humans became *honji,* while buddhas occasionally became *suijaku.* The distinction between provisional and real led to the establishment of a contrast between the buddhas' metaphysical essence and their concrete, local manifestations (not merely as *kami,* but as buddhas as well), whereas that distinction, applied to the gods, led to the bifurcation of certain deities (like Daikokuten and Benzaiten) into two forms, one threatening, the other protecting. In this more complex model, the *honji* turns out to be not an ontological essence but rather another function or trace. In other words, *honji* and *suijaku,* as roles, mutually determine each other. They are (almost) interchangeable.

The two-tiered model of Japanese religion has long outlived its usefulness and needs to be demoted from the rank of a theoretical paradigm to that of an ideological product. Although the Japanese themselves had their own two-tiered model of *honji suijaku,* to differentiate buddhas from *kami* is not the same as to oppose Buddhism to Shintō. The relationship between buddhas and *kami* is one of complementarity or tension within a single system. Furthermore, the contrast drawn between the original ground and its traces is too static. The traces do not keep still, they are active (and retroactive). For instance, applying the *honji suijaku* model to the relationship between the buddhas of Enryakuji and the *kami* of Hie Shrine does not explain the veneration of the latter by Enryakuji monks.[23] Yet the notion of a trace may still have some usefulness: it allows us to shift from the taxonomic logic of the orthodox *honji suijaku* model to a logic of dissemination that avoids the model's dualism. Instead of the two-tiered *honji suijaku* model, we have what Derrida calls a "sheaf"—that is, "an assemblage that has the complex structure of weaving, an interlacing which permits the different threads and different lines of meaning—or force—to go off again in different directions, just as it is always ready to tie itself up with others."[24] John Law, in turn, defines the assemblage as an "enactment or crafting of a bundle of ramifying relations that generate presence."[25]

Satō Hiroo has made some interesting remarks concerning the evolution of the perceived role of the buddhas and *kami* in medieval Japan. In particular, his emphasis on the idea that mundane buddhas and *kami* belong to a single category, distinct from supramundane buddhas, has heuristic value in that it blurs the sharp distinction between *kami* and buddhas. But in the end Satō reinstates a dichotomy that fails to account for the constant circulation, and the blurring of the lines, between these categories. This leads him to pay insufficient attention to such problematic categories as the wisdom kings (*myōō*), devas (*ten*), and demons of all stripes.[26] His distinction between "saving" and "wrathful" deities is heuristically useful, yet it leaves no room for gods of obstacles like Matarajin, who is clearly demonic yet is said to hold the key to salvation. What should we make, for instance, of passages like those in the *Shasekishū* in which Śākyamuni appears as a demon (under the form of Zaō Gongen 藏王権現) to devour the unconverted?[27]

An alternative model might be borrowed from the scientific notion of self-organization, which represents an optimum balance between, on the one hand, a rigid, immutable order, like that of crystal, which cannot be modified without being destroyed, and, on the other hand, a constant renewal without any stability, which evokes chaos and the unpredictable volutes of smoke.[28] This intermediary state is not fixed and reacts to unexpected disturbances through changes that are not a mere destruction of the preexisting organization, but a reorganization allowing the emergence of new properties. These properties can take the shape of a new structure, but we should not interpret these reorganizations as mere rearrangements of interconnected elements or the result of a *combinatoire*. Each rearrangement corresponds to a new organization and results from the creation of new meanings. Without that creation, we are dealing with a mere combination that would be unable to produce new functions.[29] In this sense, the *jissha* and similar phenomena may correspond to the element of randomness, or that which, by resisting the system, actually increases its complexity.

The question can be formulated as follows: are the devas *mediators* or *parasites*? In complexity theory, the two notions are not exclusive. Thus, one could say that deities like Matarajin, by posing themselves as parasites and diverting the relationship between the follower and the buddha, play the same role as ambiguous elements in information theory, thereby contributing to an increase in complexity. While they may play a negative role at the local level, that loss of information turns into an increase in diversity at the global level. The principle is that, by diminishing the information, one diminishes the constraints of the system. This, however, is a different, alternative model from that of a mediator who produces the *terms* (or terminals) of the relationship. More importantly, the dichotomy between *kami* and buddhas created a vacuum, an in-between that needed to be filled, leading to the invention of "moot" deities, hybrids, and monsters that do not fit into a clear category and defy any pigeonholing (even that of "mootness").

Admittedly, we are still faced with a system that is able to integrate any opposition. And perhaps that was the case with the *jissha,* after all—but I would like to preserve the possibility of a truly irreducible resistance, a *ligne de fuite* offered by these vanishing mediators.

HYBRIDS

Neither buddhas nor *kami,* let alone demons, the emergent medieval deities undermined simplistic distinctions. These deities were by no means marginal, nor entirely new. They have been characterized, in these pages, by their hybrid nature. The description is accurate if we take the makeshift word "hybrid" in the sense outlined by Bruno Latour, that is, not as a mixture of two pure forms, but as the basic reality from which, through a process of purification or concatenation, the "pure" forms that characterize ideological discourse may eventually emerge.[30] In other words, the traditional perception needs to be inverted. These gods constitute the coming to light of a fundamental phenomenon, the hybrid nature of the divine, from which the allegedly pure deities—whether buddhas or *kami*—were always already derived. To paraphrase Latour, instead of growing from stable extremities (buddhas and *kami*) toward the middle as intermediaries, medieval gods grow from the middle toward the extremities, which they push ever further.[31] Thus, buddhas and *kami* (not to mention Buddhism and Shintō) do not offer solid hooks onto which we can hang our interpretations; on the contrary, they are what needs to be explained.[32]

If we abandon the traditional perception, we see that the former point of encounter and division now becomes the starting point, and we no longer go from pure forms to combinatory, moot forms, but from the center to the poles. Thus, the poles are no longer the "original ground" or "pure" essence, but instead are emerging realities, provisional and purified outcomes of the central practices.[33] Yet, as Latour points out, both movements of hybridization and of purification are always at work, and both are necessary. The problem arises when only the latter is recognized, and perceived as a genuine expression of the reality rather than as the

FIGURE C.3. "Syncretistic" buddha (Mercury). Museum of East Asian Art, Cologne.

ideological production it is. In that sense, medieval religion can be defined as precisely the "reverse" of syncretism.

Even if they can manifest themselves in objects such as icons, the gods always resist objectification; they are imagined (and occasionally experienced) as an elusive presence. Forever eluding our pitifully inadequate categories (divine, demonic, human, animal—as well as male and female, young and old), they drift and fall through the cracks. Their perceived uncanniness perhaps reflects the obscure realization that the reality they represent is properly *inhuman*. Their wrathful aspect is only the blazing flame of being or becoming, also expressed in their fiery aura. Amaterasu hides herself in a cave, like the Egyptian goddess Isis. The true nature of the deity must remain hidden, as Benzaiten herself tells the shōgun who wants to see it. The goddess remains a female sphynx of sorts. The naked truth is terrible, awesome, or awful, as the shōgun finds out for himself.[34]

It is the same gesture of purification that separated the buddhas and the *kami* and hierarchized them. That gesture renders invisible the network they form, which makes them constantly pass into each other, like the background and the flying swans in M. C. Escher's woodcut "Day and Night" (1938). By way of contrast, I initially intended to take as the emblem of this book the uncanny "syncretistic buddha" of the Museum of East Asian Art in Cologne, which seems to reflect the moment of transition from classical buddha to deva, or vice versa (Fig. C.3), until I realized that it is, after all, not a buddha but an astral deity (Mercury). Too bad, but the point remains.

Transcendent buddhas and immanent gods are two contradictory expressions of the same reality, which envelop, limit, and counterbalance each other, creating a precarious equilibrium rich in potentialities. And precisely because that gesture separates buddhas and *kami,* hybrids proliferate. Buddhas and *kami* themselves owe their existence to that proliferation of hybrids, and they emerge against the background of that rich hinterland. Paradoxically, by discovering their hybrid nature, we reach the conclusion that there are only hybrids, that hybridity itself is not an accident but a quasi-essence. It follows that there are *no* hybrids, and there never were, because from the outset there were no "pure" gods or buddhas. What we find instead is a polarizing mechanism, a dialectic of purification *and* hybridization (or mediation), and both processes need at long last to be acknowledged. Yet so far only one, the purifying process, has been recognized, or misrecognized, as reflecting a natural *fait accompli.*

Animal Deities

A particularly interesting aspect of the gods' hybrid or metamorphic nature, contributing to the blurring of genres, is their proclivity to "become animal." Esoteric Buddhist iconography contains a large number of hybrid figures—usually a human body with an animal head, although a few are theoriomorphic). For example, the twelve spirit commanders that form the retinue of the buddha Yakushi are often represented with the head of a rat, ox, tiger, and so on, because of the spatiotemporal symbolism linking them with the twelve points of the compass and the twelve cyclic deities. Many astral deities among the twenty-eight lunar mansions are also animal headed.

Not all animal-headed deities are assimilation bodies (*tōrujin* 等流身) of the cosmic Buddha, however. In the iconographic manuals of Japanese esotericism, the horse-headed *mahoragas* (Mahā-uraga 'great snake') and *gandharvas,* although generally classified among the devas and perceived as demonic, look like certain representations of Hayagrīva Avalokiteśvara (J. Batō Kannon 馬頭観音), the horse-headed manifestation of Kannon.[35]

Sometimes, the animal that constitutes a submerged aspect of the deity is represented as that deity's mount. Thus Dakiniten, although she is never represented as a theriomorphic deity, is implicitly identified with the fox that serves as her mount. Amaterasu, on the other hand, is described as a fox in certain secret traditions of Ise Shrine. Bishamonten and Benzaiten are also associated with foxes, and Benzaiten appears as a snake- or dragon-headed deity in the Tenkawa Benzaiten mandala. The same is true of certain representations of Bishamonten. The child god Jūzenji of Hie (Hiyoshi) Shrine is associated with monkeys, and his protector, the god Daigyōji 大行事, is represented as an official with a monkey's head in the Hie mandala. The *tengu* Izuna Gongen rides a fox, and his face, like that of the Hindu god Garuḍa, resembles that of a bird (a kite or eagle).

A deity can be represented as an animal, in part or in toto. Representations of the "divine becoming animal" include the aforementioned Batō Kannon, the bull-headed Gozu Tennō (who sometimes is horse headed), and the elephant-headed Shōten. Often deities mounted on an ox, bull, or buffalo are partially assimilated to that animal. Now and then the deity manifests itself through an animal messenger—like the monkeys of Mount Hiei or the foxes of Mount Inari. This dangerous proximity, or even intertwining, of the divine and the animal seems to threaten the deity's "individuality." In the Tenkawa Benzaiten mandala, for instance, Benzaiten's feminine face is replaced by three reptilian heads.

What is the meaning of these hybrid figures, which are found almost everywhere in Asian religions, but especially in esoteric Buddhism? Images of the Tibetan Bardo, reproduced in *cham* dances; representations of Chinese cyclical and astral deities; figures of horse-headed *gandharvas* in Japanese iconographic compendia—these images testify to the fascinating yet threatening presence of the nonhuman in humans. They point to the dark origins of power. In Japan, even the imperial line sees its source in animals—snake or fox. The same is true for many of the great aristocratic or priestly families. On the battlefield, moreover, the panoply of the medieval warrior—in particular the helmet—is often a magical return to invincible animality.[36]

The relation between human and animal is not only a major Buddhist theme, it also provides a medium of translation between Buddhism and local cultures. Divine transcendence is expressed through metamorphosis. Gods are truly *meta*-morphic, in the sense that they constantly morph from one form into another, yet dwell in none. They conceal—and reveal—themselves by metamorphosing, circulating through identities, changing masks.[37] Yet the human mind tries to freeze them into immutable forms, and their metamorphic shimmer is ultimately reduced to static identities and contradictory appearances. A hierarchical system eventually gets elaborated, which only retains faint traces of the intensity of visions, vague echoes of the oracles, mere figments of a forgotten dream. Deleuze and Guattari, describing the "becoming-animal," focus on the case of the wolf as a pack animal. By this, however, they do not merely mean that the wolf lives in packs, but that it is itself a pack.[38] The same can be said of our medieval gods.

The "becoming-animal" of the gods is also their "becoming-demon." The multiplicity subverts the old dialectic of one/multiple that formed the basis of the classical *honji suijaku* model. The common functionality of images establishes passages across various levels of the pantheon. For instance, the images of the ox, bull, and buffalo link deities like Yama Īśāna (Śiva as a directional deity), Daiitoku Myōō, Gozu Tennō, and so on; that of the horse, Batō Kannon and the *gandharvas.* Kannon is the paradigmatic example of a deity that multiplies, deterritorializes, and reterritorializes itself, disseminating into a multitude of traces—the Eleven-faced Kannon, Thousand-armed Kannon, Six Kannon, Thirty-three Kannon, and thirty-three thousand manifestations, including theriomorphic ones. It becomes impossible to subsume all these traces under a single divine power like Śiva or Devī in Hinduism. The Buddhist tradition did try to simplify, to reduce medieval deities to a fundamental principle. In so doing, however, it emptied them from their substance and diminished their vitality, their intensity, and their metamorphic power.

THE FOURTH FUNCTION

The emergence of the medieval deities was supplemented by the reinterpretation of classical gods like Susanoo. These deities—old and new—are characterized by their profound ambiguity, their subversive nature, and their affinities with dark chaos. Certain of them are gods of obstacles or deities that control human destiny. Some are of Buddhist origin, others not; some are seen as native, others as foreign. They recall what certain scholars, in an attempt to augment Dumézil's trifunctional analysis of Indo-European ideology, have recently defined as a "fourth function." Dumézil himself, while he never ventured beyond the frame of the three functions, hinted at the need for a fourth one. Regarding the Indo-European pantheons, he was the first to admit that his trifunctional model left a "remainder" irreducible to standard explanations. It failed in particular to account for important Greek, Roman, and Indian deities such as Dionysos, Pan, Apollo, Artemis, Hecate, Saturn, Neptune, and Śiva-Rudra. Commentators have also pointed out in his work, next to deities specialized in one single function, the presence of a complementary figure, usually feminine, which embraces all three functions. Such for instance is the case with Śrī and Sarasvatī in Vedic India; or with Draupadī, the spouse of the five Paṇḍava brothers, in the Indian epics.[39] This supplementary figure (also in the Derridian sense of the *supplement*) begins to transition to what may be defined as a fourth function. Several authors, as well as Dumézil himself, have noted the frequency of quaternary series in Indo-European thought.[40] As Dumézil observed, the Buddha himself, during his contest with Māra (the self-proclaimed king of this world), rejects and transcends the three functions. In that sense, although Dumézil stops short of making it, he is a figure of the fourth function.

What is, then, this elusive fourth function? Briefly, while the three functions cover the cosmic and social order, the fourth function includes everything that is alien to the realm of order.[41] Like dark matter or energy, it has been added to the picture in an attempt to cover the universe in all its aspects—the *chaosmos,* as it were. Despite its heterogeneous nature, it can be read either as complementary or as antagonistic to the three others. It includes everything that is other, beyond, and exterior. By opposition to (but also as the source of) the realm of forms, it corresponds to the formless. As Mary Douglas suggests, "There is a power in the forms and [an] other power in the inarticulate area, margins, confused lines, and beyond the external boundaries."[42] Furthermore, in light of the fact that the Buddhist universe is said to be composed of three realms—of desire, form, and formlessness—one could argue that the fourth function is the highest. Thus, a tetrafunctional model would allow us to classify the totality of institutions, deities, qualities, and activities: those belonging strictly to the realm of order can be assigned to one or several of the three functions, while the others belong to the fourth function.[43]

Paradoxically, the marginal deities called *jissha* are said to be "mundane gods." Yet this appellation, which perhaps reflects an attempt to debase them, should not hide the fact that they dwell, by their very nature, outside the cosmic framework and the ordered pantheon, which they help to destabilize. Or rather, as typical tricksters, they straddle both the inside and the outside. In the cosmic realm as in the social realm, these figures define a field characterized by the notion of the "remainder"—although it is not itself residual, quite to the contrary.[44] The structural analogies may help to explain why these marginal gods appear in initiation rituals, since initiation corresponds to what Arnold van Gennep has defined as the liminal stage of the rites of passage, a stage that belongs precisely to the fourth function.[45]

Although Japan is not an Indo-European society, Indian Buddhism was originally an offshoot of the trifunctional ideology, so it is not surprising that vast portions of that ideology—including a fourth function—were preserved in Japan.[46] While never formulated as such, something akin to the fourth function became particularly important in medieval Japanese Buddhism through the notion of fundamental enlightenment (*hongaku*), according to which the ignorance residing in all beings is the source both of evil and of enlightenment.[47] This notion can also be seen at work in the definition of the *jissha*. The mythological figure that most thoroughly embodies it is probably Kōjin, but all the deities studied in this book are, to one degree or another, examples of it. The *hongaku* identity between ignorance and enlightenment is also exemplified in the figures of Māra, Devadatta, Susanoo, and Matarajin.[48]

THE SPANDREL

Assuming momentarily that medieval deities emerged on the margins of established religious currents, the question becomes: were these margins as marginal as we think? In the upside-down world of medieval Japan, nothing is less certain. Let us introduce here the notion of "spandrels" as proposed by Stephen Jay Gould and Richard C. Lewontin. Spandrels are secondary architectural developments imposed by the structure of a building, and therefore they do not play an important role in its evolution. The same is true, they claim, in the evolution of species.[49] The religious domain, however, looks somewhat different in that developments that once were considered spandrels often come to play a central role. A more relevant model might be that of the mandala, in which each peripheral court can in turn become central and eventually independent. Ronald Davidson argues that this model, particularly well adapted to feudal society, allowed Tantrism to become one of the dominant ideologies in India.[50]

Arguably, this was also the case in medieval Japan. One must distinguish, however, between a "disseminating" mandala that lends itself to feudal or local reappropriation and a "centripetal" mandala that becomes an instrument of centralization. As we have seen, the first phase in the development of the mandala in esoteric Buddhism was a process of collection, gathering local mandalas into macromandalas, the best example being the Vajra Realm mandala, whose nine assemblies can be traced back to specific mandalas. Yet these mandalas exploded again into a multiplicity of *besson* mandalas devoted to specific deities during the medieval period in Japan, lending themselves to localizing and pluralistic tendencies, as was also the case in medieval India.

In the ritual and mythological domains, everything is important, and a derived or late motif can move centerstage, depending on the needs of the moment. Any spandrel can become a keystone, and conversely any primary element can be relegated to the backstage. It is the constant shift between centrality and marginality—or even between orthodoxy and heterodoxy—the ceaseless fluidity of forms and functions, which characterizes medieval Japanese religion.

OUT OF THE RUT?

The prologue and epilogue (or rather, the pro-*gramme* and epi-*gramme*) of this book do not mirror each other like the two sides of a parenthesis, or the two hinges of a folding door on which guardian deities are painted. Rather, they form a kind of "parallax," to use Slavoj Žižek's expression.[51] In the process, the questions have changed, or shifted, and the answer—assuming there is one—is no longer that which was given to the initial question. It is rather a new, or renewed, question. Between the two, the relation is not simply that of the germ to the fruit, of potentiality to actuality, of essence to manifestation. A series of accidents has occurred, which, through a feedback loop, has become part of the essence.

The image that lurks behind these analyses is that of the "wild god" Kōjin, a Janus-faced deity whose capacity as a role model influenced in turn the reinterpretation of classical, and less classical, deities of the esoteric pantheon—buddhas like Yakushi, bodhisattvas like Monju, Nyoirin, and Myōken, wisdom kings like Fudō and Aizen, and devas like Daikokuten, Bishamonten, Enmaten, Shōten, Dakiniten, and Benzaiten. Behind that image lurks another, that of the earth deity (or deities)—or rather, the divine powers immanent in this world (which can be those of astral deities as well)—as opposed to the *tout autre* (or *totaliter aliter*) of transcendence. In this vision, the buddhas are brought down to earth, "cut to size." Buddhism, having settled too early for absolute transcendence, was constrained to step back and redefine itself in more humble (from *humus* 'earth'), hence earthly fashion. This model of a Janus-faced Buddhism

(Kōjin being neither a buddha nor a demon, or both at once) puts the two elements—buddha and demon—on a relatively equal standing, and is quite distinct from the *honji suijaku* hierarchy, which it subverts by transforming a vertical structure into a horizontal or oblique one. The fourth function is an (admittedly flawed) attempt to circumscribe that bundle of features. Susanoo, for instance, is no longer simply the opposite or evil twin of Amaterasu, but also the complement of Benzaiten. Significantly, Susanoo and Benzaiten are said to represent the two faces of Kōjin.

It is again the figure of Kōjin that allows us to reevaluate the polytheistic nature of Japanese religion before it became polarized into Buddhism and Shintō (and even afterward, as it continued to engender hybrids), and to imagine a counter-history that would bring back to light the forgotten tradition. It also undermines the ideological discourse of sectarian traditions, bent on establishing a clear distinction between truth and error, orthodoxy and heterodoxy. Yet, the figure of Kōjin is subject to the same tensions and evolutions, and it undergoes in turn its own moralizing, quasi-henotheistic drift. At this point, I have to confess that, in the initial conception of this book, the preceding chapters (and the preceding book) were steps toward a thorough discussion of the multifarious aspects of Kōjin. However, it became eventually clear that that discussion would far overflow the bounds of a single chapter, and it has therefore been postponed to a forthcoming book (with my apologies to the reader).

The late medieval period stands out for the resilience of these deities in the face of an increasingly strong drive toward integration and sectarian purity. That pressure resulted, in the Edo period, in a dominant tendency toward abstraction and a centralization of power, despite the resistance of local powers and the concrete genius of Japanese polytheism. The ultimate demise of the medieval gods was the result of a conjunction of factors. Among them was the transformation of Buddhism—in particular, esoteric Buddhism's loss of prestige and the weakening of its social and political support once the imperial house lost its central role, causing its gods also to lose part of their appeal (or power of deterrence). As Amino Yoshihiko has shown, the loss of prestige extended to the areas known as *muen* 無縁 (unattached), which gradually lost their privileges, and the *igyō* 異形 (heteromorphic) types—people and gods—were increasingly ostracized and relegated to the outer margins of society.[52] A number of the medieval gods were co-opted by the new urban culture, but in a tamed form like that of the Seven Gods of Fortune. Their ambiguity, the expression of esoteric Buddhism's deep psychological insight and the hallmark of medieval religion, was lost, replaced in most cases by a superficial appeal to worldly benefits. Everything fell into place: the buddhas on one side, the *kami* on the other, and a no-man's land or no-god's land in between. Both sides lost their *kōjin* characteristics, becoming increasingly benign, and Kōjin himself reformed, becoming—to a point—a moral god.

Actually, things may not have changed as much as it seems. Although the gradual estrangement of Buddhism and Shintō during the Edo period, and the brutal "separation of the gods and the buddhas" (*shinbutsu bunri* 神佛分離) during the Meiji Restoration (a misleading term if there ever was one), has had irreversible effects, hybrids continued to exist (as Bruno Latour points out in a different context), even as they were being denied in the name of ideological purism. To demonstrate this would take us too far afield. Suffice it to say that the common view of medieval Japanese religion as a field separated into Buddhism and Shintō, or buddhas and *kami,* is definitely anachronistic and misleading, not only for the medieval period but for the early modern and modern periods as well. Perhaps we could even say, paraphrasing Latour, that "Japan has never been modern."[53]

The networks of medieval esoteric Buddhism described here arise against a nonsymbolic (or nonsocial) background or reserve, which corresponds to what John Law calls a "hinterland."[54] A hinterland routinely produces certain classes of reality and reality-statements, that is, a certain religious landscape, but not others, which are made unthinkable or irrelevant.[55] What is the hinterland of Japanese religion? It has every appearance of a geography created by generations of scholars, one in which the *honji suijaku* theory has become a normative element of the landscape. Questioning its "reality" means going against the grain of established discourse, a discourse that confers on the theory the legitimacy of the institution. Likewise, Teeuwen's distinction between Shintō and the earlier royal ideology called *jindō* 神道, while making perfect sense and based on solid argumentation, encounters strong resistance on the part of even the most open-minded Japanese scholars. It is easier to stick to the traditional version until the paradigm has changed (as in the case of Kuroda's conceptions of Shintō and *kenmitsu* Buddhism). Since so much historical work is indebted to that model, it is difficult to reject it wholesale while keeping the historical data that supported it. Our current work is too entangled in our predecessors' work, and the hinterland that produces the conditions of possibility of a work is almost invisible—hard to see, let alone to reject. Indeed, it tells us not only what to see, but what *not to see*. It defines what is deemed irrelevant, or *moot*. The insights it provides are also a source of blindness, inasmuch as "what is made present depends on what is also made absent."[56] Buddhas and *kami* in this sense are masks and transformations of the invisible, since, as Lévi-Strauss puts it, "a mask is not primarily what it represents but what it transforms, as it were, what it is attempting not to show."[57] Yet changing tracks may just seem too costly. The opposite view may simply not attract sufficient interest, as Isabelle Stengers argues in the case of scientific propositions.[58] Yet hinterlands are not carved on stone, and can on occasion be significantly altered. The very recognition of their existence, like the description of what Foucault called the conditions of possibility of a certain discourse, already has a deconstructive potential.[59]

Our wandering in these networks led us to strange places, across conceptual territories called Buddhism and Shintō, which are both produced and canceled by their own symbolic and sociopolitical networks. The medieval esoteric networks link practices, objects, techniques, individuals, and institutions, rather than abstract notions like Tendai and Shingon, or even quasi-entities like the buddhas and the *kami.* Yet I continue using the latter two terms as shorthand even while remaining acutely aware of their dubious hypostatic quality.

De te fabula narratur. Beyond its cultural and historical importance, has medieval ideology a meaning for us moderns? If modernity can be characterized by its claim to have left the old behind, perhaps it could get some inspiration from the self-examination achieved by medieval Buddhism, which seems at long last to have realized that any hasty attempt to deny this world (and the local cultures that represent it) is condemned to fail. The return of the gods, and the return of Japanese Buddhists to a more polytheistic conception of reality, was perhaps a necessary step forward (if only apparently backward).

But it is time to reintroduce a space of indeterminacy. Instead of trying to tie loose ends, I leave the work open ended. In the end, any attempt to bring together the disparate elements of medieval religion is a perilous and perhaps ultimately doomed endeavor: it evokes the enigmatic painting entitled "The Murder of the Goldfish," which Georges Pérec imagined in *Life: A User's Manual*. This painting brings together all the elements (a goldfish bowl, an old primary school table, a water jug, a wall telephone) that constitute the enigmatic murder weapon—the victim having been killed by several persons when he himself was trying to commit suicide. It is impossible, however, for the viewer to connect these elements, for lack of knowing the incredible story from which they are the remainder.[60] The mystery remains.

ABBREVIATIONS

BEFEO	*Bulletin de l'École française d'Extrême-Orient*
BZS	*Bukkyō zuzō shūsei*
CEA	*Cahiers d'Extrême-Asie*
DNBZ	*Dai Nihon bukkyō zensho*
DZ	*Daozang*
GR	*Gunsho ruijū*
IBK	*Indogaku bukkyōgaku kenkyū*
JJRS	*Japanese Journal of Religious Studies*
KST	*Shintei zōho kokushi taikei*
KT	*Shinpen kokka taikan*
MN	*Monumenta Nipponica*
NKBT	*Nihon koten bungaku taikei*
NKBZ	*Nihon koten bungaku zenshū*
NSBS	*Nihon shomin bunka shiryō shūsei*
NSSS	*Nihon shomin seikatsu shiryō shūsei*
NST	*Nihon shisō taikei*
SNKBT	*Shin Nihon koten bungaku taikei*
SNKBZ	*Shinpen Nihon koten bungaku zenshū*
ST	*Shintō taikei*
T	*Taishō shinshū daizōkyō*
TASJ	*Transactions of the Asiatic Society of Japan*
TSZ	*Tendaishū zensho*
TZ	*Taishō shinshū daizōkyō zuzō*
ZGR	*Zoku gunsho ruijū*
ZNKZ	*Zoku Nihon koten zenshū*
ZSZ	*Zoku Shingonshū zensho*
ZST	*Zoku shintō taikei*
ZTZ	*Zoku Tendaishū zensho*
ZZ	*Dai Nihon zokuzōkyō*
ZZGR	*Zokuzoku gunsho ruijū*

Ch.	Chinese
J.	Japanese
K.	Korean
Skt.	Sanskrit
Tib.	Tibetan

NOTES

PROLOGUE

1. Quoted in *Koji ruien,* Shukyōbu 2: 107.
2. Quoted in Cooper 1982: 300.
3. Blacker 1986: 33.
4. Yamamoto 1998a: i–ii.
5. Yamamoto 1998a: 645.
6. The anthropologist David Gellner has attempted to rehabilitate the term, but his own use is so limiting as to lose much of its utility when applied to medieval Japanese religion. See Gellner 1997.
7. See Ruegg 1964.
8. Mark Teeuwen has drawn some strong reactions from Japanese scholars by arguing that these various strands of Japanese religion were called differently prior to the medieval period, and that the term *jindō* 神道 (not *shintō*) was used to designate official religion. See Teeuwen 2002.
9. See for example Grapard 1987: 212–220
10. Coleridge, *Bibliographia Literaria* 1: 304, quoted in Sacks 1996: 288–289.
11. Latour 2005: 153.
12. Latour 2005: 153–154.
13. The "conquest" model was made famous by Erik Zürcher's *The Buddhist Conquest of China* (2007). For a critique of that model, see Bokenkamp 2007.
14. Baxandall 1985: 58–60. See also Bokenkamp 2007: 11; and Bokenkamp 2009.
15. For a different take on this question, see David Seyfort Ruegg's notion of a "popular substratum" (1964), and Ronald Davidson's criticism of it (2002: 171–72).
16. I borrow this term from Prasenjit Duara (1988).
17. See Deleuze and Parnet 1977: 2. The English translation has "double capture."
18. Another interesting example is the assimilation of the Miwa 三輪 god Ōmononushi 大物主 (Ōkuninushi 大国主) with the esoteric Buddhist god Mahākāla, the "Great Black One" 大黒 (based on the homonymy of the Sino-Japanese reading of their names, Daikoku).
19. The model finds its sources in Chinese Buddhism, most notably with the Tiantai patriarch Zhiyi (538–597), who applied it to his hermeneutics of the *Lotus Sūtra.*

20. For an overview of the *honji suijaku* theory, see Rambelli 2004 and the introduction to Teeuwen and Rambelli 2003. See also Yoshida Kazuhiko 2006: 198–220.

21. See Tsuji Zennosuke 1964: 436–486.

22. See for instance Matsunaga 1969.

23. Hori Ichirō (1953), for instance, emphasizes the tension and resistance between the kami and the buddhas. He sees, somewhat anachronistically, Tsuji's notion of *shinbutsu shūgō* as an attempt to reconcile the two. He points out that the syncretistic process was not as linear as Tsuji thought, and that the tension continued all along. Another criticism of Tsuji came from Tamura Enchō (1995), who claims that national *kami* like Hachiman became protectors of Buddhism without ever having changed their *kami* nature, whereas local *kami* had to convert to Buddhism to get salvation. This distinction between two types of *kami* (national and local) led him to further distinguish between two types of syncretism (state-sponsored and popular). While he accepts Tsuji's notion of a fusion between buddhas and *kami,* he argues that it proved to be a difficult and incomplete one. Tamura's thesis influenced the work of Yoshie Akio (1996).

24. See Tsuda Sōkichi 1949.

25. See Umemura 1996; and Kuroda Toshio 1980b.

26. See Matsunaga 1969.

27. The word *kami* is occasionally written in *katakana* by Japanese scholars to refer to elemental spirits that have little to do with the great gods of classical Japanese mythology.

28. See Suzuki Masataka 2001: 4–5; and Satō Hiroo 2003.

29. On this distinction, see for instance Suzuki Masataka 2001. On the polysemy of the term "buddha," see Satō Hiroo 2003; on the polysemy of the term *kami,* see Iwata 1979.

30. The entire divine corpus is invoked in vows (*kishōmon*), transfers of merits (*ekō* 廻向), ceremonials (*kōshiki* 講式), and other liturgical texts. A case in point is the *Atsuta kōshiki,* in Kokubungaku kenkyū shiryōkan 1999b: 361–372. On *kōshiki,* see Gülberg 1999.

31. On this point, see Teeuwen 2000.

32. See Teeuwen 2000: 95.

33. Teeuwen 2000: 97.

34. On Jihen, see Sueki 2006–2007.

35. Deleuze and Guattari 2004: 474–477.

36. Ingold 2000: 341.

37. Ingold 2000.

38. After adopting that metaphor, I came across a mention of Ralph Linton's book, *Tree of Culture.* The image evoked by Linton's title is "not the familiar evolutionary tree with a single trunk and spreading branches, but the banyan tree of the tropics." See Ingold 2000: 426–427.

39. "Buddha's tree itself becomes a rhizome." Deleuze and Guattari 1987: 20.

40. Foucault 1977.

41. Rob Linrothe (1999) describes the process through which marginal

deities moved to the center of the mandala and were eventually elevated to a supreme status in later Tantric Buddhism. Although he distinguishes between deities that personify the bodhisattva's attributes and local deities that are tamed or converted, he does not emphasize this distinction and chooses to dwell on the "inner," psychological, or allegorical interpretation of the deities. By the same token, he leaves aside the "protectors" (*chökyong*), although the distinction between *chökyong* and *yidam* (elective deity) is very important in Tibetan Buddhism and the protectors tend to take precedence over the *yidam* in everyday worship. In so doing, he underestimates the subversive forces at work and privileges the standpoint of Buddhist orthodoxy. Some of the ambiguous deities that rose to the top of the pantheon (or moved toward the center of the mandala) were not simply a personification of some bodhisattva's attributes. By bringing these hastily converted deities into its mandalas, esoteric Buddhism was, as it were, "playing with fire." Occasionally the process backfired, permitting the development of anti-Buddhist movements like Bön (in Tibet) and Shintō (in Japan).

42. On this notion, see "Bucchō" in *Hōbōgirin* 2: 148–150.

43. I follow here Bruno Latour's distinction between *intermediary* and *mediator*. For him, an intermediary transports meaning or force without transformation, whereas a mediator "transforms, translates, distorts, and modifies the meaning of the elements it is supposed to carry." See Latour 2005: 39.

44. See Hayashi 2002; and Komine and Takahashi 2001.

45. Müller 1897, 2: 604.

46. *T.* 76, 2410: 632c.

47. Kōshū is speaking only of Kangiten here, not of the devas in general. *T.* 76, 2410: 642a.

48. *T.* 76, 2410: 630b.

49. See Kawatō 2002: 430–434.

50. Alfred Korzybski (1879–1950) developed the theme of the difference between map and territory, which was expanded by A.E. Van Vogt in his SF novels, and by Jonathan Z. Smith in Religious Studies. See Korzybski 2010; Van Vogt 2002; and Smith 1993.

51. Toothing stones, in architecture, are stones that protrude from a wall to establish a link with another wall that will be erected later. Figuratively, it is used about something in a work or a story that lets the audience think it is partly achieved and makes it expect a continuation.

CHAPTER 1: EARTHLY POWERS

1. See *T.* 21: 384b. These directional devas are: Indra (Taishakuten) in the east, Agni (Katen 火天, southeast), Yama (Enmaten, south), Rākṣasa (Rasetsuten 羅刹天, southwest), Varuṇa (Suiten 水天, west), Vāyu (Fūten 風天, northwest), Vaiśravaṇa (Tamonten 多聞天, i.e., Bishamonten, north), Īśāna (Ishanaten 伊舎那天, northeast), Brahmā (Bonten, zenith), Pṛthivi (Jiten 地天, nadir), Sūrya (Nitten 日天, the sun god), and Candra (Gatten 月天, the moon god). On the various lists of directional devas (four, eight, ten, twelve), see Wessels-Mevissen 2001. See also *Kakuzenshō*, *DNBZ* 50: 364–375; *Mikkyō daijiten,* 2: 883–884; and Tajima 1959: 128–131.

2. See "Bishamon" in *Hōbōgirin* 1: 79b.

3. The *Pishamen yigui* 毘沙門儀軌 (*T.* 1249) gives an anachronistic version of the legend, since it claims that Emperor Xuanzong 玄宗 (r. 712–756) turned to Vaiśravaṇa upon the advice of the esoteric master Yixing (684–727). In Zanning's *Dasong sengshi lüe* 大宋僧史略, *T.* 54, 2126 (quoted in *Hōbōgirin* 1: 82a), it is Amoghavajra who invokes the god on behalf of Xuanzong. On this legendary event, see also Valerie Hansen 1993: 75–113; and Granoff 1970. More recently, see Geoffrey Goble (2013), who traces the legend's origins, through the central Asian state of Khotan, to the Hellenistic world, namely, to Herodotus's *Histories*.

4. See *Nihonshoki* 21, s.v. Yōmei Tennō 用明天皇 (r. 585–587), 2nd year (587); and *Fusō ryakki* 25, s.v. Tenkei 天慶 3 (940)/11/21: prayers to Bishamon for the subjugation of Fujiwara no Sumitomo (d. 941). The *honzon* of Shigisan's Oku-no-in is said to be a statue of Bishamonten carved by Shōtoku Taishi as an ex-voto after the defeat of Monobe no Moriya 物部守屋. See *Taiheiki* 太平記 3.1, quoted in Kida 1976: 228–229.

5. The paradox is only apparent, as Bishamonten, protector of the north, came to subsume the functions of the other three deva kings to become the protector of the four cardinal points.

6. See *Keiran shūyōshū*, *T.* 76, 2410: 862b.

7. See *Azuma kagami* 吾妻鏡(東鑑), *s.v.* Kenkyū 建久 2 (1191).5; quoted in Kida 1976: 229. Just as the royal family of Khotan claimed to descend from Vaiśravaṇa, the Kusunoki lineage claimed descent from Bishamonten. As the legend has it, Masashige's mother, after praying to Bishamonten, obtained a child who was consequently named Tamon-maru 多門丸.

8. See *Hekizan nichiroku* , s.v. Kansei 2 (1461).3.3; and *Inryōken nichiroku*, s.v. Chōkyū 3 (1489).6.3.

9. See Tanaka Hisao 1996: 93–116.

10. Kida 1976: 234–235.

11. In India, the north is an auspicious direction, whereas in China it is the source of yin, and therefore inauspicious.

12. See also *Keiran shūyōshū*, *T.* 76, 2410: 790a; and *Jindaikan hiketsu*, in *ZST*, Ronsetsu-hen: Shūgō shintō, 199–200.

13. *Konjaku monogatarishū*, *NKBT* 17:44.

14. On that apocryphal scripture, see see Kitao 2001. The *Miyako meisho zue* 都名所図絵 reports that one should visit Kuramadera on the tiger day—which is the festival day (*ennichi* 縁日) of Bishamonten—and especially during the tiger month. See Ishizaki Tatsuji 1936: 40–56. The *Inryōken nichiroku* estimates the number of visitors on one occasion to 20,000. See *Inryōken nichiroku*, s.v. Chōkyū 3 (1489) 6.3; see also *Hekizan nichiroku*, s.v. Kansei 2 (1461) 3.3; and *Kanmon gyōki*, s.v. Eikyō 4 (1431) 6.3. Quoted in Kida 1976: 236.

15. For a distinction between *shōmonji* and other types of ritual specialists and outcasts, see Rath 2002: 175–192.

16. See *Shokoku zue* and *Zōtanshū*, quoted in Kida 1976: 234–235. These ritualists were also sometimes called *shiku*, a name that may derive from *shuku* and is perhaps related to the cult of the *shukujin* (on which more later).

17. On the influence of the Chinese motif of winged demons on the medieval Western iconography of hell, see Baltrušaitis 1981: 183–185.

18. In the ritual performed at Tōdaiji, for instance, it is the *nāga* king who expels the demons through the "back door" (*ushirodo* 後戸) of the monastery. See Caillet 1981a.

19. See Iwasa Kanzō 1976b; and Matsuoka Shinpei 2000b.

20. See Matsuoka Shinpei 2000b.

21. See *T.* 21, 1332: 556a.

22. See Shiga kenritsu Azuchijō kōko hakubutsukan 2011: 54. This is, however, the only known representation of this kind.

23. In the biography of Enchin 円珍 of Kiyomizudera 清水寺 in *Genkō shakusho* 元亨釈書, a history of Buddhism by the Zen priest Kokan Shiren 虎関師錬 (1278–1347), we are told that, at the time of the conquest of the north by Tamuramaro, Bishamonten and Shōgun Jizō 将軍地藏 were added to the Kannon of Kiyomizudera (a Senju Kannon 千手観音 with bow and arrows). Tamuramaro is said to have founded Kiyomizudera. After defeating the Ezo, he enshrined Bishamonten in a cave, the Takkoku no Iwaya 達谷窟 (today known as Takkoku no Iwaya Bishamondō, near Hiraizumi). After his death, he was buried in a tumulus on a hill south of Kiyomizudera, the so-called Shōgun-zuka 将軍塚, which was said to rumble when the capital is threatened. He himself came to be perceived as an avatar of Bishamonten. See *Hōbōgirin* 1: 81; and Kida 1976: 227; and Faure 2012.

24. It may be worth pointing out in this context that in the Anxi legend mentioned above, rats gnawed the bows of enemies. Note also the possible link with the rat that is the mount or emissary of Gaṇeśa/Vināyaka.

25. See Ishizaki 1936: 20–21.

26. *ST,* Jinja-hen 29, Hie: 51.

27. See *Gong'yang shier daweidetian baoen pin* 供養十二大威徳天報恩品, translated by Amoghavajra, *T.* 21, 1297: 384. The sūtra describes the benefits and calamities that follow from the twelve devas' pleasure and anger, respectively. See *T.* 21, 1297: 383c–389b.

28. Following a popular etymology, Bishamon literally "looks (*bi* = *nitari*) like a monk" (*shamon*, from the Sanskrit *śramaṇa*). The *Keiran shūyōshū* states that "when he disperses Māra's armies, he wears a *vajra* armor, but inside he wears the robe of deliverance (*kaṣāya*). This is why he resembles a monk." This *kaṣāya*, however, is compared to the placenta. See *T.* 76, 2410: 629a.

29. In Hinduism, Naḍa is described as the son of Kubera. On this god, see Shahar 2013.

30. *Hōbōgirin* 1: 81, quoting the *Beifang Pishamen tianwang suijun hufa yigui* 北方毘沙門天王随軍護法儀軌, *T.* 21, 1247.

31. On Āṭavaka, see Duquenne 1983; Iyanaga 2002a: 159–161; and Rambelli 2002–2003.

32. See the cover of the catalogue *Tenbu no shoson* (Kōyasan Reihōkan 1994); and Kōyasan Reihōkan 2002: 83, fig. 41. Another widespread representation shows him with strangely twirled hair. In spite of his frightening look, he is said to protect his followers: "Those who recite that incantation,

I will protect them day and night, like the shadow follows the body." See *Kakuzenshō* 50: 352a. See also *Shugen seiten* 修験聖典: 305a; and *Fudarakusan kenritsu shugyō nikki:* 11.

33. Jinja Daishō is sometimes identified with the ruler of the underworld Taizan Fukun. See the *Shijūjōketsu*, *T.* 75, 2408: 892a. As noted earlier, the topos of the "shadow that follows the body" is characteristic of the gods of obstacles. On Xuanzang's legend, see also *Shintōshū* 神道集, "Aridōshi Myōjin no koto" 蟻通明神の事, in *ST,* Bungaku-hen 1, *Shintōshū:* 191–194.

34. The name Tobatsu appears in the *Besson zakki* 別尊雑記 by Shinkaku 心覚 (1117–1180), but the image itself was already found in central Asia and in China. According to Rolf Stein, it derives from Tubbat (a name designating Turkestan, and more particularly Khotan). On Tobatsu Bishamon, see Granoff 1970 and Iyanaga 2002a: 391–442. The best known representations of Tobatsu Bishamon are found at Tōji, Seiryōji (10th century), Kanzeonji (9th–10th century), and at the Nara National Museum (12th century). As noted above, the Tōji exemplar was initially enshrined at the Rashōmon Gate, and it is a Chinese figure with a tiara adorned by a phoenix and other figures. The Seiryōji exemplar is of the same type, and the Nara National Museum exemplar is perhaps a copy of it. The Kanzeonji statue is the second oldest Tobatsu specimen, but it is more in line with the usual Bishamonten appearance: the statue has no tiara, and its aura is a wheel of flames. The earlier line drawing appears in the *Besson zakki.* See also Murase 2000: 30 and fig. 9.

35. This image brings to mind certain representations of the "Taking the earth as witness" (*bhūmisparṣa*) episode, in which the earth goddess half-emerges from the ground and seems to serve as a pedestal to the Buddha during his confrontation with Māra. On this episode, see Guthrie 2004: 59–99. In the *Golden Light Sūtra*, Pṛthivī protects the reciter and, conceiling her form, "lifts up his feet."

36. See *Bukkyō daijiten*, fig. 97 (statue of Tōji). According to the *Hongjiatuoye yigui* 吽伽陀野儀軌 (J. *Ungadaya giki*) (*T.* 21, 1251), Bishamonten tramples three *yakṣas,* the one in the center being either Jiten (the earth goddess) or Vināyaka. See *Hōbōgirin* 1: 83. This text is deemed by Matsumoto Bunzaburō to be a Japanese apocryphon dating from the late Heian or Kamakura period (I will therefore use the Japanese title, *Ungadaya giki,* hereafter). See Misaki 1986. The two demons are said to be the origin of the bean-throwing ritual of Setsubun. When they caused havoc, Bishamonten was called to tame them. Note also that, in some sources, the earth goddess is called Kangiten, the Bliss Deva, a name usually referring to the dual-bodied Vināyaka, and sometimes to Hārītī, also called Kangimo (Bliss Mother). Ranba (Skt. Lambā) and Niranba (Nilambā) are the first two figures in the group of ten *rākṣasīs* (Jūrasetsunyo 十羅刹女) that protect the *Lotus Sūtra* and form the retinue of the bodhisattva Samantabhadra (J. Fugen); see Fabricand-Person 2002: 346–347.

37. In the *Golden Light Sūtra*, the king is called *bhūpati* (husband of the earth). The earth goddess (Pṛthivī) vows that she will protect those who will uphold that scripture and that she will "uphold their feet." Pṛthivī also holds up the feet of Maitreya. See Granoff 1970: 164. But Granoff does not

account for the two demons, Lambā and Nilambā, who appear at the sides of the earth goddess under the feet of Vaiśravaṇa. Precedents are found in Indian mythology and art: Viṣṇu, for instance, is represented standing on Pṛthivī. The king was perceived as husband of the earth (*Śatapatha Brāhmaṇa*), image of the union between heaven and earth. The motif of the hierogamy between king (heaven) and queen (earth) seems to have been widespread throughout the Indo-European ideology of kinship. See for instance Erwin Panofsky's remark in *Essais d'iconologie* concerning the image of the king standing on his shield, lifted by the earth goddess (1967: 35).

38. See Biardeau 1991f. In the Bishamon section of the *Byakuhō kushō*, we are told that Kichijōten is identical with the earth goddess Jiten, and is consequently the mother of all buddhas and bodhisattvas. See *TZ* 7: 137c.

39. *Asabashō*, *TZ* 9: 517a.

40. See *Jindaikan hiketsu, ZST,* Ronsetsu-hen, Shūgō shintō: 200; and *Kakuzenshō*, *DNBZ* 50: 204c.

41. In the *Ungadaya giki* 吽迦陀野儀軌 (*T.* 21, 1251: 235a), a ritual text allegedly translated by Vajrabodhi but probably compiled in Japan, Vaiśravaṇa is said to trample three *yakṣa* demons: Jiten (here called Kangiten or Bliss Deva), Niranba, and Biranba. Here the earth goddess is clearly called a *yakṣa*. In the cover illustration of Ishizaki Tatsuji's book, *Tōfukuji Bishamon Tennō* (1936), the three figures trampled by Bishamonten look the same. See also *Asabashō*, *TZ* 9: 427b–c.

42. See Iwasa Kanzō 1976b. On this representation, see also Ikawa Kazuko 1963. Incidentally, one of the four deva kings, Virupākṣa (J. Kōmokuten), is represented holding a brush and a scroll, like the twin devas who attend King Yama or Taizan Fukun (var. Taisenbukun, the god of Taishan, Yama's Daoist counterpart).

43. She is also sometimes called "*yakṣa* demon." See Iyanaga 2002a: 358. Hārītī too was called "*Yakṣa*-woman Kangi," a confusion due to the appellation Kangiten for both Vināyaka and the earth goddess. In esoteric Buddhism, however, Vināyaka himself is often trampled by a Dharma protector. Granoff also points out that Tobatsu Bishamon is standing on either Pṛthivī or Gaṇeśa. See Granoff 1970: 159–160. Lalou emphasizes the confusion between Vaiśravaṇa and Gaṇeśa in Tibetan texts. As she points out, Gaṇeśa (actually Vināyaka) appears as an acolyte in some Dunhuang representations of Vaiśravaṇa. See Lalou 1946: 104.

In a Dunhuang image, the demon on the left of the earth goddess is Vināyaka, the one on the right has been replaced by the worshiper. Lalou points out that there are sometimes elephant tusks around Kubera's head. She quotes a Tibetan text that says: "You whose robust teeth narrowly follow the tongue" (Toi dont les dents robustes suivent étroitement la langue) [like the tusks of an elephant]. See Lalou 1946: 109.

44. See for instance an exemplar dated to the early 13th century, which shows Daoist influence, in Rosenfield and ten Groetenhuis, 1980: 93.

45. See Ishizaki 1936: 66 and fig. 4. A cartouche on the lower left side indicates that it was made by Sōryū 宗立 (i.e., Tamura Gesshō 田村月樵) at the age of 16.

46. The list of the five sons of Bishamonten (known as the five princes) varies. See Ishizaki 1936: 66. An infrared image of a similar mandala, the Bishamon mandala of Zentō-in 前唐院 (dated to the Edo period), is found in the catalogue *Tenbu no shoson* (Kōyasan Reihōkan 1994, fig. 12).

47. See *Bushō ga sugatta shinbutsutachi* (Shiga kenritsu Azuchijō kōko hakubutsukan 2011), figs. 40–43. The same catalogue shows two statues from Saimyōji, one the three great monasteries east of Lake Biwa (Kotō sansan 湖東三山): one represents a four-faced, twelve-armed Tohachi Bishamonten riding a lion, with a small image of the Kongōkai Dainichi 金剛界大日 above his lion diadem; the other is a triad, with a four-faced, ten-armed Bishamonten riding a tortoise, flanked by Kichijōten and Zennishi Dōji. Tohachi Bishamonten is rarely accompanied by these two figures, which are common in other Bishamonten triads. See ibid., 54–55.

48. See the catalogue *Kamigami no bi no sekai* (Kyōto kokuritsu hakubutsukan 2004), fig. 29 and p. 223. A similar representation is that of the four-faced, twelve-armed Tohachi Bishamon of Shinnō-in 親王院 (also dated to the Muromachi period) on Mount Kōya. See *Tenbu no shoson*, fig. 10 (Kōyasan Reihōkan 1994: 49). Although this Tohachi Bishamon looks very much the same, the distribution of his attendants varies somewhat. The same is true of another exemplar preserved at Chōmyōji in Shiga prefecture.

49. Tochigi kenritsu hakubutsukan 1996.

50. See the catalogue *Busshari to hōju* (Nara kokuritsu hakubutsukan 2001); the Ninnaji exemplar is reproduced in *The Fluid Pantheon,* Fig. 6.6.

51. The *Butsuzō zui* 佛像図彙 (1690, reed. 1783) by Ki no Hidenobu 紀秀信 was translated by von Siebold's assistant, Johann Joseph Hoffmann (1805–1878), as an annex to volume 5 of von Siebold's *Nippon.*

52. See *Keiran shūyōshū*, *T.* 76, 2410: 630c; and *Asabashō*, fig. 71.

53. On the Chinjō Yasha ritual performed by Saichō, see Misaki 1992. This ritual appears in the apocryphal *Ungadaya giki* (*T.* 21, 1251). Most other texts on Vaiśravaṇa in *T.* 21 are translations by Amoghavajra. In the *Asabashō*, this ritual text is credited to Vajrabodhi, while at the same time it (or its commentary) is attributed to the Tendai priest Hosshōbō 法性房 (Son'i, 859–940). As noted earlier, Son'i is also credited with the "invention" of Tohachi Bishamon. See *TZ* 9: 430a. There is a ritual with the same name in Shingon, but its content is different, as it is centered on Kongōyasha Myōō (Skt: Vajrayakṣa).

54. As we will see below, Hanten Baramon came to play an important role as a rival or evil twin of Bishamonten. Another kind of evil twin is Kokuni Dōji 黒耳童子, a goddess of misfortune, who was originally known as Kokuni tennyo 黒耳天女 (Black-eared Goddess, Skt. Kālakarmikā) and said to be the elder sister of Kichijōten. We have here a double ambivalence, in which the duality (ultramundane vs. mundane dharmas) represented by Bishamonten and Kichijōten is duplicated in two "good-evil" pairs—Bishamonten and Hanten Baramon on the one hand, and Kichijōten and Kokuniten 黒耳天 on the other—expressing the duality between Dharmatā and Ignorance.

55. See Iyanaga 2002a: 537–539. This strange image calls to mind a local deity of Hida province, the so-called Two-faced Sukuna (Ryōmen Sukuna 両面宿儺); see Robertson 2005: 206; Schnell 1999: 45; and Ozeki 2009.

56. In later Hinduism, Śrī is associated with Indra or Viṣṇu. She is also associated with Kubera (Vaiśravaṇa), the god of wealth who guards the treasures of the earth. Perhaps because of her association with elephants (as symbols of rain and fertilty) in the motif known as Gaja-Lakṣmī, she is also sometimes linked with Gaṇeśa, a *yakṣa*-type deity associated with wealth and good luck. In Buddhism, she is often presented as a daughter of Hārītī and the wife or sister of Vaiśravaṇa. See *Tuoluoni xi jing* 陀羅尼集經, *T.* 18, 901: 876a; and *Pishamentianwang jing* 毘沙門天王經, *T.* 21, 1244: 215c. In the *Sanbō ekotoba*, for instance, we are told that "Kichijō is the spouse of Bishamonten. She made a vow to fill all storehouses with the five grains and to answer all manners of prayers." See Kamens 1988: 251.

57. In the "Sōbi" 双鼻 (Two Noses, an abbreviation of Sōshin Bishamon 双身毘沙門) section of the *Jindaikan hiketsu*, Bishamonten and Kichijōten symbolize a series of nondual polarities: the two realms (Womb and Vajra), concentration and wisdom, principle (*ri* 理) and phenomena (*ji* 事), mental and material phenomena, exoteric and esoteric teachings. The nonduality of these polarities is symbolized by the one-pronged *vajra* held between their joined palms. This is why, we are told, Bishamonten is "the most secret buddha that Saichō brought back from China." ZST, Ronsetsu-hen, Shūgō shintō: 189–190.

58. See Yamamoto 1993a: 306. Of course this kind of nondual hermeneutics is commonplace in esoteric Buddhism. In the case of Bishamonten himself, it is usually read into his attributes: thus, the stūpa on his right palm symbolizes his protection of the Dharma, the trident in his left hand his taming of demons. See *Keiran shūyōshū*, *T.* 76, 2410: 629a. See also Murata Seikō 2003; and Misaki 1992: 298–318.

59. This theory was inscribed in the landscape. In Kyūshū, for instance, there are paired caves representing Bishamonten and Kichijōten.

60. *T.* 76, 2410: 629c.

61. See Lalou 1946: 103–104; and Granoff 1970. The identity between Vaiśravaṇa and Gaṇeśa has been also mentioned by Stein in his essay on the twinned nature of the divine temple gatekeepers. See Stein 1991b. It is not clear, however, whether Kubera and Vaiśravaṇa can be totally fused. Perhaps the latter simply inherited one of the functions of the former (fortune), while remaining distinct.

62. See for instance the *Jindaikan hiketsu*, in *ZST,* Ronsetsu-hen, Shūgō shintō: 189–190; of course, *bi* 'nose' is homophonous with the first syllable—and seed-letter—of Bishamonten, and, as noted above, Sōbi is merely an abbreviation of Sōshin Bishamon; but even so, the coincidence seems significant.

63. *T.* 21, 1251: 233a.

64. Lalou 1946: 111.

65. See Granoff 1970 on the two addorsed figures: Maheśvara/Nandirudra or Maheśvara/Mahākāla (as two distinct deities).

66. Foucher 1900–1905, quoted in Getty 1971: 103.

67. *T.* 76, 2410: 777c–779a.

68. By the Edo period, as can be seen in the *Sōshin Bishamon shishō* 双

身毘沙門私抄 by the Tendai priest Gyōhen 行遍, the dual-bodied Bishamon is reduced to a symbol of the usual Shingon polarities—the two mandalas, principle and wisdom, the esoteric and exoteric teachings, and so on. He has lost all his bite. His fangs are explained (away) by the fact that he "completely chews 噛む the passions of the three worlds." Similarly, the fact that his retinue, the *vajrayakṣas*, eat humans is said to signify the destructions of passions (symbolized by the human body). See Sonehara 1999.

69. *T.* 76, 2410: 38a, 629a.

70. On the legend of the Iron Tower, see Orzech 1995.

71. See "Kaen hōju kansō shari zushi" (Shinagawa, individual collection), in Nara kokuritsu hakubutsukan 2001, fig. 105. This reliquary presents the relics at its center, with Kichijōten on the left and Bishamon on the right. In the Mimurotoji mandala, in the same catalogue, the *cintāmaṇi* is flanked by Bishamonten and Kichijōten.

72. See *Keiran shūyōshū*, *T.* 76, 2410: 629b, 630c, and 778b; see also the *Bishamon zuzō* (Ninna-ji), in which Bishamonten holds a wish-fulfilling jewel in his right hand and a sword in his left.

73. In one recension of the *Golden Light Sūtra*, the *Suvarnaprabhasōttama rājasūtra*, Vaiśravaṇa appears in front of the Buddha and his assembly and teaches the *Cintāmaṇi dhāraṇī*. He adds that the recitation of this formula will make his son Zennishi 禅膩師 appear, and that Zennishi will offer one hundred gold coins per day to the Three Jewels. Vaiśravaṇa also tells the assembly that, whenever anyone paints the Buddha flanked by him and Śrī (J. Kichijōten), he will appear in the form of a youth or an old man holding a wish-fulfilling jewel and a box or a bag full of gold. See *T.* 665: 431a-cp. Quoted in *Hōbōgirin* 1: 81b; this passage, however, is missing in *T.* 663 and *T.* 664.

74. *Keiran shūyōshū*, *T.* 76, 2410: 778c.

75. *Keiran shūyōshū*, *T.* 76, 2410: 779b.

76. An ox-headed god appears among the ten great generals of Vaiśravaṇa in the *Ungadaya giki*, *T.* 21, 1251: 236c. Misaki Ryōshū (1986) emphasizes Bishamonten's relation with the pestilence god Gozu Tennō.

77. *Asabashō*, *TZ* 9: 419a.

78. *T.* 76, 2410: 778c.

79. *T.* 76, 2410: 779a.

80. *T.* 76, 2410: 779b.

81. *ST*, Ronsetsu-hen 4, Tendai shintō 2: 94, 245.

82. Mahākāla also means Great Time. Like Chronos (or rather Kronos, the homonymous Titan), he devours his children. Mahākāla is also linked with Bhairava, Śiva's blood-thirsty manifestation. Bhairava is himself associated with the Eight Mothers (Aṣṭamātṛkā), as Mahākāla is with the *ḍākinīs*. While he became very popular in India (not only in Hinduism, but also in Jainism), his cult never developed in East Asia. On this figure, see Kramrisch 1981: 250–300.

83. In the Tibetan tradition, Mahākāla, before becoming a demon tamer, has to be himself tamed by a Tantric deity (Vajrapāṇi, Hayagrīva, or Heruka, as the case may be). This taming is no ordinary feat, as he is swallowed and defecated by his formidable opponent. This myth is a variant of the widespread myth of Maheśvara's subjugation; see Iyanaga 1981–1985 and Davidson 1991.

84. This relationship with the north also led the Tendai priest Ennin to identify him with Kongōyasha, the wisdom king associated with that direction in the spatial scheme of the five *myōō*. See Iyanaga 2002b: 378.

85. See Iyanaga 1994 and 2002a. Iyanaga describes this evolution from svelte to stocky. However, if the Japanese Daikokuten is indeed lean at the beginning, he also has pot-bellied predecessors in Tibet and Yunnan. The first "Japanized" Daikokuten seems to date from the end of the tenth century, with the exemplar from Kanzeonji. A "Japanized" Daikokuten already appears in the *Bonbun Shijōkōbutchō darani shoson zue* 梵文熾盛光佛頂陀羅尼諸尊圖會 (*TZ* 4, 3012: 92, fig. 23, and p. 126, fig. 106), a work attributed to Zhikong 指空 (Dhyānabhadra), an Indian monk who traveled all the way to Korea. However, since the oldest extent text dates to 1480, the illustrations are probably Japanese. See Iyanaga 1994: 897.

86. See *Daikoku Tenjin-hō*, *T.* 21, 1287: 356a, also quoted in *Kakuzenshō*, *DNBZ* 50: 261b. This work, attributed to the Tang Chinese monk Shenkai 神愷 (J. Jingai), is a Japanese apocryphon. See Iyanaga 1994: 862.

87. See for instance *Kakuzenshō*, *DNBZ* 50: 263b. The *Kakuzenshō* quotes Jitsunin's argument that, precisely because Daikokuten lives in a dark place, he needs light, and therefore the offering he enjoys most is that of the Bright Light mantra (*kōmyō shingon* 光明真言). Ibid., 270.

88. Biardeau 1991a: 38.

89. Bouillier 1993:185.

90. *Kakuzenshō*, *DNBZ* 50: 262b.

91. See *Sādhamalā*, quoted in Lee Yu-min 1996. On stealing the vital principle, see *Kakuzenshō*, *DNBZ* 45: 90.

92. *Kakuzenshō*, *DNBZ* 50: 262.

93. Mahākāla's appearance in the Dali "Long Roll" (*Fanxiang juan*) is rather striking; see Lee Yu-min 1996. It shows the seven manifestations of Mahākāla. The main one is paired with a *nāga* deity, Fude Longnü 福德龍女, which has been associated with the local Dali goddess Baijie and with Hārītī. See Bryson 2010, chap. 3. Note that in that document Mahākāla, in spite of his wrathful appearance, is already represented as a pot-bellied figure. The motif is therefore not simply, as some have argued, a result of his transformation into a more benign god of fortune. Indeed, Bhairava, a form of Mahākāla that did not develop in East Asia as it did in India and the Himalayas, is both wrathful and pot-bellied.

94. On this question, see Iyanaga 2002a: 323–336.

95. *Varāha-purāṇa* xxvii, 34. See also Iyanaga 1994: 866.

96. For a detailed discussion of that myth, see Iyanaga 2002a: 299–336. See also Doniger 1973: 190–192; and Doniger 1975: 168–173.

97. See the illustration in *Kakuzenshō*, *DNBZ* 50: 269. In esoteric Buddhism, Mahākāla is also paired with the Buddhist ogress Hārītī, who is also connected with Vināyaka.

98. *T.* 21, 1239: 195c.

99. See *Kakuzenshō*, *DNBZ* 50: 263b–264a, 265a; and Iyanaga 2002a: 103–135.

100. *T.* 54, 2128: 366b. See also Iyanaga 1994: 865–866.

101. *T.* 8, 243, translated by Amoghavajra (705–774). See also *Kakuzenshō*, *DNBZ* 50: 268–69. On the seven or eight Mothers, see *DNBZ* 50: 265a; Iyanaga 1994: 863–864; and Iyanaga 2002a: 246–248, 584–585.

102. See *Kakuzenshō*, *DNBZ* 50: 267. The same motif is found in the representation of the astral god Rāhu. In the *Fanxiang juan* 梵像卷 from Dali 大理, one of the manifestations of Mahākāla, called "Yakṣa of Great Peace" (Da'an yecha shen 大安夜叉神), is shown standing on a diagram of the Northern Dipper. See Li Lin-ts'an 1982: 118.

103. See Yijing 2009: 38.

104. Yijing 2009: 39.

105. See *Daikoku tenjin-hō*, *T.* 21, 1287.

106. See for instance the *Yiqiejing ying* 一切經音義 (*T.* 54, 2128), quoted in *Bukkyō daijiten* 4: 3217c; and *Kakuzenshō*, *DNBZ* 50: 264b.

107. On the three-faced Daikokuten, see Iyanaga 2002a: 545–636. See also *Bukkyō daijiten* 4: 3216–3218; Sasama 1993; and Frank 1991: 207–213.

108. This would nicely illustrate the proverb "Even Kōbō Daishi (i.e., Kūkai, the greatest Japanese master of calligraphy) makes mistakes with his brush" (Kōbō mo fude no ayamari). The theory of Kūkai's error goes back to the *Chiribukuro* 塵袋 (ca. 1264). On this point, see Iyanaga, "Daikkuten," in *Hōbōgirin* 7: 912b. Daikokuten probably inherited the rat as messenger from his association with Ōkuninushi, a god who was helped at one point by a rat, as well as from his association with the north (which he protects against demons, and which corresponds in Chinese cosmology to the sign of the rat, the beginning of the sexagesimal cycle). The *Shugendō yōten* 修験要典 criticizes the assimilation of Daikokuten with Ōkuninushi as a confusion on the part of ignorant Buddhists. See *Shugendō yōten*, 279. This confusion is reminiscent of that between Chronos (Time) and Kronos (the Titan, father of Zeus)—see Panofsky 1967: 109–111.

109. This aspect had already developed in India, as can be shown by the pairing of Mahākāla and Hārītī. Ōkuninushi is a typical civilizing hero, who "created the land" (with the help of the tiny god Sukunahikona), a land he would eventually have to yield to the descendants of Amaterasu. He is also the master of agriculture and the inventor of sake. As a healer, a feature deriving from his encounter with the hare of Inaba in classical mythology, he came to be identified with the buddha Yakushi. He also represents beauty, love, and fecundity. As Daikokuten, he forms conjugal ties, and becomes a god of wealth. The affinities between Daikokuten and Ōkuninushi are particularly evident at Kiyomizudera, the temple of Kannon the giver of children, where his massive wooden statue stands in the Main Hall, adjacent to the Jishū Jinja 地主神社, a shrine dedicated to Ōkuninushi in his function as a god "who ties the knot" (*en-musubi no kami*).

110. *T.* 76, 2410: 799a. The same source quotes a text dated 1099 by Ōe no Masafusa 大江匡房 (1040–1111), in which the deity that appeared to Saichō on Mount Hiei is said to be Miwa Myōjin.

111. See *Keiran shūyōshū, T.* 76, 2410: 634b, 799a; and the text edited in Gorai 2000, 2: 119b. See also See Iyanaga 2002a; and Kida 1976: 191–192.

112. See Iyanaga 2002a: 561.

113. Stein links Mahākāla and Hārītī as "guardians of the gate." See Stein 1991b: 124–125. On Hārītī and Pañcika, see Foucher 1922, 1: 102–154.

114. See *TZ* 10: 1136.

115. *T.* 20, 1153.

116. On Mohouluo, a Buddhist deity integrated into the Tanabata 七夕 Festival, see Kobayashi Taichirō 1940–1941, pt. 2: 35. In both cases, Tanabata and Mohouluo, we find prayers to obtain children.

117. See Nishioka Hideo 1961: 128–130. The hat of Ōkuninushi (Miwa Myōjin) in Fig. 1.38 above clearly has phallic connotations. On the popular Daikoku, see also Sano 1996: 409–428.

118. The radish is also the symbol of Shōten. On Pañcika and Hārītī, see Ogawa 1973: 31–79. In Japan, Pañcika fused with Daikokuten, and Hārītī took on the look of a *rākṣasī.* Hārītī is discussed in the *Asabashō* (chap. 140), and included among the devas (chap. 146). See also *Besson zakki:* 553–554, figs. 274–275; and *Kakuzenshō*, *DNBZ* 50: 156–159.

119. It is noteworthy to recall in this respect that Śiva (Maheśvara) is represented in ithyphallic form (*linga*). On this question, see Yamabe Nobuyoshi 2013.

120. For a detailed discussion, see Iyanaga 2002a: 337–390.

121. Yamamoto 1998a: 161. On Mahākāla and the Seven Mothers, see *Rishūkyō* 理趣經 (sec. 13 of *Mahāprajñāpāramitā-naya-sūtra*), *T.* 19, 1003: 616a.

122. See *Keiran shūyōshū*, *T.* 76, 2410: 638a. On other forms of *tsubute*, see Amino 1993: 145–196.

123. In India and Tibet, Mahākāla experienced a different kind of apotheosis: he became a supreme deity, who eventually eclipsed the buddha(s) from which he had initially emanated.

124. *Keiran shūyōshū*, *T.* 76, 2410: 637c.

125. Ishana was also assimilated to Māra, the ruler of the sixth heaven—and the paradigmatic god of obstacles. On this question, see Iyanaga 1996–1997; and Itō Satoshi 2011: 118–159.

126. *Keiran shūyōshū*, *T.* 76, 2410: 636c, 640a.

127. *T.* 76, 2410: 637c. In this respect, Daikokuten is said to be identical to Kōjin.

128. See Iyanaga 2002a: 606.

129. Cited in Kida 1976: 214–215.

130. See *Kōbō daishi zenshū* 5: 319–328. See also Nakagawa 1964: 73–74. The name Dōro Shōgun (General of the Ways) suggests Daikokuten's affinities with the *dōsojin,* the crossroads deity (or deities).

131. Quoted in Duquenne, n.d.: 36. On the identity between Daikokuten and the earth deity, see Iyanaga 2002a: 235. In the *Daikoku tenjin hō*, Daikokuten is a metamorphosis of the earth deity. In the *Yiqiejing yinyi*, the earth goddess supports Mahākāla with her hands (as she did in the case of Vaiśravaṇa).

132. See Shimada and Iriya 1987: 79–80.

133. Even today, in the Daikokuten Hall at Enryakuji on Mount Hiei, little figurines of the god, some of them in gold and silver, are sold at preposterous prices.

134. This feature also characterizes deities like Hārītī (J. Kishimojin),

Vināyaka (Shōten), Śrī (Kichijōten), Sarasvatī (Benzaiten), and Yama (Enmaten). On this question, see Iyanaga 2002a: 355–359.

135. See Teiser 1994.

136. See for instance the *Yuqie jiyao Anan tuoluoni yankou guiyi jing* 瑜伽集要救阿難陀羅尼焔口軌儀経, *T.* 21, 1318 and the *Yuqie jiyao yankou shishi qijiao Anantuo yuanyou* 瑜伽集要焔口施食起教阿難陀縁由, *T.* 21, 1319, compiled by Amoghavajra.

137. Teiser 1988.

138. See the *Yaoshi rulai benyuan jing* 薬師如来本願経, *T.* 14, 449: 403c.

139. See Lincoln1991: 32–33.

140. Yama's name is said to mean "twin," but in the *Brāhmaṇas* it is also said to derive from the root *yam* 'to restrain, curb, subdue.' Yama appears as one of a pair of twins born to Vivasvant (the sun god) and Saraṇyū (the daughter of Tvaṣṭṛ, the divine artisan). The *Ṛg-veda* mentions an interesting episode, Yamī's attempt to seduce her twin brother, but the latter resists successfully this incestuous relationship. This "expurgated" version, however, seems to point to the existence of an earlier version in which the incest does take place. Indeed, in the Iranian version of the tale, Yamī argues that she and her brother already had intercourse while in the womb. See Malamoud 2002:16–17; and Siklós 1996: 168.

141. A bath in the Yamunā was said to prevent rebirth in Yama's realm; see Siklós 1996:173. Yamunā is linked with another river goddess, Sarasvatī. The latter, indeed, appears as Yama's sister in the translation of the *Golden Light Sūtra* by Yijing (635–713), and this is why she is sometimes listed among his retinue. In this scripture, Sarasvatī (whom we will encounter again under the name Benzaiten) is also called Nārāyaṇi (a name that points to her role as sister or consort of Nārāyāṇa, i.e., Viṣṇu), and she becomes a kind of transcendent mother goddess.

142. See the *Shimen zhengtong* (1237), quoted in Teiser 1994: 64. See also *Asabashō*, in *TZ* 9, 3190: 496.

143. See *Śathapatha-Brāhmaṇa* xiv, 1, 3, 4; quoted in Malamoud 2002: 17–18.

144. In northern and central India, for instance, the demonic hairstyle (*ūrdhvakeśa,* hair standing on end) has been mostly chosen for Yama, in order to emphasize his fierce nature. See Wessels-Mevissen 2001: 98.

145. See *Śathapatha-Brāhmaṇa* xiv, 1, 3, 4, cited in Malamoud 2002: 15. See also Siklós 1996: 165–189.

146. On Dizang, see Wang-Toutain 1998; Ng 2007; Soymié 1966 and 1979.

147. See van den Bosch 1982; and Wayman 1959.

148. See *Taittirīya-Brāhmana* v, 2, 3, 1, quoted in Malamoud, 2002: 26.

149. See Snodgrass 1988: 641.

150. See van den Bosch 1982; and Wayman 1959.

151. See Snodgrass 1988: 481.

152. *Usuzōshi kuketsu* 薄雙紙口訣 by Raiyu, *T.* 79, 2535: 282c. Yama also causes hindrance to the practitioner by appearing in the south in the form of a terrifying corpse; his nose is cut off, and he howls in a loud voice; he

holds a sword in one hand and drinks blood from a skull that he holds in his other hand. See Giebel 2006: 294–295.

153. See the *Da Piluzhena chengfo jing shu* 大毘盧遮那成佛經疏, *T.* 39, 1796: 684b.

154. Quoted in Snodgrass 1988: 481. In some sources, however, Yama's buffalo is white. According to Malamoud, the black color of Yama's buffalo is associated with his ink writing. Both Yama and Citragupta (his scribe, "he who preserves the diversity of good and evil actions") are linked by the use of ink. See Malamoud 2002: 138–139; on the two kinds of water buffalo, see *Usuzōshi kuketsu* by Raiyu, which states that Daiitoku's buffalo is blue, that of Enmaten, white (*T.* 79, 2535: 282).

155. See the *Dapiluzhena chengfo shenbian jiachi jing* 大毘盧遮那成佛神変加持經, *T.* 18, 848: 35a; and the *Dapiluzhena cheng fo jing shu* 大毘盧遮那成佛經疏, *T.* 39, 1796: 744a.

156. See *Da Piluzhena chengfo shenbian jiachi jing*, *T.* 18, 848: 35a; and Yixing's *Commentary*, *T.* 39, 1796: 744a (which only gives a textual description, but no diagram). According to the *Asabashō*: "One must draw this mandala to obtain *siddhis*." *TZ* 9, 3190: 504a, 505b.

157. See *TZ* 9: 497c; and Snodgrass 1988: 484.

158. See for instance *Betsugyō* 別行, *T.* 78, 2476: 178c; *Yōsonbō* 要尊法, *T.* 78, 2478: 209a; *Shoson yōshō* 諸尊要抄, *T.* 78, 2484: 319c, 329a; *Hizō konpōshō* 秘藏金宝鈔, *T.* 78, 2485: 365c; *Hishō* 秘鈔, *T.* 78, 2489: 572a; *Usuzōshi* 薄双紙, *T.* 78, 2495: 646a; and *Kakuzenshō*, in *DNBZ* 50: 306.

159. See Nakamura Teiri 2001: 75–76.

160. See Figs. 1.45 and 1.46 above.

161. On Kālāratri, see Yixing's *Commentary*: "On the west of Yamadeva, draw Yama's consort and the consort Death, who is also Yama's consort. On the east, draw the goddess Dark Night (Kokuya-shin) and the Seven Mothers." *T.* 39, 1796: 634b, quoted in *Bukkyō daijiten* 2: 1133–1134. In Hinduism, she is especially invoked to protect people from dangers peculiar to the night, and from the darkness of ignorance. Occasionally, however, she is associated with the very creatures or dangers of the night from which she is elsewhere asked to protect people. Kālarātrī, then, is not only the guardian of the night, who protects people during the dark hours of their rest, but the night itself and those things, both benign and hostile, that inhabit the night. See Kinsley 1986: 14.

162. On this tradition, see Iyanaga 1999.

163. *T.* 39, 1796: 684b.

164. In the Womb Realm mandala, they are described as black demonesses and also placed in the western section; see *Ishiyama shichishū* 石山七集, *TZ* 1: 181a. On this topic, see Mani 1995; and Miyasaka Yūshō 1990.

165. According to Ariane MacDonald, "the group of the Seven Mothers, ambivalent deities, benevolent or ogresses, seems distinct from that of the *mātṛkā* or *grahī*, which is not well fixed." See MacDonald 1962: 84.

166. Krishan 1999: 134.

167. See "Shamunda" in *Bukkyō daijiten*, 3: 2182c-2183a; and Snodgrass 1988: 499–450.

168. On Vināyaka, see Chap. 2 below.

169. On the twelve Mothers, see *Luofonu shuo jiuliao xiaoer jibing jing* 囉嚩拏說救療小兒疾病經, translated by Dharmabhadra, *T.* 21, 1330: 491c–494a; and Filliozat 1937. On the Seven Mothers and Cāmuṇḍā in medieval Japan, see *Kakuzenshō*, *DNBZ* 50: 308.

170. See *ZZ* 2b, 23, 4 (new ed., vol. 150: 381).

171. *T.* 39, 1796: 643c. On Citragupta, see also Malamoud 2002: 318.

172. The identity between Taishan Fujun and Citragupta (or the takeover of the latter by the former) is suggested by the fact that both have the same mantra. See *Asabashō*, TZ 9, 3190: 498.

173. An early sixth-century text, the *Xi Taishan wen*, notes that King Yama "determines one's basic lifespan in the august records and inspects the city registers in heaven's offices." See "Xi Taishan wen" in *Hongming ji* 弘明集, *T.* 52, 2102: 92a; quoted in Teiser 1988: 186.

174. *T.* 3, 185: 475c. The name of this god, translated by Dudbridge as "Great Knowledge" is also used in the *Asabashō*, *TZ* 9, 3190: 498b. It might also refer to the storehouse consciousness (*ālaya-vijñāna*). See Dudbridge 1996–1997: 89.

175. See Sawada 1984b: 90–91; and Dudbrige 1996–1997: 92.

176. Dudbridge 1996–1997: 92.

177. On this Great Exorcism, see Davis 2001: 112–114.

178. See Eliasberg 1984: 237–240.

179. On Siming and Silu, see Soymié 1966: 45–73.

180. On the *daṇḍa* staff, see Seidel 2003a.

181. See Seidel 2003a: 1121a.

182. See Duara 1988.

183. See Iyanaga 1999; and Faure 2006.

184. For an overview of Yama's role in India, China, and Japan, see Matsunaga 1969: 34–48. For a description of Yama as a Chinese judge, see Teiser 1994; and Frank 2000a: 82–84.

185. See Ten Grotenhuis 1999: 68.

186. Matsunaga 1969: 36–37. Thus, the duties of hell's official consist of recording debits and credits against each person's karmic account. According to the *Jingdu sanmei jing* 浄土三昧經, quoted in the *Jinglü yixiang* 經律異相: "Every month they make six reports, every year they make four investigations. . . . Those with meritorious actions have their lifespan increased, those with sinful actions have it reduced." See *T.* 53, 2121: 259c; cited in Teiser 1988: 190. In his role as granter of longevity, Enmaten becomes a cosmic deity who is sometimes identified with the buddha Yakushi. See *Kakuzenshō*, *DNBZ* 45: 90.

187. Teiser 1988: 184.

188. Teiser 1988: 185.

189. See for instance *Jindaikan hiketsu* 神代巻秘訣, in *ZST,* Ronsetsuhen, Shūgō shintō: 56.

190. See Teeuwen and van der Veere 1998: 43–44 and 75–77. See also *Nakatomi no harae chūshaku:* 243; *Reikiki:* 39; *Tenchi reikiki*: 135–139.

191. *Nakatomi no harae chūshaku:* 243.

192. On Taizan Fukun as a god of fortune, see Nishida 1976; and Nasu 2004.

193. According to H. Kern, Yama coincides with Varuṇa in his function of upholding justice and moral order (1884: 178), cited in Matsunaga 1969: 35–36.

194. Eventually, with the religious transformation of the Edo period, the sinified King Yama becomes a threatening caricature, while Bishamonten and Daikokuten are domesticated and become part of a family idyll (Daikokuten and consort, Bishamonten with Kichijōten and their son Zennishi)—thereby losing a large part of their symbolic richness and potential (although not necessarily their symbolic efficacy and their devotional appeal).

195. See *Goma kuketsu* 護摩口決, *T.* 79, 2532: 96c.

CHAPTER 2: THE ELEPHANT IN THE ROOM

1. Shōten was by no means the only supernatural ally invoked setup by emperors against the bakufu. Using the pretext of the pregnancy of the imperial consort, Go-Daigo had rituals dedicated to Butsugen 佛眼 and Ichiji Kinrin 一字金輪, the five wisdom kings, Kujaku Myōō 孔雀明王, the Seven Yakushi, the Five Kokūzō 虚空藏, the Six-letter Kannon 六字観音, the Eight-letter Monju 八字文殊, Fugen 普賢, and Kongō Dōji 金剛童子. See McCullough 1979: 12.

2. See Amino 1993: 221–223.

3. See Favret-Saada 1980: "The witch is the other."

4. Murayama Shūichi 1990: 362.

5. See De Visser 1935: 518. According to a legend, Shōten once appeared to him and gave him medicine. See *Keiran shūyōshū, T.* 76, 2410: 783c.

6. According to the *Tenjin engi* 天神縁起, this statuette was brought in 847 from China by Ennin 円仁 (794–864), who placed it at the front of the boat to overcome the demons and storms that tried to prevent his return. It was finally enshrined at Zentō-in 前唐院 on Mount Hiei. On the *Tenjin engi,* see Akiyama 1943: 38–62; and Nanri 1996.

7. On this question, see Iyanaga 1983.

8. Nanri argues that Michizane was a devotee of Vināyaka by emphasizing his relationship with the Tendai priest Annen. See Nanri 1996: 49; and Iyanaga 2003: 153–155. The *Shinki* 神記 by the Shingon priest Hōgen 法眼 (fl. Muromachi period) gives Kangiten as one of the five *honji* of Tenjin (the others being Amida, Jūichimen Kannon, Bishamonten, and Benzaiten). It adds that because Kangiten was perceived as an avatar of Daijizaiten 大自在天 (Maheśvara) at Kitano Tenjin shrine (Kyoto), he was also identified with Daikokuten (Mahākāla, a variant of Maheśvara). On the links between Daijizaiten and Tenjin, see Iyanaga 1994 and 2002a. At any rate, Shōten/Kangiten was clearly linked to Kitano Tenjin. On this question, see Makabe 1981.

9. Such rituals usually include the main altar, two *goma* altars, one altar for the twelve devas, one Shōten altar, and one altar for offerings to the gods. See Mack 2006: 152.

10. *Son'i zō sōshō den,* quoted in Yamanaka 1985–1986: 73.

11. See Groner 2002: 86. This appears to be the earliest reference to Shōten in Japan.

12. See *Byakuhō kushō, TZ* 7: 174a; and Yamanaka 1985–1986: 74.

13. On the cult in the modern period, see Holtom 1938; and Shūkyō shakaigaku no kai 1985: 38–81. There is at Hōzanji only one hall dedicated to Kangiten, and it is of course not open to the public. The temple's commercial guidebook shows no representation at all of Shōten. By contrast, Fudō is abundantly represented. As Sanford points out, the guide is aimed at persuading the reader that, contrary to popular belief, Kangiten is more interested in bringing spiritual solace than in providing worldly benefits. See Sanford 1991b: 302–309.

14. See Yamamoto 1998a: 427–428. Once restored by Echin 恵鎮 (1281–1356), Hōkaiji became a great Tendai center in Kantō. It was in particular the residence of an influential member of the *kaike* (Vinaya) tradition of the Kurodani-ryū 黒谷流 of Mount Hiei, Kenchū 謙忠, who was instrumental in the development of the Benzaiten cult at Enoshima and the author of ritual texts on Benzaiten, Daikokuten, and Kōjin.

15. See *Chōseiden* 寵誓伝, in Seki 1987: 324–325; see also the *engi* of Katsuoji in *Genkō shakusho, DNBZ* 62: 147.

16. Iyanaga Nobumi, personal communication.

17. Much has been written on the elephant-headed god. See in particular: Bakshi 1987; Biardeau 1991b; Bühnemann 1988 and 1989; Dhavalikar 1970; Duquenne 1988, 1994a; Getty 1971; Holtom 1938; Kabanoff 1994; Krishan 1999; Martin-Dubost 1997; Sanford 1991b; Stein 1991a; Sasama 1989; Shirato 1982; Yadav 1997.

18. See O'Flaherty [Doniger]'s preface to Courtright 1985: vii.

19. Quoted in Iyanaga 2003. Iyanaga demonstrates in his article, as I hope to do in this book, how Doniger's remark applies to Japan.

20. See for example Duquenne 1994a; and Renou 1937: 271–274.

21. According to Narain, there was originally an elephant god with positive features, Hastimukha, in southern India. See Narain 1991.

22. The standard view is well represented by the *Mahābhārata,* in which Gaṇeśa is the Lord who removes all obstacles. See *Mahābhārata,* Anuśāsana Parvan XIII, 151, 6, 57, quoted in Martin-Dubost 1997: 8. Gaṇeśa is also said to be the scribe of Vyāsa, the author of the *Mahābhārata.* As god of beginnings, Gaṇeśa is also the protector of the first cakra (*mūlācakra*) at the base of the backbone, the starting point of the *kuṇḍalini* energy.

23. Skanda is said to have been born from Śiva's semen, which fell into the mouth of Agni. The latter discharged it in the Ganges, which in turn threw the embryo on a bank, where it was found and raised by the six Kṛttikās (the Pleiades). Thus, strictly speaking, Skanda and Gaṇeśa are only half-brothers, since the former is the son of Śiva, the latter the "son" of Pārvatī.

24. From the theological point of view, this means that he is the guardian of the earth and the manifested world, or of the Dharma. According to Madeleine Biardeau, Pārvatī's refusal to be seen in her nudity means a refusal to join the world of deliverance, and an assertion of the value of the worldly realm. This suggests that Gaṇapati, as keeper of the goddess, is in charge of the *bhukti,* the smooth running of earthly affairs, rather than of *mukti,* deliverance. See Biardeau 1991d: 846.

25. Krishan 1999: 41–42.

26. One popular etymology is: born "without" (*vinā*) "spouse" (*nāyaka*). See Courtright 1985: 135.

27. Another example is that of the southern Indian goddess Māriamma, who, after being beheaded, receives the head of an outcast. On this goddess, see Assayag 1992.

28. For Madeleine Biardeau (1991d), who follows closely the theological interpretation, this means that *bhukti* (enjoyment of this world), without renouncing its rights, acknowledges the transcendence of *mukti* (deliverance). Initially guardian of the goddess, Gaṇeśa becomes keeper of the heavenly gate. In late Indian representations, the two consorts of Gaṇeśa, representing his two aspects, are Buddhi (Intellect) and Siddhi (spiritual power). See Lawrence Cohen 1991:132–135. Sometimes these two consorts are replaced by Sarasvatī and Śrī (known in Japan as Benzaiten and Kichijōten). According to Krishan: "In short, the spouses of Gaṇeśa are the personifications of his powers, manifesting his functional features." Krishan 1999: 62.

29. In modern India, Gaṇeśa is often found together with the goddess Durgā in the function of gatekeeper.

30. Krishan 1999: 58 and 130.

31. Significantly, it is the same Skanda who, under the erroneous transcription Weituo 韋駄, became, as gatekeeper of Chinese Buddhist monasteries, the companion of Budai 布袋, the pot-bellied "laughing Buddha," a great friend of children. Stein has argued that the figure of Gaṇeśa influenced that of Budai, so that the pairing of Budai and Weituo at the gate of Chinese monasteries is, through a strange *détour,* that of Gaṇeśa and Skanda as "gatekeepers." See Stein 1991b. On Skanda and children, see Krishan 1999: 128–129, and Strickmann 1996.

32. *Mahābhārata* 3.217; Krishan 1999: 128–129.

33. On this question, see Péri 1916.

34. Krishan 1999: 133. The pair Fugen/Monju is also related to the two-headed Aizen (ryōzu Aizen 兩頭愛染) representing Aizen and Fudō.

35. See Filliozat 1937.

36. *Brahmāṇḍa Purāṇa* 2.34.33; quoted in Krishan 1999: 21.

37. Krishan 1999: 36–38.

38. *Vāmapurāṇa,* chap. 28, 30–77, quoted in Martin-Dubost 1997.

39. From the fifth century onward, Gaṇeśa is represented at either end of panels representing the Mothers. Sometimes an eighth Mother is added (at Elephanta, for instance), and the groups of eight are often flanked by Skanda and Gaṇeśa. The motif already appears in Cave 6 of Udayagiri around the fourth century, but the first representations of the Mothers are said to date to the first century CE. Gaṇeśa is also the central deity of cave 6-A of Aurangabad. On the Aurangabad caves, see Berkson 1986: 115–21; and Huntington 1981. On the identification of the female deities, see Gupte 1963: 59–63. Another recently discovered cave shows Gaṇeśa at the center rear, with the Seven Mothers and Śiva on his right, Durgā and two buddhas on his left. See Berkson 1987: 226–228; Martin-Dubost 1997: 14. On Gaṇeśa and the Mothers, see the introduction in Robert L. Brown 1991: 7–8; Martin-Dubost 1997: 273–290; and Iyanaga 2002a: 583.

40. Krishan 1999: 131–132.

41. See *Besson zakki, TZ* 3: 504–507.

42. In a stone sculpture found at Gongxian, however, and dated 531—that is, anterior to the first Indian representations of Gaṇeśa, except that of Udayagiri—an elephant-headed figure has been found in a series of ten animal-headed deities. This form has not yet been explained. See Getty 1971 and Lancaster 1991.

43. See for instance the *Lishi apitanlun* 立世阿毘曇論, *T.* 32, 1644: 208c; and the *Fugai zhengxing suo ji jing* 福蓋正行所集經, *T.* 32, 1671: 739b.

44. See the *Mārīcīdhāraṇī-sūtra* (*Molizhitian pusa tuoluoni jing* 摩利支菩薩陀羅尼經), translated by Amoghavajra, *T.* 1255a: 257b. In this text, the members of Vināyaka's retinue have animal heads. They are to be bound with colored threads, like the demons tamed by the Gandharva king. See also *Tuoluoni jing* 陀羅尼經, *T.* 18, 901: 856c, where he is called Demon King. In the *Jinse jianabode tuoluoni jing* 金色迦那鉢底陀羅尼經 (*T.* 21, 1269: 303b), he is also the leader of ten demons with animal heads, which are perhaps related to the Gongxian stone sculpture of 531. The *Kakuzenshō,* quoting a text by the Tendai priest Kōgei 皇慶 (977–1049), mentions an unusual identification of the two embraced figures: the *female* figure is said to be Vināyaka as mother of demons (*kishimo* 鬼子母, an appellation usually reserved to Hārītī), while the *male* is a manifestation of the bodhisattva Avalokiteśvara. See *DNBZ* 50: 121.

45. Krishan 1999: 166.

46. Krishan 1999: 135.

47. Rāhu in particular became the object of an important cult, from India to Central Asia, China and Japan.

48. Courtright 1985: 134.

49. The extent of the oblivion and denial that afflicts modern India is shown by the fact that Courtright received a flurry of angry mail (including death threats) after the 2003 reedition of his 1985 book, for having emphasized the sexual and oedipal symbolism of Ganesh.

50. See Foucher 1900–1905, vol. 1, fig. 30; and Getty 1971: 31.

51. Krishan 1999: 50.

52. Krishan 1999: 79.

53. Krishan 1999: 63, 163–169, and 191–193.

54. Krishan 1999: 118.

55. See reference myths in Sanford 1991b: 297–300. Gaṇapati is also an epithet of Rudra/Śiva (or Maheśvara). "Golden Gaṇapati" is the name given to one of the four directional Vināyakas—the only one with an elephant head, actually—in the esoteric mandalas.

56. See Martin-Dubost 1997: 14.

57. Krishan 1999: 118.

58. See Krishan 1999: 166.

59. Ibid.

60. On this question, see Strickmann 1996: 310–322.

61. Vināyaka appears in a number of texts: *T.* 1266, 1267, 1270, 1273, 1274, and 2129.

62. See Yixing's *Commentary on the Mahāvairocana, T.* 39: 650a; and *Kakuzenshō, DNBZ* 50: 107. See also *Byakuhō kushō, TZ* 10: 1117b: "Vināyaka corresponds to the false thoughts of the practitioner."

63. See for instance *Kakuzenshō, DNBZ* 50: 135. On the nightmare-causing *vināyakas,* see Strickmann 1996; and Kabanoff 1994: 120.

64. The toponym Zōzu-san appears often in Japan. On this question, see Yanagita 1990d: 169–172; and Duquenne 1994.

65. See *Besson zakki, TZ* 3, 3007: 532a; *TZ* 7, 3119: 173a; and Kakuzenshō, *DNBZ* 50: 109.

66. Sasama 1989: 137–149.

67. Vināyaka is defined as "the one who discards (*vī-nī*) obstacles," Vighna-vināyaka. Gaṇeśa was also called Vighnānthaka, "the one who puts an end to all obstacles." On Vighnāntaka as destroyer of obstacles, see De Mallmann 1986: 447–448: "This deity tramples obstacles (*vighna* or Vināyaka)." Yet Buddhists regularly explain *vināyaka* as "obstacle" (*shōge* 障礙). See *T.* 21, 1796: "The Vināyakas are all those who cause obstacles. All such obstacles are produced by illusory connotations of the mind." However, as Robert Duquenne points out, the *Mahāvyutpatti* gives the opposite interpretation, "batsuja" (discarding what is nefarious)—but this may be a later interpretation. Vināyaka is not a poor devil, he is the Demon King (*Tuoluoni jing* 陀羅尼經, *T.* 18, 901: 872c) or the "King of the hundred demons" (*Suxidijieluo jing* 蘇悉地羯羅經, *T.* 18, 893: 630c). He is said to "ravish the vital breath of beings" and to cause obstacles. He is constantly on the watch, waiting for any occasion to take advantage of human weaknesses. According to the *Miaofa lianhuajing xuan zan* 妙法蓮華經玄讃, *T.* 34, 1723, for instance, Vināyaka is a demon who "ceaselessly pursues people to cause obstacles and difficulties for them." See also the *Shōten-hō engi* 聖天法縁起 in *TZ* 3: 532a; *Byakuhō kushō, TZ* 7: 173a; *Asabashō, TZ* 9: 486a; and *Kakuzenshō, DNBZ* 50: 109.

68. See *Muli mantuoluo shou jing, T.* 19, 1007: 659c; and *Azhapo guishen dajiang shangfo tuoluoni jing, T.* 21, 1238: 183b.

69. *Guanzizai pusa suixin zhu jing* (translated by Zhitong 智通 (*ca.* 627–649), *T.* 20, 1103: 458b. See also the *Foshuo Molizhitian jing* 佛説摩梨支天經, a text included in the collection known as *Tuoluoni ji jing* 陀羅尼集經 (translated in 654), where it is said that, when one performs the Molizhitian 摩梨支天 (J. Marishiten) ritual, one must expel the obstacles caused by all demons with the incantation of Gaṇapati. One fabricates the image of the King of the hundred demons, Vināyaka, with the head of a white elephant. The goal in all cases is to tie up Vināyaka—the leader of demons—by an incantation and to expel him.

70. *T.* 76, 2410: 641b.

71. See Nanri 1996.

72. See Miya 1976: 17–19; Makabe 1981; and Akiyama 1943: 38–62.

73. Makabe 1981: 40.

74. On Tenjin, see Iyanaga 1983. Iyanaga shows in particular that the image of Michizane as Tenjin merged with that of Indra/Śiva. In that sense, one could see the antagonistic relation between Shōten and Michizane/Tenjin as a reenactment of Gaṇeśa's antagonism toward Śiva.

75. *Suxidijieluo jing* 蘇悉地羯羅經, *T.* 18, 893: 630c; *Molizhi tipo huaman jing* 末利支提婆華鬘經, *T.* 21, 1254: 257b, 299c, 303b.

76. See *Keiran shūyōshū, T.* 76, 2410: 640c.

77. *TZ* 10: 1118a.

78. In some texts he is called the "heavenly youth" (*tendō* 天童).

79. *Kakuzenshō*, *DNBZ* 50: 119.

80. *See Bukkyō daijiten* 2: 1325c; *Mikkyō daijiten* 2: 685–686.

81. *Bukkyō daijiten* 2: 1330–31, *Mikkyō daijiten* 2: 662–663.

82. *Bukkyō daijiten* 2: 131, *Mikkyō daijiten* 2: 658–659. This form of Vināyaka is explicitly identified with Aizen in the *Byakuhō shō, TZ* 10: 1123a, and in the *Keiran shūyōshū, T.* 76, 2410: 642b.

83. *Bukkyō daijiten* 2: 1341; *Mikkyō daijiten* 2: 710–711. See also Sawa Ryūken 1972. In the divination rites centered on Shōten, these four Vināyakas are called Nichiō (Sun King; east), Aiō (Love King; south), Getsuai (Moon Love; west) and Gitoku (Excellent in Discussion; north). For more details, see below. See also *Dasheng Huanxi shuangshen Pinayejiatian xingxiang pin yigui* 大聖歓喜双身毘那夜迦天形像品儀軌, *T.* 21, 1274; and Manabe 2000–2001, 2: 94–115.

84. See Tajima 1959; on the four directional Vināyakas, see also *Kakuzenshō, DNBZ* 50: 117b.

85. See *Mikkyō daijiten* 2: 714.

86. The two heads, facing opposite directions, call to mind the drawing of the *Shinkō musōki,* where they are said to be to the *hun* and the *po* souls of the person.

87. See Shiga kenritsu biwako bunkakan 1998, fig. 47.

88. Of course, this evolution is not everywhere the same, and in some corners Vināyaka remained a secondary deity. See for instance, in the *Genkō shakusho,* the case of the priest Kōi 公伊 who throws a statue of Vināyaka into the river, after the latter appeared to a donor in a dream, complaining that the priest failed to worship him. See *DNBZ* 62: 122b, quoted in Kabanoff 1994: 121.

89. The Hindu poet Śaṇkara (eighth century), for instance, has a devotional poem in which he praises Vināyaka for eliminating the elephant demon. See Martin-Dubost 1997: 8.

90. The same motif is also found in India. See for instance fig. 37 in Linrothe and Watt 2004: it is a painting of the late Pala dynasty showing Acala (who will become Fudō in Japan) trampling on an elephant-headed demon (Vināyaka). See also figs. 38 and 39 in the same volume.

91. See Stein1991b. Another deity, this time a female one, shown trampling Vināyaka is Aparājita. See Bhattacharya 1968, s.v. "*sādhanā* 204."

92. Krishan 1999: 118.

93. See Linrothe 1999: 303; and Stein 1995: 140.

94. See Davis 2001: 130–131.

95. See *Mahāvairocana-sūtra, T.* 18: 12c; and Duquenne 1994b.

96. See *T.* 18: 851c–852a; *Kakuzenshō,* in *DNBZ* 50: 132; *Byakuhō kushō, TZ* 7: 177a. Gundari Myōō is said to be particularly efficient against Vināyaka's aggressions. Shōten is also said to belong to Gundari's retinue.

See also the myth of Kangiten's seduction, as told in *Kakuzenshō*. Here, Shōten is the daughter of Daijizaiten (Maheśvara). Because of her ugliness and her violent nature, she is exiled on Mount Vināyaka, where she meets a male deva who courts her. She replies that she is already married to a wrathful god, Gundari. When the deva gets angry, she tells him that she will become his wife if he mends his ways. As we can see, Shōten plays here the role of Kannon. See *Kakuzenshō, DNBZ* 50: 142; *Byakuhō kushō, TZ* 7, 3119: 177b; and Iyanaga 2002b: 218–220 and 331–333. At Dunhuang, we find a representation of Vajrapāṇi (blue) and Ucchuṣma (red) trampling two Vināyakas (one boar-headed, the other elephant-headed). In some sources, the tamer of Vināyaka, Gundari Bosatsu 軍荼利菩薩, is a goddess, and not a wisdom king. On Vināyaka and Gundari, see Iyanaga 2002b: 210–215.

97. See for instance the *Byakuhō shō* by Chōen, *TZ* 10: 1119b.

98. Hārītī resembles Vināyaka in her role as "mother of demons." She was originally a goddess of smallpox. She is usually represented as a *yakṣinī,* but the *Lotus Sūtra* identifies her with the ten *rākṣasīs.* See Péri 1917: 38–39. The *Kakuzenshō* also describes a female form of Vināyaka as Hārītī. See *DNBZ* 50: 121a.

99. See Sanford 1991b: 93.

100. According to the Chinese commentator Huanguang 含光, *kangi* ("bliss") is the translation of Gaṇapati. It is the bliss that the *vināyakas* cause by their seduction, but also the bliss through which Gaṇapati/Vināyaka in turn seduces them and tames them; finally, it is the bliss through which Vināyaka himself was seduced and tamed by Avalokiteśvara. On Kangiten, see Iyanaga 2002b: 218–220 and 331–333.

101. On that notion, see Stein 1995: 140; Duquenne 1983: 653–656; Linrothe 1990; and Linrothe 1999: 303.

102. In *Kakuzenshō,* the two figures are said to represent a female deva (Vināyaka as the mother of demons, Kishimo) and a bodhisattva (Avalokiteśvara/Kannon). *DNBZ* 50: 121a. See also *Keiran shūyōshū, T.* 76, 2410: 526a.

103. The manuscript Pelliot 4518(8), for instance, represents Kangiten as two *vināyakas* in embrace, one (the male) with an elephant head, the other (female) with a boar head. See Bibliothèque Nationale 1995, 1: 138. A similar couple appears on either side of Avalokiteśvara in a magnificent painting preserved at the Musée Guimet. According to Dhavalikar, this form results from a confusion; see also Sanford 1991b: 317. See also *Kakuzenshō, DNBZ* 50: 120. The splitting of the name Vinā/yaka into two separate names (and figures) is criticized in the *Byakuhō shō, TZ* 10: 1118b. On the symbolic affinities between elephants and pigs/boars, see Strickmann 1996: 266–272.

104. See *Zuzōshō,* Daiba-bon, *TZ* 4: 356–357.

105. This legend illustrates the Tantric notion of the "revolution by coupling" (*maithunasya parāvṛtti*), as described in the *Mahāyānasūtrālaṃkāra, T.* 1604: 605a; see also *Keiran shūyōshū, T.* 76, 2410: 526a.

106. See for example *Byakuhō kushō, TZ* 7: 181c.

107. See *Keiran shūyōshū, T.* 76, 2410: 640c

108. See *Dasheng Huanxi shuangshen dazizaitian Pinayejia-wang guiyi*

niansong gongyang fa 大聖歡喜雙身大自在天毘那夜迦王歸依念誦供養法, trans. by Śubhakarasiṃha, *T.* 21, 1270: 303b. See also Ryūkoku daigaku 1938–1940, 4: 3174.

109. See Miyasaka Yūshō 1977, 2: 27–31, quoted in Sanford 1991b: 301.

110. Apparently, as Iyanaga points out, that part of the story is indebted to the legend of the cannibalistic king Kalmāṣapāda, who also appears in the myth of Mahākāla. See Iyanaga 2002a: 139–148.

111. For a representation of Ucchiṣṭa Gaṇapati with his *śakti*, see ill. 64 (16th century, Tamilnadu) in Martin-Dubost 1997. See also Stein 1991b, and Strickmann 1996: 248, 265, 267.

112. As is well known, this unfortunate belief had led to the extermination of large numbers of African elephants, and threatens to eradicate the "roots of heaven." See Gary 1973.

113. See the image of the two-armed Vināyakī at the Völkerkunde Museum (Munich) in Martin-Dubost 1997. See also Krishan 1999: 63.

114. The distinction between the two types of Vināyaka (real and metamorphic) is already clearly made by Amoghavajra in the *Pinayejia enabode yuqie xidepin miyao by* Hanguang, *T.* 21, 1273: 322b. In this text, however, the male is also a provisional manifestation of Vairocana.

115. Among these texts, five are variants of a Vināyaka ritual contained in the *Tuoluoni ji jing* 陀羅尼集經 (*T.* 18, 901: 884c–885a) translated by the Indian monk Atikūṭa (fl. 651–654). See the description in Lancaster 1991; and Duquenne 1988. The *Sheng Huangxitian shifa* 聖歓喜天式法 (*T.* 1275), in particular, provides a typically Chinese method of divination, combining Indian gods with Chinese cosmological figures. On this question, see Kabanoff 1994. For Japanese sources, see Kabanoff 1994; and Sanford 1991b.

116. See *Tankai*: 346–347.

117. See *Chishō daishi zenshū,* 2: 1043b.

118. See Miyasaka Yūshō 1977, 2: 27–31, quoted in Sanford 1991b: 301.

119. See *Kakuzenshō, DNBZ* 50: 135 (*TZ* 5, 3022: 452a); and Iyanaga 2003.

120. This name is anachronistic in that it anticipates Shōten's later function as a Dharma protector; but it may also mean in this case that he is the deity that can "rough up" the Three Treasures (Buddha, Dharma, and Sangha)—a fair revenge for someone that has been so often trampled by Buddhist bullies.

121. The *Shibu Binayaka hō* is unfortunately no longer extent, but this passage is quoted in *Kakuzenshō, DNBZ* 50: 135; *Asabashō, TZ* 7: 174a. See also *Kangiten reigenki,* quoted in Nanri 1996: 47–52; and Iyanaga 2003: 155.

122. See "Kōjin engi," in *Shintō zatsuzatsusho* 神道雑々集 (Coll. Yamada, Tenri Library). I am indebted to Abe Yasurō for sending me a copy of the manuscript, preserved at the Ōsu bunko in Nagoya. The passage in question is also quoted in Yamamoto 1998a: 345.

123. See SZ 37.

124. *T.* 76, 2410: 642b. This astral and embryological symbolism calls to mind certain representations of the Three Devas, on which more shortly.

The relation between Vināyaka and Aizen is also mentioned in Shingon texts such as the *Shōten-hō zōshū:* "Among the four types of Vināyakas, the Vināyaka with bow and arrows is King Aizen. When respect and love (*keiai*) are nondual, all things unite harmoniously, without obstacles. All things are born from that stage." See *Byakuhō shō, TZ* 10, 3191: 1123a.

125. See *Chōseiden*: 325; and Kabanoff 1994: 116–117.

126. *Chōseiden*: 325.

127. Kabanoff 1994: 124. See also "Shōten-sama," in Seki 1987: 547.

128. Quoted in *Jindaikan hiketsu, ZST,* Ronsetsu-hen: Shūgō shintō, 60–61.

129. See Akiyama Teruo 1943: 38–62. On the *Kangiten reigenki* (a.k.a. *Tenjin engi*), see also Nanri 1996: 29–52.

130. In the *Shintōshū,* for example, Gozu Tennō and Zaō Gongen are identified with Kangiten (Vināyaka). See *ST,* Bungaku-hen 1, *Shintōshū*: 159–161; and Murayama 2000: 348. On Gozu Tennō, see Saitō 2007.

131. *Meishukushū, NSTK* 24.

132. See Itō Masayoshi 1970.

133. Quoted in Itō Masayoshi 1970 and Tanaka Nariyuki 1996. As we will see, Zenchiku's faith in Kangiten may have been overdetermined by the network of symbolic associations that he attempted to describe in his *Meishuku shū* (although the name of Kangiten itself does not seem to appear in this work).

134. See Tanaka Nariyuki 1996: 49–63.

135. The name *shaguji* can be written with various *ateji,* among which: 社宮司，左久神，作神左口神、社口神、佐護神，石神、釈護神，遮愚神、三宮神，三狐神，山護氏、射軍子、杓子、赤口神、蛇口神. See Kawaguchi Kenji 1999: 359.

136. See Yanagita 1990d: 169–172.

137. Gakkō Yoshihiro, arguing mainly from the fact that Jūichimen Kannon was the *honji* of both Shōten and the Hakusan deity, and from similarities in distribution, beliefs, appearance, etc., argues that the Shōten cult and other cults played an important role in the elaboration of the *oshira* cult. See Gakkō 1965. The *oshira* are known under various names (*oshirasama, oshiragami* オシラ神, *oshirabutsu* オシラ佛, *okonaisama* オコナイ様, etc.). Their cult is connected to that of Hakusan (and the Eleven-faced Kannon), and they are gods of the house or deities of silkworms (*kaikogami* 蚕神). They are worshipped on the 16th of the first, third, and ninth months. They are also related to Memyō Bosatsu 馬鳴菩薩, a horse-riding deity sometimes identified with Amaterasu. On the Oshira cult, see Yanagita 1990e: 201–419.

138. The winnow is said to look like an elephant ear. One of the five directional Vināyakas has a winnow among his attributes. See Krishan 1999: 178.

139. See Stein 1991b.

140. Of course the image of the gate evokes the "Yin gate," i.e., the vagina, and by extension childbirth, but this may not be sufficient.

141. On this question, see Needham 1970: 262–264; Kalinowski 1983: 309; and Nishioka Yoshifumi 2007: 11–15.

142. See *Asabashō, TZ* 9: 480 a.

143. On these four Vināyakas, see above. On the Kangiten divination board, see Nishioka 2013: 144–146.

144. See *Sheng Huanxitian shifa, T.* 21, 1275: 324c-325a.

145. See Kanagawa kenritsu Kanazawa bunko 2007b.

146. See *Shōten shiki,* in Kanagawa kenritsu Kanazawa bunko 2007b: 39–40.

147. Ibid., 43b–c.

148. Ibid., 39a.

149. See Tanaka Nariyuki 1996: 53–55; and Zenchiku, *Meishukushū,* in Omote and Katō 1974: 414b.

150. *Dasheng Huanxi shuangshen Pinayejiatian xinxiang pin yigui* 大聖歓喜双身毘那夜迦天形像品儀軌, *T.* 21, 1274: 323c.

151. *T.* 21, 1273: 322a.

152. Ibid., 322b.

153. See Miya 1976: 18.

154. *Bikisho,* in *ST,* Ronsetsu-hen 2, Shingon shintō 2: 509.

155. See Seki 1987. See also *Shiojiri,* 10: 51.

156. Seki 1987: 327.

157. On Gaṇeśa and the *navagrahas*, see Martin-Dubost 1997: 291–297; Yadav 1997: 167–171. In Japan, the Seven Mothers are also identified with the seven stars of the Northern Dipper, and by the same token Shōten, their leader, is implicitly identified with the pole star deity, Myōken.

158. *Shinbutsu ittai kanjō shō*, 156b.

CHAPTER 3: A STINK OF FOX

1. See Iyanaga 1999; Kuo 2003; Doniger 1980: 237.

2. The relation between this power and flesh eating was a widely accepted belief in medieval India among Tantric practitioners. The *Cakrasaṃvara-tantra,* for instance, teaches the virtues of consuming the concretion or bezoar (*rocanā*), found in persons "born seven times a man." See Gray 2007: 100. Likewise, the *Hevajra-tantra* teaches that, should one meet such a person, one should eat his essence, which will give you the power to fly. See Snellgrove about such "seven-timers" (*saptāvarta*): "By the mere eating of his flesh one will gain at that moment the powers of an aerial being." Snellgrove 1959, 1: 87. A "seven-timer" is any man or woman who has transmigrated in human forms throughout seven lives, but preferably, "a man who has been hanged, a warrior killed on the field of battle, and a man of irreproachable conduct who has returned seven times to human states, of the flesh of these one should partake." Ibid., 71. This passage points to ritual cannibalism by "knowing yogis," although Snellgrove finds the figurative interpretation (the beings referring to the five *skandhas,* and the flesh to their self-nature) "more acceptable." See ibid., 73n. The cult of the *ḍākinīs* may be seen to reflect the influence of marginal groups such as the Kāpālikas, which were known to worship Mahākāla.

Indeed, the Buddha's injunction in the *Hevajra-tantra* sounds rather appalling from a traditional Buddhist standpoint (or any standpoint). The East Asian tradition tried to skirt the issue by making the *ḍākinī* wait till the death of the person before eating his/her essence, or by arguing that, by "stealing the *hun* and *po spirits*" of beings, *ḍākinīs* were actually freeing them from ignorance and leading them to enlightenment.

Ḍākinīs were initially represented as birds. In the *Lankāvātara-sūtra,* however, they are described as hybrid creatures born from the union between King Kalmāṣapāda and a lioness. See Suzuki Daisetsu 1968: 16. In the representation of Śiva's subduing of the asura Andhaka, a chimera (half-bird, half-woman) is seen flying over the scene, hoping to drink some of the asura's blood. See Doniger 1973: 190–192; Doniger 1975: 168–173; and Kramrisch 1980: 50. (I am indebted to Iyanaga Nobumi for this reference.) On Andhaka, see also Kramrisch 1981: 374–383.

3. One popular etymology derives its name from the Sanskrit root *di* 'to fly.' According to Samayoga, "*Da* means sky travel, and she who is directly realized in space, that is, who has achieved [the ability] to range all throughout the sky, is called the *ḍākinī.*" Gray 2007: 101–102. The *Yogaratnamāla* (Garland of Jewel-like Yoga), a commentary on the *Hevajratantra,* derives *ḍākinī* from the root *dai* 'to fly.' See also Snellgrove 1959, 1: 135: "*Ḍakiṇī* is commonly related to the Skt verbal root *ḍī,* to fly, and represents that 'perfection which acts throughout the whole of space.'" The term was translated into Tibetan as *mkhah-'gro-ma* 'she who goes in the sky.' See Dowman 1984. The term was rendered into Chinese as *kongxingmu* 空行母 'sky-going mother,' or *xukongxingmu* 虚空行母 'space-going mother,' but the etymology remains obscure. See for instance *T.* 19: 402a. On the Tibetan *ḍākinī,* see Hermann-Pfandt 1992; and Skorupski 1997.

4. See *T.* 18: 17a; and *T.* 19, 1796: 687b; French translation in Iyanaga 1994: 858–859. See also Iyanaga 2002a. This passage, known very early on in Japan, was taken up by the Tendai priest Annen in his *Taizō kongō bodaishingi ryaku mondōshō* 胎藏金剛菩提心義略問答抄, *T.* 75, 2397: 457c. See also *Sōjishō* 総持抄 by Chōgō 澄豪 (1259–1350), *T.* 77, 2412: 76a.

The choice of Mahākāla is rather ironic given the fact that, in Hinduism, the *yoginīs/ḍākinīs* are said to originate from the goddess Kālī after she conquers the demon Mahākāla. See Shastri 1982: 53. In the *Vajraśekhara-sūtra* (J. *Kongōchōkyō* 金剛頂經, *T.* 18, 865), it is Vajrapāṇi who subjugates the *ḍākinīs.* In several variants, it is Acala (Fudō).

5. See *Dapiluzhena chengfo jing shu* 大毘盧遮那成佛經疏, *T.* 39, 1796: 687b. See also Gray 2007:100; and *Kakuzenshō, DNBZ* 50: 260–264. The *Gyōrinshō* 行林抄, quoting the *Bodaishingi,* states that the Buddha authorized the *ḍākinīs* to eat the heart of the dead, and this heart is called "human yellow," *T.* 76, 2410: 421c. The term "heart" must be understood here in the sense of "essence." Indeed, the text adds that this "heart" is actually composed of seven grains of jade on the top of the head.

6. See Tanaka Hisao 2003: 130. See *Kakuzenshō, DNBZ* 50: 264b.

7. Tanaka Hisao 2003:130.

8. The *Asabashō* 阿娑縛抄, after mentioning that rite, adds in a note: "Empower ox yellow seven times." The ox yellow used during the Shushō-e ceremony in various temples can be traced back to this rite, during which the

practitioner, imitating a fox, licks the palm of his/her left hand, as if licking blood. This gesture is actually one of Dakiniten's mudrās. See also *Dapiluzhena chengjiu yuqie jing, T.* 18, 852: 122a. On the mudrās and mantras of Dakiniten, see Sakurai 1996: 232–250.

9. This is for instance the view held by the Daigoji priest Kenjin 憲深 (1192–1263). See Itō Satoshi 2002a: 195. The term "essence-stealing demon" (*dasshōki* 奪精鬼) appears only twice in the *Keiran shūyōshū,* in connection with Mahākāla and the *ḍākinīs.* See *T.* 76, 2410: 636a and 644a. One also finds, for the *ḍākinī,* the term "deity snatching the *hun* [soul]" Dakkonjin 奪魂神, and one of Dakiniten's eight acolytes has precisely the name Datsukonpaku-ki ("Demon snatching the *hun* and *po* [souls]"). See *T.* 76, 2410: 732b; and Shirahara 1999.

10. See Manabe 1999: 50–54.

11. The wish-fulfilling jewel was also perceived as the vital essence. For instance, the *nāga* maiden of the *Lotus Sūtra* gives her jewel to the Buddha, the jewel that is her life, her vital principle—reversing the motif of the essence-stealing demon. On the symbolic equivalence between ox yellow, *śarīra*, and *cintāmaṇi,* see *T.* 76, 2410: 778c, 779c. See also *Gyōrinshō, T.* 76, 2409: 421c, which confuses "human yellow" and "ox yellow."

12. In his *Sōjishō,* the Tendai monk Chōgo (1259–1350) writes that the seven grains of white jade are located in the eight-petaled heart of a person. When they are eaten one by one by the *ḍākinī,* only Acala (Fudō) can save that person. See *T.* 77, 2412: 76a.

13. As noted above, Aizen is also invoked in that case, because he can hold the human yellow of a person in his upper left hand and protect that person from the *ḍākinī*'s attack.

14. See Lorenzen 2002: 29–30.

15. This process has been well documented by Iyanaga Nobumi (Iyanaga 1999) and Nakamura Teiri (Nakamura 2001). See also Kuo 2003; Abe Yasurō 1989: 138–188; Sasama 1988; and Tanaka 1993. On the Inari cult, see Gorai 1985a; Ōmori 1994 and 2000; Bouchy 1985; and Smyers 1999. On the fox cult, see De Visser 1908b; and Bouchy 1984.

16. See *Kakuzenshō, DNBZ* 50: 308. See also Iyanaga 1999: 57; Tajima 1959: 127; and Nakamura Teiri 2001. *Ḍākinīs* are also described as attendants to Nirṛti-rāja, a directional deity that governs the southwest. See Snodgrass 1988: 494.

17. *Keiran shūyōshū, T.* 76, 2410: 689b–c. This is due to the fact that practitioners rely on the *ḍākinī samādhi* to obtain realization (*siddhi,* J. *jōju* 成就). On this *samādhi,* see *Shijūjō ketsu* 四十帖決 by Chōen 長宴, *T.* 75, 2408: 866c and 867a.

18. Even today, this image is represented on the protective *ofuda* of the Toyokawa Dakiniten 豊川茶吉尼天.

19. Nakamura Teiri 2001: 70–71.

20. Teeuwen and Van der Veere 1998: 69.

21. On the Indo-Tibetan *ḍākinī,* see Hermann-Pfandt 1992–1993. The ingestion trope is indeed prevalent with the *ḍākinīs:* Padmasambhava is said to have been initiated by a *ḍākinī,* who swallowed him after transforming him

into the seed-syllable *hūṃ*, and kept him inside her body, before finally giving birth to him. See Young 2009; and White 2003.

22. See *Yiqiejing yinyi* 一切經音義, *T.* 54, 2128: 539c. A gloss on the apocryphal *Sūraṃgama-sūtra* explains that they are "bewitching female demons, foxes." This may be one of the first associations between *ḍākinīs* and foxes, although it did not develop in China as it did in Japan. See Kuo 2003: 1101.

23. Sanford 1991a: 15. See also the Mongolian ritual related to *ḍākinīs* in Serruys 1970; Bawden 1976 and 1978; Heissig 1970.

24. Iyanaga Nobumi, personal communication.

25. See *Kokon chōmonjū* 6, 215–216. See also *Genpei jōsuiki,* 1932: 12–15; and Kida 1976: 330–338; Tanaka Takako1993; Abe Yasurō 1989: 148. The story is taken up in the *Shirushi no sugi* しるじの杉, although its protagonist is no longer Tadazane, but a monk by the name of Daigonbō. *ST,* Jinja-hen 9, Inari: 417.

26. See *Keiran shūyōshū, T.* 76, 2410: 633b. Also significant is Ningai's association with the Gion consort, who, owing to her relation to retired emperor Shirakawa, came to wield enormous power at court. People attributed this power to the fact that, when she was a young girl, her father had sent her every day to Ningai with food offerings. See *Keiran shūyōshū, T.* 76, 2410: 633b. As Tanaka Takako points out, Ningai and the Gion consort were not contemporaries, and strong symbolic reasons must have existed for their fate to be posthumously linked; Tanaka suggests that it had to do with the cult of Dakiniten. See Tanaka Takako 1993: 231–243. See also Abe Yasurō 1989: 148; and Minobe 1982: 220–221.

27. See *Genpei jōsuiki,* 1932: 12–15, and Minobe 1982: 217–223.

28. On the Tachikawa-ryū, see Mizuhara 1931; Moriyama 1965; and Manabe 1999. For a recent critique of the "heterodox" label applied by earlier scholarship, see Iyanaga 2003; and Köck 2000 and 2007.

29. On Monkan's religious and social background, see Abe Yasurō 1989; Amino 1993; and Hosokawa 2002–2003. On Monkan's textual output, see Abe Yasurō 2010b.

30. *Hōkyōshō,* cited in Moriyama 1965: 577–579.

31. McCullough 1979: 366. The *Taiheiki* sets Monkan up as a foil against Jōkei 貞慶 (Gedatsu Shōnin, 1155–1213), whom it presents as a paragon of virtue.

32. See *Keiran shūyōshū, T.* 76, 2410: 623b.

33. See *Dakini kechimyaku,* in Kushida Ryōkō 1973: 318.

34. See Kanagawa kenritsu Kanazawa bunko 2007b: 6, 66; and Nishioka Yoshifumi 2008: 36–38.

35. *Kanazawa bunko komonjo,* 6149; quoted in Nishioka Yoshifumi 2007: 20.

36. See Heine 1994: 85. On Toyokawa Inari, see Smyers 1999: 25.

37. The Dakiniten statue was moved to Tokyo Toyokawa Inari in Asakusa in 1887. Another of the three great centers of Inari is the Saijō Inari Temple of Takamatsu 高松 in Okayama City, at the foot of Ryūō-san 竜王山, a mountain with many tumuli (*kofun*), which is also known for its rain rituals.

Inari was worshiped there as *jinushigami.* The place was also a cultic center for Kumano shugendō (Tendai). A *jingūji* 神宮寺 of the Inari shrine was eventually built there, and in 1601 a Nichiren priest, Nichien (1572–1616), restored it and renamed it "Inarisan Myōkyōji."

38. Another Sōtō Zen master, Gennō Shinshō 源翁心昭 (1329–1400), is famous for having exorcized the "killing stone," which was the abode of an old nine-tailed fox called Tamamo no Mae. In one version of the legend, this stone was eventually moved to Shinnyo-dō 真如堂 in Kyoto. This temple also has a Dakiniten Hall, and the cult of Dakiniten there is said to go back to the Kamakura period. At the beginning of the Tokugawa period, the shōgun Ieyasu 家康 made donations to it in 1615. See Kobayashi Tsukifumi 1978: 81–87.

39. See for instance the *Inari ki,* in Yamaori 1999: 360, 362; and the *Inari taisha yuishoki shūsei,* Shinkō chosaku-hen, 4.

40. Abe Yasurō 1995: 152–153.

41. *T.* 76, 2410: 633c.

42. See for instance *Tenshō daiji kuketsu,* in *ST,* Ronsetsu-hen 2, Shingon shintō 2: 499. This legend becomes the theme of the Kōwakamai "Iruka" 入鹿 (15th or 16th century). This fox was the Myōjin of Matsuoka, that is, the form of Dakiniten as Kashima Myōjin 鹿島明神 (Kasuga, var. Amaterasu). The image of Dakiniten as a fox king appears in the *Shintōshū:* see "Inari Daimyōjin no koto," in *ST,* Bungaku-hen 1, *Shintōshū:* 72–77. Great men are often said to be the offspring of a fox: we already noted the case of Kamatari. Another case in point is En no Gyōja. In the *En no Gyōja hongi* 役行者本記 (end of Muromachi), En no Gyōja's mother, significantly called Shiratōme (White Fox) became pregnant after dreaming that she swallowed a one-pronged *vajra.* In the Edo period, En no Gyōja came to be seen as the child of a fox. See also "En no Gyōja ryaku engi no koto" in the *Shugen shuyō hiketsu shū* (1521–1528). In the Kabuki play *Kuzu no ha,* it is the mother of Abe no Seimei, the ancestor of Onmyōdō, who is described as a white fox. The Tendai school relied on another foundation legend, that of the Chinese King Mu 穆 and the youth Jidō 慈童, focused on the *Lotus Sūtra.* On this question, see Abe Yasurō 1984.

43. *Sokui kanjō inmyō yūraiki,* Muromachi period, Naikaku bunko; cited in Itō Masayoshi 1980. The *Keiran shūyōshū,* however, claims that, even before the introduction of Shingon in Japan, Shōtoku Taishi had transmitted a Dakiniten ritual. See *T.* 76, 2410: 633a. This tradition, however, is not confirmed by other sources.

44. Tanaka Takako 1993: 245–246.

45. See Iyanaga 1994; Yamamoto 1993a; Tanaka Takako 1993; Nakamura Teiri 2001; Matsumoto Ikuyo 2005; and Grapard 2002–2003.

46. On this question, see Iyanaga 1999: 87–88 and 94–95, Iyanaga 2002a: 600; Sakurai 1993: 229; and Itō Masayoshi 1980, docs. 11–12; Abe Yasurō 1989; Yamamoto 1993a: 36. The ritual becomes more complex in the Tōji tradition, involving three mudrās and two mantras. In the *Jindaikan hiketsu,* we find a Joint Ritual of the Three Devas (Santen gōgyō-hō) centered on Shōten, Dakiniten, and Benzaiten. See *ZST,* Ronsetsu-hen, Shūgō shintō: 391–392.

47. The ritual was practically unknown at the time of the Tendai abbot Jien 慈円 (1155–1225). Most texts, like the *Tōji sokui hō* 東寺即位法 (1337), the *Bikisho* 鼻帰書 (1324), the *Tenshō daijin kuketsu* (1327), and the *Jindai kuketsu* 神代口決 (1436), date from the fourteenth and fifteenth century.

48. Yamamoto 1993a: 364.

49. These stories call to mind the *Pañcatantra,* or the old French folk tales about the cunning fox Goupil, rewritten by Jean de La Fontaine.

50. See for instance Amino 1993; Abe Yasurō 1984 and 1989; Iyanaga 1999; Matsumoto Ikuyo 2005; Faure 1998a and 2003a; and Ruppert 2000.

51. See Abe Yasurō 1989; and Iyanaga 1999: 98.

52. See *Keiran shūyōshū, T.* 76, 2410: 520c and 867b.

53. Nakazawa 1994: 261–262.

54. As Amino Yoshihiko and others have shown, as the imperial house lost its grip on power, it attempted to regain it at the symbolic level by connecting with marginal social strata. On this question, see Faure 2002–2003a.

55. See the definition of the *kora* and of the Three Devas in the *Jingi hishō,* in Kokubungaku kenkyū shiryōkan 1999b: 394.

56. Yamamoto 1993a: 341.

57. See *Bikisho,* in *ST,* Ronsetsu-hen 2, Shingon shintō 2: 511–513.

58. This ritual developed a little later than the Ise kanjō, and was already widespread during the Kamakura period. See Kushida 1973: 317–321; Misaki 1994: 564; *Rinnō kanjō kuketsu,* in Kanagawa kenritsu Kanazawa bunko 2007b: 56–57; and Nishioka Yoshifumi 2007: 15.

59. *Tenshō daijin kuketsu,* in *ST,* Ronsetsu-hen 2, Shingon shintō 2: 500. See also Yamamoto 1993a: 363.

60. On this question, see Breen and Teeuwen 2010: 213–214.

61. *Dapiluzhena chengfo jingshu, T.* 39, 1796: 744a. In the *Gyōrinshō, yakan* is read *kogitsune* 'small fox.' See *T.* 76, 2410: 421b.

62. This image also spread in Japan, as can be seen in the legend of Tamamo-no-mae 玉藻前. The story relates that Tamamo-no-mae appeared as a beautiful and cultivated young woman in the palace of retired emperor Toba, and seduced him. After having had intercourse with her, he became gravely ill. The Yin-Yang master Abe no Yasunari 阿部泰成 performed a divination that revealed that the young woman was the avatar of an eight-hundred-year-old fox that once lived in the Nasuno plain in Shimotsuke province. On this legend, see Faure 1996: 71.

63. Lévi 1984: 115.

64. This identification is mentioned for instance in the *Shirushi no sugi,* a compendium of Inari lore compiled by Ban Nobutomo 伴信友 (1773–1846). See *ST,* Jinja-hen 9, Inari.

65. *Bikisho,* in *ST,* Ronsetsu-hen 2, Shingon shintō 2: 511–513.

66. In Gorai Shigeru's view, the Inari cult consists of many layers, among which the most important are beliefs in a food (most notably rice) deity, in ancestor spirits, and in a deity of natural elements (in particular fire). See Gorai 1985a: 13–30; see also Bouchy 1984 and 1992.

67. See *Keiran shūyōshū, T.* 76, 520c.

68. Ibid.

69. The term appears in the *Keiran shūyōshū,* and Iyanaga translates it as "gleaming fox." Marc Teeuwen, on the other hand, translates it as "dragon fox" (probably because these foxes are flying through space). The character *shin* 辰 does mean "dragon," but it is also used in the term Hokushin 北辰, usually translated as the Northern Chronogram, namely the pole star. One of the texts clearly identifies Shinkoō with Hokushin and Myōken Bosatsu. I have therefore chosen to translate *shinko* as "astral fox." The term *guchen* 狐辰 (J. *koshin*) appears in Dunhuang manuscripts: see Kalinowski 2003: 161, 163, 189, where it refers to one of the many spirits controlling the days in the calendar method of divination. Perhaps we are putting too much freight on this anyway, as *shinko* 辰狐 may just be a homonym for *shinko* 神狐 (divine fox), a term that is often used in the same contexts.

70. See Kawaguchi 1999: 240.

71. See *Keiran shūyōshū, T.* 76, 2410: 632b.

72. In *The Fox and the Jewel,* Karen Smyers discusses this symbolic association, but unfortunately she does not trace it to medieval esoteric rituals, nor does she discuss the enthronement ritual. See Smyers 1999.

73. See Yamaori 2004b: 397–398 and 418–421. The *Inari jinja kō* points out that the fact that the Inari deity was a goddess (Toyouke) was gradually forgotten, and the Tōji tradition envisioned Inari Myōjin as a male god. This deity eventually merged with Dakiniten, however, and its female nature is mentioned in other branches of Shingon, for instance in the Hirosawa-ryū of Shukaku Hōshinnō. See *ST,* Jinja-hen 9, Inari: 472.

74. This merging calls to mind that of Ugajin with Benzaiten, which resulted in a new deity called Uga Benzaiten 宇賀弁才天. On this question, see Chap. 7 below.

75. On the Inari cult, see Naoe 1983; Kondō 1978; Bouchy 1984; and Iyanaga 1999: 59–64. See also De Visser 1908b. In the background of the Dakiniten cult at Inari, as in that of Matarajin at Kōryūji, we find the influential Hata clan of Korean ancestry. The Matarajin of Tōji was also perceived as an emissary of Inari Myōjin, due probably to the close relationships established by Kūkai between Tōji and Inari Shrine. However, the *Inari jinja kō* deplores the "mistaken identification" between Inari and Dakiniten. See Yoshino Hiroko 1980: 140; and Smyers 1999: 26.

76. See *ST,* Jinja-hen 9, Inari: 16; and Yamaori 1999: 364.

77. *ST,* Jinja-hen 45, Hizen Higo: 562.

78. See Miyake 2005: 158.

79. In the talismans sold at Inari Shrine today, the name Ugajin has replaced that of Uka no Mitama. In the upper part of the talisman are three jewels, the "three-petaled *cintāmaṇi,*" corresponding to Shōten, Benzaiten, and Dakiniten. See Miyake 2005: 151–152; and Fig. 3.16. Above the rice bags are two white snakes, a representation of Ugajin as white snake. Above them are two foxes, white and black. In the "Myōbu no koto" section of the *Inari Daimyōjin ruki* 稲荷大明神流記 (14th century), these foxes are said to represent an old fox couple that vowed to serve Inari Daimyōjin. The vixen is black, and she is called Akomachi 阿小町. The components of that talisman

(stylized jewels, snakes, and foxes, flanking the name Uka no mitama), suggest that the Inari deity, redefined during the Meiji period in purely Shintō terms, was in premodern Japan a composite deity formed of Benzaiten, Ugajin, and Dakiniten. See Kawasoe 2006: 176.

80. Tenna Shōnin, first abbot of Aizenji 愛染寺, is also known as founder of the Aizenji-ryū 愛染寺流 of Ryōbu shintō. See Kojima 1999: 336–341; and Bouchy 1985: 232–235.

81. See *Inari shūsei shinkō: chosaku-hen,* 89–96.

82. See *Ototari saimon,* in Nishioka Yoshifumi 2008: 42b.

83. *Shugen hiōshō,* quoted in Miyake 2005: 153–154.

84. See *Keiran shūyōshū, T.* 76, 2410: 633b; Tanaka Nariyuki 2003; 208–213; and Minobe 1982: 220.

85. In the *Tenchi jingi shinchin yōki* by Jihen 慈遍 (fl. 14th century), this "holy woman" is further linked with Ugajin (although here Uga Benzaiten is probably meant) and with Toyouke, the deity of the Outer Shrine of Ise. In a later text, the *Hie Sannō Gongen chishinki* 日吉山王権現知新記, she is clearly assimilated with Benzaiten (who was herself perceived as a manifestation of Nyoirin Kannon).

86. See for instance the *Dakiniten hihō* 吒枳尼天秘法, a later text that provides formulas to obtain a *cintāmaṇi,* in *Shugen seiten,* 492–500.

87. See *Dazhidulun, T.* 25, 1509: 134a; and *Keiran shūyōshū, T.* 76, 2410: 631c.

88. See Gorai 1985a: 105–106.

89. The *ofuda* shows a frontal view of the fox-riding youth on an altar. He holds a sword in his left hand, a jewel in his right. The circular aura above his head contains three jewels. Above his head is another jewel. Above the fox is printed a seal representing three jewels surrounded by an aura.

90. See for example *Shirushi no sugi,* in *NSSS* 26: 695; and *ST,* Jinja-hen 9, Inari: 418–421.

91. *ST,* Ronsetsu-hen 5, Ise Shintō 1. See also *Yamatohime no mikoto seiki* 倭姫命世記, cited in Kida 1976: 44–45.

92. Kida 1976: 48–49. Yanagita Kunio mentions the theory in *Wakun no shiori* 和訓栞 that the name *shakuji,* designating a kind of god of the limits, derives from *sankoshin,* but he eventually rejects it, arguing that the two deities coexisted. See 1990d: 28 and 171–172.

93. Yanagita has also suggested that *sankoshin* was an alternate reading (or *ateji* 当字) for the *shaguji,* a term designating a rather enigmatic deity to which we will return. See Yanagita 1990d: 27. On the view that Sankoshin is none other than the Miketsu no kami, see also p. 28. The association between Uka no Mitama and the fox already appears in the *Yamatohime no mikoto seiki.* See Ōsumi 1977: 34. Uka no Mitama was also said to be the child of Daijizaiten (Skt. Maheśvara), and she was called *tōme* 刀目 (term usually designating a fox or an old woman). According to the *Jinmei hishō* 神明秘鈔, the *kami* of the Tsuki mikura (granary of the Outer Ise Shrine) was called Sankoshin 三狐神 (or Tōme-gami 専女神). See Kokubungaku kenkyū shiryōkan 1999b. In the *Jingi fuden zuki,* Uka

no Mitama becomes one of the members of a vulpine triad (Sankoshin), in this case a "heavenly fox" (tenko). See *Tamakisan gongen engi,* in *ST,* Jinja-hen 5, Yamato no kuni: 523. See also Gorai 2000, 2: 151; and Yamamoto 1993a: 356.

94. See *Tamakisan gongen engi* 玉置山権現縁起, in Gorai Shigeru 2000, 2: 151a. See also Yamamoto 1993a: 355. For the iconography, see *Gyōrinshō, T.* 76, 2409: 164.

95. Strangely, Yama is here displaced from the subterranean world by the *dōsojin* and relegated to the demonic sphere. See also Kokubungaku kenkyū shiryōkan 1999b: 463–464.

96. Furthermore, it had bird legs, a feature perhaps inherited from the *tenko* (or *tengu*).

97. Gorai 2000, 2: 151b; Yamamoto 1993a: 356. The emblematic animal of Kumano is a three-legged crow, an ancient Chinese solar symbol. Mount Tamaki is said to owe its name to the legend according to which En no Gyōja and Kūkai had buried jewels (*tama*) on it. See *Tamakisan gongen engi,* in Gorai 2000, 2: 151b–152a.

98. See Gorai 2000, 2: 151: "Regarding the *honji* of the Sankoshin, there is a very secret oral tradition, which cannot be shown outside." See also Yamamoto 1993a: 356–358. This deity is also said to have given birth to ten "princes," some of which, the heavenly foxes, settled on Japanese mountains that became major Shugendō centers: Atago, Hira, Togakushi, Fuji, Hakusan, Ontake, Haguro, Ōyama, Mount Nikkō, and Mount Hakone. See Gorai 2000, 2: 151. These *tenko* are clearly assimilated here with *tengu* 天狗, for instance the *tengu* of Mount Atago 愛宕山, on which see Bouchy 1979. The text adds that, among the three foxes, the heavenly fox corresponds to Haguro Gongen 羽黒権現, the earthly fox to the Sankoshin of Kumano, and the human fox to the four bodhisattvas (Yoku 欲, Shoku 触, Ai 愛, and Man 慢) that form the retinue of King Aizen (Gorai 2000, 2: 151b).

99. Gorai 2000, 2: 151a. As one source quoted by Yamamoto Hiroko puts it: "Asuka Mountain is a *cintāmaṇi* peak. The white fox now dwells on it." See Yamamoto 1993a: 358. The cult of the Sankoshin spread from Ise to Kumano, and further on to Fushimi Inari and Tōji.

100. "Inari saimon," in *Inari ichiryū daiji* 稲荷一流大事, cited in Nanami 1986: 77–78.

101. See Tochigi kenritsu hakubutsukan 1996: 81, fig. 84.

102. See *Shintōshū,* in *ST,* Bungaku-hen 1, *Shintōshū*: 74.

103. Interestingly, the fox is not considered here to be a mere assimilation body, as is usually the case with animal manifestations of Buddhist deities. As to what the bird represents, I have no clue. Perhaps it is a reference to the bird standing for the "earthly fox" in the exorcistic representations of the three foxes.

104. Tanaka Nariyuki 1993: 244. Another link between Dakiniten and Aizen is the fact that the latter was called King Takki (J. Taki 吒枳, written with the same characters as Daki(niten). On this name, see *Sanmai-ryū kudenshū, T.* 77, 2411: 18c; and Goepper 1993: 58–62.

105. *Keiran shūyōshū, T.* 76, 2410: 853a. We recall that Nyoirin Kannon was identified with the pole star deity Sonjōō (Myōken Bosatsu). Shinra Myōjin is said to be an avatar of both Monju and Amaterasu. Dakiniten is also a "trace" of Monju.

106. See *Tamon dakini kyō,* quoted in Abe Yasurō 1995: 156–57.

107. See Irie 2008.

108. On the bottom right of the scroll, too, a multi-armed deity riding—exceptionally—a green ox or buffalo (like King Yama) is also labeled "King Dakini."

109. For an analysis of this scroll, see Irie 2008. In the upper part of the scroll, Monju-Dakiniten is also surrounded by another set of eight attendants. In the *Tonjō shitsuji,* one of them, "Soul stealer," is said to have the form of Tamonten (Bishamonten).

110. *Keiran shūyōshū, T.* 76, 2410: 520c–521a. See also *Bikisho, ST,* Ronsetsu-hen 2, Shingon shintō 2: 512. This motif may go back to the Chinese belief that foxes produce fire when they hit their tails. The three-tailed vulpine form of Amaterasu also calls to mind one of the protectors of Miidera, known as "Three-tailed Deity" (Mio Myōjin 三尾明神). See for instance the *Onjōji denki* 園城寺伝記: "The Great Deity Amaterasu has three tails: a red one (Amaterasu); a black one (Shinra Myōjin); and a white one (Hakusan Gongen 白山権現). The three together are called Mio Myōjin." *DNBZ* 127: 11.

111. *ST,* Ronsetsu-hen 2, Shingon shintō 2: 499; I follow Allan Grapard's translation, with slight changes. See Grapard 2002–2003:144–145. On Kamatari's legend, see also Iyanaga 1999: 96–97.

112. This demoness is mentioned in Chinese commentaries on the *Lotus Sūtra,* for example Jizang's 吉藏 *Fahua yishu* 法華義疏 (*T.* 34, 1721: 630b) and Zhiyi's *Guanyin yishu* 観音義疏 (*T.* 34, 1728: 925a). In the Tendai tradition, see Enchin's *Bodaijōkyō ryakugishaku* 菩提場經略義釈 (*T.* 61, 2230: 526b); and Kōshū's *Keiran shūyōshū, T.* 76, 2410: 632a.

113. See Iyanaga 2002a: 97.

114. See *Heike monogatari, NKZS,* 1970: 120. See also Nanami 1986: 69, 194; and Kida 1976: 252.

115. McCullough 1988: 226; and Kida 1976: 252

116. See *Keiran shūyōshū, T.* 76, 2410: 628a.

117. Nanami 1986: 79.

118. On the relation between that dream and the exclusion of women from sacred mountains (*nyonin kekkai* 女人結界), see Faure 2003: 235–249.

119. Nanami 1986: 74.

120. *Keiran shūyōshū, T.* 76, 2410: 632a.

121. The site of the Dakiniten shrine is called Hoshi no mine (Star Peak), and its *honzon* was called Shinkoō Bosatsu. His six arms were said to symbolize the six paths of rebirth.

122. *Keiran shūyōshū, T.* 76, 2410: 633a.

123. See *Hoki naiden, ST,* Ronsetsu-hen 16, Onmyōdō: 64. See also Minobe 1982: 222; and Shirahara 1999: 11.

124. See *Hoki naiden, ST,* Ronsetsu-hen 16, Onmyōdō: 64; and Minobe

1982: 222–223. On the three Benzaiten, see *Keiran shūyōshū, T.* 76, 2410: 625ab; on the four princes, see also *Shintōshū,* in *ST,* Bungaku-hen 1, *Shintōshū*: 74–75; and Shirahara 1999.

125. Kōyasan Reihōkan 1994, fig. 30.

126. See *BZS* 2216.

127. Private collection, Paris.

128. Nanami 1986: 77.

129. Nanami 1986: 77–78.

130. *Shin[ko] bosatsu kuden* 辰菩薩口伝, in Kanagawa kenritsu Kanazawa bunko 2007b: 49a. Ranba (Skt. Lambā) and Niramba (Skt. Vilambā) appear in various contexts, for instance as demons flanking the earth deity, or as companion spirits (*kushōjin*). Ranba is also represented as a snake among the fifteen demons of the *Dōjikyō.* As a "soul stealer," Dakiniten is identified with another of the ten *rākṣasīs,* the "Soul-ravishing Demoness." See infra.

131. *ST,* Bungakuhen 1, *Shintōshū*: 72–77.

132. *T.* 76, 2410: 732a. King Shintamani is said to have seven servants (a couple of foxes and their five children, who become kings of the five regions of India), and symbolize the seven jewels of the *cakravartin* king. See *T.* 76, 2410: 732a. This legend reflects the Onmyōdō notion of the five foxes as regents of the five phases.

133. See the *Shin[koō] bosatsu kuden jō kuketsu* 辰菩薩口伝上口訣, in Kanagawa kenritsu Kanazawa bunko 2007b: 50c; see also Kushida 1973: 320–321. In the apocryphal *Dakini sendari-ō kyō* 吒枳尼旃陀利王經, a female bodhisattva by the name of Byakushinko-ō 白辰狐王 (King of White Astral Foxes) springs from the ground during a Dharma assembly. The Buddha introduces her to the audience as the king of this world, from whom all earthly rulers derive their authority. See Nakazawa 1994: 247. According to the *Shirushi no sugi*, the name of that bodhisattva is an alias for Dakiniten as the "divine body" (*shintai* 神体) of Inari. See *NSSS* 26: 694; and *ST,* Jinja-hen 9, Inari: 418.

134. See *Keiran shūyōshū, T.* 76, 2410: 732a.

135. *Shintōshū,* in *ST,* Bungaku-hen 1, *Shintōshū*: 73–74.

136. See Itō Satoshi 1993: 44–45. This sūtra is another clue to the combination of the cults of Dakiniten and Ugajin. The *Keiran shūyōshū* mentions it under a slightly different title, *Sūtra of the King of the One-Letter Heart Incantation* (*Ichiji shinju-ō kyō* 一字心呪王經), and says that it was transmitted at Miidera. *T.* 76, 2410: 633b. Several apocryphal scriptures on Dakiniten (Shinkoō Bosatsu) appear in a list of Tachikawa-ryū works, among which the *Shinkoō nyoirin kyō* 辰狐王如意輪經 (Sūtra of the King of the Astral Foxes with the Wish-fulfilling Jewel) and the *Shinkoō jōju nyoi hōjū kyō* 辰狐王成就如意宝珠經 (Sutra of the King of the Astral Foxes Who Produces (or becomes) the *Cintāmaṇi*). These scriptures seem to belong to the same vein as the Ugajin apocrypha.

137. Kushida 1973: 321. See also *Tonjō shitsuji kudenshū* 頓成悉地口伝集, in Kanagawa kenritsu Kanazawa bunko 2007b: 61a.

138. See Shirahara 1999: 7–24; and Kuo 2004.

139. See *Shintōshū,* in *ST,* Bungaku-hen 1, *s*: 74; see also *Keiran shūyōshū, T.* 76, 2410: 774a.

140. *Hoki naiden, ST,* Ronsetsu-hen 16, Onmyōdō: 64. The snake-headed figures in the Tenkawa mandala are also called the "Three Princes," but they form the retinue of Benzaiten, not of Dakiniten, and their look is strikingly different. Note also the Dakiniten mandala of Ichigami Shrine (Yōkaichi), where a fox-riding, two-armed Dakiniten, wearing Ugajin on her headgear, is surrounded by ten acolytes, as well as Bishamonten (with his symbolic animal, the centipede) and Kichijōten. See Shiga kenritsu Biwako bunkakan 1991a, fig. 54.

141. See Kanagawa kenritsu Kanazawa bunko 2007b: 55b.

142. The manual translated by Antelmo Severini (Severini 1874: 34), reflecting a tradition that probably goes back to the Muromachi period, says that this deity is the "minister of Taishakuten's paradize," and that he roams the three worlds to prepare reports on their inhabitants. Taishakuten (Śakra, the Buddhist name of Indra) himself comes to inspect the beings of the Jambudvīpa three times a year (during the 1st, 5th, and 9th months). See *T.* 54, 2127: 304c.

In China, Śakra came to be related to Daoist beliefs about the *kōshin* 庚申 day (the 57th day of the sexagesimal cycle) and the three corpses (*sanshi* 三尸). See Kubo Noritada 1961: 705; and Soymié 1966. In the Buddhist tradition, he does not inspect the world himself, but receives the reports of the four deva kings, who each inspect a quarter of the world. See Frank 1998: 122–124. The locus classicus is the *Sitienwang jing* 四天王經, a text included in several *Āgamas* (*T.* 1, 1: 124–135, *T.* 2, 99: 295–296, *T.* 2, 125: 624–625). See also *Dazhidulun, T.* 25, 1509: 160a. An apocryphal *Sūtra of the Four Deva Kings,* the *Foshuo sitianwang jing* 佛說四天王經, is also included in *T.* 15, 590. See Iyanaga 1983: 764–765.

143. See *ST,* Bungaku-hen 1, *Shintōshū*: 75. Incidentally, in the legend of Kūya Shōnin 空也上人 (903–972), Monju appears as a fox.

144. The eight *dōji* are also represented in the Izuna mandala of Rinnōji, whose cartouches give us names for seven of the eight: 1) Moriya no kami 守屋神 (House-protecting deity); 2) Datsukonpakujin 奪魂魄神 (*Hun*-stealing deity); 3) Hajusojin; 4) Gonin daijin 護人大神; 5) Chōga shinnō 挑我神王 (Divine king Chōga, "Challenging Self"); 6) Misshō shinnō 未称神王 ("As yet unnamed divine king"?); and 7) Aikei daijin 愛敬大神 (Great god of love subduing). See Fig. 3.20. The same seven names are given in *ST,* Bungaku-hen 1: *Shintōshū*, 74–76. These youths call to mind the eight children (Hachi ōji 八王子 'eight princes') of Gozu Tennō; one of them, at least, is said to be the cause of diseases.

145. As is well known, in Japan the catfish is a mythical animal that is held responsible for earthquakes. See Ouwehand 1964. It is also associated with Benzaiten in the myth of origins of Chikubushima Island.

146. The name of Ototari also appears in ritual texts of Onmyōdō in relation to fox exorcisms. On this legend, see *Onmyōdō kakeru mikkyō,* 2007b: 51c.

147. The *Shintōshū* mentions eight *dōji,* but only gives the names of

seven: Moriya no kami, Datsukonpakujin, Hajusojin, Gonin daijin, Chōga shinnō, Misshō shinnō, and Aikei daijin. *ST,* Bungaku-hen 1: *Shintōshū,* 75–76; see also Kanagawa kenritsu Kanazawa bunko 2007b: 51a; Irie Tami 2008; and *BZS* 78.

148. On the ten *rākṣasīs,* see Fabricand-Person 2002.

149. See *Shintōshū,* in *ST,* Bungaku-hen 1: *Shintōshū,* 75–76.

150. See *Tonjō shitsuji hō kuketsu mondō,* in Kanagawa kenritsu Kanazawa bunko 2007b: 66b. Ton'yugyō is also said to be an avatar of Fudō, and Shuyuchisō an avatar of Aizen. As a dyad, they symbolize the Vajra and Womb realms.

151. In his *Shintōshū ryakushō* 神道集略鈔, the Pure Land monk Taichū 袋中 (1552–1639) states that the two figures are *shikigami.* But he adds that, during the twelve hours of the day, Ton'yugyō brings happiness to people, whereas Shuyuchisō steals their longevity. See Yokoyama 1970: 162.

152. Also worth mentioning as a toothing stone is the presence, among the acolytes of Dakiniten, of deities "that constantly follow [people]." That expression calls to mind the "companion spirits" (*kushōjin*) who watch people and report on their actions, thus determining their fate and longevity. Indeed, some of these acolytes are specifically described as *kushōjin.* See *ST,* Bungaku-hen 1, *Shintōshū*: 75.

153. See Shirahara 1999. The Metropolitan Museum exemplar is similar, although its facture is simpler, more stylized. The fox appears to fly on a cloud, against a background of undulated geometric patterns that evokes waves. It has no snakes coiled around its legs. There are three jewels above, a fire halo, with the moon on the left, the sun on the right.

154. See Takahashi Yusuke 2006a: 14.

155. See also *BZS* 4088. Another representation of Nyorai Kōjin shows him surrounded by eight demon attendants, including two of which are *vināyakas* (one with an elephant head, the other with a sow head). *BZS* 4087.

156. See the legend of Dakiniten in the *Keiran shūyōshū, T.* 76, 2410: 631c. The *Shintōshū* explains that Dakiniten's four acolytes, which are emanations of the Five Phases, manifest themselves in the four orients and the four seasons, and protect the twelve months and the twelve hours. *ST,* Bungaku-hen 1: *Shintōshū,* 75.

157. *Keiran shūyōshū, T.* 76, 2410: 774a. According to the *Tonjō shitsuji chiban hō shidai* 頓條成悉地地盤法次第 by a disciple of Kenna, the heavenly maiden is in the southeast (trigram *son* 巽), the red maiden in the southwest (trigram *kon* 坤), the black maiden in the northwest (trigram *kan* 乾), and Indra's emissary in the northeast (*ushitora*). See Kanagawa kenritsu Kanazawa bunko 2007b: 59a–b; and Nishioka Yoshifumi 2007: 16.

158. In the introduction to the exhibition catalogue and also in a recent article (Kanazawa bunko kenkyū 320, 2008), Nishioka complains about the lack of documentation regarding Buddhist divination on the Chinese side. This is true, but some progress has been made recently, at least in Western scholarship. Apart from Michel Strickmann's *Chinese Poetry and Prophecy* (2005), which focuses on fortune strips (J. *omikuji* 御御籤, 御神籤 from a cross-cultural perspective, there is an article by Kuo Liying (1994b) which

describes Chinese Buddhist divination boards (and Buddhist *sugoroku* games) that present similarities to our Japanese exemplars. Then there is Marc Kalinowski's edited book on Chinese divination as revealed in Dunhuang manuscripts, which describes a method of divination centered on Maheśvara (Daijizaiten) that may be related to those found in the Kanazawa bunko catalogue, centered mainly on Dakiniten and Shōten. See Kalinowski 2003.

159. On Kenna and his abbotship at Shōmyōji, see Kushida 1973: 541; and Kanagawa kenritsu Kanazawa bunko 2007b: 6–7.

160. On the *liuren* method, see Kalinowski 1983.

161. See the photograph in Hiroshima kenritsu rekishi hakubutsukan 1990, reproduced in Abe Yasurō 1995: 159. The first level (*tenban*) shows an unclear number of unknown deities; the second level, five winged deities, and the third and fourth levels (corresponding to the *chiban*), twelve deities each (representing the twelve cyclical animals and the generals of the twelve months).

162. The similarity should alert us to the fact that what we usually see as star mandalas might actually be diagrams of divination boards.

163. In a variant, the heavenly board (*tenban*) corresponds to the head, the earthly board (*chiban*) to the trunk and limbs. This is perhaps why skull bones were supposed to be placed in the *tenban,* bones of arms and legs in the *chiban.* We are reminded here of the skull ritual (also centered on Dakiniten) described in Sanford 1991a.

164. See Tohyō Nyoirin mandara, Ōsu bunko archives, box 297, 108; and *Gojikkanshō, SZ* 30: 145–147.

165. *Keiran shūyōshū, T.* 76, 2410: 732c. On the Dakiniten ritual, see Nishioka 2013: 153–155; Hayashi 1994; and Shirahara 1999.

166. See *Keiran shūyōshū, T.* 76, 2410: 732c. The term *dada* is said to come from *dada-fumi,* a ritual trampling performed at the New Year Festival to arouse the powers of the earth and push demonic forces into the ground. See Caillet 1981b: 107–109. Another etymology derives it from *danda-in* 'danda seal,' a term perhaps related to Enmaten's *daṇḍa* staff. See Caillet 1981a: 239–240.

167. To cure the disease, one must empower oneself (*kaji*) with the mantra of Fudō and the sword mudrā. In particular, when one "deposits" this mudrā in the afflicted body parts, the suffering disappears. Another mudrā to be used for empowerment is that of Mahākāla, from which the secret method for the prolongation of life beyond the six months derives.

168. *Keiran shūyōshū, T.* 76, 2410: 732c. This ritual may be related to the magic cult of the *inugami* 犬神 (dog deity), which also uses at its *honzon* the skull of a dog. One may also use the head of a live fox, or a golden or silver image (as in the enthronement ritual), or else a wooden image.

169. See *Jakushōdō kokkyōshū,* in *DNBZ* 94, 834: 155, and *Shirushi no sugi, ST,* Jinja-hen 9, Inari: 417. Adrian Snodgrass refers to the latter conception when he writes that the *ḍākinī* will eat the defilements in the hearts of men. See Snodgrass 1988: 485. This expurgated version of Dakiniten's image is belied by the representation of the mandala itself, where a *ḍākinī* devours the *membra disjecta* of a corpse. As noted above, a similar hermeneutic move,

amounting to an attempt at sorting out the doctrinal wheat from the magical chaff, was observed in the case of Mahākāla and similar dubious characters.

170. *Kiyū shōran,* 2: 310. See also *Shirushi no sugi,* in *ST,* Jinja-hen 9, Inari: 417; and Sasama 1988: 36. The same distinction is already found in India, where the beings devoured by the *ḍākinīs* are interpreted allegorically as the "five aggregates" (*skandha*) that create the illusion of a self. In Tibet, the Chöd school, created by a "flesh and blood" *ḍākinī* called Machig Labron, emphasized techniques of visualization that consisted in dismembering oneself mentally as an offering to the goddess. The Tibetans also distinguish two types of *ḍākinī:* the "Gnostic" (*ye shes*) and the flesh-eating (*sha za*)—in other words, the otherworldy and the worldly, the helpful and the harmful, the divine and the demonic. Janet Gyatso writes: "A common distinction . . . with respect to divinities, that is, between the 'worldly' (*laukika*), malevolent ones, and the enlightened ones who are 'beyond the world' (*lokottara*), is also applied to *ḍākinīs.* But the distinction easily blurs, for the same violent characteristics that originally might have made a spirit 'worldly' are just those that were assimilated into their tantric roles as enlightened, if somewhat fierce, deities." Gyatso 1999: 247. See also Kuo 2003.

171. Kanagawa kenritsu Kanazawa bunko 2007b: 56c. On the "soul-stealing" *rākṣasī* (Skt. Sarvasattvōjāhārī), see Jizang's 吉藏 *Commentary on the Lotus Sūtra, T.* 34, 1721: 630b; and Zhiyi's *Commentary* on the same scripture, *T.* 34, 1728: 925c, quoted by Enchin in *T.* 61, 2230: 526b. I am indebted to Iyanaga Nobumi for these references.

172. The two aspects are then compared to the buddhas Prabhutaratna (J. Tahōtō 多宝塔) and Śākyamuni (Shaka), dwelling like peas in a pod in their stūpa: "Prabhutaratna is the bones of the innumerable past lives of beings, Śākyamuni is the Tathāgata King of Astral Foxes (Shinkoō Nyorai) of beginningless kalpas. The motionless eating of bones is the ultimate principle of 'becoming a buddha in this very body' (*sokushin jōbutsu* 即身成仏) as expounded in the One Vehicle. Because subject and object are nondual, they dwell in one stūpa." Kanagawa kenritsu Kanazawa bunko 2007b: 50c.

173. *T.* 76, 2410: 632b.

174. See "Dakiniten to Fuku Daimyōjin," in Kida 1976: 330–338. Dakiniten merges with Ugajin: "The white fox is Ugajin" (ibid., 334). Under the name Tenko (heavenly fox), she also came to be confused with the *tengu.* This may be why Akiba Gongen, usually represented as a *tengu* riding a fox, is worshiped as a god of fortune. On Akiba Gongen, see Tamura Sadao 1998.

175. See "Inari Daimyōjin no koto" in *ST,* Bungaku-hen, *Shintōshū:* 72–77.

176. *ST,* Jinja-hen, Hizen, Higo: 570.

177. See *Jakushōdō kokkyōshū:* 154–155; Kida 1976: 333. On Izuna Myōjin, see Sasama 1988: 95–114; and Kawasoe 2006.

178. The wings call to mind those of the Three-Deva deity and suggest a Persian, or perhaps Christian, influence. I thank Hank Glassman for drawing my attention to this detail.

179. On Izuna rituals and Dakiniten rituals, see Sanford 1991a:16–18; Strickmann 2002: 271.

180. These mountains are all Shugendō sites known for their *tengu,* and it is possible that the latter's association with foxes was facilitated by the quasi-homophony between *tenko* 'heavenly fox' and *tengu.* See also *Izuna Daimyōjin engi,* in Gorai 2000, 1: 470–471; and *Tamakisan gongen engi,* in Gorai 2000, 2: 151. See also Yamamoto 1993a: 356.

181. On the Shōgun Jizō cult of Mount Atago, see Bouchy 1979. The *tengu* of Mount Atago are associated with wild boars, however, not with foxes.

182. See Gorai 2000, 1: 470–472.

183. See for instance Tominaga Nakamoto 富永仲基, *Okina no fumi* 翁の文: "The tendency peculiar to Buddhism is magic, which is now called 'sorcery' (*izuna*)." Tominaga, however, nuances this statement by a comment: "The Old Man explained things in this way, but supernatural powers (*jinzū* 神通) and sorcery (*izuna*) are two different things. Sorcery comes from magical skill (*jutsu* 術) and supernatural powers from training (*shugyō* 修行). However the Old Man was right in his arguments." Tominaga 1967: 209, in Katō Shūichi's translation (slightly modified). See also Casal 1959: 22–23. "Certain 'sorcerers' are said to employ a method of capturing their fox servants first used on Mount Izuna in Shinano, and therefore known as the *Izuna-tsukai.* Although some shrines on the mountain were dedicated to the Food-deity, *Ukemochi-no-kami,* Izuna was popularly regarded, rather, as the abode of *Dakini* (or *Dagini-ten, Daten*), also known as Kiki Tennô, 'The Heavenly King, the Venerable Fox'. . . . The mountain's name, Izuna, is itself believed to mean Embodied Sorcery."

184. Wilbur Hansen 2008: 150.

185. See Gorai 1985b: 80.

186. See Gorai 1985b: 87–111.

187. On the notion of "becoming-animal," see Deleuze and Guattari 1987: 232–309.

CHAPTER 4: FROM GODDESS TO DRAGON

1. On this mysogynistic topos, see Faure 2003a: 55–62.

2. The two- and eight-armed images are described in iconographic compendia such as the *Besson zakki*: 238–241; the *Shikeshō zuzō* 2, figs. 217–218; and the *Shoson zuzō shū,* figs. 45–47.

3. This second type derives from the eight-armed type (with a first intermediary stage, in which warrior attributes were replaced by the wish-fulfilling jewel and the key, symbols of wealth; and a second stage, in which the number of arms was reduced, and only the sword and the jewel remained.

4. Ludvik 2001: 156.

5. Ludvik 2001: 295.

6. Ludvik 2001: 70.

7. Ludvik 2001: 85.

8. *Ṛg-veda* X, 125, v. 6, in Doniger (O'Flaherty), *Rig Veda,* 1981: 63. Certain texts indeed link Durgā with Vāc (and thus, indirectly, with Sarasvatī).

9. See Ludvik 2001: 15 and 18. See also Ludvik 1998a, 1998b, and 2000.

10. Ludvik 2001: 52. In the Vedas, however, the slaying of the dragon Vṛtra is attributed to Rudra; see Doniger 1975: 74–90.

11. Dumézil writes: "In short this goddess, which her intrinsic nature (as river), part of her definition (as mother, fecundating, nourishing, etc.), and finally her links with the Aśvins locate in the third function, is nonetheless very at ease in the two higher functions: . . . destroying the enemy, she is a warrior; pure, queen of good thoughts, inspiring and channelling piety, she belongs to the realm of the sovereign gods." Dumézil 1968: 107.

12. See Dumézil 1968: 106–107.

13. Ludvik 2001: 50–51.

14. Ludvik 2001: 51 and 58.

15. Ludvik 2001: 15.

16. See *T.* 16: 437c. The main textual sources include the various translations of the *Suvarṇaprabhāsa-sūtra* (*T.* 663, 664, and 665); the *Da fangguang rulai bimi zang jing* 大方広如来秘密藏經 (*T.* 17, 821: 837), the *Mahavairocana-sūtra* (*T.* 18, 848: 1; *T.* 20, 1092: 227); and Yixing's commentary on the latter (*T.* 39, 1796: 579). See also Nobel 1958, 1: 227–268. Also noteworthy are esoteric ritual manuals like the *Yōson dōjōkan* 要尊道場観 by Shunnyū 淳祐; see *T.* 78, 2468: 39.

17. *T.* 663 ends here. It limits the gifts of Sarasvatī to eloquence and intelligence, allowing understanding of sūtras and quick achievement of awakening.

18. As Ludvik (2001) and others have pointed out, Kauṇḍinya's eulogy is borrowed from a Hindu text, the *Harivaṃsa.* See *T.* 16, 665: 437a.

19. See *T.* 18: 876a, *T.* 20: 282; *T.* 21: 215c. See also the *Sanbō ekotoba,* in Kamens 1988: 251.

20. *T.* 18, 848 and *T.* 39, 1796.

21. See *Kakuzenshō, DNBZ* 50: 305: "Private note: The *Saishōkyō* [sic] states that Benzaiten is the elder sister of Yama. This is why she is placed [in this mandala.]"

22. See Ludvik 1999–2000.

23. Yoshida 1961–1962.

24. Ludvik 2001: 4.

25. Ludvik 1999–2000: 297.

26. Unfortunately, the only study on the Tibetan Sarasvatī is a short essay by Alex Wayman. In Tibetan texts, Sarasvatī is no longer a river goddess; she is represented as a maiden of sixteen (whereas in India she is often a girl of twelve). She is also the object of various *sādhanās,* in which she is usually visualized with four arms (there is also a three-faced, six-armed form). In one case at least, she is associated with Mañjuśrī in his fierce form as the "Subduer of Yama" (Yamāntaka). See Wayman 1984.

27. *T.* 76, 2410: 620.

28. Tsunemasa in his youth had been a *chigo* at Ninnaji, where he returned the famous lute when he had to flee the capital with the Taira.

29. McCullough 1988: 226.

30. Fritsch 1996: 33–41.

31. Fritsch 1996: 33.

32. See *Lotus Sūtra,* chap. 23.

33. On the different types of *biwa* (*gagaku biwa, mōsō biwa,* and *Heike*

biwa), see James T. Araki 1964: 49; see also Bialock 2002–2003. Another goddess represented with a *biwa* is Venus (Kin'yō 金曜 or Taihaku 太白), one of the nine "seizers" of the star mandalas. On the origins of the blind monks, see *NSSS* 17: 247–248, and "Bussetsu mōsō engi" in Nishi Nihon bunka kyōkai 1993: 565–569.

34. Fritsch 1996: 63.

35. See Masuo 2001; Murata 1994: 12–40.

36. Whereas the *mōsō* of Kyūshū passed under the authority of Hieizan during the Edo period, those of Yamato were placed under the authority of Kōfukuji in Nara. Another branch, that of the *mōsō* of Tōhoku, was under the patronage of Chūsonji 中尊寺 in Hiraizumi.

37. See Fritsch 1996; and Hyōdō 2009: 159–183. On the Tōdōza, see *NSSS* 17: 231; see also Matisoff 1973: 43 ff.

38. On Semimaru, see Matisoff 1973 and Fritsch 1996: 148; on Amayo and Komiya, see Fritsch 1996: 116–130.

39. This may also explain how the blind Semimaru became a manifestation of the crossroads deity (Dōsojin). See *Jimon denki horoku:* 197b. The *Keiran shūyōshū* identifies him with Myōon Bosatsu and Benzaiten.

40. On Komiya, see Fritsch 1996: 116–130.

41. *Komiya taishi ichidaiki,* quoted in Fritsch 1996: 123–127. Here, Chikubushima is still Myōon Benzaiten's site, whereas it later became Uga Benzaiten's stronghold.

42. See Shitō Shin'yū, ed., "Shiryō Komiya taishi ichidai ki," in Tōhoku minzoku no kai, ed., *Tōhoku minzoku,* vol. 11: 32–37; quoted in Fritsch 1996: 127–128. All these variants reflect the differences in the target groups of the legend. The legend of Prince Komiya, for instance, was widespread among lower status blind monks, whereas that of Prince Saneyasu 人康 (831–872), fourth son of Ninmyō Tennō, was more widespread in aristocratic circles. See Tanigawa 2009: 367–369.

43. See Fritsch 1996: 139.

44. On Kenreimon'in, see Hyōdō 2009: 118–119; and Bialock 2002–2003: 293–303.

45. On this tradition, see Fritsch 1996: 198–231.

46. Fritsch 1996: 217. In a myth related to the blind singers, Benzaiten plays the *biwa* to make Amaterasu come out of the cave in which she has withdrawn. Here she replaces Ame no Uzume, the goddess who, through her inspired dance (said to be the origin of *sarugaku*), had made the gods roar with laughter, causing Amaterasu's curiosity.

47. Fritsch 1996: 249.

48. See Triplett 2004: 65–125; and Fritsch 1996: 29–30.

49. See for instance the *Śatapatha-Brāhmaṇa* 11:2:6:3, cited in Ludvik 2001: 65.

50. *T.* 76, 2410: 620a.

51. The identification of Benzaiten (Sarasvatī) with the *cintāmaṇi* can also be traced back to the legend of Zhiyi. This *cintāmaṇi* was defined as the "essence of the Precepts." See *Keiran shūyōshū, T.* 76, 2410: 544bc; and Yamamoto 1998a.

52. The vase is not specific to the Benzaiten cult; however, it is a ritual implement in many esoteric *sādhanās.* On this point, see for instance Beyer 1978.

53. The seed-letters of the fifteen youths (*jūgo dōji* 十五童子) that form her retinue also played an important ritual role in the initial protection of the practitioner's body (Skt. *nyāsa,* J. *fuji* 布字).

54. Colophon dated Kōan 1/7/12, at Saidaiji, by Eison and Senne.

55. *Keiran shūyōshū, T.* 76, 2410: 623.

56. *Keiran shūyōshū, T.* 76, 2410: 619c ff. On the dragon king palace as the locus of ignorance, see *T.* 76, 2410: 624b. Benzaiten's gender is occasionally questioned, however. The *Asabashō,* for instance, quoting a passage in which Benzaiten is said to have (female) consorts, asks: "Is this a male deva?" *TZ* 9: 506a. Most sources, however, refer to her as a "heavenly woman" (*tennyo* 天女)—a term that reflects a Daoist influence.

57. See Faure 2002–2003.

58. See *Tenchin jingi shinchin yōki,* in *ST,* Ronsetsu-hen, Tendai shintō 1: 466. See also Yamamoto 1998b: 58–61.

59. *Tenchin jingi shinchin yōki,* in *ST,* Ronsetsu-hen, Tendai shintō 1: 465. On the relation of Benzaiten with Sakadono, see *Bikisho,* in *ST,* Ronsetsu-hen, Shingon shintō 2: 507; and *Gengenshū* 元元集, in *ST,* Ronsetsu-hen, Tendai shintō 1: 465. In the *Gengenshū,* Sakadono is added to the six sacred sites of Benzaiten as the most secret of all (p. 466). The same source describes the eight maidens who came to earth as the eight Benzaiten who rule heaven and earth. It also identifies the last one, who temporarily remained on earth and introduced alcohol and medicine into human culture, with the "classical" goddess Ame no Uzume. In the Suwa tradition, because of the phonetic resemblance between sake and the morpheme *saku/suku,* the deity of Sakadono is identified with the deity called Shukujin.

Benzaiten's functional relation with alcohol brings to mind Dionysos. One could apply to her what Michael Pollan says about the Greek god: "Nothing better captures the paradox of Dionysos's double role as a force for domestication *and* wildness, than his involvement with grape and wine." See Pollan 2002: 38. Perhaps, like alcohol, Benzaiten, who is a both a goddess of music and a "wild god" (*kōjin*), bridging the alleged gap between culture and nature, is the kind of deity that "suffuses the world around us . . . with the warm glow of meaning" (Pollan 2002:38).

60. *Shugendō yōten*, 34–35. I translate *tennyo* as "heavenly woman" rather than "celestial maiden" because the representations of Benzaiten show her as a rather imposing woman, almost a matron. Yet, in the *Keiran shūyōshū,* she is often compared to the *nāga* maiden of the *Lotus Sūtra.*

61. See *TZ* 9: 505bc.

62. *TZ* 9: 505b.

63. See also *Hishō mondō* by Raiyu 頼瑜 (1226–1304), *T.* 79. 2536: 496c–497a, who bases his definition of Benzaiten as a *gandharva* on the *Golden Light Sūtra.*

64. *T.* 76, 2410: 624a.

65. Ludvik 2001: 85–100.

66. Ludvik 2001: 94–95.

67. See Dumézil 1929.

68. Dumézil writes: "We are therefore justified in regarding the identity of the three names Gandharva, Februo-, Kentauro-—give or take a few articulatory nuances—as a probability." See Dumézil 1988: 31.

69. In India, the famous Sarasvatī *puja* still takes place nowadays at the beginning of February.

70. *T.* 76, 2410: 772b. See also Yamamoto 1993a: 275.

71. *Shingon hiōshō,* quoted inYamamoto 1993: 280.

72. McCullough 1988: 105.

73. There was also an Itsukushima shrine in Kyoto, south of the imperial palace, built by Taira no Kiyomori for his presumed mother, the famous courtesan Gion Nyōgo 祇園女御, after his pilgrimage to the original shrine in Aki province.

74. According to Kobayashi Taichirō, however, this sūtra was not offered by Kiyomori himself in 1164, but a few years later by his concubine, an Itsukushima priestess known as Itsukushima no naishi 嚴島内侍. Kiyomori had a daughter from her, born precisely in 1164, who later became one of the consorts (*nyōgo*) of retired emperor Go-Shirakawa. See Kobayashi Taichirō 1946; and Frank 1994–1995. This illustrated *Lotus Sūtra* would represent the feminine esthetic sensibilities prevalent at court and influenced by the style of the *Genji monogatari.*

75. McCullough 1988: 132–133.

76. See McCullough 1988: 173; and Minobe 1982: 216. According to the *Gukanshō,* "the Itsukushima deity is said to be the daughter of the dragon king. In response to Kiyomori's profound reverence for her, she herself was reborn as this emperor [Antoku]." See Okami and Akamatsu 1967: 265. See also the Kakuichi-bon recension of the *Heike monogatari,* 1: 223, translated in McCullough 1988: 104–105.

77. Brown and Ishida 1979: 143. Antoku was also said to be the reincarnation of the eight-headed dragon Yamata no Orochi 八岐大蛇, who had been killed by Susanoo and who had returned to this world to recover the divine sword and take it back to the dragon palace. The dragon nature of Susanoo himself is suggested by the ritual through which the members of the Miwa clan, who claim descent from him, prayed for rain. They danced in the garden of Shinsen'en, wearing a red hat and a straw coat like Susanoo, to mime the god's pitiful exile. See Matsumoto Nobuhiro 1928: 39. Several descendants of Susanoo are also snake gods associated with thunder. On Susanoo as a thunder god, see Ouwehand 1958. See also *Taiheiki, NKBT* 33.348–349, quoted in Brown and Ishida 1979: 143n47.

78. McCullough 1979: 134–135.

79. See de Visser 1913.

80. McCullough 1988: 436.

81. On this question, see de Visser 1913; and Schafer 1980: 15–37.

82. Schafer 1980: 36.

83. See Tsuji Hidenori 1970.

84. On this question, see Ruppert 2000: 156; and Trenson 2002–2003.

85. See McCullough 1988: 93.

86. See *Ga'un nikkenroku batsuyū,* s. v. "Bun'an 4 (1447).4.17"; cited in Tanaka Takako 1993: 28.

87. *Reikiki,* in *ST,* Ronsetsu-hen, Shingon shintō 1: 206.

88. A case in point is the "spring of the *nāga* palace" (*ryūgū-sui*) near Gion Shrine, which was said to communicate with the *nāga* palace, as well as with the springs of Shinsen'en and of Kanjō-in at Tōji (two places centered on the cult of the *nāga* Zenmyō). See Inoue 1968: 70–71.

89. On this question, see Faure 1999.

90. See *Keiran shūyōshū, T.* 76, 2410: 624a.

91. Eventually, the mythical empress Jingū 神功 too was inserted into that motif, becoming a *nāgī* herself. We are told for instance that, to ensure the success of her famous expedition to Korea, Empress Jingū sent her sister to the *nāga* palace, to retrieve the *cintāmaṇi.* Incidentally, this sister, called Toyohime (an obvious doublet of Toyotama-hime 豊玉姫), was said to have had a dragon body. According to the *Taiheiki,* for instance: "Likewise it is said of the Empress Jingū of our court, that going forth against Silla she caused the waters to recede by casting a tide-ebbing pearl upon the surface of the sea, wherefore at last she was enabled to win a victory in the fighting." McCullough 1979: 290. In the *Mizu kagami* 水鏡, the story is more detailed, but the dragon sister is replaced by a deity called Kawakami Daimyōjin. See de Visser 1913: 142–143.

92. On this legend, see Triplett 2004.

93. See Fritsch 1996: 30; and Triplett 2004.

94. The fear of dragon women is well reflected in the legend of the ascetic Gaken 我見, who, when trying to have sex with a mysterious woman, has his tongue bitten off by her, upon which she regains her dragon shape. See *Hikosan ruki,* in Gorai 2000, 2: 466b.

95. Schafer 1980: 188.

96. Tanaka Takako 1992: 186–187. Benzaiten is said to have initially protected the bakufu in response to a prayer from the charismatic priest Mongaku 文覚, a supporter of Yoritomo. More specifically, Yoritomo is also said to have appealed to Benzaiten on Mongaku's advice in order to defeat Fujiwara no Hidehira 藤原秀衡. Here Benzaiten manifests herself as a warrior deity. See Kanagawa kenritsu Kanazawa bunko 2007a, text 39. On this question, see also Itō Satoshi 2007: 31–67.

97. Tanaka Takako 1992: 187. Several variants of that story can be found, in which Benzaiten, having received the teaching of Rankei, gives him as protector a female youth (*dōji*). When the rumor spreads that Rankei has an illicit relationship with the girl, the shōgun (or his consort) comes to investigate the matter. The girl then is transformed into a large snake that disappears into the temple's pond. Summoned by Rankei, she returns to her initial form. While the identity of Rankei's protector varies, in certain versions it is said to be Oto Gohō 乙護法 or Sensha Dōji 船車童子, the last-born of Benzaiten's fifteen children. On this question, see Itō Satoshi 2007. Rankei is also said to have converted Suwa Myōjin, another snake god.

98. See de Visser 1913: 169–170. Another interesting variant of the Miwa myth is found in the story of Koizumi no Kotarō 小泉小太郎: a priest follows the woman after sticking a thread in her dress, and discovers a cave where a big snake is giving birth to a child. The snake dies, and the child is washed away by a flood into a lake. Adopted by an old woman, he turns out to be of enormous strength and becomes a regional culture hero. See Ouwehand 1958: 148–149.

99. Tanaka Takako 1992: 189. This story recalls the Miwa myth, although the genders of the two protagonists are inverted: in the Miwa myth, it is a young girl who secretly follows her nighttime lover, and discovers that he is a snake god.

CHAPTER 5: FROM DRAGON TO SNAKE

1. *Kōko zōtō hishō,* in Kokubungaku kenkyū shiryōkan 1999a: 372.

2. An example of the earlier pairing is the two large clay statues of Benzaiten (the oldest extant) and Kichijōten at the Hokke-dō 法華堂 (also known as Sangatsu-dō 三月堂) of Tōdaiji.

3. On this text and the ritual it describes, see Yamamoto 1998a: 356–390. Kenchū played an important role in the development of the Benzaiten cult in Tendai. During the years 1234–1259, he resided at the Sannō-dō in Kamakura. His works include the *Benzaiten shugi hiketsu* 弁才天修儀秘決, the *Makakara-ten kushiki* 摩訶伽羅天供式, and perhaps the *Hie hongi* 日吉本紀 (1235).

4. Among them are the *Bussetsu saishō gokoku Ugaya tontoku nyoi hōju-ō darani kyō* 佛說最勝護国宇賀耶頓得如意宝珠王陀羅尼經 *(hereafter: Ugaya darani-kyō). The Bussetsu sokushin tonten fukutoku enman Uga shinshō bosatsu hakuja jigen mikka jōju kyō* 佛說即身貪転福徳円満宇賀神将菩薩白蛇示現三日成就經, and the *Bussetsu Uga shinnō fukutoku enman darani-kyō* 佛說宇賀神王福徳円満陀羅尼經. The first two were allegedly translated by Amoghavajra, the third by Kumārajīva. This trio later came to be called the "three sūtras of Benzaiten" (*sanbukyō* 三部經). See Yamamoto 1998a: 475–502. With the addition of the *Bussetsu dai ugajin kudoku Benzaiten kyō* 佛說大宇賀神功徳弁才天經 and *Daibenzaitennyo himitsu darani-kyō* 大弁才天女秘密陀羅尼經, the group came to be called the "five sūtras of Benzaiten" (*gobukyō* 五部經).

In the introduction to his Benzaiten section in the *Keiran shūyōshū,* Kōshū mentions the following scriptures: the *Enman darani kyō* 円満陀羅尼經; the *Shinshō darani kyō* 神将陀羅尼經; the *Uga chōja kyō* 宇賀長者經; the *Jūgo ōji kyō* 十五王子經; and the *Tōjime kyō* 刀自目經. See *T.* 76, 2410: 620a. Among the Uga Benzaiten-related documents cited in the *Keiran shūyōshū,* only one, the *Enman daranikyō,* is found among the texts collected in the Edo period under the titles *sanbukyō* 三部經 and *gobukyō* 五部經. Itō Satoshi has introduced two new Benzaiten-related texts from the Yoshida Library (Tenri University). These texts, however, seem to correspond to those collected in the apocryphal *Benzaiten kunō kyō* 弁才天功能經. The *Keiran shūyōshū* also mentions various works by the Tendai priest Kenchū, including the *Benzaiten daishugi.*

5. On this deity, see Bryson 2010. On the *Long Roll,* see Chapin 1972; Li 1967; and Matsumoto Moritaka 1976. Of course, *nāgas* in human form with snake-head hoods also appear in India, but the Indian *nāginī* usually looks like a half-naked *yakṣinī;* she does not wear the kind of elegant Chinese dress that Benzaiten and Fude Longnü wear. See Getty 1998: 172.

6. Bryson 2010: 118–119.

7. In his *Kūge dansō* 空華談叢, the Shingon-Ritsu priest Myōryū 妙龍 (1705–1786) emphasizes that the torii is found neither in the *Mahāvairocana-sūtra* (whose mandala only contains the two-armed Myōon) nor in the *Golden Light Sūtra* (the locus classicus for the eight-armed Benzaiten). Authors of works like the *Kūge dansō,* by arguing that deities like Kōjin or Ugajin are specific to Japan, show that they are conscious of the special nature of these deities, which appeared late and are reducible neither to the buddhas nor the *kami,* and which are consequently, from the outset, outside the binary logic of the *honji suijaku* theory.

8. One possible prototype is the Mahoraga (Mahā-uraga, "great snake"). At Rengeō-in (Sanjūsangendō 三十三間堂) in Kyoto, a statue of Mahoraga shows the deity with a snake coiled on the top of his head and playing the lute like Benzaiten. Mahoragas are usually listed among the eight classes of protectors of Buddhism, along with *devas, nāgas, yakṣas, gandharvas, asuras, garuḍas,* and *kiṃnaras.*

9. Because she is usually worshiped on the day of the snake, Benzaiten came to be identified with that calendrical deity.

10. See "Tenjin shichidai zu" 天神七代図、in Gangōji bunkazai kenkyūjo 1999: 21, fig. 48; and *BZS* 4028–4030.

11. *Shiojiri* 49, 9: 834.

12. This looks like a reference to the composite deity known as the Three Devas (Santen), about which see Chap. 6.

13. See Mukōzaka 2007: 25.

14. *T.* 76, 2410: 628a.

15. See McCullough 1988: 266.

16. See *Sange yōryaku ki*, 50–51.

17. See Itō Satoshi 2007: 46. See also *Oto Gohō kōshiki,* in *ST,* Jinja-hen, Aso, Hiko 50: 258–263.

18. See *Shugendō shōso,* 1: 575a.

19. The complete title is *Saishō gokoku Ugaya tontoku nyoi hōju-ō shugi* 最勝護國宇賀耶頓得如意宝珠修義. See Itō Satoshi 1993: 40; and Yamamoto 1998a: 482–499.

20. *Keiran shūyōshū, T.* 76, 2410: 627b.

21. *T.* 76, 2410: 628a.

22. A similar tendency appears in the interpretation of the Sannō deity as a monkey—as both a real monkey and the Chinese zodiacal monkey (*shin* 申, Ch. *shen*).

23. In one variant, Zaō is replaced by Kōjin. See *Buchū hiden,* in *Shugendō shōso,* 1: 569. Various sources point out that Yoshino, where the Zaō-dō (with its three colossal statues of the blue Zaō) is located, is in the dragon-snake (*tatsumi* 辰巳, i.e., southeastern) direction of Tenkawa, which

implies that Zaō is the kind of demonic Kōjin subjugated by Benzaiten. As the *Keiran shūyōshū* and other texts emphasize, Benzaiten's direction is the northwest (because she subjugates demons in the southeast).

24. See *ST,* Jinja-hen, Yamato: 517.

25. See Sasama 1991: 51–52. A similar representation was that of one of the animal deities, the snake (*mi*), represented as a woman in Tang dress—only with the head of a snake. Benzaiten is also associated with the fox; see Nakamura Teiri 2001.

26. The first triad is allegedly based on major Mahāyāna scriptures, the second on the oral traditions of the Tendai master Genshin 源信 (942–1017).

27. *T.* 76, 2410: 620ab.

28. Itsukushima Daimyōjin is said to be the second daughter of the *nāga* king Sāgara, and to have vowed to fulfill the three desires of beings: awakening, wisdom, and happiness.

29. A later text, the *Daibenzaiten hiketsu* 大弁才天秘訣 (1713) by Jōgon 浄嚴, gives a fourfold allegorical interpretation of Benzaiten. At the first level, the most superficial, she is considered as belonging to the "real" category (*jitsurui* 実類 = *jissha* 実者); at the second, she is perceived as a provisional manifestation (*gongen* 権現) that appears in the mandala, and whose *honji* is either Dainichi or Shaka (or other buddhas in the case of Myōon). The text adds that both *honji* and *suijaku* vary, and it is therefore difficult to perceive all of their aspects. Myōon can, for instance, as stated in the *Lotus Sūtra,* take the form of a deva, *nāga, gandharva, asura, garuḍa, kiṃnara, mahoraga,* or a human form. From that standpoint, both *jissha* and *gonsha* are identical. Finally, at the fourth, most secret level, the practitioner realizes that Benzaiten is none other than himself or herself, and that his/her own body is that of Dainichi. Likewise, all the words of common people express the goddess's eloquence. See Hiroya 1925: 87.

30. This is also true in the case of Shintō—for instance, with the demiurge Kunitokotachi 国常立, who is displaced by the yin and yang principles in Yoshida shintō 吉田神 道 and the later tradition (in particular the Suika shintō 垂加神道 of Yamazaki Ansai 山崎闇斎); see Yamamoto 1995. A good analysis of this process in the case of Tibetan goddesses can be found in Volkman 1995.

31. *T.* 76, 2410: 625a.

32. On these three torii, see *Keiran shūyōshū, T.* 76, 2410: 516a.

33. *T.* 76, 2410: 623b.

34. *T.* 76, 2410: 517c.

35. The *nāga* ordination also became important in Sōtō Zen, as we can see from a number of *kirigami.* See Ishikawa 1992: 102–105.

36. See Hiroya 1925: 119–123.

37. Hiroya 1925: 92–93. A similar viewpoint is found in Amano Sadakage's *Shiojiri:* see *Nihon zuihitsu taisei,* 9: 780 and 834, and 10: 516.

38. *T.* 76, 2410: 625b.

39. *T.* 76, 2410: 519c. See also p. 625a.

40. *T.* 76, 2410: 626b.

41. See Unno Kazutaka 1994b.

42. See Kuroda Hideo 2003: 33.

43. *Hie hongi* 日吉本紀, in *ZGR* 52: 725. See also ST, Ronsetsu-hen 4, Tendai shintō 2: 543–586.

44. This dream was reported by Chūson (1046–1138). See *TZ* 12: 26; see also *Wakō dōjin riyaku kanjō,* in *TZ* 12: 186.

45. *TZ* 12: 217–218.

46. *ST,* Jinja-hen, Hie: 448–449; see also Nanami 1986.

47. The Hōganji temple has a Kannon Hall dating from the Momoyama period, and it is one of the so-called thirty-three Kannon temples of western Japan, although its *honzon* is Benzaiten. On the architectural aspect, see Watsky 2004. On the legend of Chikubushima, see *Keiran shūyōshū, T.* 76, 2410: 624c; and Kida 1976: 240–261. The island was first perceived as an island of the immortals, on which Benzaiten eventually appeared as an emanation of Amaterasu (Kida 1976: 251). On this "small Island Sikubusima," see also Kaempfer 1906, 1: 164; Watsky 2004; and Tyler 1992. On the Nō play *Chikubushima,* see Tyler 1992: 58.

48. *T.* 76, 2410: 627a.

49. McCullough 1988: 226.

50. The association with blindness points to the spread of that legend by "blind monks" (*mōsō*).

51. The very shape of Lake Biwa is said to be that of a lute (*biwa*). The *Keiran shūyōshū* interprets the main topographical features of the lake (islands, etc.) as parts of the musical instrument. For instance, the four rivers at the southern end of the lake are identified with the four strings of the lute. *T.* 76, 2410: 625a.

52. Ryōgen was believed to be an avatar of Benzaiten. On Ryōgen and Chikubushima, see Groner 2002: 206–207. Regarding the festival, see Kageyama 1973a.

53. *T.* 76, 2410: 626a.

54. *T.* 76, 2410: 627b.

55. See Kuroda Hideo 2003.

56. *T.* 76, 2410: 626a. This pairing is typical of the *Keiran shūyōshū*'s account, intent on showing the complementarity (and equality) of Myōon and Uga Benzaiten.

57. See *Shoji engi shū* 諸寺縁起集, copied ca. 1345, and *Chikubushima engi,* in *GR* 2: 311.

58. See Royall Tyler 1992, and 1993: 58 ff.

59. The Matsuun-ji 松雲寺 in Ōmi province preserved a Namazue Benten 鯰江弁天 (Benten of the Catfish River), a form of Benzaiten that was worshiped for rain in Noto 能登, Settsu 摂津, and Iyo 伊予 provinces. It is a rather simple statue, with a large coiled Ugajin on Benzaiten's head. According to the temple legend, it was transmitted from Kōfukuji 興福寺 in the twelfth century, and it represents Benzaiten as she is said to have appeared at the Saruzawa 猿沢 Pond on the precincts of Kōfukuji. Because she was riding a catfish at the time, she came to be called Namazue Benten. The Saruzawa Pond is the place where the dragon king Zennyo 善女 is said to have dwelt before moving to Murōzan, and Benzaiten is identified with him in this legend.

60. See Ouwehand 1964 on the *namazu* myth and the *kaname-ishi* 要石 motif; see also Kuroda Hideo 2003. The motif of the *namazu* as sea monster (reminiscent of the whale in the story of Jonah) also appears in the myth of Dakiniten, whose children, on their way to Japan from India, are swallowed by a monstrous catfish and rescued by an old fisherman.

61. In his discussion of Chikubushima, the German naturalist Engelbert Kaempfer emphasizes the *omphalos* motif: "These places are not shook, because they immediately repose upon the immov'd Center of the Earth." See Kaempfer 1906, 1: 164.

62. *T.* 76, 2410: 625. See also Ouwehand 1964. The same center symbolism is found at Ise's Sakadono, another dwelling place of Benzaiten, in relation with the "August heart pillar" (*shin no mihashira*), another *axis mundi,* resting on a white snake (Benzaiten) and guarded by the dragon Kurikara (a manifestation of Fudō). The most famous *kaname-ishi* are those of Kashima Shrine (Ibaragi prefecture) and Katori Shrine (Chiba prefecture), but perhaps the belief can be traced back to Chikubushima.

63. See *Ga'un nichiroku* 臥雲日件録, s.v. "Bun'an 4.4.17."

64. On this question, see Tanaka 1993: 16–19, 38.

65. See *Azuma kagami,* s.v. "Juei 1.4.5"; cited in Nedachi 1992: 68.

66. The foundation of the Zeniarai Benzaiten shrine is traced back to a dream of the shōgun Minamoto no Yoritomo. The Benten Cave at Hasedera also enshrines a statue of Benzaiten.

67. It was during the Edo period, however, that Enoshima became a thriving pilgrimage site, in connection with the cult of nearby Mount Fuji, owing to the increased prosperity and the popularity of "worldly benefits." Increasingly Benzaiten became a deity of trade for merchants, while she remained a water deity for peasants and fishermen, and a protector against illness. See Korezawa 1955.

68. See also the *Wakan sansai zue* by Terajima Ryōan. The deity of Enoshima is an eight-armed Benzaiten, whose *honji* is Ugajin. On Mount Fuji, the last of the "six sacred places," the main deity of Asama Shrine is the goddess Konohanasakuya-hime, who came to be identified with Benzaiten.

69. *Keiran shūyōshū, T.* 76, 2410: 627a. See also *Enoshima engi;* Aizawa 1991; and Fujisawa-shi kyōiku iinkai 2000.

70. Yet another tradition reports that a white snake lived in a cave of Enoshima and fed on human flesh.

71. The temple, called Kinkizan (Golden Turtle) Shaganji, was transformed into a Shintō shrine during the Meiji separation of Shintō and Buddhism. On Enoshima and its five caves of Benzaiten, see *Tankai,* 355.

72. See for instance the statues of the Fuji Museum, Minamitsuru-gun (Yamanashi pref.), in Richie and Itō 1967: 186–187.

73. *T.* 76, 2410: 627a. According to the *Kinpusen himitsuden* 金峰山秘密伝 by Monkan 文観, Benzaiten's four cultic centers correspond to the four eloquences (*ben* 弁). Thus, Tenkawa is said to correspond to the Dharma eloquence (*hō no ben* 法の弁); Chikubushima, to the eloquence regarding the meaning (*gi no ben* 義の弁); Enoshima, to the eloquence regarding the words

(*shi no ben*); and Itsukushima, to eloquence about pure eloquence (*ben no ben* 弁の弁). The shape of her *biwa* symbolizes yin and yang, heaven and earth, as well as various other doctrinal tenets. See *Shugendō shōso,* 1: 443b–445b.

74. T. 76, 2410: 625a. The *Nihonshoki* identifies Ōnamuchi as Ōkuninushi, and Sukunamuchi as Sukunahikona: "Now Ōnamuchi no mikoto and Sukunahikona, with united strength and one heart, constructed the sub-celestial world. Then for the sake of the visible race of men as well as for beasts, they determined the method of healing diseases." See Aston 1972: 59; see also Philippi 1968: 115–117.

Benzaiten's relationship with King Tokuzen is also part of the origin story of Minoodera 箕面寺. See *Minoodera himitsu engi,* in Gorai 2000, 2: 275–286. King Tokuzen appears as a historical figure in the chronicles of Munakata Shrine in Kyūshū—that of a Korean king. This may be a clue to the Korean influences on the transmission of the Benzaiten cult.

75. This symbolism perhaps explains the emphasis on sexuality in the Tenkawa tradition, in particular the "womb symbolism" of the place and the belief that one of its treasures was the hair (specifically the pubic hair) of the court dancer Shizuka Gozen 静御前 (1165–1211), the lover of Minamoto no Yoshitsune. See Kamata 1995b: 164–180; and Kamata 2000a: 203–217.

76. See *Kinpusen himitsuden,* in *Shugendō shōso,* 1: 442b–443a.

77. *T.* 76, 2410: 626ab.

78. *T.* 76, 2410: 519c.

79. On Tenkawa Benzaiten, see Nakajima 2009.

80. Kūkai is said to have carved Kōfukuji's Benzaiten statue after his visit to Tenkawa. See *Tenkawa Benzaiten-sha monjo* 天河弁才天社文書, in Hayashiya 1995: 214–224; Nagashima 1995; Takatori 1995; Nakamura Ikuo 1995; Akai 1995; and Kamata Tōji 1995b.

81. See the *Daijōin jisha zatsuji ki* 大乗院寺社雑事記 by the abbot of Daijōin at Kōfukuji, Jinson 尋尊, s.v. Kansei 2 (1461)/3/6.

82. Actually, the present-day temple has been moved farther downstream to the bottom of the mountain, close to the site of another temple, where Shōten is said to have appeared to En no Gyōja.

83. See *Minoodera himitsu engi* 箕面寺秘密縁起, in Gorai 2000, 2: 275–277. See also *TZ* 9: 753b.

84. The same protagonists appear in the origin story of Sefurisan 背振山 in northern Kyūshū, in relation with Oto Gohō, the mountain deity that would become the last born of Benzaiten's fifteen children. According to the *Chikuzen Fudoki* 筑前風土記, Benzaiten is a Korean deity who came to dwell on Sefuri-san. See Suzuya 1987.

85. See Yamamoto 1994a: 220–221.

86. *ST,* Ronsetsu-hen, Tendai shintō 1: 466.

87. *Gochinza hongi denki,* cited in Yamamoto 1998b: 60–61. The *Bikisho* (1324) explains that the Benzaiten who dwells at Sakadono is the white snake that lies under the August Heart pillar (*shin no mihashira*). Since that pillar symbolizes Mount Sumeru, the image of the white snake merges with that of the two *nāgas* Nanda and Upananda, coiled around that cosmic mountain. See *ST,* Ronsetsu-hen, Shingon shintō 2: 507–508. On Ise as *axis mundi,* i.e.,

as center of Jambudvīpa, see *Keiranshū shūyōshū, T.* 76, 2410: 518c. The *Tenchi reikaku hishō* also identifies the deity of Sakadono, Toyo-ugame, as a heavenly maiden and as the Benzaiten of the Womb realm. See Kokubungaku kenkyū shiryōkan 1999a: 389.

88. See *Keiran shūyōshū, T.* 76, 2410: 518. This is, we are told, why Japan does not fear invasions. See also *Bikisho*, ibid., which also connects the August heart pillar (and therefore Benzaiten) with Kurikara Fudō (Fudō in the form of a dragon coiled around an erect sword). The August heart pillar is also compared with a *vajra,* said to be the true form of Japan. The diagram of Japan as a *vajra* appears in the Benzaiten chapter of the *Keiran shūyōshū.* (See Fig. 5.13.)

89. There is another Misen at Itsukushima, behind the Benzaiten Shrine.

90. See Nara kokuritsu hakubutsukan 2007, fig. 183.

91. See Kanagawa kenritsu Kanazawa bunko 2007a, fig. 5.

92. See Miyake 1985: 431.

93. These *dōji* are carved on the walls of the Benzaiten Cave at Hasedera in Kamakura.

94. *T.* 76, 2410: 783a.

95. As we will see, this number was derived from Indian conceptions about the sixteen units of time marking the phases of the moon (White 1996) or the sixteen vowels of the Sanskrit alphabet (represented by and intimately linked to the Siddhaṃ script in Japanese esoteric Buddhism). This number also brings to mind the sixteen evil deities that form the retinue of Vināyaka, or the sixteen *graha* determined by divination through a sixteen-syllable grid in a Nepalese medical book (Pal 1992). As Sylvain Lévi and Édouard Chavannes have argued regarding the sixteen *arhats*, the number sixteen can also easily be reached by the duplication of the four directional deities. See Lévi and Chavannes 1916.

96. *T.* 76, 2410: 621a. The process is also described as reflecting practice and enlightenment, seen in Tantric yoga as a process of resorption that reverts the cosmic process of emanation into an upward movement leading the energy from the bottom to the top of the body: this is why the seed-letter of the fifteenth youth, Sensha Dōji, symbolizing meditation and wisdom, is placed on the feet, whereas the seed-letter of the first one, Inkan Dōji, symbolizing enlightenment, is placed on the top of the head. Interestingly, this passage immediately precedes the section on the unity of Fudō and Aizen, and it suggests that Kōshū extracted the first and last *dōji* of the list as representatives of the entire list and its dual-nondual nature. These two *dōji* are also identified with Fudō's two acolytes, Kongara 矜羯羅 and Seitaka 制吒迦 (var. 勢多迦). At times, however, it is Oto Gohō who corresponds to Seitaka. According to a Nanbokuchō period text entitled *Rokushū ri kuyō narabini Ugajin,* when an Uga Benzaiten ritual leads to a higher *siddhi,* Benzaiten appears in her womanly form; when to a middle-level *siddhi,* she appears in her *samaya* form, the wish-fulfilling jewel, or as Inkan Dōji; when to a lower *siddhi,* in her snake form. See Kanagawa kenritsu Kanazawa bunko 2007a: 40. On the practice of *nyāsa,* see Padoux 2011.

97. Another cosmological theme, the theory of the sixteen *kāla* of the

moon, explains the disappearance of the last (here the sixteenth) child. See White 1996: 36–43.

98. The motif of the five hundred eggs is also found in the *Konjaku monogatarishū;* see Dykstra 1986. The number fifteen also calls to mind the fifteen demons that form the retinue of the Gandharva-king in the *Dōjikyō,* and who attack children. Furthermore, the fifteen *dōji* are said in at least one source to form the retinue of Shōten—and they are also often found around Dakiniten.

99. See Mukōzaka 2007.

100. See Kida 1976: 42. As we will see, Uka no Mitama, the spirit of rice—and by extension the *kami* of cereals, food, and clothing, in other words, of wealth—was identified with Benzaiten and with the dragon deity of the Miketsudono granary.

101. See Mukōzaka 2007: 22. Oto Gohō, one of Benzaiten's fifteen *dōji,* is also identified with Ton'yugyōjin.

102. See *Hoki naiden* 3; and Shirahara 1999: 11.

103. See Sasama 1991: 48.

104. *T.* 76, 2410: 628a. Several ritual texts attributed to Eison suggest that the Benzaiten cult was important in the Shingon-Ritsu school of Saidaiji. Furthermore, a Saidaiji statue of Daikokuten attributed to Eison himself was discovered to contain a copper image (*kakebotoke* 掛佛) of Benzaiten. See Iyanaga 2002a, fig. 140.

105. *T.* 76, 2410: 628.

106. See Nanami 1986; and Minobe 1982: 222.

107. See *Enkai jōroku chō,* quoted in Yamamoto 1998a: 457.

108. See *Nanto shichidaiji junreiki, DNBZ* 120: 28b, quoted in Iyanaga 1994: 906b. This text, based on records of the Fujiwara period, is dated to the second half of the fifteenth century. Because of this ritual burial, the shrine in question came to be known as "Hollow (Kubo) Benzaiten." See also Naganuma Kenkai 1931: 639; and Iyanaga 2002a: 612–613.

109. The fairly obscure details of the ritual of union between master and disciple may very well have homosexual connotations. This is very much the case with regard to the way in which the master and his disciple are supposed to intertwine their arms and legs to form the deity's *mudrā.* On this question, see Yamamoto 1998a: 164–175.

110. See Iyanaga 2002a: 611; Yamamoto 1998a: 404; *Keiran shūyōshū, T.* 76, 2410: 636c, 640a, and 864a.

111. See Nara kokuritsu hakubutsukan 1990: 97 (item no. 52), commentary on pp. 177–178.

112. See *Chikubushima engi ryaku,* quoted in Kida 1976: 251.

113. McCullough 1979: 290.

114. See *Kōbō Daishi zenshū*. On this symbolism and its relation to the wish-fulfilling jewel, see *The Fluid Pantheon,* chap. 6.

115. In the *Bussetsu saishō gokoku Ugaya tontoku nyoi hōju daranikyō ryakusho* (1687) by Chōon, not only is Benzaiten is identified with Amaterasu, but the latter is also said to subsume the three *kami* Ōhirumenomuchi 大日孁貴, Tsukuyomi 月読, and Ninigi 瓊瓊杵, who correspond in turn

to the three buddhas Birushana (Vairocana), Amida (Amitābha), and Shaka (Śākyamuni), and to the three deities Benzaiten, Dakiniten, and Uhō Dōji. See Harada 2002: 209.

116. This theory may be a minority view, however. It is attributed to the Yasakadera 八坂寺 priest Kyūkai 求海, a devotee of Myōonten. See *T.* 76, 2410: 628a.

117. This representation is not attested in any Benzaiten ritual text. At least from the seventeenth century onward, Benzaiten (and more specifically Uga Benzaiten) was said to be the protector of the Ryūkyū kingdom, or even its "original ground" (*honji*), a radical extension to the Ryūkyū archipelago of her kinship with islands. See Harada 2002: 196–197.

118. Venus is also related to Kokūzō, owing in particular to the fact that the most famous ritual centered on Kokūzō, the so-called Gumonji-hō, involves the contemplation of the planet Venus.

119. Harada 2002: 205–207.

120. Harada 2002: 204–205.

121. Marishiten is also represented holding the sun and moon in her hands. See Harada 2002: 203.

122. Quoted in *Chintaku reifujin,* 40–41. See also *Sange yoryaku ki,* in *ST,* Ronsetsu-hen, Tendai shintō 2: 76.

123. Harada 2002.

124. In the Tenkawa tradition, Benzaiten and her spouse are also identified with the two Japanese gods Ōnanji (that is, Ōnamuchi or Ōkuninushi) and Onanji (var. Sukunanji). In the Sefuri-san tradition, the two *kami* are said to be the first two children of Benzaiten. See *Keiran shūyōshū, T.* 76, 2410: 625a.

125. *DNBZ* 127: 11.

126. As we have seen, Benzaiten herself is sometimes identified as the daughter of the *nāga* king Sāgara and the sister of the *nāga* maiden of the *Lotus Sūtra.* This is not specific to medieval Japan, however: kinship ties were already emphasized in the Vedic and Purāṇic traditions, which describe Sarasvatī as the daughter or consort of Brahmā and the elder sister of Yama. As Vāc, she is both the daughter and consort of the primordial god Prajāpati. Benzaiten is also said to be the consort of King Aizen (who is sometimes identified with King Yama). One should keep in mind that, in Japanese mythology, the sister is also often the wife. Thus, many matrimonial features of the Vedic Sarasvatī seem to resurface in Benzaiten.

127. One source underscores that while Benzaiten only has fifteen children, Ugajin's progeny is numberless.

128. According to the *Daibenzaiten hiketsu,* Benzaiten is called Maiden of Bliss (Kanginyo 歓喜女), a name that calls to mind Kangiten, the Bliss Deva, and Kangimo (the Mother of Bliss, i.e., Hārītī). Kangi is said to be the translation of the Sanskrit Nanda; in this way, Sarasvatī is identified with the shepherdess Nanda who offered milk to the future Buddha after he decided to put an end to his austerities and took a bath in the river. See Hiroya 1925: 92a. Benzaiten is paired with Daikokuten as wife and husband, while Hārītī is paired with Pañcika. The figure of the latter developed along two lines: he

becomes a warrior deity by merging with Vaiśravaṇa (Bishamonten), and a god of wealth by merging with Mahākāla (Daikokuten).

129. See *Sefurisan engi,* in Gorai 2000, 2: 551–554. See also *Keiran shūyōshū, T.* 76, 2410: 782; and Suzuki Masao 1987.

130. The name of the queen, Kirisai, resonates with that of Harisai 頗梨采, the dragon consort of Gozu Tennō 牛頭天王, who bore him eight children (the Hachiōji 八王子). These eight were in turn identified with the eight dragon kings who govern the eight quarters of the compass.

131. Although Benzaiten never reached Hārītī's (let alone Kannon's or Jizō's) position as protector of childbirth, her role in this domain is suggested by a custom, still quite popular in Chikubushima (an island whose very name evokes fecundity). According to it, women inscribe a small clay cup, which they subsequently throw down a cliff, trying to make it pass through a torii below. I venture to interpret this custom as a birth ritual, in which the torii symbolizes the vulva, and the cup the fetus. Similar rituals for easy childbirth are found elsewhere in Japan; see Nakamura Teiri 1999: 43–49.

132. The motif of the five hundred eggs is also found in the *Konjaku monogatarishū.* See Dykstra 1986.

133. See Miyoshi 1975: 243.

134. Fritsch 1996: 227.

135. See *Kakuzenshō, DNBZ* 50: 226; and *Byakuhō kushō, TZ* 7: 169c.

136. Iyanaga Nobumi, personal communication.

137. See *T.* 76, 2410: 626c.

138. *Asabashō, TZ* 9: 517a

139. See for instance Fritsch 1996: 180.

140. *Shikigami* appear for instance in the ritual texts (*saimon*) of the Izanagi-ryū, as they have been transmitted till today in Monobe village (Kōchi prefecture, Shikoku). See Kōchi ken ritsu rekishi minzoku shiryōkan 1997.

141. Komatsu 1994: 173.

142. A case in point is the snake festival of Kurama, a mountain village on the northern outskirts of Kyoto. The Kurama-dera is a major cultic center for Bishamonten.

143. See the case of Daikokuten, who is identified with Ōkuninushi or Ōnamuchi (like Benzaiten herself).

144. *ST,* Jinja-hen, Higo: 450.

145. On Benzaiten as *shukujin,* see Yamada 1994: 18–26.

146. Nanami 1986: 92–94.

147. See Kuroda Hideo 2003.

148. Ortega y Gasset 1961: 111.

CHAPTER 6: THE THREE DEVAS

1. This is the definition that appears in standard Japanese language dictionaries (including the largest, the *Nihon kokugo daijiten*), as well as in Japanese Buddhist terminology dictionaries.

2. Interpicturality is a neologism based on the term "intertexuality" coined by Julia Kristeva in the 1960s. Here interpicturality should be

understood as the visual counterpart of the latter, referring to the appropriation of and allusion to one visual art object by another visual art object.

3. See *Kita-in Omuro shūyōshū* 喜多院御室拾要集 (ca. 1200), cited in Nakamura Teiri 2001: 76–77. See also *Gyoki* 御記, *T.* 78, 2493: 614a.

4. On this deity, see Iyanaga 1994: 906–909.

5. Gōhō also mentions the existence of two *yakṣas*—one male, the other female—as gatekeepers of Tōji, but these seem to be different deities. Iyanaga 1999: 66.

6. According to Nakazawa Shin'ichi, a similar statue existed at Murōji, a temple connected very early on with dragon deities and rain rituals (1994: 259–264). If one considers Kannon as being identical to Benzaiten, the image of Mount Tamaki 玉置 can be seen as a ritual synthesis of Shōten, Dakiniten, and Benzaiten. Here, too, it absorbs the form of the "celestial fox" that flies over Mount Tamaki, giving it a strange appearance, including the bird legs. See Yamamoto 1993a: 356.

7. Eizan bunko collection. Another oral tradition associates the Three Devas with the three fundamental seed-letters *a/ban/un* (Skt. *a/vaṃ/hūṃ*). See *Jingi hishō* 神祇秘抄, Tenri University Library, Yoshida bunko coll.; cited in Yamamoto 1993a: 359. These seed-letters symbolize the Womb and Vajra realms and their union in the Susiddhi realm. See also *Jingi hishō,* in Kokubungaku kenkyū shiryōkan 1999b : 394; and *Keiran shūyōshū, T.* 76, 2410: 625b.

8. See "The Three Mysteries of the Three Devas," in *Keiran shūyōshū, T.* 76, 2410: 853a. Furthermore, the Three Devas are said to be the unconditioned buddha bodies of form, mind, and action, and they are also identified with the three bodies of the Buddha Śākyamuni as described in the *Lotus Sūtra:* Shōten corresponds to the Dharma body, Dakiniten to the retribution body, and Benzaiten to the metamorphosis body. *T.* 76, 2410: 853a–b; and 606a.

9. *Keiran shūyōshū, T.* 76, 2410: 862b.

10. *ST,* Ronsetsu-hen, Tendai shintō 2: 231. The same was apparently true in Shingon, as suggested by the existence on Mount Kōya (at Hōju-in) of a text entitled "The Profound Mystery of the Joint Ritual of the Three Devas." See Kōyasan Reihōkan 2002: 168.

11. See Iyanaga 2002a: 600.

12. *Jindaikan hiketsu* 36, in *ZST,* Ronsetsu-hen, Shūgō shintō: 391–392

13. Ibid., 392. See also Sakurai Yoshirō 1993: 229; Itō Masayoshi 1980, docs. 11, 12; and Iyanaga 2002a: 601.

14. *Shake shiryō,* 5: 421.

15. See *ST,* Ronsetsu-hen, Onmyōdō: 39.

16. The Three Devas are said to be the "traces" (*suijaku*) of the wish-fulfilling jewel. See *Keiran shūyōshū, T.* 76, 2410: 853a. Regarding the three peaks of Mount Inari, see also *Jindaikan hiketsu,* according to which the Hirosawa branch of Shingon performed an *abhiṣeka* ritual (*santen gōgyō hō*) centered on the Three Devas Shōten, Dakiniten, and Benzaiten. See *ZST,* Ronsetsu-hen, Shūgō shintō: 391. See also Yamamoto 1993a: 360; Sakurai 1996: 262–263; and Smyers 1999: 154.

17. *T.* 76, 2410: 853a.

18. See *Inari kōshi*, ed. Fushimi Inari taisha kōmu honchō 1978.

19. *ST,* Jinja-hen 9, Inari: 63.

20. In the *Inari ki* 稲荷記, the five peaks of Mount Inari are said to symbolize the eight-petaled lotus of the Womb realm, that is, the seat from which the buddha Vairocana (J. Biroshana) preaches. The distribution of deities across the landscape is a little strange, however: the western peak is where King Aizen and Benzaiten manifested themselves to bring happiness to beings; the northern peak is where Fudō and the "three great deities" manifested themselves to punish faithless beings; the eastern peak is where Daiitoku, Tenshō Daijin (that is, Amaterasu), and Daten (that is, Dakiniten) manifested themselves due to their compassion for all beings; the southern peak is where Gōzanze Myōō 降三世明王, Niu Myōjin 丹生明神, and Kariteimo 訶梨帝母 manifested themselves; finally, the central peak is where the Inari deity, Amida, and the King of Heavenly Foxes (Shinkoō) dwell. See *ST,* Jinja-hen, Inari: 16.

21. *Busshin ittai kanjō shō,* 164a.

22. *Busshin ittai kanjō shō,* 56b.

23. See *Keiran shūyōshū, T.* 76, 2410: 520a, 867a. See also *ST,* Ronsetsu-hen, Tendai shintō: 424, which specifies that the astral fox is an avatar of Nyoirin Kannon. As noted elsewhere, these ritual symbols also had an embryological signification. In the *Chibasan ruki* 千葉山流記, three stones are identified with the Three Devas, and we are also told that in the Buddha's biography King Śuddhodhana corresponds to Daten (Dakiniten), Queen Māyā to Benzaiten, and the future Buddha himself, i.e., Siddhārta (or sometimes Maitreya), to Shōten. The text then identifies the Three Devas with three *kami:* Izanagi (the yang *kami*), Izanami (the yin *kami)*, and one of their three children, Tsukuyomi (the brother of Amaterasu and Susanoo). A second triad is formed by Kōjin (as Hiruko, the first-born child of Izanami and Izanagi), Daikokuten (as Susanoo), and Bishamonten (as Amaterasu). The six deities are finally equated with the Six Kannon. See *Chiba-san ruki* 千葉山流記*,* in Gorai 2000, 1: 280–281. See also Kanai 1990: 162.

24. Also of possible relevance is the fact that these shrine maidens performed a Dakiniten ritual very similar to the enthronement *abhiṣeka.* See Kokubungaku kenkyū shiryōkan 1999b: 394.

25. See *Jingi hishō,* Tenri University Library, Yoshida bunko coll.; cited in Yamamoto 1993a: 359; and Iyanaga 2002a: 605.

26. In the *dōjōkan* 道場観 (visualization of the ritual area) of the Dakiniten ritual, the practitioner visualizes an altar with a jewel on it, which transforms into a heavenly woman riding a white fox. She holds a wish-fulfilling jewel (*cintāmaṇi*) in her left hand, a sword in the right (like Benzaiten). She is flanked by three or four acolytes, who are also riding foxes.

27. See Kida 1976: 335.

28. See Kōyasan Reihōkan 1994, figs. 48 and 61.

29. The body of that snake is black, while its head is brown, which is different from the usual representations of Benzaiten as a white snake. See also the Inari Daimyōjin mandala (Fig. 6.2 below), which has also been

reproduced in Tōji hōmotsukan 1994: 63, fig. 27. Although it is said to be "the earliest representation of Inari Daimyōjin preserved at Tōji," it is clearly a representation of the Three-Deva deity.

30. See Kōyasan reihōkan 1994: 18.

31. Note that the image reproduced in the *Tōji no tenbu zō* catalogue has been reversed.

32. The exception is a late exemplar, dated to the Meiji period, in which geometrical patterns seem to represent waves.

33. See *BZS* 2226 and 2227. In the latter, the bottom of the image is occupied by Dakiniten's eight youths (*dōji*). Positioned among them is an old man carrying two bundles of rice stalks, who is patterned after Inari Myōjin.

34. See Morse and Tsuji 1998, 1: 153, plate 143.

35. As we will see shortly, some of these youths and their associated animals (fish, crane, etc.) are also found in the Tenkawa Benzaiten mandala.

36. See Kida 1976: 335; Gorai 1985b: 129; and Iyanaga 2002a: 603–604.

37. These paintings have appeared in several exhibitions. See Ōsaka shiritsu bijutsukan 2004: 160–161, figs. 169 (Nōman-in scroll by Rinken), 170 (Nōman-in scroll attributed to Takuma Hōgen), and 171 (Shinnō-in scroll), and explanatory notes on p. 318. See also Ōsaka shiritsu bijutsukan 1999: 102–103, figs. 182, 183 (Nōman-in), and 184 (Ishiyama-dera), and explanatory notes on p. 230; as well as Nara kokuritsu hakubutsukan 2007: 206, fig. 187 (Nōman-in scroll by Rinken), and explanatory note on p. 309. The Shinnō-in scroll is also found in Kōyasan Reihōkan 1994: 29, fig. 32, and explanatory note on pp. 154–155. The Ishiyama-dera scroll appears in Shiga kenritsu Biwako bunkakan 1998: 24, fig. 36, and explanatory note on pp. 107–108; and in Nara kokuritsu hakubutsukan 2002: 49, fig. 22, and explanatory note on p. 125. A fifth scroll, badly damaged, is presently exhibited in the Reihōkan of Hasedera.

38. On this deity, see Bryson 2010: 120–135; and Li 1967: 53, plates 4 and 16.

39. Bryson 2010: 157.

40. A simplified representation on woodblock print, almost identical to *BZS* 2218, exists at the Tenkawa Benzaiten Shrine. See Ōsaka shiritsu bijutsukan 2004: 318. The current *ofuda* of that shrine, however, is a traditional representation of Benzaiten and her fifteen *dōji.*

41. I am indebted to Yaara (Yagi) Morris for this suggestion.

42. See Ōsaka shiritsu bijutsukan 2004, fig. 171.

43. See the *Jippi Benzaiten shidai kuketsu* (Kōyasan), a text attributed to Kūkai's disciple Shinga but more likely dating from the early Muromachi period (Ōsaka shiritsu bijutsukan 2004, fig. 171).

44. See Ōsaka shiritsu bijutsukan 1999, fig. 185.

45. See Kōyasan Reihōkan 1994, fig. 10.

46. In at least one case, we find a group of five deities in official dress, riding flying lions whose postures are strikingly similar to those of the flying foxes of the Dakiniten mandala. The group is represented below an image of a bodhisattva-like deity, perhaps Kōjin, seated on a vase (like Aizen) and holding two jewels (red and white). See *BZS* 4088.

47. See other examples from *BZS,* e.g., 1077, 2225, and 2226.

48. Bonnefoy 1992.

49. See Faure 1998b and de Certeau 1992.

50. De Certeau 1992: 49.

51. De Certeau 1992: 51.

52. De Certeau 1992: 51.

53. De Certeau 1992: 72.

54. See Iyanaga 2002a: 600.

55. See Iyanaga 1994: 903; and Kida 1976: 72. The same story appears in the Kyōgen "Ebisu Daikoku" and in the *Jingi shūi* by Urabe no Kanemitsu 卜部兼満. See Iyanaga 1994: 880–881 and 902–910.

56. Iyanaga 1994: 902. Iyanaga has argued that the grouping of Daikokuten, Benzaiten, and Bishamonten did not appear all of a sudden in medieval Japan, and that antecedents can be found in India. He has explored the relationships of substitution that could have, in the quasi-algebraic formulas of esoteric Buddhism, contributed to the pairing of Daikokuten and Benzaiten: namely, the relationships between Daikokuten and Bishamonten, between Bishamonten and Kichijōten, and finally between Kichijōten and Benzaiten. This system of associations rests on deeper affinities, however, and in particular those between Benzaiten and Ugajin, on the one hand, and between Ugajin and Daikokuten on the other.

57. The wild boar is the mount of two other deities: Marishiten and Shōgun Jizō, as the deity of Mount Atago. On Sanmen Daikoku (as composed of Vināyaka, Ugajin, and Daikokuten), see also *Tankai,* 380.

58. Nakagawa Zenkyō 1964: 56–58.

59. See *Jindaikan hiketsu* in *ZST,* Ronsetsu-hen, Shūgō shintō: 281–282; and Abe Yasurō 1989; Ruppert 2000; and *The Fluid Pantheon,* chap. 6.

60. See for instance *Hishō mondō, T.* 79, 2536: 499b.

61. See "Shōten," box 315 #58, Kanazawa bunko.

62. See for instance *ST,* Jinja-hen, Hie: 132.

63. *ST,* Jinja-hen, Aso, Hiko: 258–263.

64. On Kyōen, see Andreeva 2006–2007: 75–78.

65. *ST,* Ronsetsu-hen, Shingon shintō 2: 483–495.

66. See Tanaka Takako 2003.

67. *Tenshō daijin kuketsu* in *ST,* Ronsetsu-hen, Shingon shintō 2: 497–504.

68. See Kojima 1999.

69. Sasama 1993: 46–55.

70. Iyanaga 2002a: 601.

71. *T.* 76, 2410: 642b. Aizen is also sometimes identified with Dakiniten, and identified as the husband of Benzaiten. See Iyanaga 2002a: 597–598.

72. According to the apocryphal *Ugaya darani-kyō* quoted in *Keiran shūyōshū, T.* 76, 853a and 909a.

73. Complete title: *Bussetsu saishō gokoku Ugaya tontoku nyoi hōju-ō darani-kyō* 仏説最勝護国宇賀耶頓得如意宝珠陀羅尼経 (hereafter *Ugaya darani kyō*). See Iyanaga 2002a: 613; Yamamoto 1998a: 478; and Kida 1976: 73–74.

74. In a fragment of the *Shinkō musōki* copied by Kenna at Shōmyōji on the basis of a vision by the Kojimadera priest Shinkō, we find a couple in sexual embrace formed by Shōten and a woman standing on an elephant-shaped rock. Shōten has a jewel on his head, while the woman (perhaps Benzaiten) has the head of a snake or dragon on hers. The text that accompanies the image says that along with the vision Shinkō received a ritual called the Tonjō shitsuji hō (Ritual of Sudden Realization), which implies that the rituals of Shōten, Benzaiten, and Dakiniten were understood to be in essence one. See Kanagawa kenritsu Kanazawa bunko 2007b: 21.

75. See Sakurai 1993: 224; and Iyanaga 1999.

76. Hegel 1956: 212.

CHAPTER 7: THE FACE OF THE SNAKE

1. Quoted in Derrida, 2008: 107–110.

2. In the rituals of Atsuta 熱田 Shrine, for instance, Benzaiten and Uga shinshō are invoked as two distinct deities. See *Atsuta kōshiki,* in *ST,* Jinja-hen, Atsuta: 27.

3. A few names are worth mentioning in this respect, those of Kōgei 皇慶 (977–1049), Kenchū (fl. mid-13th century), Kōshū (1276–1350, the compiler of the *Keiran shūyōshū*), and his disciple Unkai. It is Kōgei (a.k.a. Ikegami ajari 池上阿闍梨), in particular, who identified Ugajin with the Hie Shrine deity Jūzenji 十禅師, characterizing both as "placenta deities" (*ena kōjin*). He also authored the *Enoshima engi* 江島縁起, a work centered on Benzaiten, and he identified the Sefuri-san deity Oto Gohō as one of Benzaiten's fifteen attendants.

4. To give just an example, the Rinzai Zen master Mumon Gensen 無文元選 (1323–90) is said to have come to reside at Sanmyōji 三明寺, a place dedicated to Benzaiten, the *suijaku* of Ugajin. See *Mumon zenji goroku* 無文禅師語録, *T.* 80, 2559: 630b.

5. *Bikisho,* in *ST,* Ronsetsu-hen, Shingon shintō 2: 507–508.

6. See "Kōshū Sano Uga Daimyōjin go-yōgō mukashigoto" 江州佐野郷宇賀大明神御影向昔事, in *Sangoku denki* 三国伝記, ed. Ikegami Jun'ichi 池上洵一 (Tokyo: Miyai shoten, 1976): 222–226.

7. See Yamamoto 1998a: 340–341.

8. See Mukōzaka 2007: 25; see also *Atsuta kōshiki,* in Kokubungaku kenkyū shiryōkan 1999b: 369; and *Miwaryū shintō-hen:* 71–72. According to the apocryphal *Ugajin daranikyō,* in the Buddha's assembly there is a bodhisattva called Spirit Commander Uga (Uga shinshō 宇賀神将) and King Cintāmaṇi, who is none other than Benzaiten. See Itō Satoshi 1996: 120.

A good example of Ugajin's independence is found in the *Ugajin-ku saimon* 宇賀神供祭文, a ritual text invoking Benzaiten, the bodhisattva Spirit Commander Uga (Uga Shinshō bosatsu 宇賀神将菩薩, and their massive retinue (*kenzoku*). In addition this work lists in turn the *uga* deities (*ugajin*) of the ten directions, the fifteen princes (ōji 王子) of Uga shinshō, and finally Daibenzaitennyo 大弁才天女, Daten (i.e., Dakiniten), and Shōten "in one single body" (that is, as the composite Three-Deva deity), as well as their attendants. The *saimon* ends with an invocation of the buddhas of the five directions (Ashuku 阿閦, Hōshō 宝生, Amida, Shaka, and Dainichi). It is aimed at obtaining realization (*siddhi*) in the present and future worlds.

9. See *ZST,* Ronsetsu-hen, Shugō shintō, ill. 185.

10. King Tokuzen is usually depicted as the husband of Benzaiten, but he can also be identified with her (for instance, in the *Sefuri-san engi*). Certain sources speak of the Great King Daibenzaiten Tokuzen as one single person. See for example the *Kōkozōtō hishō,* in Kokubungaku kenkyū shiryōkan 1999a: 372.

11. See *Kōkozōtō hishō,* in Kokubungaku kenkyū shiryōkan 1999a: 369–378.

12. In a variant in which Benzaiten and Daikokuten (who is himself at times identified with Ugajin) both appear, the former is listed among buddhas and bodhisattvas, the latter among devas.

13. *Sanbōin-ryū dōsen sōjō kuketsu, SZ* 34: 155b-156a.

14. Getty 1940: 36.

15. Getty 1940: 40–41. When Emmanuel Lévinas spoke of "giving a face to the snake," he obviously had Lucifer in mind. It is strange that Getty, in her comparative mood, did not think of medieval representations of the serpent in Eden, in which Lucifer appears with a snake body and a woman's head. Of course, my references to the biblical snake in the exergue of this chapter should not be taken to mean that I always see the snake as a figure of interiority, although iconographic influences may not be entirely ruled out. On this question, see Baltrušaitis 1981.

16. Incidentally, this discovery triggered her interest in (and collection of) Mesopotamian seals, and her article on Ugajin was her last contribution on East Asian topics: as one of her friends put it, "the serpent god is responsible for shifting her interest from the Far East and India to the Near East."

17. Getty 1940: 48. The first mention of Ugajin in the West seems to have been in connection with the von Philipp Franz von Siebold Collection (cat. 235), under the inscription: "Benten as weisse Schlange." This inscription refers to a portable shrine (14.5 x 15.7 x 22.3 cm) described as a "small altar of Benzaiten in the form of a snake." Staatliches Museum für Völkerkunde, Munich.

18. *Shinkō musōki,* quoted in Manabe 1999: 166.

19. See *Ugaya daranikyō,* in Yamamoto 1998a: 478. See also Kida 1976: 73–74.

20. Yanagita 1990a: 451–458; Kida 1976: 31–60; Yamamoto 1998a: 325–502.

21. See *Santō mintan shū,* in Yanagita 1990a: 451.

22. Yanagita discusses common points between Ugajin and Ryū no Tōta 竜頭太 (lit. "Dragon head"), an avatar of the Inari deity that became the protector of Kūkai's Tōji monastery (1990a: 451). Ryūtōta was also associated with the stove god. See Komatsu 1985: 172; and Iijima 1988: 235–237.

23. See Yamamoto 1998a: 325–502; and Mukōzaka 2007.

24. For another example of this kind of anachronism, see Yoshino Hiroko 1999.

25. See *Jinnō keizu,* quoted in *Jinnō shōtōki*: 53n25. Likewise, in the

Daijingū sankeiki 大神宮参詣記 (1286–1288), the record of a pilgrimage to Ise by the Buddhist monk Tsūkai 通海, Ugajin (here, probably Uga Benzaiten) is identified with Māra, Ishana-ten 伊舎那天 (Īśāna, i.e., Mahākāla as a directional deity), and Izanagi. See Iyanaga 1996–97. On the identity between Mahākāla and Ishanaten, see also *Keiran shūyōshū, T.* 76, 2410: 637c.

26. *Mudai shō,* in *ST*, Ronsetsu-hen, Unden shintō: 354.

27. *Shiojiri*: 780, 834.

28. *Shiojiri*: 780.

29. See *Gochinza denki* and *Yamatohime no mikoto seiki* in Ōsumi 1977: 34; and the *Jinten ainōshō.* The latter source also gives the legend of Uganōhime 宇賀能売命, the deity of the Nagu Shrine in Tango province, (Takeno district), at the end of which we read: "The fact that, in the world today, one calls snakes *uga* is based on the cult in which Ugajin manifests itself as a snake." *DNBZ* 150: 87.

30. *ST,* Jinja-hen, Inari: 543.

31. See Aston 1972: 32; and Philippi 1968: 87.

32. The myth of Toyouke, reminiscent of the Hagoromo 羽衣 legend, also influenced local legends of Benzaiten as a heavenly goddess exiled to earth who, once there, taught humans the secrets of sake brewing. See for instance the *engi* of Nagu Shrine (Nagu no yashiro, in Tango Province) in *DNBZ* 150: 87. See also Teeuwen 1995: 32b–33a.

33. Teeuwen 1993: 225–245; and Teeuwen 1996: 27–84 et passim.

34. See *Yamatohime no mikoto seiki,* in Ōsumi 1977: 34.

35. See *Toyouke kōtaijin gochinza hongi,* in *ST,* Ronsetsu-hen, Ise shintō 1: 34–50. This text, one of the so-called Five Scriptures of Shintō (*shintō gobusho* 神道五部書), was dismissed as a forgery by the Edo scholar Motoori Norinaga 本居宣長 (1730–1801). See Teeuwen 1995: 23.

36. *Dakiniten-son ryaku engi* (facsimile), Shinnyodō.

37. One finds in the *Daikokuten kōshiki* a passage similar to that of the *Ugaya darani kyō,* in which Daikokuten is associated with Ugajin and other deities. See Kida 1976: 216; and Iyanaga 2002a: 614–615.

38. Yamamoto 1998a: 457.

39. On this question, see Yamaori 2004b: 397–398, 419.

40. Miyake 2007: 340–341.

41. As the *Shiojiri* puts it, "when one fabricates a snake above the [straw bag], one calls it *tawara* 俵." *Shiojiri*: 834–835.

42. See the *Jinten ainōshō*, in *DNBZ* 150: 87. In the *Shiojiri,* Ugajin is said to come from a Sanskrit word meaning "white snake." *Shiojiri,* 9: 834. The term *uraga* appears in the *Uraga-jātaka.* See also Vogel 1995.

43. The only exception is a type of albino rat snake found near Iwakuni City in Yamaguchi prefecture.

44. The *aodaisho* 青大将, for instance, is a large snake that can reach three and half meters and feeds on frogs and toads, like the *yamakagashi,* a poisonous snake. The most common poisonous snake is the *mamushi* 蝮 (viper). Also worth mentioning is the *hibakari* 熇尾蛇, of yellowish color. None of these snakes is ever explicitly related to Ugajin or Benzaiten.

45. See for instance the following passage in Shakespeare's *As You Like*

It (act 2, sc. 1, 12–14): "Sweet are the uses of adversity which, like the toad, ugly and venomous, wears yet a precious jewel in his head." The *nāgas*, too, were believed to carry a jewel in their hood. See Vogel 1995.

46. On these scriptures, see Itō Satoshi 1996c; and Mukōzaka 2007. Mukōzaka introduces four other Kanazawa Bunko documents related to Uga Benzaiten, two of which have the name Ugajin in their title. The last one, *Benzaiten hihō* 弁才天秘法, was apparently closely related to Eison's circle at Saidaiji.

47. A case in point is Myōken, who is said to become Ugajin when properly worshiped, and Kōjin (or a *kōjin*) when not. Here, however, the name Ugajin designates Benzaiten. Similar statements were made that contrasted Benzaiten with Susanoo, the archetypal *kōjin* (or *araburu kami,* "wild deity").

48. See Yamamoto 1998a: 384–385. See also the *Ugaya tontoku nyoi hōju-ō shugi,* in which the priest invokes all the *uga shinshō* of the five directions. Yamamoto 1998a: 484.

49. See Yamamoto 1998a: 365: "The *uga* of the five directions are the five dragons."

50. *ST,* Ronsetsu-hen, Shingon shintō 2: 579–581. Perhaps it is not just a coincidence that this text is followed by a "Saimon of the Stove God" (*Sōshin saimon* 竈神祭文); see pp. 582–583. Various *ugajin* also appear in *Daikoku tenjin shiki,* another text attributed to Kūkai. See Eder 1951: 265.

51. In the Liturgy of the Earth Festival (Chisai sahō 地祭作法), for instance, one explains the symbolism of the monastic robe (*kesa* 袈裟), and one describes the ritual phase during which the priest spreads the *kesa:* "If one makes the *kesa* float over the ocean, the *garuḍas* no longer harm the dragons. If one spreads it over the ground, Kenrō Jijin no longer casts curses (*tatari* 祟り) on humans. This is why, spreading on the ground the monastic robe (*kesa*) of the field of felicity, the deliverance robe, one asks for the unborn, nirvanized *samādhi.* The deity (or deities) of the earth (*chijin* 地神), water (*suijin* 水神), wind (*fūshin* 風神), space (*kokūshin* 虚空神), the wild deities (*kōjin*), the landlords (*jinushi*) of old, Taisai 大歳, Daishōgun 大将軍, all the demons individually, and in particular the disease deities and the 'fashionable deities' (*hayarigami* 流行神) of the current year, Gozu Tennō, Harisainyo 婆利采女 [his wife], [his children] the Hachiōji 八王子 and Dadokuke no kami 蛇毒気神 (the 'snake with poisoned breath'), as well as [the devas] Daishō Kangiten, Dakiniten and [her acolytes,] Taishaku's emissary (Taishaku shisha 帝釈使者), the Red Woman (Shakunyoshi 赤女子) and the Black Woman (Kokunyoshi 黒女子), two of the Hachiōji, the *shikijin* Ugajin, the seven kinds of wild foxes (*yakan*)—[all these deities receive offerings]. The invocation is followed by the Nakatomi harae." See Ōmiwa jinja shiryō, 10: 380.

52. *Kōbō Daishi zenshū* 5: 328–329; see also Nakagawa 1964: 73–74.

53. This is often the case in portable shrines (*zushi*). In a *zushi* belonging to Shinnō-in 親王院 on Mount Kōya, for instance, a female Ugajin is visible inside a crystal *cintāmaṇi* jewel. See Kōyasan Reihōkan 1994: 71, fig. 37.

54. In the Ritual of Spirit Commander Uga (Uga shinshō-hō 宇賀神将法), King Ugajin appears as a young woman holding a sword in her right hand, a jewel in her left, who turns into a white snake. In this case, however,

we seem to be dealing with a manifestation of Uga Benzaiten, rather than Ugajin as such. See Miyake 1985.

55. Seen in this light, the combination of Benzaiten and Ugajin in the figure of Uga Benzaiten seems to replicate the mythic Chinese couple. The latter is indeed mentioned in a passage related to Ugajin. On Nü Wa, see Loewe 1978: 57–59; and Schafer 1980: 37–41.

56. See *Shanhai jing*; and Strassberg 2002: 215–216, 223, 198, and 126.

57. Granet 1959: 351. This story is reminiscent of the Suwa god Takeminakata 健御名方, another snake deity traced back to the Izumo *kami* who rebelled against the heavenly *kami* and was exiled to Suwa.

58. See Stein 1990: 236. A similar passage is found in Vitiello 1984.

59. See Vitiello 1984.

60. See Gangōji bunkazai kenkyūjo 1999: 21–22 and 28.

61. Yamamoto 1998a: 96–97.

62. See *Onjōji denki* 園城寺伝記, *DNBZ* 86, 786.

63. On Indian serpent cults, see Vogel 1995.

64. This representation calls to mind the motif of Ryūmaki Daruma 龍巻達磨 (Daruma and the coiled dragon). See Faure 2011. Ugajin also appears in the Nichiren mandalas. See Frank 2000a: 110–112. In a Dakiniten painting in the Nagoya Museum, Ugajin is coiled around a skull, on which a fox is seated. See Nakamura Teiri 2001: 78–80.

65. See Williams 2005: 112–115.

66. See Wakayama kenritsu hakubutsukan 2003: 60, fig. 51. I am indebted to Elizabeth Tinsley for bringing this image to my attention. The symbolism of the white and black dogs brings to mind the black and white horses of Kibune Myōjin 貴船明神, a rain-ritual deity closely related to Niu Myōjin. The same color code is found in both cases.

67. See Caillet 1981a: 262–270. On Niu Myōjin, see also *Niu Daimyōjin giki* 丹生大明神儀軌, in *ST,* Jinja-hen: Iga, Ise, Shima no kuni: 80–84.

68. *T.* 76, 2410: 517c.

69. *T.* 76, 2410: 620b, 866b.

70. See the Kōjin mushi kaji hō 荒神虫加持法 (Kōjin Ritual of Empowerment for Insects) in the *Shugen jōyō hihōshū* 修験常用祕法集, in *Shugendō shōso,* 1: 226–228; and Tada 1985: 67–71.

71. As I have discussed in *The Fluid Pantheon* (chap. 5), the two wisdom kings Aizen and Fudō symbolize the wish-fulfilling jewel and its procreative power. Aizen's seed-letter is further analyzed as being formed by four letters (*a, ha, u, ma*). The sound *a*, being unborn, does not appear, and symbolizes Fudō. *Ha* and *u* are said to symbolize a snake (as indicated by their shapes), while *u-ha* means "Uga." *Ma* symbolizes the "space dot" (Skt. *anusvāra*) and the wish-fulfilling jewel. See Yamamoto 1998a: 418.

72. See Nara kokuritsu hakubutsukan 2007: 187, figs. 170–173.

73. See *Ugajin zō,* in Ōsu bunko, catalog ref. 99/29.

74. See *Bussetsu sokushin hinten fukatoku enman Uga shinshō bosatsu byakuja jien mikkan jōjū kyō,* in Ishihara 1990–1992, 1: 161–167.

75. See for instance Kanagawa kenritsu Kanazawa bunko 2007a, fig. 18 (Edo period); see also Frank 1991: 205, ill. 122.

76. Yamamoto 1998a.

77. The identity between the relics and the *nāga* (as Ugajin) is also mentioned in the *Keiran shūyōshū, T.* 76, 2410: 772bc and 863a.

78. On this question, see *The Fluid Pantheon,* chap. 7.

79. See also *Keiran shūyōshū, T.* 76, 2410: 863a.

80. *T.* 76, 2410: 628ab.

81. The images of the snake and the toad or frog also appeared at the Upper Suwa Shrine (Kamisha) as part of a New Year ritual that contained a frog- or toad-hunting sequence.

In a recent book, Hara Naomasa argues that the toad-deity-taming Suwa Daimyōjin, who became a great *kōjin* and brought havoc to the world, is none other than Ugajin. He quotes local sources according to which the Suwa god destroys the hole in which the toad deity lived by filling it with stones. Significantly, this hole was said to be connected to the dragon palace. See Hara Naomasa 2012: 16–27.

82. See Yamada 1994.

83. See *Kaijōshō, DNBZ* 130: 88.

84. This calls to mind a passage from the *Keiran shūyōshū*'s section on Benzaiten, according to which there exists, in the lungs of practitioners, a small snake that is their true nature. *T.* 76, 2410: 623b. See also Yamamoto 1998a: 367.

85. See *Kōfukuji ruki,* in Suzuki Masataka 2001: 209.

86. On this question, see *The Fluid Pantheon,* chaps. 4–5.

87. See *Moriya-ke shokiroku rui* 守屋家諸記録類, quoted in Hara Naomasa 2012.

88. See *Monoimi ryō* 物忌令, quoted in Hara Naomasa 2012: 62–75. This stone is reminiscent of the *kaname-ishi* pinning down the earthquake-causing catfish (*namazu* 鯰). See Ouwehand 1964.

89. Hara Naomasa 2012: 87–90.

90. Hara Naomasa 2012: 90–91.

91. See *Hōjō kyūdai ki* 北条九代記, quoted in Hara Naomasa 2012: 77.

92. See description in Hara Naomasa 2012: 16–28.

93. Quoted in Hara Naomasa 2012: 107. Related to this is Hara's observation that the topology of the Upper Shrine reproduces that of the altar used in the Benzaiten ritual (2012: 41–53).

94. The southeastern direction is also that of Fugen in the Womb Realm mandala.

95. Quoted in Hara Naomasa 2012: 180.

96. The other sites where Ugajin manifested himself as a dragon are Benzaiten's main cultic centers: Chikubushima, Mishima, Enoshima, and Itsukushima, as well as Sumiyoshi, Kashima and Katori. See Hara Naomasa 2012: 149. The importance of Suwa as it is related to Uga Benzaiten is attested by the map of Japan as a one-pronged *vajra,* contained in the Benzaiten chapter of the *Keiranshū yōshū;* see Fig. 5.13.

97. On this cosmological structure, see Stein 1990.

98. See Iyanaga 1996–1997: 30.

99. *T.* 76, 2410: 639c. See also the explanation of the gates in the *Longshu wuming lun* 龍樹五明論, *T.* 21, 1420: 958b.

100. *Sange yōryakki,* in *ST,* Ronsetsu-hen, Tendai shintō 2: 230.

101. See Yamamoto 1998a: 362.

102. Quoted in Nanami 1986: 65–66.

103. Ibid.

104. See Yamamoto 1998a: 478.

105. See Kida 1976: 216; and Iyanaga 2002a: 614–615.

106. Kida 1976.

107. See *Daikoku tenjin shiki;* Eder 1951: 265; and Fritsch 1996: 24.

108. *Kuma-gōri jinja ki,* in *ST,* Jinja-hen 45, Hizen Higo: 287.

109. See Sawa Shisei 1984: 337.

110. See *Tenchi jingi shinchin yōki* in *ST*, Tendai shintō 1: 462.

111. *Chintaku reifujin engi shūsetsu,* in Hayakawa 2000: 341b; see also p. 338a: "Again, he transforms into Maheśvara, the companion spirits (*kushōjin*), and Sanbō Kōjin; and he becomes the god Taiyi of the higher origin."

112. Hayakawa 2000: 341.

113. See *Mon'yōki* (*TZ* 11–12), s.v. "Eikyō 1" (1429), quoted in Satō Masato 1985: 53. The fact that Ugajin is the other face of Kōjin is also suggested by the latter's reptilian aspect (symbolized by the widespread straw snakes or by the spring ritual of bamboo cutting).

114. See the *Saishō gokoku Ugaya tontoku nyoi hōju-ō shugi,* in Yamamoto 1998a. See also Takahashi Yūsuke 2006a: 4; and Kanagawa kenritsu Kanazawa bunko 2007a: 60–62.

115. See Takahashi Yūsuke 2006a.

116. See Frank 1991: 281.

117. *Ugajin-ku saimon,* in Mukōzaka 2007: 27b–28a.

118. *T.* 76, 2410: *T.* 76, 2410: 639c, 772c. These three syllables also represent the three realms according to Tendai (Womb, Vajra, and Susiddhi), as well as the familial triad of father, mother, and child.

119. This passage is derived from one of the apocryphal Ugajin sūtras, the *Saishō gokoku Ugaya tontoku nyoi hōju-ō shugi* (see Yamamoto 1998a: 481–482). A similar gloss is given of the name Uga jinnō, in which the vertical line in the last character, *ō* 王 'king,' is interpreted as symbolizing communication between the three realms (heaven, man, and earth), which are of course represented by the three horizontal lines. (This sort of interpreation is also applied to the characters *san* 山 and *ō* 王 in the name of the Sannō deity.) This is why one says that Ugajin penetrates the three realms. See *T.* 76, 2410: 639c.

120. See *Ugaya daranikyō,* quoted in Kida 1976: 73–74; and Yamamoto 1998a: 478; De Visser 1911: 289; Fritsch 1996: 23.

121. See Text A, in Manabe Shunshō 2000.

122. Text from the Eizan bunko archives, cited in Iizuna rekishi fureaikan 2006: 37.

123. See the description of the *mimuro* ritual of Suwa in Shimada Kiyoshi 1990.

124. Without explaining why, Yanagita Kunio identifies the "heavenly maiden" Ugaya (female Ugajin) with the *shukujin;* see Yanagita 1990a: 455.

125. Linrothe 1990 and 1999.
126. Borges 1962: 119–126.
127. See Deleuze and Parnet 1977.

CHAPTER 8: MATRICIAL GODS

1. Since the pioneering work of Kida Teikichi (1976), Matarajin has attracted the interest of a number of scholars, among whom the most important are Kageyama Haruki (1973a); Yamamoto Hiroko (1998a), Suzuki Masataka (2001); and, more recently, William Bodiford (2006–2007), Kawamura Minato (2008), Tanigawa Ken'ichi (2009), and Hasuike Toshitaka (2009).

2. The name Yasha Daimyōjin 夜叉大明神 is also used for the protecting deity of Kiyomizu-dera in Kyoto, and talismans (*ofuda*) bearing this name are still popular today. This deity is worshiped in a small altar near the Amida Hall.

3. See *Huayan jing Puxian xingyuan pin biexing shi chao* 華嚴經普賢行願品別行疏鈔, *ZZ* 1, 7, 505; and Iyanaga 1999.

4. The same associative logic may explain why the bodhisattva Fugen 普賢 (Skt. Samantabhadra), riding an elephant (and thus loosely connected with Vināyaka), is sometimes represented in the company of the ten Rasetsunyo 羅刹女 (Skt. *rākṣasī*), flesh-eating demonesses who have affinities with the *mātṛkā.* Thus, the argument of Yamaori Tetsuo, according to which the only link between Fugen and the Rasetsunyo is their being protectors of the *Lotus Sūtra,* seems insufficient. Like his companion Monju (Mañjuśrī) and practically all esoteric deities, Fugen has a decidedly darker side. See Yamaori 1992: 76.

5. *Shiojiri* 35, 9: 604–606. Among the Kōryūji documents, we find a *Matarajin saimon* 摩多羅神祭文 dated Tenbun 18 (1549), which a priest disguised as a *yakṣa*—in imitation of Matarajin—reads at the time of the Ox Festival (*ushi matsuri* 牛祭り). There is also a *saimon* dated 1402 (Ōei 9).

6. Hasuike 2009.

7. See *Shiojiri* 35, 9: 604–606; and *Kūge dansō* 3, *DNBZ,* ed. Bussho kankōkai (1912): 451. See also Uesugi 1973, 2: 891; for a more positive view, see Hazama 1948, vol. 2.

8. On this later form of Matarajin, see Bodiford 2006–2007. Tenkai enshrined Tōshō 東照 (Tokugawa Ieyasu), Sannō, and Matarajin as the three protectors of the bakufu. See Sugahara Shinkai 1992: 30.

9. On Tenkai, see Ooms 1985. On the Matarajin of Tōshōgū, see Sugahara Shinkai 1992; and Bodiford 2006–2007. For a detailed discussion of the role of Tenkai in the promotion of Matarajin, see Kawamura 2008.

10. On the Genshi kimyōdan, see *Genshidan hishō*; Uesugi 1973; and Hazama 1948, 2: 137–180.

11. In spite of his criticism of the Genshi kimyōdan ritual, inspired by Reikū, Amano argues that this ritual is not "heretical," inasmuch as it is mentioned in the texts of the Hirosawa-ryū of Shingon and therefore has a long history. See *Shiojiri* 35, 9: 604–606.

12. For a representative Genshi kimyōdan text, see *Genshidan hishō*. See also Kageyama 1973a: 247.

13. See Kawamura 2008: 192–214.

14. Bodiford 2006–2007: 11.

15. As Sugahara Shinkai (1996b) points out, the Sannō ichijitsu shintō that Jōin inherited from Tenkai is quite different from the Sannō shintō of Mount Hiei.

16. Actually, in his *Chapter on the Cakravartin King* (*Tenrinjōō shō*, 1728), Jōin identifies Matarajin with Konpira, and gives a far-fetched explanation of the god's name in terms of the Sanskrit alphabet, based on the phonetic derivation *matara* = *mātṛkā,* Sanskrit vowels. This theory, which Bodiford does not mention, confirms the fact that Jōin's interpretation of Matarajin is a doctrinal rationalization that transforms the god into an orthodox representative of Tendai theology—thus bringing to its completion the process of domestication started (or continued) by the Genshi kimyōdan. Even in the Genshi kimyōdan movement, however, Matarajin, while reinterpreted—and domesticated—in terms of Tendai scholasticism, remained an "essence-stealing demon." Jōin's interpretation is rejected by another author, Mitsuan Sōji 密庵僧慈, who affirms in his *Saiten kaifūshō* 祭典開覆章 (1806) that Jōin "never read the *Mahāvairocana-sūtra,*" and he does not know that Matarajin designates the seven divine Mothers. He confuses Konpira and Matara and turns them into a single god. This is a theory, but not the correct one." See Yamamoto 1998a: 171.

17. See for instance Sugawara Kōji 2004.

18. Certain scholars emphasize one aspect at the expense of another. Orikuchi Shinobu, for instance, interpreted Matarajin as a *genius loci,* a representative of the powers of the ground. See Tanigawa 2009: 353–354. These two aspects, however, need not be exclusive, indeed, they are constantly intertwined—as can be seen in the cases of the Three Devas, Shinra Myōjin, Konpira Gongen, Gozu Tennō, etc. In this particular case, we are told that Shinra Myōjin is only the foreign manifestion of the Japanese god Susanoo. On this question, see Kim Sujung 2014 .

19. Yamamoto 1998a: 250–251.

20. On that point, it seems related to the *tengu odoshi* performed at the *ushirodo.* See *Keiran shūyōshū, T.* 76, 2410: 730b–c.

21. There is no extant image of the fierce Matarajin (apart from an image of Mahākāla called Matarajin in the *Bukkyō zuzō shūsei*). The image of Matarajin found on Mount Hiei has lost its fierce appearance. The representation of Matarajin's "song and dance" seems to derive from the Shushō-e context (at sites like Mōtsuji and Tōnomine), where Matarajin is shown as an old man (*shukujin*). In the rituals of Mount Hiei, however, no image is visible.

22. See *Keiran shūyōshū, T.* 76, 2410: 632c.

23. On this question, see Rhodes 1987.

24. See *Genshi kimyōdan hirokushū,* quoted in Uesugi 1973, 2: 838a. See also Yamamoto 1998a: 186.

25. On Daigenshuri, see Durt 1983.

26. On the Constantly Walking Samādhi (*jōgyō-zanmai*), see Faure 1986a.

27. See for instance *Shiojiri* 49, which calls Matarajin the form of

Mahākāla as a *yakṣa* with three faces and six arms, with which he tames the *ḍākinīs* and all the demons. See Kageyama 1973a: 255.

28. On Matarajin and the human yellow, see *Shiojiri* 35, 9: 604–605. On the human yellow, see also Moriyama 1965: 544; Iyanaga 2012: 394–395; and Faure 2015a, chap. 4.

29. *T.* 76, 2410: 633a.

30. Yamamoto 1998a: 124; and Iyanaga 1994.

31. Yamamoto 1998a: 130–131. In one source at least, Mahākāla (Daikokuten) and Matarajin are said to symbolize the two aspects, evil and good, deluded and enlightened, of all beings. This formulation calls to mind the Janus-faced Kōjin, who appears as a benign figure to the good, and as a terrible demon to the bad.

32. Yamamoto 1998a: 201.

33. *T.* 76, 2410: 632c–633a.

34. The twelve vowels, as opposed to the thirty-five consonants produced by these "mothers" to form a total of forty-seven letters. As noted above, this phonological interpretation of Matarajin is found in Jōin.

35. See Uesugi 1973, 2: 891–892; and the *Dainichikyō so ennoshō* 大日經疏演奧鈔 by Gōhō, *T.* 59: 2216, 394a.

36. *T.* 19, 1003. See also Uesugi 1973, 2: 891.

37. This interpretation also brings to mind the popular image of Jizō who "removes the nails" (Kuginuki Jizō 釘抜地蔵); this Jizō is himself represented as a pair of pliers.

38. See Tochigi kenritsu hakubutsukan 1996: 79, fig. 82; and Kawamura 2008.

39. The Seven Mothers in the retinue of Yama are: Rudrī (Jizai-nyo 自在女), Vaiṣṇavī (Biishunu-nyo), Indrāṇī (Yama-nyo), Vārāhī (Bonten-nyo 梵天女), Caurī (Taishaku-nyo 帝釈女), Kaumarī (Kumari), and Cāmuṇḍā (Shamonda).

40. The identification of the Seven Mothers with the seven stars of the Northern Dipper also brings Matarajin (qua Mahākāla) closer to Vināyaka, often represented together with the Mothers, and to Hārītī, who appears in the company of the seven stars in the Seven-star Nyoirin mandala.

41. See DesJardins 2001.

42. See *Mararajin shikō* 摩多羅神私考, quoted in Yamamoto 1998a: 213–215.

43. Apart from the parallel episodes of Ennin's encounter with Matarajin and Sekizan Myōjin, and Enchin's encounter with Shinra Myōjin, it reappears in the meeting of Saichō with Sannō Gongen, and of Ennin with the god of Sumiyoshi.

44. See Tsuji Zennosuke 1919–1931; Miyaji 1931; Kageyama 1975b; Kida 1976; Yamamoto 1998a; Kawamura 2008.

45. On the cult of the Taishan god in Japan, see Nasu 2004.

46. *DNBZ* 86, quoted in Yamamoto 1998a: 151.

47. See Kawamura 2008: 93.

48. For instance, when the controversy over the ordination platform became particularly heated during the reign of Sujaku Tennō (1036–1045), an

ominous rumbling was heard in the direction of Shinra Myōjin's shrine. See *Jimon denki hōroku,* in *DNBZ* 86: 120.

49. In a cryptic passage of Tachibana Narisue's 橘成季 *Kokon chomonjū* 古今著聞集 (A Collection of Notable Tales Old and New), we are told that Shinra Myōjin and Sannō Gongen were initially both worshipped at Miidera, but Sannō Gongen eventually returned to Mount Hiei. Quoted in Miyake 1998. In the *Aki no yo nagamonogatari* 秋夜長物語, the fight between Sanmon and Jimon (and their respective protectors) is put in a broader perspective: after the destruction of Miidera by the monks of Mount Hiei, thirty Miidera monks dream that Sannō Gongen has come to pay an official visit to Shinra Myōjin. One of the monks (in the dream) wonders about this, since the monks of Mount Hiei had destroyed Miidera. Shinra Myōjin then admonishes him: "It is hardly likely that you would know what pleases me. With the destruction of the temple and the priests' quarters there is opportunity now for merit to be earned through contributions toward its reconstruction. With the loss of the sūtras and *śāstras*, the commentaries and sacred teachings, a fate of future enlightenment may be secured by recopying them. . . . Although products of sorrow, these things are cause for joy. Sannō came here because he was also glad." See Childs 1980: 149–150. A variant of that story appears in the *Shasekishū;* see Morrell 1973: 474.

50. Yamamoto 1998a: 55.

51. See *Jitoku shū* (1344), cited in Miyake 1998. In a similar episode, Shirakawa Tennō suffers the loss of his heir after refusing to allow the Miidera priest Raigō to build an ordination platform. The death of the crown prince from smallpox in 1077 is anachronistically attributed to a curse from Raigō's resentful spirit (*onryō*), since the priest died seven years later, in 1084. See Yamamoto 1998a: 2–17.

52. Shinra Myōjin could also send illness to unworthy monks. See Morrell 1985: 87–88 and 153–154.

53. The best known example is Daruma (Bodhidharma), about which see Faure 2011. Other examples include the simian god Sarutahiko, the householder Kotan, Gozu Tennō's nemesis and double, and Yagorō-san, a giant wrathful effigy still displayed in Kyushu festivals.

54. See Kawamura 2008.

55. On this island, see Moerman 2009.

56. The date varies according to sources. According to the *Sekizan myōjin engi* (*ST,* 624), Anne built the Zen'in in 864, but the shrine to Sekizan Myōjin had to await an edict dated 868, just after Anne's death. According to the *Jikaku daishiden* 慈覺大師伝, it was erected in 888. Shiozawa Hirohito thinks that the construction of Sekizan Zen'in was started in 868 and was finished in 888. See Shiozawa 2008: 32. I am indebted to Kim Sujung for this reference.

Note that the name of that temple does not necessarily refer to Zen (Chan) meditation, as usually thought, but could also refer to the *shan* 禅 ritual that was part of the *fengshan* 封禅 sacrifices to heaven and earth. It would therefore be related to the chthonian god of Taishan (J. Taizan Fukun). See *Sekizan myōjin engi,* in *ST,* Tendai shintō 2: 623–625. On Taishan, see Chavannes 1910.

57. See *Genpei jōsuiki* 1988, 2: 69: "Sekizan is the name of a mountain in China. The god is called Sekizan Myōjin because he dwells on that mountain. He is also called Taizan Fukun." See also Minakata 1971.

58. Sekizan Myōjin's identification with Taizan Fukun probably took place in China, due to the proximity of Chishan to Mount Tai (Taishan).

59. The oldest document regarding Shinra Myōjin is the *Onjōji ryūge-e engi* 園城寺龍華会縁起 (1062), quoted in the *Honchō zoku monsui* 11. On Shinra Myōjin, see Kageyama 1975b; Miyaji 1931; and Guth 1999.

60. I am indebted to Kim Sujung for pointing this out to me. On Chang Pogo and Matarajin, see Lee Pyŏng-ro 2006: 319–341.

61. Miyai Yoshio emphasizes the relations between Ōmi province and Silla, and argues that the presence of Korean immigrants in that province explains the apparition of Shinra Myōjin. See Miyai 2004: 335–336; see also Kim Sujung 2014, chap. 5.

62. On Mio Myōjin, see Kageyama 1973a: 465–467.

63. According to the *Shinra ryakki* 新羅略記, Hannya Dōji and Shukuō Dōji were born from the two halves of the halberd that the goddess Amaterasu gave to her brother Susanoo. See *Shinra ryakki, ST,* Ronsetsu-hen 17, Shugendō: 322–325.

64. See Misaki 1992: 230–231; and Kimura 1991: 87.

65. Kuroda Satoshi (1998) has counted a total 36 representations in paintings, including Miidera mandalas.

66. See for instance Kimura 1991: 87–91.

67. See Kuroda Satoshi 2001.

68. See Miyake 2002b, and Ōsaka shiritsu bijutsukan 1999. Christine Guth argues that the statue predates the 12th century (1999: 102). Kim Sujung has suggested a link between Shinra Myōjin and of one of Mañjuśrī's acolytes, an old man identified with the Indian ascetic Vasu (Basu Sennin). See Kim Sujung 2014: 242.

69. See Kageyama 1973a: 45–46 and 471.

70. Kageyama 1973a, ill. 157.

71. See *The Fluid Pantheon*, fig. 2.18.

72. See Misaki 1992: 229, based on the *Shinra Myōjin mondō shō yōkunsho* (1344).

73. See Misaki 1992: 230.

74. *T.* 76, 2410: 853a.

75. Quoted in Eishin's 永心 *Jitōku shū* 寺徳集, in *ZGR* 18; see also Miyake 1998: 12.

76. See Yamamoto 1998a: 150–151, and Miyake 1998: 11. The same passage, with slight variations, is also found in the *Onjōji denki*, in *DNBZ* 127: 36, 49.

77. On the relation between Shinra Myōjin and Susanoo, see Miyai 1964.

78. The text adds that Shinra Myōjin has several *honji,* but the main one is Monju. It also mentions the story of Somin Shōrai 蘇民将来, apparently conflating Shinra Myōjin with Gozu Tennō and presenting him as a pestilence deity. On Shinra Myōjin, see also *Genkō shakusho* 18, section on "Immortals" (Sennin).

79. Yamamoto 1998a: 199.

80. See Yamamoto 1998a: 140–142.

81. As is well known, in the medieval Pure Land schools, Amida's saving grace was said to transcend all particular benefits and protections offered by the buddhas and *kami,* and to insure the "easy way" to salvation. From the standpoint of Matarajin's worshipers, Pure Land adepts could be criticized for failing to reckon with Matarajin. On the identity between Matarajin, Mahākāla, Dakiniten, and the gods of obstacles (*shōgejin* 障碍神), see *T.* 76, 2410: 632c–633a.

82. The same is true, *mutatis mutandis,* for Yama and the ten kings of hell, who administer a karmic retribution that, in early Buddhism, was supposedly automatic.

83. Yamamoto 1998a: 212.

84. See *Keiran shūyōshū, T.* 76, 2410: 730c.

85. See Kawamura 2008.

86. The Okina mask kept at the Jōgyō Hall of Tōnomine was worshipped as Madarajin. The same mask was worshiped as guardian of the *hinin.* It also represents Monju, a deity worshiped by lepers and other outcasts.

87. According to the *Kojitsu sōshi* 故實雙紙, for instance, the "mad dance" performed during the Shushō-e of Rinnōji was a way to discard demonic obstacles. The climax of that ritual was the greeting of Matarajin, on the third and fifth nights. See Yamaji Kōzō 1990; and Kawamura 2008: 348. The same performance took place at Izusan Shrine and at Tōnomine.

88. On the Shushō-e and the *ushirodo,* see Hattori 1973. Hattori argues that *sarugaku* actors performed series of dances in front of the statue at the time of the Shūshō-e festival.

89. Matarajin may not always have been the main protagonist of the Shūshō-e. The important exorcism (*tsuina*) that was staged on the last night of the Shūshō-e ritual involved the chasing and beating of the demon Vināyaka—depicted as the disrupter of cosmic order—by twelve guardian deities led by Ryūten 龍天 (the *nāga* king) and Bishamonten. This symbolic act was played behind closed doors to avoid contamination. See Matsuoka Shinpei 2000b.

90. Hayakawa 2000: 18–122. See also the texts edited in Uesugi 1973, 2: 831–896: *Matarajin shikō,* pp. 891–892; and *Madarijin ki,* pp. 892–895.

91. See Kageyama 1973a: 248–251.

92. See *Shintō bijutsu,* in Kageyama 1973a: 247–250.

93. As we will see, this may also be related to his role as placenta deity. Indeed, one source calls him Ina Tenjin, a name that may refer to the *ena kōjin* or placenta deity (on which see my forthcoming volume in this series, *Lords of Life*, chap. 2).

94. See for instance the criticism of the Genshi kimyōdan by Reikū Kōken, quoted in Yamamoto 1998a: 197.

95. See for instance Kageyama 1973a.

96. See the explanation of Matarajin's iconography and legend in Hazama 1948, 2: 143–144. In the *Genshi shiki,* Matara is said to be a Sanskrit term, translated into Japanese as Dainichi. Dai represents the six elements (*rokudai*

六大), Nichi, the six types of consciousness (*rokushiki* 六識). In other words, Matarajin symbolizes the mind-king (*shinnō* 心王) or ruler of the six types of consciousness. His two acolytes represent the gross mental elements of these six types of consciousness. See Uesugi 1973, 2: 843b. Likewise, according to the *Shiojiri,* the triad is said to symbolize the "three contemplations of the one mind" (*isshin sangan* 一心三觀). See Kageyama 1973a: 250–251.

97. *Genshi dan hishō,* in Hayakawa 2000: 98–99.

98. Hayakawa 2000: 63–64.

99. Hayakawa 2000: 90–91; see also Kawamura 2008: 184.

100. Hayakawa 2000: 104b. See also *Genshi jūdaishi kuketsu shisho,* quoted in Kawamura 2008: 189.

101. Yamamoto 1998a: 197–199.

102. See *Genshi kimyōdan denki,* quoted in Yamamoto 1998a: 200.

103. On this question, see Sanford 1994. In this respect, Matarajin resembles the Hie Shrine deity Jūzenji.

104. See Yamamoto 1998a: 182–183.

105. Suzuki Masataka notes the homophony between Matara, Māra (in the sense of obstacle), and *mara,* a slang word meaning penis. See Suzuki Masataka 2001: 284.

106. Eizan bunko archives. See Yamamoto 1998a: 153.

107. See *Jōgyōdō Raiyuki,* quoted in Yamamoto 1998a: 58.

108. See Kageyama 1973a: 246.

109. As Kawamura Minato (2008) points out, the *saimon* contained in the *Gunsho ruijū* and the *Dainihon bukkyō zensho* are quite different. The paradox of Matarajin reading a *saimon* addressed to himself suggests that the ox-riding figure may not be Matarajin, but simply the officiating priest. The motif of the ox (or bull) is significant: it is also the mount of Yama (Enmaten), Yamāntaka (Yama's Conqueror, J. Daiitoku), and Maheśvara (i.e., Mahākāla, J. Daijizaiten), all Indian gods that may have served as prototypes for Matarajin. In Indian texts, ox, bull, and buffalo are usually clearly distinguished as divine mounts, but in Japan this tendency tends to get lost.

110. The origin story of Kōryūji tells us that the Tendai priest Genshin 源信 (Eshin sōzu 恵心僧都) worshiped in a dream an image of the Amida of the same temple, and carved himself that image; then, in 1012, on the occasion of a *nenbutsu* assembly, he enshrined Matarajin as protector at the "back door" (*ushirodo*) of the temple, and, on the night of the twelfth of the same month, performed for this god a musical festival (*hōraku saiki*) that gave birth to a medieval performance known as Matarajin *fūryū* 風流. We are told that, later on, when the procession in that festival came to include an ox, it was called the Ox Festival. However, this explanation sounds like a rationalization that downplays the symbolic importance of the ox.

111. The mask used by the priest today is said to be the one designed by Tomioka Tessai 富岡鉄斎 when he restored the ritual in 1887. In a representation on a folding screen by Ukita Ikkei 浮田一恵 (1795–1859), which forms part of a set (the other being the representation of the Yasurai festival of Imamiya 今宮 Shrine against epidemics), the ox-riding figure, wearing a round white mask, looks strikingly alien, albeit more benign—and rather Korean. The screens

are preserved at the Hosomi Art Museum in Kyoto. The Kōryūji deity appears there as a moon-faced female riding a black ox or bull, wearing a white mask with three green leaves over her head, holding paper strips (*gohei*). Her two acolytes wear a red and green demon mask, respectively, and hold a spear. See Kyōto kokuritsu hakubutsukan 2004: 129, ill. 67. See also Tanigawa 2009: 367; and Katō 1902: 127–129. The *Miyako meisho zue* 都名所図絵 shows the god wearing a *tengu*-like mask and riding a black ox backward. See *Miyako meisho zue*: 444–445; I am indebted to Tanaka Takako for this reference. This work also dates from the Edo period, however. Another festival, called Matara kijin sai 摩多羅鬼神祭 (Festival of the Demon Matara), in Makabe 真壁 district (Ibaraki prefecture), shows the god wearing a very different mask and riding a horse. The name of that festival indicates that, at the popular level, Matarajin was still perceived as a demon (*kijin* 鬼神). On this festival, see Kawamura 2008.

112. Yamamoto 1998a: 147–148.

113. Yamamoto 1998a: 147.

114. See Orikuchi, *Nihon geinōshi josetsu,* quoted in Tanigawa 2009: 353–354.

115. The identification of Shinra Myōjin with Susanoo seems to be a later development. See *Jimon denki horoku:* 108; and Tsuji Zennosuke 1919–1931, 1: 216–217 (pp. 168–169 in the 1964 edition).

116. *Jimon denki horoku:* 113.

117. Yamamoto 1998a: 254.

118. Yamamoto 1998a: 258.

119. Kageyama 1973a: 248–250. In another tradition, the place where Saichō encountered the tutelary deity (*jinushi*) Ninomiya 二宮 in the form of an old man was called Peak of Kokūzō, and it was also believed to be the place where the seven stars (or the planet Venus) had fallen. Ninomiya is worshiped at one of the seven Upper Shrines of Hie, and these seven shrines are themselves said to be the traces on earth of the seven stars. Yamamoto Hiroko, however, denies that the Matarajin of the Genshi kimyōdan had special relations with the seven stars. She argues that the auxiliary star mentioned in this context is not Myōken, the god of the pole star, but an Indian bodhisattva of the same name. But in other ritual texts, the auxiliary star is indeed the polar Myōken. See Yamamoto 1998a: 258–260.

120. Noteworthy in this respect is the tradition related to the "fundamental" Sannō of the *jingūji.* According to the *Keiran shūyōshū,* this deity appeared to Saichō before his ordination, in the form of a goddess, also referred to as a "*yakṣa* deity" (*tennyo tenba yashajin* 天女天婆夜叉神). After receiving the tonsure, Saichō buried his hair at this spot. According to a related tradition, it was precisely at that spot that Saichō's father once prayed to the mountain god to grant him a child. It was also there that Saichō's mother, Myōtoku, spent three years after his departure for China. Later on, Saichō built a hermitage on that (overdetermined) site and enshrined an image of Jūichimen Kannon in it. The hermitage eventually became a *jingūji,* whose main deity was an image of Myōken Bosatsu, who was believed to have been a past incarnation of Myōtoku. The image of the *yakṣa* deity, which is perhaps Matarajin,

seems influenced by the legend about Saichō's mother. It also calls to mind that of Kōjin, the paradigmatic god of obstacles.

121. *ST, Tendai shintō* 2: 7.

122. See Kawamura 2008. According to the section on the "Matarajin of Nikkō-san" in the *Razan bunshū* 羅山文集 by the Edo scholar Hayashi Razan 林羅山 (1583–1657), Matarajin appeared to Saichō when the latter visited Mount Tiantai and vowed to accompany him to Japan, transmitting to him a secret ritual of the "drum beating." Saichō met him again on Mount Hiei. See Kageyama 1973a: 246. This reference to the drum beating reflects the image of Matarajin as developed in the Genshi kimyōdan.

123. During the Edo period, Jōin in particular emphasized the identity between Matarajin and Konpira. He was criticized on this point by Mitsuan Sōji 密庵僧慈, a priest of Kōun-in in Nikkō, in his *Saiten kaifūshō* (1806). For Sōji, the name Matarajin refers to the Mothers (*mātṛkās*).

124. In his manifestation as Īśāna (the first of the twelve directional devas), Mahākāla is also identified with the northeast (and with a small northeastern country called Japan, supposedly created by a *kami* called Izanagi—a transparent allusion to Īśāna in the eyes of medieval esoteric Buddhists). On this question, see Itō Satoshi 1995b, Hosokawa 1993: 85–117; and Iyanaga 1996–1997.

125. A similar symbolism was attached to the planet Venus, which mediates between day and night. It is said to come out at the hour of the tiger, becoming the sun; and again at the hour of the monkey, becoming the moon. See *Genshidan hishō:* 95a.

126. See *Keiran shūyōshū, T.* 76, 2410: 632c.

127. If the cult of Kawakatsu (and of Matarajin) was promoted by the Hata clan, that of Shinra Myōjin was sponsored mainly by another Korean immigrant group, the Ōtomo 大友. The Ōmi province, and in particular the region around Lake Biwa, has been from very early on a particularly important settlement area for Korean immigrant groups like the Hata and the Ōtomo. On this question, see Kim Sujung 2014.

128. Kawamura 2008: 80. Yamamoto, however, links this Ina Tenjin with the *ḍākinī* (1998a: 147).

129. Matsuoka Shinpei 2000b.

CODA

1. See for instance Satō Hiroo 1998 and 2003.
2. Latour 2005: 39.
3. Teuween and Rambelli 2003: 47; see also p. 25.
4. Ibid., 30.
5. Ibid., 48.
6. Ibid.
7. Ibid., 29–30. The *onryō* 怨霊 or *goryō* 御霊 were malevolent spirits thought to be bent on revenge.
8. Indeed, this paradigm is a variant of analogical thought, as described in its classical Chinese version by Marcel Granet (1999), and to which Pierre

Bourdieu opposed—as its supplement or reality—the fuzzy "logic of practice" (1990: 86–87, 261).

9. The importance of the *jissha* has recently been emphasized in Rambelli and Teeuwen 2003: 31–32.

10. The *Keiran shūyōshū* also distinguishes between *gonsha* and *jissha* types of malevolent spirits (*onryō*), recognizable by the specific pains they inflict. In the first case, where pain is caused by buddhas and bodhisattvas (!), the only remedy is repentance; in the second case, an exorcism is needed. It also distinguishes three types of *jissha*: 1) "wild gods" (*kōjin*); 2) "assimilation bodies" (*tōrujin*); and 3) devas like Shōten. The mention of the assimilation bodies is somewhat intriguing, since the latter are in principle animal manifestations of the buddha Dainichi (or of some bodhisattvas). *T.* 76, 2410: 731c. See also Yamamoto 1998a: 434–436.

11. Initially, Hachiman and Amaterasu were oracular deities, but as they were integrated into the imperial cult, they gradually lost their oracular nature.

12. See *Bukkyō daijiten*, 9: 245; *Shin honji no koto*, in *Shinshū shiryō shūsei,* 5: 82–84; *Ryūkyū shintōki*, 96–97.

13. *T.* 76, 2410: 866a.

14. See *Takachiho jūshāgū*, in *ST,* Jinja-hen: Hizen, Higo, Hyuga, Satsuma, Ōsumi no kuni: 480.

15. The *Tenshō kōtaijin giki* 天照皇大神儀軌 also distinguishes three levels. Amaterasu is the only deity at the higher level of "innate awakening." The level of "nonawakening" is occupied by deities like the "raging deities" (*araburu kami*) of Izumo. Deities of this type, which are truly deluded, are actually demons. Finally, there are gods who have reached "initial awakening" after a long slumber in the cycle of transmigration. Among them are the *kami* of Iwashimizu and Hiromine Shrines. See Kokubungaku kenkyū shiryōkan 1999a: 365; see also *Tenshō kōtaijin giki*: 65. This distinction between three types of deities, which boils down to one between good (orthodox) and evil (heterodox, lit. "perverse") deities (*jashin* 邪神), is still found in the *Jinten ainōshō*, in a passage dealing with the oracles of Ise Shrine. This passage explains why, because perverse deities imitated the oracles of the great deity Amaterasu, the latter decided to stop giving oracles. See *Jinten ainōshō*, *DNBZ* 130: 312. On Susanoo as a "trickster-figure," see Ouwehand 1958.

16. *Jindaikan hiketsu*, *ZST,* Ronsetsu-hen, Shūgō shintō: 85–86.

17. See *Jindaikan hiketsu*, *ZST,* Ronsetsu-hen, Shūgō shintō: 86–88. This typology is based on the *Reikiki*, in *ST,* Ronsetsu-hen, Shingon shintō 1: 86–87.

18. Jorge Luis Borges, "John Wilkins' Analytical Language," in Borges 1999: 231; and Foucault 1994. According to this oft-quoted passage, all animals are divided into: (a) belonging to the Emperor, (b) embalmed, (c) tame, (d) suckling pigs, (e) sirens, (f) fabulous, (g) stray dogs, (h) included in the present classification, (i) frenzied, (j) innumerable, (k) drawn with a very fine camelhair brush, (l) *et cetera,* (m) having just broken the water pitcher, (n) that from a long way off look like flies.

19. Here is how Jean-Joseph Goux describes the "universal equivalent"

in other contexts: "In each case, a hierarchy is instituted between an excluded, idealized element and the other elements, which measure their value in it." See Goux 1990: 4.

20. This point is brought home visually in the Sannō mandala (Figs. C.1 and C.2), where the two-tiered model is surreptitiously replaced by a three-tiered model, in which the buddhas themselves, instead of being the *honji,* are the emanations of the seed-letters above them, and by the same token become intermediaries (or mediators) between these primordial sounds (already written down) and the *kami* below.

21. Among the entourage, we must include the mount of the deity. This mount can signify the animal form taken by that deity (the fox for Dakiniten, the dragon for Benzaiten), or simply some of its latent aspects. In some cases—Fugen's elephant, for instance—we seem to have a mount in the ordinary sense, rather than an avatar. But even in that case, the subliminal message is sometimes apparent: in some Japanese representations, Fugen's elephants have a strongly demonic face— reminiscent of Vināyaka.

22. Deleuze 1995: 132.

23. The *honji suijaku* paradigm finds its iconographic expression in painted scrolls such as the Sannō mandala (Fig. C.1). But precisely, it is on Mount Hiei that mythological proliferation and philosophical speculation give birth to a new hybrid category of gods, which are going to put the system into question. The recent rediscovery of the underground structure of the Juge-gū of Hie Shrine, for instance, shows the complexity of the cult: *kami* were worshiped above, while buddhas were worshiped in the basement (*geden*), thereby communicating with the spring that existed there, in the process changing their nature and becoming increasingly telluric deities. The new medieval gods were not merely hypostases of some cosmic buddha; they shifted from one state or stasis to another, and flowed from one form into another.

24. Derrida 1982: 3; quoted in Law 2004: 42.

25. Law 2004: 42.

26. Satō Hiroo 2003.

27. Morrell 1973: 467.

28. I borrow the metaphor from Henri Atlan (1979).

29. See Atlan 1986: 83–84.

30. Latour 1993: 34, 41–42, 78; on hybrids, see also Ingold 2011, chap. 8.

31. Latour 1999: 74. Latour quotes William James: "The intermediaries which in their concrete particularity form a bridge, evaporate ideally into an empty interval to cross. . . ." See James 1975: 247–248.

32. See Latour 1993: 95.

33. Latour 1993: 77–79.

34. Taking his cue from Nietzsche, Pierre Hadot writes: "From the perspective of the metaphor of Nature as Sphynx, not to unveil Nature is to let the young girl's bosom, a symbol of beauty and art, hide the ferocious, terrifying beast, the symbol of Truth." See Hadot 2006: 292.

35. See for instance *Kakuzenshō*, *DNBZ* 47: 116b. On this resemblance,

see also *Jakushōdō kokkyōshū*, *DNBZ*, 280b. On Batō Kannon and horses, see *Hōbōgirin* 1: 59–60; and Lomi 2011. In popular religion, there is also an Ox-headed Kannon (Gozu Kannon) specialized in the protection of bovines. See Kyburz 1987: 228. These representations call to mind the animal-headed deities of the Tibetan "intermediary realm" (*bardo*), although the conception of the *bardo* did not develop in Japanese iconography. But Hayagrīva is, precisely, a *tōrujin*. Ox-headed deities like Gozu Tennō, while reinterpreted by the Buddhists as "traces" (*suijaku*) of a buddha, have a strong demonic nature and are typical of the *jissha* category.

36. Deleuze and Guattari comment on Dumézil's analysis of the Indo-European man of war: "The man of war has an entire becoming that implies multiplicity, celerity, ubiquity, metamorphosis and treason, the power of affect. Wolf-men, bear-men, wildcat-men, men of every animality, secret brotherhoods, animated the battlefields." Deleuze and Guattari 1987: 243.

37. Perhaps this is why Okina, in late medieval Japan, becomes the supreme god: he is above all a mask.

38. Deleuze and Guattari 1987: 249.

39. Toffin 1993: 139.

40. See Knipe 1972.

41. See Sauzeau and Sauzeau 2004; see also N. J. Allen 1987 and 1998. A case in point is that of the four Indian *varnas*, which Dumézil tried, not too convincingly, to reduce to the three functions.

42. Douglas 2002: 99.

43. On the "three plus one" figure, see Knipe 1972: 32–33; and Malamoud 1996: 145. Gérard Toffin has raised objections to the existence of a fourth function. He argues that the latter is never integrated in a series, as Dumézil required, and that it is not sustained by an organizing functional intention, as was the case with the three functions. Furthermore, he reproaches it for being too heterogeneous, covering as it does things that are very different, and at times radically opposite. In other words, it is a residual category that includes everything that does not fit the first three functions. As such, it cannot be put on the same level as the other functions. But the third function, as Dumézil himself admitted, was already quite heterogeneous and residual, and the residue or remainder is precisely a defining characteristic of the fourth function. The fact that the latter does not fit the Dumézilian model neatly, that it escapes the Procrustean bed of Indo-European ideology, might be more a strength than a weakness in the case of medieval Japan. See Toffin 1993: 160–163.

44. On this question, see Malamoud 1996: 7–22; and Derrida 2002.

45. Van Gennep 2010.

46. On this question, see Macé 2009.

47. Medieval esoteric Buddhism plays dialectically with two conceptions of evil: on the one hand, a cosmic opposition, perhaps inherited from Hinduism, between the two principles of good and evil; on the other hand, their identity or ambivalence, based on the *hongaku* theory.

48. See Takahashi Yūsuke 2006a. Māra was once seen as the ambiguous source of reality, in *hongaku* fashion, but was eventually relegated (once again) to the position of an outside enemy as a god of obstacles.

49. Gould and Lewontin 1979.

50. Davidson 2002: 131–142.

51. A parallax is usually defined as the effect by which the position or direction of an object appears to differ when viewed from different positions. See Žižek 2009: 4.

52. See Amino 1978.

53. Latour 1993. A similar argument was made, in the wake of postmodernism, by Japanese scholars such as Asada Akira and Karatani Kōjin.

54. Law 2004: 28–34. This notion calls to mind Yves Bonnefoy's "arrière-pays," yet the latter notion, which I also find attractive, is completely different, pointing, as it were, to the transcendent "silver lining" of mundane landscapes. See Bonnefoy 2003: 46–48.

55. Law 2004: 34.

56. Law 2004: 83.

57. Lévi-Strauss 1982: 144.

58. Stengers 2010–2011, vol. 1.

59. See Foucault 1982.

60. Quoted in Olivier 2008: 50.

BIBLIOGRAPHY

PRIMARY SOURCES

Ainōshō 壒嚢鈔 (1445). By Gyōyō 行誉. In *Jinten ainōshō, ainōshō* 塵添壒嚢鈔. 壒嚢鈔, ed. Hamada Atsushi 濱田敦 and Satake Akihiro 佐竹昭広 (Kyoto: Rinsen shoten, 1971).

Aizen denpu hihō daiji 愛染田夫秘法大事. In Yamamoto 1998a: 415.

Amano zatsuki 天野雑記. *ST,* Ronsetsu-hen 論説編 1, Shingon shintō 真言神道 1: 379–409.

Amaterasu kōtaijin giki 天照皇太神儀軌. In Kokubungaku kenkyū shiryōkan 1999a: 355–360.

Asabashō 阿娑縛抄. By Shōchō 承澄 (1205–1282). *TZ* 8–9, 3190; also *DNBZ* 57–60.

Asama-san engi 朝熊山縁起. In *Jisha engi* 寺社縁起: 77–88.

Atsuta kōshiki 熱田講式. In Kokubungaku kenkyū shiryōkan 1999b: 361–372.

Atsuta kōshiki 熱田講式. In *Atsuta jingū shiryō: engi yuisho-hen* 熱田神宮資料一縁起由緒編, ed. Atsuta jingū chō, 1: 107–108 (2006). See also Kokubungaku kenkyū shiryōkan 1999b: 373–402.

Atsuzōshi 厚造紙. By Genkai 元海 (1094–1157). *T.* 78, 2483.

Azhapo guishen dajiang shangfo tuoluoni jing 阿吒婆拘鬼神大将上佛陀羅尼經. *T.* 21, 1238.

Azuma kagami 吾妻鏡. Anon. *KST* 32–33.

Beifang Pishamen tianwang suijun hufa yigui 北方毘沙門天王随軍護法儀軌. Trans. Amoghavajra. *T.* 21, 1247.

Benzaiten 弁才天. In Mukōzaka 2007: 23–25.

Benzaiten hihō 弁才天秘法 (copy by Eison 叡尊). In Mukōzaka 2007: 34–35.

Benzaiten kōshiki 弁才天講式. In Yamamoto 1998a: 467–468.

Benzaiten saimon 弁才天祭文. In Yamamoto 1998a: 468.

Benzaiten-sha monjo 弁才天社文書. In Hayashiya et al. 1995: 214–224.

Benzaiten shugi 弁才天修儀. See *Saishō gokoku Ugaya tontoku nyoi hōju-ō shugi.*

Benzaiten shugi shi 弁才天修儀私. In Yamamoto 1998a: 499–502.

Besson zakki 別尊雑記 (*Gojikkanshō* 五十巻抄). By Shinkaku 心覚 (1117–1180). *TZ* 3, 3007: 57–674.

Betsugyō 別行. By Kanjo 寛助 (1052–1125). *T.* 78, 2476.

Betsugyō giki 別行儀軌. In Kanagawa kenritsu Kanazawa bunko 2007b: 68–70.

Bikisho (var. *Hanagaerisho*) 鼻歸書 (1324). By Chien 智円. *ST,* Ronsetsu-hen 論説編 2, Shingon shintō 真言神道 2: 505–522.

Bishamon kudoku kyō 毘沙門功徳經. Japanese apocryphon (Muromachi period). Quoted in Kida 1976: 234.

Bishamonten nijūhachi shisha zuzō 毘沙門天二十八使者図像. *TZ* 7: 551–566.

Biwa no shaku 琵琶の釈. *NSSS* 17: 123–124.

Bodaijōkyō ryakugishaku 菩提場經略義釈. By Enchin 円珍 (814–891). *T.* 61, 2230.

Bodaishin gishō. See *Taizō kongō bodaishin ryaku mondō shō*.

Bonbun Shijōkōbutchō darani shoson zue 梵文熾盛光佛頂陀羅尼諸尊図会. *TZ* 4, 3012.

Buchū hiden 峰中秘伝. In *Shugendō shōso,* vol. 1.

Bukkyō daijiten 佛教大辞典. Ed. Mochizuki Shinkō 望月信亨. 10 vols. Kyoto: Sekai seiten kankō kyōkai, 1960.

Bukkyō zuzō shūsei 佛教図像聚成 *(BZS)*. In Kyōto shiritsu geijutsu daigaku geijutsu shiryōkan 2004.

Buppō shintō ki 佛法神道記. *ST,* Ronsetsu-hen 論説編 1, Shingon shintō 真言神道 1: 84–90.

Bussetsu chijin daranikyō 佛説地神陀羅尼經. *NSSS* 17: 119–121.

Bussetsu chijin darani ōji kyō 佛説地神陀羅尼王子經. *NSSS* 17: 124–126.

Bussetsu chijin kyō 説地神. In *Shugen seiten*, 53–54.

Bussetsu Daibenzaitennyo kyō 説大弁才天女経. Japanese apocryphon. In Itō Satoshi 1993: 45–46.

Bussetsu Daikōjin seyo fukutoku enman darani-kyō 佛説大荒神施与福徳圓満陀羅尼經. Trans. attr. Amoghavajra. In *Shugen seiten*, 51–53.

Bussetsu Dai Uga kudoku Benzaiten-kyō 説大宇賀功徳弁才天經. In Itō Satoshi 1993: 40–46.

Bussetsu saishō gokoku Ugaya tontoku nyoi hōju darani-kyō 説最勝護国宇賀耶頓得如意宝珠陀羅尼経. In Yamamoto 1998a: 475–478.

Bussetsu shinko daiō bosatsu ichiji himitsu sokushitsu jōju shiki kyō 仏説辰狐大王菩薩一字速疾成就式經. Japanese apocryphon. In Itō Satoshi 1993: 44–45.

Bussetsu sokushin hinten fukutoku enman Uga shinshō bosatsu hakuj jigen mikka jōju-kyō 佛説即身貧転福徳円満宇賀神将菩薩白蛇示現三日成就經. In Yamamoto 1998a: 479–480.

Bussetsu Uga shinnō fukutoku enman darani-kyō 仏説宇賀神王福徳円満陀羅尼經. In Yamamoto 1998a: 481–482.

Busshin ittai kanjō shō 佛神一躰灌頂鈔. Eizan bunko archives.

Butsuga shariki 仏牙舎利記. *GR* 24: 443.

Byakuhō kushō 白宝口鈔. By Ryōson 亮尊. *TZ* 6–7, 3119.

Byakuhō shō 白宝鈔. By Chōen 澄円 (1218–ca.1290). *TZ* 10, 3191.

Chang ahan jing 長阿含經. Trans. Buddhayaśas and Zhu Fonian 竺佛念. *T.* 1, 1.

Chibukushima engi 智福嶋縁起. By Fumon 普文. *DNBZ* 86, 798: 295–297.

Chijin ku saimon 地神供祭文. *NSSS* 17: 322–323.

Chijin kyō (var. *Jijin kyō*) 地神經. *NSSS* 17: 206–207.

Chijin kyō biwa no shaku 地神經琵琶の釈. *NSSS* 17: 207–208.

Chijin mōsō engi 地神盲僧縁起. *NSSS* 17: 225–228.

Chikubushima engi 竹生島縁起. In *Shugendō shiryō shū,* 2: 26–29. Also in *GR* 25: 616–620.

Chikubushima engi ryaku 竹生島縁起略. Quoted in Kida 1976: 251.

Chintaku reifu engi shūsetsu 鎮宅霊符縁起集説. By Takuryō 沢了. *ST,* Ronsetsu-hen 論説編 16, Onmyōdō: 243–294. Also as *Chintaku reifujin engi shūsetsu,* in Hayakawa 2000: 335–364.

Chiribukuro 塵袋 (ca. 1264). Tokyo: Nihon koten zenshū kankōkai, 1934–1935.

Chishō Daishi zenshū 智証大師全集. Ed. Onjōji hensankai 園城寺編纂会. Ōtsu: Onjōji jimusho, 1918; reprint, Kyoto: Dōhōsha shuppan, 1978.

Chōseiden 寵誓伝. By Ikū Shōnin 以空上人 (d. 1670). In Seki 1987: 319–336.

Chōshū ki 長秋記 (1015–1036). By Minamoto no Morotoki 源師時. In *Zōho shiryō taisei,* vols. 16–17.

Da fangguang rulai bimizang jing 大方広如来秘密藏經. *T.* 17, 821.
Dahei tianshen fa 大黒天神法. By Shenkai 神愷. *T.* 21, 1287. See also Naganuma 1987: 209–214.
Daibenzaiten hiketsu 大弁才天秘訣. By Jōgon 淨嚴 (1639–1702). In Hiroya 1925: 87–123.
Daibenzaitennyo himitsu darani-kyō 大弁才天女秘密陀羅尼經. Quoted in Itō 1993: 40–46.
Daigoji monjo 醍醐寺文書. *Dai Nihon komonjo*, vol. 19.
Daijingū sankei ki 大神宮参詣紀 (a.k.a. *Tsūkai sankei ki* 通海参詣記). By Tsūkai 通海 (1234–1305). *ZGR,* Jingi-bu 28: 927–949.
Daijō-in jisha zatsuji 大乗院寺社雑記. By Jinson 尋尊 (1430–1508). Kyoto: Rinsen shoten, 1978.
Daikoku Tenjin-hō. See *Dahei tianshen fa.*
Daikoku tenjin keizō kō. By Shaku Seitan 釈清潭. Quoted in Sasama 1993: 36.
Daikoku tenjin shiki 大黒天神式. In *Kōbō Daishi zenshū* 弘法大師全集, vol. 5.
Dainichikyō sho ennoshō 大日經疏演奥鈔. By Gōhō 杲宝 (1306–1362). *T.* 59: 2216.
Dai Nihon bukkyō zensho 大日本佛教全書 *(DNBZ)*. Ed. Suzuki gakujutsu. 100 vols. Tokyo: Suzuki gakujutsu zaidan, 1970–1973. Earlier edition published 1912–1919 by Bussho kankōkai.
Dai Nihon komonjo 大日本古文書. Ed. Tokyo daigaku, Shiryō hensanjo. Tokyo: Tōkyō daigaku shuppankai, 1901–1940.
Dai Nihon shiryō 大日本史料. Ed. Tokyo daigaku, Shiryō hensanjo. 380 vols. Tokyo: Tōkyō daigaku shiryō hensanjo, 1901–.
Dai Nihon zokuzōkyō 大日本続藏經 *(ZZ)*. Ed. Nakano Tatsue 中野達慧. 750 vols. Kyoto: Zōkyō shoin, 1905–1912. Reprint, Taipei: Xinwenfeng, 1967–1970.
Daishō Kangi shō 大聖歓喜鈔. In Seki 1987: 217–317.
Daishō Kangiten junsei zuigan ki 大聖歓喜天順世随願記. In Seki 1987: 352–381.
Daishō Kangiten-son keisūden 大聖歓喜天尊敬崇伝. In Seki 1987: 337–349.
Dakini hō 吒枳尼法(秘). In Kanagawa kenritsu Kanazawa bunko 2007b: 70–71.
Dakini kechimyaku 吒枳尼血脈. In Kanagawa kenritsu Kanazawa bunko 2007b: 69–70.
Dakini sendari-ō kyō 吒枳尼旃陀利王經. Apocryphon. Quoted in Nakazawa 1994: 247.
Dakiniten hihō 荼吉尼天秘法. In *Shugen seiten* 修験聖典, 492–500.
Dakiniten-son ryaku engi 荼吉尼天尊略縁起 (facsimile). Shinnyodō 真如堂.
Daozang 道藏 (*DZ*). 36 vols. Beijing: Wenwu chubanshe; Shanghai: Commercial Press, 1926. See *Concordance du Tao-tsang: titres des ouvrages,* ed. K. M. Schipper, Publications de l'École Française d'Extrême-Orient 104 (Paris: École Française d'Extrême-Orient, 1975).
Dapiluzhena chengfo shenbian jiachi jing 大毘盧遮那成佛神変加持經. Trans. Śubhakarasiṃha and Yixing 一行. *T.* 18, 848.
Dapiluzhena chengjiu yuqie jing 大毘盧遮那成就儀軌.Trans. Faquan 法全. *T.* 18, 853.
Dasheng Huanxi shuangshen Pinayejiatian xingxiang pin yigui 大聖歓喜双身毘那夜迦天形像品儀規. By Jingse 憬瑟. *T.* 21, 1274.
Dasheng Huanxi dazizaitian Pinayejia-wang guiyi niansong gongyang fa 大聖歓喜天大自在天毘那夜迦王歸依念誦供養法. Trans. Śubhakarasiṃha. *T.* 21, 1270.
Dasong sengshi lue 大宋史略. By Zanning 賛寧 (919–1001). *T.* 54, 2126.
Dato hiketsu shō 駄都秘決鈔. By Gahō 我宝 (d. 1317). *SZ* 22: 179–293.

Dazhidu lun 大智度論. Attr. Nāgārjuna. *T.* 25, 1509.
Denbō kanjō shiki 伝法灌頂私記. By Kyōjun 教舜. *T.* 78, 2499.
Dengaku ki 田楽記. *ST,* Ronsetsu-hen 論説編 4, Tendai shintō 天台神道 2: 617–618.
Dengyō Daishi zenshū 伝教大師全集. Vol. 5. Tokyo: Nihon Bussho kankōkai, 1926; repr. 1975.
Denju shū 傳受集. By Kanjin 寛信 (1084–1153). *T.* 78, 2482.
Denpu-hō kuketsu 田夫法口決. Kanazawa bunko archives.
Dokōjin saimon 土公神祭文. *NSBS* 1: 230–239.
Eiga monogatari 栄華物語 (ca. 1092). *NKBT* 75–76, ed. Matsumura Hiroji 松村博司 and Yamanaka Yutaka 山中裕. English translation in McCullough and McCullough 1980.
Eizan daishi den 叡山大師傳. By Ninchū (n.d.). *ZGR* 8: 2.
En no gyōja honki 役行者本記. In *Shugendō shōso*, 3: 245–257.
Enoshima engi 江嶋縁起. By Kōgei 皇慶 (977–1049). In Kanagawa kenritsu Kanazawa bunko 2007a: 24–32.
Fahua yizhu 法華義疏. By Jizang 吉藏. *T.* 34, 1721.
Fudarakusan kenritsu shugyō nikki 補陀洛山建立修行日記. *ST,* Jinja-hen 神社編, Nikkōsan 日光 二荒山: 11–21.
Fugai zhengxing suo ji jing 福蓋正行所集經. *T.* 32, 1671.
Fusō ryakki 扶桑略記. *KST* 12.
Gangōji garan engi 元興寺伽藍縁起. In *Jisha engi*: 7–22.
Genji monogatari 源氏物語. *NKBZ* 12–17, ed. Abe Akio 阿部秋生 et al. (1970–1976). Also *NKBT* 14–18 (1958–1963).
Genkō shakusho 元亨釈書 (1322). By Kokan Shiren 虎関師錬 (1278–1346). *DNBZ* 62, 470.
Genpei jōsuiki 源平盛衰記. Tokyo: Kokumin bunko kankōkai, 1932.
Genpishō 玄祕抄. By Jichiun 実運 (1105–1160). *T.* 78, 2486.
Genshidan hishō 玄旨壇秘鈔. In Hayakawa 2000: 18–122.
Genshi kimyōdan denki 玄旨帰命壇伝記. Quoted in Yamamoto 1998a: 200.
Genshi kimyōdan hirokushū. 玄旨帰命壇玄旨歸命壇祕録集. In Uesugi 1973, 2: 838.
Gion Gozu Tennō go-engi 祇園牛頭天王御縁起. *ST,* Bungaku-hen 2, Chūsei monogatari 文学編一中世物語: 387–394.
Gochinza shidaiki shō 御鎮座次第記鈔. *ST*, Ronsetsu-hen 6, Ise shintō 2.
Gojikkanshō 五十巻鈔. By Kōzen 興然 (1120–1203). *SZ* 29–31.
Goma kuketsu 護摩口決. By Raiyu 頼瑜 (1226–1304). *T.* 79, 2532.
Gonshinshō 嚴神抄. *ZGR,* Jingi-bu 49: 636–653.
Guanyin yizhu 観音義疏. By Zhiyi 智顗 (538–597). *T.* 34, 1728.
Guanzizai pusa suixin zhu jing 観自在菩薩随心呪經. Trans. Zhitong 智通 (*ca.* 627–649). *T.* 20, 1103.
Guizimu jing 鬼子母經. Anon. *T.* 21, 1262.
Gukanshō 愚管抄. By Jien 慈円 (1155–1225). Ed. Okami Masao 岡見正雄 and Akamatsu Toshihide 赤松俊秀. Tokyo: Iwanami shoten, 1967.
Gunsho ruijū 群書類従 (*GR*). 25 vols. Zoku Gunsho ruijū kanseikai, 1959–1960.
Gyōki 御記 (ca. 1180). By Shukaku Shinnō 守覺親王 (1150–1202). *T.* 78, 2493.
Gyokuyō 玉葉. By Kujō Kanezane 九条兼実 (1149–1207). Ed. Ichishima Kenkichi 市島 謙吉. 3 vols. Tokyo: Kokusho kankōkai, 1907. See also the 1966 edition published by Sumiya shobō.
Gyōrinshō 行林抄. By Jōnen 静然 (fl. 1154). *T.* 76, 2409.
Hachiman daibosatsu 八幡大菩薩. In Kokubungaku kenkyū shiryōkan 1999b: 423–440.

Hachiman daibosatsu go-engi 八幡大菩薩御縁起. *ST,* Bungaku-hen 2, Chūsei monogatari: 49–66.
Hachiman gudōkun 八幡愚童訓. By Kaigen (d. 1469) and Urabe (Yoshida) Kanetomo (d. 1511). *ZGR*, Jingi-bu 30: 49–109. Also in *Jisha engi*: 169–206 (A) and 207–274 (B).
Hachiman Usa go-takusenshū 八幡宇佐御託宣集 (1313). By Jin'un 神吽(1230–1314). *ST,* Jinja-hen 神社編 47, Usa: 13–206.
Hakusan no ki 白山の記. In *Jisha engi*: 291–304.
Heian ibun 平安遺文. Ed. Takeuchi Rizō 竹内理三. 15 vols. Tokyo: Tōkyōdō shuppan, 1947–1980.
Heike monogatari 平家物語 (Kakuichi-bon 覚一本) (late 12th–early 13th c.). Anon. *NKBT* 32–33, ed. Takagi Ichinosuke 高木市之助 et al.
Hekizan nichiroku 碧山日録 (Blue Cliff Record; 1459–1468). By Unsen Taikyoku 雲泉太極 (ca. 1421–1486). Ed. Tsunoda Bun'ei 角田文衞 and Gorai Shigeru 五来重. *Shintei zōho shiseki shūran* 新訂増補史籍集覧 26: 235–448. Kyoto: Rinsen shoten.
Henkushō 遍口鈔. By Seigen 成賢 (1162–1231). Ed. Dōkyō 道教 (1200–1236). *T.* 78, 2496.
Hie hongi 日吉本紀 (1235). By Kenchū (d.u.). *ST,* Ronsetsu-hen 論説編, Tendai shintō 天台神道 2: 543–586. See also *ZGR,* Jingi-bu 神祇部 52: 707–749.
Hie Sannō gongen ki 日吉三王權現記. By Kakushin 覚深. *ZTZ,* Shintō 1, Sannō shintō 1: 400–410.
Hie Sannō hiden ki 日吉山王祕傳記. By Gigen 義源. *ZTZ,* Shintō 1, Sannō shintō 1: 211–221.
Hie Sannō ki 日吉山王. *ZTZ,* Shintō 1, Sannō shintō 1: 270–296.
Hie Sannō shinki. 日吉山王新記. By Kakuo 覺雄. *ZGR* 52: 751–772.
Hiesha shintō himitsuki 日吉社神道秘密記. *ST*, Jinja-hen 神社編 29, *Hie* 日吉.
Hikosan rūki 彦山流記 In Gorai 2000, 2: 463–473.
Himitsu shugen yōhō shū 祕密修験要法集. *ST,* Ronsetsu-hen 論説編 17, Shugendō: 515–542.
Hishō 祕鈔. By Shōken 勝賢 (1138–1196). Ed. Shukaku Shinnō (1150–1202). *T.* 78, 2489.
Hishō mondō 祕鈔問答. By Raiyu 頼瑜 (1226–1304). *T.* 79, 2536.
Hizō konpō shō 祕藏金寶鈔. By Jichiun 實運 (1105–1160). *T.* 78, 2485.
Hōbutsu shū 宝物集. Attr. Taira no Yasuyori 平康頼 (fl. 1190–1200). *ZGR* 32: 2.
Hōki naiden ホキ内伝. Attr. Abe no Seimei. *ST,* Ronsetsu-hen 論説編 16, Onmyōdō: 27–86. Also *ZGR* 31a: 347–414.
Hokishō ホキ抄. In *Nihon koten gisho sōkan* 日本古典偽書総観, ed. Fukazawa Tōru 深沢徹, vol. 3 (Tokyo: Gendai shichō shinsha, 2004): 163–195.
Hōkyōshō 實鏡鈔. By Yūkai 宥快 (1346–1416). *T.* 77, 2456. See also Hayakawa 2000: 1–17.
Honchō jinja kō 本朝神社考. *NSSS* 26: 79–180.
Honchō kōsōden 本朝高僧伝. By Shiban 師蠻. *DNBZ* 102–103.
Honchō monsui 本朝文粋. *NKBT* 27, 1992; *KST* 29: 2, 1965.
Honchō shinsenden 本朝神仙伝. *NST* 7; *ZGR* 8.
Honchō zoku monsui 本朝続文粋. In *Kokushi taikei* 29, 2: 1–238.
Hongjiatuoye yigui 吽伽陀野儀規 (J. *Ungadaya giki*). *T.* 21, 1251.
Hongming ji 弘明集. By Seng'you 僧祐 (445–18). *T.* 52, 2102.
Huilin yinyi 慧琳音義. See *Yiqiejing yinyi.*
Izuna Daimyōjin engi 飯縄大明神縁起. In Gorai 2000, 1: 469–472.
Inari daimyōjin engi 稲荷大明神縁起. *ST*, Jinja-hen 神社編 9, Inari 稲荷: 1–6. See also Yamaori 1999: 380–394.

Inari daimyōjin ruki 稲荷大明神流記 (14th century). In Yamaori 1999: 372–379.

Inari engi ekotoba 稲荷縁起絵詞. In Yamaori 1999: 369–371.

Inari ichiryū daiji 稲荷一流大事. See *Inari taisha yuishoki shūsei* 稲荷大社由緒記集成.

Inari jinja ki hiketsu 稲荷神社記秘決. In Yamaori 1999: 471–475.

Inari jinja kō 稲荷神社考. *ST*, Jinja-hen 神社編 9, Inari 稲荷: 437–506.

Inari jinja shiryō 稲荷神社資料. Ed. Kojima Shōsaku 小島鉦作. Kyoto: Inari jinja shamusho, 1936–1941.

Inari ki 稲荷記. *ST,* Jinja-hen 9, Inari: 7–22. See also Yamaori 1999: 359–368.

Inari kokkyō ki 稲荷谷響記. *ST,* Jinja-hen 神社編 9, Inari 稲荷: 185–233.

Inari kōshi 稲荷講志. By Tenna 天阿 (d. 1676). Ed. Fushimi Inari taisha kōmu honchō 伏見稲荷大社公務本庁 (1978).

Inari myōjin kōshiki. 稲荷明神講式. In Yamaori 1999: 467–470.

Inari-sha jijitsu kōshō ki 稲荷社事實考證記. *ST,* Jinja-hen 神社編 9, Inari 稲荷: 235–371.

Inari shūsei shinkō: chosaku-hen 稲荷集成信仰一著作篇. See Fushimi Inari taisha 1957.

Inari taisha yuishoki shūsei 稲荷大社由緒記集成. In Yamaori 1999: 358–484.

Inariyama sanrō ki 稲荷山参籠記. By Konparu Zenchiku 金春禅竹 (1405–ca. 1470). In Itō Masayoshi 伊藤正義 and Omote Akira 表章, eds., *Konparu kodensho shūsei* 金春古伝書集成 (Tokyo: Wan'ya shoten, 1970): 317–322.

Inryōken nichiroku 蔭凉軒日録 (1435). *DNBZ* 75–78, ed. Tamamura Takeji 玉村竹二 and Katsuno Takanobu 勝野隆信.

Ise nisho kōtaijin gochinza denki 伊勢二所皇太神御鎮座伝記. *ST,* Ronsetsu-hen 論説編 5, Ise shintō 1: 11–32.

Ise shintō shū 伊勢神道集. In Kokubungaku kenkyū shiryōkan 1999b.

Ishiyamadera engi 石山寺縁起. *DNBZ* 86, 791: 269–278.

Ishiyama shichishū 石山寺七集. By Junnyū 淳祐 (890–953). *TZ* 2, 2924: 137–190.

Ison shō 異尊抄. By Shukaku Shinnō 守覺親王. *T.* 78, 2490.

Izuna Daimyōjin engi 飯縄明神縁起. In Gorai 2000, 1: 469–472.

Izuna Daimyōjin yurai no engi 飯綱大明神由来之縁起. *ST,* Jinja-hen 神社編 45, Hizen 肥前: 570–571.

Jakushōdō kokkyōshū 寂照堂谷響集. By Unshō 運敞 (1614–1693). *DNBZ* 90, 823.

Jikaku daishi den 慈覚大師伝. *ZTZ, shiden* 続天台宗全書、史伝, 2: 58–76, ed. Tendai shūten hensanjo (1990).

Jikkanshō 十巻抄. See *Zuzōshō* 図像抄.

Jikki shō 實歸鈔. By Jinken 深賢 (d. 1262). *T.* 78, 2497.

Jimon denki horoku 寺門伝記補録. By Shikō 志晃 (1662–1730). *DNBZ* 86, 787: 108–157.

Jindaikan hiketsu 神代巻秘決. *ZST,* Ronsetsu-hen 論説編, Shūgō shintō 習合神道: 41–406.

Jindaikan shikenmon 神代巻私見聞. By Ryōhen 良遍 (fl. early 15th century). *ST,* Ronsetsu-hen 論説編 3, Tendai shintō 天台神道 1: 559–594.

Jingangding jing 金剛頂經 (Skt. *Vajraśekhara-sūtra*; J. *Kongōchōkyō*). Trans. Amoghavajra (Ch. Bukong 不空, 705–774). *T.* 18, 865.

Jingang feng louge yiqie yujia yuqi jing 金剛峯楼閣一切瑜伽瑜祇經. Trans. Vajrabodhi. *T.* 18, 867.

Jingdu sanmei jing 浄度三昧經. Apocryphon. Mss. Dunhuang S. 4546, 5960, and 2301. In Makita Tairyō 牧田諦亮, *Gikyō kenkyū* 疑經研究 (Kyoto: Jinbun kagaku kenkyūjo, 1976); and Makita Tairyō and Ochiai Toshinori 落合俊典,

eds., *Nanatsudera koitsu kyōten kenkyū sōsho* 七寺古逸經典研究叢書 1, Chūgoku senjutsu kyōten 中国撰述經典 1 (Tokyo: Daitō, 1994).

Jingi dōryō fuin 神祇道靈符印. *ST,* Ronsetsu-hen 論説編 9, Urabe shintō 卜部神道: 145–163.

Jingi hishō 神祇秘抄. *ST,* Ronsetsu-hen 論説編 1, Shingon shintō 真言神道 1: 175–210. Also in Kokubungaku kenkyū shiryōkan 1999b: 375–401.

Jinguangming zuishengwang jing 金光明最勝王經 (Skt. *Suvarṇaprabhāsottama-sūtra*; J. *Konkōmyō saishōōkyō*). Trans. Yijing 義浄 (635–713). *T.* 16, 665.

Jinnō keizu, Jinnō jitsuroku 神皇系図、神皇実録. In *Ise shintō shū,* 629–656.

Jinnō shōtōki 神皇正統記. By Kitabatake Chikafusa 北畠親房 (1293–1354). *NKBT* 87, ed. Iwasa Masashi 岩佐正 (1976). Also *ST*, Ronsetsu-hen 論説編 29, Kitabatake Chikafusa 北畠親房 2: 47–186.

Jinse jianabode tuoluoni jing 金色迦那鉢底陀羅尼經. Trans. Vajrabodhi. *T.* 21, 1269.

Jinten ainōshō 塵添 壒鈔 (1532). Anon. *DNBZ* 150.

Jisha engi 寺社縁起. *NST* 20, ed. Sakurai Tokutarō 桜井徳太郎, Hagiwara Tatsuo 萩原龍夫, and Miyata Noboru 宮田登. Tokyo: Iwanami shoten, 1975.

Jitoku shū 自徳集 (1344). *ZGR*, Shake-bu 釈家部, 28 (1): 1–25.

Juge no gohō 樹外の護法. *ST,* Ronsetsu-hen 論説編 4, Tendai shintō 天台神道 2: 627–652.

Jūniten keizō 十二天形像. *TZ* 7: 581–590.

Jūō kyō 十王經. *ZZ* 2, 23, 4 (new ed., vol. 150).

Jūten keizō 十天形像. *TZ* 7: 567–580.

Kakugenshō 覚源抄. Oral teachings of Kakukai 覚海 (1142–1223) and Yūgen 融源 (fl. 1160). Comp. Rendō 蓮道. *SZ* 36: 325–392.

Kakuzenshō 覚禅鈔. By Kakuzen 覚禅 (1143–1213). *DNBZ* 44–51; *TZ* 4–5, 3022.

Kamakura ibun 鎌倉遺文. Ed. Takeuchi Rizō 竹内理三. 52 vols. Tokyo: Tōkyōdō shuppan, 1971–1997.

Kanazawa bunko monjo shihai shōgyō 金沢文庫文書紙背聖教 (Kiin-bon 熙允本). In Kanagawa kenritsu Kanazawa bunko 2007b: 67–68.

Kangiten reigenki 歓喜天霊験紀 (a.k.a. *Kitano Tenjin engi* 北野天神縁起). Painted scroll (*emakimono*). Coll. Kondō family (Hyōgo prefecture). Quoted in Nanri 1996.

Kangiten shiki 歓喜天私記. In Kanagawa kenritsu Kanazawa bunko 2007b: 41–42.

Kanmon gyōki 看聞御記. By Fushiminomiya Sadafusa 伏見宮貞成. *ZGR*, Suppl. 2. Rev. ed. (Tokyo: Zoku gunsho ruijū kanseikai, 2000).

Kasuga Gongen kenki e 春日権現験記絵. *Zoku Nihon no emaki* 続日本の絵巻, vol. 13 (Tokyo: Chūō kōronsha, 1993); *Zoku Nihon emaki taisei* 続日本絵巻大成, vols. 14–15 (Tokyo: Chūō kōronsha, 1982).

Keiran shūyōshū 渓嵐拾葉集. By Kōshū 光宗 (1276–1350). *T.* 76, 2410.

Keiran shūyōshū 渓嵐拾葉集 (Kiroku-bu 記録部, Shinmei-bu 神明部, Kaike-bu 戒家部). By Kōshū 光宗 (1276–1350). *ST,* Ronsetsu-hen 論説編 4, Tendai shintō 天台神道 2: 405–428.

Kinpusen himitsuden 金峰山秘密伝. By Monkan 文観 (1278–1357). In *Shugendō shōso,* 1: 437–470. Also in *Kinpusenji shiryō shūsei* 金峰山寺資料集成 (Tokyo: Kokusho hakkōkai, 2000); and Abe Yasurō 2011: 240–248.

Kita-in Omuro shūyōshū 北院御室拾葉集 (ca. 1200). *ZGR*, Shake-bu 釈家部, 28 (2).

Kitano tenjin engi 北野天神縁起. In *Jisha engi*: 141–168.

Kiyū shōran 嬉遊笑覧 (1816). By Kitamura Nobuyo 喜多村信節 (1784–1856).

Ed. Meicho kankōkai. 4 vols. Tokyo: Meicho kankōkai, 1970. Also in *Nihon zuihitsu taisei* 日本随筆大成, vols. 7–10 (Tokyo: Yoshikawa kōbunkan, 1979).

Kōbō Daishi zenshū 弘法大師全集. Ed. Mikkyō bunka kenkyūjo 密教文化研究所. 5 vols. Kōyasan: Mikkyō bunka kenkyūjo, 1970–1977. Reprint, 1978.

Kōfukuji ruki 興福寺流記. *DNBZ* 84: 295–307.

Kōgyō Daishi senjutsu shū 興教大師撰述集. Ed. Miyasaka Yūshō 宮坂有勝. Tokyo: Sankibō busshorin, 1977.

Kojiki 古事記. *NST* 1.

Kojimadera Shinkō musō Shōten hō 小島寺真興夢想聖天法. Coll. Shōmyōji, Kōyasan. Quoted in Manabe 2000.

Koji ruien 古事類苑. Ed. Tōkyō gakushi kaiin. Tokyo: Koji ruien sankei, 1927.

Kokawadera engi 粉河寺縁起. In *Jisha engi*: 37–68.

Kokiroku (*Suwa jinja engi*) 古記録 (諏訪神社縁起). In *Suwa shiryō sōsho* 諏訪資料叢書, ed. Suwa kyōikukai 諏訪教育会, vol. 4 (Suwa-shi: Hotaru shobō, 1984).

Kokon chōmonjū 古今著聞集 (1254). By Tachibana no Narisue 橘成季. *NKBT* 84.

Kōko zōtō hishō 高庫藏等秘抄. In Kokubungaku kenkyū shiryōkan 1999a: 369–378.

Kokushi taikei 国史大系. Ed. Kuroita Katsumi 黒板勝実. 60 vols. Tokyo: Yoshikawa kōbunkan, 1929–1967.

Kongōchōkyō. See *Jingangding jing*.

Kongō himitsu Sannō denju daiji 金剛秘密山王傳授大事. By Chūjin 忠尋. *ST*, Ronsetsu-hen 論説編 4, Tendai shintō 天台神道 2: 451–504. Also *TSZ* 12 : 5–42.

Kongōzan jingikan 金剛山神祇巻. *ST*, Ronsetsu-hen 論説編 2, Shingon shintō 真言神道 2: 539–554.

Konjaku monogatari shū 今昔物語集. Anon. 5 vols. *NKBT* 22–26, ed. Yamada Yoshio 山田孝雄 et al. (1959–1963).

Kōshin shō 幸心鈔. By Kenjin 憲深 (1192–1263) and Shinkai 親快 (1215–1276). *T.* 78, 2498.

Kōyasan hiki 高野山秘記. In Kokubungaku kenkyū shiryōkan 1999c: 255–274.

Kūge dansō 空華談叢. By Myōryū 妙竜 (Teinin 諦忍, Kūge 空華). *DNBZ* 94, 836.

Kuma-gun jinja ki 球磨郡神社記. *ST*, Jinja-hen 神社編, Hizen Higo 肥前肥後: 287.

Kuramadera engi 鞍馬寺縁起. In Gorai 2000, 2: 75–79.

Liqu jing 理趣經 (Skt. *Adhyardhaśatikā-prajñāpāramitā-sūtra*, J. *Rishukyō*). By Amoghavajra. *T.* 8, 243.

Lishi apitanlun 立世阿毘曇論. Trans. by Paramārtha. *T.* 32, 1644.

Longshu wuming lun 龍樹五明論. *T.* 21, 1420.

Meishuku shū 明宿集. By Konparu Zenchiku 金春禅竹. In *Zeami, Zenchiku* 世阿弥 禅竹, *NST* 24. Also in *Konparu kodensho shūsei* 金春古伝書集成, ed. Omote Akira 表彰 and Itō Masayoshi 伊藤正義 (Tokyo: Wan'ya shoten 1969).

Mikkyō daijiten 密教大辞典. Ed. Mikkyō daijiten hensankai. Kyoto: Hōzōkan, 1969–1970.

Mine aiki 峯相記. *DNBZ* 808: 72–86.

Minōji himitsu engi 箕面寺秘密縁起. In *Shugendō shiryō shū*, 2: 275–286.

Miwa daimyōjin engi 三輪大明神縁起. *ZGR* 46: 536–543.

Miwaryū shintō-hen 三輪流神道篇. In Ōmiwa jinja shiryō 大神神社資料, vols. 5–6.

Miwa shōnin gyōjō shō 三輪上人行状抄. *ST,* Ronsetsu-hen 論説編 2, Shingon shintō 真言神道 2: 21–24.

Miyako meisho zue. By Akisato Ritō 秋里籬島 (fl. 1780–1814). Ed. Takemura Toshinori 竹村俊則. Kadokawa shoten 1976.

Molizhitian pusa tuoluoni jing 摩利支菩薩陀羅尼經. Trans. by Amoghavajra. *T.* 21, 1255a.

Molizhi tipo huaman jing 末利支提婆華鬘經. Trans. by Amoghavajra. *T.* 21, 1254.

Mon'yōki 門葉記. *TZ* 11–12, 3216.

Mōsō yūrai 盲僧由来. *NSSS* 17: 247–248.

Mudai shō 無題抄. *ST,* Ronsetsu-hen 論説編, Unden shintō 雲伝神道, 325–357.

Muli mantuoluo zhou jing 牟梨曼荼羅呪經. *T.* 19, 1007.

Mumon zenji goroku 無文禅師語録. *T.* 80, 2559.

Muromachi jidai monogatari taisei 室町時代物語大成. Ed. Yokoyama Shigeru 横山重 and Matsumoto Ryūshin 松本隆信. 13 vols. (Tokyo: Kadokawa shoten, 1973–1985).

Nakatomi harae no chūshaku 中臣祓註釈. *ST,* Koten chūshaku-hen 古典注釈編.

Nakatomi harae kunge 中臣祓訓解. In Ōsumi 1977: 39–56. Translated in Teeuwen and van der Veere 1998.

Nanto shichidaiji junreiki 南都七大寺巡礼記. *DNBZ* 120.

Nara ibun 奈良遺文. Ed. Takeuchi Rizō 竹内理三. 2 vols. Tokyo: Tōkyōdō, 1943–1944.

Nichiiki hongi 日諱貴本紀. In Kokubungaku kenkyū shiryōkan 1999a: 493–505.

Nihon koten bungaku taikei 日本古典文学大系 (*NKBT*). 100 vols. Tokyo: Iwanami shoten, 1957–1967.

Nihon koten bungaku zenshū 日本古典文学全集 (*NKBZ*). 60 vols. Tokyo: Shōgakkan, 1970–1976.

Nihon shisō taikei 日本思想大系 (*NST*). 67 vols. Tokyo: Iwanami shoten, 1970–1982.

Nihonshoki 日本書紀 (720). Ed. Toneri Shinnō 舎人親王 (676–735) et al. In *NKBT* 67–68.

Nihonshoki kan daiichi kikigaki 日本書紀巻第一聞書. By Ryōhen 良遍 (fl. early 15th century). *ST,* Ronsetsu-hen 論説編 3, Tendai shintō 天台神道 1: 515–558.

Nihon shomin bunka shiryō shūsei 日本庶民文化資料集成 (*NSBS*). 16 vols. Tokyo: San'ichi shobō, 1973–1978.

Nihon shomin seikatsu shiryō shūsei. 日本庶民生活資料集成 (*NSSS*). Ed. Miyamoto Tsuneichi 宮本常一 et al. 31 vols. Tokyo: San'ichi shobō, 1968–1984.

Nikkōsan engi 日光山縁起. In *Jisha engi*: 275–290.

Niu Daimyōjin giki 丹生大明神儀軌, in *ST*, Jinja-hen 神社編: Iga; Ise; Shima no kuni 伊賀 伊勢 志摩国, 80–84.

Okina no fumi 翁の文. By Tominaga Nakamoto 富永仲基 (1715–1746). *NKBT* 97.

Ōmiwa jinja shiryō 大神神社資料. Ed. Ōmiwa jinja shiryō henshū iinkai 大神神社資料編修委員会. 10 vols. Sakurai: Ōmiwa jinja shiryō henshu iinkai, 1968–1991.

Onjōji denki 園城寺伝記. *DNBZ* 86, 786: 56–107.

Oto Gohō kōshiki 乙護法講式. *ST,* Jinja-hen 神社編 50, Aso, Hikosan 阿蘇 英彦山: 258–263.

Ototari shinku saimon 乙足神供祭文. In Kanagawa kenritsu Kanazawa bunko 2007b: 51–52.

Pinayejia enabodi yuqie xidipin miyao. By Hanguang 含光. *T.* 21, 1273.
Pishamen tianwang jing 毘沙門天王經. Trans. Amoghavajra. *T.* 21, 1244.
Pishamen tianwang jing 毘沙門天王經. Trans. Fatian 法天. *T.* 21, 1245.
Pishamen yigui 毘沙門儀規. Trans. Amoghavajra. *T.* 1249.
Reiki kanjō (*shi*) 麗氣灌頂私. *ST,* Ronsetsu-hen 論説編 2, Shingon shintō 真言神道 2: 25–36.
Reikiki 麗氣記. In *ST,* Ronsetsu-hen 論説編, Shingon shintō 真言神道 1: 1–117. *ZGR* 59: 92–136.
Reiki kikigaki 麗氣聞書. *ST,* Ronsetsu-hen 論説編 1, Shingon shintō 真言神道 1: 213–274.
Reikiki shō 麗氣記抄. *ST,* Ronsetsu-hen 論説編 1, Shingon shintō 真言神道 1: 275–326.
Reikiki shūi shō 麗氣記拾遺鈔. *ST,* Ronsetsu-hen 論説編 1, Shingon shintō 真言神道 1: 167–174
Reiki seisaku shō 麗氣制作抄. *ST,* Ronsetsu-hen 論説編 1, Shingon shintō 真言神道 1: 151–166.
Rinnō kanjō kuketsu 輪王灌頂口決 (Kenna-bon 釼阿本). In Kanagawa kenritsu Kanazawa bunko 2007b: 56–57.
Rokugō kaisan Ninmon bosatsu hongi 六郷開山仁聞大菩薩本紀. In *Jisha engi*: 305–325.
Ryōin ketsu 了因決. By Ryōe 了惠 (n.d.). *T.* 77, 2414.
Ryūkyū shintō ki 琉球神道記. By Taichū Ryōtei 袋中良定 (1552–1639). See Yokoyama 1970.
Saishō gogoku Ugaya tontoku nyoi hōju-ō shugi 最勝護国宇賀耶頓得如意宝珠王修儀. By Kenchū 謙忠. In Yamamoto 1998a: 482–499.
Sanbōe kotoba 三宝絵詞. By Minamoto no Tamenori 源為憲 (d. 1010). Ed. Eguchi Takao 江口孝夫. 2 vols. Tokyo: Gendai Shichosha. Also in Tōyō bunko 513 (Tokyo: Heibonsha).
Sanbōin-ryū dōsen sōjō kuketsu 三宝院流洞泉相承口決. By Dōchō 動潮 (n.d.) and Ryūō 隆応 (n.d.). *SZ* 34: 155b–156a
Sange sairyakki 山家最略記. *ZTZ*, Shintō 1: Sannō shintō, 167–180.
Sange yoryakki ki 山家要略記. *ST*, Ronsetsu-hen 論説編 4, Tendai shintō 天台神道 2: 137–262; also *ZTZ*, Shintō 1, Sannō shintō 山王神道: 1–148.
Sangoku denki 三国伝記. By Gentō (fl. first half of 15th century). *DNBZ* 1, 92. Also in 2 vols., ed. Ikegami Jun'ichi 池上洵一 (Tokyo: Miyai shoten, 1976).
Sangyō sōō Miwa Sannō 三業相應三輪山王. *ST,* Ronsetsu-hen 論説編 4, Tendai shintō 2: 523–527.
Sanmai-ryū kudenshū 三昧流口伝集. By Ryōyū 良祐. *T.* 77, 2411.
Sanmon shibun kiroku ryakki 山門四分記漉錄略記. *ZTZ,* Shintō 1, Sannō shintō: 149–166.
Sannō hiki 山王秘記. *ST,* Ronsetsu-hen 論説編 4, Tendai shintō 天台神道 2: 587–602; also *ZTZ,* Shintō 1, Sannō shintō 山王神道: 222–234.
Sannō mitsuki (bonji) 山王密記（梵字). *ZTZ,* Shintō 1, Sannō shintō 山王神道: 181–188.
Sannō mitsuki 山王密記. *ZTZ*, Shintō 1, Sannō shintō 山王神道: 235–269.
Sannō yurai 山王由来. *ST,* Ronsetsu-hen 4, Tendai shintō 天台神道 2: 603–612.
Santen gōgyō-hō 三天合行法 . Eizan bunko collection.
Santō mintan shū 山島民譚集. In *Yanagita Kunio Zenshū* 柳田国男全集, 5: 55–484.
Sarugaku dangi 猿楽談義 (Talks on Sarugaku). By Zeami 世阿弥 (1363–1443). In *Karonshū nōgakuronshū* 歌論集能楽論集. Hisamatsu Sen'ichi 久松潜一 and Nishio Minoru 西尾実, eds. *NKBT* 65. Tokyo: Iwanami shoten 1961.

Sefuri-san engi 背振山縁起. In *Shugendō shiryō shū*, 2: 551–553.

Seigaku mondō 聖学問答 (1736). By Dazai Shundai 太宰春台 (1680–1747). In *Sorai gakuha* 徂徠学派, ed. Rai Tsutomu 頼惟勤, *NSTK* 37: 57–135.

Seiryō gongen onkoto 清瀧権現御事. *ST*, Ronsetsu-hen 論説編 2, Shingon shintō 真言神道 2: 537–538.

Sekizan Myōjin engi 赤山明神縁起. *ST*, Ronsetsu-hen 論説編 4, Tendai shintō 天台神道 2: 623–626.

Shake shiryō 社家資料. In *Suwa shiryō sōsho* 諏訪資料叢書, ed. Suwa kyōiku-kai 諏訪教育会 (Suwa-shi: Hotaru shobō, 1984).

Shakujin mondō 石神問答 (var. *Ishigami mondō*). In *Yanagita Kunio zenshū* 柳田国男全集, vol. 13.

Shaku Nihongi 釈日本紀. By Urabe Kanekata 兼方. *ST*, Koten chūshaku-hen 5, *Shaku Nihongi* 釈日本紀.

Shanhai jing 山海經. *DZ* 675–676. Reprint, Taiwan: Yiwen yinshuguan, 1963.

Shasekishū 砂石集. By Mujū Ichien 無住一円 (1226–1312). *NKBT* 85.

Sheng Huangxitian shifa 聖歓喜天式法. By Prajñācakra. *T.* 21, 1275.

Shichisha ryakki 七社略記. By Zonshin 存心. *TZ* 12: 225–232.

Shigisan engi 信貴山縁起. In *Jisha engi*: 23–28.

Shijō hiketsu 四帖祕決. By Jien 慈円 (1155–1225). *ZTZ*, Mikkyō 3: 291–423.

Shijūjō ketsu 四十帖決. By Chōen 長宴 (1016–1081). *T.* 75, 2408.

Shikeshō zuzō 四家鈔図像. *TZ* 3: 749–916.

Shinbutsu ittai kanjō shō 神佛一体灌頂鈔. Archives of the Eizan bunko.

Shingon reikiki 真言麗氣記. *ST*, Ronsetsu-hen 論説編 1, Shingon shintō 真言神道 1: 65.

Shin honji no koto 神本地之事. In *Shinshū shiryō shūsei* 真宗資料集成, ed. Mori Ryūkichi 森龍吉 (Kyoto: Dōhōsha), 5: 82–84.

Shin[koō] bosatsu kuden 辰菩薩口伝. In Kanagawa kenritsu Kanazawa bunko 2007b: 49–50.

Shin[koō] bosatsu kuden jō kuketsu 辰菩薩口伝上口決. In Kanagawa kenritsu Kanazawa bunko 2007b: 50–51.

Shinko daiō jōjukyō 佛狐大王成就經 (full title: *Bussetsu shinko daiō daibosatsu ichiji himitsu shissō jōjukyō* 仏説辰狐大王大菩薩一字秘密疾走成就經). In Itō Satoshi 1993: 44–45.

Shinkō musōki 真興夢想記. By Shinkō 真興 (934–1004). See Manabe 1999: 166–168.

Shin Nihon koten bungaku taikei 新日本古典文学大系 (*SNKBT*). 100 vols. Iwanami shoten, 1989–.

Shinnyokan 真如観. In *Tendai hongakuron* 天台本覚論. *NST* 9.

Shinpen kokka taikan 新編国歌大観 (*KT*). 20 vols. Kadokawa shoten, 1983–1992.

Shinpen Nihon koten bungaku zenshū 新編日本古典文学全集 (*SNKBZ*). 88 vols. Tokyo: Shōgakkan, 1994–.

Shinra Myōjin mondō shō yōkunsho 新羅明神問答抄用訓書 (1344). In *Jitoku shū*: 14–25.

Shinra no ki 新羅記. In *Shinra no kiroku* 新羅の記録 (1646). Ed. Shindo 2005.

Shinra ryakki 新羅略記. *ST*, Ronsetsu-hen 論説編 17, Shugendō: 319–358.

Shin sarugaku ki 新猿楽紀. By Fujiwara no Akihira 藤原明衡 (ca. 989–1066). Koten bunko 66. Tokyo: Gendai shichosha.

Shinshō tōtsūki 神将東通記. In Itō Satoshi 2011: 269–270.

Shintei zōho kokushi taikei 新訂増補国史大系 (*KST*). 66 vols. Tokyo: Yoshikawa kōbunkan, 1929–1966.

Shintō kanpaku-ryū zatsubu 神道関白流雑部. In Itō Satoshi 2011: 408–411.

Shintōshū 神道集. *ST*, Bungaku-hen: *Shintōshū*.

Shintōshū ryakushō 神道集略鈔. By Taichū Ryōtei 袋中良定 (1552–1639). In Yokoyama 1970.

Shintō taikei 神道大系 (*ST*). 123 vols. Ed. Shintō taikei hensankai 神道大系編纂会. Tokyo: Shintō taikei hensankai, 1977–1994.

Shintō zatsuzatsushū 神道雑々集. Yamada Collection, Tenri Library (Yoshida bunko).

Shiojiri 塩尻. By Amano Nobukage 天野信景 (1661–1733). In *Nihon zuihitsu taisei* 日本随筆大成, 3rd ed., vols. 9–10 (Tokyo: Kawase shoten, 1930).

Shirushi no sugi しるしの杉. By Ban Nobutomo 伴信友 (1775–1846). *ST,* Jinja-hen 神社編 9, Inari 稲荷: 375–436; also *NSSS* 26: 673–704.

Shitennō zō 四天王像. *TZ* 7: 529–534.

Shoji engishū 諸寺縁起集. Ed. Kunaichō shoryōbu 宮内庁書陵部. Tokyo: Meiji shoin, 1970.

Shoson yōshō 諸尊要抄. By Jichiun 實運 (1105–1160). *T.* 78, 2484.

Shoson zuzō 諸尊図像. By Shinkaku 心覺. *TZ* 3, 3008: 675–748.

Shōten (Kojima yume no ki) 聖天 (小島夢記). In Kanagawa kenritsu Kanazawa bunko 2007b: 56a.

Shōten shiki 聖天式. In Kanagawa kenritsu Kanazawa bunko 2007b: 39–40.

Shōten shikiban kessa-hō 聖天式盤結作法. In Kanagawa kenritsu Kanazawa bunko 2007b: 42–43.

Shōwa teihon Nichiren shōnin ibun 昭和定本日蓮上人遺文. Ed. Risshō daigaku Nichiren kyōgaku kenkyūjo. 4 vols. Minobu: Minobusan Kuonji, 1989.

Shozan engi 諸山縁起. In *Jisha engi*: 89–140.

Shugendō shiryō shū 修験道資料集. See Gorai 2000.

Shugendō shōso 修験道章疏. Ed. Nihon daizōkyō hensankai 日本大藏經編纂会. 4 vols. Tokyo: Nihon daizōkyō hensankai, 1916–1919. Reprint, Tokyo: Kokusho hakkōkai, 2000.

Shugendō shuyō hiketsu shū 修験道修要秘決集 (1521–1528). In *ST, Ronsetsu-hen* 論説編 17, *Shugendō:* 242–318.

Shugendō yōten 修験道要典. Ed. Hattori Nyojitsu 服部如実. Tokyo: Sanmitsudō shoten, 1972.

Shugen hio-shō 修験祕奥鈔. By Kyokuren 旭蓮. In *Shugendō shōso,* 1: 385–432.

Shugen seiten 修験聖典. Ed. Shugen seiten hensankai 修験聖典編纂会. Tokyo: Daigakudō shoten, 1927. Reprint, 1938.

Shugen shūshi sho 修験宗旨書. *ST, Ronsetsu-hen* 論説編 17, *Shugendō*: 1–46.

Sitianwang jing 佛説四天王經. Trans. Zhiyan 智嚴 and Fayun 法雲. *T.* 15, 590.

Sōgi shokoku monogatari 宗祇諸国物語. Ed. Kinsei bungaku shoshi kenkyūkai 近世文学書誌研究会. Tokyo: Benseisha, 1977.

Sōjishō 總持抄. By Chōgō 澄豪 (1259–1350). *T.* 77, 2412.

Song gaoseng zhuan 宋高僧伝. By Zanning 贊寧 (919–1001). *T.* 50, 2061.

Suidai ki 水台記. In *ST,* Jinja-hen 神社編 9, Inari 稲荷: 23–66.

Supohu tongzi qingwen jing 蘇婆呼童子請問經 (Skt. *Subāhuparipṛcchā*). Trans. Śubhakarasiṃha. *T.* 18, 895.

Suwa Daimyōjin go-honji 諏訪大明神御本地. *ST*, Bungaku-hen 文学編 2, Chūsei monogatari 中世物語: 333–386.

Suxidijieluo jing 蘇悉地羯羅經. Trans. Śubhakarasiṃha. *T.* 18, 893.

Taiheiki 太平記. *NKBT* 34–36.

Taishō shinshū daizōkyō 大正新脩大藏經 (*T*). Ed. Takakusu Junjirō and Watanabe Kaigyōku. 85 vols. Tokyo: Issaikyō kankōkai and Daizō shuppan, 1924–1932.

Taishō shinshū daizōkyō zuzō 大正新修大蔵経 (*TZ*). Ed. Takakusu Junjirō and Watanabe Kaigyōku. 12 vols. Tokyo: Taishō issaikyō kankōkai, 1924–1935.

Taizan Fukun saimon 泰山府君祭文. *NSSS* 17: 324–327.
Taizō kongō bodaishin ryaku mondōshō 胎藏金剛菩提心義略問答抄. By Annen 安然. *T.* 75, 2397.
Takachiho jūshāgū 高千穂十社宮. *ST, Jinja-hen* 神社編 45, *Hizen Higo Hyūga Satsuma Ōsumi no kuni* 肥前、肥後、日向、薩摩，大隅國: 475–481.
Tamakisan gongen engi 玉置山権現縁起. *ST, Jinja-hen* 神社編 5, *Yamato no kuni*: 520–527. Also in Gorai 2000, 2: 148–154.
Takao kuketsu 高雄口決. By Shinzei 眞濟. *T.* 78, 2466.
Takushō 澤鈔. By Kakujō 覺成 (1126–1198). *T.* 78, 2488.
Tamon dakini kyō 多聞荼吉尼經. See Tatchū 塔中 Coll., box 3, in Nara kokuritsu bunkazai kenkyūjo 1958.
Tankai 談海. By Tsumura Masayuki 津村正恭. Tokyo: Kokusho kankōkai, 1970.
Tenbu keizō 天部形像. *TZ* 7: 591–626.
Tenchi jingi shinchin yōki 天地神祇審鎮要記. By Jihen 慈遍 (fl. 14th century). *ST,* Ronsetsu-hen 論説編 3, Tendai shintō 天台神道 1: 403–474. See also *TSZ* 12: 187–224.
Tenchi reikiki 天地麗氣記. *ST,* Ronsetsu-hen 論説編 1, Shingon shintō 真言神道 1: 135–139; also in Ōsumi 1977: 69–78.
Tendaishū zensho 天台宗全書 (*TSZ*). Ed. Tendai shūten kankōkai (1935–1937). Reprint, Tokyo: Daiichi shobō, 1974.
Tenkawa Benzaiten-sha monjo 天天河弁才天社文書. In Hayashiya et al. 1995: 214–224.
Tenshō daijin kuketsu 天照太神口決 (1327). By Kakujō 覚乗 (1273–1363). *ST,* Ronsetsu-hen 論説編 2, Shingon shintō 真言神道 2: 497–504.
Tenshō kōtaijin giki 天照皇太神儀軌. In Kokubungaku kenkyū shiryōkan 1999a: 357–360.
Tō-bon Shitennō zō 唐本四天王像. *TZ* 7: 523–528.
Tōdō shinshikimoku 当道新式目. *NSSS* 17: 241–247.
Tōdō yōshū 当道要集. *NSSS* 17: 229–241.
Tonjō shitsuji banpō shidai 頓成悉地盤法次第. In Kanagawa kenritsu Kanazawa bunko 2007b: 58–61.
Tonjō shitsuji daiji tō 頓成悉地大事等. By Kenna 釼阿 and Shūhan 秀範. In Kanagawa kenritsu Kanazawa bunko 2007b: 54–55.
Tonjō shitsuji hō 頓成悉地法 (copied by Shūhan 秀範). In Kanagawa kenritsu Kanazawa bunko 2007b: 47–49.
Tonjō shitsuji hō kuketsu mondō 頓成悉地法口決問答 (Kiin-bon 熙允本). In Kanagawa kenritsu Kanazawa bunko 2007b: 66.
Tonjō shitsuji kudenshū 頓成悉地口伝集 (Kiin-bon 熙允本). In Kanagawa kenritsu Kanazawa bunko 2007b: 61–65.
Tonjō shitsuji kuketsu mondō 頓成る悉地口訣問答. In Kanagawa kenritsu Kanazawa bunko 2007b: 66.
Tonjō shitsuji saishi hō 頓成悉地祭祀法 (Shūhan-bon 秀範本). In Kanagawa kenritsu Kanazawa bunko 2007b: 43–45.
Tsuiki 追記. By Shukaku Hōshinnō 守覺法親王. *T.* 78, 2494.
Tsukubasan ruki 筑波山流記. In *Shugendō shiryō shū,* 1: 266–297.
Tuoluoni ji jing 陀羅尼集經. *T.* 18, 901.
Ugajin-ku saimon 宇賀神供祭文. In Mukōzaka Takuya 2007: 25–29.
Ugajin kunō kyō 宇賀神功能經. Japanese apocryphon. In Itō Satoshi 1996: 133–149.
Ugajin nenju shidai 宇賀神念誦次第. In Mukōzaka Takuya 2007: 33.
Ugajin saimon, Kamadogami saimon 宇賀神祭文、竈神祭文. *ST,* Ronsetsu-hen 論説編 2, Shingon shintō 真言神道 2: 579–583.

Ugajin zō 宇賀神像. Ōsu Library, catalog ref. 99/29.
Ungadaya giki 吽伽陀野儀軌. See *Hongjiatuoye yigui.*
Ususama myōō shu senrei yōroku 烏樞沙摩明王修仙霊要録. In Hayakawa 2000: 365–391.
Usuzōshi 薄雙紙. By Seigen 成賢 (1162–1213). *T.* 78, 2495.
Usuzōshi kuketsu 薄草子口決. By Raiyu 頼瑜 (1226–1304). *T.* 79, 2535.
Wagō saimon 和合祭文. *NSSS* 17: 347–349.
Wakan sansai zue 和漢三才圖絵 (1712). By Terajima Ryōan 寺島良安 (n.d.). 2 vols. Tokyo: Wakan sansai zue kankō iinkai, 1970.
Wakō dōjin riyaku kanjō 和光同塵利益灌頂. *ST,* Ronsetsu-hen 論説編 4, Tendai shintō 天台神道 2: 505–522. Also *TSZ* 12: 179–187.
Yako kaji hihō 野狐加持秘法. In Yamaori 1999: 395–402.
Yamatohime no mikoto seiki 倭姫命世記. *ST,* Ronsetsu-hen 論説編 5, Ise shintō 伊勢神道 1: 71 –108. See also *ZGR,* Jingi-bu 神祇部 3: 48–65.
Yamato Katsuragi hōzanki 大和葛城宝山記. In Ōsumi 1977: 57–68.
Yamato no kuni Tenkawa Benzaiten engi 大和国天河弁才天縁起. *ST,* Jinja-hen 神社編, Yamato no kuni 大和国: 516–518.
Yaoshi rulai benyuan jing 薬師如来本願經. Trans. Dharmagupta. *T.* 14, 449.
Yiqiejing yinyi 一切經音義. By Huilin 慧琳. *T.* 54, 2128.
Yōsonbō 要尊法. By Yōgen 永嚴. *T.* 78, 2478.
Yōson dōjōkan 要尊道場観. By Junnyū 淳祐 (890–953). *T.* 78, 2468.
Yōtenki 耀天記 (1223). *ZGR,* Jingi-bu 48: 581–635; also in *ST,* Jinja-hen 神社編 29, Hie 日吉.
Yuqie jiyao Anan tuoluoni yankou guiyi jing 瑜伽集要救阿難陀羅尼焔口軌儀經. Trans. Amoghavajra. *T*. 21, 1318.
Yuqie jiyao yankou shishi qijiao Anantuo yuanyou 瑜伽集要焔口施食起教阿難陀縁由. Trans. Amoghavajra. *T*. 21, 1319.
Yuqi jing (J. *Yugi kyō;* abbr. of *Jingangfeng louge yiqie yujia yuqi jing* 金剛峯楼閣一切瑜伽瑜祇經). Attr. Vajrabodhi. *T.* 867.
Zōho shiryō taisei 增補資料大成. Ed. Zōho shiryō taisei kankōkai 增補資料大成刊行会. 48 vols. Kyoto: Rinsen shoten, 1965.
Zoku gunsho ruijū 続群書類従 *(ZGR).* Ed. Hanawa Hokiichi 塙保己一. 37 vols. and 3 supplementary vols. Zoku gunsho ruijū kanseikai, 1959–1960.
Zoku Nihon koten zenshū 続日本古典全集 (*ZNKZ*). Tokyo: Gendai shinchōsha, 1979–1981.
Zoku Shingonshū zensho 続真言宗全書 (*ZSZ*). Ed. Zoku Shingonshū kankōkai 続真言宗全書刊行会. Kōyasan: Zoku Shingonshū kankōkai, 1977–1988.
Zoku shintō taikei 続神道体系 (*ZST*). Ed. Shintō taikei hensankai 神道体系編纂会. Tokyo: Shintō taikei hensankai.
Zoku Tendaishū zensho 続天台宗全書 (*ZTZ*). Tendai shūten hensanjo 天台宗典編纂所. Tokyo: Shunjūsha, 1987–.
Zokuzoku gunsho ruijū 続続群書類従 (*ZZGR*). Ed. Kokusho kankōkai 国書刊行会. 16 vols. Tokyo: Kokusho kankōkai, 1906–1909. Reprint, Kosho hozonkai 古書保存会, Tokyo: Zoku gunsho ruijū kanseikai, 1978.
Zōtanshū 雑談集 (1305). By Mujū Ichien 無住一円. In *Chūsei no bungaku* 中世の文学, ed. Yamada Shōzen 山田昭全 and Miki Sumito 三木紀人 (Tokyo: Miyai shoten, 1973).
Zuzōshō 図像図抄 (a.k.a. *Jikkanshō* 十巻抄). By Ejū 慧什 (fl. 1135). *TZ* 3, 3006.
Zuzō shū 図像集. *TZ* 4, 3020.

REFERENCES

Abe Mika 阿部美香. 2005. "Daigoji Enma-dō no zuzōgaku-teki kōsatsu" 醍醐寺焔魔堂の図像学的考察. In Manabe Shunshō 真鍋俊照, ed., *Bukkyō bijutsu to rekishi bunka* 佛教美術と歴史文化, 273–290. Kyoto: Hōzōkan.

Abé, Ryūichi. 1999. *The Weaving of Mantra: Kūkai and the Construction of Esoteric Buddhist Discourse.* New York: Columbia University Press.

Abe Shinji 阿部真司. 1981. *Hebigami denjōron josetsu* 蛇神伝承論序説. Tokyo: Dentō to gendaisha.

Abe Yasurō 阿部泰郎. 1980. "'Iruka' no seiritsu" 「入鹿」の成立. *Geinō kenkyū* 芸能研究 69: 16–38.

———, ed. 1983. *Chūsei Kōyasan engi no kenkyū* 中世高野山縁起の研究. Nara: Gangōji bunkazai kenkyūjo.

———. 1984. "Jidō setsuwa no keisei 慈童説話の形成." *Kokugo kokubun* 国語国文 600–601, 1–29: 30–56.

———. 1989. "Hōju to ōken: chūsei to mikkyō girei" 宝珠と王権一中世と密教儀礼. *Iwanami kōza tōyō shisō 16: Nihon shisō* 岩波講座東洋思想 16一日本思想 *2,* 115–169. Tokyo: Iwanami shoten.

———. 1995. "Irokonomi no kami: Dōsojin to aihōjin" 色好みの神一道祖神と愛法神. In Yamaori 1995–1996, 1: 121–172.

———. 2010b. "Monkan chosaku shōgyō no saihakken: Sanzon gōgyō no tekusuto fuchi to sono isō" 文観著作聖教の再発見一三尊合行法のテクスト布置とその位相. In Abe Yasurō, ed., *Chūsei shūkyō tekusuto taikei no fukugenteki kenkyū: Shinpukuji shōgyō tenseki no saikōchiku* 中世宗教テクスト体系の復元的研究一真福寺聖教典籍の再構築, 121–144. Nagoya: Nagoya daigaku daigakuin bungaku kenkyūka.

———. 2011. "Shugen ni okeru shūkyō tekusuto no rinkaku: sono engi to zuzō o megutte oboegaki" 修験における宗教テクストの輪郭一その縁起と図像をめぐって覚書. In Kawasaki 2011: 229–248.

Agatsuma Matashiro 上妻又四郎. 1982. "Chūsei shintō ni okeru Bonten-ō shisō" 中世佛教神道における梵天王思想. *Terakoya gogaku bunka kenkyūjo ronsō* 寺子屋語学文化研究所論叢 1: 45–59.

Agrawala, Prithvi Kumar. 1967. *Skanda-Kārttikeya: A Study in the Origin and Development*. Varanasi: Benares Hindu University.

Agrawala, Vasuveda Kumar. 1970. *Ancient Indian Folk Cults*. Varanasi: Prthiv Prakashan.

Aizawa Masahiko 相澤正彦. 1991. "Enoshima engi no sekai" 江島縁起の世界. In *Zusetsu Fujisawa no rekishi* 図説ふじさわの歴史. Fujisawa: Fujisawa-shi monjokan.

Akai Tatsurō 赤井達郎. 1995. "Tenkawa no bijutsu" 天天河の美術. In Hayashiya et al. 1995: 151–162.

Akiyama Teruo 秋山光夫. 1943. *Nihon bijutsu shi ronkō* 日本美術史論攷. Tokyo: Daiichi shobō.

Allen, Michael. 1975. *The Cult of Kumārī: Virgin Worship in Nepal*. Delhi: Motilal Banarsidass.

Allen, N.J. 1987. "The Ideology of the Indo-Europeans: Dumézil's Theory and the Idea of a Fourth Function." *International Journal of Moral and Social Studies* 2: 28–39.

———. 1998. "Varnas, Colours and Functions," *Zeitschrift für Religionswissenschaft* 6: 163–177.

Amino Yoshihiko 網野良彦. 1978. *Muen, kugai, raku: Nihon chūsei no jiyū to heiwa* 無縁・公界・楽一日本中世の自由と平和. Tokyo: Heibonsha.

———. 1993. *Igyō no ōken* 異形の王権. Heibonsha raiburarii. Tokyo: Heibonsha.
Andreeva, Anna. 2006. "Saidaiji Monks and Esoteric Kami Worship at Ise and Miwa." *JJRS* 33, 2: 349–377.
———. 2006–2007. "The Origin of the Miwa Lineage." *CEA* 16: 71–89.
Araki Hiroyuki 荒木博之. 1979. "Mōsō no denshō bungei" 盲僧の伝承文芸. In Gorai Shigeru 五来重 et al., eds., *Minkan shūkyō bungei* 民間宗教文芸, 156–177. Nihon no minzoku shūkyō 7. Tokyo: Kōbundō.
———. 1997. *Jishin mōsō shiryō shū* 地神盲僧資料集. Denjō bunka shiryō shūsei 19. Tokyo: Miyai shoten.
Araki, James T. 1964. *The Ballad Drama of Medieval Japan*. Berkeley and Los Angeles: University of California Press.
Arichi, Meri. 2006. "*Sannō Miya Mandara*: The Iconography of Pure Land on This Earth." *JJRS* 33, 2: 319–347.
Assayag, Jackie. 1992. *La colère de la déesse décapitée. Traditions, cultes et pouvoir dans le sud de l'Inde*. Paris: CNRS Éditions.
Assmann, Jan. 2008. *Of God and Gods: Egypt, Israel, and the Rise of Monotheism.* Madison: University of Wisconsin Press.
Aston, W. G., trans. 1972 (1956). *Nihongi: Chronicles of Japan from the Earliest Times to A.D. 697.* Rutland, VT: Charles E. Tuttle Company.
Atlan, Henri. 1979. *Entre le cristal et la fumée: Essai sur l'organisation du vivant.* Paris: Éditions du Seuil.
———. 1986. *À Tort et à raison: intercritique de la science et du mythe.* Points Science. Paris: Seuil.
Augé, Marc. 1988. *Le dieu-objet.* Paris: Flammarion.
Bagchi, P. C. 1940. "New Materials for the Study of the *Kumāra-tantra* of Rāvaṇa." *Indian Culture* 7: 269–286.
Bakshi, Dwijendra Nath. 1987. *Iconography of the Buddha Images in Japan: A Comparative Study, Japan-India.* Calcutta: Centre of Japanese Studies.
Baltrušaitis, Jurgis. 1981. *Le Moyen Age fantastique: antiquités et exotismes dans l'art gothique.* Paris: Flammarion.
Banerjea, Jitendra Nath. 1938. "Some Folk Goddesses of Ancient and Mediaeval India." *Indian Historical Quarterly* 14: 101–109.
———. 1956. *The Development of Hindu Iconography.* Calcutta: University of Calcutta.
Bawden, Charles R. 1976. "The 'Offering of the Fox' Again." *Zentralasiatische Studien* 10: 439–473.
———. 1978. "An Oirat Manuscript of the 'Offering of the Fox.'" *Zentralasiatische Studien* 12: 7–34.
Baxandall, Michael. 1985. *Patterns of Intention: On the Historical Explanation of Pictures*. New Haven, CT: Yale University Press.
Béguin, Gilles, and Sylvie Colinart. 1994. "Vaiśravaṇa, dieu des richesses, dieu des armées: A propos d'un Thang-ka du Musée Guimet." *Artibus Asiae* 54, 1–2: 137–155.
Benická, Jana. 2009. "Distant Journeys and Roaming into Immortality, or: There is No Better Place than Earth." In Raoul D. Findeisen et al., eds., *At Home in Many Worlds: Reading, Writing and Translating from Chinese and Jewish Cultures,* 179-188. Wiesbaden: Harrassowitz.
Berkson, Carmel. 1987. *The Caves at Aurangabad: Early Buddhist Tantric Art in India.* Seattle: University of Washington Press.
Berkson, Carmel. 1995. *The Divine and the Demoniac: Mahisa's Heroic Struggle with Durga.* Oxford: Oxford University Press.
Beyer, Stephan. 1978. *The Cult of Tārā: Magic and Ritual in Tibet.* Berkeley: University of California Press.

Bhattacharya, B., ed. 1968. *Sādhanamāla*. Bharoda: Oriental Institute.

Bialock, David T. 2002–2003. "Outcasts, Emperorship, and Dragon Cults in *The Tale of the Heike*." *CEA* 13: 227–310.

———. 2007. *Eccentric Spaces, Hidden Histories: Narrative, Ritual, and Royal Authority from the Chronicles of Japan to the Tale of the Heike*. Stanford, CA: Stanford University Press.

———. 2013. "Biwa Masters and Musical Hierophanies in the *Heike monogatari* and Other Medieval Texts." *Journal of Religion in Japan* 2: 119–151.

Biardeau, Madeleine. 1991a (1981). "The *Yūpa* (Sacrificial Post) in Hinduism." In Bonnefoy 1991: 37–39.

———. 1991b. "The Mythologies of Hindu India." In Bonnefoy 1991: 34–36.

———. 1991c. "Rudra/Śiva and the Destruction of the Sacrifice." In Bonnefoy 1991: 39–43.

———. 1991d. "Deva/Asura: Celestial Gods and 'Demons' in Hinduism." In Bonnefoy 1991: 52–53.

———. 1991e. "Gaṇapati." In Bonnefoy 1991: 90–92.

———. 1991f. "Symbols of the Earth in Indian Religion." In Yves Bonnefoy, ed., *Asian Mythologies*, 99–101.

Bibliothèque Nationale. 1995. *Catalogue des manuscrits chinois de Touen-houang. Fonds Pelliot chinois de la Bibliothèque Nationale*. Vol. 5, nos. 4001–6040. Paris: École Française d'Extrême-Orient.

Birrell, Anne, trans. 1999. *The Classic of Mountains and Seas*. Penguin Classics. London: Penguin Books.

Bischoff, F. A. 1956. *Ārya Mahābala-nāma-mahāyānasūtra: Contribution à l'étude des divinités mineures du bouddhisme tantrique*. Paris: Paul Geuthner.

Blacker, Carmen. 1986 (1975). *The Catalpa Bow: A Study of Shamanistic Practices in Japan*. London: G. Allen and Unwin.

Bodiford, William M. 2006–2007. "Matara: A Dream King between Insight and Imagination." *CEA* 16: 233–262.

Bokenkamp, Stephen R. 2007. *Ancestors and Anxiety: Daoism and the Birth of Rebirth in China*. Berkeley: University of California Press.

———. 2009. "The Silkworm and the Bodhi Tree: The Lingbao Attempt to Replace Buddhism in China and Our Attempt to Place Lingbao Daoism." In John Lagerwey, ed., *Ancient and Medieval China*, 317–339. Vol. 1 of *Religion and Chinese Society*. Hong Kong: Chinese University of Hong Kong Press and École Française d'Extrême-Orient.

Bonnefoy, Yves, ed. 1991. *Asian Mythologies*. Trans. Wendy Doniger. Chicago: University of Chicago Press.

———. 1992. *L'Improbable et autres essais*. Paris: Gallimard.

———. 2003 (1972). *L'Arrière-pays*. Paris: Gallimard.

Borges, Jorge Luis. 1962. *Labyrinths: Selected Stories and Other Writings*. New York: New Directions.

———. 1999. *Selected Non-Fictions*. Ed. Eliot Weinberger. New York: Viking.

Bouchy, Anne-Marie (Anne). 1979. "Comment fut révélée la nature véritable de la divinité du Mont Atago." *Cahiers d'études et de documents sur les religions du Japon* 1: 9–48.

———. 1984. "Le renard: élément de la conception du monde dans la tradition japonaise." *Études mongoles et sibériennes* 15, *Le renard: Tours, détours et retours*, 17–70.

———. 1985. "Inari shinkō to miko" 稲荷信仰と巫覡. In Gorai 1985a: 171–305.

———. 1992. *Les oracles de Shirataka: ou la sibylle d'Osaka*. Paris: Editions Philippe Picquier.

Bouillier, Véronique. 1993. "Mahâdev himalayen." In Bouillier and Toffin 1993: 173–187.

Bouillier, Véronique, and Gérard Toffin, eds. 1993. *Classer les dieux? Des panthéons en Asie du Sud.* Purushartha 15. Paris: Éditions de l'EHESS.

Bourdieu, Pierre. 1990. *The Logic of Practice*. Trans. Richard Nice. Stanford: Stanford University Press.

Brancaccio, Pia. 2013. *The Buddhist Caves at Aurangabad: Transformations in Art and Religion.* Leiden: Brill.

Breen, John, and Mark Teeuwen, eds. 2000. *Shinto in History: Ways of the Kami.* Honolulu: University of Hawai'i Press.

———. 2010. *A New History of Shinto.* Oxford: Wiley-Blackwell.

Brown, Delmer M., and Ishida Ichirō, trans. 1979. *The Future and the Past: A Translation and Study of the Gukanshō, an Interpretive History of Japan Written in 1219.* Berkeley: University of California Press.

Brown, Robert L., ed. 1991. *Ganesh: Studies of an Asian God.* Albany, NY: SUNY Press.

Bryson, Megan. 2010. "The Transformation of Baijie Shengfei: Gender and Ethnicity in Chinese Religion." PhD diss., Stanford University.

———. "Mahākāla Worship in the Dali Kingom (937–1253) : A Study of the *Dahei tianshen daochang yi.*" *Journal of the International Association of Buddhist Studies* 35, 1–2: 3–69."

Bühnemann, Gudrun. 1988. *The Worship of Mahāgaṇapati according to the Nityosatva.* Wichtrach: Institut für Indologie.

———. 1989. *Forms of Gaṇeśa: A Study Based on Vidyārṇavatantra.* Wichtrach: Institut für Indologie.

Caillet (Berthier), Laurence. 1981a. *Syncrétisme au Japon. Omizutori: le rituel de l'eau de Jouvence*. Paris: Presses Orientales de France.

———, ed. 1981b. *Fêtes et rites des 4 saisons au Japon*. Paris: Presses Orientalistes de France.

Casal, U. A. 1959. "The Goblin Fox and Badger and Other Witch Animals of Japan." *Folklore Studies* 18: 1–94.

Chandra, Lokesh. 1992. "Sarasvatī in Japanese Art." In Tara Chandrika, ed., *Cultural Horizons of India*, 2: 23–39. New Delhi: International Academy of Indian Culture.

———. 1999–2005. *Dictionary of Buddhist Iconography.* 14 vols. New Delhi: Aditya Prakashan.

Chapin, Helen B. 1972. *A Long Roll of Buddhist Images*. Rev. Alexander Soper. Ascona: Artibus Asiae.

Chatterjee, Asim Kumar. 1970. *The Cult of Skanda-Kārttikeya in Ancient India.* Calcutta: Punthi Pustak.

Chavannes, Édouard. 1910. *Le T'ai chan: Essai de monographie d'un culte chinois.* Paris: Librairie Ernest Leroux.

Childs, Margaret. 1980. "*Chigo monogatari*: Love Stories or Buddhist Sermons?" *MN* 35, 2: 127–151.

Cohen, Lawrence, 1991. "The Wives of Gaṇeśa." In Robert L. Brown 1991: 115–140.

Cohen, Richard. 1998. "Nāga, Yaksinī, Buddha: Local Deities and Local Buddhism at Ajanta." *History of Religions* 37, 4: 1–19.

Coomaraswamy, Ananda K. 1997 (1928). *Yakṣas: Essays in the Water Cosmology.* Ed. Paul Schroeder. Oxford: Oxford University Press.

Cooper, Michael. 1982. *They Came to Japan*. Berkeley: University of California Press.

Courtright, Paul B. 1985. *Gaṇeśa, Lord of Obstacles, Lord of Beginnings*. New York: Oxford University Press.

Dang Yan'ni 黨燕妮. 2005. "Pishamen Tianwang xinyang zai Dunhuang de liuchuan." 毗沙門天王信仰在敦煌的流傳. *Dunhuang yanjiu* 敦煌研究 3: 99–104.

Daniels, F. J. 1960. "Snake and Dragon Lore of Japan." *Folklore* 71: 145–164.

Das Gupta, Shashibusan. 1976 (1946). *Obscure Religious Cults as a Background to Bengali Literature*. Calcutta: Firma KLM.

Davidson, Ronald M. 1991. "Reflections on the Maheśvara Subjugation Myth: Indic Materials, Sa-skya-pa Apologetics, and the Birth of Heruka." *Journal of the International Association of Buddhist Studies* 14, 2: 197–225.

———. 2002. *Indian Esoteric Buddhism: A Social History of the Tantric Movement.* New York: Columbia University Press.

Davis, Edward L. 2001. *Society and the Supernatural in Song China.* Honolulu: University of Hawai'i Press.

de Certeau, Michel. 1992. *The Mystic Fable: The Sixteenth and Seventeenth Centuries.* Chicago: University of Chicago Press.

Deleuze, Gilles. 1995 (1968). *Difference and Repetition.* Trans. Paul Patton. New York: Columbia University Press.

Deleuze, Gilles, and Félix Guattari. 1987. *A Thousand Plateaus: Capitalism and Schizophrenia.* Trans. Brian Massumi. Minneapolis: University of Minnesota Press.

———. 1996. *What Is Philosophy?* Trans. Hugh Tomlinson and Graham Burchell. New York: Columbia University Press.

Deleuze, Gilles, and Claire Parnet. 1977. *Dialogues.* Trans. Hugh Tomlinson and Barbara Habberjam. New York: Columbia University Press.

de Mallmann, Marie-Thérèse. 1973. "Un aspect de Sarasvatī dans le tāntrisme bouddhique." *BEFEO* 53: 369–374.

———. 1986 (1975). *Introduction à l'iconographie du tântrisme bouddhique.* Paris: Adrien Maisonneuve.

Derrida, Jacques. 1980a. "Structure, Sign, and Play in the Discourse of the Human Sciences." In Jacques Derrida, *Writing and Difference,* 278–294. Trans. Alan Bass. Chicago: University of Chicago Press.

———. 1980b. "The Supplement of Copula." In Josué V. Harrari, ed., *Textual Strategies: Perspectives in Post-Structuralist Criticism.* Ithaca, NY: Cornell University Press.

———. 1982. *Margins of Philosophy.* Chicago: University of Chicago Press.

———. 1983 (1972). "Plato's Pharmacy." In Jacques Derrida, *Dissemination,* 67–186. Trans. Barbara Johnson. Chicago: University of Chicago Press.

———. 1985. *Margins of Philosophy.* Trans. Alan Bass. Chicago: University of Chicago Press.

———. 1998 (1976). *Of Grammatology.* Trans. Gayatri Chakravorti Spivak. Baltimore: Johns Hopkins University Press.

———. 2002. "Reste—le maître, ou le supplément d'infini." In Lyne Bansat-Boudon and John Scheid, eds., *Le Maître et ses disciples: pour Charles Malamoud,* 25–63. Paris: Seuil.

———. 2008. *The Animal That Therefore I Am.* Ed. Marie-Louise Mallet. Trans. David Wills. New York: Fordham University Press.

Descola, Philippe. 2005. *Par-delà nature et culture.* Paris: Gallimard.

DesJardins, Marc. 2001. "*Mahāmāyūrī:* explorations sur la création d'une écriture prototantrique." PhD diss., McGill University.

Detienne, Marcel, and Gilbert Hamonic, eds. 1995. *La Déesse Parole: quatre figures de la langue des dieux.* Idées et Recherches. Paris: Flammarion.

Devi, Shanti. 1984. "Kompira Daigongen: Kami or hotoke?" *Transactions of the International Conference of Orientalists in Japan* 28–29: 40–51.

De Visser, Marinus Willem. 1908a. "The Tengu." *TASJ* 36, 2: 25–99.

———. 1908b. "The Fox and the Badger in Japanese Folklore." *TASJ* 36, 3: 1–159.

———. 1911. "The Snake in Japanese Superstition." *Mitteilungen des Seminars für Orientalische Sprachen* 41, 1: 267–322.

———. 1913. *The Dragon in China and Japan*. Amsterdam: Johannes Müller.

———. 1935. *Ancient Buddhism in Japan: Sūtras and Ceremonies*. 2 vols. Leiden: Brill.

Dhavalikar, M. K. 1970. "Gaṇeśa beyond the Indian Frontiers." In Lokesh Chandra, ed., *India's Contribution to World Thought and Culture*, 1–16. Madras, Vivekananda Rock Memorial Committee.

Diény, Jean-Pierre. 1994. *Le symbolisme du dragon dans la Chine antique.* Paris: Collège de France, Institut des Hautes Études Chinoises.

Dobbins, James C., ed. 1996. "The Legacy of Kuroda Toshio." *JJRS* 23, 3–4: 217–232.

Doniger (O'Flaherty), Wendy. 1973. *Ascetism and Eroticism in the Mythology of Śiva.* London: Oxford University Press.

———, trans. 1975. *Hindu Myths: A Sourcebook.* Harmondsworth: Penguin.

———. 1980. *Women, Androgynes, and Other Mythical Beasts.* Chicago: University of Chicago Press.

———, trans. 1982. *The Rig Veda: An Anthology of One Hundred Eight Hymns.* London: Penguin Classics.

———. 1998. *The Implied Spider: Politics and Theology in Myth.* New York: Columbia University Press.

Douglas, Mary. 2002 (1966). *Purity and Danger: An Analysis of the Concepts of Pollution and Taboo*. Routledge Classics. London: Routledge.

Dowman, Keith, trans. 1984. *Sky Dancer: The Secret Life and Songs of Lady Yeshe Tsogel*. London: Routledge & Kegan Paul.

Duara, Prasenjit. 1988. "Superscribing Symbols: The Myth of Guandi, Chinese God of War." *Journal of Asian Studies* 47, 4: 778–795.

Dudbridge, Glen. 1996–1997. "The General of the Five Paths in Tang and Pre-Tang China." *CEA* 9: 85–98.

Dumézil, Georges. 1929. *Le problème des Centaures: Étude de mythologie comparée indo-européenne.* Annales du Musée Guimet. Paris: Paul Geuthner.

———. 1968. *Mythe et épopée: 1. L'idéologie des trois fonctions dans les épopées des peuples indo-européens.* Bibliothèque des sciences humaines. Paris: Gallimard.

———. 1988. *Mitra-Varuna: An Essay on Two Indo-European Representations of Sovereignty.* Trans. Derek Coltman. New York: Zone Books.

Duquenne, Robert. n.d. "Le sac à malices dans la peinture Zen." *Les Voix* 59: 36–37.

———. 1983. "Daiitoku Myōō" 大威徳明王. *Hōbōgirin* 6: 652–670.

———. 1988. "Gaṇapati Rituals in Chinese." *BEFEO* 77: 321–352.

———. 1994a. "Pérégrinations entre l'Inde et le Japon: du 'Mont en Tête d'Eléphant' et d'autres montagnes sacrées." In Fukui Fumimasa and Gérard Fussman, eds., *Bouddhisme et cultures locales: Quelques cas de réciproques adaptations,* 199–223. Paris: École Française d'Extrême-Orient.

———.1994b. "Dairiki-daigo-myōhi" 大力大護明妃. *Hōbōgirin* 7: 947–953.

Durt, Hubert. 1983. "Daigenshuri Busa" 大権修利菩薩. *Hōbōgirin* 6: 599–609.

Dykstra, Yoshiko K., trans. 1986. *The Konjaku Tales, Indian Section: From a Medieval Japanese Collection*. Osaka: Kansai Gaidai University.

———, trans. 1998–2003. *The Konjaku Tales, Japanese Section: From a Medieval Japanese Collection.* 3 vols. Osaka: Kansai Gaidai University.

Eder, Matthias. 1951. "Figürliche Darstellungen in der japanischen Volksreligion." *Folklore Studies* 10, 2: 197–280.

Eliasberg, Danielle. 1984. "Quelques aspects du grand exorcisme No à Touen-houang." In Michel Soymié, ed., *Contributions aux études de Touen-houang*, 3: 237–253. Paris: École Française d'Extrême-Orient.

Emmerick, R. E., trans. 1970. *The Sūtra of Golden Light: Being a Translation of the Suvarṇabhāsottamasūtra*. London: Luzac and Company.

Fabricand-Person, Nicole. 2002. "Demonic Female Guardians of the Faith." In Barbara Ruch, ed., *Engendering Faith: Women and Buddhism in Premodern Japan,* 343–382. Ann Arbor: Center for Japanese Studies, University of Michigan.

Faure, Bernard. 1986a. "The Concept of One-Practice *Samādhi* in Early Ch'an." In Peter N. Gregory, ed., *Traditions of Meditation in East Asian Buddhism,* 99–128. Studies in East Asian Buddhism 4. Honolulu: University of Hawai'i Press.

———. 1986b. "Bodhidharma as Textual Paradigm." *History of Religions* 25, 3: 187–198.

———. 1991. *The Rhetoric of Immediacy: A Cultural Critique of Chan/Zen Buddhism.* Princeton, NJ: Princeton University Press.

———. 1996. *Visions of Power: Imagining Medieval Japanese Buddhism.* Princeton, NJ: Princeton University Press.

———. 1998a. *The Red Thread: Buddhist Approaches to Sexuality.* Princeton, NJ: Princeton University Press.

———. 1998b. "The Buddhist Icon and the Modern Gaze." *Critical Inquiry* 24, 3: 768–813.

———. 1999. "Relics, Regalia, and the Dynamics of Secrecy in Japanese Buddhism." In Eliot R. Wollfson, ed., *Rending the Veil: Concealment and Secrecy in the History of Religions,* 271–287. New York: Seven Bridges Press.

———. 2000. "Japanese Tantra, the Tachikawa-ryū, and Ryōbu Shintō." In David G. White, ed., *Tantra in Practice,* 543–556. Princeton, NJ: Princeton University Press.

———, ed. 2002–2003a. "Buddhist Priests, Kings, and Marginals: Studies on Medieval Japanese Buddhism." *CEA* 13.

———. 2002–2003b. "Une perle rare: la 'nonne' Nyoi et l'idéologie médiévale." *CEA* 13: 177–196.

———. 2003a. *The Power of Denial: Buddhism, Purity, and Gender.* Princeton, NJ: Princeton University Press.

———. 2003b (1995). "Quand l'habit fait le moine: The Symbolism of the *Kaṣāya* in Sōtō Zen." In Bernard Faure, ed., *Chan Buddhism in Ritual Context,* 211–249. London: Routledge Curzon.

———. 2003c. "Dato" 駄都. *Hōbōgirin* 8: 1127–1158.

———. 2006. "The Elephant in the Room: The Cult of Secrecy in Japanese Tantrism." In Scheid and Teeuwen 2006: 255–268.

———. 2007. "Kegon and Dragons: A Mythological Approach to Huayan Doctrine." In Imre Hamar, ed., *Reflecting Mirrors: Perspectives on Huayan Buddhism.* 297–308. Wiesbaden: Harrassowitz Verlag.

———. 2009. "Vers une nouvelle approche de la religion japonaise: le cas du Japon médiéval." *Historia religionum* 1: 105–113.

———. 2011. "From Bodhidharma to Daruma: The Hidden Life of a Zen Patriarch." *Japan Review* 23: 45–71.

———. 2012. "The God Daishōgun: From Calendar to Cult." *CEA* 21: 201–221.

———. 2013a. "Indic Influences on Chinese Mythology: King Yama and His Acolytes as Gods of Destiny." In John Kieschnick and Meir Shahar, eds., *India in the Chinese Imagination: Myth, Religion, and Thought*, 36–50. Philadelphia: University of Pennsylvania Press.

———. 2013b. "The Cultic World of the Blind Monks: Benzaiten, Jūzenji, and Shukujin." *Journal of Religion in Japan* 2: 171–194.

———. 2015a. *The Fluid Pantheon*. Vol. 1 of *Gods of Medieval Japan*. Honolulu: University of Hawai'i Press.

———. 2015b. "Buddhism Ab Ovo: Aspects of Embryological Discourse in Medieval Japanese Buddhism." In Anna Andreeva and Dominic Steavu, eds., *Enlightenment in Utero: Embryological and Reproductive Symbolism in East Asian Religions*. Leiden: Brill.

———. Forthcoming. *Rogue Gods*. Vol. 3 of *Gods of Medieval Japan*. Honolulu: University of Hawai'i Press.

———. Forthcoming. *Lords of Life*. Vol. 4 of *Gods of Medieval Japan*. Honolulu: University of Hawai'i Press.

Favret-Saada, Jeanne. 1980. *Deadly Words: Witchcraft in the Bocage*. Cambridge: Cambridge University Press.

Filliozat, Jean. 1937. *Étude de démonologie indienne: Le* Kumāratantra *de Rāvaṇa et les textes parallèles indiens, tibétains, chinois, cambodgien et arabe*. Cahiers de la Société Asiatique. Paris: Imprimerie Nationale.

Foucault, Michel. 1977. "What Is an Author?" Trans. Donald F. Bouchard and Sherry Simon. In Donald F. Bouchard, ed., *Language, Counter-Memory, Practice*, 124–127. Ithaca, NY: Cornell University Press.

———. 1982 (1969). *The Archaeology of Knowledge*. New York: Vintage.

———. 1994 (1966). *The Order of Things: An Archeology of the Human Sciences*. New York: Vintage.

Foucher, Alfred. 1900–1905. *Étude sur l'iconographie bouddhique de l'Inde*. 2 vols. Paris: Librairie Ernest Leroux.

———. 1922. *L'Art gréco-bouddhique du Gandhâra: Étude sur les origines de l'influence classique dans l'art bouddhique de l'Inde et de l'Extrême-Orient*. 2 vols. Paris: Imprimerie Nationale.

Frank, Bernard. 1981–1982. "Résumé de cours et travaux: Civilisation Japonaise." In *Annuaire du Collège de France*, 587–611. Paris: Collège de France.

———. 1986. "Vacuité et 'corps actualisé': le problème de la présence des 'Personnages Vénérés' dans leurs images selon la tradition du bouddhisme japonais." In *Le Temps de la réflexion: Corps des dieux*, 7: 141–170. Reprinted in *Journal of the International Association of Buddhist Studies* 11, 2 (1988): 53–86.

———. 1990. "Les *deva* de la tradition bouddhique et la société japonaise: l'exemple d'Indra/Taishakuten." In Alain Forrest, Eiichi Katō, and Léon Vandermeersch, eds., *Bouddhisme et sociétés asiatiques: clergés, sociétés et pouvoirs*, 61–74. Paris: Editions L'Harmattan. Reprinted in Frank 2000b.

———. 1991. *Le panthéon bouddhique au Japon: Collections d'Émile Guimet*. Paris: Réunion des Musées Nationaux.

———. 1994–1995. "Civilisation japonaise." In *Annuaire du Collège de France*, 749–762. Paris: Collège de France.

———. 1998 (1958). *Kata-imi et kata-tagae: Étude sur les interdits de direction à l'époque Heian*. Paris: Collège de France, Institut des Hautes Études Japonaises.

———. 2000a. *Dieux et Bouddhas au Japon.* Paris: Éditions Odile Jacob.

———. 2000b. *Amour, colère, couleur: Essais sur le bouddhisme au Japon.* Paris: Collège de France, Institut des Hautes Études Japonaises.

Fritsch. Ingrid. 1991. "Benzaiten, die Göttin mit der Laute." In Eva Bachmayer, Wolfgang Huber, Sepp Linhart, eds., *Japan, von Aids biz Zen*, 155–164. Vienna: Institut für Japanologie.

———. 1996. *Japans blinde Sänger: im Schutz der Gottheit Myōon-Benzaiten.* Munich: Iudicium Verlag.

Fujisawa-shi kyōiku iinkai 藤沢市教育委員会, ed. 2000. *Enoshima engi emaki* 江ノ島縁起絵巻. Fujisawa: Fujisawa-shi kyōiku iinkai.

Fushimi Inari taisha 伏見稲荷大社, ed. 1957. *Inari taisha yuishoki shūsei: shinkō chosaku hen* 稲荷大社由緒記集成ー信仰著作篇. Kyoto: Fushimi Inari taisha shamusho.

———, ed. 1972. *Inari taisha yuishoki shūsei: kenkyū chosaku hen* 稲荷大社由緒記集成：研究著作篇. Kyoto: Fushimi Inari taisha shamusho.

Fushimi taisha 伏見大社, ed. 1951. *Inari no shinkō* 稲荷の信仰. Kyoto: Inari taisha.

Gaboriau, Marc. 1993. "Des dieux dans toutes les directions: Conception indienne de l'espace et classification des dieux." In Bouillier and Toffin 1993: 23–42.

Gakkō Yoshihiro 月光善弘. 1965. "Tōhoku ni okeru oshira shinkō to Kangiten to no ruijisei" 東北貳おけるオシラ信仰説歓喜天戸の類似性. *Nihon minzokugaku* 日本民俗学 37: 13–17.

Gangōji bunkazai kenkyūjo 元興寺文化財研究所, ed. 1999. *Shintō kanjō: wasurareta shinbutsu shūgō no sekai* 神道灌頂ー忘られた神佛習合の世界. Nara: Gangōji.

Gary, Romain. 1973. *The Roots of Heaven.* London: White Lion Publishers.

Gellner, David. 1997. "For Syncretism: The Position of Buddhism in Nepal and Japan Compared." *Social Anthropology* 5: 277–290.

Germano, David, and Janet Gyatso. "Longchenpa and the Possession of the Dākinī." In White 2000a: 239–265.

Getty, Alice. 1940. "Uga-jin: The Coiled-Serpent God with a Human Head." *Artibus Asiae* 8, 1: 36–48.

———. 1971 (1936). *Gaṇeśa: A Monograph on the Elephant-Faced God.* Oxford: Clarendon Press.

———. 1998. *The Gods of Northern Buddhism: Their History and Iconography.* New York: Dover Publications.

Ghosh, Niranjan. 1984. Śrī Sarasvatī in Indian Art and Literature. Delhi: Sri Satguru Publications.

Giebel, Rolf W., trans. 2001. *Two Esoteric Sutras: The Adamantine Pinnacle Sutra/The Susiddhikara Sutra.* Berkeley: Numata Center for Buddhist Translation & Research.

———, trans. 2006. *The Vairocanābhisaṃbodhi Sutra.* Berkeley: Numata Center for Buddhist Translation and Research.

Goble, Geoffrey. 2013. "The Legendary Siege of Anxi: Myth, History, and Truth in Chinese Buddhism." *Pacific World* 15: 1–32.

Goepper, Roger. 1993. *Aizen-myōō: The Esoteric King of Lust; An Iconological Study.* Artibus Asiae. Zurich: Museum Rietberg.

Gorai Shigeru 五来重, ed. 1985a. *Inari shinkō no kenkyū* 稲荷信仰の研究. Kyoto: San'yō shinbun-sha.

———. 1985b. "Inari shinkō to bukkyō: Dakiniten o chūshin to shite" 稲荷信仰と佛教ー荼吉尼天を中心として. In Gorai 1985a: 75–170.

———, ed. 2000 (1983–1984). *Shugendō shiryō shū* 修験道史料集. 2 vols. Tokyo: Meicho shuppan.

Gould, Stephen Jay. 1996. *Full House: The Spread of Excellence from Plato to Darwin*. New York: Three Rivers Press.

Gould, Stephen Jay, and Richard C. Lewontin. 1979. "The Spandrels of San Marco and the Panglossian Paradigm: A Critique of the Adaptationist Programme." *Proceedings of the Royal Society of London* 205, 1161: 581–598.

Goux, Jean-Joseph. 1990. *Symbolic Economies: After Marx and Freud*. Trans. Jennifer Curtis Gage. Ithaca, NY: Cornell University Press.

Granet, Marcel. 1959. *Danses et légendes de la Chine ancienne*. Paris: Presses Universitaires de France.

———. 1999 (1934). *La pensée chinoise*. Paris: Albin Michel.

Granoff, Phyllis. 1970. "Tobatsu Bishamon: Three Japanese Statues in the U.S. and an Outline of the Rise of this Cult in East Asia." *East and West*, n.s. 20: 144–168.

———. 1979. "Maheśvara/Mahākāla: A Unique Buddhist Image from Kaśmīr." *Artibus Asiae* 41, 1: 64–82.

Grapard, Allan. 1987. "Linguistic Cubism: A Singularity of Pluralism in the Sannō Cult." *JJRS* 14: 211–234.

———. 1998a. "*Keiranshūyōshū:* A Different Perspective on Mt. Hiei in the Medieval Period." In Payne 1998: 55–69.

———. 2002–2003. "Of Emperors and Foxy Ladies." *CEA* 13: 127–150.

Gray, David B. 2005. "Eating the Heart of the Brahmin: Representations of Alterity and the Formation of Identity in Tantric Buddhist Discourse." *History of Religions* 45, 1: 45–69.

———. 2007. *Cakrasamvara Tantra (The Discourse of Śrī Heruka) (Śrīherukābhidhāna)*. New York: American Institute of Buddhist Studies at Columbia University.

Groner, Paul. 2002. *Ryōgen and Mount Hiei: Japanese Tendai in the Tenth Century*. Studies in East Asian Buddhism 15. Honolulu: University of Hawai'i Press.

Gülberg, Niels. 1999. *Buddhistische Zeremoniale (Kōshiki) und ihre Bedeutung für die Literatur des japanischen Mittelalters*. Münchener ostasiatische Studien 76. Stuttgart: Franz Steiner Verlag.

Gummer, Nathalie Dawn. 2000. "Articulating Potency: A Study of the *Suvarṇa(pra)bhāsottamasūtra*." PhD diss., Harvard University.

Gupte, Ramesh Shankar. 1963. "An Interesting Panel from the Aurangabad Caves." *Marathwada University Journal* 3, 2: 59–63.

Guth (Kanda), Christine M. E. 1999. "Mapping Sectarian Identity: Onjōji's Statue of Shinra Myōjin." *Res* 35: 108–124.

Guthrie, Elizabeth. 2004. "A Study of the History and Cult of the Buddhist Earth Deity in Mainland Southeast Asia." PhD diss., University of Canterbury, Christchurch, NZ.

Gyatso, Janet. 1999. *Apparitions of the Self: The Secret Autobiographies of a Tibetan Visionary*. Princeton, NJ: Princeton University Press.

Hadot, Pierre. 2006. *The Veil of Isis: An. Essay on the History of the Idea of Nature*. Trans. Michael Chase. Cambridge, MA: Harvard University Press.

Hall, David A. 2014. *The Buddhist Goddess Marishiten: A Study of the Evolution and Impact of Her Cult on the Japanese Warrior*. Leiden: Global Oriental.

Hamilton, Roy W. "The Goddess of Rice." 2003. In Roy W. Hamilton, ed. *The Art of Rice: Spirit and Sustenance in Asia*, 255–271. Los Angeles, CA: UCLA Fowler Museum of Cultural History.

Hansen, Valerie. 1993. "Gods on Walls: A Case of Indian Influence on Chinese Lay Religion?" In Patricia Buckley Ebrey and Peter N. Gregory, eds., *Religion and Society in T'ang and Sung China*, 75–113. Honolulu: University of Hawai'i Press.

Hansen, Wilbur. 2008. *When Tengu Talk: Hirata Atsutane's Ethnography of the Other World*. Honolulu: University of Hawai'i Press.

Hara Katsuaki 原克昭. 1999. "'Chūsei Nihongi' kenkyūshi" 「中世日本紀」研究史. *Kokubungaku kaishaku to kanshō* 国文学ー解釈と鑑賞 814: 174–184.

———. 2012. *Chūsei Nihongi ronkō: chūshaku no* 中世二本紀論考ー注釈の思想史. Kyoto: Hōzōkan.

Hara Naomasa 原直正. 2012. *Suwa Daimyōjin no chūsei-teki tenkai* 諏訪大明神中世的展開. Nagoya: Ningensha.

Harada Nobuo 原田禹雄. 2002. "Ryūkyū o shugo-suru kami" 琉球を守護する神. *Jinbun gakuhō* 人文学報 86: 191–211.

Harper, Katherine Anne. 1989. *The Iconography of the Saptamatrikas: Seven Hindu Goddesses of Spiritual Transformation*. Lewiston, N.Y.: Edwin Mellen Press.

Hashimoto Akihiko 橋本章彦. 2008. *Bishamonten: Nihon-teki tenkai no shosō* 毘沙門天ー日本的展開の諸相. Tokyo: Iwata shoin.

Hasuike Toshitaka 蓮池利隆. 2009. "Jōgyōdō no shugojin Matarajin" 常行堂の守護神・摩多羅神. Bukkyōgaku kenkyū 佛教学研究 65: 78–104.

Hatakeyama Yutaka. 2014. "*Ofuda* aux images de Kōshin, de la divinité du ver à soie et de la divinité du sol." In Kyburz 2014: 233–245.

Hatta Tatsuo 八田達男. 1989. "Zaō Gongen shinkō no denpan ni tsuite" 藏王権現信仰の伝播について. In Hiramatsu Reizō sensei koki kinen sha 平松令三先生古稀記念会, ed., *Nihon no shūkyō to bunka* 日本宗教の文化, 155–175. Kyoto: Dōhōsha.

Hatta Yukio 八田幸雄. 1991. *Kamigami to hotoke no sekai: shinbutsu shūgō o kataru* 神々と佛の世界ー神佛習合を語る. Tokyo: Hirakawa shuppansha.

Hattori Yukio 服部幸雄. 1973. "Ushirodo no kami: geinōshin shinkō ni kansuru ichi kōsatsu" 後戸の神ー藝能神信仰に関する一考察. *Bungaku* 41, 7: 73–85.

———. 2009. *Shukujin-ron: Nihon geinōmin shinkō no kenkyū* 宿神論ー日本芸能民信仰の研究. Tokyo: Iwanami shoten.

Hayakawa Junzaburō 早川純三郎, ed. 2000 (1915). *Shinkō sōsho* 信仰叢書. Tokyo: Hachiman shoten.

Hayashi On 林温. 1994. "Dakiniten mandara ni tsuite" 陀枳尼天曼荼羅について. *Bukkyō geijutsu* 佛教芸術 217: 10–11, 92–108.

———. 2002. "Besson mandara" 別尊曼荼羅. *Nihon no bijutsu* 日本の美術 433. Tokyo: Shibundō.

Hayashiya Tatsusaburō 林屋辰三郎 et al., eds. 1995. *Tenkawa* 天河. Tokyo: Heibonsha.

Hazama Jikō 硲慈弘.1948. *Nihon bukkyō ni tenkai to sono kichō* 日本佛教の展開とその基調. 2 vols. Tokyo: Sanshōdō.

Hegel, G. W. F. 1956. *Philosophy of History*. Trans. J. B. Sibree. New York: Dover.

Heine, Steven. 1994. "Sōtō Zen and the Inari Cult: Symbiotic and Exorcistic Trends in Buddhism and Folk Religious Amalgamations." *The Pacific World* 10: 75–101.

———. 1999. *Shifting Shape, Shaping Text: Philosophy and Folklore in the Fox Koan*. Honolulu: University of Hawai'i Press.

Heissig, Walter. 1970. "Zur Morphologie der 'Fuchsopfer': Gebete." *Zentralasiatische Studien* 10: 475–519.

Hermann-Pfandt, Adelheid. 1992. *Ḍākiṇīs: Zur Stellung und Symbolik des Weiblichen in den Tantrischen Buddhismus*. Bonn: Indica und Tibetica 20.

———. 1992–1993. "*Ḍākiṇīs* in Indo-Tibetan Tantric Buddhism: Some Results of Recent Research." *Studies in Central and East Asian Religions* 5–6: 45–63.

Hess, Daniel C. 2004. "Critiquing the Language of Syncretism: A Case Study of Hārītī," MA thesis, University of California-Santa Barbara.

Hillebrand, Alfred. 1981 (1891–1902). *Vedic Mythology*. Trans. Sreeramula Rajeswara Sarma. 2 vols. Delhi: Motilal Banarsidass.

Hiroshima kenritsu rekishi hakubutsukan: 広島県立歴史博物館, ed. 1990. *Chūsei no minshū to majinai*: *Heisei ninen haru no kikakuten* 中世の民衆とまじない一平成二年春の企画展. Hiroshima: Hiroshima kenritsu rekishi hakubutsukan tomo no kai.

Hiroya Yūtarō 廣谷雄太郎, ed. 1925. *Kinsei bukkyō shūsetsu* 近世佛教集說. Tokyo: Kokusho kankōkai.

Hiruta Genshirō 昼田原四郎. 1985. *Ekibyō to kitsune-tsuki: kinsei shomin no iryō jijō* 疫病と狐憑一近世庶民の医療事情. Tokyo: Misuzu shobō.

Hōbōgirin: Dictionnaire encyclopédique du bouddhisme d'après les sources chinoises et japonaises. 1927–. Vols. 1–8. Paris: Adrien Maisonneuve.

Holtom, D. C. 1938. "Japanese Votive Pictures (The Ikoma Ema)." *MN* 1, 1: 154–164.

Hori Ichirō 堀一郎. 1953. "Shinbutsu shūgō ni kansuru ichi kōsatsu." 神佛習合に関する一考察. Reprinted in Hori 1963.

———. 1963. *Shūkyō, shuzoku no seikatsu kisei* 宗教・習俗の生活規制. Nihon shūkyōshi kenkyū 日本宗教史研究 2. Tokyo: Miraisha.

Hosokawa Ryōichi 細川涼一. 1993. *Itsudatsu no Nihon chūsei: Kyōki, tōsaku, ma no sekai* 逸脱の日本中世一狂気・倒錯・魔の世界. Tokyo: JICC shuppankyoku.

———. 2002–2003. "Emperor Go-Daigo's Rule and the Monks of the *Vinaya* School: Sonkyō of Chōfukuji and Kyōen of Tōshōdaiji." Trans. Sango Asuka. *CEA* 13: 197–209.

Huntington, John C. 1975. "The Tendai Iconographic Model Book *Shosonzuzō*, Dated 1858." *Studies in Indo-Asian Art and Culture* 4: 121–424.

———. 1981. "Cave Six at Aurangabad: A Tantrayāna Monument?" In Joanna Williams, ed., *Kalādarśana: American Studies in the Art of India,* 47–55. Leiden: E. J. Brill.

Hyōdō Hiromi 兵藤裕己. 2009. *Biwa hōshi: 'ikai' o kataru hitobito* 琵琶法師一<異界>を語る人びと. Iwanami shinsho 1184. Tokyo: Iwanami shoten.

Iijima Yoshiharu 飯島吉晴. 1988. *Rikuzen no kamadogami shinkō: Kamadogami no seikaku to girei o chūshin ni* 陸前の竈神信仰一竈神の性格と儀礼を中心に. Tokyo: Yūzankaku shuppan.

Iizuna rekishi fureaikan いいづな歴史ふれあい館, ed. 2006. *Iizuna shinkō: habataku Iizunasaburō tengu* 飯綱信仰一羽ばたく飯綱三郎天狗. Nagano: Iizuna rekishi fureaikan.

Ikawa Kazuko 猪川和子. 1963. "Jiten ni sasaerareta Bishamonten chōzō: Tobatsu Bishamon ni tsuite no ichi kansatsu" 地天に支えられた毘沙門天彫像一兜跋毘沙門についての一観察. *Bijutsu kenkyū* 美術研究 229: 53–73.

Imai Jōen 今井淨圓. 2000. "Bishamonten ni kansuru kenkyū nōto" 毘沙門天に関する研究ノート. *Mikkyō shiryō kenkyūjo kiyō* 密教資料研究所紀要 3: 59–86.

Inaya Yūsen 稲谷祐宣, ed., 1993. *Shingon shintō shūsei: Tōmitsu jisō kuketsu shūsei* 真言神道集成一東密事相口訣集成 3. Osaka: Seizansha.

Ingold, Tim. 2000. *The Perception of the Environment: Essays in Livelihood, Dwelling and Skill.* London: Routledge.

———. 2011. *Being Alive: Essays on Movement, Knowledge and Description.* London: Routledge.

Inoue Yoritoshi 井上頼寿, ed. 1968. *Kyōto minzokushi* 京都民俗志. Tokyo: Heibonsha.

Irie Tami 入江多美. 2008. "Dakiniten (Shinko-ō bosatsu) ni kansuru ichi shiron: Nikkōsan Rinnōji-zō 'Izuna mandara-zu' o chūshin to shite" ダキニ天(辰狐王菩薩)に関する一試論ー　日光山輪王寺蔵「伊頭那(飯縄)曼荼羅図」を中心として. *Bijutsushi ronshū* 美術史論集 8: 94–110.

Ishihara Yasuo 石原康夫. 1990–1992. *Shikō Benzaiten-ki* 私考弁才天記. 2 vols. Musashino shi (private publisher).

Ishikawa Rikizan 石川力山. 1992. Chūsei Sōtōshū kirigami no bunrui shiron (20): girei (jukai, tengen, segaki, sono hoka) kankei o chūshin to shite中世曹洞宗切紙の分類試論（二十）ー儀礼(授戒、点眼、施餓鬼、その他）関係を中心として. *Komazawa daigaku bukkyō gakubu ronshū* 駒沢大学佛教学部論集 23: 95–126.

Ishizaki Tatsuji 石崎達二. 1936. *Tōfukuji Bishamon Tennō* 東福寺毘沙門天王. Kyoto: Tōfukuji Bishamondō Shōrin-an.

Itō Masayoshi 伊藤正義. 1970. *Konparu Zenchiku no kenkyū* 金春禅竹の研究. Tokyo: Akao shobundō.

———. 1972. "Chūsei *Nihongi* no rinkaku: *Taiheiki* ni okeru Urabe no Kanekazusetsu o megutte" 中世日本紀の輪郭ー太平記における卜部兼員説をめぐって. *Bungaku* 40, 10: 28–48.

———. 1980. "Jidō setsuwa kō" 慈童説話考. *Kokugo kokubun* 国語国文 49, 11: 1–32.

Itō Satoshi 伊藤聡. 1993. "Yoshida bunko shozō no Benzaiten kankei gikyō ni tsuite: sono honkoku to shokai." 吉田文庫所藏の弁財天関係偽經についてーその翻刻と紹介. *Muromachi* むろまち 2: 40–46.

———. 1995a. "Tenshō Daijin, Kūkai dōtai-setsu o megutte: toku ni Sanbōin-ryū o chūshin to shite" 天照大神空海同体説を巡ってｰ特に三宝院流を中心として. *Tōyō no shisō to shūkyō* 東洋の思想と宗教 12: 112-131.

———. 1995b. "Dairokuten Maō-setsu no seiritsu: toku ni *'Nakatomi harae kunge'* no shosetsu o chūshin to shite" 第六天魔王説の成立—特に『中臣祓訓解』の所説を中心として. *Nihon bungaku* 日本文学 44, 7: 67–77.

———. 1996. "Ōsu bunko shozō *Ugajin kudoku kyō*" 大須文庫藏『宇賀神功徳経』. *Kokugakuin daigaku Nihon bunka kenkyūjo kiyō* 77: 117–149.

———. 1997. "*Hokkekyō* to chūsei jingi-sho: tokuni Kamakura-ki ryōbu shintō-sho ni okeru Bonten-ō setsu o megutte"「法華經」と中世神祇書ー特に鎌倉期兩部神道書における梵天王説を巡って. *Kokubungaku: kaishaku to kanshō* 国文学ー解釈と鑑賞 790: 50–57.

———. 2002a. "Chōgen to hōju" 重源と宝珠. *Bukkyō bungaku* 佛教文学 26: 10–26.

———. 2002b. "Dai Nihon ni okeru taiyō shinkō: tokuni Amaterasu ōmikami to Aizen Myōō no shūgō o megutte" 大日本における太陽信仰ー特に天照大神と愛染明王の習合を巡って. In Matsumura Kazuo 松村一男 and Watanabe Kazuko 渡辺和子, eds, *Taiyōshin no kenkyū* 太陽神の研究, 1: 191–208.

———. 2002c. "Chūsei mikkyō ni okeru shintō sōjō ni tsuite: tokuni Reirei-ki kanjō kechimyaku o megutte" 中世密教における神道相承についてー特に麗気記灌頂相承血脈をめぐって. In Imatani Akira 今谷明, ed., *Ōken to jingi* 王権と神祇, 219–243. Tokyo: Shibunkaku shuppan.

———. 2005. "Denpu Aizen-hō o megutte" 田夫愛染法をめぐって. In Fukui Fumimasa hakushi koki taishaku kinenkai 福井文雅博士古稀・退職記念論集刊行会, ed., *Ajia bunka no shisō to girei* アジア文化の思想と儀礼, 821–840. Fukui Fumimasa hakushi koki kinen ronshū. Tokyo: Shunjūsha.

———. 2007. "'Yoritomo no saiki' ni okeru Benzaiten honshin kendan o megutte"『頼朝之最期』における弁才天本身顕現譚を巡って. In Setsuwa to setsuwa bungaku no kai, ed., *Setsuwa ronshū* 説話論集 16: 31–67. Tokyo: Seibundō.

———. 2011. *Chūsei Tenshō daijin shinkō no kenkyū* 中世天照大神信仰の研究. Kyoto: Hōzōkan.

Iwasa Kanzō 岩佐貫三. 1976a. "Daishōgun shinkō ni tsuite: Biwa-ko shuhen no daijoko-matsuri to no kanren (1)" 大将軍信仰について一琵琶湖周辺のダイジョコまつりとの関連. *Tōyōgaku kenkyū* 東洋学研究 10: 37–47.

———. 1976b. "Shiten no jaki to hōsōki: oni no shisō kenkyū (3)" 四天の邪鬼と方相鬼一鬼の思想研究・その三. *IBK* 25, 1: 387–390.

Iwasa Masashi 岩佐正 et al., eds. 1976. *Jinnō shōtōki・Masukagami* 神皇正統記・増鏡. *NKBT* 87. Tokyo: Iwanami shoten.

Iwata Keiji 岩田慶治. 1979. "Kami to kami." In *Kōza Nihon to minzoku shūkyō* 講座日本と民俗宗教, 3: 45–67.

Iyanaga Nobumi 彌永信美. 1981–1985. "Récits de la soumission de Maheśvara par Trailokyavijaya—d'après les sources chinoises et japonaises." In Strickmann 1981–1985, 3: 633–745.

———. 1983. "Daijizaiten (Maheśvara)" 大自在天. *Hōbōgirin* 6: 713–765.

———. 1994. "Daikoku-ten" 大黒天. *Hōbōgirin* 7: 839–920.

———. 1996–1997. "Le Roi Māra du Sixième Ciel et le mythe médiéval de la création du Japon." *CEA* 9: 323–396.

———. 1999. "Dākinī et l'Empereur: Mystique bouddhique de la royauté dans le Japon médiéval." *Versus: Quaderni di studi semiotici* 83–84: 41–111.

———. 2002a. *Daikokuten hensō: bukkyō shinwagaku 1* 大黒天変相 一佛教神話学 1. Kyoto: Hōzōkan.

———. 2002b. *Kannon hen'yōdan: bukkyō shinwagaku 2* 観音変容談一佛教神話学 2. Kyoto: Hōzōkan.

———. 2003. "*Honji suijaku* and the Logic of Combinatory Deities: Two Case Studies." In Teeuwen and Rambelli 2003a: 145–176.

———. 2006. "Secrecy, Sex, and Apocrypha: Remarks on Some Paradoxical Phenomena." In Scheid and Teeuwen 2006: 204–228.

———. 2006–2007. "Medieval Shintō as a Form of 'Japanese Hinduism': An Attempt at Understanding Early Medieval Shintō." *CEA* 16: 263–303.

———. 2012. "La 'possession' des esprits animaux (*tsukimono*) au Japon et la mythologie bouddhique." *CEA* 21: 387–403.

James, William. 1975 (1907). *Pragmatism*. Cambridge, MA: Harvard University Press.

Kabanoff, Alexander M. 1994. "The Kangi-ten (Gaṇapati) Cult in Medieval Japanese Mikkyō." In Ian Astley, ed., *Esoteric Buddhism in Japan*, 99–126. SBS Monographs 1. Copenhagen: Seminar for Buddhist Studies.

Kaempfer, Engelbert. 1906 (1690–1692). *The History of Japan: Together with a Description of the Kingdom of Siam*. London: J. MacLehose and Sons.

Kageyama Haruki 影山春樹. 1962. *Shintō bijutsu no kenkyū* 神道美術の研究. Tokyo: Yamamoto Koshū shashin kōgeibu.

———, ed. 1967. "Shintō bijutsu" 神道美術. *Nihon no bijutsu* 日本の美術 18. Tokyo: Shibundō.

———. 1971. *Shintai-san: Nihon no genshi shinkō o saguru* 神体山一日本の原始信仰を探る. Tokyo: Gakuseisha.

———. 1973a. *Shintō bijutsu: sono shosō to tenkai* 神道美術一その諸相と展開. Tokyo: Yūzankaku Shuppan.

———. 1973b. *The Arts of Shinto.* Trans. Christine Guth. New York: Weatherhill/Shibundo.

———. 1975b. "Matarajin shinkō to sono ihō" 摩多羅神信仰とその異法. In Maruyama Shūichi 村山修一, ed., *Hieizan to Tendai bukkyō no kenkyū* 比叡山と天台佛教の研究, 317–340. Sangaku shūkyōshi kenkyū sōsho 2. Tokyo: Meichō shuppan.

———. 1975c. "Kazuragawa Myōō-in to Jishū jinja." In Murayama Shūichi 村山修一, ed., *Hieizan to Tendai bukkyō no kenkyū* 比叡山と天台佛教の研究, 427–462. Tokyo: Meicho shuppan.

———. 1973 (1958). "Chikubushima sairei zu" 竹生島祭禮圖. In Kageyama 1973a: 328–336.

Kalinowski, Marc. 1983. "Les instruments astro-calendériques des Han et la méthode *liu ren.*" *BEFEO* 72: 309–419.

———, ed. 2003. *Divination et société dans la Chine médiévale: Étude des manuscrits de Dunhuang de la Bibliothèque Nationale de France et de la British Library*. Paris: Bibliothèque Nationale de France.

Kamata Tōji 鎌田東二. 1995a. "Kami to hotoke no topogurafii" 神と佛のトポグラフィー. In Yamaori 1995–1996, 1: 209–252. Tokyo: Heibonsha.

———. 1995b. "Tenkawa shinkō to shizen sūhai" 天河信仰と自然崇拝. In Hayashiya et al. 1995: 164–180.

———. 2000a. *Kami to hotoke no seishin-shi: shinshin shūgō-ron josetsu* 神と佛の精神史: 神神習合論序説. Tokyo: Shunjūsha.

Kamens, Edward. 1988. *The Three Jewels: A Study and Translation of Minamoto Tamenori's Sanboe*. Michigan Monograph Series in Japanese Studies. Chicago: University of Michigan, Center for Japanese Studies.

Kamstra, Jacques. 1987. "Who Was First, the Fox or the Lady? The God of Fushimi in Kyōto." In Dirk van der Plas, ed., *Effigies Dei*, 97–111. Leiden: E. J. Brill.

———. 1989a. "The Goddess Who Grew into a Bodhisattva Fox: Inari." In Irmela Hijiya-Kirschnereit, ed., *Festschrift für Bruno Lewin*, 2: 189–214. Bochum: Brockmeyer.

———. 1989b. "The Religion of Japan: Syncretism or Religious Phenomenalism." In J. D. Gort et al., eds., *Dialogue and Syncretism: An Interdisciplinary Approach*, 134–145. Grand Rapids, MI: William B. Eerdmans Publishing Co.

Kanagawa kenritsu Kanazawa bunko 神奈川県立金沢文庫, ed. 2004. *Mihotoke to goriyaku* みほとけとごりやく. Yokohama: Kanazawa bunko.

———, ed. 2007a. *Benzaiten: sono sugata to riyaku* 弁財天一その姿と利益. Yokohama: Kanazawa bunko.

———, ed. 2007b. *Onmyōdō kakeru mikkyō* 陰陽道X密教. Yokohama: Kanazawa bunko.

———, ed. 2011. *Aizen Myōō: Ai to ikari no hotoke* 愛染明王一愛と怒りのほとけ. Yokohama: Kanazawa bunko.

Kanai Kiyomitsu 金井清光. 1990. "Fukujin Kyōgen no keisei" 福神狂言の形成. In Ōshima Tatehiko 大島建彦 ed., *Daikoku shinkō* 大黒信仰. Tokyo: Yūzankaku shuppan.

Kang Xiaofei. 2006. *The Cult of the Fox: Power, Gender, and Popular Religion in Late Imperial and Modern China*. New York: Columbia University Press.

Katō Kumaichirō 加藤熊一郎, ed. 1902. *Nihon shūkyō fūzokushi* 日本宗教風属し. Tokyo: Morie shoten.

Kawaguchi Kenji 川口謙二, ed. 1999. *Nihon no kamigami yomitoki jiten* 日本の神々読み解き事典. Tokyo: Kashiwa shobō.

Kawakatsu Masatarō 川勝政太郎. 1941. "Hebidoshi ni chinamu Ugajin to Benzaiten" 蛇年にちなむ宇賀神と弁才天. *Shiseki to bijutsu* 史跡と美術 122: 34–38.

Kawamura Minato 川村湊. 2007. *Gozu Tennō to Somin Shōrai densetsu: kesareta ijin tachi* 牛頭天王と蘇民将来伝説ー消された異神たち. Tokyo: Sakuinsha.

———. 2008. *Yami no Matarajin: hengen-suru ijin no nazo o ou* 闇の摩多羅神ー変幻する異神の謎を追う. Tokyo: Kawade shobō shinsha.

Kawasaki Tsuyoshi 川崎剛志, ed. 2011. *Shugendō no Muromachi bunka* 修験道の室町文化, 229–248. Tokyo: Iwata shoin.

Kawasoe Hideki 川副秀樹. 2006. *Sukyandarasuna kamigami: yōjutsu Iizuna no hō to kudagitsune, reiko to tengu no gattai daimajin* スキャンダラスな神々ー妖術・飯縄の法とクダ狐・霊狐と天狗の合体大魔神. Nagano: Ryūhō shobō.

Kawatō Masashi 河東仁. 2002. *Nihon no yume shinkō: shūkyōgaku kara mita Nihon seishinshi* 日本の夢信仰ー宗教学から見た日本精神史. Machida: Tamagawa daigaku shuppanbu.

Kelsey, W. Michael. 1981. "Salvation of the Snake, the Snake of Salvation: Buddhist-Shinto Conflict and Resolution." *JJRS* 8, 1–2: 83–113.

Kern, H. 1884. *The Saddharma Puṇḍarika or the Lotus of the True Law*. Sacred Books of the East 21. Oxford: Clarendon Press. Reprint, New York: Dover, 1963.

Kida Teikichi (Sadakichi) 喜田貞吉.1975. *Tsukimono* 憑物. Ed. Yamada Norio 山田野理夫. Tokyo: Hōbunkan.

———. 1976. *Fukujin* 福神. Ed. Yamada Norio. Tokyo: Hōbunkan.

Kieschnick, John, and Meir Shahar. 2013. *India in the Chinese Imagination: Myth, Religion, and Thought*. Philadelphia: University of Pennsylvania Press.

Kim Sujung 金秀廷. 2014. "Transcending Locality and Creating Identity: Shinra Myōjin, a Japanese Deity from Korea." PhD diss., Columbia University.

Kimura Hirokazu 木村博. 1991. "Yōsan shugojin to shite no Kokūzō Bosatsu" 養蚕守護神としての虚空藏菩薩. In Sano Kenji 佐野賢治., ed., *Kokūzō shinkō* 虚空藏信仰, 85–91. Tokyo: Yūzankaku shuppan.

Kinsley, David. 1986. *Hindu Goddesses: Visions of the Divine Feminine in the Hindu Religious Tradition*. Berkeley: University of California Press.

Kitagawa Masahiro 北川正寛. 2002. "*Keiran shūyōshū* ni okeru jōdo shisō" 『渓嵐拾葉集』における浄土思想. *Mikkyō bunka* 密教文化 208: 1–32.

———. 2004. "*Keiran shūyōshū* ni okeru Tō-Tai ryōmitsu no kōshō" 『渓嵐拾葉集』における東台両密の交渉. *Mikkyōgaku kenkyū* 密教学研究 36: 65–80.

Kitao Ryūshin 北尾隆心. 2001. "Shingon mikkyō ni miru 'Daijō Bishamon kudoku-kyō'" 真言密教に見る「大乗毘沙門功徳經」. *Shūchiin daigaku mikkyō shiryō kenkyūjo kiyō* 種智院大学密教資料研究所紀要 4, 14: 1–14.

Klein, Susan Blakeley. 1990. "When the Moon Strikes the Bell: Desire and Enlightenment in the Noh Play *Dōjōji*." *Journal of Japanese Studies* 17, 2: 291–322.

———. 1995. "Woman as Serpent: The Demonic Feminine in the Noh Play Dōjōji." In Jane Marie Law, ed., *Religious Reflections on the Human Body*, 100–136. Bloomington: Indiana University Press.

Knipe, David M. 1972. "One Fire, Three Fires, Five Fires: Vedic Symbols in Transformation." *History of Religions* 12: 28–41.

Kobayashi Taichirō 小林大市郎. 1940–1941. “Tanabata to Magora kō (1)” 七夕と摩睺羅考. *Shina bukkyō shigaku* 支那佛教史學 4, 3: 1–34; 4: 30–53.
———. 1946. *Yamato-e shiron* 大和絵史論. Osaka: Zenkoku shobō.
Kobayashi Tsukifumi 小林月史. 1970. *Benzaiten kenkyū sōsho* 弁財天研究叢書, vol. 1. Kyoto: Kanshōe jimusho.
———. 1978. *Gennō zenjiden* genshutsu to shinnyodō shinkō: Gennō zenji to fushigi na deai『玄翁禪師伝』現出と真如堂信仰 一玄翁禅師と不思議な出合. Kyoto: Shinnyodō kenkyūkai.
———. 1981. *Ryūjin to Benzaiten* 竜神と弁財天. Kyoto: Shinnyodō kenkyūkai.
Kobori Kōsen 小堀光詮. “Benzaiten no shinkō to shuhō: chie, fukutoku no sonten” 弁財天の信仰と修法一知恵, 福徳の尊天. *Tendai gakuhō* 天台学報 6: 32–40.
Kōchi ken ritsu rekishi minzoku shiryōkan 高知県立歴史民俗資料館, ed. 1997. *Izanagiryū no uchū: kami to hito no monogatari* いざなぎ流の宇宙一神と人のものがたり. Kōchi: Kenritsu rekishi minzoku shiryōkan.
Köck, Stefan. 2000. “The Dissemination of the Tachikawa-ryū and the Problem of Orthodox and Heretic Teachings in Shingon Buddhism.” *IBK* 7: 69–83.
———. 2007. “Das *Juhō-yōjin-shū* (Sammlung von der Wachsamkeit beim Empfangen buddhistischer Lehren) des Mönches Shinjō als Apologie der Shingon-Schule gegenüber konkurrierenden Lehren in der Provinz Echizen um 1270.” PhD diss., Ruhr-Universität Bochum.
Kojima Shōsaku 小島鉦作. 1999. “Tenna shōnin to Inari shintō” 天阿上人と稲荷神道. In Yamaori 1999: 336–341.
Kokubungaku kenkyū shiryōkan 国文学研究資料館, ed. 1999a. *Ryōbu shintō shū* 両部神道集. Shinpukuji zenpon sōkan 真福寺善本叢刊, 2nd ser., vol. 6. Tokyo: Rinsen shoten.
———, ed. 1999b. *Chūsei Nihongi shū* 中世日本紀集. Shinpukuji zenpon sōkan, 2nd ser., vol. 7. Tokyo: Rinsen shoten.
———, ed. 1999c. *Chūsei Kōyasan engi shū* 中世高野山縁起集. Shinpukuji zenpon sōkan, 2nd ser., vol. 9. Tokyo: Rinsen shoten.
———, ed. 2006. *Chūsei sentoku chosaku shū* 中世先徳著作集. Shinpukuji zenpon sōkan, 2nd ser., vol. 3. Tokyo: Rinsen shoten.
Komatsu Kazuhiko 小松和彦. 1985. *Kamigami no seishin-shi* 神々の精神史. Tokyo: Hokuto shuppan.
———. 1994. *Hyōrei shinkō ron* 憑霊信仰論. Kōdansha gakujutsu bunko 1115. Tokyo: Dentō to gendaisha.
Komine Michihiko 小峰彌彦 and Takahashi Hisao 高橋尚夫, eds. 2001. *Zukai besson mandara: mikkyō zuzō o yomu* 図解・別尊曼荼羅一密教図像をよむ. Tokyo: Daihōrinkaku.
Kondō Yoshihiro 近藤喜博. 1961. “Heike biwa izen” 平家琵琶以前. *Bungaku* 文学 29, 9: 69–80.
———. 1966. *Nihon no oni: Nihon bunka tankyū no shikaku* 日本の鬼一日本文化探究の視角. Tokyo: Ōfūsha.
———. 1978. *Inari shinkō* 稲荷信仰. Hanawa shinsho 52. Tokyo: Hanawa shobō.
Korezawa Kyōzō 是澤恭三. 1955. *Enoshima Benzaiten no shinkō shi* 江の島弁財天の信仰史. Tokyo: Tokyo shidanka.
Korzybski, Alfred. 2010. *Selections from Science and Sanity*. Fort Worth, TX: New Non-Aristotelian Library.
Koyama Satoko 小山聡子. 1999. “Hokkekyō ni miru gohō dōji: *Dainihonkoku hokkekyō kenki* o chūshin to shite” 法華信仰にみる護法童子一『大日本国法華経験記』を中心として. *Nihon shūkyō bunkashi kenkyū* 日本宗教分化史研究 3, 1: 104–117.

———. 2000. "Chūsei zenki no Shōren-in monzeki ni okeru gohō dōji shinkō no juyō" 中世前期の青蓮院門跡における護法童子信仰の受容. *Nihon shūkyō bunkashi kenkyū* 日本宗教分化史研究 4, 1: 38–62.

———. 2003. *Gohō Dōji shinkō no kenkyū* 護法童子信仰の研究. Kyoto: Jishōsha shuppan.

Kōyasan Reihōkan 高野山霊宝館, ed. 1994. *Tenbu no shoson* 天部の諸尊. Kōyasan: Kōyasan Reihōkan.

———, ed. 2002. *Sacred Treasures of Mount Kōya: The Arts of Japanese Shingon Buddhism.* Kōyasan: Kōyasan Reihōkan.

Kramrisch, Stella. 1980. *Manifestations of Śiva.* Philadelphia: Philadelphia Museum of Art.

———. 1981. *The Presence of Śiva.* Princeton, NJ: Princeton University Press.

Krishan, Yuvraj. 1982. "The Origins of Gaṇeśa." *Artibus Asiae* 43, 4: 285–301.

———. 1991–1992. "Vināyaka as *vighnakarta* (Causer of Obstacles) in the *Ranavagṛhya-sūtra* and *Yajñāvalkyasmṛti*: A Comparative Study." *Annals of the Bandarkar Oriental Research Institute* 72–73: 363–367.

———. 1992. "A New Interpretation of 'Pañca-Gaṇeśa' Sculptures." *Artibus Asiae* 52, 1–2: 47–53

———. 1999. *Gaṇeśa: Unravelling an Enigma.* Delhi: Motilal Banarsidass.

Kubo Noritada 窪徳忠. 1961. *Kōshin shinkō no kenkyū* 庚申信仰の研究. Tokyo: Nihon gakujutsu shinkōkai.

Kubota Osamu 久保田收. 1959. *Chūsei shintō no kenkyū* 中世神道の研究. Kyoto: Shintōshi gakkai.

———. "Tenshō Daijin to Uhō Dōji: Asama-san no shinkō o chūshin to shite" 天照大神と雨宝童子—朝熊山の信仰を中心として. In Hagiwara Tatsuo 萩原龍夫, ed., *Ise Shinkō* 伊勢信仰1, 142–158. Minshū shūkyōshi sōsho 1. Tokyo: Yūzankaku. Reprinted in Kubota 1973: 412–432.

———. 1973. *Shintōshi no kenkyu* 神道史の研究. Ise: Kōgakkan daigaku shuppanbu.

———. 2002. "Itsukushima jinja ni okeru shinbutsu kankei" 嚴島神社における神佛関係. In Nosaka Genryō 野坂元良, ed. *Itsukushima shinkō jiten* 嚴島信仰辞典, 242–255. Tokyo: Ebisu kōshō shuppan.

Kuo Liying. 1994a. *Confession et contrition dans le bouddhisme chinois du Ve au Xe siècle.* Paris: École Française d'Extrême-Orient.

———. 1994b. "Divination, jeux de hasard et purification dans le bouddhisme chinois." In Fumimasa Fukui and Gérard Fussman, eds., *Bouddhismes et cultures locales: Quelques cas de réciproques adaptations*, 145–167. Paris: École Française d'Extrême-Orient.

———. 2003. "Dakini" 荼吉尼. *Hōbōgirin* 8: 1095–1106.

Kuroda Hideo 黒田日出男. 1986. *Kyōkai no chūsei, zōchō no chūsei* 境界の中世・像徴の中世. Tokyo: Tōkyō daigaku shuppankai.

———. 2003. *Ryū no sumu Nihon* 龍の棲む日本. Iwanami shinsho 831. Tokyo: Iwanami shoten.

Kuroda Satoshi 黒田智. 1998. "Shinra Myōjin to Fujiwara no Kamatari" 新羅明神と藤原鎌足. *Bukkyō geijutsu* 佛教芸術 238:15–33.

———. 2001. "Shiryō shōkai: '*Shinra Myōjin ki*'" 資料紹介—『新羅明神記』. *Tōkyō daigaku shiryō hensanjo kiyō* 東京大学資料編纂所紀要11: 75–98.

Kuroda Toshio. 1975. *Nihon chūsei no kokka to shūkyō* 日本中世の国家と宗教. Tokyo: Iwanami shoten.

———. 1980a. *Jisha seiryoku* 寺社勢力. Tokyo: Iwanami shoten.

———. 1980b. "Shintō in the History of Japanese Religion." Trans. James C. Dobbins and Suzanne Gay. *Journal of Japanese Studies* 7, 1: 1–21.

———. 1989. "Historical Consciousness and *Hon-jaku* Philosophy in the Medieval Period on Mount Hiei." Trans. Allan Grapard. In George Tanabe and Willa Tanabe, eds., *The Lotus Sūtra in Japanese Culture,* 143–158. Honolulu: University of Hawai'i Press.

———. 1990. *Nihon chūsei no shakai to shūkyō* 日本中世の社会と宗教. Tokyo: Iwanami shoten.

———. 1996. "The Development of the *Kenmitsu* System as Japan's Medieval Orthodoxy." Trans. James C. Dobbins. *JJRS* 23, 3–4: 233–269.

Kushida Ryōkō 櫛田良洪. 1973 (1964). *Shingon mikkyō seiritsu katei no kenkyū* 真言密教成立過程の研究. Tokyo: Sankibō busshorin.

———. 1979. *Zoku Shingon mikkyō seiritsu katei no kenkyū* 続真言密教成立過程の研究. Tokyo: Sankibō busshorin.

Kushida Ryōkō hakushi shōju kinenkai 櫛田良洪博士頌寿記念会, ed. 1973. *Kōsōden no kenkyū: Kushida hakushi shōju kinen* 高僧伝の研究一櫛田博士頌寿記念. Tokyo: Sankibō Busshorin.

Kyburz, Joseph A. 1987. *Cultes et croyances au Japon. Kaida, une commune dans les montagnes du Japon central*. Paris: Maisonneuve et Larose.

———. 2007. "Histoires d'amulettes: le Taishaku-ten de Shibamata." In Arnaud Brotons and Christian Galans, eds., *Japon pluriel 7: Actes de la Société française des études japonaises,* 335–342. Paris: Éditions Philippe Picquier.

———. 2014. *Ofuda: Amulettes et talismans du Japon. Ofuda—On Japanese Charms*. Paris: Collège de France, Institut des Hautes Études Japonaises.

Kyōto kokuritsu hakubutsukan 京都国立博物館, ed. 1998. *Ōchō no butsuga to girei* 王朝の佛画と儀礼. Kyoto: Kyoto National Museum.

———, ed. 2004. *Kamigami no bi no sekai* 神々の美の世界. Kyoto: Kyoto National Museum.

———, ed. 2005. *Saichō to Tendai no kokuhō* 最澄と天台国宝. Kyoto: Kyoto National Museum.

Kyōto shiritsu geijutsu daigaku geijutsu shiryōkan 京都市立芸術大学芸術資料館, ed. 2004. *Rokkakudō Nōman-in butsuga funpon, Bukkyō zuzō shūsei* 六角堂能満院仏画粉本・佛教図像聚成. 2 vols. Kyoto: Hōzōkan.

Lalou, Marcelle. 1946. "Mythologie indienne et peintures de Haute-Asie: 1. Le dieu bouddhique de la fortune." *Artibus Asiae* 9: 97–110.

Lamotte, Étienne, trans. 1949–1976. *Le Traité de la grande vertu de sagesse de Nāgārjuna.* 4 vols. Louvain: Institut Orientaliste, Université de Louvain.

———. 1960. "Mañjuśrī." *T'oung Pao* 48, 1–3: 1–96.

———. 1966. "Vajrapāṇi en Inde." In Paul Demiéville, *Mélanges de Sinologie offerts à Monsieur Paul Demiéville,* 113–159. Paris: Presses Universitaires de France.

Lancaster, Lewis R. 1991. "Gaṇeśa in China: Methods of Transforming the Demonic." In Robert L. Brown 1991: 277–286.

Latour, Bruno. 1993. *We Have Never Been Modern.* Trans. Catherine Porter. Cambridge, MA: Harvard University Press.

———. 1999. *Pandora's Hope: Essays on the Reality of Science Studies.* Cambridge, MA: Harvard University Press.

———. 2005. *Reassembling the Social: An Introduction to Actor-Network Theory.* Oxford: Oxford University Press.

———. 2010. *On the Modern Cult of the Factish Gods; followed by Iconoclash.* Durham, NC: Duke University Press.

Law, John. 1992. "Notes on the Theory of the Actor-Network: Ordering, Strategy, and Heterogeneity." *Systems Practice* 5, 4: 379–393.

———. 2004. *After Method: Mess in Social Science Research.* London: Routledge.

Le Le Win. 2003. "Chūsei Nihon ni okeru ryū no hyōzō to kokudokan: 'Gyōki zu' o megutte" 中世日本における龍の表象と国土観一「行基図」をめぐって. *Zeami* 世阿弥 2: 174–197.

Lee Pyŏng-ro 李炳魯. 2006. "Ilbon esŏ ūī Sillashin gwa Chang Pogo: Chŏksan Myŏngshin gwa Silla Myŏngshin ŭl chŭngshim ŭro" 일본에서의 신라신과 장보고: 적산명신과 신라명신을 중심으로. *Tongbuk'a munhwa yŏn'gu* 10: 319–341.

Lee Yu-min. 1996. "An Iconographic Study of Mahākāla Imagery in Yunnan: From the Ninth to Thirteen Centuries." In Kokusai kōryū bijutsushi kenkyūkai 国際交流美術史研究会, ed., *Bukkyō bijutsushi kenkyū ni okeru 'zuzō to gishiki'* 佛教美術史研究における「図像と儀式」, 99–113. Kobe: Kōbe daigaku.

Lévi, Jean. 1984. "Le renard, la morte et la courtisane dans la Chine antique." In "Le Renard: Tours, détours et retours." *Études Mongoles… et sibériennes* 15: 111–139.

Lévi, Sylvain, and Édouard Chavannes. 1916. "Les seize *arhat* protecteurs de la loi." *Journal Asiatique* 11, 8: 5–50 and 189–304.

Lévi-Strauss, Claude. 1982 . *The Way of the Masks.* Trans. Sylvia Modelski. Seattle: University of Washington Press.

Li Lin-ts'an (Li Lincan) 李霖燦. 1967. "Zhongguo mozhu huafa de duandai yanjiu" 中國墨竹畫法的斷代研究. *Gugong jikan* 故宮季刊 (*National Palace Museum Quarterly*) 1, 4.

———. 1982. *Nanzhao Dali guo xin ziliao de zonghe yanjiu* 南詔大理國新資料的綜合研究 (A Study of the Nan-chao and Ta-li Kingdoms in the Light of Art Materials Found in Various Museums). Taipei: National Palace Museum.

Lincoln, Bruce. 1991. *Death, War, and Sacrifice: Studies in Ideology and Practice.* Chicago: University of Chicago Press.

Linrothe, Rob. 1990. "Beyond Sectarianism: Towards Reinterpreting the Iconography of Esoteric Buddhist Deities Trampling Hindu Gods." *Indian Journal of Buddhist Studies* 2, 2: 16–25.

———. 1999. *Ruthless Compassion: Wrathful Deities in Early Indo-Tibetan Esoteric Buddhist Art.* Boston: Shambhala.

Linrothe, Rob, and Henrik H. Sørensen, eds. 2001. *Embodying Wisdom: Art, Text and Interpretation in the History of Esoteric Buddhism.* SBS Monographs 6. Copenhagen: Seminar for Buddhist Studies.

Linrothe, Rob, and Jeff Watt, eds. 2004. *Demonic Divine: Himalayan Art and Beyond.* New York: Rubin Museum of Art.

Loewe, Michael. 1978. "Man and Beast: The Hybrid in Early Chinese Art and Literature." *Numen* 25, 2: 97–117.

Lomi, Benedetta. 2011. "The Precious Steed of the Buddhist Pantheon: Ritual, Faith and Images of Batō Kannon in Japan." PhD diss., School of Oriental and African Studies, University of London.

Lorenzen, David N. 2002. "Early Evidence for Tantric Religion." In Katherine Anne Harper & Robert L. Brown, eds. *The Roots of Tantra,* 25–36. Albany, NY: SUNY Press.

Ludvik, Catherine. 1998a. "The Barter for Soma: Vāc, Women's Love of Music, and Sarasvatī's *Vīṇā.*" *Annali dell'istituto orientale di Napoli* 58, 3–4: 347–358.

———. 1998b. "The Origin of the Conception of Sarasvatī as Goddess of Knowledge." *IBK* 47, 1: 507–510.

———. 1999–2000. "La Benzaiten à huit bras—Durgā déesse guerrière sous l'apparence de Sarasvatī." *CEA* 11: 292–338.

———. 2000. "Sarasvatī-Vāc: The Identification of the River with Speech." *Asiatische Studien/Études Asiatiques* 54, 1: 119–130.

———. 2001. "From Sarasvatī to Benzaiten." PhD diss., University of Toronto.

———. 2006. "Recontextualizing the Praises of a Goddess." *Occasional Papers* 10, Kyoto: Italian School of East Asian Studies.

———. 2007. *Sarasvatī, Riverine Goddess of Knowledge: From the Manuscript-carrying* Vīṇā*-player to the Weapon-wielding Defender of the Dharma*. Leiden: Brill.

Lyle, Emily B. 1982. "Dumézil's Three Functions and Indo-European Cosmic Structure." *History of Religions* 22, 1: 25–44.

Macdonald, Ariane, ed. and trans. 1962. *Le Maṇḍala du Mañjuśrīmūlakalpa*. Paris: Adrien Maisonneuve.

Macé, François. 2009. "Dumézil et la mythologie japonaise." In Jean-Noël Robert and Jean Leclant, eds., *150e anniversaire de l'établissement des relations diplomatiques entre le Japon et la France,* 37–47. Paris: AIBL–Diffusion de Boccard.

Mack, Karen. 2006. "The Function and Context of Fudō Imagery from the Ninth to Fourteenth Century in Japan." PhD diss., University of Kansas.

Makabe Toshinobu 真壁俊信. 1981. "Tenjin engi shikō: Kangiten reikenki no saikentō" 天神縁起私考ー歓喜天霊験記の再検討. *Kokugakuin zasshi* 国学院雑誌 82, 5: 39–43.

Malamoud, Charles. 1992. "Histoire des religions et comparatisme: la question indo-européenne." *Revue de l'histoire des religions* 208, 2: 115–121.

———. 1996 (1989). *Cooking the World: Ritual and Thought in Ancient India.* Trans. David G. White. New York: Oxford University Press.

———. 2002. *Le Jumeau solaire.* La Librairie du XXIe siècle. Paris: Seuil.

Manabe Shunshō 真鍋俊照. 1999. *Jakyō Tachikawa-ryū* 邪教立川流. Tokyo: Chikuma shobō.

———. 2000. "Shingon mikkyō to jakyō Tachikawa-ryū" 真言密教と邪教立川流. *Kokubungaku: kaishaku to kyōzai no kenkyū* 国文学ー解釈と教材の研究 45, 12: 110–117.

———. 2000–2001. *Mikkyō zuzō to giki no kenkyū* 密教図像と儀軌の研究. 2 vols. Kyoto: Hōzōkan.

Mani, V. R. 1995. *Saptamātṛkās in Indian Religion and Art*. New Delhi: Mittal Publications.

Martin-Dubost, Paul. 1997. *Gaṇeśa: L'enchanteur des trois mondes*. Mumbai: Project for Indian Cultural Studies.

Masuo Shin'ichirō 増尾伸一郎. 2001. "*Chijinkyō* hensō: chijin mōsō to Chōsen no biwa koji・kyōfu to no aida"『地神経』変奏ー地神盲僧と朝鮮の琵琶居士・經巫とあいだ. *Kokubungaku: kaishaku to kyōzai no kenkyū* 国文学ー解釈と教材の研究 8: 65–72.

Matisoff, Susan. 1973. *The Legend of Semimaru, Blind Musician of Japan.* New York: Columbia University Press.

Matsumoto Eiichi 松本榮一. 1956. "Tonkōbon Hakutaku seikai zukan" 敦煌本白沢精怪図巻. *Kokka* 国華770: 135–147.

Matsumoto Ikuyo 松本郁代. 2005. *Chūsei ōken to sokui kanjō*中世王権と即位灌頂. Tokyo: Shinwasha.

Matsumoto Kōichi 松本公一. 1991. "Go-Sanjō Tennō to jingi shinkō: tokuni Hiezan to Hie-sha o chūshin to shite" 後三条天皇と神祇思想ーとくに比叡山と日吉社を中心として. *Jinbun kagaku* 人文科学 11: 109–133.

Matsumoto Moritaka. 1976. "Chang Sheng-wen's Long Roll of Buddhist Images: A Reconstruction and Iconology." PhD diss., Princeton University.

Matsumoto Nobuhiro. 1928. *Essai sur le mythe japonais*. Paris: Paul Geuthner.

Matsunaga, Alicia. 1969. *The Buddhist Philosophy of Assimilation: The Historical Development of the* Honji-Suijaku *Theory*. Tokyo: Sophia University.

Matsuoka Hisato 松岡久人 and Gotō Yōichi 後藤陽一. 2002. "Itsukushima shinkō no rekishi" 嚴島信仰の歴史. In Nosaka Genryō 野坂元良, ed., *Itsukushima shinkō jiten* 嚴島信仰辞典, 54–77. Tokyo: Ebisu kōshō shuppan.

Matsuoka Shinpei 松岡心平. 1999. "Shinbutsu shūgō to Okina" 神佛習合と翁. *Kokubungaku: kaishaku to kyōzai no kenkyū* 国文学―解釈と教材の研究 44, 8: 38–44.

———, ed. 2000a. *Oni to geinō: Higashi Ajia no engeki keisei* 鬼と芸能―東アジアの演劇形成. Tokyo: Shinwasha.

———. 2000b. "Binayaka kō: Okina no hassei josetsu" 毘那夜迦考―翁の発生序説. In Matsuoka 2000a: 221–252. Tokyo: Shinwasha.

Mayer-König, Birgit. 1997. "Das Böse als das Göttliche: Betrachtungen am Beispiel Bhairavas und der ḍākinīs." *Hōrin* 4: 109–125.

McCullough, Helen Craig, trans. 1979 (1959). *The Taiheiki: A Chronicle of Medieval Japan.* Rutland, VT: Charles E. Tuttle Company.

———. 1988. *The Tale of the Heike.* Stanford, CA: Stanford University Press.

Michael, S. M. "The Origin of the Ganapati Cult." *Asian Folklore Studies* 42: 91–116.

Minakata Kumagusu 南方熊楠. 1971. "Sekizan Zen-in no koto" 赤山禅院のこと. In *Minakata Kumagusu zenshū* 南方熊楠全集 3: 195–196. Tokyo: Heibonsha.

Minobe Shigekatsu. 1982. "The World View of *Genpei Jōsuiki*." *JJRS* 9, 2–3: 213–233.

Misaki Ryōshū 三崎良周. 1986. "Yakushi shinkō to Gozu Tennō" 薬師信仰と午頭天王. *Tendai gakuhō* 天台学報 29: 17–28.

———. 1992. *Mikkyō to jingi shisō* 密教と神祇思想. Tokyo: Sōbunsha.

———. 1994. *Taimitsu no ronri to jissen* 台密の論理と実践. Tokyo: Sōbunsha.

Misra, Om Prakash. 1989. *Iconography of the Saptamātrikās*. Delhi: Agam Kala Prakashan.

Mitter, Partha. 1992 (1977). *Much Maligned Monsters: A History of European Reactions to Indian Art*. Chicago: University of Chicago Press.

Miya Tsugio 宮次男. 1976. "Kangiten reikenki shikō" 歓喜天霊験記私考. *Bijutsu kenkyū* 美術研究 305: 1–19.

Miyai Yoshio 宮井義雄. 2004 (1964). "Susanoo no mikoto to Shinra Myōjin" 素菱鳴尊と新羅明神. In Mishina Shōei 三品彰英, ed., *Nihonshoki kenkyū* 日本書紀研究. Tokyo: Hanawa shobō, 1964. Reprinted in Ōbayashi Taryō 大林太良, ed., *Susanoo shinkō jiten* スサノオ信仰事典, 331–340. Shinbutsu shinkō jiten shirīzu 7. Tokyo: Ebisu kōshō shuppan.

Miyaji Naokazu 宮地直一. 1931. "Heian-chō ni okeru Shinra Myōjin" 平安朝における新羅明神. In Tendaishū Jimon-ha goonki jimukyoku天台宗寺門派御遠忌事務局, ed., *Onjōji no kenkyū* 園城寺之研究, 321–382. Kyoto: Hoshino shoten.

Miyake Hitoshi 宮家準. 1971. *Shugendō girei no kenkyū* 修験道儀礼の研究. Tokyo: Shunjūsha.

———, ed. 1984. *Yama no matsuri to geinō* 山の祭りと芸能. 2 vols. Tokyo: Hirakawa shuppansha.

———. 1985. *Shugendō shisō no kenkyū* 修験道思想の研究. Tokyo: Shunjūsha.

———. 1993. "Shugendō to Fudō Myōō" 修験道と不動明王. In Tanaka Hisao 1993: 47–58.

———. 1995. "Shinbutsu shūgō-ron: Shugendō o chūshin ni" 神佛習合論一修験道を中心に. In Takasaki Jikidō 高崎直道 and Kimura Kiyotaka 木村清孝 eds., *Nihon bukkyō-ron: Higashi Ajia no bukkyō shisō* 日本佛教論一東アジアの佛教思想, 3: 165–203. Higashi Ajia bukkyō 東アジア佛教 4. Tokyo: Shunjūsha.

———. 2002a. "Gozu Tennō shinkō to shugendō" 牛頭天王信仰と修験道. *Kokugakuin zasshi* 国学院雑誌 103, 11: 233–248.

———. 2002b. "Shinra Myōjin shinkō to En no gyōja zō" 新羅明神信仰と役行者像. *Shintō shūkyō* 神道宗教 188: 1–33.

———. 2005a. *The Mandala of the Mountain: Shugendō and Folk Religion*. Trans. Gaynor Sekimori. Tokyo: Keiō University Press.

———. 2005b. "Inari shinkō no tenkai to shugen: Gofu o chūshin ni" 稲荷信仰の展開と修験一護符を中心に. Reprinted in Miyake 2007: 336–368.

———. 2007. *Shintō to shugendō: Minzoku shūkyō shisō no tenkai* 神道と修験道: 民俗宗教思想の展開. Tokyo: Shunjūsha.

Miyamoto Kesao 宮本袈裟雄, ed. 1987. *Fukujin shinkō* 福神信仰. Minshū shūkyō sōsho 20. Tokyo: Yūzankaku.

———. 1989. *Tengu to shugendō: sangaku shinkō to sono shūhen* 天狗と修験道一山岳信仰とその周辺. Kyoto: Jinbun shoin.

Miyasaka Mitsuaki 宮坂光昭. 1975. "Jatai to sekibō no shinkō: Suwa misagujin to genshi shinkō" 蛇体と石棒の信仰一諏訪御佐口神と原始信仰. In Kobuzoku kenkyūkai 古部族研究会, ed., *Kodai Suwa to mishaguji sai seitai no kenkyū* 古代諏訪とミシャグジ祭政体の研究, 74–88. Tokyo: Nagai shuppan.

Miyasaka Yūshō 宮坂宥勝, ed. 1977. *Kōgyō Daishi senjutsushū* 興教大師撰述集. Tokyo: Sankibō busshorin, 1977.

———. 1990. "*Saptamātṛkā* to mikkyō: *mātṛkā* kō" (*Saptamātṛkā* と密教一*mātṛkā* 考). *Chisan gakuhō* 智山学報 39: 1–27.

Miyata Noboru 宮田登. 1979. *Kami no minzokushi* 神の民俗誌. Iwanami shinsho 97. Tokyo: Iwanami shoten.

———. 1987a. "Fukujin shinkō no keifu" 福神信仰の系譜. In Miyamoto Kesao 宮本袈裟雄, ed., *Fukujin shinkō* 福神信仰, 33–45. Tokyo: Yūzankaku.

———. 1987b. "Benten shinkō" 弁天信仰. In Miyamoto 1987: 261–267.

———. 1993. *Edo no hayarigami* 江戸のはやり神. Chikuma gakugei bunko 980. Tokyo: Chikuma shobō.

Miyoshi Kazunari 三好一成. 1975. "Iida-goze nakama no seikatsu shi" 飯田瞽盲仲間の生活誌. In *Kikan Yanagita Kunio kenkyū: minzoku no shisō o saguru* 季刊柳田國男研究 一民俗の思想を探る 8, 226–251.

Mizuhara Gyōhei 水原尭栄. 1931. *Jakyō Tachikawa-ryū no kenkyū* 邪教立川流の研究. Kyoto: Shibundō.

Moerman, D. Max. 2009. "Demonology and Eroticism: Islands of Women in the Japanese Buddhist Imagination." *JJRS* 36, 2: 351–380.

Moriyama Seishin 守山聖真. 1965. *Tachikawa jakyō to sono shakaiteki haikei no kenkyū* 立川邪教とその社会的背景の研究. Tokyo: Kokusho kankōkai.

Morrell, Robert E. 1973. "Mujū Ichien's Shinto-Buddhist Syncretism: *Shasekishū*, Book 1." *MN* 28, 4: 447–488.

———. 1982. "Passage to India Denied: Zeami's *Kasuga Ryūjin*." *MN* 37, 2: 179–200.

———, trans. 1985. *Sand and Pebbles (Shasekishū): The Tales of Mujū Ichien, a Voice for Pluralism in Kamakura Japan*. Albany, NY: SUNY Press.

Morse, Anne Nishimura, and Nobuo Tsuji, eds. 1998. *Japanese Art in the Museum of Fine Arts, Boston.* 2 vols. Boston: Museum of Fine Arts.

Mukōzaka Takuya 向坂卓也. 2007. "Shōmyōji shōkgō ni miru Ugajin kankei shiryō ni tsuite" 称名寺聖教に見る宇賀神関係資料について. *Kanazawa bunko kenkyū* 金沢文庫研究 318: 22–35.

Müller, Friedrich Max. 1883. *India: What Can It Teach Us?* London: Longmans, Green, and Co.

———. 1897. *Contributions to the Science of Mythology.* 2 vols. London: Longmans, Green, and Co.

Murase, Miyeko. 2000. *Bridge of Dreams: The Mary Griggs Burke Collection of Japanese Art.* New York: Metropolitan Museum of Art.

Murata Hiroshi 村田熙. 1994. *Mōsō to minkan shinkō* 盲僧と民間信仰. Murata Hiroshi senshū 1. Tokyo: Daiichi shobō.

Murata Seikō 村田靖子. 2003. "Sōshin Bishamonten shōzō no shōsō" 双身毘沙門天小像の諸相. *Mikkyō zuzō* 密教図像 22: 1–16.

Murayama Shūichi 村山修一. 1942. "Muromachi jidai no bukkyō kyōka to rekishi ishiki" 室町時代の佛教教化と歴史意識. *Shina bukkyō shigaku* 支那佛教史学 6, 2: 60–82.

———. 1957. *Shinbutsu shūgō shichō* 神佛習合思潮. Sāra sōsho 6. Kyoto: Heirakuji shoten.

———. 1976. *Kodai bukkyō no chūsei-teki tenkai* 古代佛教の中世的展開. Kyoto: Hōzōkan.

———. 1979. "Nihon ni okeru kami to hotoke no kōshō" 日本における神と佛の交渉. *Bukkyō shishōshi* 佛教思想史 1: 225–253.

———. 1983. *Tenjin shinkō* 天神信仰. Tokyo: Yūzankaku.

———. 1984. "Gion-sha no goryōshin-teki hatten" 祇園社の御霊神的発展. In Shibata Minoru, ed., *Goryō shinkō* 御霊信仰, 207–215. Minshū shūkyō sōsho 5. Tokyo: Yūzankaku.

———. 1987a. *Nihon onmyōdō shiwa* 日本陰陽道史話. Asahi Culture Books 71. Osaka: Ōsaka shoseki.

———. 1987b. *Shugō shisō-shi ronkō* 習合思想史論考. Tokyo: Hanawa shobō.

———. 1990. *Henbō-suru kami to hotoke-tachi: Nihonjin no shūgō shisō* 変貌する神と佛たち一日本人の習合思想. Kyoto: Jinbun shoin.

———. 1994. *Hieizan shi: tatakai to inori no seiiki* 比叡山史一闘いと祈りの聖域. Tokyo: Tōkyō bijutsu.

———. 1996. *Tenjin goryō shinkō* 天神御霊信仰. Tokyo: Hanawa shobō.

———. 1997. *Shugen, Onmyōdō to shaji shiryō* 修験·陰陽道と社寺資料. Kyoto: Hōzōkan.

———. 2000 (1981). *Nihon onmyōdō-shi sōsetsu* 日本陰陽道史総説. Tokyo: Hanawa shobō.

Murayama Shūichi 村山修一 et al., eds. 1993. *Onmyōdō sōsho* 陰陽道叢書. 4 vols. Tokyo: Meicho shuppan.

Mure Hitoshi 牟禮仁. 2000. *Chūsei shintōsetsu keisei ronkō* 中世神道説形成論考. Tokyo: Kōgakkan daigaku shuppanbu.

Nagano Sadako 長野禎子. 1988. "*Konkōmyōkyō* ni okeru 'Benzaiten' no seikaku" 『金光明經』における「弁才天」の性格 . *IBK* 72: 235–239.

Naganuma Kenkai 長沼賢海. 1931. *Nihon shūkyōshi no kenkyū*日本宗教史の研究. Tokyo: kyōiku kenkyū kai.

———. 1987. "Daikokuten kō" 大黒天考. In Miyamoto 1987: 209–230.

Nagao Kayoko 長尾佳代子. "Yasha" 夜叉. *Bukkyō bungaku* 佛教文学 22: 1–13.

Nagar, Shantilal. 1989. *Composite Deities in Indian Art and Literature*. New Delhi: Criterion Publications.

———. 1997. *The Cult of Vināyaka*. New Delhi: Intellectual Publishing House.

Nagasaka Ichirō 長坂一郎. 2004. *Shinbutsu shūgō zō no kenkyū* 神佛習合像の研究. Tokyo: Chūōkōron bijutsu.

Nagashima Fukutarō 永島福太郎. 1986. "Kasuga Wakamiya ni tsuite" 春日若宮について. *Shintō koten kenkyū* 神道古典研究 8: 13–31.

———. 1995. "Tenkawa no rekishi" 天河の歴史. In Hayashiya et al. 1995: 90–110.

Nakagawa Zenkyō 中川善教. 1964. *Daikoku tenjin kō* 大黒天神考. Kōyasan: Shinnōin.

Nakajima Ayaka 中島彩花. 2009. "Chūsei Benzaiten mandara ni miru shinbutsu no kagen" 中世弁才天曼荼羅にみる神佛の化現. *Joshi bijutsu daigaku kiyō* 女子美術大学紀要 39: 128–138.

Nakamaki Hirochika. 1983. "The 'Separate' Existence of Kami and Hotoke: A Look at Yorishiro." *JJRS* 10, 1: 65–86.

Nakamura Ikuo 中村生雄. 1994. *Nihon no kami to ōken* 日本の神と王権. Kyoto: Hōzōkan.

———. 1995. "Tenkawa no Nō" 天河の能. In Hayashiya et al. 1995: 130–150.

Nakamura, Kyoko Motomochi, trans. 1973. *Miraculous Stories from the Japanese Buddhist Tradition: The Nihon Ryōiki of the Monk Kyōkai.* Cambridge, MA: Harvard University Press.

Nakamura Teiri 中村禎里. 1999. *Ena no inochi* 胞衣の生命. Tokyo: Kaimeisha.

———. 2001. *Kitsune no Nihon shi: Kodai, chūsei-hen* 狐の日本史ー古代·中世篇. Tokyo: Nihon editā sukūru shuppanbu.

Nakano Teruo 中野照男, ed. 1992. "Enma, Jūō zō" 閻魔·十王像. *Nihon no bijutsu* 日本の美術 313. Tokyo: Shibundō.

———. 1998. "Jūni shinshō zō" 十二神将像. *Nihon no bijutsu* 381. Tokyo: Shibundō.

Nakazawa Shin'ichi 中沢新一. 1994. *Akutō-teki shikō* 悪党的思考. Heibonsha raiburarii. Tokyo: Heibonsha.

Nanami Hiroaki 名波弘彰. 1984a. "*Heike monogatari* ni arawareru Hie jinja kankei setsuwa no kōsatsu: Chūsei Hie jinja ni okeru miyagomori to jugesō" 『平家物語』に現れる日吉神社関係説話の考察ー中世日吉神社における宮籠りと樹下僧. *Bungei gengo kenkyū: bungei-hen*文芸言語研究ー文芸編 9: 63–113.

———. 1986. "Nanto-bon 'Heike monogatari' Tsunemasa Chikubushima mōde to Hie-sha Seijogū no biwa hōshi: Eizan shinkō-ken ni okeru Uga Benzaiten shinkō o megutte" 南都本『平家物語』經正竹生島詣と日吉社聖女宮の琵琶法師ー叡山信仰圏における宇賀弁才天信仰をめぐって. *Bungei gengo kenkyū: bungei-hen* 文芸言語研究ー文芸篇11: 59–99.

Nanri Michiko 南里みち子. 1980. "'Hoki naiden' nōto: Gozu Tennō engi setsuwa to no kanren kara" 『ホキ内伝』ノートー牛頭天王縁起説話との関連から. *Fukuoka joshi daigaku tandai kiyō* 福岡女子大学短大紀要 19: 119–128.

———. 1996. *Onryō to shugen no setsuwa* 怨霊と修験の説話. Tokyo: Perikansha.

Naoe Hiroji 直江廣治, ed. 1983. *Inari shinkō* 稲荷信仰. Minshū shūkyōshi sōsho 3. Tokyo: Yūzankaku.

Nara kokuritsu bunkazai kenkyūjo 奈良国立文化財研究所, ed. 1958. *Ninnaji shōgyō komonjo mokuroku* 仁和寺聖教古文書目録. Nara: Nara kokuritsu bunkazai kenkyūjo.

Nara kokuritsu hakubutsukan 奈良国立博物館, ed. 1964. *Suijaku bijutsu* 垂迹美術. Tokyo: Kadokawa shoten.

———, ed. 1975. *Shaji engi-e* 社寺縁起絵. Tokyo: Kadokawa shoten.

———, ed. 1990. *Nara kokuritsu hakubutsukan no meihō* 奈良国立博物館の名宝. Nara: Nara National Museum.

———, ed. 2000. *Myōō: ikari to itsukushimi no hotoke* 明王一怒りと慈しみの佛. Nara: Nara National Museum.

———, ed. 2001. *Busshari to hōju: Shaka o shitau kokoro* 佛舎利と宝珠一釈迦を慕う心. Nara: Nara National Museum.

———, ed. 2002. *Kannon no mitera: Ishiyamadera* 観音のみてら石山寺. Nara: Nara National Museum.

———, ed. 2007. *Shinbutsu shūgō: kami to hotoke ka orinasu shinkō to bi* 神仏習合一神と佛か織りなす信仰と美. Nara: Nara National Museum.

Narain, A.K. 1991. "Gaṇeśa: A Protohistory of the Idea and the Icon." In Robert L. Brown 1991: 19–48. Albany: SUNY Press.

Narazaki Muneshige 楢崎宗重. 1952. "Enoshima Benzaiten zō oyobi Enoshima engi emaki ni tsuite" 江の島弁才天像及江島縁起絵巻について. *Kokka* 国華 724: 217–227.

Nasu Eisho. 2004. "Introduction of the Chinese God of the Dead into Medieval Japanese Religious Culture: A Study of Taizanfukun-sai (Rites Honoring T'ai-shan Fu-chün)." In *Bukkyō to ningen shakai no kenkyū* (Asaeda Zensho hakushi kanreki kinen ronbunshū), 277–299.

Nedachi Kensuke 根立研介, ed. 1992. "Kichijō, Benzaiten zō" 吉祥·弁才天像. *Nihon no bijutsu* 日本の美術 317. Tokyo: Shibundō.

———, ed. 1997. "Aizen myōō zō" 愛染明王像. *Nihon no bijutsu* 日本の美術 376. Tokyo: Shibundō.

Needham, Joseph. 1970. *Science and Civilization in China*. Vol. 4, Pt. 1., *Physics and Physical Technology*. Cambridge: Cambridge University Press.

Ng, Zhiru. 2007. *The Making of a Savior Bodhisattva: Dizang in Medieval China*. Studies in East Asian Buddhism 21. Honolulu: University of Hawai'i Press.

Nishida Naojirō 西田直次郎. 1976. "Fukujin to shite no Taizan Fukon" 福神としての泰山府君. In Kida 1976: 423–431.

Nishimura Chie 西村智恵. 1987. "Bishamonten to fuku" 毘沙門天と福. In Miyamoto Kesao 宮本袈裟雄, ed., *Fukujin shinkō* 福神信仰, 241–260. Tokyo: Yūzankaku.

Nishi Nihon bunka kyōkai 西日本文化協会, ed. 1993. *Fukuoka-kenshi* 福岡県史. Fukuoka: Fukuoka-ken

Nishioka Hideo 西岡秀雄. 1961. *Nihon seishin-shi* 日本性神史. Tokyo: Takahashi shoten.

Nishioka Yoshifumi 西岡芳文. 1989a. "Kanazawa bunko hokan shikisen kankei shiryō ni tsuite" 金沢文庫保管式占関係資料について. *Kanazawa bunko kenkyū* 金沢文庫研究 282: 39–48.

———. 1989b. "Shaku" 赤口. In Amino Yoshihiko 網野善彦, ed., *Kotoba no Bunkashi: Chūsei* ことばの文化史一中世, vol. 3. Tokyo: Heibonsha.

———. 2002. "Rikujin shikisen to konrō no miura" 六壬式占と軒廊御卜. In Imatani Akira 今谷明, ed., *Ōken to jingi* 王権と神祇. Kyoto: Shibunkaku Shuppan.

———. 2007. "Shikiban o matsuru shuhō: Shōten shikihō, tonjō shitsuji-hō, dakini-hō" 式盤をまつる修法: 聖天式法・頓成悉地法・ダキニ法. *Kanazawa bunko kenkyū* 318: 11–21.

———.2008. "Kanazawa Shōmyōji ni okeru tonjō shitsuji-hō: kikakuten 'Onmyōdō kakeru mikkyō' hoi" 金沢称名寺における頓成悉地法一企画展「陰陽道X密教」補遺. *Kanazawa bunko kenkyū* 金沢文庫研究 320: 35–47.

———. 2012. "Aspects of *Shikiban*-Based Mikkyō Rituals." *CEA* 21: 137–162.

Nobel, Johannes, trans. 1958. *Suvarṇaprabhāsottama-sūtra: das Goldglanz-Sūtra, ein Sanskrittext des Mahāyāna-Buddhismus*. Vol. 1. Leiden: E.J. Brill.

Nomoto Kakujō 野本覚成. 2008. "Hie Sannō-shin no rekishi kubun (zenpen)" 日吉山王神の歴史区分（全編）. *Tendai gakuhō* 天台学報 50: 29–37.

Nōtogawa seinen kaigisho 能登川青年会議所, ed. 1989. *Ōmi no kakurebotoke: Echi sanjūsanbutsu junrei* 近江の隠れれ佛ーえち三十三佛巡礼. Kyoto: Hōzōkan.

Notomi Jōten 納富常天. 1972. "Enoshima ni kansuru ni, san no shiryō" 江の島に関する二,三の資料. *Kanazawa bunko kenkyū* 金沢文庫研究 18, 4: 9–17.

———. 1985. "Kamakura jidai no shari shinkō" 鎌倉時代の舎利信仰. *IBK* 33, 2: 32–36.

Nozaka Motoyoshi 野坂元良, ed. 2002. *Itsukushima shinkō jiten* 嚴島信仰事典. Tokyo: Ebisu kōshō shuppan.

Odaira Mika 小平美香. 2014. "Chūsei no Ama no Iwato to dōji shinkō: Jingū Chōkokan-bon 'Ise sankei mandara'" 中世の天岩戸と童子信仰ー神功徴古館本「伊勢参詣曼荼羅」. In Sano Midori 佐野みどり et al., eds., *Chūsei kaiga no matorikkusu II* 中世絵画のマトリックス 2: 276–294. Tokyo: Seikansha.

Ogawa Kan'ichi小川, 貫弌. 1973. *Bukkyō bunkashi kenkyū* 佛教文化史研究. Kyoto: Nagata bunshodō.

Okami Masao 岡見正雄 and Akamatsu Toshihide 赤松俊秀, eds. 1967. *Gukanshō* 愚管抄. *NKBT* 86. Tokyo: Iwanami Shoten.

Olivier, Laurent. 2008. *Le sombre abîme du temps: Mémoire et archéologie*. Paris: Éditions du Seuil.

Ōmori Keiko 大森惠子. 1994. *Inari shinkō to shūkyō minzoku* 稲荷信仰と宗教民俗. Nihon shūkyō minzokugaku sōsho 1. Tokyo: Iwata shoin.

———. 2000. "Aihōjin, seiaijin to Inari shinkō: tokuni megitsune to josei, miko o chūshin ni shite" 愛法神・性愛神と稲荷信仰: 特に、女狐と女性・神子を中心にして. *Sangaku shugen* 山岳修験 25: 1–17.

———. 2010. "Miidera no Benzaiten shinkō no kakudai to mōjin geinōsha no kakawari: toku ni, bessho no Kinshōji to Seki Kiyomizu Semimaru Daimyōjin o chūshin ni" 三井寺の弁財天信仰の拡大と盲人芸能者の関わりー特に、別所の近松寺と関清水蝉丸大明神を中心にー. *Sangaku shugen* 山岳修験 45: 62–82.

Omote Akira 表章 and Katō Shūichi 加藤周一, eds. 1974. *Zeami Zenchiku* 世阿弥禅竹. *NST* 24. Tokyo: Iwanami shoten.

Onodera Masato 小野寺正人. 1977. "Kinkazan shinkō no tenkai" 金華山信仰の展開. In Gakkō Yoshihiro, ed., *Tōhoku reizan to shugendō* 東北霊山と修験道. Sangaku shūkyōshi kenkyū sōsho 7. Tokyo: Meicho shuppan.

Ooms, Herman. 1985. *Tokugawa Ideology: Early Constructs, 1570–1680*. Princeton, NJ: Princeton University Press.

Orikuchi Shinobu 折口信夫. 2012. *Nihon geinōshi josetsu* 日本芸能史序説. In *Orikuchi Shinobu geinō ronshū* 折口信夫芸能論集, vol. 3. Kōdansha bungei bunko. Tokyo: Kōdansha.

Ortega y Gasset, José. 1961 (1941). *History as a System and Other Essays: Toward a Philosophy of History*. New York: W.W. Norton.

Orzech, Charles D. 1995. "The Legend of the Iron Stūpa." In Donald S. Lopez, Jr., ed., *Buddhism in Practice*. Princeton, NJ: Princeton University Press.

Ōsaka shiritsu bijutsukan 大坂市立美術館, ed. 1999. *En no gyōja to shugendō no sekai* 役行者と修験道の世界. Osaka: Ōsaka shiritsu bijutsukan.

———, ed. 2004. *Inori no michi: Yoshino, Kumano, Kōya no meihō* 祈りの道ー吉野・熊野・高野の名宝. Osaka: Mainichi shinbunsha.

Ōshima Tatehiko 大島建彦, ed. 1990. *Daikoku shinkō* 大黒信仰. Tokyo: Yūzankaku shuppan.

———. 1992. "Benten shinkō to minzoku" 弁天信仰と民俗. *Nihon no bijutsu* 日本の美術 317: 85–93.

———. 1998. "Shichi fukujin no denshō" 七福神の伝承. In Miyata Noboru 宮田登, ed., *Shichi fukujin shinkō jiten* 福神信仰辞典, 308–316. Tokyo: Ebisu kōshō shuppan.

Ōsumi Kazuo 大隅和雄, ed. 1977. *Chūsei shintō ron* 中世神道論. *NSTK* 19. Tokyo: Iwanami shoten.

Ōtsu-shi rekishi hakubutsukan 大津市歴史博物館, ed. *Kaihōgyō to seichi Katsuragawa* 回峰行と聖地葛川. Ōtsu: Ōtsu-shi rekishi hakubutsukan.

———. 2006. *Tendai o mamoru kamigami: Sannō mandara no shosō* 天台を守る神々一山王曼荼羅の諸相. Ōtsu: Ōtsu-shi rekishi hakubutsukan.

Ouwehand, Cornelius. 1958. "Some Notes on the God Susa-no-o." *MN* 14: 138–161. Reed. in P. E. de Josselin De Jong, ed., *Structural Anthropology in the Netherlands*, 338–358. The Hague: Martinus Nijoff, 1977.

———. 1964. *Namazu-e and Their Themes: An Interpretive Approach to Some Aspects of Japanese Folk Religion.* Leiden: E. J. Brill.

Ōwa Iwao 大和岩雄. 1993. *Hata-shi no kenkyū: Nihon no bunka to shinkō ni fukaku kan'yoshita torai shūdan no kenkyū* 秦氏の研究—日本の文化と信仰に深く関与した渡来集団の研究. Tokyo: Yamato shobō.

Ōyama Kōjun 大山公淳. 1956. *Himitsu bukkyō Kōyasan Chūin-ryū no kenkyū* 秘密佛敎高野山中院流の研究. Kōyasan: Ōyama kyōju kinen shuppankai.

———. 1975. *Shinbutsu kōshō-shi* 神佛交渉史. Kyoto: Rinsen shoten.

Ozeki Akira 尾関章. 2009. *Ryōmen no kishin: Hida no Sukuna denjō no nazo* 両面の鬼神一飛騨の宿儺伝承の謎. Tokyo: Mensei shuppan.

Padoux, André. 2011. *Tantric Mantras: Studies on Mantraśastra.* London: Routledge.

Pal, Pratapaditya. 1992. *Arts of the Himalaya: Treasures from Nepal and Tibet.* New York: Hudson Hills.

Panofsky, Erwin. 1939. *Studies in Iconology.* Oxford: Oxford University Press.

———. 1967. *Essais d'iconologie: Les thèmes humanistes dans l'art de la Renaissance.* Paris: Gallimard.

Payne, Richard K., ed. 1998. *Re-Visioning "Kamakura" Buddhism.* Studies in East Asian Buddhism 11. Honolulu: University of Hawai'i Press.

Pedersen, Hillary Eve. 2010. "The Five Great Space Repository Bodhisattvas: Lineage, Protection and Celestial Authority in Ninth-Century Japan." PhD diss., University of Kansas.

Péri, Noël. 1916. "Le dieu Wei-t'ouo." *BEFEO* 16, 3: 41–56.

———. 1917. "Hārītī la Mère-de-démons." *BEFEO* 17, 3: 1–102.

Philippi, Donald L., trans. 1968. *Kojiki.* Tokyo: University of Tokyo Press.

Pollan, Michael. 2002. *The Botany of Desire: A Plant's Eye View of the World.* New York: Random House.

Rambelli, Fabio. 1996. "Religion, Ideology of Domination, and Nationalism: Kuroda Toshio on the Discourse of *Shinkoku.*" *JJRS* 23, 3–4: 387–426.

———. 2000. "Tantric Buddhism and Chinese Thought in East Asia." In David G. White 2000a: 361–380.

———. 2002. "The Ritual World of Buddhist 'Shintō': The *Reikiki* and Initiations on Kami-Related Matters *(Jingi kanjō)* in Late Medieval and Early-Modern Japan. *JJRS* 29, 3–4: 265–297.

———. 2002–2003. "The Emperor's New Robes: Processes of Resignification in Shingon Imperial Rituals." *CEA* 13: 427–453.

———. 2004. "Shintō (*Honji Suijaku*) and Buddhism," in Robert E. Buswell, Jr., *Encyclopedia* of *Buddhism,* 767–771. New York: Macmillan, 2004.

———. 2007b. "Interactions between Buddhism and Local Cults: Considerations from the Perspective of Cultural Semiotics." *Sapporo daigaku sōgō ronsō* 札幌大学総合論叢 23: 35–55.

———. 2009. "Before the First Buddha: Medieval Japanese Cosmogony and the Quest for the Primeval Kami." *MN* 64, 2: 235–271.

Rath, Eric C. 2002. "Chanters at the Gate: Ritual/Performing Arts of the Fifteenth-Century Japanese Outcasts." In Joëlle Rollo-Koster, ed., *Medieval and Early Modern Ritual: Formalized Behavior in Europe, China, and Japan.* Leiden: Brill.

Rawlinson, Andrew. 1986. "Nāgas and the Magical Cosmology of Buddhism." *History of Religions* 16, 2: 135–153.

Reischauer, Edwin O. 1940. "The Thunder-Weapon in Ancient Japan." *Harvard Journal of Asiatic Studies* 5, 2: 137–141.

———. 1955a. *Ennin's Diary: The Record of a Pilgrimage to China in Search of the Law.* New York: Reginald Press.

———. 1955b. *Ennin's Travels in T'ang China.* New York: Reginald Press.

Renou, Louis. 1937. "Note sur les origines védiques de Gaṇeśa." *Journal Asiatique* 229: 271–274.

Renou, Louis, and Jean Filliozat, eds. 1985 (1947). *L'Inde classique: Manuel des études indiennes.* 2 vols. Paris: Librairie d'Amérique et d'Orient.

Richie, Donald, and Kenkichi Itō. 1967. *The Erotic Gods: Phallicism in Japan.* Tokyo: Zufushinsha.

Rhodes, Robert F. 1987. "The *Kaihōgyō* Practice of Mt. Hiei." *JJRS* 14, 2–3: 185–202.

Robertson, Jennifer Ellen. 2005. *A Companion to the Anthropology of Japan.* Oxford: Blackwell.

Rosenfield, John M., and Elizabeth ten Groetenhuis. 1980. *Journey of the Three Jewels: Japanese Buddhist Paintings from Western Collections.* New York: Asia Society.

Ruegg, David Seyfort. 1964. "Sur les rapports entre le bouddhisme et le 'substrat religieux' indien et tibétain." *Journal Asiatique* 252, 1: 77–95.

Ruppert, Brian. 2000. *Jewel in the Ashes: Buddha Relics and Power in Early Medieval Japan.* Cambridge, MA: Harvard University Press.

Ryūkoku daigaku 龍谷大学, ed. 1938–1940. *Bukkyō daijii* 佛教大辞彙. Tokyo: Fuzanbō.

Sacks, Oliver. 1996. *An Anthropologist on Mars.* New York: Vintage.

Saga Jun'ichi 佐賀純一. 1992. *Kangiten no nazo: himerareta aiyoku no keifu* 歓喜天の謎—秘められた愛欲の系譜. Tokyo: Tosho shuppansha.

Saitō Hideki 斎藤英喜. 2007. *Onmyōdō no kamigami* 陰陽道の神々. Kyoto: Bukkyō Daigaku tsūshin kyōikubu, shinbunkaku shuppan.

Sakaki Taijun 榊泰純. 1974. "Matarajin to kayō: Shushō-e no ennen" 摩多羅神と歌謡—修正会の延年. *Bukkyō to minzoku* 佛教と民俗 11: 40–50.

Sakurai Yoshirō 桜井好朗, ed. 1985. *Kami to hotoke: bukkyō juyō to shinbutsu shūgō no sekai* 神と佛—佛教受容と神佛習合の世界. Tokyo: Shunjūsha.

———. 1993. *Saigi to chūshaku: Chūsei ni okeru kodai shinwa* 祭儀と注釈—中世における古代神話. Yoshikawa kōbunkan.

———. 1996. *Girei kokka no kaitai: Chūsei bunkashi ronshū* 儀礼国家の解体—中世文化史論集. Tokyo: Yoshikawa kōbunkan.

———. 2000 (1976). *Kamigami no henbō: Shaji engi no sekai kara* 神々の変貌—社寺縁起の世界から. Chikuma gakugei bunko. Tokyo: Chikuma shobō.

———. 2002–2003. "The Myth of Royal Authority and Shinbutsu-Shūgō (Kami-Buddha Amalgamation)." *CEA* 13: 85–100.

Sanford, James H. 1991a. "The Abominable Tachikawa Skull Ritual." *MN* 46, 1: 1–20.

———. 1991b. "Literary Aspects of Japan's Dual Gaṇeśa Cult." In Robert L. Brown 1991: 287–335.

———. 1994. "Breath of Life: The Esoteric Nenbutsu." In Ian Astley, ed., *Esoteric Buddhism in Japan*, 65–98. SBS Monographs 1. Copenhagen: Seminar for Buddhist Studies.

———. 1997. "Wind, Water, Stupas, Mandalas: Fetal Buddhahood in Shingon." *JJRS* 24, 1–2: 1–38.

Sano Kenji 佐野賢治. 1996. *Kokūzō Bosatsu shinkō no kenkyū* 虚空藏菩薩信仰の研究. Tokyo: Yoshikawa kōbunkan.

Sasama Yoshihiko 笹間良彦. 1988. *Dakini shinkō to sono zokushin* ダキ二信仰とその俗信. Tokyo: Daiichi shobō.

———. 1989. *Kangiten (Shōten) shinkō to zokushin* 歓喜天 (聖天) 信仰と俗信. Tokyo: Yūzankaku.

———. 1991. *Benzaiten shinkō to zokushin* 弁才天信仰と俗信. Tokyo: Yūzankaku.

———. 1993. *Daikokuten shinkō to zokushin* 大黒天信仰と俗信. Tokyo: Yūzankaku.

Saso, Michael. 1990. *Tantric Art and Meditation*. Honolulu: University of Hawai'i Press.

Satō Hiroo 佐藤弘夫. 1998. *Kami, hotoke, ōken no chūsei* 神、佛、王権の中世. Kyoto: Hōzōkan.

———. 2003. "Wrathful Deities and Saving Deities." In Teeuwen and Rambelli 2003: 95–114.

———. 2007. "'Shinbutsu shūgō' ron no keisei no shiteki haikei" 「神仏習合」'論の形成の史的背景. *Shūkyō kenkyū* 宗教研究 353: 211–234.

Satō Masato 佐藤真人. 1985. "Sannō shintō keiseishi no ippan: Sannō shichisha, Hokuto shichishō dōtaisetsu no seiritsu o megutte" 山王神道形成史の一班一山王七社、北斗七星同体説をめぐって. *Shūkyō kenkyū* 宗教研究 266: 28–53.

Satō Torao 佐藤虎雄. 1966. "Kinpusen himitsuden no kenkyū" 金峰山秘密伝の研究. *Tenri gakuhō* 天理学報 17, 1: 119–136.

Sauzeau, Pierre, and André Sauzeau. 2004. "La quatrième fonction: Pour un élargissement du modèle dumézilien." In "Mythe et mythologie dans l'Antiquité gréco-romaine," *Europe* 904–905: 231–253.

Sawada Mizuho 澤田瑞穂. 1984a. *Chūgoku no juhō* 中国の呪法. Tokyo: Hirakawa shuppansha.

———. 1984b. *Jigoku-hen: Chūgoku no meikai-seitsu* 地獄編一中国の冥界説. Tokyo: Hirakawa shuppansha.

Sawa Ryūken 佐和隆研, ed. 1972. *Omuro-ban ryōbu mandara, sonzō-shū* 御室版両部曼荼羅, 尊像集. Kyoto: Hōzōkan.

Sawa Shisei 沢史生. 1984. *Tōzasareta kamigami: ōsenkoku to wajinden* 閉ざされた神々ー黄泉国と倭人伝. Tokyo: Sairyūsha.

Schafer, Edward H. 1980. *The Divine Woman: Dragon Ladies and Rain Maidens*. San Francisco: North Point Press.

Scheid, Bernhard, and Mark Teeuwen, eds. 2006. *The Culture of Secrecy in Japanese Religion*. London: Routledge.

Schnell, Scott. 1999. *The Rousing Drum: Ritual Practice in a Japanese Community*. Honolulu: University of Hawai'i Press.

Schönberger, Sarah-Allegra. 2012. "Kriegsglück und Reichtum: Zur iconographischen Transformation Bishamon-ten's. Indien - Japan." MA Thesis, Vienna University.

Seidel, Anna. 2003a. "Danda" 檀拏. *Hōbōgirin* 8: 1113–1125.
———. 2003b. "Datsueba" 奪衣婆. *Hōbōgirin* 8: 1159–1169.
Seki Shōdō 関尚道, ed. 1987. *Waga kuni ni okeru Shōten shinkō* わが国における聖天信仰. Tokyo: Hirai Shōten Tōmyōji.
Sekiguchi Jōyū 関口静雄. "Itsukushima shinkō to bungei" 嚴島信仰と文芸. *Kokubungaku: kaishaku to kanshō* 国文学一解釈と鑑賞 1993: 97–101.
Serruys, Henry. 1970. "Offering of the Fox: A Shamanistic Text from Ordos." *Zentralasiatische Studien* 4: 311–325.
Severini, Antelmo. 1874. "Notizie di Astrologia Giapponese." In *Atsume-gusa*. Geneva: H. Georg.
Shahar, Mair. 2013. "Indian Mythology and the Chinese Imagination: Nezha, Nalakūbara, and Kṛṣṇa." In Kieschnick and Shahar 2013: 11–35.
Shastri, Biswanaryan, ed. 1982. *Yoginī Tantra*. Delhi: Bharatiya Vidya Prakashan.
Shaw, Miranda. 2006. *Buddhist Goddesses of India*. Princeton, NJ: Princeton University Press.
Shiga kenritsu Azuchijō kōko hakubutsukan 滋賀県安土城考古博物館. 2011. *Bushō ga sugatta shinbutsutachi* 武将が縋った神佛たち. Hachiman: Shiga kenritsu Azuchi kōko hakubutsukan.
Shiga kenritsu Biwako bunkakan 滋賀県立琵琶湖文化館, ed. 1991a. *Daikokuten to Benzaiten mokuroku*. 大黒天と弁才天目録. Ōtsu: Shiga kenritsu Biwako bunkakan.
———. 1991b. *Hiyoshi Sannō gongen: kami to hotoke no bijutsu: kaikan sanjisshūnen kinen tokubetsuen* 日吉山王権現一神と佛の美術一開館三十周年記念特別展. Ōtsu: Shiga kenritsu Biwako bunkakan.
———. 1998. *Tenjōkai no hotoke-tachi* 天上界のほとけたち. Ōtsu: Shiga kenritsu Biwako bunkakan.
Shimada Isao 島田勇雄 et al., eds. 1985–1991. *Wakan sansai zue* 和漢三才図会 (1712). Tokyo: Heibonsha.
Shimada Kiyoshi 島田潔. 1990. "Mimuro saishi to ōhori: Chūsei Suwa saishi" 御室祭祀と大祝一中世の諏訪祭祀. *Kokugakuin daigaku daigakuin kiyō bungaku kenkyū shiryō* 21: 93–117.
Shimada Shujirō 島田修二郎, and Iriya Yoshitaka 入矢義高. 1987. *Zenrin gasan: chūsei suibokuga o yomu* 禅林画賛一中世水墨画を読む. Tokyo: Mainichi shinbunsha.
Shimaji Daitō 島地大. 1931. "Marishiten ron" 摩利支天論. In Shimaji Daitō 島地大等, ed., *Kyōri to shiron* 教理と史論, 151–174. Tokyo: Meiji Shoin.
Shinbutsu imasu Ōmi jikkō iinkai 神佛います近江実行委員会, ed. 2011. *Shinbutsu imasu Ōmi* 神佛います近江. Miho Museum, Shiga kenritsu kindai bijutsukan, Ōtsu-shi rekishi hakubutsukan.
Shindo Tōru 新藤透. 2005. "*Shinra no kiroku* to Shinra Myōjin shiryō" 『新羅之記録』と新羅明神史料. *Toshokan jōho media kenkyū* 図書館情報 メディア 研究 3, 1: 19–28.
Shiozawa Hirohito 塩沢裕仁. 2008. "Sekizan-jin ni tsuite" 赤山神について. In Suzuki Yasutami 鈴木靖民 ed., *Kodai Nihon no ibunka kōryū* 古代日本の異文化交流, 28–47. Tokyo: Bensei shuppan.
Shirahara Yukiko 白原由起子. 1999. "'Fushimi Inari mandara' kō: Kojin-bon 'Dakinitenmandara'niokeruiken" 「伏見稲荷曼陀羅」考一個人本「吒枳尼天曼荼羅」二対する異見. *Museum* (Tokyo National Museum) 560, 3–4: 7–23.
Shirato Kaisho 白戸快昇. 1982. "Shōten shinkō." 聖天信仰. *Tendai gakuhō* 天台学報 6: 41–47.
Shirayama Raigen 志羅山頼玄. 1979. "Hiraizumi Mōtsuji ennen to bukkyō" 平

泉毛越寺延年と佛教. In Gorai Shigeru et al., eds., *Shūkyō minzoku geinō* 宗教民俗芸能, 190–207. Kōza: Nihon minzoku shūkyō 6. Tokyo: Kōbundō.
Shūkyō shakaigaku no kai 宗教社会学の会, ed. 1985. *Ikoma no kamigami: Gendai toshi no minzoku shūkyō* 生駒の神々: 現代都市の民俗宗教. Osaka: Sōgensha.
Siklós, Bulcsu. 1996. "The Evolution of the Buddhist Yama." In T. Skorupski, ed., *The Buddhist Forum* 4 :165–190. London: Routledge.
Skorbyski, Alfred. 2010. *Selections from Science and Sanity: An Introduction to Non-Aristetolian Systems and General Semantics*. Fort Worth, TX: Institute of General Semantics.
Skorupski, Tadeusz. 1997. "In Praise of the Ḍākinīs." In Samten Karmey and Philippe Sagant, eds., *Les habitants du toit du monde: Études recueillies en hommage à Alexander W. Macdonald,* 309–324. Nanterre: Société d'ethnologie.
Smith, Jonathan Z. 1993. *Map Is Not Territory: Studies in the History of Religions.* Chicago: University of Chicago Press.
Smits, Ivo. 1996. "An Early Anthropologist? Ōe no Masafusa's *A record of fox spirits*." In P. F. Kornicki and I. J. McMullen, eds., *Religion in Japan: Arrows to Heaven and Earth*, 78–89. Cambridge University Press.
Smyers, Karen A. 1999. *The Fox and the Jewel: Shared and Private Meanings in Contemporary Japanese Inari Worship*. Honolulu: University of Hawai'i Press.
Snellgrove, David L., ed. and trans. 1959. *The Hevajra Tantra: A Critical Study.* 2 vols. London Oriental Series 6. London: Oxford University Press.
Snodgrass, Adrian. 1988. *The Matrix and Diamond World Mandalas in Shingon Buddhism.* 2 vols. New Delhi: Aditya Prakashan.
Sonehara Satoshi 曽根原理. 1999. "Kike to mikkyō: Gyōhen o megutte" 記家と密教一行遍をめぐって. In Sonoda Kōyū 薗田香融, ed., *Nihon bukkyō no shiteki tenkai* 日本佛教の史的展開, 300–315. Tokyo: Hanawa shobō.
Souyri, Pierre F. 2001. *The World Turned Upside Down: Medieval Japanese Society.* Trans. Käthe Roth. New York: Columbia University Press.
Soymié, Michel. 1966. "Notes d'iconographie chinoise: les acolytes de Ti-tsang (1)." *Arts Asiatiques* 14: 45–73.
———. 1979. "Les dix jours de jeûne de Kṣitigarbha." In Michel Soymié, ed., *Contributions aux études sur Touen-houang*, 135–159. Geneva: Librairie Droz.
Stein, Rolf A. 1970. "La légende du foyer dans le monde chinois." In Jean Pouillon and Pierre Maranda, eds., *Échanges et communications: Mélanges offerts à Claude Lévi-Strauss à l'occasion de son 60ème anniversaire,* 1280–1305. Paris: Mouton.
———. 1990. *The World in Miniature: Container Gardens and Dwellings in Far Eastern Religious Thought.* Trans. Phyllis Brooks. Stanford, CA: Stanford University Press.
———. 1991a (1981). "Buddhist Mythology." In Bonnefoy 1991: 119–121.
———. 1991b (1981). "The Guardian of the Gate: An Example of Buddhist Mythology, from India to Japan." In Bonnefoy 1991: 122–136.
———. 1995. "La soumission de Rudra et autres contes tantriques." *Journal Asiatique* 283, 1: 121–160.
Stengers, Isabelle. 2010–2011. *Cosmopolitics*. Trans. Robert Bononno. 2 vols. Posthumanities 9–10. Minneapolis: University of Minnesota Press.
Stevenson, Daniel B. 1986. "The Four Kinds of Samādhi in Early T'ien-t'ai

Buddhism." In Peter N. Gregory, ed., *Traditions of Meditation in Chinese Buddhism*, 45–97. Studies in East Asian Buddhism 4. Honolulu: University of Hawai'i Press.

Stone, Jacqueline I. 1995. "Medieval Tendai Hongaku Thought and the New Kamakura Buddhism: A Reconsideration." *JJRS* 22, 2: 17–48.

———. 1999. *Original Enlightenment and the Transformation of Medieval Japanese Buddhism.* Studies in East Asian Buddhism 12. Honolulu: University of Hawai'i Press.

———. 2002–2003. "Do Kami Ever Overlook Pollution? *Honji suijaku* and the Problem of Death Defilement." *CEA* 16: 203–232.

Strassberg, Richard E., ed. 2002. *A Chinese Bestiary: Strange Creatures from the Guideway through Mountains and Seas*. Berkeley: University of California Press.

Strickmann, Michel. 1996. *Mantras et Mandarins: Le bouddhisme tantrique en Chine.* Paris: Gallimard.

———. 2002. *Chinese Magical Medicine.* Ed. Bernard Faure. Stanford, CA: Stanford University Press.

———. 2005. *Chinese Poetry and Prophecy: The Written Oracle in East Asia.* Ed. Bernard Faure. Stanford, CA: Stanford University Press.

Sueki Fumihiko 末木文美士. 2003. *Chūsei no kami to hotoke* 中世の神と佛. Tokyo: Yamakawa shuppansha.

———. 2006–2007. "La place des divinités locales, des bouddhas et du *tennō* dans le shintō médiéval: en particulier la théorie de Jihen." *CEA* 16: 343–373.

———. 2007. "De la nature des liens entre kami et bouddhas." In Arnaud Brotons and Christian Galans, eds., *Japon pluriel 7: Actes de la Société française des études japonaises*, 493–512. Paris: Editions Philippe Picquier.

Sugahara Kōji 菅原浩二. 2004. "Matarajin ni tsuite: Kurokawa nō to no kanrensei no kentō" 摩多羅神について一黒川能との関連性の検討. *Shintō koten kenkyūjo kiyō* 神道古典研究所紀要 10: 61–74.

Sugahara Shinkai 菅原信海. 1992. *Sannō shintō no kenkyū* 山王神道の研究. Tokyo: Shunjūsha.

———. 1996a. *Nihon shisō to shinbutsu shūgō* 日本思想と神佛習合. Tokyo: Shunjūsha.

———. 1996b. "The Distinctive Features of Sannō Ichijitsu Shintō." *JJRS* 23, 1–2: 61–84.

Sundara, A. 1987. "Early Sculptural Forms of Gaṇeśa in North Karnataka." In M. S. Nagaraja Rao, ed., *Kusumāñjali: New Interpretation of Indian Art and Culture; Sh. C. Sivaramamurti Commemoration Volume,* 2: 255–262. Delhi: Agam Kala Prakashan.

Suzuki Daisetsu (D. T.) 鈴木大拙. 1968 (1932). *The Lankāvātara Sūtra: A Mahāyana Text.* London: Routledge and Kegan Paul.

Suzuki Masataka 鈴木正崇. 2001. *Kami to hotoke no minzoku* 神と佛の民俗. Nihon rekishi minzoku sōsho. Tokyo: Yoshikawa kōbunkan.

Suzuki Shōhei 鈴木昭英. 2004. *Reizan mandara to shugen miko: Shugendō rekishi minzoku ronshū 2* 霊山曼荼羅と修験巫女一修験道歴史民俗論集. Kyoto: Hōzokan.

———. 2009. "The Development of *Suijaku* Stories about Zaō Gongen." *CEA* 18: 139–166.

Suzuki, Takayasu. 2008. "The Characteristics of 'The Five Chapters on the Various Gods and Goddesses' in *Suvarṇaprabhāsa*." *IBK* 56, 3: 66–73.

Suzuki, Yui. 2012. *Medicine Master Buddha: The Iconic Worship of Yakushi in Heian Japan.* Leiden: Brill.

Suzuya Masao 鈴谷正男. 1987. "Oto gohō kō (sono ichi)" 乙護法考 (その一). *Sangaku shugen* 3: 71–77.

Swanson, Paul L., and Clark Chilson, eds. 2006. *Nanzan Guide to Japanese Religion.* Honolulu: University of Hawai'i Press.

Tada Kōsei 多田孝正. 1985. "Tendaishū no Kishimojin shinkō" 天台宗の鬼子母神信仰. In Miyazaki Eishū 宮崎英修, ed., *Kishimojin shinkō* 鬼子母神信仰, 63–92. Minshū shūkyōshi sōsho 9. Tokyo: Yūzankaku.

Tajima Ryūjun. 1959. *Les deux grands maṇḍalas et la doctrine de l'ésotérisme Shingon.* Tokyo: Nakayama shobō busshorin.

Takahashi Gyōshō 高橋堯昭. 1994. "Ryūjin shinkō to bukkyō no hōyōsei" 龍神信仰と佛教の包容性. *IBK* 43, 2: 187–193.

Takahashi Nariaki 高橋平明. 2006. "Izuna-san no shinkō to Izuna gongen-zō" 飯縄山の信仰と飯縄権現像. In Iizuna rekishi fureaikan 2006: 15–20.

Takahashi Yūsuke 高橋悠介. 2006a. "Kōjin no engi to saishi" 荒神の縁起と祭祀. *Junreiki kenkyū* 巡礼研究 3: 1–22.

———. 2006b. "*Meishuku shū* chūshaku kō (1)" 『明宿集』注釈稿. *Zeami: chūsei no geijutsu to bunka* 世阿弥—中世の芸術と文化 4: 172–188.

———. 2012. "Kōjin no zuzō ni tsuite: Nyorai Kōjin o chūshin ni" 荒神の図像について—如来荒神を中心に. In Tsuda Tetsuei, ed., *Zuzōgaku* 図像学, 1: 334–349.

———. 2014. *Zenchiku nōgakuron no sekai* 禅竹能楽論の世界. Tokyo: Keio gijuku daigaku shuppankai.

Takatori Masao 高取正男. 1995. "Shinkō no fūdo: Tenkawa Benzaiten o chūshin ni" 信仰の風土—天河弁才天を中心に. In Hayashiya et al. 1995: 111–128.

Tamamuro Fumio (Bun'yu) 圭室文雄. 1987. "Enoshima no shihai to Benzaiten shinkō" 江の島の支配と弁才天信仰. In Miyamoto Kesao 宮本袈裟雄, ed. 1987. *Fukujin shinkō* 福神信仰, 269–284. Minshū shūkyō sōsho 20. Tokyo: Yūzankaku.

Tamura Enchō 田村円澄. 1995 (1954). "Shinbutsu kankei no ichi kōsatsu" 神佛関係の一考察. In Sone Masato 曽根正人, ed., *Kamigami to Nara bukkyō* 神々と奈良佛教. Ronshū Nara bukkyō 論集奈良佛教4. Tokyo: Yūzankaku.

Tamura Sadao 田村貞雄, ed. 1998. *Akiba shinkō* 秋葉信仰. Minshū shūkyōshi sōsho 31. Tokyo: Yūzankaku.

Tanabe, George J., ed. 1999. *Religions of Japan in Practice.* Princeton, NJ: Princeton University Press.

Tanaka Hisao 田中久夫, ed. 1993. *Fudō shinkō* 不動信仰. Minshū shūkyōshi sōsho 25. Tokyo: Yūzankaku.

———. 1996. *Kingindōtetsu denshō to rekishi no michi* 金銀銅鉄伝承と歴史の道. Minzokugaku sōsho 9. Tokyo: Iwata shoin.

Tanaka Nariyuki 田中成行. 1990. "Yōkyoku 'Tōru' no ba: Kawara-in no Shōten shinkō" 謡曲「融」の場—河原院の聖天信仰. *Chūsei bungaku ronsō* 中世文学論叢 8: 19–41.

———. 1996. "Yōkyoku 'Teika' to Kangiten shinkō" 謡曲「定家」と歓喜天信仰. *Ryōjin: kenkyū to shiryō* 梁塵—研究と資料 14: 49–63.

Tanaka Takako 田中貴子. 1992. *Akujo ron* 悪女論. Tokyo: Kinokuniya shoten.

———. 1993. *Gehō to aihō no chūsei* 外法と愛法の中世. Tokyo: Sunakoya shobō.

———. 1995. "Torai suru kami to dochaku suru kami" 渡来する神と土着する神. In Yamaori 1995–1996, 1: 173–208.

———. 2003. Keiran shūyōshū *no sekai* 『渓嵐拾葉集』の世界. Nagoya: Nagoya daigaku shuppankai.

Tanigawa Ken'ichi 谷川健一. 2009. *Senmin no ijin to geinō: Sannin, urōjin, hinin* 賤民の異神と芸能：山人・浮浪人・非人. Tokyo: Kawade shobō shinsha.
Taniguchi Takuhisa 谷口卓久. 1987. "*Heike monogatari* no katari: Biwa hōshi no henbō" 『平家物語』の語り一琵琶法師の変貌. *Nihon bungaku shiyō* 日本文学誌要 38: 57–71.
Teeuwen, Mark J. 1993. "Attaining Union with the Gods: The Secret Books of Watarai Shintō." *MN* 48, 2: 225–245.
———. 1995. *Motoori Norinaga's The Two Shrines of Ise: An Essay of Split Bamboo (Ise Nikū Sakitake no Ben).* Izumi: Quellen, Studien und Materialen zur Kultur Japans 3. Wiesbaden: Harrassowitz Verlag.
———. 1996. *Watarai Shintō: An Intellectual History of the Outer Shrine in Ise.* CNWS Publications 52. Leiden: Research School CNWS.
———. 2000. "The Kami in Esoteric Buddhist Thought and Practice." In John Breen and Mark Teeuwen, eds., *Shinto in History: Ways of the Kami,* 95–116. Honolulu: University of Hawai'i Press.
———. 2002. "From *Jindō* to Shinto: A Concept Takes Shape." *JJRS* 29, 3–4: 233–263.
Teeuwen, Mark, and Fabio Rambelli, eds. 2003. *Buddhas and Kami in Japan: Honji Suijaku as a Combinatory Paradigm.* London. Routledge Curzon.
Teeuwen, Mark J., and Hendrik van der Veere. 1998. *Nakatomi Harae Kunge: Purification and Enlightenment in Late-Heian Japan.* Buddhismus-Studien 1. Munich: Iudicium-Verlag.
Teiser, Stephen F. 1988. *The Ghost Festival in Medieval China.* Princeton, NJ: Princeton University Press.
———. 1992. "Having Once Died and Returned to Life: Representations of Hell in Medieval China." *Harvard Journal of Asiatic Studies* 48, 2: 433–464.
———. 1994. *The Scripture on the Ten Kings and the Making of Purgatory in Medieval Chinese Buddhism.* Studies in East Asian Buddhism 9. Honolulu: University of Hawai'i Press.
Ten Grotenhuis, Elizabeth. 1999. *Japanese Mandalas: Representations of Sacred Geography.* Honolulu: University of Hawai'i Press.
Tochigi kenritsu hakubutsukan 栃木県立博物館, ed. 1996. *Nikkōsan Rinnōji no butsuga* 日光山輪王寺の佛画. Utsunomiya: Tochigi kenritsu hakubutsukan.
Toffin, Gérard. 1993. *Le Palais et le Temple: La fonction royale dans la vallée du Népal.* Paris: CNRS Éditions.
Tōji hōmotsukan 東寺宝物館, ed. 1994. *Tōji no tenbuzō* 東寺の天部像. Kyoto: Tōji hōmotsukan.
Tominaga Nakamoto. 1967 (1746). "*Okina no fumi*: The Writings of an Old Man." Trans. Katō Shūichi. *MN* 22, 1–2: 177–193.
Trenson, Steven. 2002–2003. "Une analyse critique de l'histoire du *Shōugyōhō* et du *Kujakukyōhō:* rites ésotériques de la pluie dans le Japon de l'époque de Heian." *CEA* 13: 455–495.
———. 2012. "Shingon Divination Board Rituals and Rainmaking." *CEA* 21: 107–134.
Triplett, Katja. 2004. *Menschenopfer und Selbstopfer in den japanischen Legenden: das Frankfurter Manuskript der Matsura Sayohime-Legende.* Studies in Modern Asian Religions 2. Münster: LIT Verlag.
Tsuda Sōkichi 津田左右吉. 1949. *Nihon no shintō* 日本の神道. Tokyo: Iwanami shoten.
Tsuda Tetsuei, ed. 2012. *Zuzōgaku 1: imēji no seiritsu to denshō (mikkyō, suijaku)*" 図像学 1 一イメージの成立と伝承伝承（密教、垂迹）. Bukkyō bijutsu ronshū 1. Tokyo: Chikurinsha.
Tsuji Hidenori 逵日出典. 1970. *Murōji oyobi Hasedera no kenkyū* 室生寺及び長谷寺の研究. Kyoto: Seika gakuen.

Tsuji Zennosuke 辻善之助. 1919–1931. *Nihon bukkyōshi no kenkyū* 日本佛教史の研究. Tokyo: Kinkōdō shoseki.

———. 1964. *Nihon bukkyōshi* 日本佛教. Vol. 1. Tokyo: Iwanami shoten.

Tyler, Royall. 1990a. *The Miracles of the Kasuga Deity.* New York: Columbia University Press.

———. 1990b. "Kōfukuji and the Mountains of Yamato." *Japan Review* 1: 153–223.

———. 1992. "'The Path of My Mountain': Buddhism in Nō." In James H. Sanford, William R. Lafleur, and Masatoshi Nagatomi, eds., *Flowing Traces: Buddhism in the Literary and Visual Arts of Japan*, 149–179. Princeton, NJ: Princeton University Press.

———, trans. 1993. *Japanese Nō Dramas*. Penguin Classics.

———. 2007. "The True History of Shido Temple." *Asian Folklore Studies* 66, 1–2: 55–82.

Tyler, Susan. 1989. "Honji Suijaku Faith." *JJRS* 16, 2–3: 227–250.

Uesugi Bunshū 上杉文秀. 1973 (1935). *Nihon Tendai shi* 日本天台史. 2 vols. Tokyo: Kokusho kankōkai.

Umemura Takashi 梅村喬, ed. 1996. *Isewan to kodai no tōkai* 伊勢湾と古代の東海. Tokyo: Meicho shuppan.

Unno Kazutaka. 1994a. "Cartography in Japan." In J. B. Harley and David Woodward, eds., *Cartography in the Traditional East and Southeast Asian Societies*, vol. 2, bk. 2: 346–477. Chicago: University of Chicago Press.

———. 1994b. "Maps of Japan Used in Prayer Rites or as Charms." *Imago Mundi* 46: 65–83.

Ushio Michio 牛尾三千夫. 1981. "Bingo no kōjin kagura ni tsuite" 備後の荒神神楽について. In Gorai Shigeru, ed., *Shugendō no bijutsu, geinō, bungaku* 修験道の美術、芸能、文学 *2*, 205–231. Sangaku shūkyōshi kenkyū sōsho 15. Tokyo: Meicho shuppan.

van den Bosch, Lourens P. 1982. "Yama, the God on the Black Buffalo." In H. G. Kippenberg, L. P. van den Bosch, and L. Leertouwer, eds., *Commemorative Figures*, 21–61. Leiden: E.J. Brill.

van Gennepp, Arnold. 2010. *The Rites of Passage*. London: Routledge.

Van Vogt, A. E. 2002. *The World of Nul-A*. New York: Orb Books.

Vitiello, Giovanni. 1984. "Pan Gu: per lo studio del tema mitico dell'uovo cosmico e dell'uomo cosmico nell'area sino-tibetana." *Cina* 19: 7–27.

Vogel, Jean Philippe. 1995. *Indian Serpent Lore: or, The Nāgas in Hindu Legend and Art*. New Delhi: Asian Educational Services.

Volkmann, Rosemarie. 1995. "Female Stereotypes in Tibetan Religion and Art: The Genitrix/ Progenitress as the Exponent of the Underworld." In Ria Kloppenborg and Wouter J. Hanegraaf, eds., *Female Stereotypes in Religious Traditions*, 171–211. Leiden: E. J. Brill.

von Siebold, Philipp Franz. 1897. *Nippon: Archiv zur Beschreibung von Japan*. 2 vols. Würzburg: L. Woerl.

Wada Tetsujō 和田徹城. 1918. *Inshi to jashin* 淫祠と邪神. Tokyo: Hakubunkan.

Wakabayashi Haruko. 1995. "Tengu: Images of the Buddhist Concepts of Evil in Medieval Japan." PhD diss., Princeton University.

———. 1999. "From Conqueror of Evil to Devil King: Ryōgen and Notions of *Ma* in Medieval Japanese Buddhism." *MN* 54, 4: 481–507.

———. 2002. "The Dharma for Sovereign and Warriors: Onjō-ji's Claim for Legitimacy in *Tengu zōshi*." *JJRS* 29, 1–2: 35–66.

Wakayama kenritsu hakubutsukan 和歌山県立博物館, ed. 2003. *Amano no rekishi to geinō: Niutsuhime jinja to Amano no meihō* 天野の歴史と

芸能一丹生都比売神社と天野の名宝. Wakayama: Wakayama kenritsu hakubutsukan.

Wang-Toutain, Françoise. 1998. *Le Bodhisattva Kṣitigarbha en Chine du Ve au XIIIe siècle*. Paris: École Française d'Extrême-Orient.

Wang Yao. 1994. "The Cult of Mahākāla and a Temple in Beijing." *Journal of Chinese Religions* 22: 117–126.

Watanabe Morimichi 渡辺守順. 1974. *Ōmi no densetsu* 近江の伝説. Tokyo: Daiippōki shuppan.

Watanabe Shujun 渡邊守順. 2006. "*Chikubushima engi* no Tendai" 『竹生島縁起』の天台. *Tendai gakuhō* 天台学報 48: 1–6.

Watsky, Andrew M. 2004. *Chikubushima: Deploying the Sacred Arts in Momoyama Japan*. Seattle: University of Washington Press.

Wayman, Alex. 1959. "Studies in Yama and Māra." *Indo-Iranian Journal* 3: 44–73, 112–131.

———. 1984. "The Goddess Sarasvatī: From India to Tibet." In Alex Wayman, *Buddhist Insight: Essays by Alex Wayman*, ed. George Elder, 431–439. Delhi: Motilal Banarsidass.

Wehmeyer, Ann, trans. 1997. *Kojiki-den, Book 1, by Motoori Norinaga*. Cornell East Asia Series. Ithaca, NY: East Asia Program, Cornell University.

Weng Tu-chien, ed. 1925. *Combined Indices to the Authors and Titles of Books in Two Collections of Taoist Literature.* Harvard-Yenching Institute Sinological Index Series 25. Beijing: Yanjing University.

Wessels-Mevissen, Corinna. 2001. *The Gods of the Directions in Ancient India: Origins and Early Development in Art and Literature.* Monographien zur indischen Archäologie, Kunst und Philologie 14. Berlin: Dietrich Reimer Verlag.

White, David G. 1996. *The Alchemical Body: Siddha Traditions in Medieval India*. Chicago: University of Chicago Press.

———, ed. 2000a. *Tantra in Practice*. Princeton, NJ: Princeton University Press.

———. 2000b. "Tantra in Practice: Mapping a Tradition." In David G. White 2000a: 3–38.

———. 2003. *The Kiss of the Yoginī: 'Tantric Sex' in its South Asian Contexts*. Chicago: University of Chicago Press.

Wilkinson, Christopher. 1991. "The Tantric Gaṇeśa: Texts Preserved in the Tibetan Canon." In Robert L. Brown 1991: 235–275.

Williams, Duncan Ryūken. 2005. *The Other Side of Zen: A Social History of Sōtō Zen Buddhism in the Tokugawa Period.* Princeton, NJ: Princeton University Press.

Willis, Janice Dean. 1987. "*Dākiṇī*: Some Comments on Its Nature and Meaning." *Tibet Journal* 12, 4: 19–37.

Yabu Motoaki 籔元晶. 2002. *Amagoi girei no seiritsu to tenkai* 雨乞儀礼の成立と展開. Tokyo: Iwata shoin.

Yadav, Nirmala. 1997. *Gaṇeśa in Indian Art and Literature*. Jaipur: Publication Scheme.

Yamabe Nobuyoshi. 2013. "Indian Myth Transformed into Chinese Apocryphal Text: Two Stories on the Buddha's Hidden Organ." In Kieschnick and Shahar 2013: 51–70.

Yamada Yūji 山田雄司. 1994. "Benzaiten no seikaku to sono juyō: shukujin no kanten kara" 弁財天の性格とその受容ー宿神の観点から. *Nihonshigaku shūroku* 日本史学集録 17: 8–26.

Yamaji Kōzō 山路興造. 1990. *Okina no za : geinōmin-tachi no chūsei* 翁の座：芸能民たちの中世. Tokyo: Heibonsha.

Yamamoto Hiroko 山本ひろこ. 1984. “Chūsei Hie-sha no Jūzenji shinkō to ninaite shudan: Eizan, reidō, fugeki no sansō kōzō o megutte” 中世日吉社の十禅師信仰と担い手集団—叡山・霊童・巫覡の三層構造をめぐって. *Terakoya gogaku bunka kenkyūjo ronsō* 寺子屋語学文化研究所論叢 3.

———. 1989. “Hie-sha Ninomiya engi to ‘Kobie no sugi’: *Yōtenki* shoshū engi o megutte” 日吉社二宮縁起と「小比叡ノ杉」—『耀天記』所収縁起をめぐって. *Gekkan hyakka* 324: 12–21.

———. 1991. “Setsuwa no toposu: Chūsei Eizan o meguru shinwa to gensetsu o megutte” 説話のトポス—中世叡山をめぐる神話と言説をめぐって. In Honda Giken 本田義憲 et al., eds., *Setsuwa to wa nanika* 説話とはなにか, 271–302. Setsuwa no kōza 1. Tokyo: Benseisha.

———. 1993a. *Henjō fu: Chūsei shinbutsu shūgō no sekai* 変成譜—中世神佛習合の世界. Tokyo: Shunjūsha.

———. 1993b. *Daikōjin ju* 大荒神頌. Tokyo: Iwanami shoten.

———. 1994a. “Watarai shi no seishuku shinkō: *Kōkozōtō hishō* o megutte” 度会氏の星宿信仰—『高庫蔵等秘抄』をめぐって. In Sano Kenji 佐野賢治, ed., *Hoshi no shinkō: Myōken, Kokūzō* 星の信仰—妙見、虚空藏, 217–234. Tokyo: Keisuisha.

———. 1994b. “Ijin no zōyō: Gozu Tennō shimawatari saimon no sekai” 異神の像容—午頭天王島渡り祭文の世界. In Yamaori Tetsuo 山折哲雄 and Miyata Noboru 宮田登, eds., *Nihon rekishi minzoku ronshū 8: Hyōhaku no minzoku bunka* 日本歴史民俗論集8—漂白の民俗文化, 80–149. Tokyo: Yoshikawa kōbunkan.

———. 1994c. “Hana-matsuri no keitaigaku: ōkagura no shikai kara” 花祭の形態学—大神楽の視界から. *Kamigatari kenkyū* 神語り研究 4: 128–141.

———. 1994d. “Jōdo kagura saimon: shi no kuni he no gyanbitto” 浄土神楽祭文—死の国へのギャンビット. *Yurika* ユリカ 26: 258–266.

———. 1995. “Henbō-suru kamigami: reikakusha-tachi no chūsei he” 変貌する神々—霊覚者たちの中世へ. *Kokubungaku: kaishaku to kanshō* 国文学—解釈と鑑賞 60: 6–18.

———. 1997. “Kagura no girei uchū: ōkagura kara hana-matsuri he” 神楽の儀礼宇宙—大神楽花祭 (1). *Shisō* 877: 134–159.

———. 1998a. *Ijin: Chūsei Nihon no hikyō-teki sekai* 異神—中世日本の秘教的世界. Tokyo: Heibonsha.

———. 1998b. *Chūsei shinwa* 中世神話. Iwanami shinsho 593. Tokyo: Iwanami shoten.

———. 2003. *Ijin: Chūsei Nihon no hikyō-teki sekai* 異神—中世日本の秘教的世界. 2 vols. Tokyo: Chikuma shobō.

Yamanaka Seiji 山中清次. 1985–1986. “Shōten (Kangiten) shinkō ni tsuite: Kita Kantō no jirei o chūshin ni shite” 聖天（歓喜天）信仰について—北関東の事例を中心にして. *Nihon minzokugaku* 171: 73–98.

Yamaori Tetsuo 山折哲雄, ed. 1992. *Nihon ni okeru josei* 日本における女性. Tokyo: Meicho kankōkai.

———. 1994. “Buddha-s and Kami-s: About the Syncretic Relationship between Shintō and Buddhism.” In Fukui Fumimasa and Gérard Fussman, eds., *Bouddhisme et cultures locales: Quelques cas de réciproques adaptations*, 179–198. Paris: École Française d’Extrême-Orient.

———, ed. 1995–1996. *Nihon no kami* 日本の神. 3 vols. Tokyo: Heibonsha.

———, ed. 1999. *Inari shinkō jiten* 稲荷信仰事典. Shinbutsu shinkō jiten shirīzu 3. Tokyo: Ebisu kōshō shuppan.

———. 2004a. *Wandering Spirits and Temporary Corpses: Studies in the History of Japanese Religious Tradition*. Nichibunken Monograph Series 7. Kyoto: Nichibunken.

———. 2004b. "Buddha, Okina, and Old Woman: Representations of Divinity in Maturation and Aging." In Yamaori 2004a: 383–423.

Yanagita Kunio 柳田國男. 1969. "Shuku no mono to shugūjin to no kankei" 宿の物と宿神との関係. In *Teihon Yanagita Kunio shū* 定本柳田国男集 9, 385–399. Tokyo: Chikuma shobō.

———. 1984. "Raijin shinkō no hensen: Haha no kami to ko no kami" 雷神信仰の変遷一母の神と子の神. In Shibata Minoru, ed., *Goryō shinkō* 御霊信仰, 269–287. Minshū shūkyō sōsho 5. Tokyo: Yūzankaku.

———. 1985. "The Evolution of Japanese Festivals: From *Matsuri* to *Sairei*." In Victor Koschmann, Ōiwa Keibō, and Yamashita Shinji, eds., *International Perspectives on Yanagita Kunio and Japanese Folklore Studies,* 167–202. Cornell University East Asia Papers 37. Ithaca, NY: Cornell University.

———. 1990a. *Santō mintan shū* 山島民譚集. In *Yanagita Kunio zenshū* 柳田国男全集, 5: 55–484.

———. 1990b. "Kami o tasuketa hanashi." 神を助けた話. In *Yanagita Kunio zenshū* 柳田国男全集, 7: 353–492.

———. 1990c "Ke bōzu kō." 毛坊主考. In *Yanagita Kunio zenshū* 柳田国男全集, 11: 419–546.

———. 1990d. *Shakujin mondō* (*Ishigami mondō*) 石神問答. In *Yanagita Kunio zenshū* 柳田国男全集, 15: 7–200.

———. 1990e. *Oshiragami kō* 大白神考. In *Yanagita Kunio zenshū* 柳田国男全集, 15: 201–417.

———. 1990f. *Yanagita Kunio zenshū* 柳田國男全集. Ed. Yanagita Tamemasa 柳田為正 et al. 32 vols. Tokyo: Chikuma shobō.

Yatsuzuka Shunji 八塚春児. 1992. "Hiyoshi Sannō-sai ni tsuite no nōto: 'uma no shinji' o megutte" 日吉山王祭について一「牛の神事」を巡って. *Momoyama rekishi, chiri* 桃山歴史地理 26–27: 1–9.

Yijing (I-Tsing). 2009 (1970). *A Record of the Buddhist Religion as Practised in India and the Malay Archipelago (A.D. 671–695).* Memphis, TN: General Books LLC.

Yokoyama Shigeru 横山重, ed. 1970. *Ryūkyū shintō ki: Benren sha Taichū shū* 琉球神道記一弁蓮社袋中集. Tokyo: Kadokawa shoten.

Yoshida Atsuhiko 吉田敦彦. 1961–1962. "La mythologie japonaise: Essai d'interprétation structurale." *Revue d'Histoire des Religions* 160: 47–66; 161: 25–44; 163: 225–245.

Yoshida Kazuhiko 吉田一彦. 2006. "Suijaku shisō no juyō to kaiten: honji suijaku no seiritsu katei" 垂迹思想の受容と開展一本地垂迹の成立過程. In Hayami Tasuku 速水侑, ed., *Nihon shakai ni okeru hotoke to kami* 日本社会における佛と神, 198–220. Tokyo: Yoshikawa Kōbunkan.

Yoshie Akio 義江彰夫. 1996. *Shinbutsu shūgō* 神佛習合. Iwanami shinsho 453. Tokyo: Iwanami shoten.

Yoshino Hiroko吉野裕子. 1975. *Kakusareta kamigami: kodai shinkō to on'yō gogyō* 隠された神々一古代信仰と陰陽五行. Kyoto: Jinbun shoin.

———. 1980. *Kitsune: Onmyōdō gogyō to Inari shinkō* 狐一陰陽道五行と稲荷信仰. Mono to ningen no bunkashi 39. Tokyo: Hōsei daigaku shuppankyoku.

———. 1999. Hebi: *Nihon no hebi shinkō* 蛇一日本の蛇信仰. Kōdansha gakujutsu bunko 1378. Tokyo: Kōdansha.

Young, Serinity. 2004. *Courtesans and Tantric Consorts: Sexualities in Buddhist Narrative, Iconography, and Ritual*. London: Routledge.

———. 2009. "Apsaras, Ḍākinīs, and Yoginīs: Aerial Women and Buddhist Utilizations of Sexuality." In Devangana Desai and Arundhati Banerji, eds. *Kalādarpaṇa: The Mirror of Indian Art*, 298–322. New Delhi: Aryan Books International.

Žižek, Slavoj. *The Parallax View*. Cambridge, MA: MIT Press.

Zürcher, Erik. 2007. *The Buddhist Conquest of China: The Spread and Adaptation of Buddhism in Early Medieval China.* Leiden: E. J. Brill.

INDEX

Aizenji, 238, 263, 278
Aizen Myōō, 36, 105, 112, 118, 142, 224, 226–227, 248, 262, 265; Peasant Aizen, 285
Ākāśagarbha. *See* Kokūzō
Akiba Gongen, 158, 161, 394n174
ālaya-vijñāna, 54, 72
Ama no Iwato, 216
Amano Sadakage, 198, 276, 300–301
Amaterasu, 216, 226; Ame no Uzume, 54, 105, 293; *aramitama* of, 72; and Benzaiten, 226; and Dainichi, 4–5; and Dakiniten, 144; and Enmaten, 72; and the fox, 127, 133, 144; and Shōten, 105, 113
Amida, 296, 306, 319, 323, 340
Amino Yoshihiko, 75, 350
Andhaka (demon), 46–47
Anira (spirit commander), 196–197
Annen, 77, 104, 118
Asabashō, 34, 41, 43, 109, 180, 231, 307
Ashibiki no miya, 212
Ashikaga Takauji, 77
Ashikaga Yoshimitsu, 183
Ashikaga Yoshinori, 75
Aśoka, 33
Aśvins, 165, 396n11
Baijie (Shengfei). *See* Fude Longnü
Banko, King, 148, 232. *See also* Pan Gu
Baozhi (J. Hōshi), 340
Batō Kannon, 345–346, 432n35
Baxandall, Michael, 4
Benzaiten, 238; and Daikokuten, 225–226; and Dakiniten, 144–148; and Durgā, 168, 170–171; as earth deity, 231–232; fifteen attendants (*dōji*) of, 36, 146, 214, 216, 218–224; as *gonsha,* 403n29; as *jissha,* 403n29; and Kichijōten, 33–34; live body of, 203–204, 210; and Myōken, 28; naked Benzaiten, 192, 213–214; as warrior deity, 170–171
Benzaiten shugi, 194, 201, 280
besson, 6, 7–8
besson mandala, 8–9, 349
Biancaitian, 231. *See also* Benzaiten
Biardeau, Madeleine, 33, 45, 373n28
Bikisho, 112, 125, 127, 133, 232, 271
Bishamonten: and Buddha relics, 43; and Dakiniten, 142–143; as god of fortune, 23–27; and Kangiten, 41; and the North, 28–29; as ox-king, 43; as protector, 18–22; three-faced, 260–261; Tobatsu, 360n34; Tohachi, 36, 258; and the wish-fulfilling jewel, 43
biwa hōshi, 145, 166, 173–175, 177–178, 195, 233, 263
Bodiford, William, 301–302, 304
Bosch, Hieronymus, 251–252, 259
Brahmā, 9, 164, 178, 179
Brāhmaṇas, 178
Buddhi, 102
Byakuhō kushō, 231
Byakuhō shō, 53, 89

cakravartin king, 254; ordination of, 127, 132, 172
Cāmuṇḍā, 66–69, 71
Certeau, Michel de, 259
Chang Pogo, 313, 315
Chiba, Prince, 176
Chikubushima, 145, 176–177, 192, 200, 205, 210–212, 214, 217
Chikubushima (Nō play), 211
Chinshō Yasha (ritual), 22, 39–40. *See also* Bishamonten
Chintaku reifujin, 228. *See also* Myōken
Chōseiden, 113
Chūjin (1065–1138), 228

cintāmaṇi (wish-fulfilling jewel), 118, 140, 154, 207, 236, 278; *dhāraṇi,* 286. *See also* Shintamani, King
Citragupta, 65–66, 69
Coleridge, Samuel, 3

dada-byō, 156, 393n66. *See also* fox(es): possession by
Daigyōji, 29, 345
Daiitoku Myōō, 44
Daikokuten, 45–46, 293; as *jissha,* 54–56; as protector of monasteries, 49–54; running, 218
Daikoku Tenjin-hō, 45
Daikokuten kōshiki, 55–56, 293
Dainipponkoku, 6, 209
ḍakini(s), 47, 56, 68, 84, 117–121, 124, 132–133, 155–156, 162, 203, 300, 305–307, 309
Dakiniten, 306; as assimilation body (*tōrūjin*), 141–142; as *jissha,* 156; and Monju, 142; and the Mothers, 300; two types of, 156
Dakiniten mandala, 240, 247
Danuo (Great Exorcism), 70
Dasheng Fude Longnü. *See* Fude Longnü
dasshōki, 45, 156–157, 305, 309, 382n9
Daten, 144, 148, 199, 237, 238. *See also* Dakiniten
Deleuze, 4, 297. *See also* Deleuze and Guattari
Deleuze and Guattari, 6–7, 12, 346
Detienne, Marcel, 13
devas, 5, 9–10, 12, 15; directional, 55, 292, 357n1; twelve, 9. *See also* Santen
Dōchi, 189
dōji: fifteen, 218–224; sixteen, 205
Dōjikyō, 81
Dokōjin, 149. *See also* Dokū
Dokū (Dokku), 231
Dōsojin (or *dōsojin*), 102, 106–107, 233, 293
Doumu (Dipper Mother), 227
dragon(s), 39, 111, 145
dragon fox(es), 133–135, 138–139
Dumézil, 181, 228, 347; on the *gandharva,* 181, 399n68; on Sarasvatī, 396n11; on the three functions, 73, 107, 165, 168–169
Durgā, 168, 190

earth deity (deities), 19, 33–35, 44, 49, 56, 74, 171, 173, 175, 231–232, 265, 349
earth goddess, 32, 35, 47, 73, 98, 166, 360n37. *See also* earth deity
Eison (1201–1290), 52, 178, 215, 226
embryological symbolism, 13, 42–43, 323. *See also* Ena Kōjin
Emishi, 28
Ena Kōjin, 151, 200, 267, 327
Enchin (814–891), 71, 104, 149, 237, 282, 305, 311, 314, 316
Enmaten, 15, 56–72, 110, 325; acolytes of, 151. *See also* Silu, Siming
Enmaten mandala, 83, 84, 94, 119, 309
Ennin, 88, 210, 237, 303–304, 313, 318
En no Gyōja, 34, 202, 210, 215–216, 272, 315
Enoshima, 145, 183–184, 187, 189, 192, 213–214, 225, 263
Enoshima engi, 200, 262
Enoshima engi emaki, 213
Enryakuji, 50, 145, 176, 211, 311, 318, 325, 341

fangxiangshi (J. *hōsōshi*), 26–27
Fanxiang juan (*Long Roll of Buddhist Images*), 195, 365n93
fengshan (ritual), 425n56
fengtan (wind altar), 60, 65
Foucault, Michel, 7, 338, 351–352
fox(es), 132–134, 278; astral, 133; earthly, 239; heavenly, 239; possession by, 156 (see also *dada-byō*); and snake(s), 135–138; Three, 138–141
Fritsch, Ingrid, 166, 169, 173
Fude Longnü, 195, 251, 365n93
Fudō Myōō, 18, 42, 56, 75, 77, 99, 111, 118, 160, 209, 239, 304; as Kurikara, 186, 199
Fujiwara (regents, *sekkanke*), 125
Fujiwara no Akihira, 76. See also *Shin sarugaku ki*
Fujiwara no Hidehira, 213
Fujiwara no Hidesato (Tawara Tōda), 188
Fujiwara no Kamatari (614–669), 149. *See also* Kamatari
Fujiwara no Moronaga, 173
Fujiwara no Tadazane (1078–1162), 121
Fujiwara no Teika, 106
Fujiwara no Yorinaga, 76

Fushimi Inari (Shrine), 36, 137–139, 238. *See also* Inari: Mount; Inari: Shrine
Fu Xi, 197–198, 280, 282, 296. *See also* Nü Wa

Gajāsura, 46, 81, 94
Gakuenji, 305
gaṇa, 79, 81, 86, 87, 112
Gaṇapati, 78–79, 81, 85, 102, 112. *See also* Gaṇeśa
gandharva, 180–181, 346
Gandharva king, 26, 81
Gaṇeśa, 41–42, 47, 69, 77–86, 100, 102, 108, 115, 373n28
Genkō shakusho. See Kokan Shiren
Genko Shikei, 56
Genpei jōsuiki, 145, 224
Genshi kimyōdan, 301–302, 303, 306–307, 319–324, 327
Getty, Alice, 273
Go-Daigo, Emperor (Tennō), 22, 75, 77, 215
Godō Daijin (great deity of the five paths), 69, 72
Gōhō (1306–1362), 300
gohō (Dharma protectors), 42, 152, 237. See also *gohō dōji;* Oto Gohō
gohō dōji, 218
Golden Light Sūtra (*Suvarṇaprabāsottama-sūtra*), 18, 19, 22, 33–34, 165–166, 170, 192, 195, 218, 227–228, 231, 279, 302
gongen, 336. See also *gonsha*
Gonggong, 281
gonsha (provisional manifestations), 74, 203–204, 336–339. See also *jissha*
goryō, 335. See also *onryō*
Go-Sanjō (Tennō), 124–125, 311–312
Gould, Stephen Jay, 348
Goyuigō daiji, 39. *See also* Monkan
Gōzanze Myōō, 286
goze, 177, 231
Gozu Tennō, 44, 105, 311, 326–327, 340
Guifeng Zongmi (780–841), 300
Gyōki, 207, 210

Hachiman, 3, 5, 183, 315, 337; Tsurugaoka, 77, 213
Hachiman gudōkun, 288
Hanjun (1038–1112), 261, 266
Hanten Baramon, 40–41, 362n54
Hārītī (J. Kariteimo), 25, 53, 98, 108, 166, 223, 229–230, 247, 266, 309. *See also* Kishimojin
Hasuike Toshikata, 300
Hata (clan), 135–136, 138, 151, 276, 279, 315, 328
Hata no Kawakatsu, 44, 327
Hata no Otorari, 137, 151
Hayagrīva. *See* Batō Kannon
Heike (clan), 183, 212, 288
Heike monogatari, 144–145, 173, 175–177, 179, 182–183, 185–186, 187, 200, 210, 233
Heike nōkyō, 182
Hekija-e, 26
Hekija hen, 301
Hirata Atsutane, 161
Hirō Gongen, 325
Hōjō (regents), 77, 184, 288
Hōjō Kanazawa, 123
Hōjō Sadaaki, 123
Hōjō Takatoki, 77, 184
Hōjō Tokimasa, 183
Hōjō Tokiyori, 272
Hōju-in, 240–241
Hōjuin monjo, 242
Hōkaiji, 77, 372
Hoki naiden, 145, 238
Hokushin (Northern Chronogram), 28, 149. *See also* Myōken
Hōkyōshō, 122
hongaku, 6, 40, 55, 77, 113, 203, 266, 286–287, 291, 297, 322, 337–338, 348
honji suijaku, 1, 4–7, 141, 197–198, 332–336, 338–342
Hōrai (Ch. Penglai), 179, 206, 210
Hotei (Ch. Budai), 54
Huilin (737–820), 47–48, 119
"human yellow" (*ninnō*), 117–118, 124, 142, 155, 156, 305
hyakki yakō (var. *yagyō*), 325

Ichiji Kinrin, 8, 55, 227
Idaten, 81
ijin, 2
Ikoma, Mount, 76–77, 111
Ikū Shōnin, 113
Inari (deity), 14, 73, 106, 132, 209; Daimyōjin, 137; and Dakiniten, 134–135; mandala, 37, 142; Mount, 121, 133–134, 137, 238–239; Myōjin, 134, 201; Shrine, 238, 277–278; and Ugajin, 277–279, 293. *See also* Fushimi Inari; Toyokawa Inari
Inari Daimyōjin saimon, 137, 148
Inari jinja kō, 134, 310
Inari kechimyaku, 122
Inari saimon, 141
Ina Tenjin, 325, 327
Indra (J. Taishakuten), 9, 57, 86, 125, 149, 165

Indra's emissary, 150, 243. *See also* Taishaku shisha
Ingold, Tim, 7
In'yaku Dōji, 223
Īśāna, 223. *See* Ishana-ten
Ise (Shrine), 5, 127, 139, 180, 216–218, 271, 338–339, 345. See also *kora; shin no mihashira*
Ise kanjō, 144
Ishana-ten, 45, 55, 94, 275, 292
Itsukushima, 105, 182–183, 186, 187, 192, 205–206, 212
Iyanaga (Nobumi), 45, 54, 89, 231, 260, 264–265, 267
Izanagi, 72, 102, 275, 292; and Izanami, 239, 275, 276
Izuna, Mount, 159
Izuna Gongen, 157–161, 296, 345
Izuna magic, 160, 395n183
Izuna mandala, 39, 43, 141–143, 151, 247

Jade Woman (J. Gyokujo), 111, 148, 191, 246
Jakushōdō kokkyōshū, 156
Japan: as *vajra,* 206–208
jewel (wish-fulfilling), 285–286. See also *cintāmaṇi*
Jihen (fl. 14th century), 6, 180, 209
Jimon, 142, 311. *See also* Sanmon
Jimon denki horoku, 311, 316, 318, 326
Jindaikan hiketsu, 237, 263, 338
jindō, 351, 355n8
Jingse (Tang dynasty), 112
Jingū, Empress, 400n91
jingūji, 288–289, 384
Jinja Daishō, 29–31, 44, 98
Jinten ainōshō, 276
jishin mōsō, 173, 175, 232
jissha, 1, 55, 74, 89, 156, 204, 332. See also *gongen; gonsha*
Jiten, 166, 231. *See also* earth deity
Jitsurui. See *jissha*
Jizō (Skt. Kṣitigarbha), 8, 71, 72, 202; Jizō Benten, 214; Shōgun Jizō, 159, 160
Jōgon (1639–1702), 204–205
Jōgyōdō, 156, 301, 303–304, 318–319, 320–321, 324
Jōgyōzanmai-dō, 318, 324. *See also* Jōgyōdō
Jōin (1682–1739), 301–302, 423n16
Jōjusen (Siddhavidhādhara), 119
Jūni shinshō (twelve spirit commanders), 197, 279, 287, 326–327, 345
Jūzenji, 105, 176, 200, 262, 292, 345

Kakujin, 119, 300, 307, 310
Kakuzenshō, 45–46, 65, 86–87, 91–92, 99, 102, 104, 180, 231–232
Kālāratri (J. Kokuanten), 45, 60, 369n161
Kālī, 45–46, 381n4. *See also* Mahākālī
kamadogami (stove god), 275
Kamatari, 125–126, 144, 315. *See also* Fujiwara no Kamatari
kaname-ishi, 212
Kangiten, 10, 34–35, 41–42, 72, 76, 77, 88–89, 93, 94, 98, 99–104, 105–108, 109–111, 113, 198, 236, 239, 263, 265, 296, 337. *See also* Shōten; Vināyaka
Kangiten mandala, 95–98
Kangiten reigenki, 88, 104–105, 112
Kanzan Giin (1217–1300), 123
Kanze Motomasa (d. 1432), 215
Kariba Myōjin, 282–283
Kasuga (deity), 144, 183, 239, 247
Kasuga Inari mandala, 152
Kasuga Shrine, 152, 248–249
Katen (Skt. Agni), 109, 247, 256
Katsuoji, 77, 113, 216, 263
Keien (1140–1223). *See* Kyōen
Keiran shūyōshū, 6, 9, 42, 43, 45, 55, 88, 120, 124, 125, 133, 137–138, 142, 144–145, 149, 152, 156–157, 171, 178–179, 180–181, 189, 193, 199–206, 208, 210, 214, 225, 231–232, 236, 238–239, 262, 283–284, 292, 294–295, 304–305, 307, 337. *See also* Kōshū
Kenchū (fl. 14th century), 193, 200–201
Ken'i (1072–?), 87
Kenna, 110, 123, 153, 266. *See also* Shōmyōji
Kenreimon'in (imperial consort), 176–177, 185
Kenrō Jijin (earth deity), 44–41, 49, 153, 191, 225
Ketu, 227. *See also* Rāhu
Kichijōten, 28, 33–35, 40, 166, 192–193,

212, 231, 251, 256, 260
Kida (Teikichi), 23, 274–275, 301
Kinpusen, 139, 255
Kinpusen himitsuden, 214–215, 218
Kishimojin, 53, 98–99, 166, 230, 247, 251, 309, 325. *See also* Hārītī
Kiyū shōran, 53, 156
Kōen (fl. early 14th century), 225, 278
Kōfukuji, 145, 176, 214–215, 226, 227, 287, 296
Kōgei (977–1049), 103, 200, 202, 262, 292
Kojima Kōjin, 152, 216, 218, 261, 267. See also Ena Kōjin; Kōjin; Sanbō Kōjin
Kōjin, 44, 49, 77, 84, 104–105, 160, 216, 228, 232, 267, 279, 289–292, 294–295, 318, 327–328, 348–350. See also *kōjin*
kōjin, 44, 115, 200, 204, 225, 233, 273, 286–287, 289–292, 319, 327
Kōjin Mound, 238
Kokan Shiren, 359n23
Kokuni Dōji, 40, 362n54
Kokūzō, 8, 72, 200, 296, 326; Five, 86
Komiya, Prince, 175–176
Kongō Dōji, 76, 98, 219
Konpira, 28, 304, 326–327
kora (Ise priestess*),* 127, 139, 239. *See also* Ise
Kōryūji, 303, 324
Kōshū, 6, 40, 122, 162, 186, 200–201, 204, 206–207, 209–211, 214–215, 221, 223, 227–228, 262, 295, 305, 310. See also *Keiran shūyōshū*
Kōson Shōnin, 138
Kubera, 23, 25, 28, 41–42, 326
Kūkai, 3, 39, 43, 51, 77, 104, 127, 137–138, 186, 206, 237, 261, 278, 283
kushōjin, 34, 43, 57, 70, 112, 151–152, 294
Kusunoki Masashige, 22
Kyōen (1140–1223), 189, 262, 267
kyōryōrinshin (wheel-commanding body), 226, 319
Kyūkai, 201

Latour, Bruno, 3, 11, 332, 343, 351, 357n43
Law, John, 342, 351
Lévi, Jean, 133
Lévi-Strauss, Claude, 12, 78, 275, 351
Linrothe, Rob, 297, 356–357n41
Liqu jing (J. *Rishūkyō*), 48
Liqu shi, 309
Ludvik, Catherine, 164–165, 168–171, 190

Madarijin, 54, 307, 309–310, 324
Mahākāla, 15, 17, 45–49, 51–54, 56, 68, 73, 117–118, 144, 195, 228, 248, 260, 264–265, 305–307, 309–310
Mahākālī, 310
Mahāvairocana, 119, 156, 179, 226, 336. *See also* Dainichi
Mahāvairocana-sūtra, 60, 68, 83, 87, 117, 133, 166
Maheśvara, 9, 45, 55, 83, 87, 101, 112, 228. *See also* Śiva
Maō (Demon King), 29, 35. *See also* Māra
Māra, 29
Matarajin, 156–157, 198, 236, 265–266, 296–297, 299–311, 318–329; acolytes of, 303
mātṛkā (Mothers), 47, 68–69, 82–84, 300, 307, 309. *See also* Mothers
Meishuku shū, 106, 237, 331. *See also* Zenchiku
Meizan (1021–1106), 288
Michizane (Sugawara no), 76, 88
Miidera (Onjōji), 105, 145, 282, 310–311; ordination platform of, 311–312, 315
Mii mandala, 316
Minamoto (clan), 22, 171, 183
Minamoto no Yoriie, 189
Minamoto no Yoritomo, 183, 213, 272
Minō, 215–216, 230
Minoodera, 263, 272
Mio Myōjin, 312, 315–316
Misen, 205, 214, 217, 251, 255. *See also* Sumeru
Mithra, 300
Miwa daimyōjin engi, 52
Miwa Myōjin, 52–53, 326
Miwa-ryū, 262–263
Mongaku (d.u.), 213
Monju (Skt. Mañjuśrī), 118, 120, 134, 141–142, 228, 315
Monkan (Kōshin, 1281–1357), 39, 121–122, 214, 262. See also *Goyuigō daiji; Kinpusen himitsuden*
Mononobe no Moriya, 22, 44
Mothers, 47–48, 60, 65, 68–71, 80–83, 300, 307, 309–310, 318, 326–330. See also *mātṛkā*

Mōtsuji, 305, 321
Mudōji, 209
Mulian (J. Mokuren), 57
Müller, Friedrich Max, 9, 112
Munakata: deities of, 212, 226
Murō, Mount, 39, 189, 262–263
Murōji, 186, 263. *See also* Murō
Myōan Eisai (1141–1215), 232
Myōe (1173–1232), 324
Myōgonji, 123, 126
myōkanzatchi, 179
Myōken, 8, 28, 72, 142, 155, 200, 227–228, 264, 277, 293–294, 314–315. *See also* Sonjōō
Myōon Bosatsu, 173
Myōonten, 171, 173–177, 178, 192–193, 200–202, 210, 231
Myōson (971–1063), 315

Naḍa (Ch. Nezha), 29
nāga, 179, 184–189, 197, 233 (*see also* dragon); goddess, 195; king(s), 27, 36, 183, 217; maiden, 212; palace, 180–181, 187–188, 205; princess, 177
Nāgakanyā, 120
Nāgārjuna, 289, 340. *See also* Ryūju
namazu, 137, 211
navagrahas, 82, 84, 113
nenbutsu, 15, 303–304, 320–321, 324; esoteric, 323
Nichirin Benzaiten, 336
nidānas (twelve), 303, 320
Nijō (Tennō), 312
Nikkō, 326; Shugendō, 31. *See also* Rinnōji
Ningai (951–1046), 121, 125, 137, 261, 288
Ninshō (Ryōkan Shōnin, 1216–1303), 145, 225, 278
Nitta Yoshisada, 226
Niu (Niutsuhime) Myōjin, 283
Nōman-in (Kyoto), 146, 152, 246
Nōman-in (Nara prefecture), 250–251, 253–256
Northern Dipper, 28, 55, 111, 238, 303, 314, 318, 323, 325–326. *See also* seven stars
nuo (exorcism), 27. *See also* Danuo
Nü Wa, 197–198, 281–282, 296, 419n55
nyāsa (J. *fuji*), 223
Nyoirin Kannon, 105, 137, 140, 144, 155, 177, 181, 200, 209

Ōhori, 289–291
Okame. *See* Ame no Uzume
Okina, 112, 296, 302–303, 309, 320–321, 328–329
Ōkuninushi, 50–51, 54, 326, 366n109. *See also* Miwa
Ōnamuchi (var. Ōnanji), 214
Onjōji. *See* Miidera
Onjōji denki, 228, 311
Onmyōdō, 10, 106, 109, 111, 122, 145, 149, 150, 152–154, 230, 232, 246, 280
onryō, 76, 88, 312. See also *goryō*
Orikuchi Nobuo, 325
Ortega y Gasset, José, 234
Oshirasama, 107, 231, 315, 379n137
Oto Gohō, 200–201, 221, 230, 262
Otorari no saimon, 151
Ototari shinku saimon, 137
Pan Gu, 280. *See also* Banko
panjiao (doctrinal classification), 3
Penglai, 179–180, 210. *See also* Hōrai
Pérec, Georges, 352
Piṇgala, 230
Prajāpati, 164, 409n126

Rāhu, 227. *See also* Ketu
Raigō (d. 1084), 311–312
rākṣasī (J. *rasetsunyo*), 144, 210, 230. See also *rasetsunyo*
Rambelli, Fabio, 334–335
Rankei Dōryū (1213–1278), 189, 289
Rasetsuten, 109, 110
Reikū Kōken (1652–1739), 301
Rendōbō Hōkyō (fl. 13th century), 262
Rinken (fl. ca. 1546), 250–253, 266
Rinnōji, 39, 43, 309. *See also* Izuna mandala
Rokuji karin-hō, 156
Rokuji Myōō, 153, 264
Ryōgen (912–985), 210
Ryōkan Shōnin. *See* Ninshō
Ryūju (Nāgārjuna), 215–216, 221, 230, 272, 286, 340

sādhanā, 178
Sāgara, *nāga* king, 183, 187
Saichō (767–822), 17, 50, 52, 145, 178, 225, 236, 260, 304, 326, 328
Saijō Inari, 136–137, 161
Sakagami (Sagami), 177
Sakodono (Ise Shrine), 180, 216, 232, 277
Sanbō-in, 273
Sanbōin-ryū, 137
Sanbō Kōjin, 104, 295,

318–319, 323, 327. *See also* Kōjin
Sanford, James, 100
Sanmen Daikoku, 50–52, 260–261, 264
Sanmon, 311, 425n49. *See also* Jimon
Sannō-dō, 200–201
Sannō Gongen, 50, 301, 311, 316, 425n49
Sannō ichijitsu shintō, 301, 326
Sannō mandala, 332, 334
Santen (Three Devas), 235–267
santen gōgyō-hō, 236–237, 267
Sanzon gōgyō-hō, 237, 267
Sarasvatī, 33, 86, 163–166, 168–171, 173, 178–181, 190, 191, 195, 210, 228, 231
sarugaku, 44, 176, 263, 302, 320–321
Sarutahiko, 105, 107, 293
Satō Hiroo, 342
Sefuri-san, 200, 221, 262. *See also* Oto Gohō
Seijo-gū, 137, 145, 209
Seison (1012–1074), 124, 288
Sekhmet, 268
Sekizan Myōjin, 310–315, 318
Sekizan Zen'in, 311, 313–314
Senāyaka, 10, 89, 99–101, 337. *See also* Vināyaka
Sensha Dōji, 218–220, 223
seven Hie shrines, 326
seven stars, 142, 148–149, 153, 157, 249, 316, 321–323, 323, 326. *See also* Northern Dipper
sexual symbolism, 35, 41–42, 53–54, 78, 89, 99–100, 102–103, 105, 107–108, 118–120, 125–126, 134, 180, 226, 293, 301, 321–324
Shanhai jing, 280–281
Sheng Huanxitian shifa, 108–110
Shijōkō-hō, 227
shikiban (divination board), 105, 108–111, 153–155
shikigami, 111, 152, 221, 232
shinbutsu bunri, 4, 351
Shinbutsu ittai kanjō shō, 113
shinbutsu shūgō, 4, 365n23
Shinjō (ca. 1215–1268), 120
Shinkō (934–1004), 152, 216, 261–262, 266, 267
shinko (astral fox), 132–133, 139–140, 146, 239, 278, 316, 386n69
Shinkō musōki, 266, 273, 296
Shinkoō (Bosatsu), 122–123, 134, 144, 148–149, 153, 156–157, 162, 236, 238, 263
Shinkō sōsho, 321
shin no mihashira (August Heart Pillar), 217, 271
Shinomiya, 233
Shinra Myōjin, 13, 142, 282, 310–312, 314–319, 326, 328
Shinran (1173–1263), 209
Shin sarugaku ki, 76
Shintamani, King, 133, 138, 140, 148–150, 156, 162
Shintōshū, 44, 149, 151, 159, 238
Shinzei (d.u.), 211
Shirahige Myōjin, 315, 328
shitennō (four deva kings), 9, 22
Shitennōji, 22
Shōgun Jizō, 159–160
Shōken (1083–1147), 261
Shōkū (d. 1007), 262
Shōmyōji, 109, 122–123, 151, 153, 263, 266, 393n159, 415n74
Shōson (d.u.), 76
Shōten, 14, 42, 75–116, 154, 161, 236–240, 243–244, 246, 248–249, 261–262, 273, 280, 296, 305. *See also* Kangiten; Vināyaka
Shugendō, 31, 34, 160, 200, 213, 215, 239, 256, 263, 303, 315, 325. *See also* En no Gyōja
Shukaku Hōshinnō, 236, 261, 299–300
Shukujin, 106, 112–113, 115, 232–233
shukujin, 296, 309, 321–322. *See also* Shukujin
Shukuō Bosatsu, 315
Shukuō Dōji, 315
Shushō-e, 26–27, 303, 320–321, 326
Shuyuchisō (Dakiniten's acolyte), 151–152
Siddhi, 102. *See also* Buddhi
siddhi (J. *shitsuji, shijji*), 110, 199
Siebold, Philipp Franz von, 39
Silu (Shiroku), 66, 70, 112, 309. *See also* Siming
Siming (J. Shimei), 18, 66, 70, 112, 309. *See also* Silu
Śiva, 9, 17, 44–47, 58, 78–83, 94, 203, 228, 265–266, 346–347. *See also* Maheśvara
Skanda, 41–43, 69–70,

78–83, 81, 107–108. *See also* Weituo
Skull ritual, 119–120
Soga monogatari, 223, 230
Soga no Iruka, 125
Sōji-in (Hieizan), 203, 227
sokui kanjō, 123–124, 237
Soma, 180
Son'en Hōshinnō, 295
Son'i, 75–76, 88, 145, 209
Sonjōō, 142, 315–316. *See also* Myōken
Sōō (831–918), 209, 304, 313–314
Sōshin Bishamon, 22, 39–41, 108
Śrī (Lakṣmī), 25, 33, 42, 166, 231, 347, 363n56. *See also* Kichijōten
Stein, Rolf, 41, 79–80, 99, 107–108, 267
Strickmann, Michel, 79, 100, 102
Suiten (varuna), 110, 181, 247, 256
Sumeru, Mount, 18, 154, 205, 211, 217
Susanoo, 72, 112, 282, 285, 287, 310–311, 316, 318, 326–327, 338–339, 348, 350, 399n77
Suvarṇaprabhāsa-sūtra. See *Golden Light Sūtra*
Suwa, 15, 237, 270, 288–292
Suwa Daimyōjin, 288–291
Suzuki Masataka, 328
swastika, 152
syncretism, 2–3, 132, 233, 344

Tachikawa-ryū, 100, 119, 121–122, 262, 301, 323
Taiheiki, 42, 122, 183, 226
Taira (clan), 173, 186–187. *See also* Heike
Taira no Kiyomori, 22, 121, 182, 212, 224
Taira no Masakado, 75, 88
Taira no Nariyori, 183
Taira no Tsunemasa, 145, 171, 183
Taishaku shisha, 150–152, 243
Taishakuten, 110. *See also* Indra
Taishan Fujun, 57, 66, 69–70, 313, 318. *See also* Taizan Fukun
Taiyi, 72, 148, 277
Taizan Fukun, 57, 309–310, 313–314, 318. *See also* Taishan Fujun
Takakura, Retired Emperor, 182–183
Takeminakata, 288
Tamonten, 18–19, 40–41, 43, 144. *See also* Bishamonten; *Shitennō*
Tamuramaro (Sakanoue no), 28, 359n23
Tankai (1629–1716), 76–77, 89, 99, 111
Tankai, 103
Teeuwen, Mark, 334–335, 338, 351
tengu, 140, 150–151, 159–161, 320–321, 325, 345
tengu odoshi, 320–321, 324
Tenkai (1536–1643), 301, 309, 326
Tenkawa, 145, 192, 200, 205–209, 214–215, 217–218, 266
Tenkawa Benzaiten, 214–215, 225, 272, 336
Tenkawa Benzaiten mandala, 195, 250–259, 266, 345–346
Tenko. See fox(es): heavenly
Tenko-ō, 139
Tenna, 136, 238, 263
Tenshō daijin kuketsu, 144, 263
Three Contemplations (*sangan*), 203
Three-Deva deity, 235, 238, 240–241, 259
three truths (*santai*), 202–203, 236, 264, 323
Tiantong, Mount, 304–305
Tobatsu Bishamon, 29, 32–36, 42, 49, 98
Tōdōza, 175–176
Togakushi, 159–160, 301
Tohachi Bishamon, 36–39, 44, 142, 144, 258
Tōji, 14, 198, 236–237
Tōkai Gieki, 123
Tokugawa Ieyasu, 301
Tokuzen, King, 214, 216, 230, 272
tonjō shitsuji (sudden realization), 154, 262
Tonjō shitsuji kuketsu mondō, 122
Tōnomine, 305, 309, 320
Ton'yugyō, 151–152
tōrujin (assimilation body), 99, 141
Tōshōgū, 301
Toyokawa Inari, 123, 161
Toyotomi Hideyoshi, 228
Toyouke, 134–135, 180, 209, 216, 274–275, 277, 293, 339
Tsuda Sōkichi, 5
Tsuji Zennosuke, 5, 356n23
Tyler, Royall, 211

Uga Daimyōjin engi, 271
Ugahime, 280
Ugajin, 14–16, 56, 123, 135–136, 146, 149–150, 159,

197–198, 227–228, 244, 248, 265, 267, 269–298, 286–287, 327; and Aizen, 285; apocrypha, 286; and Benzaiten, 191, 194, 197–200, 203, 209, 271–273; and Daikokuten, 225–226; and Inari, 277–279, 293; and Kōjin, 232–233, 295; and Myōken, 294–295; and Suwa, 288–292; *ugajin,* 280
Ugajin darani kyō, 105, 296
Ugajin-ku saimon, 199, 224, 292
Ugaya tontoku nyoi hōju daranikyō, 271
Uhō Dōji, 226
Uka no Mitama, 14, 134–136, 138–139, 216, 224, 275–278, 285, 296
Ukemochi, 135, 224, 276–277
Unkai, 201, 262–263. *See also* Kōshū
ushi matsuri, 324–325

Vajrapāṇi, 45, 98, 108
Varuṇa, 73, 181. *See also* Suiten
Vināyaka, 10, 12, 14, 27, 47, 68–69, 77–79, 81–84, 285, 327–328, 375n27; as demon, 81–84; dual-bodied, 112 (*see also* Kangiten); as god of obstacles, 86–89; and the Mothers, 82–84; and Skanda, 107–108; in Vajra mandala, 91–93. *See also* Shōten
vināyakas (demons), 19, 42, 69; directional, 91–93, 109, 111, 112, 117
Vināyakī, 102
Voltaire, 13

Weituo, 81, 108, 373n31. *See also* Idaten; Skanda
Wutai shan, 313

Xuanwu (Dark Warrior), 28
Xuanzang, 29–31

yakan, 133. *See also* fox(es)
Yakushi, 8, 28, 197, 211, 228, 340; seven, 211. *See also* Jūni shinshō
Yama, 18, 34, 56, 60, 68–74, 83–84, 118, 213, 265, 309. *See also* Enmaten
yamabushi, 239. *See also* Shugendō
Yamamoto Hiroko, 2, 127, 204, 275, 303, 309, 310, 312, 320, 322, 325
Yamāntaka. *See* Daiitoku Myōō
Yamī, 57–58, 166
Yanagisawa Myōjin, 282–284
Yanagita Kunio, 106, 274–275
Yijing (635–713), 49, 165–166, 170
Yiqiejing yinyi, 47. *See also* Huilin
Yixing (683–727), 60, 68–69, 117, 133, 166, 309
yoginī, 119–120
Yoshida Atsuhiko, 169
Yoshida Kanemitsu, 52

Zaō Gongen, 202, 219, 256, 342
Zeami (Motokiyo), 106, 327
Zenchiku (Konparu), 106, 112, 115–116, 327, 331
Zeniarai Benzaiten, 213, 272
Zennyo (*nāga*-king), 186, 189
Zhiyi (538–597), 178
Zhong Kui (J. Shōki), 26, 70
Zuikei Shūhō, 187, 212
Zürcher, Erik, 4

ABOUT THE AUTHOR

Bernard Faure, who received his Ph.D. (Doctorat d'Etat) from Paris University, is interested in various aspects of East Asian Buddhism, with an emphasis on Chan/Zen and Tantric or esoteric Buddhism. His work, influenced by anthropological history and cultural theory, has focused on topics such as the construction of orthodoxy and heterodoxy, the Buddhist cult of relics, iconography, sexuality, and gender. He has published a number of books in French and English. His English-language publications include: *The Rhetoric of Immediacy: A Cultural Critique of Chan/Zen Buddhism* (1991), *Chan Insights and Oversights: An Epistemological Critique of the Chan Tradition* (1993), *Visions of Power: Imagining Medieval Japanese Buddhism* (1996), *The Red Thread: Buddhist Approaches to Sexuality* (1998), *The Power of Denial: Buddhism, Purity, and Gender* (2003), and *Double Exposure* (2004). *Protectors and Predators* is the second in a planned four-volume work that explores the mythico-ritual system of esoteric Buddhism and its relationships with medieval Japanese religion. Faure has taught at Cornell University and Stanford University and is presently Kao Professor in Japanese Religion at Columbia University.